Writing About Literature

Eleventh Edition

Edgar V. Roberts

PEARSON
Prentice
Hall

Upper Saddle River, New Jersey 07458

Library of Congress Cataloging-in-Publication Data

Roberts, Edgar V.
  Writing about literature/Edgar V. Roberts.—11th ed.
    p. cm.
  Includes index.
  ISBN 0-13-154057-2
  1. English language—Rhetoric. 2. Literature—History and criticism—Theory, etc.
3. Criticism—Authorship. 4. Academic writing. I. Title.
  PE1479.C7R59 2006
  808'.0668—dc22

                                                              2005018792

Editorial Director: Leah Jewell
Acquisitions Editor: Vivian Garcia
Editorial Assistant: Melissa Casciano
Director of Marketing: Brandy Dawson
Assistant Marketing Manager: Andrea Messineo
Prepress and Manufacturing Buyer: Brian Mackey
Cover Art Director: Jayne Conte
Cover Design: Kiwi Design
Cover Art: © Royalty-Free/Corbis
Interior Design: John P. Mazzola
Composition/Full-Service Project Management: Kari Callaghan Mazzola and John P. Mazzola
Printer/Binder: Courier Companies, Inc.
Cover Printer: Phoenix Color Corp.

This book was set in 10/12 Palatino.

*Grateful acknowledgment is made to the copyright holders on page 412, which is hereby
a continuation of this copyright page.*

Pearson Education LTD.
Pearson Education Singapore, Pte. Ltd
Pearson Education, Canada, Ltd
Pearson Education–Japan
Pearson Education Australia PTY, Limited

Pearson Education North Asia Ltd
Pearson Educación de Mexico, S.A. de C.V.
Pearson Education Malaysia, Pte. Ltd
Pearson Education, Upper Saddle River, NJ

10 9 8 7 6 5 4 3 2 1
ISBN 0-13-154057-2

Contents

Chapter 3 Writing About Character: *The People in Literature*   64

Chapter 4 Writing About Point of View: *The Position or Stance of the Work's Narrator or Speaker*   77

Chapter 5 Writing About Plot and Structure: *The Development and Organization of Narratives and Drama*   93

Chapter 6 Writing About Setting: *The Background of Place, Objects, and Culture in Literature*   109

Chapter 7 Writing About an Idea or a Theme: *The Meanings and the Messages in Literature*   119

Chapter 8 Writing About Imagery: *The Literary Work's Link to the Senses*   129

Chapter 12 Writing About a Problem: *Challenges to Overcome in Reading* 175

Chapter 13 Writing About Prosody: *Sound, Rhythm, and Rhyme in Poetry* 182

Chapter 14 Writing Essays of Comparison-Contrast and Extended Comparison-Contrast: *Learning by Seeing Literary Works Together* 207

Chapter 15 Writing a Review Essay: *Developing Ideas and Evaluating Literary Works for General or Particular Audiences*   222

Chapter 16 Writing About a Work in Its Historical, Intellectual, and Cultural Context   232

Chapter 17 Writing About Film: *Drama on the Silver Screen, Television Set, and Computer Monitor*   243

To the Instructor

In this eleventh edition of *Writing About Literature,* I have kept and strengthened those features that so many of you have valued over the years. As in the past, I base my approach not on genres, with specific assignments to be determined, but rather on topics for full-length essays on texts in any genre. While the constant emphasis is on writing complete essays about literature, the chapters may also be used as starting points for classroom study and discussion, and thus may also be adapted for shorter writing assignments. In a one-semester course the book offers selective choices for study and writing; whereas in a two- or three-semester sequence, it is extensive enough to offer the possibility of complete or close-to-complete use.

The various chapter discussions may actually be considered as essay assignments, for that is how they were developed. Many years ago, when I was just starting out as a teacher of literature, and, inevitably, as a teacher of writing, I learned that there was a direct connection between the ways I made my assignments and the quality of student work. The more I described to students what I wanted, and the longer I took in explaining things, the better their final essays turned out to be. Soon, however, I found myself spending close to entire classroom periods in assigning essays, and it was then that I began to write and hand out my directions, thus saving much valuable classroom time. I tried and tested each assignment in a number of separate classes, and I made innumerable changes and improvements based on both student questions and student writing. When I was able to put everything together, *Writing Themes About Literature,* now *Writing About Literature,* was the result, first published in 1964.

Organization

As in each past edition of *Writing About Literature,* each chapter consists of two parts. The first is a discussion of a literary approach, and the second consists of suggestions for writing, together with an illustrative essay or essays showing how students might deal with the approach.

A major characteristic preserved in this edition is that, after the preliminary discussion in Chapter 1, the chapters are arranged in a loose order of increasing difficulty. Beginning with Chapter 2, which helps students develop skill in detailed reading, the chapters contain topics relevant to all the genres. The comparison-contrast chapter, for example (Chapter 14), illustrates the ways in which the earlier techniques may be focused on any of the chapter-title topics in the book. This chapter also demonstrates how an extensive comparison-contrast technique may be applied simultaneously to fiction, poetry, and drama. The later chapters, such as those on prosody, film, and research (Chapters 13, 17, and 18), are increasingly detailed and complex, but they also build on the various techniques of analysis presented in the earlier chapters.

Although you might assign the chapters in sequence throughout your course, you may also choose them according to your objectives and needs. One instructor, for example, might pass over the earlier chapters and go directly to the later ones. Another might choose the chapter on comparison-contrast for separate assignments such as comparative studies of symbolism, structure, character, and point of view. Still another might use just a few of the chapters, assigning them two or more times until students overcome initial difficulties. No matter how the chapters are used, the two parts—discussion and illustration—enable students to improve their skills as readers and writers.

The demonstrative parts of the chapters—the illustrative essays—are presented in the belief that the word *imitation* need not be preceded by adjectives like *slavish* and *mere*. The illustrative essays represent suggestions and guidance for thematic development, and therefore represent a full treatment of each of the various topics. Nevertheless, they have been kept within the approximate lengths of most assignments in undergraduate courses. Even though the illustrative essays treat three or more aspects of particular topics, there is nothing to prevent assigning only one aspect, either for an impromptu or for an outside-class essay. Thus, using the chapter on setting, you might assign a paragraph about the use of setting in only the first scene of a story, or a paragraph about descriptions of interior settings, colors, or shades of color and light.

I emphasize that the purpose of the illustrative essays is to show what *might* be done—not what *must* be done—on particular assignments. Students writing about literary works are facing a complex task. First, they must read a work for the first time; second, they must attempt to understand it; and third, they must apply new or unfamiliar concepts to that work as they write about it. By guiding them in developing a thematic form in which to express their ideas, the illustrative essays are intended to help them overcome the third difficulty. *Guidance* is the key here, *not* prescription. At first, of course, some students may follow the illustrative essays closely, whereas others may adapt them or else use them as points of departure. My hope is that students will free themselves to go their own ways as they gain more writing experience.

Following the illustrative essays are commentaries, something that students recommended I include in the fourth edition, and that I have kept ever since. These are designed to connect the precepts in the first parts of the chapters to the interpretive writing in the second parts.

Additions, Revisions, Other Changes, and Retentions

All changes in the eleventh edition of *Writing About Literature* are designed to help students read, study, think, plan, draft, and write. A number of chapters are extensively revised; some are almost entirely rewritten. This is particularly true of the revisions in Chapter 1, "Preliminary." Of particular note, at the earnest advice of a number of readers, is the inclusion once again of the chapter on imagery (Chapter 8). Also restored, on the same advice, is Chapter 13, on prosody. One instructor insisted that his students enjoyed developing the schemes for rhythms and sounds needed in prosodic analysis, and that they developed a more vital understanding and appreciation of poetry through the close analysis of sounds than they had previously gained in their years as readers. An additional restoration is Chapter 16, "Writing About a Work in Its Historical, Intellectual, and Cultural Context," which has been extensively rewritten. More and more commentators on the book have asked for an essay type that more fully reflects the increasing pluralization of our society, and it is my hope that Chapter 16 will answer their needs. Of special interest is Chapter 15, "Writing a Review Essay," which was first included in the ninth edition and is continued here. The rationale for this chapter is a practical one: Of all the writing skills about literature that students might possibly need in their lives and future careers, the writing of a review is the most likely, whether for general audiences or for audiences united by a common concern.

Another major change is the repositioning of Chapters 2 through 7. These six chapters, all of which are suitable for fiction and three of which are suitable for drama, are now arranged in the order of *close reading, character, point of view, plot and structure, setting,* and *idea or theme.* In this edition the description of the extended comparison-contrast essay in Chapter 14 is continued at the request of reviewers of the tenth edition. This chapter and the full chapter on research (Chapter 18) make for two challenging extended assignments that instructors might give students.

There are many other features designed to improve the eleventh edition. In making the many revisions, alterations, repositionings, and additions (as well as subtractions), I have tried to clarify, improve, and freshen the underlying information and examples. Many of the titles, headings, and subheadings have been retained as complete sentences so as to make them encapsulate the discussions they precede. My hope is that these informative headings will assist students in their understanding of the various topics. In a number of the chapters, the writing sections headed "Raise Questions to Develop Ideas" are augmented, and in the various "Special Writing Topics" sections, I have kept the topics designed to help students do library research.

Of the ancillary material, Appendix A is worthy of note. This appendix contains descriptions of important critical approaches such as New Criticism, structuralism, feminism, deconstructionism, and reader-response criticism. Also of major importance in the eleventh edition are the lists of "Special Topics for Studying and Discussing" at the ends of the chapters. These are mainly keyed to the works anthologized in Appendix C, but you can adapt them to the selections in whatever anthologies you are using. In several chapters, there are related topics that are boxed and shaded to set them apart for emphasis. These discussions are designed as short notes to help students think about and develop their own writing. Users of previous editions have found these short boxed discussions helpful for their students.

Aside from the extensive revisions and improvements, the chapters are internally different because of a number of changes in Appendix C ("Works Used for References and Illustrative Essays"). This book is not designed as an anthology, but even so, the selections (on which most of the discussions and questions are based) are intended to be as representative as possible. Accordingly, additions to Appendix C are Coleman's "Unfinished Masterpieces," Twain's "Luck," Brooks's "We Real Cool," Browning's "My Last Duchess," Browning's "Porphyria's Lover," Donne's "Good Friday, 1613, Riding Westward," Frost's "The Road Not Taken," Hughes's "Theme for English B," Masefield's "Cargoes," Salinas's "In a Farmhouse," and Wordsworth's "Stepping Westward." Also, a small number of poems included in the tenth edition have been omitted. To accompany these changes, there are many changes in the topics of the illustrative essays. I hope that these will make the book richer and, within the confines of the short number of selections, timely. With all the changes, the eleventh edition of *Writing About Literature* remains a comprehensive guide for composition courses in which literature is introduced, and also for literature courses at any level.

An innovation of the sixth edition that has been retained in all subsequent editions is the glossary, which is based on the terms set in boldface in the text. The increasing number of students taking entrance examinations and the GRE has justified this continuation. To help students acquaint themselves with important literary terms and concepts, the glossary includes brief definitions together with text page numbers for further reference.

An extra word is in order about the works in Appendix C. At one time I believed that clarifying references could be drawn from a pool of works commonly known by advanced high school and college students, and I therefore thought that no reference anthology was necessary. I presented a small number of works in the second edition, keyed to some, but not all, of the illustrative essays, but reviewers recommended against it for later editions. Recently, however, readers have emphasized that references to unknown works, even complete and self-explanatory ones, do not fully explain and clarify. Therefore, after the fifth edition, I made the book almost completely self-contained with the increased number of works in Appendix C.* The result is that both references and illustrative essays may be easily verified by a reading of the works included in the book. Experience has shown that the unity and coherence provided by these works help students develop and improve their writing.

Writing and Literature

The eleventh edition brings into focus something that has been true of *Writing About Literature* since it first appeared in 1964. The book is primarily a practical guide for writing; the stress throughout is on how the reading of literature

---

*For Chapter 12, however, I assume that students are somewhat acquainted with Shakespeare's *Hamlet;* and for Chapter 17 I assume that they might know Welles's *Citizen Kane.*

may improve writing. This emphasis is made to help students not only in composition and literature but also in most of their classes. In other subjects such as psychology, economics, sociology, biology, and political science, instructors use texts and ask students to develop essays from raw data. Writing is based on external, written materials, not on the student's own experiences or on opinions. Writing is about reading.

Yet instructors of writing and literature face the problems we have always faced. Throughout all of our colleges and universities, the demand for good student writing has gone beyond a requirement and a goal, and now has reached a clamor. The needs of other departments have been brought into strong focus by the creation of programs for writing across the curriculum. Such demands have correspondingly imposed a wide diversification of subject matter, straining the general knowledge of English department staffs and also creating topical and thematic pressure on composition and literature courses. Writing programs that stress internalized subject matter, such as personal experiences or occasional topic materials, have little bearing on writing for other courses. We as English faculty, with a background in literature, have the task of meeting the service needs of our institutions without compromising our own disciplinary commitment.

The approach in this book is aimed at these problems. English teachers can work within their own discipline—literature—while also fulfilling their primary and often required responsibility of teaching writing that is externally, not internally, directed. The book thus keeps the following issues in perspective:

- The requirement for composition by our institutions.
- The need of students to develop writing skills based on written texts.
- The responsibility of the English faculty to teach writing while still working within their own expertise.

It is therefore gratifying to claim that, for the past four decades, *Writing About Literature* has been offering assistance to meet these needs. The approach works, but I believe it is still novel. It gives coherence to the sometimes fragmented composition course. It also provides for adaptation and, as I have stressed, variety. Using the book, you can develop a virtually endless number of new topics for essays. One obvious benefit is the possibility of entirely eliminating not only the traditional "theme barrels" of infamous memory but also the newer interference from "enterprises" that provide critical and research essays on the Internet. I do not have words to express my contempt for such disingenuous businesses.

Although *Writing About Literature* is designed, as I have said in the past, as a rhetoric of practical criticism for students, it is based on profoundly held convictions. I believe that true liberation in a liberal arts curriculum is achieved only through clearly defined goals. Just to make assignments and let students do with them what they can is to encourage frustration and mental enslavement. If students develop a deep knowledge of specific approaches to subject material, however, they can begin to develop some of that expertness that is essential to freedom. As Pope said in *An Essay on Criticism,*

> True Ease in Writing comes from Art, not Chance,
> As those move easiest who have learn'd to dance.

It is almost axiomatic that the development of writing skill in one area (in this instance, the interpretation of literature) has an enabling effect for skills in other areas. The search for information with a particular goal in mind; the asking of pointed questions; the testing, rephrasing, and developing of ideas—all these and more are transferable skills for students to build on throughout their college years and beyond.

I have one concluding article of faith. Those of us who have devoted ourselves to the study of literature are committed to our belief in its value. The study of literature is valid in and of itself, but literature as an art form employs techniques and creates problems for readers that can be dealt with only through analysis, and analysis means work. Thus the immediate aim of *Writing About Literature* is to help students to read and write about individual literary works. The primary objective—the ultimate objective—is to promote the lifelong pleasurable study and love of literature.

Acknowledgments

As I complete the eleventh edition of *Writing About Literature,* I renew my deepest thanks to all of you who have been loyal to the earlier editions. Your approval of the book is a great honor. As I think about the revisions for the eleventh edition, I am impressed by how much *Writing About Literature* has been influenced by the collective wisdom of many students and teachers. The following reviewers of this edition have been particularly helpful: H. George Hahn II, Towson University; Barbara Thompson, Columbus State Community College; David Pink, Rock Valley College; Cynthia Tucker, Mississippi College; and Bryant Creel, University of Tennessee–Knoxville. Discussions with many others have influenced my changes in innumerable and immeasurable ways.

I thank Vivian Garcia, English Editor of Prentice Hall, for her thoughtfulness, encouragement, and helpfulness. Thanks are also due to Phil Miller of Prentice Hall, who gave me firm and friendly support for many years. In addition, I thank Kari Callaghan Mazzola of Big Sky Composition for all her hard work and graciousness. I also thank Dana Chicchelly, who copyedited the manuscript and who offered many corrections and improvements. I am deeply grateful to her. I particularly thank Jonathan Roberts for his skilled and unfailing help in preparing the manuscripts and disks of the halting and tentative drafts leading to the final copy. Thank you each and every one.

Edgar V. Roberts

1

Preliminary

The Process of Reading, Responding to, and Writing About Literature

The following chapters introduce a number of analytical approaches important in the study of literature, along with guidance for writing informative and well-focused essays based on these approaches. The chapters will help you fulfill two goals of composition and English courses: (1) to write good essays, and (2) to understand and assimilate great works of literature.

The premise of the book is that no educational process is complete until you can *apply* what you study. That is, you have not learned something, really *learned* it, until you talk or write about it. This does not mean that you retell a story, state an undeveloped opinion, or describe an author's life, but rather that you deal directly with topical and artistic issues about individual works. The need to write requires that you strengthen your understanding and knowledge through the recognition of where your original study might have fallen short. Thus, it is easy for you to read the chapter on point of view (Chapter 4), and it is also easy to read Ambrose Bierce's story "An Occurrence at Owl Creek Bridge." Your grasp of point of view as a concept will not be complete, however, nor will your appreciation of the technical artistry of this story be complete, until you have prepared yourself to write about the technique. As you do so, you will need to reread parts of the work, study your notes, and apply your knowledge to the problem at hand; you must check facts, grasp relationships, develop insights, and try to express yourself with as much exactness and certainty as possible.

Primarily, then, this book aims to help you improve your writing skills through the use of literature as subject matter. After you have finished a number of essays derived from the following chapters, you will be able to approach just about any literary work with the confidence that you can understand it and write about it.

What Is Literature, and Why Do We Study It?

We use the word **literature**, in a broad sense, to mean compositions that tell stories, dramatize situations, express emotions, and analyze and advocate ideas. Before the invention of writing thousands of years ago, literary works were necessarily spoken or sung, and they were retained only as long as living people continued to repeat them. In some societies, the oral tradition of literature still exists, with many poems and stories designed exclusively for spoken delivery. Even in our modern age of writing and printing, much literature is still heard aloud rather than read silently. Parents delight their children with stories and poems; poets and storywriters read their works directly before live audiences; plays and scripts are interpreted on stages and before movie and television cameras for the benefit of a vast public.

No matter how we assimilate literature, we gain much from it. In truth, readers often cannot explain why they enjoy reading, for goals and ideals are not easily articulated. There are, however, areas of general agreement about the value of systematic and extensive reading.

Literature helps us grow, both personally and intellectually. It opens doors for us. It stretches our minds. It develops our imagination, increases our understanding, and enlarges our power of sympathy. It helps us see beauty in the world around us. It links us with the cultural, philosophical, and religious world of which we are a part. It enables us to recognize human dreams and struggles in different places and times. It helps us develop mature sensibility and compassion for all living beings. It nurtures our ability to appreciate the beauty of order and arrangement—gifts that are also bestowed by a well-structured song, a beautifully painted canvas, or a well-chiseled piece of sculpture. It enables us to see worthiness in the aims of all people. It exercises our emotions through interest, concern, sympathy, tension, excitement, regret, fear, laughter, and hope. It encourages us to assist creative and talented people who need recognition and support. Through our cumulative experience in reading, literature shapes our goals and values by clarifying our own identities—both positively, through acceptance of the admirable in human beings, and negatively, through rejection of the sinister. It enables us to develop perspectives on events occurring locally and globally, and thereby it gives us understanding and control. It is one of the shaping influences of life. It makes us human.

Types of Literature: The Genres

Literature may be classified into four categories or *genres:* (1) prose fiction, (2) poetry, (3) drama, and (4) nonfiction prose. Usually the first three are classified as **imaginative literature**.

The genres of imaginative literature have much in common, but they also have distinguishing characteristics. **Prose fiction**, or **narrative fiction**, includes **myths, parables, romances, novels**, and **short stories**. Originally, *fiction* meant anything made up, crafted, or shaped, but today the word refers to prose stories based in the imaginations of authors. The essence of fiction is **narration**, the relating or recounting of a sequence of events or actions. Fictional works usually focus on one or a few major characters who change and grow (in their ability to make decisions, their awareness or insight, their attitude toward others, their sensitivity, and their moral capacity) as a result of how they deal with other characters and how they attempt to solve their problems. Although fiction, like all imaginative literature, can introduce true historical details, it is not real history, for its main purpose is to interest, stimulate, instruct, and divert, not to create a precise historical record.

If prose is expansive, **poetry** tends toward brevity. It offers us high points of emotion, reflection, thought, and feeling in what the English poet Wordsworth called "narrow room[s]." Yet in this context, it expresses the most powerful and deeply felt experiences of human beings, often awakening deep responses of welcome recognition: "Yes, I know what that's like. I would feel the same way." Poems make us think, make us reflect, and generally instruct us. They can also arouse our emotions, surprise us, make us laugh or cry, and inspire us. Many poems become lifelong friends, and we visit them again and again for insight, understanding, laughter, or the quiet reflection of joy or sorrow.

Poetry's power lies not only in its words and thoughts, but also in its music, using rhyme and a variety of rhythms to intensify its emotional impact. Although poems themselves vary widely in length, individual lines are often short because poets distill the greatest meaning and imaginative power from their words through rhetorical devices such as **imagery** and **metaphor**. Poetry often requires many **formal** and **metrical** restrictions but it is paradoxically the very restrictiveness of poetry that provides poets with great freedom. Traditionally important poetic forms include the fourteen-line sonnet, **ballads**, blank verse, **couplets**, elegies, epigrams, hymns, limericks, odes, **quatrains**, songs or **lyrics**, tercets or triplets, villanelles, and the increasingly popular **haiku**. Many songs or lyrics have been set to music, and some were written expressly for that purpose. Some poems are long and discursive, like many poems by the American poet Walt Whitman. **Epic** poems, such as those by Homer and Milton, contain thousands of lines. Since the time of Whitman, many poets have abandoned rhymes and regular rhythms in favor of free verse, a far-ranging type of poetry growing out of content and the natural rhythms of spoken language.

Drama is literature designed for stage or film presentation by people (actors) for the benefit and delight of other people (an audience). The essence of drama is the development of **character** and situation through speech and action. Like fiction, drama may focus on a single character or a small number of characters, and it enacts fictional (and sometimes historical) events as if they were happening right before our eyes. So the audience is a witness to the ways in which characters are influenced and changed by events and by other characters. Although most modern plays use prose dialogue (the conversation of two or more characters), on the principle that the language of drama should resemble the language of ordinary people as much as possible, many plays from the past, such as those of ancient Greece and Renaissance England, are in poetic form.

Nonfiction prose consists of news reports, feature articles, essays, editorials, textbooks, historical and biographical works, and the like, all of which describe or interpret facts and present judgments and opinions. The goal of nonfiction prose is to present truths and conclusions about the factual world.

Imaginative literature, although also grounded in facts, is less concerned with the factual record than with the revelation of truths about life and human nature. Recently another genre has been emphasized within the category of nonfiction prose. This is **creative nonfiction**, a type of literature that is technically nonfiction, such as essays, articles, diaries, and journals, but which nevertheless introduces carefully structured form, vivid examples, relevant quotations, and highly creative and imaginative insights.

Reading Literature and Responding to It Actively

Sometimes after reading a work it is difficult to express thoughts about it and to answer questions about it. But more active and thoughtful reading gives us the understanding to develop well-considered answers. Obviously, we need to follow the work and to understand its details, but just as importantly, we need to respond to the words, get at the ideas, and understand the implications of what is happening. We rely on our own fund of knowledge and experience to verify the accuracy and truth of situations and incidents, and we try to articulate our own emotional responses to the characters and their problems.

To illustrate active responding, we will examine "The Necklace" (1884), by the French writer Guy de Maupassant.[1] "The Necklace" is included here with marginal notes like those that any reader might make during original and follow-up readings. Many notes, particularly at the beginning, are *assimilative;* that is, they record details about the action. But as the story progresses, the marginal comments are more concerned with conclusions about the story's meaning. Toward the end, the comments are full rather than minimal; they result not only from first responses but also from considered thought.

---

[1] Henri-René-Albert-Guy de Maupassant (1850–1893) is considered one of the major nineteenth-century French naturalist writers. Scion of an aristocratic Norman family, he received his baccalaureate degree from a lycée at Le Havre, after which he began studying law. When the Franco-Prussian War broke out he served in the French army, including battlefield duty. After leaving the military he became a minor bureaucrat, first in the Ministry of Marine and then in the Ministry of Education (also the workplace of Loisel, the husband of "The Necklace").

As a youth Maupassant was an energetic oarsman, swimmer, and boatman—a power that he also devoted to his career as a writer. During the 1870s in Paris he had regularly submitted his literary efforts to the novelist Gustave Flaubert (1821–1880), a family friend who regarded him as a son and whose criticism both improved and encouraged him. In Maupassant's thirties, after the death of his mentor Flaubert, his career flourished. His first published volume was a collection of poems (*Des Vers,* 1880), which he had to withdraw after it created a scandal and a lawsuit because of its sexual openness. After this time, until his death in 1893, he produced thirty volumes—novels, poems, articles, travel books, and three hundred short stories. In addition to "The Necklace," a few of his better-known stories are "The Ball of Fat," "Mademoiselle Fifi," and "A Piece of String."

Maupassant was a meticulous writer, devoting much attention to the reality of everyday existence (hence his status as a naturalist writer). A number of his stories are about events occurring during the Franco-Prussian War. Some are about life among bureaucrats, some about peasant life in Normandy, and a large number, including "The Necklace," about Parisian life. His major stories are characterized by strong irony; human beings are influenced by forces they cannot control, and their wishes are often frustrated by their own defects. Under such circumstances, Maupassant's characters exhibit varying degrees of weakness, hypocrisy, vanity, insensitivity, callousness, and even cruelty, but those who are victimized are viewed with understanding and sympathy.

Guy de Maupassant (1850–1893)

The Necklace (1884)

Translated by Edgar V. Roberts

She was one of those pretty and charming women, born, as if by an error of destiny, into a family of clerks and copyists. She had no dowry, no prospects, no way of getting known, courted, loved, married by a rich and distinguished man. She finally settled for a marriage with a minor clerk in the Ministry of Education.

"She" is pretty but poor, and has no chance in life unless she marries. Without connections, she has no entry into high society and marries an insignificant clerk.

She was a simple person, without the money to dress well, but she was as unhappy as if she had gone through bankruptcy, for women have neither rank nor race. In place of high birth or important family connections, they can rely only on their beauty, their grace, and their charm. Their inborn finesse, their elegant taste, their engaging personalities, which are their only power, make working-class women the equals of the grandest ladies.

She is unhappy.

A view of women who have no chance for an independent life and a career. In 1884, women had nothing more than this. Sad.

She suffered constantly, feeling herself destined for all delicacies and luxuries. She suffered because of her grim apartment with its drab walls, thread-bare furniture, ugly curtains. All such things, which most other women in her situation would not even have noticed, tortured her and filled her with despair. The sight of the young country girl who did her simple housework awakened in her only a sense of desolation and lost hopes. She daydreamed of large, silent anterooms, decorated with oriental tapestries and lighted by high bronze floor lamps, with two elegant valets in short culottes dozing in large armchairs under the effects of forced-air heaters. She imagined large drawing rooms draped in the most expensive silks, with fine end tables on which were placed knickknacks of inestimable value. She dreamed of the perfume of dainty private rooms, which were designed only for intimate tête-à-têtes with the closest friends, who because of their achievements and fame would make her the envy of all other women.

She suffers because of her cheap belongings, wanting expensive things. She dreams of wealth and of how other women would envy her if she could display finery. But such luxuries are unrealistic and unattainable for her.

When she sat down to dinner at her round little table covered with a cloth that had not been washed for three days, in front of her husband who opened the kettle while declaring ecstatically, "Ah, good old boiled beef! I don't know anything better," she

Her husband's taste is for plain things, while she dreams of expensive gourmet food. He has adjusted to his status. She has not.

dreamed of expensive banquets with shining place settings, and wall hangings portraying ancient heroes and exotic birds in an enchanted forest. She imagined a gourmet-prepared main course carried on the most exquisite trays and served on the most beautiful dishes, with whispered gallantries that she would hear with a sphinxlike smile as she dined on the pink meat of a trout or the delicate wing of a quail.

5   She had no decent dresses, no jewels, nothing. And she loved nothing but these; she believed herself born only for these. She burned with the desire to please, to be envied, to be attractive and sought after.

    She had a rich friend, a comrade from convent days, whom she did not want to see anymore because she suffered so much when she returned home. She would weep for the entire day afterward with sorrow, regret, despair, and misery.

She lives for her unrealistic dreams, and these increase her frustration.

She even thinks of giving up a rich friend because she is so depressed after visiting her.

    Well, one evening, her husband came home glowing and carrying a large envelope.

"Here," he said, "this is something for you."

She quickly tore open the envelope and took out a card engraved with these words:

A new section in the story.

> The Chancellor of Education
> and Mrs. George Ramponneau
> request that Mr. and Mrs. Loisel
> do them the honor of coming to dinner
> at the Ministry of Education
> on the evening of January 8.

An invitation to dinner at the Ministry of Education. A big plum.

10   Instead of being delighted, as her husband had hoped, she threw the invitation spitefully on the table, muttering:

"What do you expect me to do with this?"

"But honey, I thought you'd be glad. You never get to go out, and this is a special occasion! I had a lot of trouble getting the invitation. Everyone wants one. The demand is high and not many clerks get invited. Everyone important will be there."

She looked at him angrily and stated impatiently:

"What do you want me to wear to go there?"

15   He had not thought of that. He stammered:

"But your theater dress. That seems nice to me . . ."

He stopped, amazed and bewildered, as his wife began to cry. Large tears fell slowly from the corners of her eyes to her mouth. He said falteringly:

"What's wrong? What's the matter?"

It only upsets her.

Loisel really doesn't understand her. He can't sympathize with her unhappiness.

She declares that she hasn't anything to wear.
He tries to persuade her that her theater dress might do for the occasion.

But with a strong effort she had recovered, and she answered calmly as she wiped her damp cheeks:

"Nothing, except that I have nothing to wear and therefore can't go to the party. Give your invitation to someone else at the office whose wife will have nicer clothes than mine."

Distressed, he responded:

"Well, all right, Mathilde. How much would a new dress cost, something you could use at other times, but not anything fancy?"

She thought for a few moments, adding things up and thinking also of an amount that she could ask without getting an immediate refusal and a frightened outcry from the frugal clerk.

Finally she responded tentatively:

"I don't know exactly, but it seems to me that I could get by on four hundred francs."

He blanched slightly at this, because he had set aside just that amount to buy a shotgun for Sunday lark-hunts the next summer with a few friends in the Plain of Nanterre.

However, he said:

"All right, you've got four hundred francs, but make it a pretty dress."

As the day of the party drew near, Mrs. Loisel seemed sad, uneasy, anxious, even though her gown was all ready. One evening her husband said to her:

"What's the matter? You've been acting funny for several days."

She answered:

"It's awful, but I don't have any jewels to wear, not a single gem, nothing to dress up my outfit. I'll look like a beggar. I'd almost rather not go to the party."

He responded:

"You can wear a corsage of cut flowers. This year it's all the rage. For only ten francs you can get two or three gorgeous roses."

She was not convinced.

"No . . . there's nothing more humiliating than looking shabby in the company of rich women."

But her husband exclaimed:

"God, but you're silly! Go to your friend Mrs. Forrestier, and ask her to lend you some jewelry. You know her well enough to do that."

She uttered a cry of joy:

"That's right. I hadn't thought of that."

The next day she went to her friend's house and described her problem.

Margin notes:

20

Her name is Mathilde.
He volunteers to pay for a new dress.

She is manipulating him.

25

The dress will cost him his next summer's vacation. (He doesn't seem to have included her in his plans.)

A new section, the third in the story. The day of the party is near.

30

Now she complains that she doesn't have any nice jewelry. She is manipulating him again.

35

She has a good point, but there seems to be no way out.

He proposes a solution: Borrow jewelry from Mrs. Forrestier, who is apparently the rich friend mentioned earlier.

40

Mrs. Forrestier went to her mirrored wardrobe, took out a large jewel box, opened it, and said to Mrs. Loisel:

"Choose, my dear."

Mathilde has her choice of her friend's jewels.

She saw bracelets, then a pearl necklace, then a Venetian cross of finely worked gold and gems. She tried on the jewelry in front of a mirror, and hesitated, unable to make up her mind about each one. She kept asking:

45 "Do you have anything else?"

"Certainly. Look to your heart's content. I don't know what you'd like best."

Suddenly she found a superb diamond necklace in a black satin box, and her heart throbbed with desire for it. Her hands shook as she picked it up. She fastened it around her neck, watched it gleam at her throat, and looked at herself ecstatically.

A "superb" diamond necklace. This is what the story has been building up to.

Then she asked, haltingly and anxiously:

"Could you lend me this, nothing but this?"

This is what she wants, just this.

50 "Why yes, certainly."

She jumped up, hugged her friend joyfully, then hurried away with her treasure.

She leaves with the "treasure." Things might be looking up for her.

The day of the party came. Mrs. Loisel was a success. She was prettier than anyone else, stylish, graceful, smiling and wild with joy. All the men saw her, asked her name, sought to be introduced. All the important administrators stood in line to waltz with her. The Chancellor himself eyed her.

A new section.

The party. Mathilde is a huge success.

She danced joyfully, passionately, intoxicated with pleasure, thinking of nothing but the moment, in the triumph of her beauty, in the glory of her success, on cloud nine with happiness made up of all the admiration, of all the aroused desire, of this victory so complete and so sweet to the heart of any woman.

Another judgment about women. Does the author mean that only women want to be admired? Don't men want admiration, too?

She did not leave until four o'clock in the morning. Her husband, since midnight, had been sleeping in a little empty room with three other men whose wives had also been enjoying themselves.

Loisel, with other husbands, is bored, while the wives are literally having a ball.

55 He threw, over her shoulders, the shawl that he had brought for the trip home—a modest everyday wrap, the poverty of which contrasted sharply with the elegance of her evening gown. She felt it and hurried away to avoid being noticed by the other women who luxuriated in rich furs.

Ashamed of her shabby everyday shawl, she rushes away to avoid being seen. She is forced back into the reality of her true situation. Her glamour is gone.

Loisel tried to hold her back:

"Wait a minute. You'll catch cold outdoors. I'll call a cab."

But she paid no attention and hurried down the stairs. When they reached the street they found no carriages. They began to look for one, shouting at cabmen passing by at a distance.

They walked toward the Seine, desperate, shivering. Finally, on a quay, they found one of those old night-going buggies that are seen in Paris only after dark, as if they were ashamed of their wretched appearance in daylight.

A comedown after the nice evening. They take a wretched-looking buggy home.

It took them to their door, on the Street of Martyrs, and they sadly climbed the stairs to their flat. For her, it was finished. As for him, he could think only that he had to begin work at the Ministry of Education at ten o'clock.

"Street of Martyrs." Is this name significant? 60

She took the shawl off her shoulders, in front of the mirror, to see herself once more in her glory. But suddenly she cried out. The necklace was no longer around her neck!

Loisel is down-to-earth.

SHE HAS LOST THE NECK-LACE!

Her husband, already half undressed, asked:

"What's wrong?"

She turned toward him frantically:

"I . . . I . . . I no longer have Mrs. Forrestier's necklace." 65

He stood up, bewildered:

"What! . . . How! . . . It's not possible!"

And they looked in the folds of the gown, in the folds of the shawl, in the pockets, everywhere. They found nothing.

They can't find it.

He asked:

"You're sure you still had it when you left the party?" 70

"Yes. I checked it in the vestibule of the Ministry."

"But if you'd lost it in the street, we would've heard it fall. It must be in the cab."

"Yes, probably. Did you notice the number?"

"No. Did you see it?"

"No." 75

Overwhelmed, they looked at each other. Finally, Loisel got dressed again:

"I'm going out to retrace all our steps," he said, "to see if I can find the necklace that way."

And he went out. She stayed in her evening dress, without the energy to get ready for bed, stretched out in a chair, drained of strength and thought.

He goes out to search for the necklace.

Her husband came back at about seven o'clock. He had found nothing.

But is unsuccessful. 80

He went to Police Headquarters and to the newspapers to announce a reward. He went to the small

He really tries. He's doing his best.

cab companies, and finally he followed up even the slightest hopeful lead.

She waited the entire day, in the same enervated state, in the face of this frightful disaster.

Loisel came back in the evening, his face pale and haggard. He had found nothing.

"You'll have to write to your friend," he said, "that you broke a clasp on her necklace and that you're having it fixed. That'll give us time to look around."

She wrote as he dictated.

85   By the end of the week they had lost all hope.

And Loisel, looking five years older, declared:

"We'll have to see about replacing the jewels."

The next day they took the case that had contained the necklace and went to the jeweler whose name was inside. He looked at his books:

"I wasn't the one, Madam, who sold the necklace. I only made the case."

90   Then they went from jeweler to jeweler, searching for a necklace like the other one, racking their memories, both of them sick with worry and anguish.

In a shop in the Palais-Royal, they found a necklace of diamonds that seemed to them exactly like the one they were looking for. It was priced at forty thousand francs. They could buy it for thirty-six thousand.

They got the jeweler to promise not to sell it for three days. And they made an agreement that he would buy it back for thirty-four thousand francs if the original were recovered before the end of February.

Loisel had saved eighteen thousand francs that his father had left him. He would have to borrow the rest.

He borrowed, asking a thousand francs from one, five hundred from another, five louis° here, three louis there. He wrote promissory notes, undertook ruinous obligations, did business with finance companies and the whole tribe of loan sharks. He compromised himself for the remainder of his days, risked his signature without knowing whether he would be able to honor it; and, terrified by anguish over the future, by the black misery that was about to descend on him, by the prospect of all kinds of physical deprivations and moral tortures, he went to get the new necklace, and put down thirty-six thousand francs on the jeweler's counter.

95   Mrs. Loisel took the necklace back to Mrs. Forrestier, who said with an offended tone:

Loisel's plan to explain delaying the return. He takes charge; he is resourceful.

Things are hopeless.

Note that Loisel does not even suggest that they explain things to Mrs. Forrestier. They hunt for a replacement.

A new diamond necklace will cost 36,000 francs, a monumental amount.

They make a deal with the jeweler. (Is Maupassant hinting that things might work out for them?)
It will take all of Loisel's inheritance . . .
. . . plus another 18,000 francs that must be borrowed at enormous rates of interest.

°*louis:* a gold coin worth twenty francs.

"You should have brought it back sooner; I might have needed it."

She did not open the case, as her friend feared she might. If she had noticed the substitution, what would she have thought? What would she have said? Would she not have taken her for a thief?

Mrs. Forrestier is offended and complains about Mathilde's delay.

Is this enough justification for not telling the truth? It seems to be for the Loisels.

Mrs. Loisel soon discovered the horrible life of the needy. She did her share, however, completely, heroically. That horrifying debt had to be paid. She would pay. They dismissed the maid; they changed their address; they rented an attic flat.

A new section, the fifth.

She learned to do the heavy housework, dirty kitchen jobs. She washed the dishes, wearing away her manicured fingernails on greasy pots and en- crusted baking dishes. She handwashed dirty linen, shirts, and dish towels that she hung out on the line to dry. Each morning, she took the garbage down to the street, and she carried up water, stopping at each floor to catch her breath. And, dressed in cheap housedresses, she went to the fruit dealer, the gro- cer, the butchers, with her basket under her arms, haggling, insulting, defending her measly cash penny by penny.

They suffer to repay their debts. Loisel works late at night. Mathilde accepts a cheap attic flat, and does all the heavy housework herself to save on domestic help.

She pinches pennies, and haggles with the local tradesmen.

They had to make installment payments every month, and, to buy more time, to refinance loans.

They struggle to meet payments. 100

The husband worked evenings to make fair copies of tradesmen's accounts, and late into the night he made copies at five cents a page.

And this life lasted ten years.

Mr. Loisel moonlights to make extra money.
For ten years they struggle, but they endure.

At the end of ten years, they had paid back everything—everything—including the extra charges imposed by loan sharks and the accumulation of compound interest.

Another new section, the sixth of the story.
The Loisels have successfully paid back the loans. They have been quite virtuous.

Mrs. Loisel looked old now. She had become the strong, hard, and rude woman of poor households. Her hair unkempt, with uneven skirts and rough, red hands, she spoke loudly, washed floors with large buckets of water. But sometimes, when her husband was at work, she sat down near the win- dow, and she dreamed of that evening so long ago, of that party, where she had been so beautiful and so admired.

Mrs. Loisel (why does the narrator not say "Mathilde"?) is rough- ened and aged by the work. But she has behaved "heroically" (paragraph 98), and has shown her mettle.

What would life have been like if she had not lost that necklace? Who knows? Who knows? Life is so peculiar, so uncertain. How little a thing it takes to destroy you or to save you!

A moral? Small, uncertain things 105 *shape our lives; we hang by a thread.*

Well, one Sunday, when she had gone for a stroll along the Champs-Elysées to relax from the cares of the week, she suddenly noticed a woman walking with a child. It was Mrs. Forrestier, still youthful, still beautiful, still attractive.

Mrs. Loisel felt moved. Would she speak to her? Yes, certainly. And now that she had paid, she could tell all. Why not?

She walked closer.

"Hello, Jeanne."

110 The other gave no sign of recognition and was astonished to be addressed so familiarly by this working-class woman. She stammered:

"But . . . Madam! . . . I don't know. . . . You must have made a mistake."

"No. I'm Mathilde Loisel."

Her friend cried out:

"Oh! . . . My poor Mathilde, you've changed so much."

115 "Yes. I've had some tough times since I saw you last; in fact hardships . . . and all because of you! . . ."

"Of me . . . how so?"

"You remember the diamond necklace that you lent me to go to the party at the Ministry of Education?"

"Yes. What then?"

"Well, I lost it."

120 "How, since you gave it back to me?"

"I returned another exactly like it. And for ten years we've been paying for it. You understand this wasn't easy for us, who have nothing. . . . Finally it's over, and I'm damned glad."

Mrs. Forrestier stopped her.

"You say that you bought a diamond necklace to replace mine?"

"Yes, you didn't notice it, eh? It was exactly like yours."

125 And she smiled with proud and childish joy.

Mrs. Forrestier, deeply moved, took both her hands.

"Oh, my poor Mathilde! But mine was only costume jewelry. At most, it was worth only five hundred francs! . . ."

The seventh part of the story, a scene on the Champs-Elysées. Mathilde sees Jeanne Forrestier for the first time in the previous ten years.

Jeanne notes Mathilde's changed appearance.

Mathilde tells Jeanne everything.

SURPRISE! The lost necklace was not made of real diamonds, and the Loisels have slaved for no reason at all. But hard work and sacrifice probably brought out better qualities in Mathilde than she otherwise might have shown. Is this the moral of the story?

Reading and Responding in a Notebook or Compu

The marginal comments printed with "The Necklace" demonstrate the active reading-responding process you should apply to everything you read. Use the margins in your text similarly to record your comments and questions, but plan also to record your more lengthy responses in a notebook, on note cards, on separate sheets of paper, or in a computer file. Be careful not to lose anything; keep all your notes. As you progress from work to work, you will find that your written or saved comments will be immensely important to you as your record, or journal, of your first impressions, together with your more carefully considered and expanded thoughts.

In keeping your notebook, your objective should be to learn assigned works inside and out and then to say perceptive things about them. To achieve this goal, you need to read the work more than once. Develop a good note-taking system so that as you read, you will create a "memory bank" of your own knowledge. You can make withdrawals from this fund of ideas when you begin to write. As an aid in developing your own procedures for reading and "depositing" your ideas, you may wish to begin with the following *Guidelines for Reading*. Of course, you will want to modify these suggestions and add to them as you become a more experienced and disciplined reader.

Guidelines for Reading

1. Observations for basic understanding
   a. Explain words, situations, and concepts. Write down words that are new or not immediately clear. Use your dictionary, and record the relevant meanings in your notebook. Write down special difficulties so that you can ask your instructor about them.
   b. Determine what is happening in the work. For a story or play, where do the actions take place? What do they show? Who is involved? Who is the major figure? Why is he or she major? What relationships do the characters have with one another? What concerns do the characters have? What do they do? Who says what to whom? How do the speeches advance the action and reveal the characters? For a poem, what is the situation? Who is talking, and to whom? What does the speaker say about the situation? Why does the poem end as it does and where it does?

2. Notes on first impressions
   a. Make a record of your reactions and responses. What did you think was memorable, noteworthy, funny, or otherwise striking? Did you worry, get scared, laugh, smile, feel a thrill, learn a great deal, feel proud, find a lot to think about?
   b. Describe interesting characterizations, events, techniques, and ideas. If you like a character or an idea, explain what you like, and do the same for characters and ideas you don't like. Is there anything else in the

work that you especially like or dislike? Are parts easy or difficult to understand? Why? Are there any surprises? What was your reaction to them? Be sure to use your own words when writing your explanations.

3. Development of ideas and enlargement of responses

a. Trace developing patterns. Make an outline or a scheme: What conflicts appear? Do these conflicts exist between people, groups, or ideas? How are the conflicts resolved? Is one force, idea, or side the winner? How do you respond to the winner or to the loser?

b. Write expanded notes about characters, situations, and actions. What explanations need to be made about the characters? What is the nature of the situations (e.g., young people discover a damaged boat, and themselves, in the spring; a prisoner tries to hide her baby from cruel guards, and so on)? What is the nature of the actions (e.g., a mother and daughter go shopping, a series of strangers intrude upon the celebration of a Christening, a woman is told that her husband has been killed in a train wreck, a group of children are taken to a fashionable toy store, and so on)? What are the people like, and what are their habits and customs? What sort of language do they use?

c. Memorize important, interesting, and well-written passages. Copy them in full on note cards, and keep these in your pocket or purse. When walking to class, riding public transportation, or otherwise not occupying your time, learn them by heart. Please take memorization seriously.

d. Always write down questions that come up during your reading. You may raise these in class, and trying to write out your own answers will also aid your own study.

Sample Notebook Entries on Maupassant's "The Necklace"

The following entries illustrate how you can use the guidelines in your first thoughts about a work. You should try to develop enough observations and responses to be useful later, both for additional study and for developing essays. Notice that the entries are not only comments but also questions.

Early in the story, Mathilde seems to be spoiled. She and her husband are not well off, but she is unable to face her own situation.

She is a dreamer but seems harmless. Her daydreams about a fancy home, with all the expensive belongings, are not unusual. It would be unusual to find people who do not have such dreams.

She is embarrassed by her husband's taste for plain food. The storyteller contrasts her taste for trout and quail with Loisel's cheaper favorites.

When the Loisels get the invitation to the ball, Mathilde becomes difficult. Her wish for an expensive dress (the cost of Loisel's shotgun) creates a problem, and she creates another problem by wanting to wear fine jewelry.

Her change in character can be related to the places in the story: the Street of Martyrs, the dinner party scene, the attic flat. Also she fills the places she daydreams about with the most expensive things she can imagine.

[handwritten margin note: Nancy is left in the end. Save her. Situation alone, left on the outside]

Her success at the party shows that she has the charm the storyteller talks about in paragraph 2. She seems never to have had any other chance to exert her power.

The worst part of her personality is shown in rushing away from the party because she is ashamed of her shabby everyday shawl. It is Mathilde's unhappiness and unwillingness to adjust to her modest means that cause the financial downfall of the Loisels. This disaster is her fault.

Borrowing the money to replace the necklace shows that both Loisel and Mathilde have a strong sense of honor. Making up the loss is good, even if it destroys them financially.

There are some nice touches, like Loisel's seeming to be five years older (paragraph 86) and his staying with the other husbands of women enjoying themselves (paragraph 54). These are well done.

It's too bad that Loisel and Mathilde don't confess to Jeanne that the jewels are lost. Their pride or their honor stops them—or perhaps their fear of being accused of theft.

Their ten years of slavish work (paragraphs 98–102) show how they have come down in life. Mathilde does all her work by hand, so she really does pitch in and is, as the narrator says, heroic.

The attic flat is important. Mathilde becomes loud and frumpy when living there (paragraph 99), but she also develops strength. She does what she has to. The earlier apartment and the elegance of her imaginary rooms had brought out her limitations.

The setting of the Champs-Elysées also reflects her character, for she feels free there to tell Jeanne about the disastrous loss and sacrifice (paragraph 121), producing the surprise ending.

The narrator's statement "How little a thing it takes to destroy you or to save you!" (paragraph 105) is full of thought. The necklace is little, but it makes a huge problem. This creates the story's irony.

Questions: Is this story more about the surprise ending or about the character of Mathilde? Is she to be condemned or admired? Does the outcome stem from the little things that make us or break us, as the narrator suggests, or from the difficulty of rising above one's economic class, which seems true, or both? What do the speaker's remarks about women's status mean? (Remember, the story was published in 1884.) This probably isn't relevant, but wouldn't Jeanne, after hearing about the substitution, give the full value of the necklace to the Loisels, and wouldn't they then be pretty well off?

These are reasonable—and also fairly full—remarks and observations about "The Necklace." Use your notebook or journal similarly for all reading assignments. If your assignment is simply to learn about a work, general notes like these should be enough. If you are preparing for a test, you might write pointed observations more in line with what is happening in your class, and also write and answer your own questions (see Chapter 19, "Writing Examinations on Literature"). If you have a writing assignment, observations like these can help you focus more closely on your topic—such as character, idea, or setting. Whatever your purpose, always take good notes, and put in as many details and responses as you can. The notes will be invaluable to you as a mind refresher and as a wellspring of thought.

Writing Essays on Literary Topics

Finished writing is the sharpened, focused expression of thought and study. It begins with the search for something to say—an idea. Not all ideas are equal; some are better than others, and getting good ideas is an ability that you will develop the more you think and write. As you discover ideas and explain them in words, you will also improve your perceptions and increase your critical faculties.

In addition, because literature itself contains the subject material (though not in a systematic way) of philosophy, religion, psychology, sociology, and politics, learning to analyze literature and to write about it will also improve your capacity to deal with these and other disciplines.

Writing Does Not Come Easily—for Anyone

A major purpose of your being in college, of which your composition and literature course is a vital part, is to develop your capacity to think and to express your thoughts clearly and fully. However, the process of creating a successfully argued essay—the actual process itself of writing—is not automatic. Writing begins in uncertainty and hesitation, and it becomes certain and confident—accomplished—only as a result of great care, applied thought, a certain amount of experimentation, the passage of time, and much effort. When you read complete, polished, well-formed pieces of writing, you might assume, as many of us do, that the writers wrote their successful versions the first time they tried and never needed to make any changes and improvements at all. In an ideal world, perhaps, something like this could happen, but not in this one.

If you could see the early drafts of writing you admire, you would be surprised and startled—and also encouraged—to see that good writers are also human and that what they first write is often uncertain, vague, tangential, tentative, incomplete, and messy. Good writers do not always like their first drafts; nevertheless, they work with their efforts and build upon them. They reconsider their ideas and try to restate them, discard some details, add others, chop paragraphs in half and reassemble the parts elsewhere, throw out much (and then maybe recover some of it), revise or completely rewrite sentences, change words, correct misspellings, sharpen expressions, and add new material to tie all the parts together in a smooth, natural flow.

The Goal of Writing: To Show a Process of Thought

As you approach the task of writing, you should constantly realize that your goal should always be to *explain* the work you are analyzing. You should never be satisfied simply to restate the events in the work. Too often students fall easily into a pattern of retelling a story or play, or of summarizing the details of a poem. But nothing could be further from what is expected from good writing. You need to demonstrate your thought. Thinking is an active process that does not happen accidentally. Thinking requires that you develop ideas, draw conclusions, exemplify them and support them with details, and connect everything in a coherent manner. Your goal should constantly be to explain the results of your thinking—your ideas, your play of mind over the materials of a work, your insights, your conclusions. This is the ideal.

Approach each writing assignment with the following thoughts in mind: You should consider your reader as a person who has read the work, just as you have done. This person knows what is in the work, and therefore does not need you to restate what she or he already knows. Instead, your reader wants to learn from you what to think about it. Therefore, always, your task as a writer is to explain something about the work, to describe the thoughts that you can develop about it. Let us consider the story we have just read, Maupassant's "The Necklace." We have recognized that the main character, Mathilde Loisel, is a young Parisian housewife who is married to a minor clerk in the Ministry of Education. We know this, but if we are reading an essay about the story we will want to learn more. Let us then suppose that a first goal of one of your paragraphs is to explain the deep dissatisfaction Mathilde feels in the early part of the story. Your paragraph might go as follows:

> In the early part of the story Maupassant establishes that Mathilde is deeply dissatisfied with her life. Her threadbare furniture and drab walls are a cause of her unhappiness. Under these circumstances her daydreams of beautiful rooms staffed by "elegant valets," together with a number of rooms for intimate conversations with friends, multiply her dissatisfaction. The meager meals that she shares with her husband make her imagine sumptuous banquets that she feels are rightfully hers by birth but that are denied her because of her circumstances. The emphasis in these early scenes of the story is always on Mathilde's discontentment and frustration.

Notice here that your paragraph ties the story's events to the idea of Mathilde's unhappiness. The events are there, but you are explaining to us, as readers, that the events are directly related to Mathilde's unhappiness. The paragraph illustrates a process of thought. Here is another way in which you might use a thought to connect the same materials:

> In the early part of the story Maupassant emphasizes the economic difficulty of Mathilde's life. The threadbare furniture and ugly curtains, for example, highlight that there is no money to purchase better things. The same

sparseness of existence is shown by the meager meals that she shares with her husband. With the capacity to appreciate better things, Mathilde is forced by circumstances to make do with worse. Her dreams of sumptuous banquets are therefore natural, given her level of frustration with the life around her. In short, her unhappiness is an understandable consequence of her aversion to her plain and drab apartment and the tightness of money.

Here the details are substantially the same as in our first paragraph, but they are unified by a different idea, namely the economic constraints of Mathilde's life. What is important is that neither paragraph tells only the details. Instead the paragraphs illustrate the goal of writing with a purpose. Whenever you write, you should always be trying, as in these examples, to use a dominating thought or thoughts to shape the details in the work you are analyzing.

Three Major Stages in Thinking and Writing: Discovering Ideas, Making Initial Drafts, and Completing the Essay

For both practiced and beginning writers alike, there are three basic stages of composition, and in each of these there are characteristic activities. In the beginning stage, writers try to find the details and thoughts that seem to be right for eventual inclusion in what they are hoping to write. The next (or middle) stage is characterized by written drafts, or sketches—ideas, sentences, paragraphs. The final or completion stage is the forming and ordering of what has previously been done—the creation and determination of a final essay. Although these stages occur in a natural order, they are not separate and distinct, but merge with each other and in effect are fused together. Thus, when you are close to finishing your essay you may find that you need something else, something more, and something different. At this point you can easily recreate an earlier stage to discover new details and ideas. You might say that your work is always tentative until you regard it as finished or until you need to turn it in.

Discovering Ideas ("Brainstorming")

With the foregoing general goal in mind, let us assume that you have read the work about which you are to write and have made notes and observations on which you are planning to base your thought. You are now ready to consider and plan what to include in your essay. This earliest stage of writing is unpredictable and somewhat frustrating because you are on a search. You do not know quite what you want, for you are reaching out for ideas and you are not yet sure what they are and what you might say about them. This process of searching and discovery, sometimes also called brainstorming, requires you to examine any and every subject that your mind can produce.

Just as you are trying to reach for ideas, however, you also should try to introduce purpose and resolution into your thought. You have to zero in on something specific, and develop your ideas through this process. Although what you first write may seem indefinite, the best way to help your thinking is to put your mind, figuratively, into specific channels or grooves, and then to confine your thoughts within these boundaries. What matters is to get your mind going on a particular topic and to get your thoughts down on paper or onto a computer screen. Once you can see your thoughts in front of you, you can work with them and develop them. The following drawing can be helpful to you as an illustration of the various facets of a literary work, or ways of talking about it.

Consider the work you have read—story, poem, play—as the central circle, from which a number of points, like the rays of a star, shine out, some of them prominently, others less so. These points, or rays, are the various subjects, or topics, that you might decide to select in exploration, discovery, and discussion. Notice also that the points grow larger as they get nearer to the work, suggesting that once you select a point of discussion you may amplify that point with details and your own observations about the work.

You can consider literary works in many ways, but for now, as a way of getting started, you might choose to explore (1) the work's characters; (2) its historical period and background; (3) the social and economic conditions it depicts; (4) its major ideas; or (5) any of its artistic qualities.[2] These topics, of course, have many subtopics, but any one of them can help you in the concentration you will need for beginning your essay (and also for classroom discussion). All you need is one topic, just one; don't try everything at the same time. Let us see how our illustration can be revised to account for these topics. This time the number of points is reduced to illustrate the points or approaches we have just raised (with an additional and unnamed point to

---

[2]Together with additional topics, these critical approaches are discussed in more detail in Appendix A.

represent all the other approaches that might be used for other studies). These points represent your ways of discovering ideas about the work.

Study the Characters in the Work

You need not be a practicing psychologist to discuss the persons or characters that you find in a work (see also Chapter 3). You need only to raise issues about the characters and what they do and what they represent. What are the characters like at the work's beginning? What happens to them? Do they do anything that causes them to change, and how are they changed? Are the changes for good or for bad? Why do the characters do the things they do? What do they do correctly? What do they do incorrectly? Why? For example, Mathilde is wrong not to tell Jeanne about her losing the necklace. Such an immediate admission of truth would save her and her husband ten years of hardship and deprivation. But Mathilde doesn't tell the truth. Why not? What do we learn about her character because she avoids or ignores this admission? Is her avoidance understandable? Why?

In discussing character, you might also wish to raise the issue of whether the people in the work do or do not do what might normally be expected from people in their circumstances. Do they correspond to type? The idea here is that certain attitudes and behaviors are typical of people at particular stages of life (e.g., children behaving like children, lovers dealing with their relationship, a young couple coping with difficult finances). Thus we might ask questions about whether the usual circumstances experienced by the characters affect them, either by limiting them in some way or by freeing them. What attitudes seem typical of the characters? How do these attitudes govern what the characters do, or don't do? For example, one of the most typical circumstances of life is marriage. According to the positive and ideal type of marriage, a husband and wife should be forthcoming with each other; they should tell each other things and should not conceal what is on their minds. If they have problems, they should discuss them and try to solve them together. In "The Necklace" we see that Mathilde and Loisel do not show these desired qualities, and their absence of communication can be seen as an

THE NEED TO PRESENT AN ARGUMENT WHEN WRITING ESSAYS ABOUT LITERATURE

As you write about literature, you should always keep trying to connect your explanations to a specific **argument**; that is, you are writing about a specific work, but you are trying to *prove*—or *demonstrate*—a point or idea about it. This book provides you with a number of separate subjects relating to the study of literature. As you select one of these and begin writing, however, you are not to explain just that such-and-such a story has a character who changes and grows, or that such-and-such a poem contains the thought that nature creates great beauty. Rather, you should demonstrate the importance of your topic to the work as a whole in relation to a specific point or argument. One example of an argument might be that a story's first-person point of view permits readers to draw their own conclusions about the speaker's character. Another argument might be that the poet's thought is shown in a poem's details about the bustling sounds and sights of animals in springtime.

Let us therefore repeat and stress that your writing should always have an argumentative edge—a goal of demonstrating the truth of your conclusions and clarifying and illuminating your idea about the topic and also about the work. It is here that the accuracy of your choices of details from the work, the soundness of your conclusions, and the cumulative weight of your evidence are essential. You cannot allow your main ideas to rest on one detail alone, but must support your conclusions by showing that the bulk of material leads to them and that they are linked in a reasonable chain of fact and logic. It is such clarification that is the goal of argumentation.

element in their financial catastrophe. However, during their long years of trouble they work together, for they share a typical quality of honesty, and in this respect they fulfill their role, or type, as a married couple.

An analysis of typical attitudes themselves can also furnish you with material for discussion. For example, Mathilde, who is a member of the lower commercial class, has attitudes that are more appropriate to the upper or leisure class. She cannot bridge this gap, and her frustration causes her to nag her husband to give her enough money to live out her dream, if only for a moment.

Determine the Work's Historical Period and Background

An obvious topic is the historical circumstances of the work. When was the work written? How well does it portray details about life at the time it appeared? What is historically unique about it? To what degree does it help you learn something about the past that you did not previously know? What actions in the work are like or unlike actions going on at the present time? What truthfulness to life do you discover in the work? In "The Necklace," for example, which was published more than a century ago, Mathilde's duty is to stay at home as a housewife—a traditional role—while her husband is the family breadwinner. After the loss of the necklace she can no longer afford domestic help, and she is compelled to do all her own housework and her own shopping. She has none of today's home conveniences such as a refrigerator, dishwasher, microwave, or car. Her husband, a clerk or secretary-copyist, spends his working day copying business records by hand, for at the period of the story there were no typewriters or word processors. Discussing matters like these might also help you with works written during modern times, because our own assumptions, artifacts, and habits will bear analysis and discussion.

Describe the Social and Economic Conditions Depicted in the Work

Closely related to the historical period, an obvious topic to pursue in many works is the social and economic condition of the characters. To what level of life, economically, do the characters belong? How are events in the work related to their condition? How does their money, or lack of it, limit what they do? How do their economic circumstances either restrict or liberate their imaginations? How do their jobs and their apparent income determine their way of life? If we ask some of these questions about "The Necklace," as we have seen, we find that Mathilde and her husband are greatly burdened by their lack of money, and also that their obligation to repay their huge loan drives them into economic want and sacrifice.

An important part of the social and economic analysis of literature is the consideration of female characters and what it means to be a woman. This is the feminist analysis of literature, which asks questions like these: What role is Mathilde compelled to take as a result of her sex and family background? How does Jeanne's way of life contrast with that of Mathilde? What can Mathilde do with her life? To what degree is she limited by her role as a housewife? Does she have any chance of an occupation outside the home? How does her economic condition cause her to yearn for better things? What causes her to borrow the necklace? What is her contribution, as a woman, to the repayment of the loans? Should Mathilde's limited life in "The Necklace" be considered as a political argument for greater freedom for women? Once you start asking questions like these, you will find that your thinking is developing along with your ideas for writing.

The feminist approach to the interpretation of literature has been well established, and it will usually provide you with a way to discuss a work. It is also possible, of course, to analyze what a work says about the condition of being a man, or being a child. Depending on the work, many of the questions important in a feminist approach are not dissimilar to those you might use if you are dealing with childhood or male adulthood.

One of the most important social and economic topics is that of race and ethnicity. What happens in the work that seems to occur mainly because of the race of the characters? Is the author pointing out any deprivations, any absence of opportunity, any oppression? What do the characters do under such circumstances? Do they succeed or not? Are they negative? Are they angry? Are they resolute and determined? Your aim in an inquiry of this type should be to concentrate on actions and ideas in the work that are clearly related to race.

Explain the Work's Major Ideas

One of the major ways of focusing on a work is to zero in on various ideas and values or issues to be discovered there. What ideas might we gain from the story of the lengthy but needless sacrifice and drudgery experienced by Mathilde and her husband? One obvious and acceptable idea is presented by the speaker, namely, that even the smallest, most accidental incident can cause immense consequences. This is an idea that we might expand and illustrate in an entire essay. Here are some other ideas that we also might pursue, all of them based on the story's actions.

- Many actions have unforeseeable and uncontrollable consequences.
- Lack of communication is a major cause of hardship.
- Adversity brings out a character's good qualities.
- Mutual effort enables people to overcome difficulties.

These ideas are all to be found in Maupassant's story. In other works, of course, we may find comparable ideas, in addition to other major ideas and issues.

Learn About and Describe the Work's Artistic Qualities

A work's artistic qualities provide many possible topics for studying, but basically here you may consider matters such as the work's plan or organization and the author's narrative method, writing style, or poetic techniques. Thus, in "The Necklace," we observe that almost the entire story develops with Mathilde at the center (narrative method; see also Chapter 4, on point of view). At first, the story brings us close to Mathilde, for we are told of her dissatisfaction and impatience with her surroundings. As the story progresses, the storyteller/speaker presents her person and actions more objectively and also more distantly. Another artistic approach would be to determine the story's pattern of development—how, chronologically, the loss of the necklace brings financial misfortune to the Loisels. We might also look for the author's inclusion of symbols in the story, such as the name of the street where the Loisels originally live, their move to an attic flat, or the roughness of Mathilde's hands as a result of her constant housework. There are many other ways to consider the formal aspects of a literary work.

Assembling Materials and Beginning to Write

By this time you will already have been focusing on your topic and will have assembled much that you can put into your essay. You should now aim to develop paragraphs and sketches of what you will eventually include. You should think constantly of the point or argument you want to develop, but invariably digressions will occur, together with other difficulties—false starts, dead ends, total cessation of thought, digressions, despair, hopelessness, and general frustration. Remember, however, that it is important just to start. Jump right in and start writing anything at all—no matter how unacceptable your first efforts may seem—and force yourself to deal with the materials. The writing down of ideas does not commit you. You should not think that these first ideas are untouchable and holy just because you have written them on paper or on your computer screen. You can throw them out in favor of new ideas, you can make cross-outs and changes, and you can move paragraphs or even sections around as you wish. However, if you do not start writing, your first thoughts will remain locked in your mind and you will have nothing to work with. You must learn to accept the uncertainties in the writing process and make them work *for* you rather than *against* you.

Build on Your Original Notes

You need to get your mind going by mining your notebook or computer file for useful things you have already written. Thus, let us use an observation in our original set of notes—"The attic flat is important," in reference to the poorer rooms where Mathilde and her husband live while they are paying back their creditors. With such a note as a start, you might develop a number of ideas to support an argument about Mathilde's character, as in the following:

> The attic flat is important. Early in the story, in her apartment, Mathilde is dreamy and impractical. She seems delicate, but after losing the necklace, she is delicate no longer. She becomes a worker after they move to the flat. She does a lot more when living there.
>
> In the flat, Mathilde has to sacrifice. She gives up her servant, washes greasy pots, climbs stairs carrying buckets of water, sloshes water around to clean floors, and does all the clothes washing by hand.
>
> When living in the flat she gets stronger, but she also becomes loud and common. She argues with shopkeepers to get the lowest prices. She stops caring for herself. There is a reversal here, from incapable and well groomed to capable but coarse.

In this way, even in an assertion as basic as "The attic flat is important," the process of putting together details is a form of concentrated thought that leads you creatively forward. You can express thoughts and conclusions that you could not express at the beginning. Such an exercise in stretching your mind leads you to put elements of the work together in ways that create ideas for good essays.

Trace Patterns of Action and Thought

You can also discover ideas by making a list or scheme for the story or main idea. What conflicts appear? Do these conflicts exist between people, groups, or ideas? How does the author resolve them? Is one force, idea, or side the winner? Why? How do you respond to the winner or to the loser? Using this method, you might make a list similar to this one:

> At the beginning, Mathilde is a fish out of water. She dreams of wealth, but her life is drab and her husband is dull.
>
> Fantasies make her even more dissatisfied; she punishes herself by thinking of a wealthy life.
>
> When the Loisels get the dinner invitation Mathilde pouts and whines. Her husband feels discomfort when she manipulates him into buying her an expensive party dress.
>
> Her world of daydreams hurts her real life when her desire for wealth causes her to borrow the necklace. Losing the necklace is just plain bad luck.

These arguments all focus on Mathilde's character, but you may wish to trace other patterns you find in the story. If you start planning an essay about another pattern, be sure to account for all the actions and scenes that relate to your topic. Otherwise, you may miss a piece of evidence that could lead you to new conclusions.

Raise and Answer Your Own Questions

A habit you should always cultivate is to raise and answer questions as you read. The *Guidelines for Reading* will help you formulate questions (pages 13–14), but you can raise additional questions like these:

- What is happening as the work unfolds? How does an action at the work's beginning bring about the work's later actions and speeches?
- Who are the main characters? What seems unusual or different about what they do in the work?
- What conclusions can you draw about the work's actions, scenes, and situations? Explain these conclusions.
- What are the characters and speakers like? What do they do and say about themselves, their goals, the people around them, their families, their friends, their work, and the general circumstances of their lives?
- What kinds of words do the characters use: formal or informal words, slang or profanity?
- What literary conventions and devices have you discovered, and how do these affect the work? (When an author addresses readers directly, for example, that is a convention; when a comparison is used, that is a device, which might be either a metaphor or a simile.)

Of course, you can raise other questions as you reread the piece, or you can be left with one or two major questions that you decide to pursue.

Use the Plus-Minus, Pro-Con,
or Either-Or Method for Putting Ideas Together

A common and very helpful method of discovering ideas is to develop a set of contrasts: plus-minus, pro-con, either-or. Let us suppose a plus-minus method of considering the following question about Mathilde: Should she be "admired" (plus) or "condemned" (minus)?

Plus: Admired?	Minus: Condemned?
After she cries when they get the invitation, she recovers with a "strong effort"—maybe she doesn't want her husband to feel bad.	She wants to be envied and admired only for being attractive and intriguing, not for more important qualities. She seems spoiled and selfish.
She scores a great victory at the dance. She really does have the power to charm and captivate.	She wastes her time in daydreaming about things she can't have, and she whines because she is unhappy.
Once she loses the necklace, she and her husband become poor and deprived. But she does "her share . . . completely, heroically" (paragraph 98) to make up for the loss.	Even though the Loisels live poorly, Mathilde manipulates her husband into giving her more money than they can afford for a party dress.
Even when she is poor, she dreams about that marvelous, shining moment at the great ball. This is pathetic, because Mathilde gets worse than she deserves.	She assumes that her friend Jeanne would think her a thief if she admitted losing the necklace. Shouldn't she have had more confidence in Jeanne?
At the end, after everything is paid back, and her reputation is secure, Mathilde confesses the loss to Jeanne.	She becomes loud and coarse and haggles about pennies, thus undergoing a cheapening of her person and manner.

By putting contrasting observations side by side in this way, you will find that ideas will start to come naturally and will be helpful to you when you begin writing, regardless of how you finally organize your essay. It's possible, for example, that you might develop either column as the argumentative basis of an essay, or you might use your notes to support the idea that Mathilde is too complex to be either wholly admired or wholly condemned. You might also want to introduce an entirely new topic of development, such as that Mathilde should be pitied rather than condemned or admired. In short, arranging materials in the plus-minus pattern is a powerful way to discover ideas—a truly helpful habit of promoting thought—that can lead to ways of development that you do not at first realize.

Use Your Writing to Develop Your Thinking

You should always write down what you are thinking for, as a principle, unwritten thought is incomplete thought. Make a practice of writing your observations about the work, in addition to any questions that occur to you. This is an exciting step in preliminary writing because it can be useful when you write later drafts. You will discover that looking at what you have written not only can enable you to correct and improve the writing you have done, but also can lead you to recognize that you need more. The process goes just about like this: "Something needs to be added here—important details that my reader will not have noticed, new support for my argument, a new idea that has just occurred to me, a significant connection to link my thoughts." If you follow such a process, you will be using your own written ideas to create new ideas. You will be advancing your own abilities as a thinker and writer.

The processes just described of searching for ideas, or brainstorming, are useful for you at any stage of composition. Even when you are fairly close to finishing your essay, you might suddenly recognize that you need to add something more (or subtract something you don't like). When that happens, you may return to the discovery or brainstorming process to initiate and develop new ideas and new arguments.

Drafting Your Essay

As you use the brainstorming and focusing techniques, you are also in fact beginning your essay. You will need to revise your ideas as connections among them become clearer and as you reexamine the work to discover details to support the argument you are making. By this stage, however, you already have many of the raw materials you need for developing your topic.

Base Your Essay on a Central Idea or Central Argument

By definition, an essay *is an organized, connected, and fully developed set of paragraphs that expand on a* **central idea** *or* **central argument**. All parts of an essay should contribute to the reader's understanding of the idea. To achieve unity and completeness, each paragraph refers to the argument and demonstrates how selected details from the work relate to it and support it. The central idea helps you control and shape your essay, just as it also provides guidance for your reader.

A successful essay about literature is a brief but thorough (not exhaustive) examination of a literary work in light of topics like those we have already raised, such as character, background, economic conditions, circumstances of gender, major ideas, artistic qualities, or any additional topic such as point of view and symbolism. Central ideas or arguments might be (1) that a character is strong and tenacious; or (2) that the story shows the unpredictability of action; or (3) that the point of view makes the action seem "distant and objective"; or (4) that a major symbol governs the actions and thoughts of the major characters. In essays on these topics, all materials must be tied to such central ideas or arguments. Thus, it is a fact that Mathilde in "The Necklace" endures ten years of slavish work and sacrifice as she and her husband accumulate enough money to repay their monumental debt. This we know, but it is not relevant to an essay on her character unless you connect it by a central argument showing how it demonstrates one of her major traits—her growing strength and perseverance.

Look through all of your ideas for one or two that catch your eye for development. In all the early stages of preliminary writing, the chances are that you have already discovered at least a few ideas that are more thought provoking, or more important, than the others.

Once you choose an idea you think you can work with, write it as a complete sentence that is essential to the argument of your essay. A simple phrase such as "setting and character" does not focus thought the way a sentence does. A sentence moves the topic toward new exploration and discovery because it combines a topic with an outcome, such as "The setting of 'The Necklace' reflects Mathilde's character." You can choose to be even more specific: "Mathilde's strengths and weaknesses are reflected in the real and imaginary places in 'The Necklace.'"

Now that you have phrased a single, central idea or argument for your essay, you also have established a guide by which you can accept, reject, rearrange, and change the ideas you have been planning to develop. You can now draft a few paragraphs (which you may base on some of the sketches you have already made; always use as much as you can of your early observations) to see whether your idea seems valid, or you can decide that it would be more helpful to make an outline or a list before you do more writing. In either case, you should use your notes for evidence to connect to your central idea. If you need to bolster your argument with more supporting details and ideas, go once again to the techniques of discovery and brainstorming.

Using the central idea that the changes in the story's settings reflect Mathilde's character might produce a paragraph like the following, which presents an argument about her negative qualities:

> The original apartment in the Street of Martyrs and the dream world of wealthy places both show negative sides of Mathilde's character. The real-life apartment, though livable, is shabby. The furnishings all bring out her discontent. The shabbiness makes her think only of luxuriousness, and having one servant girl causes her to dream of having many servants. The luxury of her dream life heightens her unhappiness with what she actually has.

In such a preliminary draft, in which the purpose is to connect details and thoughts to the major idea, many details from the story are used in support. In the final draft, this kind of support is essential.

WRITING BY HAND, TYPEWRITER, OR WORD PROCESSOR

Thinking and writing are interdependent processes. If you don't get your thoughts into writing in some way, your thinking will be incomplete. It is therefore vital for you to use the writing process as the means of developing your ideas. For many students, it is a psychological necessity to carry out this process by pencil, pen, or typewriter. If you are one of these students, make your written or typed responses on only one side of your paper or note cards. This strategy will enable you to spread your materials out and get an actual physical overview of them when you begin writing. Everything will be open to you; none of your ideas will be hidden on the back of the paper.

Today, word processing is thoroughly established as an indispensable tool for writers. The word processor can help you develop ideas, for it quickly enables you to eliminate unworkable thoughts and replace them with others. You can move sentences and paragraphs into new contexts, test how they look, and move them somewhere else if you choose.

In addition, with the rapid printers now available, you can print even the initial and tentative stages of writing. Using the printed draft, you can make additional notes, corrections, and suggestions for further development. With the marked-up draft as a guide, you can go back to the word processor and fill in your changes and improvements, repeating this procedure as often as you can. This facility makes the machine an incentive for improvement, right up to your final draft.

Word processing also helps you in the final preparation of your essays. Studies have shown that errors and awkward sentences are frequently found at the bottoms of pages prepared by hand or with a conventional typewriter. The reason is that writers hesitate to make improvements when they get near the end of a page because they shun the dreariness of starting the page over. Word processors eliminate this difficulty completely. Changes can be made anywhere in the draft, at any time, without damage to the final appearance of your essay.

Regardless of your writing method, you should always remember that unwritten thought is incomplete thought. You cannot lay everything out at once on the word processor's screen. You can see only a small part of what you are writing. Therefore, somewhere in your writing process, you need to prepare a complete draft of what you have written. A clean, readable draft permits you to gather everything together and to make even more improvements through revision.

Create a Thesis Sentence

With your central idea or argument as your focus, you can decide which of the earlier observations and ideas can be developed further. Your goal is to establish a number of major topics to support your argument and to express them in a **thesis sentence**—an organizing sentence that contains the major topics you plan to treat in your essay. Suppose you choose three ideas from your discovery stage of development. If you put the central idea at the left and the list of topics at the right, you have the shape of the thesis sentence. Note that the first two topics below are taken from the discovery paragraph.

Central Idea	Topics
The setting of "The Necklace" reflects Mathilde's character.	1. First apartment 2. Dream-life mansion rooms 3. Attic flat

This arrangement leads to the following thesis statement or thesis sentence.

> Mathilde's character growth is related to her first apartment, her dream-life mansion rooms, and her attic flat.

You can revise the thesis sentence at any stage of the writing process if you find that you do not have enough evidence from the work to support it. Perhaps a new topic will occur to you, and you can include it, appropriately, as a part of your thesis sentence.

As we have seen, the central idea or central argument is the *glue* of the essay. The thesis sentence lists the parts to be fastened together—that is, the topics in which the central idea is to be demonstrated and argued. To alert your readers to your essay's structure, the thesis sentence is usually placed at the end of the introductory paragraph, just before the body of the essay.

Writing a First Draft

To write a first draft, you support the points of your thesis sentence with your notes and discovery materials. You can alter, reject, and rearrange ideas and details as you wish, as long as you change your thesis sentence to account for the changes (a major reason why many writers write their introductions last). The thesis sentence just shown contains three topics (it could be two, or four, or more) to be used in forming the body of the essay.

Begin Each Paragraph with a Topic Sentence

Just as the organization of the *entire essay* is based on the thesis, the form of each *paragraph* is based on its **topic sentence**. A topic sentence is an assertion about how a topic from the predicate of the thesis statement supports the argument contained or implied in the central idea. The first topic in our example is the relationship of Mathilde's character to her first apartment, and the resulting paragraph should emphasize this relationship. If your topic is the coarsening of her character during the ten-year travail, you can then form a topic sentence by connecting the trait with the location, as follows:

The attic flat reflects the coarsening of Mathilde's character.

Beginning with this sentence, the paragraph will present details that argue how Mathilde's rough, heavy housework changes her behavior, appearance, and general outlook.

Select Only One Topic—No More—for Each Paragraph

You should treat each separate topic in a single paragraph—one topic, one paragraph. However, if a topic seems especially difficult, long, and heavily detailed, you can divide it into two or more subtopics, each receiving a separate paragraph of its own—two or more subtopics, two or more separate paragraphs. Should you make this division, your topic then is really a section, and each paragraph in the section should have its own topic sentence.

Use Your Topic Sentence as the Basis of Your Paragraph Development

Once you choose a topic sentence, you can use it to focus your observations and conclusions. Let us see how our topic about the attic flat can be developed in a paragraph of argument:

The attic flat reflects the coarsening of Mathilde's character. Maupassant emphasizes the burdens Mathilde endures to save money, such as mopping floors, cleaning greasy and encrusted pots and pans, taking out the garbage, and washing clothes and dishes by hand. This work makes her rough and coarse, an effect also shown by her giving up care of her hair and hands, wearing the cheapest dresses possible, haggling with the local shopkeepers, and becoming loud and penny-pinching. If at the beginning she is delicate and attractive, at the end she is unpleasant and coarse.

Here, details from the story are introduced to provide support for the topic sentence. All the subjects—the hard work, the lack of personal care, the wearing of cheap dresses, and the haggling with the shopkeepers—are introduced not to retell the story but rather to exemplify the argument the writer is making about Mathilde's character.

Developing an Outline

So far we have been creating an **outline**—that is, a skeletal plan of organization. Some writers never use any outline but prefer informal lists of ideas; others always rely on outlines. Still others insist that they cannot make an outline

USING VERB TENSES
IN THE DISCUSSION OF LITERARY WORKS

Literary works spring into life with each and every reading. You may thus assume that everything happening takes place in the present, and when writing about literature you should use the *present tense of verbs*. It is correct to say, "Mathilde and her husband *work* and *economize* [not *worked* and *economized*] for ten years to pay off the 18,000-franc debt they *undertake* [not *undertook*] to pay for the lost necklace."

When you consider an author's ideas, the present tense is also proper, on the principle that the words of an author are just as alive and current today (and tomorrow) as they were at the moment of writing, even if this same author has been dead for hundreds or even thousands of years.

Because it is incorrect to shift tenses inappropriately, you may encounter a problem when you refer to events that happened before a story's principal action. An instance is Bierce's Civil-War tale "An Occurrence at Owl Creek Bridge," in which a separate section leads us to conclude that Farquhar, a Southerner, was caught by Union forces when attempting an act of sabotage. When you consider situations such as this one, it is important to keep details straight, and thus you can use past tenses as long as you make the connection clear between past and present, as in this example: "The Union soldiers *execute* [present tense] Farquhar by hanging because he *tried* [past tense] to burn the Owl Creek Bridge." This mixing of tenses in the same sentence is correct because it traces the cause-and-effect relationship brought out in the story.

until they have finished writing, and then they use the outline for revising. Regardless of your preference, your final essay should have a tight structure. Therefore, you should use a guiding outline to develop and shape your essay.

The outline we are concerned with here is the **analytical sentence outline**. This type is easier to create than it sounds. It consists of (1) an introduction, including the central idea and the thesis sentence; together with (2) topic sentences that are to be used in each paragraph of the body; followed by (3) a conclusion. When applied to the subject we have been developing, such an outline looks like this:

Title: Setting in "The Necklace" Is Connected to Mathilde's Character

1. **Introduction**
    a. *Central idea:* Maupassant uses setting to show Mathilde's character.
    b. *Thesis statement:* Her character growth is brought out by her first

A problem also arises when you introduce historical or biographical details about a work or author. It is appropriate to use the *past tense* for such details if they genuinely do belong to the past. Thus it is correct to state, "Shakespeare *lived* from 1564 to 1616," or that "Shakespeare *wrote* his tragedy *Hamlet* in about 1600–1601." It is also permissible to mix past and present tenses when you are treating historical facts about a literary work and are also considering it as a living text. Of prime importance is to keep things straight. Here is an example showing how past tenses (in bold) and present tenses (in italic) may be used when appropriate:

> Because *Hamlet* **was** first **performed** in about 1601, Shakespeare most probably **wrote** it shortly before this time. In the play, a tragedy, Shakespeare *treats* an act of vengeance, but more importantly he *demonstrates* the difficulty of ever learning the exact truth. The hero, Prince Hamlet, *is* the focus of this difficulty, for the task of revenge *is assigned* to him by the Ghost of his father. Though the Ghost *claims* that his brother, Claudius, *is* his murderer, Hamlet *is* not able to verify this claim.

Here, the historical details are in the past tense, while all details about the play *Hamlet*, including Shakespeare as the creating author whose ideas and words are still alive, are in the present.

As a general principle, you will be right most of the time if you use the present tense exclusively for literary details and the past tense for historical details. When in doubt, however, *consult your instructor.*

      apartment, her daydreams about elegant rooms in a mansion, and her attic flat.

2. **Body:** *Topic sentences* a, b, and c (and d, e, and f, if necessary)
   a. Details about her first apartment explain her dissatisfaction and depression.
   b. Her daydreams about mansion rooms are like the apartment because they too make her unhappy.
   c. The attic flat reflects the coarsening of her character.

3. **Conclusion**
   a. *Topic sentence:* All details in the story, particularly the setting, are focused on the character of Mathilde.

The *conclusion* may be a summary of the body; it may evaluate the main idea; it may briefly suggest further points of discussion; or it may be a reflection on the details of the body.

Use the Outline in Developing Your Essay

The illustrative essays included throughout this book are organized according to the principles of the analytical sentence outline. To emphasize the shaping effect of these outlines, all central ideas, thesis sentences, and topic sentences are underlined. In your own writing, you can underline or italicize these "skeletal" sentences as a check on your organization. Unless your instructor requires such markings, however, remove them in your final drafts.

The Use of References and Quotations in Writing About Literature

In establishing evidence for the points you make in your essays and essay examinations, you constantly need to refer to various parts of stories, plays, and poems. You also need to include shorter and longer quotations and to keep the time sequences straight within the works you are writing about. In addition, you may need to refer to biographical and historical details that have a bearing on the work or works you are studying. So that your own writing may flow as accurately and naturally as possible, you must be able to integrate these references and distinctions of time clearly and easily.

Integrating Passages and Ideas into Your Essay

Your essays should reflect your own thought as you study and analyze the characteristics, ideas, and qualities of an author's work. In a typical discussion of literature, you are constantly introducing brief summaries, quotations, general interpretations, observations, and independent applications of everything you are discussing. It is not easy to keep these various elements integrated and to keep confusion from arising.

Tread Carefully to Distinguish Your Thoughts from Those of Your Author

Often a major problem is that it is hard for your reader to figure out when *your* ideas have stopped and your *author's* have begun. You must therefore arrange your sentences to make the distinctions clear, but you must also blend your materials so that your reader may follow you easily. Let us see an example of how such problems may be handled. Here, the writer being discussed is the Victorian poet Matthew Arnold (1822–1888). The passage moves from reference to Arnold's ideas to the essay writer's independent application of the ideas.

[1] In his poem "Dover Beach," Arnold states that in past times religious faith was accepted as absolute truth. [2] To symbolize this idea he refers to the ocean, which surrounds all land, and the surf, which constantly rushes onto the earth's shores. [3] According to this symbolism, religious ideas are as vast as the ocean and as regular as the surf, and these ideas at one time constantly and

irresistibly replenished people's lives. [4] Arnold's symbol of the flowing ocean changes, however, to a symbol of the ebbing ocean, thus illustrating his idea that belief and religious certainty were falling away. [5] It is this personal sense of spiritual emptiness that Arnold is associating with his own times, because what he describes, in keeping with the symbolism, is that in the present time the "drear" shoreline has been left vacant by the "melancholy long withdrawing roar" of retreat and reduction (lines 25–27).

This specimen paragraph combines but also separates paraphrase, interpretation, and quotation, and it thereby eliminates any possible confusion about the origin of the ideas and also about who is saying what. In the first three sentences the writer uses the phrases "Arnold states," "To symbolize this idea," and "According to this symbolism," to show clearly that interpretation is to follow. Although the fourth sentence marks a new direction of Arnold's ideas, it continues to separate restatement from interpretation. The fifth sentence indicates, through the phrase "in keeping with the symbolism," to explain what seems to the writer to be the major idea of "Dover Beach."

Integrate Material by Using Quotation Marks

It is often necessary, and also interesting, to use short quotations from your author to illustrate and reinforce your ideas and interpretations. Here the problem of separating your thoughts from the author's is solved by quotation marks. In such an internal quotation, you may treat prose and poetry in the same way. If a poetic quotation extends from the end of one line to the beginning of another, however, indicate the line break with a virgule (/), and use a capital letter to begin the next line, as in the following:

> In "Lines Written in Early Spring" Wordsworth describes a condition in which his speaker is personally and ethically united with the natural world. Nature is a combination of the "thousand blended notes" of joyful birds (line 1), the sights of "budding twigs" (line 17), and the "periwinkle" (line 10). In the exact words of the speaker, these "fair works" form a direct "link" to "The human soul that through me ran," and the speaker goes on to state that "much it grieved my heart to think / What man has made of man" (lines 5–8)/.

Blend Quotations into Your Own Sentences

Using internal quotations still creates the problem of blending materials, however, for quotations should never be brought in unless you prepare your reader for them in some way. *Do not*, for example, use quotations in the following manner:

> Wordsworth's woodland grove is filled with the sounds of birds, the sights of flowers, and the feeling of the light wind, making for the thought that creatures of the natural world take pleasure in life. "The birds around me hopped and played."

This abrupt quotation throws the reader off balance because it is not blended into the previous sentence. It is necessary to prepare the reader to move from your discussion to the quotation, as in the following revision:

> Wordsworth's woodland scene is made joyful by the surrounding flowers and the gentle breeze, causing his speaker, who states that "The birds around me hopped and played," to conclude that the natural world has resulted from a "holy plan" created by Nature.

Here the quotation is made an actual part of the sentence. This sort of blending is satisfactory, provided that the quotation is brief.

Indent and Block Long Quotations

The standard for how to place quotations should be not to quote within a sentence any passage longer than twenty or twenty-five words (but consult your instructor, for the allowable number of words may vary). Quotations of greater length demand so much separate attention that they interfere with your own sentence. It is possible but not desirable to have one of your sentences conclude with a quotation, but you should never make an extensive quotation in the *middle* of a sentence. By the time you finish such an unwieldy sentence, your reader will have lost sight of how it began. When your quotation is long, you should make a point of introducing it and setting it off separately as a block.

The physical layout of block quotations should be as follows: Leave three blank lines between your own discourse and the quotation. Double-space the quotation (like the rest of your essay), and indent it five spaces from your left margin to distinguish it from your own writing. You might use fewer spaces for longer lines of poetry, but the standard should always be to create a balanced, neat page. After the quotation, leave a three-line space again, and resume your own discourse. Here is a specimen, from an essay about Wordsworth's "Lines Written in Early Spring":

> In "Lines Written in Early Spring" Wordsworth develops an idea that the world of nature is linked directly to the moral human consciousness. He speaks of no religious systems or books of moral values. Instead, he derives his ideas directly from his experience, assuming that the world was made for the joy of the living creatures in it, including human beings ("man"), and that anyone disturbing that power of joy is violating "Nature's holy plan" itself. Wordsworth's moral criticism, in other words, is derived from his faith in the integrity of creation:
>
>> If this belief from heaven be sent,
>> If such be Nature's holy plan,
>> Have I not reason to lament
>> What man has made of man?
>>   (lines 21–24)

The concept that morality and life are joined is the most interesting and engaging aspect of the poem. It seems to encourage a live-and-let-live attitude toward others, however, not an active program of direct outreach and help.

When quoting lines of poetry, always remember to quote them *as lines*. Do not run them together as though they were continuous prose. When you create such block quotations, as in the preceding example, you do *not* need quotation marks.

Today, computer usage is becoming a more established means of preparing papers, and therefore computer styling has become prominent in the handling of the matters discussed here. If you have style features in your menu, such as "Poem Text" or "Quotation," each of which sets block quotations apart from "Normal" text, you may certainly make use of the features. Explain to your instructor, however, to make sure that your computer corresponds to the styles established for your class.

Use Three Spaced Periods (an Ellipsis) to Show Omissions

Whether your quotation is long or short, you will often need to change some of the material in it to conform to your own sentence requirements. You might wish to omit something from the quotation that is not essential to your point or to the flow of your sentence. Indicate such omissions with three spaced periods, as follows:

Under the immediate threat of death, Farquhar's perceptions are sharpened and heightened. In actuality there is "swirling water . . . racing madly beneath his feet," but it is his mind that is racing swiftly, and he accordingly perceives that a "piece of dancing driftwood . . . down the current" moves so slowly that he believes the stream is "sluggish."

If your quotation is very brief, however, do not use spaced periods, as they might be more distracting than helpful. For example, do not use the spaced periods in a quotation like this:

Keats asserts that ". . . a thing of beauty . . ." always gives joy.

Instead, make your quotation without the ellipsis:

Keats asserts that "a thing of beauty" always gives joy.

Use Square Brackets to Enclose Words That You Add Within Quotations

If you add words of your own to integrate the quotation into your own train of discourse or to explain words that may seem obscure, put square brackets around these words, as in the following passage:

In "Lines Written in Early Spring," Wordsworth refers to a past experience of extreme happiness, in which Nature seemed to "link / The human soul that through . . . [him] ran." He is describing a state of mystical awareness in which "pleasant thoughts / Bring [him] sad thoughts," and make him "lament" moral and political cruelty (lines 2–8).

Do Not Overquote

A word of caution: *Do not use too many quotations.* You will be judged on your own thought and on the continuity and development of your own essay. It is tempting to include many quotations on the theory that you need to use examples from the text to illustrate and support your ideas. Naturally, it is important to introduce examples, but you should realize that too many quotations can disturb the flow of your own thought. If your essay consists of many illustrations linked together by no more than your introductory sentences, how much thinking have you actually shown? Try, therefore, to create your own discussion, using appropriate examples to connect your thought to the text or texts you are analyzing.

Do Not Change Spellings in Your Source

Always reproduce your source exactly. Sometimes the works of British authors may include words like *tyre, defence, honour,* and *labour.* Duplicate these as you find them. Although most anthologies modernize the spelling of older writers, you may often encounter "old-spelling" editions in which all words—such as *entring, Shew, beautie, ore* (for "over"), *witte* (for "wit"), *specifick, 'twas, guaranty* (for "guarantee"), or *determin'd*—are spelled and capitalized exactly as they were centuries ago. Your principle should be *to duplicate everything exactly as you find it,* even if this means spelling words like *achieve* as *atchieve, music* as *Musick,* or *joke* as *joak.* A student once changed the word *an* to "and" in the construction "an I were" in a Shakespeare play. The result was misleading, because in introductory clauses *an* really meant "if" (or "and if") and not "and." Difficulties like this one are rare, but you can avoid them if you reproduce the text as you find it. Should you think that something is either misspelled or confusing as it stands, you may do one of two things:

1. Clarify or correct the confusing word or phrase within brackets, as in the following:

    In 1714, fencing was considered a "Gentlemany [i.e., gentlemanly] subject."

2. Use the word *sic* (Latin for *thus,* meaning "it is this way in the text") in brackets immediately after the problematic word or obvious mistake:

    He was just "finning [sic] his way back to health" when the next disaster struck.

Illustrative Essay (First Draft)

The following illustrative essay is a first draft of the subject we have been developing. It follows our outline, and it includes details from the story in support of the various topics. It is by no means, however, as good a piece of writing as it could be. The draft omits a topic, some additional details, and some new insights that are included in the second draft, which follows (pages 49–51). It therefore reveals the need to make improvements through additional brainstorming and discovery-prewriting techniques.

How Setting in "The Necklace" Is Related to the Character of Mathilde

[1] In "The Necklace," Guy de Maupassant does not give much detail about the setting. He does not even describe the necklace itself, which is the central object in his plot, but he says only that it is "superb" (paragraph 47). <u>Rather, he uses the setting to reflect the character of the central figure, Mathilde Loisel.</u>° All his details are presented to bring out her traits. <u>Her character growth is related to her first apartment, her dream-life mansion rooms, and her attic flat.</u>*

[2] <u>Details about her first apartment explain her dissatisfaction and depression.</u> The walls are "drab," the furniture "threadbare," and the curtains "ugly" (paragraph 3). There is only a simple country girl to do the housework. The tablecloth is not changed daily, and the best dinner dish is boiled beef. Mathilde has no evening clothes, only a theater dress that she does not like. These details show her dissatisfaction about her life with her low-salaried husband.

[3] <u>Her dream-life images of wealth are like the apartment because they too make her unhappy.</u> In her daydreams about life in a mansion, the rooms are large, filled with expensive furniture and bric-a-brac, and draped in silk. She imagines private rooms for intimate talks, and big dinners with delicacies like trout and quail. With dreams of such a rich home, she feels even more despair about her modest apartment on the Street of Martyrs in Paris.

[4] <u>The attic flat reflects the coarsening of Mathilde's character.</u> Maupassant emphasizes the burdens she endures to save money, such as mopping floors, cleaning greasy and encrusted pots and pans, taking out the garbage, and washing clothes and dishes by hand. This work makes her rough and coarse, a fact also shown by her giving up care of her hair and hands, wearing the cheapest dresses possible, haggling with local shopkeepers, and becoming loud and penny-pinching. If at the beginning she is delicate and attractive, at the end she is unpleasant and coarse.

°Central idea.
*Thesis sentence.

[5] <u>In summary, Maupassant focuses everything in the story, including the set-</u>
<u>ting, on the character of Mathilde.</u> He does not include anything extra. Thus
he says little about the big party scene, but emphasizes the necessary detail that Mathilde was a great "success" (paragraph 52). It is this detail that
brings out some of her early attractiveness and charm (despite her more
usual unhappiness). Thus in "The Necklace," Maupassant uses setting as a
means to his end—the story of Mathilde and her needless sacrifice.

Developing and Strengthening
Your Essay Through Revision

After finishing a first draft like this one, you may wonder what more you can
do. You have read the work several times, used discovery and brainstorming
techniques to establish ideas to write about, made an outline of your ideas, and
written a full draft. How can you do better?

The best way to begin is to observe that a major mistake writers make
when writing about literature is to do no more than retell a story or summarize an idea. Retelling a story shows only that you have read it, not that you
have thought about it. Writing a good essay requires you to arrange a pattern
of argument and thought.

Use Your Own Order of References

One way to escape the trap of summarizing stories and to set up a pattern of
development is to stress your own order when referring to parts of a work. Rearrange details to suit your own central idea or argument. It is often important to write first about the conclusion or middle. Should you find that you
have followed the chronological order of the work instead of stressing your
own order, you can use one of the preliminary writing techniques to figure out
new ways to connect your materials. The principle is that you should introduce details about the work *only* to support the points you wish to make. Details for the sake of detail are unnecessary.

Use Literary Material as Evidence Supporting Your Argument

When you write, you are like a detective using clues as evidence for building
a case, or a lawyer citing evidence to support an argument. Your goal is to
convince your readers of your knowledge and the reasonableness of your conclusions. It is vital to use evidence convincingly so that your readers can follow your ideas. Let us look briefly at two drafts (on page 41) of a new example
to see how writing can be improved by the pointed use of details. These are
from drafts of an essay on the character of Mathilde.

Paragraph 1

The major extenuating detail about Mathilde is that she seems to be isolated, locked away from other people. She and her husband do not talk to each other much, except about external things. He speaks about his liking for boiled beef, and she states that she cannot accept the big invitation because she has no nice dresses. Once she gets the dress, she complains because she has no jewelry. Even when borrowing the necklace from Jeanne Forrestier, she does not say much. When she and her husband discover that the necklace is lost, they simply go over the details, and Loisel dictates a letter of explanation, which Mathilde writes in her own hand. Even when she meets Jeanne on the Champs-Elysées, Mathilde does not say a great deal about her life but only goes through enough details about the loss and replacement of the necklace to make Jeanne exclaim about the needlessness of the ten-year sacrifice.

Paragraph 2

The major flaw of Mathilde's character is that she is withdrawn and uncommunicative, apparently unwilling or unable to form an intimate relationship. For example, she and her husband do not talk to each other much, except about external things such as his taste for boiled beef and her lack of a party dress and jewelry. With such an uncommunicative marriage, one might suppose that she would be more open with her close friend, Jeanne Forrestier, but Mathilde does not say much even to her. This flaw hurts her greatly, because if she were more open she might have explained the loss and avoided the horrible sacrifice. This lack of openness, along with her self-indulgent dreaminess, is her biggest defect.

A comparison of these paragraphs shows that the first has more words than the second (156 compared to 119) but that it is more appropriate for a rough than a final draft because the writer does little more than retell the story. Paragraph 1 is cluttered with details that do not support any conclusions. If you try to find what it says about Maupassant's actual use of Mathilde's solitary traits in "The Necklace," you will get little help. The writer needs to revise the paragraph by eliminating details that do not support the central idea.

On the other hand, the details in paragraph 2 actually do support the declared topic. Phrases such as "for example," "with such," and "this lack" show that the writer of paragraph 2 has assumed that the audience knows the story and now wants help in interpretation. Paragraph 2 therefore guides readers by connecting the details to the topic. It uses these details as evidence, *not* as a retelling of actions. By contrast, paragraph 1 recounts a number of relevant actions but does not connect them to the topic. More details, of course, could have been added to the second paragraph, but they are unnecessary because the paragraph develops the argument with the details used. Good writing has many qualities, but one of the most important is shown in a comparison of the two paragraphs: *In good writing, no details are included unless they are used as supporting evidence in a pattern of thought and argument.*

Always Keep to Your Point; Stick to It Tenaciously

To show another distinction between first- and second-draft writing, let us consider a third example. The following *unrevised* paragraph, in which the writer assumes an audience that is interested in the relationship of economics to literature, is drawn from an essay on the idea of economic determinism in "The Necklace." In this paragraph the writer is trying to argue the point that economic circumstances underlie a number of incidents in the story. The idea is to assert that Mathilde's difficulties result not from character but rather from financial restrictions.

> More important than chance in governing life is the idea that people are controlled by economic circumstances. Mathilde, as is shown at the story's opening, is born poor. Therefore she doesn't get the right doors opened for her, and she settles down to marriage with a minor clerk, Loisel. With a vivid imagination and a burning desire for luxury, seeming to be born only for a life of ease and wealth, she finds that her poor home brings out her daydreams of expensive surroundings. She taunts her husband when he brings the big invitation, because she does not have a suitable (read "expensive") dress. Once she gets the dress it is jewelry she lacks, and she borrows that and loses it. The loss of the necklace means great trouble because it forces the Loisels to borrow heavily and to struggle financially for ten years.

This paragraph begins with an effective topic sentence, indicating that the writer has a good plan. The remaining part, however, shows how easily writers can be diverted from their objective. The flaw is that the material of the paragraph, while accurate, is not clearly connected to the topic. Once the second sentence is under way, the paragraph gets lost in a retelling of events, and the promising topic sentence is forgotten. The paragraph therefore shows that the use of detail alone will not support an intended meaning or argument. *Writers must do the connecting themselves, to make sure that all relationships are explicitly clear.* This point cannot be overstressed.

Let us see how the problem can be treated. If the ideal paragraph can be schematized with line drawings, we might say that the paragraph's topic should be a straight line, moving toward and reaching a specific goal (the topic or argument of the paragraph), with an exemplifying line moving away from the straight line briefly to bring in evidence, but returning to the line to demonstrate the relevance of each new fact. Thus, the ideal scheme looks like the figure at the top of page 43, with a straight line touched a number of times by an undulating line.

Notice that the exemplifying line, waving to illustrate how documentation or exemplification is to be used, always returns to the topic line. A scheme for the faulty paragraph on "The Necklace," however, would look like this, with the line never returning but flying out into space.

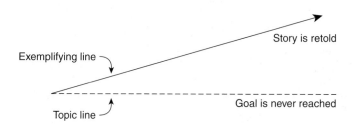

How might the faulty paragraph be improved? The best way is to remind the reader again and again of the topic and to use examples from the text in support.

As our model wavy-line diagram indicates, each time a topic is mentioned, the undulating line merges with the straight, or central-idea line. This relationship of argument to illustrative examples should prevail no matter what subject you write about, and you have to be tenacious in forming these connecting relationships. If you are analyzing *point of view,* for example, you should keep connecting your material to the speaker, or narrator, and the same applies to topics such as character, theme, or setting. According to this principle, we might revise the paragraph on economic determinism in "The Necklace" as follows. (Parts of sentences stressing the relationship of the examples to the topic of the paragraph are underlined.)

> *More important than chance in governing life is the idea that people are controlled by economic circumstances.* <u>As illustration,</u> the speaker begins by emphasizing that Mathilde, the main character, is born poor. Therefore she doesn't get the right doors opened for her, and she settles down to marriage with a minor clerk, Loisel. <u>In keeping with the idea,</u> her vivid imagination and burning desire for luxury feed on her weakness of character as she feels deep unhappiness and depression because of the contrast between her daydreams of expensive surroundings and the poor home she actually has. <u>These straitened economic circumstances</u> inhibit her relationship with her husband, and she taunts him when he brings the big invitation because she does not have a suitable (read "expensive") dress. As a merging of her unrealistic dream life with actual reality, <u>her borrowing of the necklace suggests the impossibility</u>

of overcoming economic restrictions. In the context of the idea, the ten-year
sacrifice to pay for the lost necklace <u>demonstrates that being poor keeps people down, destroying their dreams and hopes of a better life.</u>

The paragraph now successfully develops the argument promised by the topic
sentence. While it has also been lengthened, the length has been caused not
by inessential detail but by phrases and sentences that give form and direction. You might object that if you lengthened all your paragraphs in this way,
your essays would grow too bulky. The answer is to reduce the number of
major points and paragraphs, on the theory that *it is better to develop a few topics pointedly than to develop many pointlessly.* Revising for the purpose of
strengthening central and topic ideas requires that you either throw out some
topics or else incorporate them as subpoints in the topics you keep. To control
your writing in this way can result only in improvement.

Checking Development and Organization

It bears repeating over and over again that the first requirement of a good
essay is to introduce a central idea or argument and then stick to it. Another
major step toward excellence is to make your central idea expand and grow.
The word *growth* is a metaphor describing the disclosure of ideas that were
not at first noticeable, together with the expression of original, new, and fresh
interpretations.

Try to Be Original

In everything you write, now and in the future, it is important that you try to
be original. You might claim that originality is impossible because you are
writing about someone else's work. "The author has said everything," might
be the argument, "and therefore I can do little more than follow the story." This
claim rests on the mistaken assumption that you have no choice in selecting
material and no opportunity to have individual thoughts and make original
contributions.

But you do have choices and opportunities to be original. You really do.
One obvious area of originality is the development and formulation of your
central idea. For example, a natural first response to "The Necklace" is "The
story is about a woman who loses a borrowed necklace and endures hardship
to help pay for it." But this response does not promise an argument because it
refers only to events in the story and not to any idea. You can turn the sentence toward an argument, however, if you call the hardship "needless." Just
this word alone demands that you explain the differences between needed and
unneeded hardships, and your application of these differences to the heroine's
plight would produce an original essay. Even better and more original insights
could result if the topic of the budding essay were to connect the dreamy, withdrawn traits of the main character to her misfortunes. A resulting central idea

might be "People themselves create their own difficulties." Such an argument would require you to define not only the personal but also the representative nature of Mathilde's experiences, an avenue of exploration that could produce much in the way of a fresh, original essay about "The Necklace."

You can also develop your ability to treat your subject originally if you plan the body of the essay to build up to what you think is your most important and incisive idea. As examples of such planning, the following brief outline suggests how a central idea can be widened and expanded:

Subject: Mathilde Grows as a Character in "The Necklace"

1. She has normal daydreams about a better life.
2. In trying to make her daydreams seem real, she takes a risk but then loses.
3. She develops by facing her mistake and working hard to correct it.

The list shows how a subject can be enlarged if you treat your exemplifying topic in an increasing order of importance. In this case, the order moves from Mathilde's habit of daydreaming to her growing strength of character. The pattern shows how you can meet two primary standards of excellence in writing—organization and growth.

Clearly, you should always try to develop your central idea or argument. Constantly adhere to your topic, and constantly develop it. Nurture it and make it grow. Admittedly, in a short essay you will be able to move only a short distance with an idea or argument, but you should never be satisfied to leave the idea exactly where you found it. To the degree that you can learn to develop your ideas, you will receive recognition for increasingly original writing.

Write with Specific Readers in Mind

Whenever you write, you must decide how much detail to discuss. Usually you base this decision on your judgment of your readers. For example, if you assume that they have not read the work, you will need to include a short summary as background. Otherwise, they may not understand your argument.

Consider, too, whether your readers have any special interests or concerns. If they are particularly interested in politics, sociology, religion, or psychology, for example, you may need to select and develop your materials along one of these lines.

Your instructor will let you know who your audience is. Usually, it will be your instructor or your fellow students. They will be familiar with the work and will not expect you to retell a story or summarize an argument. Rather, they will want you to explain and interpret the work in the light of your main assertions about it. Thus, you can omit details that do not exemplify and support your argument, even if these details are important parts of the work. What you write should always be based on your developing idea together with your assessment of your readers.

Using Exact, Comprehensive, and Forceful Language

In addition to being original, organized, and well developed, the best writing is exact, comprehensive, and forceful. At any stage of the composition process, you should try to correct and improve your earliest sentences and paragraphs, which usually need to be rethought, reworded, and rearranged.

Try to make your sentences meaningful. First, ask yourself whether your sentences mean what you really intend, or whether you can make them more exact and therefore stronger. For example, consider these two sentences from essays about "The Necklace":

1. It seems as though the main character's dreams of luxury cause her to respond as she does in the story.
2. This incident, although it may seem trivial or unimportant, has substantial significance in the creation of the story; by this I mean the incident that occurred is essentially what the story is all about.

These sentences are inexact and vague and therefore are unhelpful. Neither of them goes anywhere. Sentence 1 is satisfactory up to the verb *cause,* but then it falls apart because the writer has lost sight of a thematic or argumentative purpose. It would be better to try to describe what the response *is* rather than to say nothing more than that some kind of response exists. To make the sentence more exact, we might try the following revision.

> Mathilde's dreams of luxury make her dissatisfied with her own possessions, and therefore she goes beyond her financial means to attend the big party.

With this revision, the writer could readily go on to consider the relationship of the early part of the story to the later parts. Without the revision, it is not clear where the writer might go.

Sentence 2 is vague because the writer has lost all contact with the main thread of argument. If we adopt the principle of trying to be exact, however, we can create more meaning and more promise:

> The accidental loss of the necklace, which is trivial though costly, supports the narrator's claim that major turns in life are produced not by earthshaking events but rather by minor ones.

In addition to working for exactness, try to make sentences—all sentences, but particularly thesis and topic sentences—complete and comprehensive. Consider the following sentence:

> The idea in "The Necklace" is that Mathilde and her husband work hard to pay for the lost necklace.

Although this sentence promises to describe an idea, it does no more than summarize the story's major action. It needs additional rethinking and rephrasing to make it more comprehensive, as in these two revisions:

1. In "The Necklace," Maupassant brings out the necessity to overcome mistakes through hard work and responsibility.
2. Maupassant's surprise ending in "The Necklace" symbolizes the need for always being truthful.

Both new sentences are connected to the action described by the original phrasing, "Mathilde and her husband work hard to pay for the lost necklace," although they point toward differing treatments. The first sentence concerns the virtue shown by the Loisels in their sacrifice. Because the second sentence includes the word *symbolizes,* an essay stemming from it would stress the Loisels' mistake in not confessing the loss. In dealing with the symbolic meaning of their failure, an essay developed along the lines of the second sentence would focus on the negative aspects of their characters, and an essay developed from the first sentence would stress their positive aspects. Both of the revised sentences, therefore, are more comprehensive than the original sentence and thus would help a writer get on the track toward a thoughtful and analytical essay.

Of course creating fine sentences is never easy, but as a mode of improvement, you might use some self-testing mechanisms:

*   *For treating story materials.* Always relate the materials to a point or argument. Do not say simply, "Mathilde works constantly for ten years to help pay off the debt." Instead, blend the material into a point, like this: "Mathilde's ten-year effort shows her resolution to overcome the horror of indebtedness," or "Mathilde's ten-year effort brings out her strength of character."
*   *For responses and impressions.* Do not say simply, "The story's ending left me with a definite impression." Where does that sentence take you? Your readers want to know what your impression is, and therefore you need to describe it, as in the following: "The story's ending surprised me and also made me sympathetic to the major character," or "The story's ending struck me with the fact that life is unpredictable and unfair."
*   *For ideas.* Make the idea clear and direct. Do not say, "Mathilde is living in a poor household," but rather use the story material to bring out an idea, as follows: "Mathilde's story shows that economic deprivation hurts the quality of life."
*   *For critical commentary.* Do not be satisfied with a statement such as "I found 'The Necklace' interesting." All right, the story is interesting, but what does that tell us? Instead, try to describe *what* was interesting and *why* it was interesting, as in this sentence: "I found 'The Necklace' interesting because it shows how chance and bad luck may either make or destroy people's lives."

USING THE NAMES OF AUTHORS

For both men and women writers, you should include the author's *full name* in the *first sentence* of your essay. Here are model first sentences.

> Ambrose Bierce's "An Occurrence at Owl Creek Bridge" is a story featuring both suspense and pathos.
>
> "An Occurrence at Owl Creek Bridge," by Ambrose Bierce, is a story featuring both suspense and pathos.

For all later references, use only last names, such as *Bierce, Chekhov, Lawrence,* or *Hardy.* However, for "giants" of literature, you should normally use only the last names including the first occurrence. For writers like Shakespeare and Milton, for example, there is no need to include *William* or *John.*

In spite of today's informal standards, do not use an author's first name, as in "*Ambrose* skillfully creates suspense and pathos in 'An Occurrence at Owl Creek Bridge.'" Also, do not use a familiar title before the names of dead authors, such as "*Mr.* Bierce's 'An Occurrence at Owl Creek Bridge' is a suspenseful and pathetic story," or "*Mr.* Shakespeare's idea in *Hamlet* is that information is uncertain." Use the last names alone.

As with all conventions, of course, there are exceptions. If you are referring to a childhood work of a writer, the first name might be appropriate, but be sure to shift to the last name when referring to the writer's mature works. If your writer has a professional or a noble title, such as "*Lord* Byron" or "*Queen* Elizabeth," it is not improper to use the title. Even then, however, the titles are commonly omitted for males, so that most references to Lord Byron and Alfred, Lord Tennyson, should usually be simply "Byron," "Tennyson," and the like.

Referring to living authors is somewhat problematical. Some journals and newspapers often use the respectful titles *Mr.* and *Ms.* in their reviews. However, scholarly journals, which are likely to remain on library shelves and Internet sites for many decades, follow the general principle of beginning with the entire name and then using only the last name for subsequent references.

Good writing begins with attempts, like these, to rephrase sentences to make them really say something. If you always name and pin down descriptions, responses, and judgments, no matter how difficult the task seems, your sentences can be strong and forceful because you will be making them exact and comprehensive.

Illustrative Essay (Revised Draft)

If you refer again to the first draft of the essay about Maupassant's use of setting to illustrate Mathilde's character (pages 39–40), you might notice that several parts of the draft need extensive reworking and revising. For example, paragraph 2 contains a series of short, unconnected comments, and the last sentence of that paragraph implies that Mathilde's dissatisfaction relates mainly to her husband rather than to her general circumstances. Paragraph 4 focuses too much on Mathilde's coarseness and not enough on her sacrifice and cooperation. The draft also ignores the fact that the story ends in another location, the Champs-Elysées, where Maupassant continues to demonstrate the nature of Mathilde's character. Finally, there is not enough support in this draft for the contention (in paragraph 5) that everything in the story is related to the character of Mathilde.

To discover how these issues can be more fully considered, the following revision of the earlier draft creates more introductory detail, includes an additional paragraph, and reshapes each of the paragraphs to stress the relationship of the central idea or argument to the topics of the various paragraphs. Within the limits of a short assignment, the essay illustrates all the principles of organization and unity that we have been discussing here.

How Maupassant Uses Setting in "The Necklace" to Show the Character of Mathilde

[1] In "The Necklace," Guy de Maupassant uses setting to reflect the character and development of the main character, Mathilde Loisel.° As a result, his setting is not particularly vivid or detailed. He does not even describe the ill-fated necklace—the central object in the story—but states only that it is "superb" (paragraph 47). In fact he includes descriptions of setting only if they illuminate qualities about Mathilde. Her changing character can be connected to the first apartment, the dream-life mansion rooms, the attic flat, and the public street.*

[2] Details about the modest apartment of the Loisels on the Street of Martyrs indicate Mathilde's peevish lack of adjustment to life. Though everything is serviceable, she is unhappy with the "drab" walls, "threadbare" furniture, and "ugly" curtains (paragraph 3). She has domestic help, but she wants more servants than the simple country girl who does the household chores in the apartment. Her embarrassment and dissatisfaction are shown by details of her irregularly cleaned tablecloth and the plain and inelegant boiled beef that her husband adores. Even her best theater dress, which is appropriate for apartment life but which is inappropriate for more wealthy

---

°Central idea.
*Thesis sentence.

surroundings, makes her unhappy. All these details of the apartment establish that Mathilde's major trait at the story's beginning is maladjustment.
She therefore seems unpleasant and unsympathetic.

[3] Like the real-life apartment, the impossibly wealthy setting of her daydreams about owning a mansion strengthens her unhappiness and her
avoidance of reality. All the rooms of her fantasies are large and expensive,
draped in silk and filled with nothing but the best furniture and bric-a-brac.
Maupassant gives us the following description of her dream world:

> She imagined a gourmet-prepared main course carried on the
> most exquisite trays and served on the most beautiful dishes, with
> whispered gallantries that she would hear with a sphinxlike smile
> as she dined on the pink meat of a trout or the delicate wing of a
> quail. (paragraph 4)

With such impossible dreams, her despair is complete. Ironically, this despair, together with her inability to live with reality, brings about her undoing. It makes her agree to borrow the necklace (which is just as unreal as
her daydreams of wealth), and losing the necklace drives her into the reality of giving up her apartment and moving into the attic flat.

[4] Also ironically, the attic flat is related to the coarsening of her character
while at the same time it brings out her best qualities of hard work and honesty. Maupassant emphasizes the drudgery of the work Mathilde endures
to maintain the flat, such as walking up many stairs, washing floors with
large buckets of water, cleaning greasy and encrusted pots and pans, taking out the garbage, washing clothes by hand, and haggling loudly with
local shopkeepers. All this reflects her coarsening and loss of sensibility,
also shown by her giving up hair and hand care and by wearing cheap
dresses. The work she performs, however, makes her heroic (paragraph
98). As she cooperates to help her husband pay back the loans, her
dreams of a mansion fade, and all she has left is the memory of her triumphant appearance at the Minister of Education's party. Thus the attic flat
brings out her physical change for the worse at the same time that it also
brings out her psychological change for the better.

[5] Her walk on the Champs-Elysées illustrates another combination of traits—
self-indulgence and frankness. The Champs-Elysées is the most fashionable
street in Paris, and her walk to it is similar to her earlier indulgences in her
daydreams of upper-class wealth. But it is on this street where she meets
Jeanne, and it is her frankness in confessing to Jeanne that makes her completely honest. While the walk thus serves as the occasion for the story's concluding surprise and irony, Mathilde's being on the Champs-Elysées is totally
in character, in keeping with her earlier reveries about luxury.

[6] Other details in the story also have a similar bearing on Mathilde's character. For example, the story presents little detail about the party scene beyond the statement that Mathilde is a great "success" (paragraph 52)—a
judgment that shows her ability to shine if given the chance. After she and
Loisel accept the fact that the necklace cannot be found, Maupassant includes details about the Parisian streets, about the visits to loan sharks,

and about the jewelry shops in order to bring out Mathilde's sense of honesty and pride as she "heroically" prepares to live her new life of poverty. Thus, in "The Necklace," Maupassant uses setting to highlight Mathilde's maladjustment, her needless misfortune, her loss of youth and beauty, and finally her growth as a responsible human being.

Commentary on the Essay

Several improvements to the first draft are seen here. The language of paragraph 2 has been revised to show more clearly the inappropriateness of Mathilde's dissatisfaction. In paragraph 3, the irony of the story is brought out, and the writer has connected the details to the central idea in a richer pattern of ideas, showing the effects of Mathilde's despair. Paragraph 5—new in the improved draft—includes additional details about how Mathilde's walk on the Champs-Elysées is related to her character. In paragraph 6, the fact that Mathilde is able "to shine" at the dinner party is interpreted according to the central idea. Finally, the conclusion is now much more specific, summarizing the change in Mathilde's character rather than saying simply that the setting reveals "her needless misfortune." In short, the second draft reflects the complexity of "The Necklace" better than the first draft. Because the writer has revised the first-draft ideas about the story, the final essay is tightly structured, insightful, and forceful.

Essay Commentaries

Throughout this book, the illustrative essays are followed by short commentaries that show how the essays embody the chapter instructions and guidelines. For each essay that has a number of possible approaches, the commentary points out which one is employed, and when an essay uses two or more approaches, the commentary makes this fact clear. In addition, each commentary singles out one of the paragraphs for more detailed analysis of its argument and use of detail. The commentaries will hence help you develop the insights necessary to use the essays as aids in your own study and writing.

To sum up, follow these guidelines whenever you write about a story or any kind of literature:

- Never just retell the story or summarize the work. Bring in story materials only when you can use them as support for your central idea or argument.
- Throughout your essay, keep reminding your reader of your central idea.
- Within each paragraph, make sure that you stress your topic idea.

- Develop your subject. Make it bigger than it was when you began.
- Always make your statements exact, comprehensive, and forceful.
- And remember, never just retell the story or summarize the work.

Special Topics for Studying
and Discussing the Writing Process

1. Write a brainstorming paragraph on the topic of anything in a literary work that you find especially good or interesting. Write as the thoughts occur to you; do not slow yourself down in an effort to make your writing seem perfect. You can make corrections and improvements later.

2. Using marginal and notebook notations, together with any additional thoughts, describe the way in which the author of a particular work has expressed important ideas and difficulties.

3. Create a plus-minus table to list your responses about a character or ideas in a work.

4. Raise questions about the actions of characters in a story or play in order to determine the various customs and manners of the society out of which the work is derived.

5. Analyze and explain the way in which the conflicts in a story or play are developed. What pattern or patterns do you find? Determine the relationship of the conflicts to the work's development, and fashion your idea of this relationship as an argument for a potential essay.

6. Basing your ideas on your marginal and notebook notations, select an idea and develop a thesis sentence from it, using your idea and a list of possible topics for an argument or central idea for an essay.

7. Using the thesis sentence you write for exercise 6, develop a brief topical outline for a full essay.

8. What effect do the minor characters in "The Necklace" (Loisel and Jeanne Forrestier) have on your perception of Mathilde?

9. A critic has said that the disaster befalling Mathilde and Loisel results not so much from their losing the necklace as from their concealing the truth. How true is this judgment? Be sure to consider what they themselves think might have happened to them if they had confessed the loss to Jeanne.

10. Write a brief story of your own in which you show how an apparently chance event has a major impact on the lives of your character or characters. In what ways is your chance event similar to or different from what happens to Mathilde? What view of life and reality do you think is represented by the consequences of the chance event?

2

Writing About a Close Reading

Analyzing Entire Short Poems or Selected Short Passages from Fiction, Longer Poems, and Plays

An essay on a close reading is a detailed study of an entire short work, usually a poem, or else a passage of prose or verse that is part of a longer work. This type of essay is specific because it focuses on the selected poem or passage. It is also general because you do not consider only a single topic such as the nature of a character or the meaning of a particular idea, but rather deal with all the elements you think are important. If the passage describes a person, for example, you might naturally want to discuss character. You might also want to stress the actions described in the passage, or noteworthy ideas or expressions of emotion, or descriptions of the location of an action, if you decide that these matters are important. In other words, the content of a close-reading essay is variable. The passage you are studying governs what you write.

The Purpose and Requirements of a Close-Reading Essay

Writing a close-reading essay magnifies your abilities and increases your skills. Think of these implications: If you can read and assimilate a single paragraph, you have then developed your power to read and assimilate an entire book. And if you can follow and appreciate a single poem, you will have acquired the skill to comprehend other poems. In addition, if you can understand a single speech by a dramatic character—any speech—you can go on to do the same for the entire play. This is not to say that writing a close-reading essay gives you the magic power instantly to understand every work you read, but what it does give you is the development of abilities on which you can build— an approach toward your comprehension and appreciation of other works.

The essay is designed as an explanation of what is in the assigned passage. General content is the objective, together with anything else that is noteworthy. To write the essay, you do not need to undertake a detailed analysis of diction, grammar, or style. Instead, you should analyze and discuss what you consider the most important aspects of the passage. Although you are free to consider special words and phrases, and should do so if you find them important, your aim is primarily to get at the content of your passage.

53

The Location of the Passage in a Longer Work

Close-reading essays about portions of a work should demonstrate how the passage is connected to the rest of the work. The principle is that all parts are equally important and essential. Analyzing an individual part, therefore, should bring out not only the meaning of the part but also the function of the part within the larger structure of the work.

Expect an Early Passage to Get Things Going

You may reasonably assume that in the early portions of a poem, play, or story, the author is setting things in motion, introducing you to the characters and ideas, and explaining the situations and problems that are going to be dealt with in the work. Therefore, you should try to discover how such early ideas, characterizations, insights, and descriptions are related to later developments. Always assume that everything you find there is connected to everything else in the work, and then analyze and explain that connection.

Expect a Midpoint Passage to Include
Anticipations of the Work's Conclusion

In a passage at the work's midpoint, the story or idea usually takes a particular turn—either expected or unexpected. If the change is unexpected, you should explain how the passage focuses the various themes or ideas and then propels them toward the forthcoming conclusion or climax. It may be that the work features surprises, and the passage thus acquires a different meaning on second reading. It may be that the speaker has one set of assumptions while the readers have others, and that the passage marks the speaker's increasing self-awareness. In short, your task is to determine the extent to which the passage (a) builds on what has happened previously; and (b) prepares the way for the outcome.

Expect Things to Come Together in a Passage at or near the Conclusion

A passage at or near the work's end is designed to solve problems or be a focal point or climax for all the cumulative situations and ideas. You will thus need to show how the passage brings together all details, ideas, and themes. In a narrative work, what is happening? Is any action described in the passage a major action or a step leading to the major action? Has everything in the passage been prepared for earlier, or are there any surprises? In a longer narrative poem, such as an epic, what is happening to the topics and ideas introduced earlier in the poem?

Writing About the Close Reading of a Passage in a Prose Work, Drama, or Longer Poem

Focus on the general meaning and impact of the passage or poem. By raising and answering a number of specific questions, you can gather materials for shaping your essay. Once you create answers, write them into a form that you can adapt in your essay. Try to reach specific and focused conclusions:

Raise Questions to Discover Ideas

- Does the passage (1) describe a scene; (2) develop a character; (3) present an action; (4) reveal a character's thoughts; (5) advance an argument; or (6) introduce an idea?
- What is the situation in the work? Who is the speaker? Who is being addressed? What does the speaker want? What ideas are in the work?
- What is the thematic content of the passage? How representative is it of the work as a whole? How does the passage relate to earlier and later parts of the entire text? (To deal with this question, you may assume that your reader is familiar with the entire work.)
- What noticeable aspects of diction and ideas are present in the passage? Do speeches or descriptions seem particularly related to any characterizations or ideas that appear elsewhere in the work?

Organize Your Essay on a Close Reading

Introduction   Because the close-reading essay is concerned with details, you might have a problem developing a thematic structure. You can overcome this difficulty if you begin to work with either a generalization about the passage or a thesis based on the relationship of the passage to the work. Suppose, for example, that the passage is factually descriptive or that it introduces a major character or raises a major idea. Any one of these observations may serve as a central idea.

Body   Develop the body of the essay according to what you find in the passage. For a passage of character description, analyze what is disclosed about the character together with your analysis of what bearing this information has on the story or play as a whole. For a passage presenting an idea or ideas, analyze the idea, and also demonstrate how the idea is important for the rest of the work. In short, your aim in this kind of essay is double: First, discuss the passage itself; and second, show how the passage functions within the entire work.

Conclusion   To conclude, stress the important details of your analysis. In addition, you may want to deal with secondary issues that arise in the passage but do not merit full consideration. The passage may contain specific phrases or underlying assumptions that you have not considered in the body

---

NUMBER THE PASSAGE FOR EASY REFERENCE

In preparing your essay, prepare a copy of the entire passage just as it appears in the text from which you are making your selection. Copy it exactly. Include your copy at the beginning of your essay, as in the following illustrative essays. For your reader's convenience, number the lines in poetry and the sentences in prose.

---

of your essay. The conclusion is the place to mention these matters, without developing them fully.

Illustrative Essay

Reading a Passage in Mark Twain's "Luck"°

[1] The battle was awfully hot; the allies were steadily giving way all over the field. [2] Our regiment occupied a position that was vital; a blunder now must be destruction. [3] At this crucial moment, what does this immortal fool do but detach the regiment from its place and order a charge over a neighboring hill where there wasn't a suggestion of an enemy! [4] "There you go!" I said to myself; "this is the end at last."

[5] And away we did go, and were over the shoulder of the hill before the insane movement could be discovered and stopped. [6] And what did we find? [7] An entire and unsuspected Russian army in reserve! [8] And what happened? [9] We were eaten up? [10] That is necessarily what would have happened in ninety-nine cases out of a hundred. [11] But no; those Russians argued that no single regiment would come browsing around there at such a time. [12] It must be the entire English army, and that the sly Russian game was detected and blocked; so they turned tail, and away they went, pell-mell, over the hill and down into the field, in wild confusion, and we after them; they themselves broke the solid Russian center in the field, and tore through, and in no time there was the most tremendous rout you ever saw, and the defeat of the allies was turned into a sweeping and splendid victory! [13] Marshall Canrobert looked on, dizzy with astonishment, admiration, and delight; and sent right off for Scoresby, and hugged him, and decorated him on the field in presence of all the armies!

[1]   Appearing close to the end of "Luck," these two paragraphs are vital in Twain's satiric puncturing of the character of Scoresby, a widely recognized

---

°For the text of this story, see Appendix C, pages 360–363.

and decorated British hero who is no better than a lucky incompetent. The paragraphs come as a climax of the story's actions. By presenting a brief account of a decisive battle in the Crimean War, in which Scoresby's regiment figures prominently, they bring out his stupidity and luck to the highest degree. Although the passages are narrative, the mark of Twain's style is to underscore how the hero's blunders are always saved by luck.* In every respect—description, word level, use of general and abstract words, grammatical patterns, and the narrator's involvement—the passage carries out Twain's satiric and comic goal.[†]

[2] The descriptions in the paragraphs are directed toward the blundering nature of the main character. In fact, the descriptions are not about the battle at all. The military matter presented in the thirteen sentences is that the allies are giving way, that Scoresby orders a charge, and that the Russians turn tail and dash away. There is no report of clashing soldiers and dying men and horses beyond the claim that the Russians themselves "tore through" their own ranks, and there are no vivid words, beyond these, describing the circumstances of victory. Indeed, the descriptions are minimal, containing just enough to exemplify Scoresby's luck, but no more. The paragraphs would be unsuccessful as an account of a battle, but as part of this story they superbly serve Twain's purposes.

[3] In keeping with the exposé, Twain uses vocabulary of mostly common words. What could be more ordinary, for example, than words like *battle, awfully, steadily, occupied, discovered, stopped, argued,* and *victory?* It may be that *splendid, astonishment, pell-mell, immortal,* and *crucial* are not common in everyday speech, but in this context they are appropriate, for they fall within the vocabulary of responses to battle. Because of their aptness, they enable the reader to focus on the subject and on the narrator's expressions of humor, and in this respect they fit within an ordinary range of words.

[4] Not only is the range ordinary, but a number of words are also uncomplimentary, in accord with the intention of the story to debunk Scoresby. The "allies were steadily giving way," for example, and the "movement" of many individuals is described as "insane." Such words are fitting for groups and mass actions, but not for specific individuals. When the Russians conclude from Scoresby's senseless charge that their "game" is "detected," they turn "tail" and run "pell-mell," dashing in such "wild confusion" that there is "the most tremendous rout you ever saw," resulting in "sweeping and splendid victory"—all basically negative words. Even the "hero," Scoresby, is not detailed anywhere as a specific leader and fighter; it is as though he is less significant than the gigantic forces of blind stupidity he unleashes. The last sentence of the two paragraphs, the thirteenth, continues in this mode with the abstract but worshipful responses of the commander, Marshall Canrobert, who is described as "dizzy with astonishment, admiration, and delight." These broad words reflect the public renown of Scoresby, which we, as the narrator's listeners, know to be untrue. These comically negative descriptions thus jell perfectly with Twain's debunking humor.

---

*Central idea.
[†]Thesis sentence.

[5] Grammatically, as well, there is great emphasis on the contrast between Scoresby's stupidity and his success. Twain's first two sentences are neatly balanced with contrasting ideas: Sentence 1 tells us that the battle is "hot" (part 1) and that the allies are losing (part 2). Sentence 2 tells us that the regiment is important (part 1) and that a mistake would be disastrous (part 2). But as the battle descends into the sweeping chaos caused by the charge of Scoresby's regiment, the grammar takes on the same chaotic pattern. Sentence 12, containing all the battle details, is eighty-one words long. It is broken up by semicolons and commas into a series of separate statements and structures describing the pell-mell Russian retreat and British victory. In other words, the sentence has the same wildness, sweep, and madness of the events being described—a blending of language and subject.

[6] The major quality of Twain's style in the passage, however, is the amused, debunking language contributed directly by the narrator. The narrator's ideas keep the passage short, and his words frame the suspense and anti-climax of the battle, as is shown in the first paragraph (sentences 1–4). He tells us (sentence 3) that the "immortal fool" orders a mistaken charge. His lamenting prediction, "this is the end at last" (sentence 4), is designed for full dramatic and suspenseful effect. The narrator's involvement is also shown by his simply phrased questions just before he tells about the results of the charge: "And what did we find?" "And what happened?" "We were eaten up?" His continual effect on the language is apparent in his reconstruction of the military logic of the Russians, and his attitude is most amusingly shown by the word "browsing" (sentence 11), which suggests grazing animals, not charging armies. This word emphasizes the dimwittedness of Scoresby's command to attack. Throughout the paragraphs, the speaker thus lends his own comic daggers to the language.

[7] In all respects, the passage is a model of the right use of words in the right places. If the writing were about an actual military combat, it would be poor. But because it is part of a comic exposé of a lucky fool, it is hard to imagine a better way to put things. Twain's speaker gives us what we need to know: namely that Scoresby has a Midas touch in everything he does, no matter how potentially disastrous. The sentences are clear and direct, and convey the facts about Scoresby that show his imbecility. Even the longest and most confused sentence, the twelfth, is appropriate to the confusion that Scoresby converts to triumph. For these reasons, the paragraphs are examples of accurate and sharp writing.

Work Cited

Twain, Mark. "Luck." Edgar V. Roberts. *Writing About Literature*. 11th ed. Upper Saddle River: Prentice Hall, 2006. 360–363.

Commentary on the Essay

This essay is unified from paragraph to paragraph by transitions such as "Not only is the range ordinary, but a number of words are also . . ." "in keeping with the exposé," "as well," and "in all respects." These transitional phrases enable reader concentration to move smoothly from one topic to the next.

The introduction demonstrates the importance of relating the passage being studied to the work as a whole. Because the central idea is connected to Twain's debunking objective, the point is made that diction and satiric intention are merged and integrated. The thesis sentence indicates five aspects of style to be considered in the essay. Any one of these, if necessary, could be separately developed.

In the body, paragraph 2 treats the absence of specifically descriptive words, explaining this lack by reference to the satiric subject. Paragraph 3 treats the neutral diction, making the point that this language is appropriate because it permits a direct focus on the asinine blunders of the major character. Twain's use of general and abstract language is treated in paragraph 4, the point being that this language is appropriate because the story exposes the emptyheadedness of Scoresby. In paragraph 5, the subject is the grammar of the passage, indicating that the movement from balance to chaos complements the chaos of the battle.

Paragraph 6, the last of the body, is designed as the high point of the discussion, asserting that the most important aspect of the writing is the narrative speaker. It is this speaker whose ideas and words permit Twain to keep the narrative brief while emphasizing his hero's blundering stupidity. Theoretically, details about a battle description might be more detailed, particularly if the goal is descriptive reality. Since the topic is a general one, however, the paragraph demonstrates that the effect of the narrator is to provide only enough details to be consistent with the story's thesis. Thus the layout of the battle, the questions, and the characterization of the British army as "browsing" are the most significant aspects of Twain's paragraphs. The concluding paragraph, 7, is a tribute to Twain's style, emphasizing again how his satiric objective governs word choices.

Writing an Essay on the Close Reading of a Poem

The close reading of a poem does not mean that you need to explain everything you find in the poem. Theoretically, a complete or total explication would require you to explain the meaning and implications of each word and every line—a technique that obviously would be exhaustive (and exhausting). It would also be self-defeating, for writing about everything in great detail would prohibit you from using your judgment and deciding what is important.

A more manageable and desirable technique is therefore to devote attention to the meaning of individual parts in relationship to the entire work. You might think of your essay as your explanation or "reading" of the poem. You will need to be selective and to consider only those details that you think are significant and vital to the thematic development of your essay.

Raise Questions to Discover Ideas

- What does the title contribute to the reader's understanding?
- Who is speaking? Where is the speaker when the poem is happening or unfolding?
- What is the situation? What has happened in the past, or what is happening in the present, that has brought about the speech?
- What difficult, special, or unusual words does the poem contain? What references need explaining? How does an explanation assist in the understanding of the poem?
- How does the poem develop? Is it a personal statement? Is it a story?
- What is the main idea of the poem? What details make possible the formulation of the main idea?

Organize Your Essay on the Close Reading of a Poem

In this close-reading essay you should plan to (1) follow the essential details of the poem; (2) understand the issues and the meaning the poem reveals; (3) explain some of the relationships of content to technique; and (4) note and discuss especially important or unique aspects of the poem.

Introduction   In your introduction, use your central idea to express a general view of the poem, which your essay will bear out. A close reading of Arnold's "Dover Beach," for example, might bring out the speaker's understanding that philosophical and religious certainty have been lost and that therefore people can find certainty only within trusting individual relationships. In the following illustrative essay describing Hardy's "The Man He Killed," the central idea is that war is senseless.

Body   In the body of your essay, first explain the poem's content—not with a paraphrase but with a description of the poem's major organizing elements. Hence, if the speaker of the poem is a first-person "I," you do not need to reproduce this voice yourself in your description. Instead, *describe* the poem *in your own words*, with whatever brief introductory phrases you find necessary, as in the second paragraph of the following illustrative essay.

Next, explain the poem's development or growth in relation to your central idea. Choose *your own* order of discussion, depending on your topics. You should, however, keep stressing your central idea with each new topic. Thus, you might wish to follow your description by discussing the poem's meaning, or even by presenting two or more possible interpretations. You might also wish to refer to significant techniques. For example, in Dudley Randall's "Ballad of Birmingham," a noteworthy technique is the unintroduced quotations (i.e., quotations appearing without any "she said" or "he said" phrases) as the ballad writer's means of dramatizing the dialogue between mother and "baby."

You might also introduce unique topics, such as the understatements in stanza two of "Ballad of Birmingham" that instruments of violence "Aren't good for a little child." Such a reference to the mother's language underscores adult attempts to shield children from the potential violence of the outside world, and it therefore makes the event described in the poem's conclusion especially ironic. In short, discuss those aspects of meaning and technique that bear upon your central idea.

Conclusion   In your conclusion, you may repeat your major idea to reinforce your essay's thematic structure. Because your essay reflects a general but not an exhaustive reading, there will be parts of the poem that you will not have covered. You might therefore mention what might be gained from a more complete discussion of various parts of the poem (do not, however, begin an extensive discussion in your conclusion). The last stanza of Hardy's "The Man He Killed," for example, contains the words "quaint and curious" in reference to war. These words are unusual, particularly because the speaker might have chosen *hateful, senseless, destructive,* or other similarly descriptive words. Why did Hardy have his speaker make such a choice? With brief attention to such a problem, you may conclude your essay.

Illustrative Essay

A Close Reading of Thomas Hardy's "The Man He Killed"°

[1] Hardy's "The Man He Killed" exposes the senselessness of war.* It does this through a silent contrast between the needs of ordinary people, as represented by a young man—the speaker—who has killed an enemy soldier in battle, and the antihuman and unnatural deaths that happen in combat. Of major note in this contrast are the speaker's circumstances, his language, his sense of identity with the dead man, and his concerns and wishes.†

[2] The speaker begins by contrasting the circumstances of warfare with those of peace. He does not identify himself, but his speech reveals that he is common and ordinary—a person, one of "the people"—who enjoys drinking in a bar and who prefers friendship and helpfulness to violence. If he and the man he killed had met in an inn, he says, they would have shared many drinks together, but because they met on a battlefield they shot at each other, and he killed the other man. The speaker tries to justify the killing but can produce no stronger reason than that the dead man was his "foe." Once he states this reason, he again thinks of the similarities between himself and the dead man, and then he concludes that warfare is "quaint and curious" (line 17) because it forces a man to kill another man whom he would have befriended if they had met during peacetime.

°See pages 371–372 for this poem.
*Central idea.
†Thesis sentence.

[3]   To make the irony of warfare clear, the poem uses easy, everyday language
to bring out the speaker's ordinary qualities. His manner of speech is conversational, as in "We should have sat us down" (line 3), and "'list" (for "enlist," line 13), and his use of "you" in the last stanza. Also, his word choices,
shown in words like "nipperkin," "traps," and "fellow" (lines 4, 15, and 18),
are common and informal, at least in British usage. This language is important because it establishes that the speaker is an average man who has
been thrown by war into an unnatural role.

[4]   As another means of stressing the stupidity of war, the poem makes clear
that the two men—the live soldier who killed and the dead soldier who was
killed—were so alike that they could have been brothers or even twins.
They had identical ways of life, identical troubles with money, identical wishes to help other people, and identical motives in enlisting in the army. Symbolically the "man he killed" is so much like the speaker himself that the
killing seems like a form of suicide. The poem thus raises the question of
why two people who are so much like each other should be shoved into opposing battle lines in order to kill each other. This question is rhetorical, for
the obvious answer is that there is no good reason.

[5]   Because the speaker (and also, very likely, the dead man) is shown as a
person embodying the virtues of friendliness and helpfulness, Hardy's
poem represents a strong disapproval of war. Clearly, political justifications
for violence as a political policy are irrelevant to the characters and concerns of the men who fight. They, like the speaker, would prefer to follow
their own needs rather than remote and vague ideals. The failure of complex but irrelevant political explanations is brought out most clearly in the
third stanza, in which the speaker tries to give a reason for shooting the
other man. Hardy's use of punctuation—the dashes—stresses the fact that
the speaker has no commitment to the cause he served when killing. Thus
the speaker stops at the word "because—" and gropes for a reason (line 9).
Not being articulate, he can say only "Because he was my foe. / Just so: my
foe of course he was; / That's clear enough" (lines 10–12). These short
bursts of words indicate that he cannot explain things to himself or to anyone else except in the most obvious and trite terms, and in apparent embarrassment he inserts "of course" as a way of emphasizing hostility even
though he felt none toward the man he killed.

[6]   A close reading thus shows the power of the poem's dramatic argument.
Hardy does not establish closely detailed reasons against war as a policy
but rather dramatizes the idea that all political arguments are unimportant
in view of the central and glaring brutality of war—killing. Hardy's speaker is
not able to express deep feelings; rather he is confused because he is an
average sort who wants only to live and let live and to enjoy a drink in a bar
with friends. But this very commonness stresses the point that everyone is
victimized by war—not only those who die but also those who pull the trig-
gers and push the buttons.

Work Cited

Hardy, Thomas. "The Man He Killed." Edgar V. Roberts. *Writing About Literature.*
11th ed. Upper Saddle River: Prentice Hall, 2006. 371–372.

Commentary on the Essay

This close-reading essay begins by stating a central idea about "The Man He Killed," then indicates the topics to follow that will develop the idea. Although nowhere does the poem's speaker state that war is senseless, the essay takes the position that the poem embodies this idea. A more detailed examination of the poem's themes might develop the idea by discussing the ways in which individuals are caught up in social and political forces, or the contrast between individuality and the state. In this essay, however, the simple statement of the idea is enough.

Paragraph 2 describes the major details of the poem, with guiding phrases like "The speaker begins," "he says," and "he again thinks." Thus the paragraph explains how things in the poem occur, as is appropriate for a close reading. Paragraph 3 is devoted to the speaker's words and idioms, with the idea that his conversational manner is part of the poem's method of argument.

Paragraph 4 extends paragraph 3 inasmuch as it points out the similarities of the speaker and the man he killed. If the situation were reversed, the dead man might say exactly the same things about the present speaker. This affinity underscores the suicidal nature of war. Paragraph 5 treats the style of the poem's fourth stanza. In this context, the treatment is brief. The last paragraph reiterates the main idea and concludes with a tribute to the poem as an argument.

The entire essay therefore represents a reading and explanation of the poem's high points. It stresses a particular interpretation and briefly shows how various aspects of the poem bear it out.

Special Topics for Studying and Discussing the Close Reading of Literary Works

1. For an Entire Poem
   a. Blake's "The Tyger" or Frost's "Desert Places." Try to establish how the poems bring out the speaker's ideas about evil or spiritual blankness.
   b. Keats's "On First Looking Into Chapman's Homer." How does Keats convey his sense of intellectual excitement and discovery?
2. For a Paragraph from a Story or Longer Poem (You Choose)
   a. Bierce's "An Occurrence at Owl Creek Bridge." Try to show the connection between the protagonist's imagination and his real death agony.
   b. Hardy's "The Three Strangers." Emphasize the connections between the details and the work's admiration of the shepherds living in the vicinity of Higher Crowstairs.
3. For a Single Speech or a Passage of Dialogue from a Play (You Choose)
   a. Glaspell's *Trifles*. Demonstrate how the speech (or speeches) shows the relationship between men and women.
   b. Chekhov's *The Bear*. How does the speech or passage create character as it also conveys the play's humor?

3

Writing About Character
The People in Literature

Writers of fiction create narratives that enhance and deepen our understanding of human character and human life. Under the influences of
such pioneers as Freud, Jung, and Skinner, the science of psychology has influenced both the creation and the study of literature. It is well known that
Freud buttressed some of his psychological conclusions by referring to literary
works, especially plays by Shakespeare. Widely known films such as *Spellbound*
(1945) and *The Snake Pit* (1948) have popularized the relationships between literary character and psychology. Without doubt, the presentation and understanding of character is a major aim of fiction (and literature generally).

In literature, a **character** is a verbal representation of a human being.
Through action, speech, description, and commentary, authors portray characters who are worth caring about, cheering for, and even loving, although
there are also characters you may laugh at, dislike, or even hate.

In a story or play emphasizing a major character, each action or speech is
part of a presentation of the complex combination of the inner and outer self that
constitutes a human being. Whereas in life things may "just happen," in literature all actions, interactions, speeches, and observations are deliberate. Thus, you
read about important actions like a long period of work and sacrifice (Maupassant's "The Necklace" [Chapter 1]), acts of quiet protest (Hardy's "The Three
Strangers"), or a young father's dream of freedom (Bierce's "An Occurrence at
Owl Creek Bridge"). By making such actions interesting, authors help you understand and appreciate not only their major characters but also life itself.

Character Traits

In studying a literary character, try to determine the character's outstanding
traits. A **trait** is a quality of mind or habitual mode of behavior that is evident
in active and passive ways, such as never repaying borrowed money, giving
moral support to loved ones, being a person on whom people always rely, listening to the thoughts and problems of others, avoiding eye contact, taking the
biggest portions, or always thinking oneself the center of attention.

Sometimes, of course, the traits we encounter are minor and therefore negligible, but often a trait may be a person's *primary* characteristic (not only in fiction but also in life). Thus, characters may be ambitious or lazy, serene or anxious, aggressive or fearful, thoughtful or inconsiderate, open or secretive, confident or self-doubting, kind or cruel, quiet or noisy, visionary or practical, careful or careless, impartial or biased, straightforward or underhanded, "winners" or "losers," and so on. With this sort of list, to which you may add at will, you can analyze and develop conclusions about character. For example, Mathilde in Maupassant's "The Necklace" indulges in dreams of unattainable wealth and comfort and is so swept up in her visions that she scorns her comparatively good life with her reliable but dull husband. It is fair to say that this denial of reality is her major trait. It is also a major weakness, because Maupassant shows that her dream life harms her real life. A contrast is seen in the speaker of Lowell's poem "Patterns," who is realistically facing the truth that her hopes for happiness have been destroyed because of her fiancé's battlefield death. By similarly analyzing the thoughts, actions, and speeches of the literary characters you encounter, you can also draw conclusions about their nature and their qualities.

Distinguish Between Circumstances and Character Traits

When you study a fictional person, distinguish between circumstances and character, for circumstances have value *only if you show that they demonstrate important traits*. Thus, if our friend Sam wins a lottery, let us congratulate him on his luck; but the win does not say much about his *character*—not much, that is, unless you also point out that for years he has been regularly spending hundreds of dollars each week for lottery tickets. In other words, making the effort to win a lottery *is* a character trait but winning (or losing) *is not*.

Or, let us suppose that an author stresses the neatness of one character and the sloppiness of another. If you accept the premise that people care for their appearance according to choice—and that choices develop from character—you can use these details to make conclusions about a person's self-esteem or the lack of it. In short, when reading about characters in literature, look beyond circumstances, actions, and appearances, and attempt to determine what these things show about character. Always try to get from the outside to the inside, for it is the internal qualities of character that determine external behavior.

How Authors Disclose Character in Literature

Basically, authors rely on five ways of bringing characters to life. Remember that you must use your own knowledge and experience to make judgments about the qualities of the characters.

The Actions of Characters Reveal Their Qualities

What characters *do* is our best clue to understanding what they *are*. For example, the character Farquhar in Bierce's "An Occurrence at Owl Creek Bridge" tries to sabotage the Union army's railway system near his country estate. This action shows both loyalty (to the Confederate cause) and personal bravery, despite the fact that he is caught. Often characters are unaware of the meanings and implications of their actions. Smirnov in Chekhov's play *The Bear*, for example, would be a fool to teach Mrs. Popov to use her dueling pistol because she has threatened to kill him with it. Even before he recognizes his love for her, he is subconsciously aware of this love, and his potentially self-destructive action shows that his loving nature has overwhelmed his instinct for self-preservation.

Like ordinary human beings, fictional characters do not necessarily understand how they may be changing or why they do the things they do. The strong inner conflict experienced by the two women in Glaspell's short play *Trifles* brings out their character strength. Theoretically, they have an overriding obligation to the law, but they discover that they have an even stronger personal obligation to the accused killer, Minnie. Hence they show their adaptability and their willingness to alter their behavior as a result of the things they discover in the farmhouse kitchen.

The Author's Descriptions Tell Us About Characters

Appearance and environment reveal much about a character's social and economic status, and they also tell us about character traits. Mathilde in Maupassant's "The Necklace" dreams about wealth and unlimited purchasing power. Although her unrealizable desires destroy her way of life, they also cause her character strength to emerge. The descriptions of country folkways in Hardy's "The Three Strangers" are independently interesting and unique, but they also make plain the personal loyalty of the peasants and their social stability and solidity.

What Characters Say Reveals What They Are Like

Although the speeches of most characters are functional—essential to keeping the action moving along—they provide material from which you may draw conclusions. When the second traveler of Hawthorne's "Young Goodman Brown" speaks, for example, he reveals his devious and deceptive nature even though ostensibly he appears friendly. The lawmen in *Trifles* speak straightforwardly but without much understanding of the women in the story. Their speeches suggest that their characters are similarly straightforward, although their constant belittling of the two women indicates their inability to understand others.

Often, characters use speech to obscure their motives. The Federal scout in Bierce's "An Occurrence at Owl Creek Bridge" is masquerading as a Confederate soldier, and in speaking with the major character Farquhar, who is a landowner and a Confederate loyalist, he speaks confidentially but deceivingly. The result of the scout's lies is that Farquhar is led to believe that he can safely burn the nearby bridge at Owl Creek. Farquhar makes the attempt, and of course he is caught by the Union troops. Comparably, in Hardy's "The Three Strangers" the first stranger, Timothy Summers, speaks easily and comfortably in order to keep the natives—and the second stranger, the Hangman—from knowing his true identity. Even when he is alone with the Hangman he speaks easily but ambiguously so that the hangman will have no clue about who he really is.

What Others Say Tells Us About a Character

By studying what characters say about each other, you can enhance your understanding of the character being discussed. For example, the major character in Glaspell's *Trifles* is the farmwoman Minnie Wright. But Minnie never appears as a character, and we learn about her only through the conversations between Mrs. Hale and Mrs. Peters. It is from them that her character is revealed as an oppressed woman who has finally snapped and turned on her oppressor, her husband.

Ironically, speeches often indicate something other than what the speakers intend, perhaps because of prejudice, stupidity, or foolishness. Nora, in O'Connor's "First Confession" tells about Jackie's lashing out at her with a butter knife, but in effect she describes the boy's individuality just as she also discloses her own spitefulness.

The Author, Speaking as a Storyteller or an Observer, May Present Judgments About Characters

What the author, speaking as a work's authorial voice, says about a character is usually accurate, and the authorial voice can be accepted factually. However, when the authorial voice interprets actions and characteristics, as in Hawthorne's "Young Goodman Brown," the author himself or herself assumes the role of a reader or critic, whose opinions are therefore open to question. For this reason, authors frequently avoid interpretations and devote their skill to arranging events and speeches so that readers can draw their own conclusions.

Types of Characters: Round and Flat

No writer can present an entire life history of a protagonist, nor can each character in a story get "equal time" for development. Accordingly, some characters grow to be full and alive, while others remain shadowy. The British novelist and critic E. M. Forster, in *Aspects of the Novel*, calls the two major types "round" and "flat."

Round Characters Are Three-Dimensional and Lifelike

The basic trait of **round** characters is that we are told enough about them to permit the conclusion that they are three-dimensional, rounded, authentic, memorable, original, and true to life. They are the centers of our attention in most works of fiction. Their roundness and fullness are characterized by both individuality and unpredictability. It is true that, like all human beings, round characters have inherent qualities that the circumstances of a story bring out, and therefore their full realization as characters is directly connected to the stories in which they live their lives. Jackie, of O'Connor's "First Confession," is round and dynamic. We learn from his adult narration that he has been a normal and typical child, trying to maintain his sense of individuality amid what he considers to be embarrassing family circumstances. His thoughts about "solutions" to his problems are of course greatly in excess, but when the time comes for him to confess his "sins," he does not evade them but dutifully states everything that he has been thinking. As amusing as his story is, his confession about the truth of his inner thoughts constitutes the type of adjustment that characterizes him as a round character.

A complementary quality about round characters is that they are often **dynamic**. Dynamic characters *recognize, change with,* or *adjust to* circumstances. The reverse side of this coin is that circumstances may also bring a dynamic character to ruin. Such changes may be shown in (1) an action or actions; (2) the realization of new strength and therefore the affirmation of previous decisions; (3) the acceptance of new conditions and the need for making changes; (4) the discovery of unrecognized truths; or (5) the reconciliation of the character with adverse conditions. We may consider Minnie, in Glaspell's *Trifles*, as dynamic. We learn that as a young woman she was happy and musical, though shy, but that she has been deprived and blighted by her thirty-year marriage. Finally, however, a particularly cruel action by her husband so enrages her that she breaks out of her subservient role and commits an act of violence. In short, her action shows her as a dynamic character capable of radical and earthshaking change. This is not to say that only round characters are dynamic, for less significant characters in a story may also be altered because of circumstances.

Because a round character plays a major role in a story, he or she is often called the **hero** or **heroine**. Some round characters are not particularly heroic, however, so it is preferable to use the more neutral word **protagonist** (the "first actor"). The protagonist is central to the action, moves against an **antagonist** (the "opposing actor"), and exhibits the ability to adapt to new situations.

Flat Characters Are Simple and One-Dimensional

Unlike round characters, **flat characters** are not complex, but are simple and one-dimensional. They may have no more than a single role to perform in a story, or they may be associated with no more than a single dominating idea. Most flat characters end pretty much where they begin, and for this reason we may think of them as **static**, not dynamic. Often their absence of growth or development results from lack of knowledge or understanding, or even from stupidity or insensitivity. Flat characters are not worthless in fiction, however, for they highlight the development of the round characters, as with the lawmen in Glaspell's *Trifles* and the characters whom Goodman Brown meets in Hawthorne's "Young Goodman Brown."

Usually, flat characters are minor (e.g., relatives, acquaintances, functionaries), but not all minor characters are necessarily flat. Sometimes flat characters are prominent in certain types of literature, such as cowboy, police, and detective stories, where the focus is less on character than on performance. Such characters might be lively and engaging, even though they do not undergo significant change and development. They must be strong, tough, and clever enough to perform recurring tasks such as solving a crime, overcoming a villain, or finding a treasure. The term **stock character** is often used to describe characters in these repeating situations. To the degree that stock characters have many common traits, they are **representative** of their class or group. Such characters, with variations in names, ages, and sexes, have been constant in literature since the ancient Greeks. Some regular stock or representative characters are the insensitive father, the interfering mother, the sassy younger sister or brother, the greedy politician, the harassed boss, the resourceful cowboy or detective, the overbearing or henpecked husband, the submissive or nagging wife, the absent-minded professor, the angry police captain, the lovable drunk, and the town do-gooder.

Stock characters are usually also flat as long as they do no more than perform their roles and exhibit conventional and unindividual traits. When they possess no attitudes except those of their class, they are often called **stereotype** characters, because they all seem to have been cast in the same mold.

But when authors bring characters into focus, no matter what roles they perform, the characters emerge from flatness and move into roundness. For example, Louise Mallard of Chopin's "The Story of an Hour" is a traditional housewife, and if she were no more than that she would be flat and stereotypical. But after receiving the news that her husband has died, the roundness of her character is brought out by her sudden and unexpected exhilaration at the prospect of being widowed and free. One may compare Louise with the title character of Mansfield's "Miss Brill." At first Miss Brill seems dull. She almost literally has no life, and as a character she is flat. But the story demonstrates that she protects herself by indulging in her remarkable inner life of imagination and creativity, and for this reason she is to be judged as round. In sum, the ability to grow and develop and adjust to changing circumstances makes characters round and dynamic. Absence of these traits makes characters flat and static.

Reality and Probability: Verisimilitude

Characters in fiction should be true to life. Therefore their actions, statements, and thoughts must all be what human beings are *likely* to do, say, and think under the conditions presented in the literary work. This is the standard of

verisimilitude, **probability**, or **plausibility**. One may readily admit that there are people *in life* who perform tasks or exhibit characteristics that are difficult or seemingly impossible (such as always leading the team to victory, always getting A+'s on every test, always being cheerful and helpful, or always understanding the needs of others). However, such characters in fiction would not be true to life because they do not fit within normal or usual behavior.

You should therefore distinguish between what characters may *possibly* do and what they *most frequently* or *most usually* do. Thus, in Maupassant's "The Necklace," it is possible that Mathilde could be truthful and tell her friend Jeanne Forrestier about the lost necklace. In light of Mathilde's pride and sense of self-respect, however, it is more in character for her and her husband to hide the loss and borrow money for a replacement, even though they must endure the harsh financial consequences for ten years. Granted the possibilities of the story (either self-sacrifice or the admission of a fault or a possible crime), the decision she makes with her husband is the more *probable* one.

Nevertheless, probability does not rule out surprise or even exaggeration. The sudden and seemingly impossible changes concluding *The Bear*, for example, are not improbable because Chekhov early in the play shows that both Mrs. Popov and Smirnov are emotional, somewhat foolish, and impulsive. Even in the face of their unpredictable embraces closing the play, these qualities of character dominate their lives. For such individuals, surprise may be accepted as a probable condition of life.

Writers render probability of character in many ways. Works that attempt to mirror life—realistic and naturalistic stories not unlike Maupassant's "The Necklace"—set up a pattern of ordinary, everyday probability. Less realistic conditions establish different frameworks of probability, in which characters are *expected* to be unusual, as in Hawthorne's "Young Goodman Brown." Because a major way of explaining this story is that Brown is having a nightmarish psychotic trance, his bizarre and unnatural responses are probable. Equally probable is the way the doctors explain Louise Mallard's sudden death at the end of Chopin's "The Story of an Hour" even though their smug analysis is totally and comically wrong.

You might also encounter works containing *supernatural* figures such as the second traveler in "Young Goodman Brown." You may wonder whether such characters are probable or improbable. Usually, gods and goddesses embody qualities of the best and most moral human beings, and devils like Hawthorne's guide take on attributes of the worst. However, you might remember that the devil is often given dashing and engaging qualities so that he can deceive gullible sinners and then drag them screaming into the fiery pits of hell. The friendliness of Brown's guide is therefore not an improbable trait. In judging characters of this or any other type, your best criteria are probability, consistency, and believability.

Writing About Character

Usually your topic will be a major character in a story or drama, although you might also study one or more minor characters. After your customary overview, begin taking notes. List as many traits as you can, and also determine how the author presents details about the character through actions, appearance, speeches, comments by others, or authorial explanations. If you discover unusual traits, determine what they show. The following suggestions and questions will help you get started.

Raise Questions to Discover Ideas

- Who is the major character? What do you learn about this character from his or her actions and speeches? From the speeches and actions of other characters? How else do you learn about the character?
- How important is the character to the work's principal action? Which characters oppose the major character? How do the major character and the opposing character(s) interact? What effects do these interactions create?
- What actions bring out important traits of the main character? To what degree is the character creating events, or just responding to them?
- Describe the main character's actions: Are they good or bad, intelligent or stupid, deliberate or spontaneous? How do they help you understand her or him? What do they show about the character as a person?
- Describe and explain the traits, both major and minor, of the character you plan to discuss. To what extent do the traits permit you to judge the character? What is your judgment?
- What descriptions (if any) of how the character looks do you discover in the story? What does this appearance demonstrate about him or her?
- In what ways is the character's major trait a strength—or a weakness? As the story progresses, to what degree does the trait become more (or less) prominent?
- Is the character round and dynamic? How does the character recognize, change with, or adjust to circumstances?
- If the character you are analyzing is flat or static, what function does he or she perform in the story (for example, by doing a task or by bringing out qualities of the major character)?
- If the character is a stereotype, to what type does he or she belong? To what degree does the character stay in the stereotypical role or rise above it? How?
- What do any of the other characters do, say, or think to give you understanding of the character you are analyzing? What does the character say or think about himself or herself? What does the storyteller or narrator say? How valid are these comments and insights? How helpful in providing insights into the character?
- Is the character lifelike or unreal? Consistent or inconsistent? Believable or not believable?

Organize Your Essay About Character

Introduction   Identify the character you are studying, and refer to noteworthy problems in determining this character's qualities.

Body   Use your central idea and thesis sentence to create the form for the body of your essay. Consider one of the following approaches to organize your ideas and form the basis for your essay.

1. **Develop a central trait or major characteristic**, such as "the habit of seeing the world only on one's own terms" (Miss Brill of Mansfield's "Miss Brill"). This kind of structure should be organized to show how the work brings out the trait. For example, one story might use dramatic speeches to bring the character to life (Minnie of *Trifles*). Another story might employ just the character's speech and actions (the Third Stranger of Hardy's "The Three Strangers"). Studying the trait thus enables you to focus on the ways in which the author presents the character, and it also enables you to focus on separate parts of the work.

2. **Explain a character's growth or change.** This type of essay describes a character's traits at the work's beginning and then analyzes changes or developments. It is important to stress the actual alterations as they emerge, but at the same time to avoid retelling the story. Additionally, you should not only describe the changing traits but also analyze how they are brought out within the work, such as the dream of Goodman Brown or Minnie Wright's long ordeal.

3. **Organize your essay around central actions, objects, or quotations that reveal primary characteristics.** Key incidents may stand out (such as using a breadknife to strike out against a person), along with objects closely associated with the character being analyzed (such as a broken birdcage). There may be important quotations spoken by the character or by someone else in the work. Show how such elements serve as signposts or guides to understanding the character. (See the following illustrative essay for an illustration of this type of development.)

4. **Develop qualities of a flat character or characters.** If the character is flat (such as the sheriff and county attorney in *Trifles* or the servants in *The Bear*), you might develop topics such as the function and relative significance of the character, the group the character represents, the relationship of the flat character to the round ones, the importance of this relationship, and any additional qualities or traits. For a flat character, you should explain the circumstances or defects that keep the character from being round, as well as the importance of these shortcomings in the author's presentation of character.

Conclusion   When bringing your essay to a close, show how the character's traits are related to the work as a whole. If the person was good but came to a bad end, does this misfortune make him or her seem especially worthy? If the person suffers, does the suffering suggest any attitudes about the class or type of which he or she is a part? Or does it illustrate the author's general view of human life? Or both? Do the characteristics explain why the person helps or hinders other characters? How does your essay help to clear up first-reading misunderstandings?

Illustrative Essay

The Character of Minnie Wright in Susan Glaspell's *Trifles*°

[1] Minnie Wright is Susan Glaspell's major character in *Trifles*. We learn about her, however, not from seeing and hearing her, for she is not a speaking or an acting character in the play, but rather from the secondhand evidence provided by the speaking characters. Lewis Hale, a neighboring farmer, tells about Minnie's behavior after the dead body of her husband, John, was found. Mrs. Hale, Hale's wife, tells about Minnie's young womanhood and about how she became alienated from her nearest neighbors because of John's stingy and unfriendly ways. Both Mrs. Hale and Mrs. Peters, the sheriff's wife, make observations about Minnie based on the condition of her kitchen. From this information we get a full portrait of Minnie, who has changed from passivity to destructive assertiveness.* Her change in character is indicated by her clothing, her dead canary, and her unfinished patchwork quilt.†

[2] The clothes that Minnie has worn in the past and in the present indicate her character as a person of charm who has withered under neglect and contempt. Martha mentions Minnie's attractive and colorful dresses as a young woman, even recalling a "white dress with blue ribbons" (399, speech 134). Martha also recalls that Minnie, when young, was "sweet and pretty, but kind of timid and—fluttery" (398, speech 107). In light of these recollections, Martha observes that Minnie had changed, and changed for the worse, during her long years of marriage with John Wright, who is characterized as "a raw wind that gets to the bone" (398, speech 104). As more evidence for Minnie's acceptance of her drab life, Mrs. Peters says that Minnie asks for no more than an apron and a shawl when under arrest in the sheriff's home. This modest clothing, as contrasted with the colorful dresses of her youth, suggests how her spirit has been suppressed.

[3] The end of this suppression of spirit and also the emergence of Minnie's rage is shown by the discovery of her dead canary. We learn that Minnie, who when young had been in love with music, has endured her cheerless farm home for thirty years. During this time her husband's contempt has made her life solitary, cheerless, unmusical, and depressingly impoverished. But her buying the canary (397, speech 87) suggests the

---

°See pages 392–400 for this play.
*Central idea.
†Thesis sentence.

reemergence of her love of song, just as it also suggests at least a degree of self-assertion. That her husband wrings the bird's neck may thus be seen as the cause not only of her immediate sorrow, shown by the dead bird in a "pretty box" (398, speech 109), but also of the anger that marks her change from a stock, obedient wife to a person angry enough to kill.

[4]   Like her love of song, her unfinished quilt indicates her creativity. In her dreary and abused years on the farm, never having had children, she has had nothing creative to do except for needlework like the quilt. Mrs. Hale comments on the beauty of Minnie's log-cabin design (396, speech 72) and observes the colorful patches of cloth in her sewing basket (396, speech 71, S.D.). The inference is that even though Minnie's life has been bleak, she has been able to indulge her characteristic love of color and form—and also of warmth, granted the purpose of a quilt.

[5]   Ironically, the quilt also shows Minnie's creativity in the murder of her husband. Both Mrs. Hale and Mrs. Peters interpret the breakdown of her stitching on the quilt as signs of her distress about the dead canary and also of her nervousness in planning revenge. Further, even though nowhere in the play is it said that John is strangled with a quilting knot, no other conclusion is possible. Both Mrs. Hale and Mrs. Peters agree that Minnie probably intended to knot the quilt rather than sew it in a quilt stitch, and Glaspell pointedly causes the men to learn this detail even though they scoff at it and ignore it. In other words, we learn that Minnie's only outlet for creativity—needlework—has enabled her to perform the murder in the only way she can, by strangling John with a slip-proof quilting knot. Even though her plan for the murder is deliberate—Mrs. Peters reports that the arrangement of the rope was "strange," and a "funny way to kill" (396, speech 65)—Minnie is not cold or remorseless. Her passivity after the crime demonstrates that planning to evade guilt, beyond simple denial, is not in her character. She is not so diabolically creative that she plans or even understands the irony of strangling her husband in a way similar to the way he killed the bird. Glaspell, however, makes this irony plain.

[6]   It is important to emphasize again that we learn about Minnie from others. Nevertheless, Minnie is fully realized, round, and poignant. For all her adult life, she has patiently accepted her drab and colorless marriage. In the dreary surroundings of the Wright farm, she suppresses her grudges, just as she suppresses her prettiness, colorfulness, and creativity. In short, she has been nothing more than a flat character. The killing of the canary, however, causes her to change and to destroy her husband in an assertive rejection of her stock role as the suffering wife. She is a patient woman whose patience finally reaches the breaking point.

Work Cited

Glaspell, Susan. *Trifles*. Edgar V. Roberts. *Writing About Literature*. 11th ed. Upper Saddle River: Prentice Hall, 2006. 392–400.

Commentary on the Essay

The strategy of the argument of this essay is to use details from the story to support the central idea that Minnie Wright is a round, developing character. Hence the essay illustrates strategy 3 described on page 72. Other plans of organization could also have been chosen, such as the qualities of acquiescence, fortitude, and potential for anger (strategy 1); the change in Minnie from submission to vengefulness (strategy 2); or the reported actions of Minnie's singing, knotting quilts, and sitting in the kitchen on the morning after the murder (another way to use strategy 3).

Because Minnie does not appear in the story but is described only in the words of the major characters, the introductory paragraph of the illustrative essay deals with the way we learn about her. The essay thus highlights how Glaspell uses methods 2 and 4 (see page 72) as the ways of rendering the story's main character, while omitting strategies 1, 3, and 5.

The essay's argument is developed through inferences made from details in the story, namely Minnie's clothing (paragraph 2), her canary (paragraph 3), and her quilt (paragraphs 4 and 5). The last paragraph summarizes a number of these details, and it also considers how Minnie transcends the stock qualities of her role as a farm wife and gains roundness as a result of her outbreak against her husband.

As a study in composition, paragraph 3 demonstrates how discussion of a specific character trait, together with related details, can contribute to the essay's main argument. The trait is Minnie's love of music (shown by her canary). The connecting details, selected from study notes, are the loss of music in her life, her isolation, her lack of pretty clothing, the contemptibility of her husband, and her grief when putting the dead bird into the box. In short, the paragraph weaves together enough material to show the relationship between Minnie's trait of loving music and the crisis of her developing anger—a change that marks her as a round character.

Special Topics for Studying and Discussing Character

1. Compare the ways in which actions and speeches are used to bring out the character traits of Farquhar of "An Occurrence at Owl Creek Bridge" and of Goodman Brown of "Young Goodman Brown."
2. Write a brief essay comparing the changes or developments of two major or round characters in stories or plays included in Appendix C. You might deal with issues such as what the characters are like at the beginning; what conflicts they confront, deal with, or avoid; or what qualities are brought out that signal the changes or developments.
3. Compare the qualities and functions of two or more flat characters (e.g., the men in *Trifles* or the secondary characters in "The Story of an Hour").

How do they bring out qualities of the major characters? What do you discover about their own character traits?

4. Using Miss Brill ("Miss Brill"), Minnie Wright (*Trifles*), and Farquhar ("An Occurrence at Owl Creek Bridge") as examples, describe the effects of circumstance on character. Under the rubric "circumstance" you may consider elements such as education, family, economic and social status, wartime conditions, and geographic isolation.

5. Write a brief story about an important decision you have made (e.g., picking a school, beginning or leaving a job, declaring a major, or ending a friendship). Show how your own qualities of character (to the extent that you understand them), together with your own experiences, have gone into the decision. You may write more comfortably if you give yourself another name and describe your actions in the third person.

6. Topics for paragraphs or short essays:

    a. What characteristics of the speaker are brought out by Amy Lowell in "Patterns"? Should the classifications "round" and "flat" even apply to her? Why or why not?

    b. Why does the speaker of Matthew Arnold's "Dover Beach" philosophize about the darkness and the pounding surf nearby? What qualities of character do his thoughts reveal?

    c. Consider this proposition: To friends who haven't seen us for a time, we are round, but to ourselves and most other people, we are flat.

4

Writing About Point of View

The Position or Stance of the Work's Narrator or Speaker

The term **point of view** refers to the **speaker**, **narrator**, **persona**, or **voice** created by authors to tell stories, present arguments, and express attitudes and judgments. Point of view involves not only the speaker's physical position as an observer and recorder, but also the ways in which the speaker's social, political, and mental circumstances affect the narrative. For this reason, point of view is one of the more complex and subtle aspects of literary study.

Authors try not only to make their works interesting but also to bring their presentations alive. The presentation is similar to a dramatic performance: In a play, the actors are themselves, but in their roles they *impersonate* and temporarily *become* the characters they act. In fictional works, not only do authors impersonate characters who do the talking, but also they *create* these characters. One such character is Jackie, the narrator of Frank O'Connor's "First Confession," who is telling about events that occurred when he was a child. Because he is the subject as well as the narrator, he has firsthand knowledge of the actions, even though he also indicates that he, as an adult, has not fully assimilated his childhood experience. We may also note the unnamed narrator of Hardy's "The Three Strangers." Hardy arranges the narrative to make us sympathetic to his speaker's opinions about the permanence and strength of the rough and unpolished shepherds as opposed to the intrusively obnoxious second stranger.

Because of the ramifications of creating a narrative voice, point of view may also be considered as the centralizing or guiding intelligence in a work—the mind that filters the fictional experience and presents only the most important details to create the maximum impact. It may be compared to the perspectives utilized by painters: The way we understand the reality presented in painted pictures—the point of view or guiding intelligence presented by the painter—determines our perceptions and understanding of the painter's ideas. Similarly, the point of view or guiding intelligence created by the author of a literary work determines how we read, understand, and respond, as with the unnamed narrator of Poe's "The Masque of the Red Death." Although this narrator might be expected to have strong opinions about the haughty and headstrong behavior of his principal character, he does not overtly state any opinions, but instead arranges the narrative to make his views apparent to us.

An Exercise in Point of View: Reporting an Accident

As an exercise to show that point of view is derived from lifelike situations, let us imagine that there has been an auto accident. Two cars, driven by Alice and Bill, have collided, and the after-crash scene is represented in the drawing below. How might this accident be described? What would Alice and Bill say?

Now assume that Frank, who is Bill's best friend, and Mary, who knows neither Bill nor Alice, were witnesses. What might Frank say about who was responsible? What might Mary say? Additionally, assume that you are a reporter for a local newspaper and are sent to report on the accident. You know none of the people involved. How will your report differ from the other reports? Finally, to what degree are all the statements designed to persuade listeners and readers that the details and claims made in the respective reports are true?

The likely differences in the various reports may be explained by reference to point of view. Because both Alice and Bill are deeply involved—each of them is a major participant or what may be called a **major mover**—they will likely arrange their words to make themselves seem blameless. Frank, because he is Bill's best friend, will report things in Bill's favor. Mary will favor neither Alice nor Bill, but let us assume that she did not look up to see the colliding cars until she heard the crash. Thus, she did not see the accident happening but saw only the immediate aftereffects. Amid all this mixture of partial and impartial views of the action, to whom should we attribute the greatest reliability?

Each person's report will have the "hidden agenda" of making herself or himself seem honest, objective, intelligent, impartial, and thorough. Thus, although Alice and Bill may be truthful to the best of their abilities, their reports will not be reliable because they both have something to gain from avoiding responsibility for the accident. Also, Frank may be questionable as a witness because he is Bill's friend and may report things to Bill's advantage. Mary could be reliable, but she did not see everything; therefore she is unreliable not because of motivation but rather because of her location as a witness. Most likely, *your* account as an impartial reporter will be the most reliable and objective of all, because your major interest is to learn all the details and to report the truth accurately, with no concern about the personal interests of either Alice or Bill.

As you can see, the ramifications of describing actions are far-reaching, and the consideration of the various interests and situations is subtle. Indeed, of all the aspects of literature, point of view is the most complex because it is so much like life itself. On the one hand, point of view is intertwined with the many interests and wishes of humanity at large; on the other, it is linked to the enormous difficulty of uncovering and determining truth.

Conditions That Affect Point of View

As this exercise in observation and expression demonstrates, point of view depends on two major factors. The first factor is *the physical situation of the narrator, or speaker, as an observer*. How close to the action is the speaker? Is the speaker a major mover or major participant or no more than a witness, either close or distant? How much is he or she privileged to know? How accurate and complete are his or her reports? How do the speaker's characteristics emerge from the narration? What are his or her qualifications or limitations as an observer?

The second factor is *the speaker's intellectual and emotional position*. How might the speaker gain or lose from what takes place in the story? Are the speaker's observations and words colored by these interests? Does he or she have any persuasive purpose beyond being a straightforward recorder or observer? What values does the speaker impose upon the action?

POINT OF VIEW AND OPINIONS

Because *point of view* is often popularly understood to mean ideas, opinions, or beliefs, it must be stressed that the term is not directly synonymous with any of these. Point of view refers to a work's mode of narration, comprising narrator, language, audience, and perceptions of events and characters, whereas opinions and beliefs are thoughts and ideas that may or may not have anything to do with a narration.

One may grant, however, that the position from which people see and understand things (e.g., established positions of political party, religion, social philosophy, and morality) has a most definite bearing on how they think and therefore on their opinions and beliefs. Opinions also affect how people view reality, and opinions affect, if not control, what they say about their perceptions of the world around them. Therefore, opinions stem out of point of view and at the same time have an influence on point of view. A four-star general and a buck private will have different things to say about what happens on a wartime battlefield.

For our purposes in this chapter, however, a discussion of point of view should emphasize how the narration and dramatic situation of a work create and shape the work. If ideas seem to be important in a story, your objective should be not to analyze and discuss the ideas as ideas, but rather to consider whether and how these ideas affect what the narrator concludes and says about the story's actions and situations.

In a story, as in many poems using narrative, authors take into account all these subtleties. For example, O'Connor's narrator, Jackie, in "First Confession" tells about boyhood family problems and his first experience with the sacrament of confession, but he has not yet fully separated himself from some of his childhood antagonisms. The narrator/speaker of Wagner's poem "The Boxes" is a mother describing the horror of searching for her lost son, who has drowned, and the anguish of her feelings in the years after the death. For these reasons, these narrators show their own involvement and concern about the events they describe. As readers, we need to determine how such varying modes of presentation determine the effects of these and all other stories and narrative poems.

Determining a Work's Point of View

In your reading you will encounter a wide variety of points of view. To begin your analysis, first determine the work's grammatical voice (i.e., first, second, or third person). Then study the ways in which the subject, characterization, dialogue, and form interact with the point of view.

In the First-Person Point of View, the Narrator Tells About Events He or She Has Personally Witnessed

If the voice of the work is an "I," the author is using the **first-person point of view**—the impersonation of a fictional narrator or speaker who may be named or unnamed. In our hypothetical accident reports, both Alice and Bill are first-person speakers who are named. Similarly, the narrator of O'Connor's "First Confession" is named and identified. By contrast, the narrators of Arnold's "Dover Beach" and Coleridge's "Kubla Khan" are both unnamed first-person speakers, as are the speakers of Poe's "The Masque of the Red Death" and Lowell's "Patterns." In Twain's "Luck," there are two unnamed first-person speakers (the first "I" introduces the second "I").

First-person speakers report events as though they have acquired their knowledge in a number of ways.

- What they themselves have done, said, heard, and thought (firsthand experience).
- What they have observed others doing and saying (firsthand witness).
- What others have said to them or otherwise communicated to them (secondhand testimony and hearsay).
- What they are able to infer or deduce from the information they have discovered (inferential information).
- What they are able to conjecture about how a character or characters might think and act, given their knowledge of a situation (conjectural, imaginative, or intuitive information).

There Are Many Different Kinds of First-Person Speakers Of all the points of view, the first person is the most independent of the author, because, as we have seen, the first-person speaker may have a unique identity, with name, job, and economic and social position. Often, however, the author creates a more anonymous but still independent first-person speaker, as with the unnamed speaker-narrator of Poe's "The Masque of the Red Death." Such a first-person plural point of view lends reliability to the narrative, as in Wagner's poem "The Boxes," because the characters included as "we," even if they are unidentified by the speaker, may be considered additional witnesses.

Some First-Person Speakers Are Reliable, but Others Are Unreliable When you encounter a first-person narrative (whether a story or narrative poem), determine the narrator's position and ability, prejudices or self-interest, and judgment of his or her readers or listeners. Most first-person speakers describing their own experiences are to be accepted as **reliable** and authoritative. But sometimes first-person speakers are **unreliable** because they may have interests or limitations that lead them to mislead, distort, or even lie. There is reason, for example, to question the reliability of the narrator of O'Connor's "First Confession." As an adult he is describing the events within his family and his after-school preparation sessions prior to his attending his first confession, but he is giving us his childhood memories, and he is not including the potential views of others about the ways in which things happened. Whether first-person speakers are reliable or unreliable, however, they are one of the means by which authors confer an authentic, lifelike aura to their works.

In the Second-Person Point of View, the Narrator Is Speaking to Someone Else Who Is Addressed as "You"

The **second-person point of view,** the least common of the points of view, and the most difficult for authors to manage, offers two major possibilities. In the first, a narrator (almost necessarily a first-person speaker) tells a listener what he or she has done and said at a past time. The actions might be a simple retelling of events, as when a parent tells a child about something the child did during infancy, or when a doctor tells a patient with amnesia about events before the causative injury. Also, the actions might also be subject to dispute and interpretation, as when a prosecuting attorney describes a crime for which a defendant is on trial or when a spouse lists grievances against an alienated spouse in a custody or divorce case. Still another situation of the second-person point of view might occur when an angry person accuses the listener of a betrayal or some other wrong. In such instances, it is worth bearing in mind that the point of view may be considered first person rather than second, for the speaker is likely to be speaking subjectively about his or her own perception or analysis of the listener's actions.

The second possibility is equally complex. Some narrators are obviously addressing a "you" but are instead referring mainly to themselves—and to listeners only tangentially—in preference to an "I," as in the last lines of Hardy's poem "The Man He Killed." In addition, some narrators follow the usage—not uncommon in colloquial speech—of the indefinite "you." In this use of point of view, the *you* (or *thou*) refers not to a specific listener but rather to anyone at all. In this way the writer avoids the more formal use of such words as *one, a person*, or *people*. (Incidentally, the selection of *you* is non-gender-specific because it eliminates the need for the pronouns *he, she; she/he; he/she;* or *he or she*.)

It is not unusual for some narrators to address a listening audience as "you," and to this degree the situation may be categorized at least partially as second person. Coleman's "Unfinished Masterpieces" is such a work, in which the narrator not only brings readers or listeners into her confidence, but also speaks to the two major characters of the story as though they are still present. It is common in poetry for the speaker to include a "you" as a person being addressed. In addition to "The Man He Killed," we see the "you" listener in Arnold's "Dover Beach" (the "love") Keats's "Bright Star" (a distant star, likely the North Star), and Rossetti's "Echo" (the "love"). Shakespeare imagines a listening person in Sonnets 30 and 73. In these works, which are strongly dramatic, the mythical second-person listener is significantly involved in prompting and interacting with the speaker.

In the Third-Person Point of View, the Speaker
Emphasizes the Actions and Speeches of Others

If events in the work are described in the third person (*he, she, it, they*), the author is using the **third-person point of view**. It is not always easy to characterize the voice in this point of view. Sometimes the speaker uses an "I," as in Poe's "The Masque of the Red Death," and may seemingly be identical with the author, but at other times the author creates a distinct **authorial voice**, as in Mansfield's "Miss Brill." There are three variants of the third-person point of view: *dramatic* or *objective, omniscient,* and *limited omniscient.*

The Dramatic or Objective Point of View Is the Most Basic Method of Narration The most direct presentation of action and dialogue is the dramatic or objective point of view (also called third-person objective). It is the basic method of rendering action and speech that all the points of view share. The narrator of the dramatic point of view is an unidentified speaker who reports things in a way that is analogous to a hovering or tracking video camera or to what some critics have called "a fly on the wall (or tree)." Somehow, the narrator/speaker is always on the spot—in rooms, forests, village squares, moving vehicles, or even in outer space—to tell us what is happening and what is being said.

The dramatic presentation is limited *only* to what is said and what happens. The writer does not overtly draw conclusions or make interpretations, because the premise of the dramatic point of view is that readers, like a jury, can form their own judgments if they are shown the right evidence. Thus Randall's "Ballad of Birmingham" is a short and powerful poem illustrating the dramatic point of view. It dramatizes a brief and poignant dialogue between a child and her mother, and it follows the mother to the scene of the bombed-out church to which the mother had sent the child. We, the readers, draw a number of conclusions about the situation (i.e., that racism is evil, that brutal violence is inexplicable, that innocent suffering is heartrending), but because of the dramatic point of view Randall does not *state* any of these conclusions for us.

The Narrator of the Omniscient Point of View Can See All, Know All, and Potentially Disclose All The third-person point of view is **omniscient** (all-knowing) when the speaker not only presents action and dialogue but also reports the thoughts and reactions of the characters. In our everyday world, we never know what other people are thinking—their minds are closed to us. However, we always make assumptions about the thoughts of others, and these assumptions are the basis of the omniscient point of view. Authors use it freely but judiciously to explain responses, thoughts, feelings, and plans—an additional dimension that aids in the development of character. For example, in Maupassant's "The Necklace," the speaker takes an omniscient stance to explain the responses and thoughts of the major character and also, though to a small degree, of her husband. However, even in an omniscient point of view story, relatively little description is actually devoted to the thoughts of the characters, for most of the narration must necessarily be taken up with objective descriptions.

The Narrator or Speaker in the Limited or Limited-Omniscient Point of View Focuses on Thoughts and Deeds of a Major Character   More common than the omniscient and dramatic points of view is the **limited third person** or **limited-omniscient third person**, in which the author concentrates on or *limits* the narration to the actions and thoughts of a major character. In our accident case, Frank, being Bill's friend, would be sympathetic to Bill. Thus Frank's report of the collision would likely be third-person limited, with Bill as the center of interest. Depending on whether a narration focuses on action or motivation, the limited third-person narrator may explore the mentality of the major character either lightly or in depth. The name given to the central figure on whom the third-person omniscient point of view is focused is the **point-of-view character**. Thus, Peyton Farquhar in "An Occurrence at Owl Creek Bridge," Miss Brill in "Miss Brill," Louise in Chopin's "The Story of an Hour," and Goodman Brown in Hawthorne's "Young Goodman Brown" are all point-of-view characters. Almost everything in these stories is there because the point-of-view characters see it, hear it, respond to it, think about it, imagine it entirely, do it or share in it, try to control it, or are controlled by it.

Mingling Points of View

In some works, authors mingle points of view in order to imitate reality. For example, many first-person narrators use various types of the third-person point of view during much of their narration. Authors may also vary points of view to sustain interest, create suspense, or put the burden of response entirely upon readers. Such shifting occurs at the end of Hawthorne's "Young Goodman Brown," where the narrator objectively and almost brutally summarizes Brown's loveless and morose life after his nightmare about evil. Similar changes occur in Bierce's "An Occurrence at Owl Creek Bridge," when the narrative shifts from close identification with the major character, Farquhar, to a remote and objective view of him at the story's conclusion. In poetry, the speaker of Arnold's "Dover Beach" speaks mainly for himself, but he also shifts to the "you" whom he is addressing, and also to "we" in the concluding lines, in reference both to himself and the "you." There is a comparable shift in Hardy's "The Man He Killed," in which the speaker shifts from "I" to include the listener as "you," meaning "you" and "I" together.

Summary: Guidelines for Point of View

The following guidelines summarize and further classify the types of points of view. Use them to see differences and shades of variation in stories and poems.

1. **First person** (*I, my, mine, me,* and sometimes *we, our,* and *us*). First-person speakers are involved to at least some degree in the actions of the work.

Such narrators may have (1) complete understanding; (2) partial or incorrect understanding; (3) no understanding at all; or (4) complete understanding with the motive to mislead or lie. Although the narrators described in guidelines 1 through 3 are usually **reliable** and tell the truth, they may also sometimes be **unreliable**. The only way to tell is to study the story closely. Obviously, 4 is by nature unreliable, but nevertheless the mode might possibly be accepted (although critically) on matters of detail.

   a. *Major participant*

      i.   Who tells his or her own story and thoughts as a major mover.

      ii. Who tells a story about others and also about herself or himself as one of the major movers.

      iii. Who tells a story mainly about others, and about himself or herself only tangentially.

   b. *Minor participant,* who tells a story about events experienced and witnessed.

   c. *Nonparticipating but identifiable speaker,* who learns about events in other ways (e.g., listening to participants through direct conversation, overhearing conversation, examining documents, hearing news reports, imagining what might have occurred). The narrative of such a speaker is a combination of fact and conjectural reconstruction.

2. **Second person** (*you,* or possibly *thou*). A point of view that authors use often enough to justify our knowing about it. Its premise is that the speaker knows more about the actions of a character (the "you") than the character himself or herself. (a) It is used when the speaker (e.g., lawyer, spouse, friend, sports umpire, psychologist, parent, angry person) talks directly to the other person and explains that person's past actions and statements. More generally, and in a colloquial and informal style, the speaker may also use "you" to mean (b) himself or herself; (c) the reader; or (d) anyone at all.

3. **Third person** (she, he, it, they). The speaker is outside the action and is mainly a reporter of actions and speeches. Some speakers may have unique and distinguishing traits even though no separate identity is claimed for them ("the unnamed third-person narrator"). Other third-person speakers who are not separately identifiable may represent the words and views of the authors themselves ("the authorial voice").

   a. *Dramatic or third-person objective.* The narrator reports only what can be seen and heard. The thoughts of characters are included only if they are spoken or written (dialogue, reported or overheard conversation, letters, reports, etc.).

   b. *Omniscient.* The omniscient speaker knows all, sees all, reports all, and when necessary, reveals the inner workings of the minds of any or all characters. Even an omniscient speaker, however, makes a mostly dramatic presentation.

   c. *Limited, or limited omniscient.* The focus is on the actions, responses, thoughts, and feelings of a single major character. Although the narration may concentrate on the character's actions, it may simultaneously probe deep within the consciousness of the character.

POINT OF VIEW AND VERB TENSE

As demonstrated in this chapter, point of view refers to the ways narrators and speakers perceive and report actions and speeches. In the broadest sense, however, point of view may be considered as a total way of rendering truth, and for this reason the *tense* chosen by the narrators is important. Most narratives rely on the past tense: The actions happened in the past, and they are now over.

But the introduction of dialogue, even in a past-tense narration, dramatically brings the story into the present. Such dramatic rendering is accomplished by the dialogue concluding Maupassant's "The Necklace," for example, which emphasizes the immediacy of Mathilde's problems.

The narrator of a past-tense narrative may also introduce present-tense commentary during the narration—a strong means of signifying the importance of past events. Examples are in O'Connor's "First Confession" in which the narrator Jackie makes personal comments about the events he is describing, and in Hardy's "The Three Strangers," in which the narrator both begins and ends his past-tense narrative in the present tense. It is also significant to note that the narrators of parables and fables use past-tense narratives as vehicles for teaching current lessons in philosophy and religion.

In recent years a number of writers have used the present tense as their principal time reference. With the present tense, the narrative story or poem is rendered as a virtual drama that is unfolded moment by moment. In Wagner's "The Boxes," for instance, the speaker employs the present tense to emphasize that her pain is a constant part of her life.

Some writers intermingle tenses to show how time itself can be merged within the human mind, because our consciousness never exists only in the present but instead is a composite made up of past memories cresting upon a never-ending wave carrying us into the future. Thus at the end of Bierce's "An Occurrence at Owl Creek Bridge," the past-tense narration shifts into the present tense to demonstrate the vividness of the main character's perceptions just before his death (paragraph 36).

Writing About Point of View

In your essay on point of view you should explain how point of view contributes to making the work exactly as it is. As you prepare to write, therefore, consider language, authority and opportunity for observation, the involvement or detachment of the speaker, the selection of detail, interpretive commentaries, and narrative development. The following questions will help you get started.

Raise Questions to Discover Ideas

- How is the narration made to seem real or probable? Are the actions and speeches reported authentically, as they might be seen and reported in life?
- Is the narrator/speaker identifiable? What are the narrator's qualifications as an observer? How much of the story seems to result from the imaginative or creative powers of the narrator?
- How does the narrator/speaker perceive the time of the actions? If the predominant tense is the past, what relationship, if any, does the narrator establish between the past and the present (e.g., providing explanations, making conclusions)? If the tense is present, what effect does this tense have on your understanding of the story?
- To what extent does point of view make the work interesting and effective?

First-Person Point of View

- What prompts the speaker to tell the story? What does the story tell us about the experience and interests of the narrator/speaker?
- Is the speaker talking to the reader, a listener, or herself? How does her audience affect what she is saying? Is the level of language appropriate to her and the situation? How much does she tell about herself?
- To what degree is the narrator involved in the action (i.e., as a major participant or major mover, minor participant, or nonparticipating observer)? Does he make himself the center of humor or admiration? How? Does he seem aware of changes he undergoes?
- Does the speaker criticize other characters? Why? Does she seem to report fairly and accurately what others have told her?
- How reliable is the speaker? Does the speaker seem to have anything to hide? Does it seem that he may be using the story for self-justification or exoneration? What effect does this complexity have on the story?

Second-Person Point of View

- What situation prompts the use of the second person? How does the speaker acquire the authority to explain things to the listener? How directly involved is the listener? What is the relationship between the speaker and listener? If the listener is indefinite, why does the speaker choose to use "you" as the basis of the narration?

Third-Person Point of View

- Does the author speak in an authorial voice, or does it seem that the author has adopted a special but unnamed voice for the work?
- What is the speaker's level of language (e.g., formal and grammatical, informal or intimate and ungrammatical)? Are actions, speeches, and explanations made fully or sparsely?
- From what apparent vantage point does the speaker report action and speeches? Does this vantage point make the characters seem distant or close? How much sympathy does the speaker express for the characters?

- To what degree is your interest centered on a particular character? Does the speaker give you thoughts and responses of this character (limited third person)?
- If the work is third-person omniscient, how extensive is this omniscience (e.g., all the characters or just a few)? Generally, what limitations or freedoms can be attributed to this point of view?
- What special kinds of knowledge does the narrator assume that the listeners or readers possess (e.g., familiarity with art, religion, politics, history, navigation, music, current or past social conditions)?
- How much dialogue is used in the story? Is the dialogue presented directly, as dramatic speech, or indirectly, as past-tense reports of speeches? What is your perception of the story's events as a result of the use of dialogue?

Tense

- What tense is used predominantly throughout the story? If a single tense is used throughout (e.g., present, past), what is the effect of this constant use of tense?
- Does the story show a mixture of tenses? Why are the tenses mixed? What purpose is served by these variations? What is the effect of this mixture?
- Is any special use made of the future tense? What is the effect of this use on the present and past circumstances of the characters?

Organize Your Essay About Point of View

Throughout your essay, you should develop your analysis of how the point of view determines such aspects as situation, form, general content, and language. The questions in the preceding section should help you decide how the point of view interacts with these other elements.

Introduction   Begin by briefly stating the major influence of the point of view on the work. (*Examples*: "The omniscient point of view permits many insights into the major character," or "The first-person point of view permits the work to resemble an exposé of back-room political deals.") How does the point of view make the work interesting and effective? How will your analysis support your central idea?

Body   An excellent way to build your argument is to explore how a different point of view might affect the presentation of the work. Hardy's poem "Channel Firing," for example, uses a first-person speaker—a skeleton long buried in a churchyard cemetery near the ocean. This speaker is awakened by the noise of nearby naval guns, a bizarre situation prompting ironic humor that could not be duplicated with a third-person point of view. Hardy's first-person point of view is essential because we learn, firsthand, about the speaker's feelings. Indeed, the poem is totally dependent on this speaker. Conversely, Mansfield's "Miss Brill" employs the third-person limited point of view, with the speaker presenting an intimate portrait of the major character while also preserving an objective and ironic distance. If Miss Brill herself were the narrator, we would get the intimacy that encourages us to sympathize with her, but we would lose the distance that permits us to see her objectively.

You can see that this approach requires creative imagination, for you must speculate about a point of view that is not present. Considering alternative points of view deeply, however, will greatly enhance your analytical and critical abilities.

Conclusion   In your conclusion, evaluate the success of the point of view. Is it consistent, effective, truthful? What does the writer gain or lose (if anything) by the selection of point of view?

Illustrative Essay

Bierce's Control of Point of View in "An Occurrence at Owl Creek Bridge"°

[1]   Ambrose Bierce's control over point of view in "An Occurrence at Owl Creek Bridge" is essential to his success in showing the human mental capacity to register an immense length of perceived time and action in no more than an instant of real time.* The story is based on the idea that it is an individual's mind, not the actual passage of time, that governs time perception. Ordinarily, time seems steady and unvarying, like the ticking of a clock (paragraph 5); but at certain heightened instances of perception—in the story, the moment just before death—a person may fully imagine experiences that take much longer than the measurable, real time. Bierce brings this idea to life by using a narrative in the dramatic point of view as the frame of a narrative in the third-person limited omniscient point of view.†

[2]   The story is framed, at both the opening and closing, by materials narrated from the dramatic point of view. The opening is an objective account of the story's basic circumstances: During the Civil War, Peyton Farquhar, a Southern loyalist, is about to be hanged by the Union army, apparently for the attempted sabotage of the railroad bridge spanning Owl Creek, a stream in northern Alabama. Bierce changes from the objective point of view in the fourth paragraph, and he then centers on Farquhar through the limited omniscient point of view. The second section of the story, which views Farquhar objectively, explains how Farquhar got to the point of hanging. Almost the entire third section—twenty descriptive paragraphs—focuses exclusively on Farquhar's last moments of life. Beginning with the reality of his drop, he perceives that the rope breaks and that he falls into the water, avoids the rifle and cannon fire of the Union soldiers, swims to shore, walks home, and is greeted by his wife. This dream of happiness is ended in paragraph 37, the

---

°For the text of this story, see pages 317–322.
*Central idea.
†Thesis sentence.

last, which marks an abrupt and brutal return to the dramatic point of view with which the story opens:

> Peyton Farquhar was dead; his body, with a broken neck, swung gently from side to side beneath the timbers of the Owl Creek bridge.

[3] The best part of the story, the "framed" part, is Bierce's use of a limited third-person narration to render Farquhar's mental perceptions. We first encounter this method in the narrator's ironic statement about Farquhar: "The arrangement [i.e., the apparatus for hanging] commended itself to his judgment as simple and effective" (paragraph 4). Bierce carefully explains how the rest of the story is to be told. First, he states that Farquhar's "thoughts, which have here to be set down in words, were flashed into the doomed man's brain" (paragraph 7). He also states that the agony of the man being hanged heightens his understanding: "Something in the awful disturbance of his organic system" exalts and refines his physical senses so that they record things "<u>never before perceived</u>" (paragraph 20, underlining added). On this principle of narration, Bierce's narrator plumbs the depths of Farquhar's dying consciousness—an entire narrative of escape that flashes through Farquhar's mind during his last moments.

[4] The escape, which forms the narrative of the third section, seems to be happening plausibly and realistically in just the way that the reader, naturally sympathetic to Farquhar, wants it to happen. <u>The power of the story results from this tension between desire and actuality.</u> Bierce's limited omniscient narrator is careful in the very second sentence of the third section to fuse together the two elements of time and perception so vital to the story's development: "ages later, it seemed to him" (paragraph 18). All the details about Farquhar's dreams of escape stem out of the words <u>ages</u> and <u>seemed.</u> Under special circumstances, in other words, human perception can fit almost a lifetime of detail into no more than fractions of a second.

[5] <u>Therefore the dying man's perception of detail is the story's major emphasis.</u> At first, the narrator's descriptions indicate that Farquhar's imagination is sharp enough even to record the eye color of one of the Union soldiers. Farquhar's mind soon gets weaker, however, and his perceptions become more dreamlike and impressionistic. By describing the road bordered by "black bodies" of trees forming "a straight wall on both sides, terminating on the horizon in a point," Bierce's narrator demonstrates Farquhar's dimming consciousness and increasing distortion of reality (paragraph 34). Paragraph 36, which changes the narrative from the past to the present tense, contains Farquhar's vision during the last split second of his life. His final mental image is that his wife "<u>steps</u> down from the verandah to meet him," and "<u>stands waiting</u>" for him (present tenses are underlined). It is then that his life is ended by the very realistic "blow upon the back of the neck."

[6] <u>Even though the events are told through Farquhar's hopeful vision of escape, however, this realistic blow reminds us that the narrative constantly reveals his physical agony.</u> A number of times we are told that Farquhar is feeling "pain," that he is "suffocating," that he feels a "sharp pain in his wrist," and that "his neck ached horribly; his brain was on fire" (paragraphs 18, 19, 35). We

may take as equally real Farquhar's sensation that his "visible world" seems to be wheeling "slowly round" (paragraph 21), for this perception is consistent with the sensations of a hanging, dying man. In other words, just as the narrative concentrates on Farquhar's understanding of reality, it also demonstrates the true reality of his final death pangs.

[7] Without doubt, the merging of Bierce's narrative voice with the consciousness of the dying man makes the story unique. <u>No other method could give the story its credibility and power, which depend on the disclosure of what is happening in the protagonist's mind.</u> For example, the use of the dramatic point of view, with which the story opens and closes, does not permit access to the internal thoughts of a character. In much the same way, the first-person point of view—focusing on an unconscious and dying man—does not permit any recording of what is happening. It is therefore clear that Bierce's limited omniscient point of view is the right one for this story. The method permits him to make the events seem both realistic and convincing and also to create sympathy for Farquhar because of the hopelessness of his situation.

[8] <u>Such masterly control over point of view is a major cause of Bierce's success in "An Occurrence at Owl Creek Bridge."</u> His narrative method is to establish a frame of normal reality and normal time, and then to render contrasting interior perceptions of perceived reality and perceived time. He is so successful that a casual reader might at first conclude that Farquhar's escape is real. The reality is not in the events, however, but in the perceptions. Without Bierce's mingling of the dramatic and the limited points of view, it would not be possible to claim such success for the story.

Work Cited

Bierce, Ambrose. "An Occurrence at Owl Creek Bridge." Edgar V. Roberts. *Writing About Literature*. 11th ed. Upper Saddle River: Prentice Hall, 2006. 317–322.

Commentary on the Essay

The strategy of this essay is to explain how Bierce's use of the limited omniscient point of view is fundamental to his success in demonstrating how time may be compressed in heightened moments of awareness. Words of tribute throughout the essay are "success," "control," "dominating," and "masterly."

The introductory paragraph sets out two major areas of investigation for the essay: first, the use of the dramatic point of view as a frame, and, second, the limited omniscient point of view as the center of concentration.

The first part of the essay (paragraph 2) is relatively brief. Only enough is brought out about the dramatic point of view to establish that Bierce uses it as a beginning and an ending frame for the deep examination of the narration happening in the protagonist's mind.

The second part of the body (paragraphs 3 to 7) emphasizes how Bierce delves into the dying protagonist's mind. The goal of paragraphs 3 to 5 is to show how the narrator's point of view virtually merges with that of Farquhar.

Paragraph 6 is designed as a defense of the narrative method because throughout the narration, Bierce reports the immense pain that Farquhar is feeling. In other words, the story faithfully and truthfully renders the perception of both agony and extended time. Continuing the thread of the argument, paragraph 7 examines other narrative possibilities for presenting Farquhar's vision and concludes that Bierce's actual choices are the best that could have been made.

The concluding paragraph (8) emphasizes how Bierce's success is attributable to his use of both the dramatic and the limited omniscient points of view.

Special Topics for Studying and Discussing Point of View

1. Write a short narrative from the first-person point of view of one of these characters:
   a. Mathilde Loisel in "The Necklace": How I ruined ten years of my life by not telling the truth.
   b. The baker in "Miss Brill": My favorite customer.
   c. The Red Death in "The Masque of the Red Death": Now, why is that foolish man in that tasteless costume running toward me?
   d. Faith in "Young Goodman Brown": I don't understand why my husband is so sour and sullen all the time.
   e. Nora in "First Confession": My terrible younger brother.

2. How would Hawthorne's story "Young Goodman Brown" be affected if told by a narrator with a different point of view (different knowledge, different interests, different purposes for telling the story), such as the narrators of "The Three Strangers" or "An Occurrence at Owl Creek Bridge"?

3. Recall a childhood occasion on which you were punished. Write an explanation of the punishment as though you were the adult who was in the position of punishing you. Be sure to consider your childhood self objectively, in the third person. Present things from the viewpoint of the adult, and try to determine how the adult would have learned about your action, judged it, and decided on your punishment.

4. Write an essay about the proposition that people often have something to gain when they speak and that therefore we need to be critical about what others tell us. Are they trying to change our judgments and opinions? Are they telling the truth? Are they leaving out any important details? Are they trying to sell us something? In your discussion, you may strengthen your ideas by referring to stories that you have been reading.

5. In the reference section of your library, find two books on literary terms and concepts. How completely and clearly do these works explain the concept of point of view? With the aid of these books, together with the materials in this chapter, describe the interests and views of the narrators in O'Connor's "First Confession," Bierce's "An Occurrence at Owl Creek Bridge," Hardy's "The Man He Killed," Keats's "On First Looking into Chapman's Homer," or another work of your choice.

5

Writing About Plot and Structure

The Development and Organization of Narratives and Drama

Stories, plays, and many poems are made up mostly of actions or incidents that follow one another in chronological order. The same is also true of life, but there is a major difference, and that is that fiction must make sense even though life itself does not always seem to make sense. Finding a sequential or narrative order is therefore only a first step in our consideration of fiction. What we depend on for the sense or meaning of fiction is **plot**, or the elements governing the unfolding of the actions.

Plot: The Motivation and Causation of Narratives and Plays

The English novelist E. M. Forster, in *Aspects of the Novel*, presents a memorable illustration of plot. To illustrate a bare set of actions, he proposes the following: "The king died, and then the queen died." Forster points out that this sequence does not form a plot because it lacks *motivation* and *causation*; it's too much like life itself to be fictional. Thus he introduces motivation and causation in his next example: "The king died, and then the queen died of grief." The phrase "of grief" shows that one thing (grief) controls or overcomes another (the normal desire to live), and motivation and causation enter the sequence to form a plot. In a well-plotted story or play, one thing precedes or follows another not simply because time ticks away but because *effects* follow *causes*. In a good work of fiction, nothing is irrelevant or accidental; everything is related and causative.

Determine the Conflict and Conflicts in a Story

The controlling impulse in a connected pattern of causes and effects is **conflict**, which refers to people or circumstances that a character must face and try to overcome. Conflicts bring out extremes of human energy, causing characters to engage in the decisions, actions, responses, and interactions that make up fictional literature.

In its most elemental form, a conflict is the opposition of two people. Their conflict may take the shape of anger, hatred, envy, argument, fighting, avoidance, political or moral opposition, gossip, lies, and many other attitudes and actions. Conflicts may also exist between groups, although conflicts between individuals are more identifiable and therefore more suitable for stories. Conflicts may also be abstract, such as when an individual opposes larger forces such as natural objects, ideas, modes of behavior, or public opinion. A difficult or even impossible *choice*—a **dilemma**—is a natural conflict for an individual person. A conflict may also be brought out in ideas and opinions that clash. In short, conflict shows itself in many ways.

Conflict Is Directly Related to Doubt, Tension, and Interest   Conflict is the major element of plot because opposing forces arouse *curiosity*, cause *doubt*, create *tension*, and produce *interest*. The same responses are the lifeblood of athletic competition. Consider which kind of athletic event is more interesting: (1) One team gets so far ahead that the outcome is no longer in doubt or (2) both teams are so evenly matched that the outcome is uncertain until the final seconds. Obviously, games are uninteresting unless they develop as contests between teams of comparable strength. The same principle applies to conflicts in stories and dramas. There should be uncertainty about a protagonist's success or failure. Unless there is doubt, there is no tension, and without tension there is no interest.

Find the Conflicts to Determine the Plot   To see a plot in operation, let us build on Forster's description. Here is a simple plot for a story of our own: "John and Jane meet, fall in love, and get married." This sentence contains a plot because it shows cause and effect (they get married *because* they fall in love), but with no conflict, the plot is not interesting. However, let us introduce conflicting elements into this common "boy meets girl" story:

> John and Jane meet in college and fall in love. They go together for a number of years and plan to marry, but a problem arises. Jane first wants to establish herself in a career, and after marriage she wants to be an equal contributor to the family. John understands Jane's wishes for equality, but he wants to get married first and let her finish her studies and have her career after they have children. Jane believes that John's plan is unacceptable because she thinks of it as a trap from which she might not escape. As they discuss their options they find themselves increasingly more irritated and unhappy with each other. Finally they bring their plans to an end, and they part in both anger and sorrow. Their love is not dead, however, but both go on to marry someone else and build separate lives and careers. In their new lives, neither is totally happy even though they like and respect their spouses. The years pass, and, after children and grandchildren, Jane and John meet again. He is now divorced and she is a widow. Because their earlier conflict is no longer a barrier, they rekindle their love, marry, and try to make up for the past. Even their new happiness, however, is tinged with regret and reproach because of their earlier conflicts, their unhappy decision to part, their lost years, and their increasing age.

Here we find a true plot because our original "boy meets girl" topic now contains a major conflict from which a number of related complications develop.

These complications embody disagreements, choices, arguments, and ill feelings that produce tension, uncertainty, rupture, and regret. When we learn that John and Jane finally join together at the end we might still find the story painful to contemplate because it does not give us a "happily ever after" ending. Nevertheless, the story makes sense—as a story—because its plot brings out the plausible consequences of the understandable aims and hopes of John and Jane during their long relationship. It is the imposition of necessary causes and effects upon a series of events in time that creates the story's plot.

Writing About the Plot of a Story or Play

An essay about plot is an analysis of the conflict and its developments. The organization of the essay should not be modeled on sequential sections and principal events, however, because these invite only a retelling of the story. Instead, the organization is to be developed from the important elements of conflict. As you look for ideas about plot, try to answer the following questions.

Raise Questions to Discover Ideas

- Who are the major and minor characters, and how do their characteristics put them in conflict? How can you describe the conflict or conflicts?
- How does the story's action grow out of the major conflict?
- If the conflict stems from contrasting ideas or values, what are these, and how are they brought out?
- What problems do the major characters face? How do the characters deal with these problems?
- How do the major characters achieve (or not achieve) their major goal(s)? What obstacles do they overcome? What obstacles overcome them or alter them?
- At the end, are the characters successful or unsuccessful, happy or unhappy, satisfied or dissatisfied, changed or unchanged, enlightened or ignorant? How has the resolution of the major conflict produced these results?

Organize Your Essay About Plot

To keep your essay brief, be selective. Rather than describe everything a major character does, for example, stress the major elements in his or her conflict. Thus, an essay on Chopin's "The Story of an Hour" might emphasize how Louise develops a conflict between her grief over her supposedly dead husband and her relief at realizing that for the first time, she may be free to do as she pleases. When there is a conflict between two major characters, the obvious approach is to focus equally on both. For brevity, however, emphasis might be placed on just one. An essay on the plot of Glaspell's *Trifles*, for example, might stress the things we learn about the major character, Minnie Wright, that are vital to her being the major participant in the play's conflict.

The plot may be analyzed more broadly in terms of impulses, goals, values, issues, and historical perspectives. Thus, you might emphasize the elements of chance working against Mathilde in Maupassant's "The Necklace" (Chapter 1) as a contrast to her dreams about wealth. A discussion of the plot of Poe's "The Masque of the Red Death" might stress the haughtiness of Prospero, the major character, because the plot could not develop without his egotism and pride.

The conclusion may contain a brief summary of the points you have made. It is also a fitting place to consider the effect or *impact* produced by the conflict. Additional ideas might focus on whether the author has arranged actions and dialogue to direct your favor toward one side or the other or whether the plot is possible or impossible, serious or comic, fair or unfair, or powerful or weak.

Illustrative Essay (on Plot)

Conflicting Values in Thomas Hardy's "The Three Strangers"°

[1]   At the beginning of Hardy's "The Three Strangers," the nature of the plot is not immediately clear. There seems to be no protagonist, no single major character, but rather a number of characters, and there is no apparent conflict. The first candidate for being the story's major character is Shepherd Fennel, but he stands out only as the cooperative host and opener of doors for the strangers entering his home. The first stranger might then seem to be the choice as major character, and this possibility is strengthened because of the jarring and obnoxious second stranger. Here the story establishes the beginning of a conflict, but a puzzling one because it seems no more than a contrast of personalities. The third stranger to enter the cottage does not seem to be a protagonist either, for he leaves almost as quickly as he enters. However, it is clear, once all the characters have been involved in the story, that Hardy's plot stems not so much from the conflict of individual characters as from a conflict between aspects of legality and the law. <u>On one side is justice and on the other injustice.</u>* <u>This opposition can be analyzed according to the characters on each side.</u>†

[2]   <u>In the order in which Hardy interweaves the opposing parts of his plot, the unjust side—the side opposing the people at the Fennels' cottage—is represented by the second stranger, the Hangman.</u> The cruelty of the hangman's duties is underlined by his selfishness, egotism, and arrogance. He drinks all the mead in the large common cup, never caring about what anyone else wants. He sings a merry song about his grisly job as hangman. He is obnoxious when he commands the guests to chase the third stranger. He shows his contempt for the people by calling them "simple-minded souls, you know, stirred up to anything in a moment" (337, paragraph 125). To emphasize just

---

°See pages 326–340 for this story.
*Central idea.
†Thesis sentence.

how terrible the hangman is, Hardy compares him to the devil (335, paragraph 87). In short, the Hangman, because of these qualities, is the story's cruel and thoughtless antagonist, and for this reason he represents the negative part of Hardy's plot.

[3]   By far the most powerful aspect of the plot is the positive and just side, represented by the Fennels, their guests, and the first and third strangers. They are ordinary, good folk, no more and no less, and their feelings about life are best shown by their celebration of the christening of the daughter of the Fennels. With regard to law, the story makes clear that such people favor fairness and compassion above strict punishment. Thus, when one of the guests explains that Timothy Summers (the first stranger) has been sentenced to be hanged because he had stolen a sheep when his "family were astarving" (paragraph 81), the other guests fall silent. Further, when the Hangman starts pushing them to start a search, they are slow and unwilling, and when they go out looking, they produce the wrong man. As we learn, the first stranger is really the fugitive Summers, whose crime is justifiable in the eyes of the people, and the third stranger is the fugitive's brother, who flees not because he is guilty but because he wants to deflect suspicion from Summers. These are the characters toward whom Hardy directs our understanding, admiration, and sympathy. Any attempt to sentence anyone harshly, as the law has done with Summers, brings out the hesitation and resistance of the natives.

[4]   An integral aspect of Hardy's plot is the countryside itself, which during the search becomes an almost active opponent against the legal capriciousness represented by the Hangman. The treacherous hill, containing the "flint slopes" of the hog's-back elevation near Higher Crowstairs, causes the searchers to stumble and tumble and make mistakes (337, paragraph 130). After the initial search for Summers proves fruitless, the people and the countryside unite to foil the thoughtlessly harsh law. The "woods and fields and lanes," together with the "lofts and outhouses" (339, paragraph 160), furnish hiding places for Summers, so that this man, the first stranger, is "never recaptured" (340, paragraph 161).

[5]   This side of rightness represented by the people is shown by Hardy as not just occasional but rather eternal. He carefully sets the story in the framework of "the lapse of centuries" (326, paragraph 1), and he includes references to the ancient figures Timon and Nebuchadnezzar, as though the happenings at the Fennels' party are as ageless as human history (327, paragraph 2). Beyond this, Hardy compares the activities of the shepherds to the movements of the universe itself, for the energetic dancing moves "in their planet-like courses, direct and retrograde, from apogee to perigee" (328, paragraph 10). When the third stranger is discovered, he steps out from behind an ash tree that was "probably sown there by a passing bird some fifty years before" (337, paragraph 131). Hardy's concluding paragraph places the entire story in the fabric of history and myth, thus stressing the continuum from the past to the present, a common humanity that is as old as time.

[6]   This brief description of the major conflict making up the plot of "The Three Strangers" does not account for the story's power. Hardy skillfully paints a sympathetic picture of the shepherds and their way—a way of friendliness and good will in which the literal and harsh application of law has little place.

His contrasting antagonist, the Hangman, personally violates the shepherd's home just as the law he represents violates the concept of justice felt by the people there. Admittedly, the complete intermeshing of the plot does not seem certain until the circumstances are explained by the brother of Timothy Summers—an explanation that makes clear the opposition between the people's justice and the Hangman's injustice. <u>Hardy's plot in "The Three Strangers" is strong because it is real and because the people themselves are presented as a collective force for fairness and justice over an application of law that is unfair and unjust.</u>

Work Cited

Hardy, Thomas. "The Three Strangers." Edgar V. Roberts. *Writing About Literature.* 11th ed. Upper Saddle River: Prentice Hall, 2006. 326–340.

Commentary on the Essay

Because the subject is plot, this essay emphasizes the conflicting elements in Hardy's "The Three Strangers"—the forces of understanding and humanity, on the one hand, and of harshness and cruelty, on the other. The first paragraph demonstrates how this conflict emerges in the story after a somewhat hesitant opening. Throughout the body of the essay, the conflict is stressed as the major element of Hardy's plot.

Note that the essay assumes that readers know the story already. Hence the essay is not a plot summary but is instead an analysis of the elements making up the plot. The only summary included here occurs in paragraph 6, in which the explanations by the third stranger are cited to show how Hardy does not make all aspects of his plot clear until near the story's end.

In the body of the essay, paragraph 2 deals with the characteristics of the antagonist, the Hangman. Following this, the greater portion of the body considers the collective (not individual) protagonist arrayed against the Hangman and the harsh law he represents. Thus the human protagonists are the people and the first and third strangers (paragraph 3), the geographical protagonist is the countryside around Higher Crowstairs (paragraph 4), and the historical protagonist is time itself (paragraph 5).

The last paragraph summarizes the conflicts of the plot and concludes with a final reference to the central idea, that the story exalts fairness and justice and deplores legal rigidity and injustice.

Structure: The Organization of Fiction, Poetry, and Drama

Structure refers to the ways in which writers arrange materials in accord with the general ideas and purposes of their works. Unlike plot, which is concerned with conflict or conflicts, structure defines the layouts of works—the ways the story, play, or poem is shaped. Structure is about matters such as placement, balance, recurring themes, true and misleading conclusions, suspense, and the imitation of models or forms such as reports, letters, conversations, or confessions. A work might be divided into numbered sections or parts, or it might begin in a countryside (or one state) and conclude in a city (or another state), or it might develop a relationship between two people from their first introduction to their falling in love.

Formal Categories of Structure

Many aspects of structure are common to all genres of literature. Particularly for stories and plays, however, the following aspects form a skeleton, a pattern of development.

The Exposition Provides the Materials
Necessary to Put the Plot into Operation

Exposition is the laying out, the putting forth, of story materials—the main characters, their backgrounds, their characteristics, interests, goals, limitations, potentials, and basic assumptions. Exposition is not limited to the beginning of the work, where it is most expected, but may be found anywhere. Thus, intricacies, twists, turns, false leads, blind alleys, surprises, and other quirks may be introduced to interest, intrigue, perplex, mystify, and please readers. Whenever something new arises, to the degree that it is new it is a part of exposition.

The Complication Marks the Beginning and the Growth of the Conflict

The **complication** is the onset and development of the major conflict—the plot. The major participants are the protagonist and antagonist, together with whatever ideas and values they represent, such as good or evil, freedom or oppression, independence or dependence, love or hate, intelligence or stupidity, or knowledge or ignorance.

The Crisis Marks the Decisions Made to End the Conflict

The **crisis** (a separating, distinguishing, or turning point) marks that part of the action where the conflict reaches its greatest tension. During the crisis, a decision or an action to resolve the conflict is undertaken, and therefore the crisis is the point at which curiosity, uncertainty, and tension are greatest. Usually the crisis is followed closely by the next stage, the *climax*. Often, in fact, the two are so close together that they are considered the same.

The Climax Is the Conclusion of the Conflict

Because the **climax** (Greek for "ladder") is a consequence of the crisis, it is the story's *high point* and may take the shape of a decision, an action, an affirmation or denial, or an illumination or a realization. It is the logical conclusion of the preceding actions; no new major developments follow it. In most stories, the climax occurs at the end or close to it. For example, in Hardy's "The Three Strangers" the climax is the friendly meeting between the first and second strangers after the natives have gone out to arrest the third stranger (paragraphs 118–129). Everything that happens prior to this meeting (which might have become a dangerous confrontation) leads to it: the story of Timothy Summers's theft, incarceration, and escape; the obnoxiousness of the second stranger; the developing sympathy of the shepherds for the escaped man; the suspicious behavior of the third stranger. Even though the loose threads still need tying together, this meeting is the story's climax because it establishes that Summers has escaped the law and that he will never be under the threat of the hangman.

The Resolution or Dénouement Finishes the Work and Releases the Tension

The **resolution** (a releasing or an untying) or **dénouement** ("untying") is the completing of the story or play after the climax, for once the climax has occurred, the work's tension and uncertainty are finished, and most authors conclude quickly to avoid losing their readers' interest. For instance, the dénouement of "Miss Brill" comprises a few short details about the major character's returning home, sitting down, and putting away her muff. Poe ends "The Masque of the Red Death" by asserting that the "illimitable" power of the Red Death has overcome the earth and all its occupants. Bierce ends "An Occurrence at Owl Creek Bridge" brusquely after the main character has dreamed that he has just come home to his wife and family. O'Connor ends "First Confession" with a short conversation between the brother and sister. In other words, after the story's major conflicts are finished, the job of the dénouement is to tie things up as quickly as possible.

Formal and Actual Structure

The structure just described is a *formal* one, an ideal pattern that moves directly from beginning to end. Few narratives and dramas follow this pattern exactly, however. Thus a typical mystery story holds back crucial details of exposition (because the goal is to mystify); a suspense story keeps the protagonist ignorant but provides readers with abundant details in order to maximize concern and tension about the outcome.

More realistic stories might also contain structural variations. For example, Hardy's "The Three Strangers" produces a *double take* because of unique structuring. Toward the story's end, Hardy raises the suspicion that the fugitive prisoner is the third stranger to enter the peasant household. At the end, however, Hardy makes clear that the fugitive is really the first stranger, who is already present when the third stranger enters and leaves. This complication introduces and emphasizes a new understanding of the position of the first stranger as both a righteous person and also a brave one. "The Three Strangers" is just one example of how a structural variation maximizes the impact of a work.

There are many other possible variants in structure. One of these is called **flashback,** or **selective recollection**, in which present circumstances are explained by the selective introduction of past events. The moment at which the flashback is introduced may be a part of the resolution of the plot, and the flashback might lead you into a moment of climax but then go from there to develop the details that are more properly part of the exposition. Let us again consider our brief story about John and Jane (page 94) and use the flashback method of structuring the story:

> Jane is now old, and a noise outside causes her to remember the argument that forced her to part with John many years before. They were deeply in love, but their disagreement about her wishes for a career and equality split them apart. Then she pictures in her mind the years she and John have spent happily together after they married. She then contrasts her present happiness with her memory of her earlier, less happy marriage, and from there she recalls her youthful years of courtship with John before their disastrous conflict developed. Then she looks over at John, reading in a chair, and smiles. John smiles back, and the two embrace. Even then, Jane realizes that she is crying.

In this structure the action begins and remains in the present. Important parts of the past flood the protagonist's memory in flashback, though not in the order in which they happened. Memory might be used structurally in other ways. An example is Wagner's poem "The Boxes," which is a narrative spoken by a mother to her dead son. The events of the poem are disclosed through the speaker's memories of the past, but the poem's conclusion depends on the speaker's temporary consideration that time has changed to a point before the death, so that she can speak to her son as though he is still living. The poem thus searingly illustrates the poignancy and finality of the situation. In short, a technique like selective recollection permits a unique narrative that departs significantly from a strictly formal and chronological structural pattern.

Each narrative or drama has a unique structure. Some stories may be structured according to simple geography or room arrangements, as in Irving Layton's poem "Rhine Boat Trip" (meditation upon castles observed by a tourist on the Rhine leading to thoughts of cattle cars during the World War II Holocaust), or in Maupassant's "The Necklace" (movement from a modest apartment, to an attic flat, to a local street), or in Poe's "The Masque of the Red Death" (a progressive movement through a series of rooms). A story may unfold in an apparently accidental way, with the characters making vital discoveries about the major characters, as in Glaspell's *Trifles*. Additionally, parts of a work may be set out as fragments of conversation, as in O'Connor's "First Confession," or as a ceremony, as in Hawthorne's "Young Goodman Brown," or as an announcement of a party, as in Maupassant's "The Necklace." The possible variations in structuring literary works are almost literally infinite.

As an exercise, you might imagine that a certain part of the work you are studying has been taken away. You might then ask what is wrong with the work remaining. Does it make sense? Does it seem truncated? Why should the missing part be returned? As you answer these questions, you are dealing with the logical necessity of structural wholeness. For example, let us suppose that the second stanza of Frost's "The Road Not Taken" is missing. The poem immediately becomes illogical because it omits the chronological event leading to the conclusion, and it also omits the logic of the speaker's choice of the road he selected. If you attempt similar imaginative exercises with other works, you can help yourself in determining whether these works are organic wholes.

You might also aid yourself by drawing a scheme or plan to explain, graphically, the structure of the work you are analyzing. The story "Miss Brill," by Katherine Mansfield, for example, may be conveniently compared with a person running happily along a narrow path deep within a dark forest and making a turn only to plunge suddenly and unexpectedly off a steep cliff. You might graph this comparison like this:

In writing an essay about the structure of "Miss Brill," you could employ this scheme as a guide. This is not to say that the structure of the story could not be profitably analyzed in another way but that such a scheme might help you to give insight, meaning, and form to your essay.

Sometimes the use of an illustration can create an insight or series of insights that might at first not have been clear to you. For example, Shakespeare's "Sonnet 73: That Time of Year Thou Mayst in Me Behold" has three quatrains and a concluding rhymed couplet. Here is the sonnet:

Quatrain I

That time of year thou mayst in me behold,
   When yellow leaves, or none, or few do hang
Upon those boughs which shake against the cold,
   Bare ruined choirs, where late the sweet birds sang.

Quatrain II

In me thou seest the twilight of such day
   As after sunset fadeth in the West,
Which by and by black night doth take away,
   Death's second self that seals up all in rest.

Quatrain III

In me thou seest the glowing of such fire,
  That on the ashes of his youth doth lie,
As the death bed, whereon it must expire,
  Consumed with that which it was nourished by.

Couplet

  This thou perceiv'st, which makes thy love more strong.
  To love that well, which thou must leave ere long.

We can see a number of links connecting the quatrains and the couplet. Each quatrain refers both to the speaker's present state and also to conditions that are passing or will pass—specifically, autumn, sunset, and a dying fire. In addition, the quatrains are grammatically parallel. Each one includes the phrase "in me," together with the parallel phrases "thou mayst behold," "thou seest," and "thou seest" again. In the couplet the phrase "thou perceiv'st" and the word "that" as a pronoun referring to the speaker appear, so that each major unit contains references to the speaker and his listener. In each of the quatrains, death is a common topic. It is spelled out specifically in quatrains two and three, and quatrain one refers to barren branches from which dying and yellowing leaves have fallen. The speaker states that he is in just such circumstances, so that his concluding statement "To love that well, which thou must leave ere long" in the concluding couplet is a fitting resumé of the poem.

We might make these links vivid through a graph, not unlike the well-known method of the Venn Diagram plan of using ellipses to show connections among sets (after John Venn [1834–1923], an English logician). Allowing for the fact that each part must be independent and distinct as well as connected, a plan or graph might be made of four overlapping triangles, with a list of common elements included within the triangles as a "key":

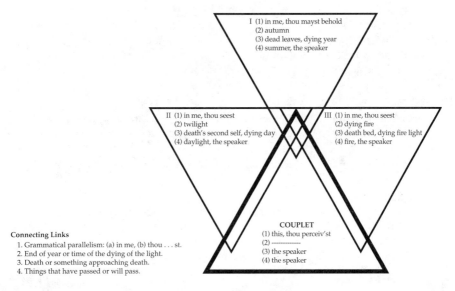

I (1) in me, thou mayst behold
(2) autumn
(3) dead leaves, dying year
(4) summer, the speaker

II (1) in me, thou seest
(2) twilight
(3) death's second self, dying day
(4) daylight, the speaker

III (1) in me, thou seest
(2) dying fire
(3) death bed, dying fire light
(4) fire, the speaker

COUPLET
(1) this, thou perceiv'st
(2) ------------
(3) the speaker
(4) the speaker

Connecting Links
1. Grammatical parallelism: (a) in me, (b) thou . . . st.
2. End of year or time of the dying of the light.
3. Death or something approaching death.
4. Things that have passed or will pass.

In our sketch, interconnecting triangles show the structure of parallels and common topics, but in analyzing another work you might prefer circles, lines, planes, other geometric figures, or a drawing like the figure falling off the hill (page 102). If you wish, you might make a list, and you always have the option of simply studying carefully and taking good notes. What is important is that you attempt to look at the work you are studying as a structure of some sort so that you may write an essay about this structure. Making a drawing or a graph has the virtue of giving you a visual grasp of the fact that the parts of a unified work are distinct and connected—important discoveries both for your understanding of the work and your writing of an essay.

Writing About Structure in Fiction, Poetry, and Drama

Your essay should concern arrangement and shape. In form, the essay should not restate or summarize the part-by-part unfolding of the narrative or argument. Rather, it should explain why things are where they are: "Why is this here and not there?" is the fundamental question you need to answer. Thus it is possible to begin with a consideration of a work's crisis, and then to consider how the exposition and complication have built up to it. A vital piece of information, for example, might have been withheld in the earlier exposition, as in Bierce's "An Occurrence at Owl Creek Bridge" and Hardy's "The Three Strangers," and introduced only at or near the conclusion. Therefore the crisis might be heightened because there would have been less suspense if the detail had been introduced earlier. Consider the following questions in planning to write about the story's structure.

Raise Questions to Discover Ideas

- If spaces or numbers divide the story into sections or parts, what is the structural importance of these parts?
- If there are no marked divisions, what major sections can you find? (You might make divisions according to places where actions occur, various times of day, changing weather, or increasingly important events.)
- If the story departs from the formal structure of exposition, complication, crisis, climax, and resolution, what purpose do these departures serve?
- What variations in chronological order, if any, appear in the story (e.g., gaps in the time sequence, flashbacks or selective recollection)? What effects are achieved by these variations?
- Does the story delay any crucial details of exposition? Why? What effect is achieved by the delay?
- Where does an important action or a major section (such as the climax) begin? End? How is it related to the other formal structural elements, such as the crisis? Is the climax an action, a realization, or a decision? To what degree does it relieve the work's tension? What is the effect of the climax on your understanding of the characters involved in it? How is this effect related to the arrangement of the climax?

Organize Your Essay About Structure

Introduction   Your essay should show why a narrative is arranged the way it is—to reveal a character's situation, create surprise, evoke sympathy, reveal nobility (or depravity) of character, unravel puzzles, express philosophical or political values, or bring out humor. You might also explain the structure of no more than a part of the story, such as the climax or the complication.

Body   The essay is best developed in agreement with what the work contains. The location of scenes is an obvious organizing element. Thus, essays on the structure of Hawthorne's "Young Goodman Brown" and Mansfield's "Miss Brill" might be based on the fact that both take place outdoors (a dark forest for one and a sunny public park for the other). An essay might explore the structure of Maupassant's "The Necklace" by contrasting the story's indoor and outdoor locations. An essay on Glaspell's *Trifles* might trace the structural importance of the various parts of a kitchen in an early twentieth-century Iowa farmhouse.

Other ways to consider structure may be derived from a work's notable aspects, such as the revelations about the "sinfulness" of Goodman Brown's father and neighbors in Hawthorne's "Young Goodman Brown," or the increasing defiance by the major character in Poe's "The Masque of the Red Death."

Conclusion   The conclusion should highlight the main parts of your essay. You may also deal briefly with the relationship of structure to the plot. If the work you have analyzed departs from chronological order, you might explain the causes and effects of this departure. Your aim should be to focus on the success of the work as it has been brought about by the author's choices in development.

Illustrative Essay (on Structure)

Conflict and Suspense in Thomas Hardy's "The Three Strangers"°

[1]   Hardy's "The Three Strangers" is a finely woven story of conflict and suspense. The suspense is essential to the conflict, which is an opposition of right and wrong when applied to criminal justice. Hardy controls the structure to develop this opposition, which embodies the idea that the letter of the law is insignificant when compared with the spirit of the law.* The application of strict legality in Hardy's story is made wrong, while understanding and forgiveness, even if nominally illegal, is made to seem right. As the basis of this idea, Hardy builds the story toward a major incident that presents a conflict for his Wessex shepherds between (1) duty toward law and (2) duty toward a human being who has been legally condemned but whose crime seems justifiable. Hardy develops his conflict and brings out his idea by showing the lives of his country people positively, by portraying his Hangman negatively, and by creating suspense about his first stranger, who is the legally condemned "criminal."†

°See pages 326–340 for this story.
*Central idea.
†Thesis sentence.

[2]   Although readers may not be aware of it during the early part of the story,
      Hardy arranges events to demonstrate a generous view of right and wrong.
      The first one-sixth of the story is an exposition of the way of life of the natives
      of Higher Crowstairs, who are shown to be warm and human. But in the ser-
      vice of his idea, Hardy is actually building up one side of the conflict by
      demonstrating that his natives are such nice, ordinary folks that their judg-
      ments on matters of life and death are to be trusted. This is the positive side
      of Hardy's narratively presented argument.

[3]   When Hardy does engage both sides of the conflict—a complication occurring
      about midway through the story—by introducing the second stranger (the
      Hangman), he has already established the grounds for his case, but he solidi-
      fies his argument by presenting this ghoulish figure as brash, selfish, and ob-
      noxious. When the natives learn that the second stranger is a hangman, they
      are startled "with suppressed exclamations" (334, paragraph 80). The excla-
      mations apparently take the form that if men like the hangman are associated
      with the letter of the law, the natives—along with the reader—will prefer the
      spirit even if the spirit may lead people to support apparently illegal actions.
      This reaction could not be sustained if the crime of the escaped criminal had
      been a violent one, but the "crime" was really the theft of a sheep to feed his
      starving family (334, paragraph 81). One may grant that Hardy is softening the
      crime here, but the conflict is not between right when it is right and wrong
      when it is wrong, but rather between legality when it is wrong and illegality
      when it is right. As Hardy structures the events in the story, it is not possible to
      disagree with the judgment of the natives at the end that the intended hanging
      of the thief "was cruelly disproportioned to the transgression" (339, paragraph
      160), for even if a reader wanted to disagree with Hardy's argument on legal
      grounds, the emotional thrust of the story leads toward extenuation.

[4]   Critical to this extenuation is Hardy's creation of suspense about the identity of
      the first stranger as Timothy Summers, the escaped prisoner. Because
      throughout the story readers have assented to the values and way of life of
      Shepherd Fennel and his guests, Hardy's crisis and climax forestall a purely le-
      galistic reaction. Hardy puts Summers before the eyes of both country folk and
      readers as a brave and witty human being, not as a fugitive who has just es-
      caped hanging. The revelation at the end therefore causes a second view of
      Summers. In retrospect, readers join the natives in admiring this first stranger's
      "marvelous coolness and daring in hob-and-nobbing with the hangman" (339,
      paragraph 160) and consequently would be indignant if such a person were ac-
      tually to be hanged. As a result of Hardy's judicious withholding and disclosing
      of detail, he leads readers to deny the law when it is used unfairly.

[5]   Related to the major conflict are a number of lesser but still important con-
      flicts that Hardy includes in the narrative. At crucial points, for example, he
      establishes that the natives living marginally "in the country about Higher
      Crowstairs" (340, paragraph 162) are uneasy and fearful about the law.
      When they realize that the second stranger is the hangman, they start
      "back," and one of them begins trembling (334, paragraph 79). Hardy invites
      readers to conclude that the natives view the conviction of Summers as a
      threat also to themselves. In a comic vein, Hardy contrasts the law with the
      ineptness of the shepherds who are called on to enforce it (336–338, para-
      graphs 106–134). He makes the law so remote from their lives that when

they finally do make an arrest—of the third stranger—their language is not that of lawmen, but rather, comically, of highwaymen and also of priests (338, paragraphs 132–134). As an ironic dénouement of the story, Hardy tells us that the shepherds, resisting the legal but troubling Hangman and magistrate, diligently search for Summers everywhere but where they know he can be found (339, paragraph 160).

[6]   In addition, Hardy includes other little but human contrasts in order to develop sympathy for the folk and therefore to strengthen his argument. Although the Fennels have twenty guests in their home, Mrs. Fennel is alarmed about giving them too much food and drink, and she is disturbed when the Hangman selfishly depletes her store of prized mead. There is a small family disagreement on this score. Another minor and amusing conflict is set up by Hardy when Mrs. Fennel asks the musicians to stop playing, but they continue because they have been bribed by the amorous shepherd, Oliver Giles. There are also some noticeable contrasts in age among couples. Beyond these contrasts or opposites, which are vital to the story's structure, the technique of suspense is a conflict in itself, for it forces readers to consider and evaluate elements of the story a second time. <u>These are all conflicts that Hardy employs in developing his major conflict between the right of the spirit and the wrong of the letter in "The Three Strangers."</u>

Work Cited

Hardy, Thomas. "The Three Strangers." Edgar V. Roberts. *Writing About Literature*. 11th ed. Upper Saddle River: Prentice Hall, 2006. 326–340.

Commentary on the Essay

As expressed in paragraph 1, this essay focuses on how Hardy structures character and action in "The Three Strangers" to achieve a contrast between right and wrong. The discussion of all events leading to the people's unspoken acquittal of the fugitive is seen not as narrative but as a contributing part of Hardy's argument. The essay thus argues that the parts of the story are arranged as parts of Hardy's argumentative plan. To emphasize this aim, the writer uses words and phrases such as "arranges events," "engage both sides of the conflict," "structures the events," "creation of suspense," "establishes," and "in order to develop sympathy." All these expressions are intended as reminders that the subject of the essay is the way in which Hardy puts the story together.

In the body, paragraph 2 explains how Hardy introduces the natives and their guests at the Fennels' cottage to illustrate their qualities of warmth and humanity. Paragraph 3 stresses the negative reaction of the country folk when they learn that the second stranger is the Hangman. Together, then, paragraphs 2 and 3 serve to explain the underlying causes of Hardy's arrangement of the narrative.

In paragraph 4 the essay explains Hardy's delay in identifying the fugitive. This delay lets Hardy elaborate on his positive picture of the country folk and their values, and it also helps him in persuading readers of the story to concur in the decision for justice that the natives make. Paragraph 5 states that other conflicts in the story show that the natives are uneasy with the law and fearful of it—attitudes that reinforce their decision to favor the first stranger. The last paragraph argues that additional "but human" contrasts are placed so as to augment Hardy's favorable portraits of the Fennels and their guests.

Special Topics for Studying and Discussing Plot and Structure

1. What kind of story might "The Three Strangers" be, structurally, if the first stranger were named and identified when he first enters the cottage, before the entrance of the other strangers?

2. Consider the surprises in "An Occurrence at Owl Creek Bridge," "The Story of an Hour," "The Necklace," *The Bear*, and "The Three Strangers." How much preparation is made for the surprises? In retrospect, to what degree are the surprises not surprises at all, but rather are necessary outcomes of the preceding parts of the works?

3. Compare the use of interior scenes in "The Story of an Hour," "First Confession," and *Trifles*. How do these scenes bring out various conflicts? How do characters in the interiors contribute to plot developments? What is the relationship of these characters to the major themes of the works?

4. Compare "The Story of an Hour" and "Young Goodman Brown" as stories developing plots about clashing social or religious values. In what ways are the plots similar and different?

5. Compare the ways in which attitudes toward law are presented in Glaspell's *Trifles* and Hardy's "The Three Strangers." How do these works structure your responses toward the people representing the law? Toward the people who have violated the law?

6. Select a circumstance in your life that caused you doubt, difficulty, and conflict. Making yourself anonymous (give yourself a fictitious name and put yourself in a fictitious location), write a brief story about the occasion, stressing how your conflict began, how it affected you, and how you resolved it. You might describe the details in chronological order, or you might begin the story in the present tense and then introduce details in flashback.

7. Write contrasting paragraphs about a character (whom you know or about whom you have read). In the first, try to make your reader like the character. In the second, try to create a hostile response to the character. Write an additional paragraph explaining the ways in which you tried to create these opposite responses. How fair would it be for a reader to dislike your negative paragraph even though your hostile portrait is successful?

8. Write a brief episode or story that takes place in a historical period you believe you know well, being as factually accurate as you can. Introduce your own fictional characters as important "movers and shakers," and deal with their public or personal affairs or both. You may model your characters and episodes on historical persons, but you are free to exercise your imagination completely and construct your own characters.

6

Writing About Setting
The Background of Place,
Objects, and Culture in Literature

Like all human beings, literary characters do not exist in isolation. Just as they become human by interacting with other characters, they gain identity because of their cultural and political allegiances, their possessions, their jobs, and where they live, and move, and have their being. They are usually involved deeply with their environments, and their surroundings are causes of much of their motivation and many of their possible conflicts. Plays, stories, and many poems must therefore necessarily include descriptions of places, objects, and backgrounds—the **setting.**

What Is Setting?

Setting is the natural, manufactured, political, cultural, and temporal environment, including everything that characters know and own. Characters may be either helped or hurt by their surroundings, and they may fight about possessions and goals. Further, as characters speak with each other, they reveal the degree to which they share the customs and ideas of their times.

Authors Use Three Basic Types of Settings

1. Private Homes, Public Buildings, and Various Possessions Are Important in Literature, as in Life   To reveal or highlight qualities of character, and also to make literature lifelike, authors include many details about objects of human manufacture and construction. Houses, both interiors and exteriors, are common, as are possessions such as walking sticks, garden paths, park benches, Christmas trees, necklaces, boxes, pistols, clocks, and hair ribbons. In Maupassant's "The Necklace," the loss of a comfortable home brings out the best in the major character by forcing her to adjust to her economic reversal. In Mansfield's "Miss Brill" the return of the major character to her shabby room brings out both the economic and emotional poverty of her life. The discovery of a quilt in the process of being sewed explains the major character's feelings and actions in Glaspell's *Trifles.*

Objects also enter directly into literary action and character. A broken birdcage reveals the pathetic and abusive husband–wife relationship in *Trifles*. The dress worn by the speaker in Lowell's "Patterns" enters into her thoughts as she contemplates the sudden news of her bereavement.

2. Outdoor Places Are Scenes of Many Literary Actions   The natural world is an obvious location for the action of many narratives and plays. It is therefore important to note natural surroundings (hills, shorelines, valleys, mountains, meadows, fields, trees, lakes, streams), living creatures (birds, dogs, horses, snakes), and also the times, seasons, and conditions in which things happen (morning or night, summer or winter, sunlight or cloudiness, wind or calmness, rain or shine, sunlight or darkness, snowfall or blizzard, heat or cold)—any or all of which may influence and interact with character, motivation, and conduct.

3. Cultural and Historical Circumstances Are Often Prominent in Literature Just as physical setting influences characters, so do historical and cultural conditions and assumptions. O'Connor's "First Confession" is written for an audience of readers who understand the role of the Catholic Church in twentieth-century Irish life. In Arnold's "Dover Beach," the speaker assumes an understanding of the religious skepticism that developed in the nineteenth century. In Chekhov's *The Bear*, the action takes place on an isolated late nineteenth-century Russian estate, and the characters therefore see life that is vastly different from current circumstances. The broad cultural setting of Layton's poem "Rhine Boat Trip" brings out the contrast between the beauty of German scenery and mythology, on the one hand, and the ugliness and depravity of German atrocities in World War II, on the other.

The Importance of Setting in Literature

Authors use setting to create meaning, just as painters include backgrounds and objects to render ideas. Such a use of setting is seen in Hawthorne's "Young Goodman Brown," where a woodland path that is difficult to follow and that is filled with obstacles is a major topographical feature. The path is of course no more than ordinary, granted the time and conditions in the story, but it also conveys the idea that life is difficult, unpredictable, and mysterious. Similarly, in Glaspell's *Trifles*, the fixtures and utensils in the kitchen of the Wright farm indicate that Midwestern homesteads early in the twentieth century were bleak and oppressive.

Setting Is Often Essential and Vital in the Story

To study the setting in a narrative (or play), discover the important details and then try to explain their function. Depending on the author's purpose, the amount of detail may vary. Poe provides many graphic and also impressionistic details in "The Masque of the Red Death," so that we can follow, almost visually, the bizarre action at the story's end. In some works the setting is so intensely present, like the countryside in Hardy's "The Three Strangers," that it is a virtual participant in the story's outcome.

Setting Augments a Work's Realism and Credibility

One of the major purposes of literary setting is to establish **realism,** or **verisimilitude.** As the description of location and objects becomes particular and detailed, the events of the work become more believable. Maupassant places "The Necklace" in real locations in late nineteenth-century Paris, and for this reason the story has all the semblance of having actually happened. Even futuristic, symbolic, and fantastic stories, as well as ghost stories, seem more believable if they include places and objects from everyday experience. Hawthorne's "Young Goodman Brown" and Poe's "The Masque of the Red Death" are such stories. Although these works make no pretense to portray everyday realism, their credibility is enhanced because they take place in settings that are based in reality.

Setting May Accentuate Qualities of Character

Setting may intersect with character as a means by which authors underscore the influence of place, circumstance, and time on human growth and change. Glaspell's setting in *Trifles* is the kitchen of the lonely, dreary Wright farm. This kitchen is a place of such hard work, oppression, and unrelieved joylessness that it explains the loss of Minnie's early brightness and promise and also helps us understand her angry act. (A blending of setting and character as seen in Maupassant's "The Necklace" is explored in the two drafts of the illustrative essay in Chapter 1.)

The way characters respond and adjust to setting can reveal their strength or weakness. Peyton Farquhar's scheme to make an escape from his fate, even when it is almost literally hanging before him, suggests his character strength (Bierce's "An Occurrence at Owl Creek Bridge"). In contrast, Goodman Brown's Calvinistic religious conviction that human beings are totally depraved, which is confirmed to him by his nightmarish encounter in the forest, indicates the weakness and gullibility of his character just as it alienates him from family and community (Hawthorne's "Young Goodman Brown").

Setting Is a Means by Which Authors Structure and Shape Their Works

Authors often use setting as one of the means of organizing their stories, as in Maupassant's "The Necklace." The story's final scene is believable because Mathilde leaves her impoverished home to take a nostalgic stroll on the Champs-Elysées, the most fashionable street in Paris. Without this change of setting, she could not have encountered Jeanne Forrestier again, for their usual ways of life would no longer bring them together. In short, the structure of the story depends on a normal, natural change of scene.

Another organizational application of place, time, and object is the **framing** or **enclosing setting**, when an author opens with a particular description and then returns to the same setting at the end. An example is Hardy's "The Three Strangers," which both begins and ends with a description of the lonely English countryside containing a solitary cottage ("Higher Crowstairs") where the main action takes place. The use of objects as a frame is seen in Mansfield's "Miss Brill," which opens and closes with references to the heroine's shabby fur piece. In such ways, framing creates a formal completeness, just as it may underscore the author's depiction of the human condition.

Various Settings May Be Symbolic

If the scenes and materials of setting are highlighted or emphasized, they also may be taken as symbols through which the author expresses ideas. The horse Toby in Chekhov's *The Bear* is such a symbol. Mrs. Popov has made caring for the horse, which was her dead husband's favorite, a major part of her memorial obligations. When she tells the servants not to give oats to this horse, Chekhov is using this ordinary animal to indicate that new commitments replace old ones. In Arnold's poem "Dover Beach," the light that gleams from across the English Channel and that is soon "gone" may be understood as a symbol of the extinguishing of intellectual and religious faith that Arnold believed had taken place during the nineteenth century.

Setting Contributes to Atmosphere and Mood

Most actions *require* no more than a functional description of setting. Thus, taking a walk in a forest needs just the statement that there are trees. However, if you find descriptions of shapes, light and shadows, animals, wind, and sounds, you may be sure that the author is creating an **atmosphere** or **mood** for the action, as in Hawthorne's "Young Goodman Brown." There are many ways to develop moods. Descriptions of bright colors (red, orange, yellow) may contribute to a mood of happiness. The same colors in dim or eerie light, like the rooms in Poe's "The Masque of the Red Death," invoke gloom or augment hysteria. References to smells and sounds bring the setting to life further by asking additional sensory responses from the reader. The setting of a story in a small town or large city, in green or snow-covered fields, or in middle-class or lower-class residences may evoke responses to these places that contribute to the work's atmosphere.

Setting May Underscore a Work's Irony

Just as setting may reinforce character and theme, so it may establish expectations that are the opposite of what occurs, not only in fiction but also in plays and poems. The colorful and orderly garden described in Lowell's "Patterns" emphasizes the irony of the deeply sad and anguished speaker. The dueling pistols in Chekhov's *The Bear* bring out the irony of the developing relationship between the major characters. These guns, which are designed for death, in fact become the means that prompt the characters to fall in love. A heavily ironic situation is created by Hardy in the poem "Channel Firing," when the noise of large guns at sea wakens the skeletons buried in an English churchyard. The irony is that those engaged in the gunnery practice, if "red war" gets still redder, will soon join the skeletons in the graveyard.

Writing About Setting

In preparing to write about setting, determine the number and importance of locations, artifacts, and customs. Ask questions like the following.

Raise Questions to Discover Ideas

- How extensive are the visual descriptions? Does the author provide such vivid and carefully arranged detail about surroundings that you could draw a map or plan? Or is the scenery vague and difficult to imagine?
- What connections, if any, are apparent between locations and characters? Do the locations bring characters together, separate them, facilitate their privacy, make intimacy and conversation difficult?
- How fully are objects described? How vital are they to the action? How important are they in the development of the plot or idea? How are they connected to the mental states of the characters?
- How important to plot and character are shapes, colors, times of day, clouds, storms, light and sun, seasons of the year, and conditions of vegetation?
- Are the characters poor, moderately well-off, or rich? How does their economic condition affect what happens to them, and how does it affect their actions and attitudes?
- What cultural, religious, and political conditions are brought out in the story? How do the characters accept and adjust to these conditions? How do the conditions affect the characters' judgments and actions?
- What is the state of houses, furniture, and objects (e.g., new and polished, old and worn, ragged and torn)? What connections can you find between these conditions and the outlook and behavior of the characters?
- How important are sounds or silences? To what degree is music or other sound important in the development of character and action?
- Do characters respect or mistreat the environment? If there is an environmental connection, how central is it to the story?
- What conclusions do you think the author expects you to draw as a result of the neighborhood, culture, and larger world of the story?

Organize Your Essay About Setting

Introduction　Begin by making a brief description of the setting or scenes of the work, specifying the amount and importance of detail. Continue by describing the topics you plan to develop.

Body   As you prepare the body of your essay, you may need to combine your major approach with one or more of the others. Whatever topics for development you choose, be sure to consider setting not as an end in itself but rather as illustration and evidence for claims you are making about the particular story.

1. **Setting and Action.** Explore the importance of setting in the work. How extensively is the setting described? Are locations essential or incidental to the actions? Does the setting serve as part of the action (e.g., places of flight or concealment; public places where people meet openly, or hidden places where they meet privately; natural or environmental conditions; seasonal conditions such as searing heat or numbing cold; customs and conventions)? Do any objects cause inspiration, difficulty, or conflict (for example, a bridge, a walking stick, a necklace, a mailbox, a gaudy room, a hair ribbon, an ordinary box, a dead bird)? How directly do these objects influence the action?

2. **Setting and Organization.** How is the setting connected to the various parts of the work? Does it undergo any changes as the action develops? Why are some parts of the setting more important than others? Is the setting used as a structural frame or enclosure for the story? How do objects, such as money or property, influence the characters? How do descriptions made at the start become important in the action later on?

3. **Setting and Character.** (For examples of this approach, see the two drafts of the illustrative essay in Chapter 1.) Analyze the degree to which setting influences and interacts with character. Are the characters happy or unhappy where they live? Do they get into discussions or arguments about their home environments? Do they want to stay or leave? Do the economic, philosophical, religious, or ethnic aspects of the setting make the characters undergo changes? What jobs do the characters perform because of their ways of life? What freedoms or restraints do these jobs cause? How does the setting influence their decisions, transportation, speech habits, eating habits, attitudes about love and honor, and general behavior?

4. **Setting and Atmosphere.** To what extent does setting contribute to mood? Does the setting go beyond the minimum needed for action or character? How do descriptive words paint verbal pictures and evoke moods through references to colors, shapes, sounds, smells, or tastes? Does the setting establish a mood, say, of joy or hopelessness, plenty or scarcity? Do events happen in daylight or at night? Do the locations and activities of the characters suggest permanence or impermanence (like a return home, the creation of figures out of mud, the repair of a battered boat, the description of ocean currents, the building of a fence)? Are things warm and pleasant, or cold and harsh? What connection do you find between the atmosphere and the author's expressed or apparent thoughts about existence?

5. **Setting and Other Aspects of the Work.** Does the setting reinforce the story's meaning? Does it establish irony about the circumstances and ideas in the story? If you choose this approach, consult the introductory paragraph on "The Literary Uses of Setting" earlier in this chapter. If you want to write about the symbolic implications of a setting, consult Chapter 10.

Conclusion   To conclude, summarize your major points or write about related aspects of setting that you have not considered. Thus, if your essay treats the relationship of setting and action, your conclusion might mention connections of the setting with character or atmosphere. You might also point out whether your central idea about setting also applies to other major aspects of the work.

Illustrative Essay

Poe's Use of Interior Setting to Augment the Eeriness of "The Masque of the Red Death"°

[1] In "The Masque of the Red Death," Poe uses details of setting to create an eerie atmosphere.* The story is about the foolishness and impossibility of trying to evade death. Poe's Prince Prospero is the example of this idea. He believes that he can lock himself away in his castle, with a thousand followers, and avoid the infectious "Red Death" raging outside. At the end, however, Death invades the castle in person and destroys all the people. Poe uses interior setting to underscore this irony, and also to make Prospero's pride seem pointless and insane. The prevailing eerie mood is brought out through Poe's use of graphic description, geographical direction, evocative color, and sepulchral sound.†

[2] The height of Poe's graphic description is the story's extensive fourth paragraph, where he describes Prince Prospero's bizarre suite of seven rooms. These rooms have different colors, each one suggesting differing moods, from subdued, to garish, to somber. The blue room is in the east, and, moving westward in an order of varying depressiveness, the next six rooms are purple, green, orange, white, violet, and finally black. The moods are determined by the narrator's explanation that each room is lighted by a "brazier of fire" throwing light through a stained glass window that provokes awe by casting a glaring, grisly light.

[3] These rooms are not only vividly described, but they are spatially arranged to complement the certainty of death. The direction of east to west suggests a movement away from life. One might observe that the blue room, in the east, is on the side of the rising sun—an optimistic idea of blue skies and new beginnings of new days. On the other hand the westernmost room, the black one, is the direction of the setting sun and the end of the day at midnight, when Death takes over. If one doubts that Poe intended this geographical direction to have meaning, it is important to note that Prospero's charge against the ghostly figure of the Red Death takes him directly from east to west—from blue to black, from life to death—on his demented dash toward doom.

°See pages 356–360 for this story.
*Central idea.
†Thesis sentence.

[4] <u>The most weird and garish room is the black one, on which Poe devotes
     the most evocative description.</u> The room is hung with black velvet tapes-
     tries, but its darkness is made flamboyant by the scarlet, "deep blood" light
     (Poe avoids the more neutral word "red" here). The narrator states that the
     room is "ghastly in the extreme" and that it produces a look of wildness
     (paragraph 4). Visually, this room evokes feelings of wildness, evil, and an
     almost ghoulish delight in blood. It is a sinister room, designed not to relax
     but to disturb and distress.

[5] <u>To these ominous locations, Poe adds the eeriness of sepulchral sounds
     by including a "gigantic clock of ebony" in the black room.</u> He devotes an
     entire paragraph (the fifth) to this weird clock, and this paragraph is there-
     fore the focal point of the story's setting. Poe's words hint that the clock is
     vaguely alive. It is not <u>placed</u> or <u>set</u> against the west wall, but is <u>standing</u>
     there (Poe's word is "stood"), as though living, and its massive pendulum
     is in constant, "monotonous" motion (like the beating of a ghostly heart?).
     Poe's implication is that the clock represents death, because every hour
     the "clang" from its "brazen lungs" chillingly ends another period of life.
     Poe's narrator points out that the clock's musical but eerie sounds stop all
     revelry and create a distressed silence among the merrymakers (Poe uses
     the word "disconcert" twice in the paragraph to describe the clock's effect).
     This use of sound, having its source in this mysteriously living clock, is de-
     signed to make readers as uneasy, unsettled, and anxious as Prospero's
     companions.

[6] Thus Poe's interior setting is both descriptive and evocative. The major ac-
     tion takes place in the rooms—the costume party attended by all Pros-
     pero's friends, except the one uninvited guest, the Red Death himself, who
     instantly kills all the party-goers. Prospero's last movement takes him
     through all the rooms, in a ritual passage from morning to midnight, from
     life to death. <u>In this way, Poe uses his setting to show the folly of trying to
     escape death, and also to suggest that the attempt is not only foolish but
     also bizarre and insane.</u> The events of the story, the sustained mood, the
     consistent idea, are all tied together by Poe's masterly control of setting.

Work Cited

Poe, Edgar Allan. "The Masque of the Red Death." Edgar V. Roberts. *Writing
     About Literature*. 11th ed. Upper Saddle River: Prentice Hall, 2006. 356–360.

Commentary on the Essay

Because it treats the relationship of setting to mood or atmosphere, this essay
illustrates the fourth approach described on page 113. The essay considers
those aspects of setting needed for the story, and then stresses how Poe's descriptions build the eerie mood, the irony of the major character's pretensions,
and the folly of his pride. The thesis sentence announces four topics for further development.

In the body, paragraph 2 describes the physical layout of Prospero's suite of rooms, and it also points out the eerie suggestiveness of Poe's descriptions of color and light. Paragraph 3 treats Poe's geographical arrangement of the rooms, suggesting that this arrangement complements the story's movement from life to death.

Paragraphs 4 and 5 treat the last and most sinister of the rooms. Paragraph 4 stresses the mood brought out by the colors black and scarlet or "deep blood." Paragraph 5, because it deals with the clock, on which Poe lavishes great detail, is the high point of the essay's body. Throughout the paragraph, the topic idea is that the clock, because of its seemingly living connection with the malign world of death, is Poe's major means of achieving an atmosphere complementary to the eerie action.

The conclusion summarizes the central idea, stressing that Poe goes beyond simple description to heighten the eerie, macabre atmosphere of his story.

Special Topics for Studying and Discussing Setting

1. Compare and contrast how details of setting are used to establish the qualities and traits of the following characters: Mrs. Popov of *The Bear*; Miss Brill of "Miss Brill"; the speakers of "Patterns," "Rhine Boat Trip," or "Dover Beach"; or Prince Prospero of "The Masque of the Red Death."

2. In what ways might we say that the events of both "The Story of an Hour" and "The Masque of the Red Death" are governed by the settings of the stories? To answer this question, consider the relationship of character to place and circumstance. How could the actions of the stories happen without the locations in which they occur?

3. Compare and contrast how details of setting establish qualities and traits of the following female characters: Faith of "Young Goodman Brown," Miss Brill of "Miss Brill," Nora of "First Confession," and Louise of "The Story of an Hour." To add to your comparison, you might introduce details about women in paintings or works of sculpture that you know.

4. Choose a story included in Appendix C and rewrite a page or two, taking the characters out of their setting and placing them in an entirely new setting, or in the setting of another story (you choose). Then write a brief analysis dealing with these questions: How were your characters affected by their new settings? Did you make them change slowly or rapidly? Why? As a result of your rewriting, what can you conclude about the uses of setting in fiction?

5. Write a short narrative as though it is part of a story (which you may also wish to write for the assignment), using options a and/or b.

   a. Relate a natural setting or type of day to a mood—for example, a nice day to happiness and satisfaction, or a cold, cloudy, rainy day to sadness. Or create irony by relating the nice day to sadness or the rainy day to happiness.

b. Indicate how an object or a circumstance becomes the cause of conflict or reconciliation (such as the lost necklace in "The Necklace," the dead canary in *Trifles,* or the trip through the forest in "Young Goodman Brown").

6. In your library locate two books on the career of Edgar Allan Poe. On the basis of the information you find in these sources, write a brief account of Poe's uses of setting and place to evoke atmosphere and to bring out qualities of human character.

7

Writing About an Idea or a Theme
The Meanings and the Messages in Literature

The word **idea** refers to the result or results of general and abstract thinking. Synonymous words are *concept, thought, opinion,* and *principle.*[1] In literary study the consideration of ideas relates to *meaning, interpretation, explanation,* and *significance.* Although ideas are usually extensive and complex, separate ideas can be named by single words, such as *right, good, love, piety, causation, wilderness,* and, not surprisingly, *idea* itself.

Ideas and Assertions

Although single words can name ideas, we must put these words into operation in *sentences* or *assertions* before they can advance our understanding. Good operational sentences about ideas are not the same as ordinary conversational statements such as "It's a nice day." An observation of this sort can be true, but it gives us no ideas and does not stimulate our minds. Rather, a sentence asserting an idea should initiate a thought or argument about the day's quality, such as "A nice day requires light breezes, blue sky, a warm sun, relaxation, and happiness." Because this sentence makes an assertion about the word *nice,* it allows us to consider and develop the idea of a nice day.

In studying literature, always express ideas as assertions. For example, you might state that an idea in Chekhov's *The Bear* is "love," but it would be difficult to discuss anything more unless you make an assertion promising an argument, such as "This play demonstrates the idea that love is irrational and irresistible." This assertion could lead you to explain the unlikely love that bursts out in the story. Similarly, for Bierce's "An Occurrence at Owl Creek Bridge," an assertion like the following would advance further argument: "Farquhar embodies the idea that perception is produced in human beings more by hope than by reality."

Although we have noted only one idea in these two works, most stories contain many ideas. When one of the ideas seems to turn up over and over again throughout a work, it is called the **theme.** In practice, the words *theme* and *major idea* are the same.

---

[1]See also Chapter 1 (page 18). **119**

Ideas and Values

Literature embodies **values** along with ideas. *Value,* of course, commonly refers to the price of something, but in the realm of ideas and principles, it is a standard of what is desired, sought, esteemed, and treasured. For example, *democracy* refers to our political system, but it is also a complex idea of representative government that we esteem most highly, and so also do we esteem concepts like honor, cooperation, generosity, and love. A vital idea/value is *justice,* which, put most simply, involves equality before the law and also the fair evaluation of conduct that is deemed unacceptable or illegal. Such an idea of justice is a major topic of Glaspell's play *Trifles.* Glaspell dramatizes the story of a farm wife who for thirty years has endured her husband's intimidation and her abject circumstances of life, but finally has risen up against him in his sleep. By a rigid concept of justice as guilt-conviction-punishment, the wife, Minnie Wright, is guilty and should be convicted and punished. But justice as an idea also involves a full and fair consideration of the circumstances and motivation of wrongdoing, and it is such a consideration that the two women in the story make during their examination of Minnie's kitchen. Many of their speeches showing their sympathy to Minnie are equivalent to a jurylike deliberation. Their final decision is like a verdict, and their final covering up of Minnie's crime is evidence for their idea that justice, to be most highly valued, should be tempered with understanding—even if they do not use these exact words in their discussions of Minnie's situation. In short, the idea of justice underlying Glaspell's *Trifles* also involves a deeply felt value.

The Place of Ideas in Literature

Because writers of poems, plays, and stories are usually not systematic philosophers, it is not appropriate to go "message hunting" as though their works contained nothing but ideas. Indeed, there is great benefit and pleasure to be derived from just savoring a work—following the patterns of narrative and conflict, getting to like the characters, understanding the work's implications and suggestions, and listening to the sounds of the author's words, to name only a few of the reasons for which literature is treasured.

Nevertheless, ideas are vital to understanding and appreciating literature: Writers have ideas and want to communicate them. For example, in *The Bear,* Chekhov directs laughter at two unlikely people suddenly and unpredictably falling in love. The play is funny, however, not only because it is preposterous but also because it is based on the *idea* that love takes precedence over other resolutions that people might make. Blake in "The Tyger" describes the "fearful symmetry" of a wild tiger in "the forests of the night," but the poem also embodies *ideas* about the inexplicability of evil, the mystery of life, and the unsearchability of divine purpose in the universe.

Distinguish Between Ideas and Actions

As you analyze works for ideas, it is important to avoid the trap of confusing ideas and actions. Such a trap is contained in the following sentence about O'Connor's "First Confession": "The major character, Jackie, misbehaves at home and tries to slash his sister with a breadknife." This sentence successfully describes a major action in the story, but it does not express an *idea* that connects characters and events, and for this reason it obstructs understanding. Some possible connections might be achieved with sentences like these: "'First Confession' illustrates the idea that family life may produce anger and potential violence" or "'First Confession' shows that compelling children to accept authority may cause effects that are the opposite of adult intentions." A study based on these connecting formulations could be focused on ideas and would not be sidetracked into doing no more than retelling O'Connor's story.

Distinguish Between Ideas and Situations

You should also make a distinction between situations and ideas. For example, in Lowell's poem "Patterns," the narrator describes what is happening to her as a result of her fiancé's death. Her plight is not an idea, but a situation that brings out ideas, such as that future plans may be destroyed by uncontrollable circumstances, or that fate strikes the fortunate as well as the unfortunate, or that human institutions often seem arbitrary, capricious, and cruel. If you are able in such ways to distinguish a work's various situations from the writer's major idea or ideas, you will be able to focus on ideas and therefore sharpen your own thinking.

How to Find Ideas

Ideas are not as obvious as characters or setting. To determine an idea, you need to consider the meaning of what you read and then to develop explanatory and comprehensive assertions. Your assertions need not be the same as those that others might make. People notice different things, and individual formulations vary. In Chopin's "The Story of an Hour," for example, an initial expression of some of the story's ideas might take any of the following forms: (1) Even in a good marriage, husbands and wives can have ambivalent feelings about their married life. (2) An accident can bring out negative but previously unrecognized thoughts in a wife or husband. (3) Even those closest to a person may never realize that person's innermost feelings. Although any one of these choices could be a basic idea for studying "The Story of an Hour," they all have in common the main character's unexpected feelings of release when she is told that her husband has been killed. In discovering ideas, you should follow a similar process—making a number of formulations for an idea and then selecting one for further development.

As you read, be alert to the different ways in which authors convey ideas. One author might prefer an indirect way through a character's speeches, whereas another may prefer direct statement. In practice, authors can employ any or all of the following methods.

Study the Authorial Voice

Although authors mainly render action, dialogue, and situation, they sometimes state ideas to guide us and deepen our understanding. In the second paragraph of Maupassant's "The Necklace," for example, the authorial voice presents the idea that women have no more than charm and beauty to get on in the world. Ironically, Maupassant uses the story to show that for the major character, Mathilde, nothing is effective, for her charm cannot prevent disaster. Hawthorne, in "Young Goodman Brown," uses the following words to express a powerful idea: "The fiend in his own shape is less hideous than when he rages in the breast of man" (paragraph 53). This statement is made as authorial commentary just when the major character, Goodman Brown, is speeding through "the benighted wilderness" on his way to the satanic meeting. Although the idea is complex, its essential aspect is that the causes of evil originate within human beings themselves, with the implication that we alone are responsible for all our actions, whether good or evil.

Study the Character and the Words of the First-Person Speaker

First-person narrators or speakers frequently express ideas along with their depiction of actions and situations, and they also make statements from which you can make inferences about ideas. (See also Chapter 4, on point of view.) Because what they say is part of a dramatic presentation, their ideas can be right or wrong, well-considered or thoughtless, good or bad, or brilliant or half-baked, depending on the speaker. The I/we (first-person) speaker of Arnold's "Dover Beach," for example, laments the diminution of vital ideas from the past, concluding that this loss is accompanied by increasing ignorance, uncertainty, and violence in today's world. In Hardy's "Channel Firing," the speaker—a skeleton suddenly awakened by the nearby noise of naval gunfire at sea—implies that warfare has been a constant menace from ancient days to the present. Even if the speaker is of dubious character, or is making a confession about personal shortcomings—as the speaker of Frost's "Desert Places" is doing—you may nevertheless study and evaluate the work's ideas.

Study the Statements Made by Characters

In many stories, characters express their own views, which can be right or wrong, admirable or contemptible. When you consider such dramatic speeches, you must do considerable interpreting and evaluating yourself. In Chekhov's *The Bear*, both Smirnov and Mrs. Popov express many silly ideas about love and duty as they begin speaking to each other, and it is the sudden force of their love that reveals to us how wrongheaded their previous ideas have been. The men in Glaspell's *Trifles* express conventional masculine ideas about the need for men to control women. The play itself, however, demonstrates the shortcomings and pomposity of their thought.

Study the Work's Figures of Speech

Figurative language is one of the major components of poetry, but it also abounds in prose fiction (see also Chapter 9). In the sonnet "Bright Star," for example, Keats symbolizes the idea of constancy with his references to a fixed star (such as the North Star). Much metaphorical language is also to be found in both narratives and drama, as at the opening of Mansfield's "Miss Brill" where a sunny day is compared to gold and white wine. This lovely comparison suggests that the world is a place of beauty and happiness, an idea that contrasts ironically with the indifference and cruelty that Miss Brill experiences. Another notable figure occurs in Glaspell's *Trifles*, when one of the characters compares John Wright, the murdered husband, with "a raw wind that gets to the bone" (speech 103). With this figurative language, Glaspell conveys the idea that bluntness, indifference, and cruelty create great personal damage.

Study How Characters Represent Ideas

Characters and their actions can often be equated with certain ideas and values. For example, Mathilde, in Maupassant's "The Necklace," represents the idea that unrealizable dreams can damage the real world. Two diverse or opposed characters can embody contrasting ideas, as with Louise and Josephine of Chopin's "The Story of an Hour." Each woman can be taken to represent differing views about the role of women in marriage. In effect, characters who stand for ideas can assume symbolic status, as in Hawthorne's "Young Goodman Brown," where the protagonist symbolizes the alienation that inevitably accompanies zealousness. Such characters can be equated directly with particular ideas, and to talk about them is a shorthand way of talking about the ideas.

Study the Work Itself as an Embodiment of Ideas

One of the most important ways in which authors express ideas is to interlock them within all parts and aspects of the work. The art of painting is instructive here, for a painting can be taken in with a single view that comprehends all the aspects of color, form, action, and expression, each of which can also be considered separately. In the same way, when a work is considered in its totality, the various parts collectively can embody major ideas, as in the third section of Bierce's "An Occurrence at Owl Creek Bridge" (paragraphs 18–36), which is based on the idea that under great stress the human mind operates with lightning speed. Most works represent ideas in a similar way. Even "escape literature," which ostensibly enables readers to forget immediate problems, contains conflicts between good and evil, love and hate, good spies and bad, earthlings and aliens, and so on. Thereby, such works *do* embody ideas, even though their avowed intention is not to make readers think but rather to help them forget.

Writing About a Major Idea in Literature

You will probably write about what you consider the work's major idea or theme, but you may also get interested in a subsidiary idea. As you begin brainstorming and developing your first drafts, consider questions such as those that follow.

Raise Questions to Discover Ideas

General Ideas

- What ideas do you discover in the work? How do you discover them (through action, character depiction, scenes, language)?
- To what do the ideas pertain? To the individuals themselves? To individuals and society? To religion? To social, political, or economic justice?
- How balanced are the ideas? If a particular idea is strongly presented, what conditions and qualifications are also presented (if any)? What contradictory ideas are presented?
- Are the ideas limited to members of any groups represented by the characters (age, race, nationality, personal status)? Or are the ideas applicable to general conditions of life? Explain.
- Which characters in their own right represent or embody ideas? How do their actions and speeches bring these ideas out?
- If characters state ideas directly, how persuasive is their expression, how intelligent and well considered? How applicable are the ideas to the work? How applicable to more general conditions?
- With children, young adults, or the old, how do the circumstances express or embody an idea?

A Specific Idea

- What idea seems particularly important in the work? Why? Is it asserted directly, indirectly, dramatically, ironically? Does any one method predominate? Why?
- How pervasive in the work is the idea (throughout or intermittent)? To what degree is it associated with a major character or action? How does the structure of the work affect or shape your understanding of the idea?
- What value or values are embodied in the idea? Of what importance are the values to the work's meaning?
- How compelling is the idea? How could the work be appreciated without reference to any idea at all?

Organize Your Essay on a Major Idea or Theme

In well-written stories, poems, and plays, narrative and dramatic elements have a strong bearing on ideas. In this sense, an idea is like a key in music or a continuous thread tying together actions, characters, statements, symbols, and dialogue. As readers, we can trace such threads throughout the entire fabric of the work.

As you write about ideas, you may find yourself relying most heavily on the direct statements of the authorial voice or on a combination of these and your interpretation of characters and action, or you might focus exclusively on a first-person speaker and use his or her ideas to develop your analysis. Always make clear the sources of your details and distinguish the sources from your own commentary.

Introduction   As you begin, state your general goal of describing an idea and of showing its importance in the work. Your brief statement of the idea will be your central idea for your essay.

Body   Each separate work will invite its own approach, but here are a number of strategies you might use to organize your essay.

1. **Analyze the idea as it applies to characters.** Example: "Minnie Wright embodies the idea that living with cruelty and insensitivity leads to alienation, unhappiness, despair, and maybe to violence." (Glaspell's *Trifles*)

2. **Show how actions bring out the idea.** Example: "That Mrs. Popov and Smirnov fall in love rather than go their rather foolish and fruitless ways indicates Chekhov's idea that love literally rescues human lives." (*The Bear*)

3. **Show how dialogue and separate speeches bring out the idea.** Example: "The priest's responses to Jackie's confession embody the idea that kindness and understanding are the best means to encourage religious and philosophical commitment." (O'Connor's "First Confession")

4. **Show how the work's structure is determined by the idea.** Example: "The idea that horror can affect a nation's beauty and tradition leads Layton to introduce and conclude the poem by referring to aspects of the World War II Holocaust." ("Rhine Boat Trip")

5. **Treat variations or differing manifestations of the idea.** Example: "The idea that zealousness leads to harm is shown in Brown's nightmarish distortion of reality, his rejection of others, and his dying gloom." (Hawthorne's "Young Goodman Brown")

6. **Deal with a combination of these (together with any other significant aspect).** Example: "Chekhov's idea in *The Bear* that love is complex and contradictory is shown in Smirnov's initial scorn of Mrs. Popov, his self-declared independence of character, and his concluding embrace." (Here the idea is traced through speech, character, and action.)

Conclusion   Your conclusion might begin with a summary, together with your evaluation of the validity or force of the idea. If you have been convinced by the author's ideas, you might say that the author has expressed the idea forcefully and convincingly, or else you might show the relevance of the idea to current conditions. If you are not persuaded by the idea, you should demonstrate the idea's shortcomings or limitations. If you wish to mention a related idea, whether in the story you have studied or in some other story, you might introduce that here, but be sure to stress the connections.

Illustrative Essay

The Idea of Love's Power in Chekhov's *The Bear*°

[1] In the one-act farce *The Bear,* Anton Chekhov shows a previously unac-
quainted man and woman, less than an hour after they first meet, falling passionately in love. With such an unlikely main action, ideas may seem
unimportant, but the play nevertheless contains a number of ideas. Some of
these are that responsibility to life is stronger than to death, that people may
justify even the most stupid and contradictory actions, that love makes people
do foolish things, and that lifelong commitments may be made with hardly
any thought at all. <u>One of the play's major ideas is that love and desire are
powerful enough to overcome even the strongest obstacles.</u>* <u>This idea is
shown as the force of love conquers commitment to the dead, renunciation of
womankind, unfamiliarity, and anger.</u>†

[2] Commitment to her dead husband is Mrs. Popov's obstacle to love. She
states that she has made a vow never to see daylight because of her mourning (384, speech 4), and she wallows in her own self-righteousness. Her devotion is so intense that she claims to be almost dead herself out of
sympathy for her husband:

> My life is already ended. He lies in his grave; I have buried myself in
> these four walls . . . we are both dead. (384, speech 2)

In her, Chekhov has created a strong obstacle so that he might show the
power of all-conquering love. By the play's end, Mrs. Popov's embracing
Smirnov is a visual example of the idea (392, speech 151, S.D.).

[3] Renunciation of women is Smirnov's obstacle. He tells Mrs. Popov that women
have made him bitter and that he no longer gives "a good goddamn" about
them (388, speech 69). These words seem to make him an impossible candidate for love; but, in keeping with Chekhov's idea, Smirnov soon confesses his
sudden and uncontrollable love at the peak of his anger against Mrs. Popov.
Within him, the force of love operates so strongly that he would even claim
happiness at being shot by her "little velvet hands" (391, speech 140).

[4] As if these personal causes were not enough to stop love, a genuine obstacle is that the two people are strangers. Not only have they never met, but
they have never even heard of each other. According to the main idea, however, this unfamiliarity is no major problem. Chekhov is dramatizing the power
of love, and shows that it is strong enough to overcome even the lack of familiarity or previous friendship.

[5] Anger and the threat of violence, however, make the greatest obstacle. The
two characters get so irritated about Smirnov's demand for payment that, as

---

°See pages 384–392 for this play.
*Central idea.
†Thesis sentence.

an improbable climax of their heated words, Smirnov challenges Mrs. Popov, a woman, to a duel! He shouts:

> And do you think just because you're one of those romantic creations, that you have the right to insult me with impunity? Yes? I challenge you! (390, speech 105)

Along with their own personal barriers against loving, it would seem that the threat of shooting each other, even if poor Luka could stop them, would cause lifelong hatred. Yet love knocks down all these obstacles, in line with Chekhov's idea that love's power is as irresistible as a flood.

[6]   The idea of love's power is not new or unusual. It is the subject of popular songs, stories, other plays, movies, and T.V. shows. What is surprising about Chekhov's use of the idea is that love in *The Bear* overcomes such unlikely conditions, and wins so suddenly. These conditions bring up an interesting and closely related idea: Chekhov is showing that intensely negative feelings may lead not to hatred but rather to love. The speeches of Smirnov and Mrs. Popov contain disappointment, regret, frustration, annoyance, anger, rage, and potential destructiveness. Yet at the high point of these negative feelings, love takes over. It is as though hostility finally collapses because it is the nature of people to prefer loving to hating. *The Bear* is an uproarious dramatization of the power of love, and it is made better because it is founded on a truthful judgment of people as they really are.

Work Cited

Chekhov, Anton. *The Bear.* Edgar V. Roberts. *Writing About Literature.* 11th ed. Upper Saddle River: Prentice Hall, 2006. 384–392.

Commentary on the Essay

This essay follows strategy 6 (page 125) by showing how various components from the play collectively exhibit the pervasiveness of the idea. Throughout, dialogue, situations, soliloquies, and actions are evidence for the various conclusions. Transitions between paragraphs are effected by phrases like "these personal causes" (paragraph 4), "greatest obstacle" (paragraph 5), and "the idea" (paragraph 6), all of which emphasize the continuity of the topic.

Paragraph 1, the introduction, notes that the play contains a number of ideas, the major one being that love has the power to surmount great obstacles. The thesis sentence lists the four obstacles to be explored in the body.

As the operative aspects of Chekhov's idea, paragraphs 2 through 5 detail the nature of each of the obstacles. The obstacle of paragraph 2, Mrs. Popov's commitment to her husband's memory, is "strong." The one in paragraph 3, Smirnov's dislike of women, is seemingly "impossible." The one in paragraph 4, their being total strangers, is a "genuinely real" difficulty. In paragraph 5, the obstacle of anger is more likely to produce "hatred" than love.

Paragraph 6, beyond providing a brief summary, suggests another related and important idea, namely that people cannot long sustain potentially destructive anger. Obviously this second idea is a broad generalization and could bear extensive treatment in its own right. Even though the topic would require greater development if it came at the beginning, it is effective as a part of the conclusion. The final sentence blends the two ideas, thereby looking both inward into the essay and outward toward the consideration of new ideas.

Special Topics for Studying and Discussing Ideas

1. Compare the ideas in two works containing similar themes. *Examples:* Arnold's "Dover Beach" and Hardy's "Channel Firing," Keats's "Bright Star" and Rossetti's "Echo," Frost's "Desert Places" and Hawthorne's "Young Goodman Brown," Layton's "Rhine Boat Trip" and Poe's "The Masque of the Red Death," or Chopin's "The Story of an Hour" and Chekhov's *The Bear.* For help in developing your essay, consult Chapter 14 on the technique of comparison-contrast.

2. Consider Maupassant's "The Necklace" in terms of the idea of economic determinism. That is, to what degree are the circumstances and traits of the characters, particularly Mathilde, controlled and limited by their economic status? According to the idea, how likely is it that the characters could ever rise above their circumstances?

3. Write an essay criticizing the ideas in a work (from Appendix C) that you dislike or to which you are indifferent. With what statements in the work do you disagree? What actions? What characters? How do your own beliefs and values cause you to dislike the work's ideas? How might the work be changed to illustrate ideas with which you would agree?

4. Select an idea that particularly interests you, and outline a brief story showing how characters may or may not live up to the idea. If you have difficulty getting started, try one of these ideas:
   a. Interest and enthusiasm are hard to maintain for long.
   b. Fortune has often given people an abundance of worldly things, but few people ever believe they have received enough.
   c. When people reach adulthood, they put away childish things.
   d. It is awkward to confront another person about a grievance.
   e. Making romantic or career decisions are difficult because they demand fundamental and complete changes in life's directions.

5. Using books that you discover in the card or computer catalogue in your college or local library, search for discussions of only one of the following topics, and write a brief report on what you find.
   a. Thomas Hardy on the power of the working classes.
   b. Nathaniel Hawthorne on the significance (good and bad) of religion.
   c. Keats on the significance of intuition and imagination as creative power.
   d. The ideas underlying Poe's concept of the short story as a form.

8

Writing About Imagery
The Literary Work's Link to the Senses

In literature, **imagery** refers to words that trigger your imagination to recall and recombine **images**—memories or mental pictures of sights, sounds, tastes, smells, sensations of touch, and motions. The process is active and even vigorous, for when words or descriptions produce images, you are using your personal experiences with life and language to help you understand the works you are reading. In effect, you are recreating the work *in your own way* through the controlled stimulation produced by the writer's words. Imagery is therefore one of the strongest modes of literary expression because it provides a channel to your active imagination, and along this channel, writers bring their works directly to you and into your consciousness.

For example, reading the word *lake* may bring to your mind your literal memory of a particular lake. Your mental picture—or image—may be a distant view of calm waters reflecting blue sky, a nearby view of gentle waves rippling in the wind, a close-up view of the sandy lake bottom from a boat, or an overhead view of a sun-drenched shoreline. Similarly, the words *rose, apple, hot dog, malted milk,* and *pizza* all cause you to recollect these objects, and, in addition, may cause you to recall their smells and tastes. Active and graphic words like *row, swim,* and *dive* stimulate you to picture moving images of someone performing these actions.

Responses and the Writer's Use of Detail

In studying imagery, we try to comprehend and explain our imaginative reconstruction of the pictures and impressions evoked by the work's images. We let the poet's words simmer and percolate in our minds. To get our imaginations stirring, we might follow Coleridge in this description from his poem "Kubla Khan" (lines 37–41):

A damsel with a dulcimer
In a vision once I saw:
It was an Abyssinian maid,

And on her dulcimer she played
Singing of Mount Abora.

We do not read about the color of the young woman's clothing, or anything else about her appearance except that she is playing a dulcimer—an old-fashioned stringed instrument—and that she is singing a song about a mountain in a foreign, remote country. But Coleridge's image is enough. From it we can imagine a vivid, exotic picture of a young woman from a distant land singing, together with the loveliness of her song (even though we never hear it or understand it). The image lives.

The Relationship of Imagery to Ideas and Attitudes

Images do more than elicit impressions. By the *authenticating* effects of the vision and perceptions underlying them, they give you new ways of seeing the world and of strengthening your old ways of seeing it. Shakespeare's speaker in "Sonnet 73: That Time of Year Thou Mayst in Me Behold" (pages 102–103), for example, emphasizes that he is getting older and therefore closer to the time of his death. Rather than stating this idea so uninterestingly, however, Shakespeare dramatizes it through the introduction of images of autumn, evening, and a dying fire. In the second quatrain, for example, the speaker describes the approaching evening of life:

In me thou seest the twilight of such day
    As after sunset fadeth in the West,
Which by and by black night doth take away,
    Death's second self that seals up all in rest.

This expanded image, like those in the two other quatrains, forms an easily recognized and affirmable link with the experiences of readers. Such uses of imagery comprise one of the strongest means by which literature reinforces ideas.

Types of Imagery

Visual Imagery Is the Language of Sight

Human beings are visual. Sight is the most significant of our senses, for it is the key to our remembrance of other sense impressions. Therefore, the most frequently occurring literary imagery is to things we can visualize either exactly or approximately—**visual images**. In "Cargoes," Masefield asks us to recreate mental pictures or images of ocean-going merchant vessels from three periods of human history. He refers to a large ancient sailing vessel, a quinquereme, which he associates with the Biblical King Solomon. Then he turns to a "stately Spanish galleon," and finally refers to a modern British ship caked with salt, carrying grubby and cheap freight over the English

Channel. His images are vivid as they stand and need no further amplification. For us to reconstruct them imaginatively, we do not need ever to have seen the ancient biblical lands or waters, or ever to have seen or handled the cheap commodities on a modern merchant ship. We have seen enough in our lives both in reality and in pictures to *imagine* places and objects like these, and hence Masefield is successful in fixing his visual images in our minds.

Auditory Imagery Is the Language of Sound

Auditory images trigger our experiences with sound. For such images, let us consider Wilfred Owen's "Anthem for Doomed Youth," which is about the death of soldiers in warfare and the sorrow of their loved ones. The poem begins with the question of "what passing-bells" may be tolled for "those who die as cattle." Owen's speaker is referring to the traditional tolling of a parish church bell to announce the burial of a parishioner. Reference to the sounds of such a ceremony suggests a period of peace and order, when there is time to pay respect to the dead. But the poem then points out that the only sound for those who have fallen in battle is the "rapid rattle" of "stuttering" rifles—in other words, not the solemn, dignified sounds of peace, but the horrifying noises of war. Owen's auditory images evoke corresponding sounds in our imaginations, and they help us to experience the poem and to hate the uncivilized depravity of war.

Olfactory, Gustatory, and Tactile Imagery Refer to Smell, Taste, and Touch

In addition to sight and sound, you will also find images from the other senses. An **olfactory image** refers to smell, a **gustatory image** to taste, and a **tactile image** to touch. A great deal of love poetry, for example, includes *olfactory images* about the fragrances of flowers.

Images derived from and referring to taste—*gustatory images*—are also common, though less frequent than those referring to sight and sound. Lines 5 and 10 of Masefield's "Cargoes," for example, includes references to "sweet white wine" and "cinnamon." Although the poem refers to these commodities as cargoes, the words themselves also register in our minds as gustatory images because they evoke our sense of taste.

Tactile images of touch and texture are not as common because touch is difficult to render except in terms of effects. The speaker of Lowell's "Patterns" (pages 375–377), for example, uses tactile imagery when imagining a never-to-happen embrace with her fiancé, who we learn has been killed on a wartime battlefield. Her imagery records the effect of the embrace ("bruised"), whereas her internalized feelings are expressed in metaphors ("aching, melting") (lines 51–52):

And the buttons of his waistcoat bruised my body as he clasped me
Aching, melting, unafraid.

Tactile images are not uncommon in love poetry, where references to touch and feeling are natural. Usually, however, love poetry deals with yearning and hope rather than sexual fulfillment (as in Keats's "Bright Star").

Kinetic and Kinesthetic Imagery Refers to Motion

References to movement are also images. Images of general motion are **kinetic** (remember that *motion pictures* are called "cinema"; note the closeness of *kine* and *cine*), whereas the term **kinesthetic** is applied to human or animal movement. Imagery of motion is closely related to visual images, for motion is most often seen. Masefield's "British coaster," for example, is a visual image, but when it goes "Butting through the channel," the motion makes it also kinetic. When Hardy's skeletons sit upright at the beginning of "Channel Firing," the image is kinesthetic, as is the action of Amy Lowell's speaker walking in the garden after hearing about her fiancé's death.

The areas from which kinetic and kinesthetic imagery can be derived are too varied and unpredictable to describe. Occupations, trades, professions, businesses, recreational activities—all these might furnish images. One poet introduces references from gardening, another from money and banking, another from modern real estate developments, another from the falling of leaves in autumn, another from life in the jungle. The freshness, newness, and surprise of much poetry result from the many and varied areas from which writers draw their images.

Writing About Imagery

Raise Questions to Discover Ideas

In preparing to write, you should develop a set of thoughtful notes dealing with issues such as the following:

- What type or types of images prevail in the work? Visual (shapes, colors)? Auditory (sounds)? Olfactory (smells)? Tactile (touch and texture)? Gustatory (taste)? Kinetic or kinesthetic (motion)? Or is the imagery a combination of these?
- To what degree do the images reflect the writer's actual observation or the writer's reading and knowledge of fields such as science or history?
- How well do the images stand out? How vivid are they? How is this vividness achieved?
- Within a group of images, say visual or auditory, do the images pertain to one location or area rather than another (e.g., natural scenes rather than interiors, snowy scenes rather than grassy ones, loud and harsh sounds rather than quiet and civilized ones)?
- What explanation is needed for the images? (Images might be derived from the classics or the Bible, the Revolutionary War or World War II, the behaviors of four-footed creatures or birds, and so on.)

- What effect do the circumstances described in the work (e.g., conditions of brightness or darkness, warmth or cold, etc.) have upon your responses to the images? What poetic purpose do you think the poet achieves by controlling these responses?
- How well are the images integrated within the poem's argument or development?

Answering questions like these should provide you with a sizable body of ready-made material that you can convert directly to the body of your essay.

Organize Your Essay About Imagery

Introduction Connect a brief overview of the work to your plan of development, such as that the writer uses images to strengthen ideas about war, character, or love, or that the writer relies predominantly on images of sight, sound, and action.

Body You might deal exclusively with one of the following aspects, or, equally likely, you may combine your approaches, as you wish.

1. **Images suggesting ideas and/or moods.** Such an essay should emphasize the effects of the imagery. What ideas or moods are evoked by the images? (The auditory images beginning Owen's "Anthem for Doomed Youth," for example, all point toward a condemnation of war's brutal cruelty.) Do the images promote approval or disapproval? Cheerfulness? Melancholy? Are the images drab, exciting, vivid? How? Why? Are they conducive to humor or surprise? How does the writer achieve these effects? Are the images consistent, or are they ambiguous? (For example, the images in Masefield's "Cargoes" first indicate approval and then disapproval, with no ambiguity.)

2. **The types of images.** Here the emphasis is on the categories of images themselves. Is there a predominance of a particular type of image (e.g., visual or auditory images), or is there a blending? Is there a bunching of types at particular points in the poem or story? If so, why? Is there any shifting as the work develops, as, for example, in Owen's "Anthem for Doomed Youth" (page 378), in which the auditory images first describe loudness and harshness, but later images describe quietness and sorrow? Are the images appropriate, granting the nature and apparent intent of the work? Do they assist in making the ideas seem convincing? If there seems to be any inappropriateness, what is its effect?

3. **Systems of images.** Here the emphasis should be on the areas from which the images are drawn. This is another way of considering the appropriateness of the imagery. Is there a pattern of similar or consistent images, such as brightness changing to darkness (Mansfield's "Miss Brill")? Do all the images adhere consistently to a particular frame of reference, such as a sunlit garden (Lowell's "Patterns"), an extensive recreational forest and garden (Coleridge's "Kubla Khan"), a church graveyard (Hardy's "Channel Firing"), the sea in various stages of light (Masefield's "Cargoes"), or

a darkened forest (Blake's "The Tyger")? What is unusual or unique about the set of images? What unexpected or new responses do they produce?

Conclusion   Your conclusion, in addition to recapitulating your major points, is the place for additional insights. It would not be proper to go too far in new directions here, but you might briefly take up one or more of the ideas that you have not developed in the body. In short, what have you learned from your study of imagery in the work?

Illustrative Essay

The Images of Masefield's "Cargoes"°

[1]   In the three-stanza poem "Cargoes," John Masefield uses imagery skillfully to create a negative impression of modern commercial life.* There is a contrast between the first two stanzas and the third, with the first two idealizing the romantic, distant past and the third demeaning the modern, gritty, grimy present. Masefield's images are thus both positive and lush, on the one hand, and negative and stark, on the other.†

[2]   The most evocative and pleasant images in the poem are in the first stanza. The speaker asks that we imagine a "Quinquereme of Nineveh from distant Ophir" (line 1), one of the ocean-going, many-oared vessels in use in the ancient times of the biblical King Solomon. As Masefield identifies the cargo, the visual images are rich and romantic (lines 3 to 5):

> With a cargo of ivory,
> And apes and peacocks,
> Sandalwood, cedarwood, and sweet white wine.

Ivory suggests richness, which is augmented by the exotic "apes and peacocks" in all their spectacular strangeness. The "sandalwood, cedarwood, and sweet white wine" evoke pungent smells and tastes. The "sunny" light of ancient Palestine (line 2) not only illuminates the imaginative scene (visual), but invites readers to imagine the sun's warming touch (tactile). The references to animals and birds also suggest the sounds that these creatures would make (auditory). Thus, in this lush first stanza, images derived from all the senses are introduced to create impressions of a glorious past.

[3]   Almost equally lush are the images of the second stanza, which completes the poem's first part. Here the visual imagery evokes the royal splendor of a tall-masted, full-sailed galleon (line 6) at the height of Spain's commercial power in the sixteenth century. The galleon's cargo suggests wealth, with sparkling diamonds and amethysts, and Portuguese "gold moidores"

°See page 377 for this poem.
*Central idea.
†Thesis sentence.

gleaming in open chests (line 10). With cinnamon in the second stanza's bill of lading (line 10), Masefield includes the image of a pleasant-tasting spice.

[4] The negative imagery of the third stanza is in stark contrast to the first two stanzas. The visual image is a modern "Dirty British coaster" (line 11), which draws attention to the griminess and suffocation of modern civilization. This spray-swept ship, caked in sea-salt, is loaded with materials that pollute the earth with noise and smoke. The smoke-stack of the coaster (line 11) and the firewood it is carrying suggest choking smog. The Tyne Coal (line 13) and road rails (line 14) suggest the noise and smoke of puffing railroad engines. As if this were not enough, the "pig-lead" (line 14) to be used in various industrial processes indicates not just more unpleasantness, but also something poisonous and deadly. In contrast to the lush and stately imagery of the first two stanzas, the images in the third stanza invite the conclusion that people now, when the "Dirty British coaster" butts through the English Channel, are surrounded and threatened by visual, olfactory, and auditory pollution.

[5] The poem thus establishes a romantic past and ugly present through images of sight, smell, and sound. The images of motion also emphasize this view: In the first two stanzas, the quinquereme is "rowing" and the galleon is "dipping." These kinetic images suggest dignity and lightness. The British coaster, however, is "butting," an image indicating bull-like hostility and stupid force. These, together with all the other images, focus the poem's negative views of modern life. The facts that existence for both the ancient Palestinians and the Renaissance Spaniards included slavery (of those men rowing the quinquereme) and piracy (by those Spanish "explorers" who robbed and killed the natives of the Isthmus) should probably not be emphasized as a protest against Masefield's otherwise valid contrasts in images. His final commentary may hence be thought of as the banging of his "cheap tin trays" (line 15), which makes a percussive climax of the oppressive images filling too large a portion of modern lives.

Work Cited

Masefield, John. "Cargoes." Edgar V. Roberts. *Writing About Literature.* 11th ed. Upper Saddle River: Prentice Hall, 2006. 377.

Commentary on the Essay

This essay illustrates the first strategy for writing about imagery, using images to develop ideas and moods. All the examples—derived directly from the poem—emphasize the qualities of Masefield's images. This method permits the introduction of imagery drawn from all the senses in order to demonstrate Masefield's ideas about the past and the present. Other approaches might have concentrated exclusively on Masefield's visual images, or upon his images drawn from trade and commerce. Because Masefield uses auditory and gustatory images, but does not develop them extensively, sound or taste might be appropriately treated in short, paragraph-length essays.

The introductory paragraph of the illustrative essay presents the central idea that Masefield uses his images climactically to lead to his negative view of modern commercialism. The thesis sentence indicates that the topics to be developed are those of (1) lushness and (2) starkness.

Paragraphs 2 and 3 form a unit stressing the lushness and exoticism of the first stanza and the wealth and colorfulness of the second stanza. In particular, paragraph 2 uses words like "lush," "evocative," "rich," "exotic," "pungent," and "romantic" to characterize the pleasing mental pictures that the images invoke. Although the paragraph indicates enthusiastic responses to the images, it does not go beyond the limits of the images themselves.

Paragraph 4 stresses the contrast of Masefield's images in the third stanza with those of the first two stanzas. To this end, the paragraph illustrates the imaginative reconstruction needed to develop an understanding of this contrast. The unpleasantness, annoyance, and even the danger of the cargoes mentioned in the third stanza are therefore emphasized as the qualities evoked by the images.

The last paragraph demonstrates that the imagery of motion—not much stressed in the poem—is in agreement with the rest of Masefield's imagery. As a demonstration of the need for fair, impartial judgment, the conclusion introduces the possible objection that Masefield may be slanting his images by including not a full but rather a partial view of their respective historical periods. Thus the concluding paragraph adds balance to the analysis illustrated in paragraphs 2, 3, and 4.

Special Topics for Studying and Discussing Literary Imagery

1. Compare the images of home in "Anthem for Doomed Youth" (page 378) and "An Occurrence at Owl Creek Bridge" (pages 317–322). Describe the differing effects of the images. How are the images used? How effectively do these images aid in the development of the attitudes toward war expressed in each poem? How is your reading of the poems affected by the knowledge that both Owen and Bierce were killed in war?

2. On the basis of the poems in Appendix C by Arnold, Blake, Coleridge, Frost, and Layton, write an essay discussing the poetic use of images drawn from the natural world. What sorts of references do the poets make? What attitudes do they express about the details they select? What is the relationship between the images and religious views? What judgments about God and nature do the poets show by their images?

3. Considering the imagery of Hardy's "Channel Firing," Shakespeare's "Sonnet 73: That Time of Year Thou Mayst in Me Behold," or Blake's "The Tyger," write an essay explaining the power of imagery. As you develop your thoughts, be sure to consider the dramatic nature of the images in

the poem you choose and to account for the impressions and ideas that they create. You may also wish to introduce references to images from other poems that are relevant to your points.

4. Write a short poem describing one of the following:

   a. Athletes who have just completed an exhausting run

   b. Children getting out of school for the day

   c. The antics of your dog, cat, horse, turtle, or other pet

   d. A cat that always sits down on your schoolwork, and then purrs

   e. A particularly good meal you had recently

   f. The best concert that you ever attended

   g. Driving to work/school on a rainy/snowy day

   Then, write an analysis of the images you selected for your poem, and explain your choices. What details stand out in your mind? What do you recall best—sight, smell, sound, action? What is the relationship between your images and the ideas you express in your poem?

5. Write an essay considering the graphic or pictorial nature of the imagery in Coleridge's "Kubla Khan," Keats's "On First Looking Into Chapman's Homer," and Rossetti's "Echo," along with other works that you may wish to include. What similarities and differences do you find in subject matter, treatment, arrangement, and general idea? On the basis of your comparison, what relationships do you perceive between sight and literary imagery?

6. Use the retrieval system (computer or card catalogue) in your library to research the topic of imagery in Shakespeare (see *imagery* or *style and imagery*). How many titles do you find? Over how many years have these works been published? Take one of the books out, and write a brief report on one of the chapters. What topics are discussed? What types of imagery are introduced? What relationship does the author make between imagery and content?

9

Writing About Metaphor and Simile
A Source of Depth and Range in Literature

Figures of speech, **metaphorical language**, **figurative language**, **figurative devices**, and **rhetorical figures** are terms describing organized patterns of comparison that deepen, broaden, extend, illuminate, and emphasize meaning. First and foremost, the use of figures of speech is a major characteristic by which great literature provides us with fresh and original ways of thinking, feeling, and understanding. Although metaphorical language is sometimes called "ornate," as though it were unnecessarily decorative, it is not uncommon in conversational speech, and it is essential in literary thought and expression.

Unlike the writing of the social and "hard" sciences, imaginative literature does not purport to be direct and absolute, offering a direct correspondence of words and things. Yes, literature often presents specific and accurate descriptions and explanations, but it also moves in areas of implication and suggestiveness through the use of metaphorical language, which enables writers to amplify their ideas while still employing a relatively small number of words. Such language is therefore a *sine qua non* in imaginative literature, particularly poetry, where it compresses thought, deepens understanding, and shapes response.

There are many metaphorical figures, some of which are *paradox, anaphora, apostrophe, personification, synecdoche* and *metonymy, pun* (or *paronomasia*), *synesthesia, overstatement*, and *understatement*. All these figures are modes of comparison, and they may be expressed in single words, phrases, clauses, or entire structures. The two most important and easily recognized figures of speech, with which we will be concerned here, are *metaphors* and *similes*.

Metaphors and Similes: The Major Figures of Speech

A Metaphor Shows That Something Unknown Can Be Understood Because It Is Identical to Something Known

A **metaphor** (a "carrying out [*phor*]a change [*meta*]") *equates* known objects or actions with something that is unknown or to be explained (e.g., "Your words are *music* to my ears," "You are the *sunshine* of my life," "My life is *a squirrel* *cage"*). The equation of the metaphor not only explains and illuminates the thing—let us choose Keats's star in the poem "Bright Star"—but also offers distinctive and original ways of seeing it, applying it, and thinking about it. Thus Keats draws his metaphor of the star because of its constancy in the heavens, for the star has kept its identical location from year to year and age to age. Keats applies this quality to his speaker's wish for love that is unchanging and permanent—both a natural and an appropriate equation of celestial star and human desire.

Metaphors are inseparable from language. In a heavy storm, for example, trees may be said to *bow* constantly as the wind blows against them. *Bow* is a metaphor because the word usually refers to performers' bending forward to acknowledge the applause of an audience and to indicate their gratitude for the audience's approval. The metaphor therefore asks us to equate our knowledge of theater life (something known) to a weather occurrence (something to be explained). A comparable reference to theater life creates one of the best-known metaphors to appear in Shakespeare's plays: "All the world's a stage, / And all the men and women merely players." Here, Shakespeare's character Jacques (JAY-queez) from Act 2, scene 7 of *As You Like It*, equates human life directly with stage life. In other words, the things said and done by stage actors are also said and done by living people in real life. It is important to recognize that Shakespeare's metaphor does not state that the world is *like* a stage but that it literally *is* a stage.

A Simile Shows That Something Unknown Can Be Understood Because It Is Similar to Something Known

A **simile** (a "showing of likeness or resemblance") illustrates the *similarity* or *comparability* of the known to something unknown or to be explained. Whereas a metaphor merges identities, a simile focuses on resemblances (e.g., "Your words are *like music* to me," "You are *like sunshine* in my life," "I feel *like a squirrel in a cage"*). Similes are distinguishable from metaphors because they are introduced by *like* with nouns and *as* (also *as if* and *as though*) with clauses. If Keats had written that his speaker's desire for steadfastness is *like* the bright star, his comparison would have been a simile.

Let us consider one of the best-known similes in poetry, from "A Valediction: Forbidding Mourning" by the seventeenth-century poet John Donne. This is a dramatic poem spoken by a lover about to go on a trip. His loved one is sorrowful, and he attempts to console her by claiming that even when he is gone, he will remain with her in spirit. The following stanza contains a famous simile embodying this idea.

> Our two souls therefore, which are one,
> Though I must go, endure not yet

A breach,° but an expansion
Like gold to airy thinness beat.

The simile compares the souls of the speaker and his loved one to gold, a metal both valuable and malleable. By the simile, the speaker asserts that the impending departure will not be a separation but rather a thinning out, so that the relationship of the lovers will remain constant and rich even as the distance between them increases. Because the comparison is introduced by "Like," the emphasis of the figurative language is on the *similarity* of the lovers' love to gold (which is always gold even when it is thinned out by the goldsmith's hammer), not on the *identification* of the two.

Characteristics of Metaphors and Similes

Metaphors and similes are based in imagery, which is the means by which literature is made graphic and vivid (see Chapter 8). That is, by using words that convey images the writer prompts us to recall memories (images) of sights, sounds, tastes, smells, sensations, and visualization of motion. Metaphors and similes go beyond literal imagery to introduce perceptions and comparisons that can be unusual, unpredictable, and surprising, as in Donne's simile comparing the lovers' relationship to gold. The comparison emphasizes the bond between the two lovers; the reference to gold shows how valuable the bond is; the unusual and original comparison is one of the elements that make the poem striking and memorable.

To see metaphorical language in further operation, let us take a commonly described condition—happiness. In everyday speech, we might use the sentence "She was happy," to state that a particular character was experiencing joy and excitement. The sentence is of course accurate, but it is not interesting. A more vivid way of saying the same thing is to use an image of action, such as "She jumped for joy." But another and better way of communicating joy is the following simile: "She felt as if she had just won the lottery." Because readers easily understand the disbelief, excitement, exhilaration, and delight that such an event would bring, they also understand—and feel—the character's happiness. It is the *simile* that evokes this perception and enables each reader to personalize the experience, for no simple description could help a reader comprehend the same degree of emotion.

As a parallel poetic example, let us look at Keats's famous sonnet "On First Looking into Chapman's Homer," which Keats wrote soon after reading the translation of Homer's great epics *The Iliad* and *The Odyssey* by the Renaissance poet George Chapman. Keats, one of the greatest of all poets himself, describes his enthusiasm about Chapman's successful and exciting work.

---

3 *breach:* break, separation.

John Keats (1795–1821)

On First Looking into Chapman's Homer° (1816)

Much have I travell'd in the realms of gold,°
    And many goodly states and kingdoms seen:
    Round many western islands° have I been
Which bards in fealty to Apollo° hold.
Oft of one wide expanse° had I been told   5
    That deep-brow'd Homer ruled as his demesne;°
    Yet did I never breathe its pure serene°
Till I heard Chapman speak out loud and bold:
Then felt I like some watcher of the skies
    When a new planet swims into his ken;°   10
Or like stout Cortez° when with eagle eyes
    He star'd at the Pacific—and all his men
Look'd at each other with a wild surmise°—
    Silent, upon a peak in Darien.

As a first step in understanding the power of metaphorical language, we can briefly paraphrase the sonnet's content.

> I have enjoyed much art and read much poetry, and I have been told that Homer is the best writer of all. However, I did not appreciate his works until I first read them in Chapman's clear and forceful translation. This discovery was exciting and awe-inspiring.

If all Keats had written had been a paragraph like this one, we would pay little attention to it, for it conveys no excitement or wonder. But the last six lines of the sonnet contain two memorable similes ("like some watcher of the skies" and "like stout Cortez") that stand out and demand a special effort of imagination. To appreciate these similes fully, we need to imagine what it would be like to be an astronomer as he or she discovers a previously unknown planet, and what it would have been like to be one of the first European explorers to see the Pacific Ocean. As we imagine ourselves in these

---

On First Looking into Chapman's Homer: George Chapman (c. 1560–1634) published his translations of Homer's *Iliad* in 1612 and *Odyssey* in 1614–1615.
1 *realms of gold:* the world of great art.   **3** *islands:* ancient literature.   **4** *bards . . . Apollo:* writers who are sworn subjects of Apollo, the Greek god of light, music, poetry, prophecy, and the sun.   **5** *expanse:* epic poetry.   **6** *demesne:* realm, estate.   **7** *serene:* a clear expanse of air; also grandeur, clarity; rulers were also sometimes called "serene majesty."   **10** *ken:* range of vision. **11** *Cortez:* Hernando Cortés (1485–1547), a Spanish general and the conqueror of Mexico. Keats confuses him with Vasco de Balboa (c. 1475–1519), the first European to see the Pacific Ocean (in 1510) from Darien, an early name for the Isthmus of Panama.   **13** *surmise:* conjecture, supposition.

Vehicle and Tenor

To describe the relationship between a writer's ideas and the metaphors and similes chosen to objectify them, two useful terms have been coined by I. A. Richards (in *The Philosophy of Rhetoric*, 1929). First is the **vehicle**, or the specific words of the metaphor or simile. Second is the **tenor**, which is the totality of ideas and attitudes not only of the literary speaker but also of the author. For example, the tenor of Donne's simile in "A Valediction: Forbidding Mourning" is the inseparable love and unbreakable connection of the two lovers; the vehicle is the hammering of gold "to airy thinness." Similarly, the tenor of the similes in the sestet of Keats's sonnet is awe and wonder; the vehicle is the description of astronomical and geographical discovery.

roles, we get a sense of the amazement, excitement, exhilaration, and joy that would accompany such discoveries. With that experience comes the realization that the world—the universe—is far bigger and more astonishing than we had ever dreamed.

Metaphorical language therefore makes strong demands on our creative imaginations. It bears repeating that as we develop our own mental pictures under the stimulation of metaphors and similes, we also develop appropriately associated attitudes and feelings. Let us consider once more Keats's metaphor "realms of gold," which invites us both to imagine brilliant and shining kingdoms and also to join Keats in valuing and loving not just poetry but all literature. The metaphorical "realms of gold" act upon our minds, liberating our imaginations, directing our understanding, and evoking our feelings. In such a way, reading and responding to the works of writers like Keats produces both mental and emotional experiences that were previously hidden to us. Writers constantly give us something new, widening our comprehension, increasing our knowledge, and deepening our imagination.

Writing About Metaphors and Similes

Begin by determining the use, line by line, of metaphors or similes. Obviously, similes are the easiest figures to recognize because they introduce comparisons with *like* or *as*. Metaphors can be recognized because the topics are discussed not as themselves but as other topics. If the poems speak of falling leaves or law courts but the subjects are memory or increasing age, you are looking at metaphors.

Raise Questions to Discover Ideas

- What metaphors and/or similes does the work contain? Where do they occur? Under what circumstances? How extensive are they?

- How do you recognize them? Are they signaled by a single word or phrase, such as "desert places" in Frost's "Desert Places" (page 369), or are they more extensively detailed, as in Shakespeare's "Sonnet 30: When to the Sessions of Sweet Silent Thought" (page 380)?

- How vivid are the metaphors and similes? How obvious? How unusual? What kind of effort is needed to understand them in context?

- Structurally, how are the metaphors and similes developed? How do they rise out of the situation envisioned in the work? To what degree are they integrated into the work's development of ideas? How do they relate to other aspects of the work?

- Is one type of figure used in a particular section while another type predominates in another section? Why?

- If you have discovered a number of metaphors, what relationships can you find among them, such as the judicial and financial connections in Shakespeare's "When to the Sessions of Sweet Silent Thought" (page 380)?

- How do the metaphors or similes broaden, deepen, or otherwise assist in making the ideas in the poem forceful?

- In general, how appropriate and meaningful is the metaphorical language in the poem? What effect does this language have on the poem's tone, and on your understanding and appreciation of the poem?

Organize Your Essay About Metaphors and Similes

Introduction In the introduction, relate the quality of the figures of speech to the general nature of the work. Thus, metaphors and similes of suffering might be appropriate to a religious, redemptive work, while those of sunshine and cheer might be right for a romantic one. If there is any discrepancy between the metaphorical language and the topic, you could consider that contrast as a possible central idea, for it would clearly indicate the writer's ironic perspective. Suppose that the topic of the poem is love, but the figures put you in mind of darkness and cold. What would the writer be saying about the quality of love? You should also try to justify any claims that you make about the figures. For example, the major metaphor of Lowell's "Patterns" is that people are virtually compelled to live their lives controlled by many habits, restrictions, customs, expectations, duties, roles, and services—"patterns." How is this metaphor to be taken? As an outcry for personal freedom? As an expression of rage against restrictions? As a suggestion that customs that restrict may also be customs that provide solace? How do you explain your answer or answers? Your introduction is the place to establish ideas and justifications of this sort.

Body   The following approaches for discussing rhetorical figures are not mutually exclusive, and you may combine them as you wish. Most likely, your essay will bring in most of the following classifications.

1. **Interpret the meaning and effect of the metaphorical language**. Here you explain how the metaphors and/or similes enable you to make an interpretation. In lines 17 to 19 of "Kubla Khan" (page 367), for example, Coleridge introduces the following simile:

   And from this chasm, with ceaseless turmoil seething,
   As if this earth in fast thick pants were breathing,
   A mighty fountain momently was forced.

   Coleridge's simile of "fast thick pants" almost literally animates the earth as a moving, working power, panting as it forces the fountain out of the chasm. The idea is that the phenomena of Nature are not dead, but vigorously alive. A directly explanatory approach, such as this, requires that metaphors and similes be expanded and interpreted, including the explanation of necessary references and allusions.

2. **Analyze the frames of reference and their appropriateness to the subject matter**. Here you classify and locate the sources and types of references and determine the appropriateness of these to the poem's subject matter. Ask questions similar to these: Does the writer refer extensively to nature, science, warfare, politics, business, reading (e.g., Shakespeare's metaphor equating personal reverie with courtroom proceedings in Sonnet 30)? Does the metaphor seem appropriate? How? Why?

3. **Focus on the interests and sensibilities of the poet**. In a way this approach is like strategy 2, but the emphasis here is on what the selectivity of the writer might show about his or her vision and interests. You might begin by listing the figures in the work and then determining the sources. But then you should raise questions like the following: Does the writer use figures derived from one sense rather than another (i.e., sight, hearing, taste, smell, touch)? Does he or she record color, brightness, shadow, shape, depth, height, number, size, slowness, speed, emptiness, fullness, richness, drabness? Has the writer relied on the associations of figures of sense? Do metaphors and similes referring to green plants and trees, to red roses, or to rich fabrics, for example, suggest that life is full and beautiful, or do references to touch suggest amorous warmth? This approach is designed to help you draw conclusions about the author's taste or sensibility.

4. **Examine the effect of one figure on the other figures and ideas of the work.** The assumption of this approach is that each literary work is unified and organically whole, so that each part is closely related and inseparable from everything else. Usually it is best to pick a figure that occurs at the beginning of the work and then determine how this figure influences your perception of the remainder. Your aim is to consider the relationship of part to parts and part to whole. The beginning of Frost's poem "Desert Places," for example, describes "snow falling and night

falling." What is the effect of this opening on the poem's metaphor of human "desert places"? To help you with questions like this, you might substitute a totally different detail, such as, for this poem, the rising sun on a beautiful day, or playing with a kitten, rather than the onset of cold and night. Such suppositions, which would clearly be out of place, may help you understand and then explain the poet's figures of speech.

Conclusion   In your conclusion, summarize your main points, describe your general impressions, try to describe the impact of the figures, indicate your personal responses, or show what might further be done along the lines you have been developing. If you know other works by the same writer, or other works by other writers who use comparable or contrasting figures, you might explain the relationship of the other work or works to your present analysis.

Illustrative Essay

Shakespeare's Metaphors in "Sonnet 30: When to the Sessions of Sweet Silent Thought"°

[1]   In this sonnet Shakespeare stresses the sadness of remembering past regrets and misfortunes, but he states that a person with such heavyheartedness may be cheered by present thoughts about a good friend. His metaphors present new and fresh ways of seeing personal life in this perspective.* He creates metaphors drawn from the public and business world of law courts, money, and banking or money-handling.†

[2]   In the first four lines, Shakespeare presents a metaphor of law and the courtroom to show that memories of past experience are constantly present and influential. Like a judge commanding defendants to appear in court, Shakespeare's speaker "summon[s]" his memory of "things past" to appear on trial before him. This metaphor suggests that people are their own judges and that their ideals and morals are actual laws by which they measure themselves. The speaker finds himself guilty of wasting his time in the past. Removing himself, however, from the strict punishment that a real judge might require, he does not condemn himself for his "dear time's waste" but instead laments it (line 4). The metaphor is thus used to indicate that a person's consciousness is made up just as much of self-doubt and reproach as of more positive qualities.

°See page 380 for this poem.
*Central idea.
†Thesis sentence.

[3]   By introducing a closely related metaphor of money in the next group of four lines, Shakespeare implies that living is a lifelong process of continued investment. According to this metaphor, living requires the spending of emotions and commitment to others. When friends move away and loved ones die, it is as though this expenditure has been lost. Thus, the speaker's dead friends are "precious" because he invested time and love in them, and the "sights" that have "vanished" from his eyes make him "moan" because he went to great emotional "expense" for them (line 8).

[4]   Like the money metaphor, the metaphor of banking or money-handling that Shakespeare creates in the next four lines emphasizes that memory is a bank in which life's experiences are deposited. The full emotions surrounding experience are recorded there, and they may be withdrawn in moments of "sweet silent thought" just as a depositor may withdraw money. Thus the speaker states that he counts out the sad parts of his experience—his woe—just as a merchant or banker counts money: "And heavily from woe to woe tell o'er" (line 10). Because strong emotions still accompany his memories of past mistakes, the metaphor extends to borrowing and the payment of interest. The speaker thus says that he pays again with "new" woe the accounts that he had already paid with old woe. The metaphor implies that the past is so much a part of the present that a person never stops feeling pain and regret.

[5]   The legal, financial, and money-handling metaphors combine in the last two lines to show how a healthy present life may overcome past regrets. The "dear friend" being addressed in these lines has the resources (financial) to settle all the emotional judgments that the speaker as a self-judge has made against himself (legal). It is as though the friend is a rich patron who rescues him from emotional bankruptcy (legal and financial) and the doom resulting from a sentence of emotional misery and depression (legal).

[6]   In these metaphors, therefore, Shakespeare's references are drawn from everyday public and business actions, but his use of them is creative and freshly unusual. In particular, the idea of line 8 ("And moan th'expense of many a vanished sight") stresses that people spend much emotional energy on others. Without such personal commitment, one cannot have precious friends and loved ones. In keeping with this metaphor of money and investment, one could measure life not in months or years, but in the spending of emotion and involvement in personal relationships. By inviting readers to explore the nature of love and friendship brought out by his metaphors, Shakespeare gives previously unrealized insights into the value of life.

Work Cited

Shakespeare, William. "Sonnet 30: When to the Sessions of Sweet Silent Thought." Edgar V. Roberts. *Writing About Literature.* 11th ed. Upper Saddle River: Prentice Hall, 2006. 380.

Commentary on the Essay

This essay treats the three classes of metaphors that Shakespeare introduces in Sonnet 30. It thus illustrates strategy 2 described on page 144. But the aim of the discussion is not to explore the extent and nature of the comparison between the metaphors and the personal situations described in the sonnet. Instead, the goal is to explain how the metaphors develop Shakespeare's meaning. This essay therefore also illustrates strategy 1, which is described on page 144.

In addition to providing a brief description of the sonnet, the introduction brings out the central idea and the thesis sentence. Paragraph 2 deals with the meaning of Shakespeare's courtroom metaphor. His money metaphor is explained in paragraph 3. Paragraph 4 considers the banking or money-handling figure. Paragraph 5 shows how Shakespeare's last two lines bring together the three strands of metaphor. The conclusion comments generally on the creativity of Shakespeare's metaphors, and it also amplifies the way in which the money metaphor leads toward an increased understanding of life.

Throughout the essay, transitions are brought about by the linking words in the topic sentences. In paragraph 3, for example, the words "closely related" and "next group" move the reader from paragraph 2 to the new content. In paragraph 4, the words effecting the transition are "Like the money metaphor" and "the next four lines." The opening sentence of paragraph 5 refers collectively to the subjects of paragraphs 2, 3, and 4, thereby focusing them on the new topic of paragraph 5.

Special Topics for Studying
and Discussing Metaphors and Similes

1. Consider some of the metaphors and similes in the works (poems, stories, plays) included in Appendix C. Write an essay that answers the following questions. How effective are the figures you select? What insights do the figures provide within the contexts of their respective poems? How appropriate are they? Might they be expanded more fully, and if they were, what would be the effect? You might choose any of the following topics:
    *   The "darkling plain" simile in Arnold's "Dover Beach"
    *   The metaphor of the knot in Glaspell's *Trifles*
    *   Metaphor in Blake's "The Tyger"
    *   The metaphor of the Rhine in Layton's "Rhine Boat Trip"
    *   Similes in Owen's "Anthem for Doomed Youth" or Coleridge's "Kubla Khan"
    *   The metaphor of "red war" in Hardy's "Channel Firing"

- The use of similes in Hughes's "Negro"
- The horse Toby as a metaphor in Chekhov's *The Bear*

2. Write a poem in which you create a governing metaphor or simile. An example might be: My girlfriend/boyfriend is like (a) an opening flower; (b) a difficult book; (c) an insoluble mathematical problem; (d) a bill that cannot be paid; (e) a slow-moving chess game. Another example: Teaching a person how to do a particular job is like (a) shoveling heavy snow; (b) climbing a mountain during a landslide; (c) having someone force you underwater when you're gasping for breath. When you finish, describe the relationship between your comparison and the development and structure of your poem.

3. In your library's reference section, find the third edition of J. A. Cuddon's *A Dictionary of Literary Terms and Literary Theory* (1991) or some other dictionary of literary terms. Study the entries for *metaphor* and *simile*, and write a brief report on these sections.

10

Writing About Symbolism and Allegory
Keys to Extended Meaning

Symbolism and **allegory**, like metaphors and similes (see Chapter 9) are modes that expand meaning. They are literary devices developed from the connections that real-life people make between their own existence and particular objects, places, or occurrences, through experience, reading, and memory. By highlighting details as *symbols*, and stories or parts of stories as *allegories*, writers expand their meaning while keeping their works within reasonable lengths. As examples, let us realize that a bereaved mother may associate personal grief with household boxes and containers. A young man may, upon seeing the North Star, dedicate himself to constant love. A beloved animal may cause a widow to remember her love for her departed husband. A distant view of a vanishing light may cause a man to think that traditional ideas are being lost. The significance of details like these can be meaningful not only at the time they occur but also throughout life. It is as though the memory of such things alone can be the same as pages of explanation and analysis, for merely bringing them to mind or speaking about them unlocks their meanings, implications, and consequences. They become **symbols**, as they in fact are in Wagner's "The Boxes," Keats's "Bright Star," Chekhov's *The Bear*, and Arnold's "Dover Beach."

Symbolism

The words *symbol* and *symbolism* are derived from the Greek word meaning "to throw together" (*syn*, "together," and *ballein*, "to throw"). A symbol creates a direct equation between (1) a specific object, scene, character, or action; and (2) ideas, values, persons, or ways of life. In effect, a symbol is a *substitute* for the elements being signified, much as the flag stands for the ideals of the nation.

When we first see a symbol in literature, it may seem to carry no more weight than its surface meaning. It can be a description of a character, an object, a place, an action, or a situation, and it may function usefully in this capacity. What makes a symbol symbolic is its capacity to signify additional levels of meaning—major ideas, simple or complex emotions, or philosophical or religious qualities or values. There are two types of symbols—*cultural* and *contextual*.

Cultural Symbols Are Derived from Our Cultural and Historical Heritage

Many symbols are generally recognized and are therefore **cultural** (also called **universal**). They embody ideas and emotions that writers and readers share as heirs of the same historical and cultural tradition. When using cultural symbols, a writer assumes that readers know what the symbols represent. An example is the character Sisyphus of ancient Greek myth. As a punishment for trying twice to overcome death, Sisyphus is doomed by the underworld gods to roll a large boulder up a high hill forever. Just as he gets the boulder to the top, it rolls down, and then he must roll it up again, and again, and again, because the boulder always rolls back. The plight of Sisyphus has been interpreted as a symbol of the human condition: In spite of constant struggle, a person rarely if ever completes anything. Work must always be done over and over from day to day and from generation to generation, and the same problems confront humanity throughout all time. Because of such fruitless effort, life seems to have little or no meaning. Nevertheless, there is hope: People who confront their tasks, as Sisyphus does, stay involved and active, and their tasks make their lives meaningful. A writer referring to Sisyphus would expect us to understand that this ancient mythological figure symbolizes these conditions.

Similarly, ordinary water, because living creatures cannot live without it, is recognized as a symbol of life. It has this meaning in the ceremony of baptism, and it conveys this meaning and dimension in a variety of literary contexts. Thus, a spouting fountain might symbolize optimism (as upwelling, bubbling life), and a stagnant pool might symbolize the pollution and diminution of life. Water is also a universal symbol of sexuality, and its condition or state can symbolize various romantic relationships. For instance, stories in which lovers meet near a turbulent stream, a roaring waterfall, a mud puddle, a beach with high breakers, a stormy sea, a calm lake, or a wide and gently flowing river symbolically represent love relationships that range from uncertainty to serenity.

Contextual Symbols Are Symbolic Only in Individual Works

Objects and descriptions that are not universal symbols can be symbols *only if they are made so within individual works*. These are **contextual**, **private**, or **authorial** symbols. Unlike cultural symbols, contextual symbols derive their meanings from the context and circumstances of individual works. As an example, the "shady seat" mentioned in Amy Lowell's "Patterns" (line 86) takes on powerful symbolic value, for we learn that it was where the speaker and her fiancé had planned, before he was sent off to war, to make love in the open air. As a symbol, the shady seat suggests a wished-for liberation from confining and stultifying cultural expectations, and for a total union of love and a desire for personal freedom. A symbolic object from a story is the large standing clock in Poe's "The Masque of the Red Death," which not only marks the passage of time but also ushers in the sinister and relentless force of death.

Like Lowell's shady seat, Poe's clock is a major contextual symbol. But there is not necessarily any carryover from one work to the next. In other works, a shady seat and a clock are not symbolic unless the authors who include them give them deliberately symbolic meaning. Further, if such objects actually are introduced as symbols, they can be given meanings that are different from those in the works by Lowell and Poe.

Determine What Is Symbolic (and Not Symbolic)

In determining whether an object, action, or character is a symbol, you need to judge the importance that the author gives to it. If the element is prominent and also maintains a consistency of meaning, you can justify interpreting it as a symbol. For example, in Hardy's "The Three Strangers" the mead given by the Fennels to their guests is ostensibly nothing more than a celebratory drink. But because the threatening and obnoxious second stranger consumes much more than his share, the mead takes on symbolic value in the story, suggesting that the imposition of law on people like the Fennels is arbitrary and capricious, and also punitive. At the beginning of Wagner's "The Boxes," the speaker refers to "boxes in the house," including footlockers, hampers, and a trunk. Readers will note that such large containers would easily conceal a small boy. But at the story's end, the speaker says that she still visits the cemetery where her son is buried. The box she mentions at the end is thus a coffin, and for this reason the "Boxes" of the poem's title may be construed as a contextual symbol of death.

Allegory

An allegory is like a symbol because it transfers and broadens meaning. The term is derived from the Greek word *allegorein*, which means "to say something beyond what is commonly understood" (from *allos*, "other" and *agoreuein*, "to speak in public"). But allegory is more sustained than symbolism. An allegory is to a symbol as a motion picture is to a still picture. In form, an allegory is a complete and self-sufficient narrative, but it also signifies another series of conditions or events. Some stories are allegories from beginning to end, but many stories that are not allegories can contain brief sections or episodes that are *allegorical*. Allegories are often concerned with morality and with religion, but we may also find political and social allegories. To the degree that literary works are true not only because of the lives of their main characters but also because of life generally, one might maintain that much literature may be considered allegorical even though the authors did not plan their works as allegories.

Understand the Applications and Meaning of Allegory

Allegories and the allegorical method are more than literary exercises. Without question, readers and listeners learn and memorize stories and tales more easily than moral lessons, and therefore allegory is a favorite method of teaching morality. In addition, thought and expression have not always been free and safe. The threat of censorship and the danger of political or economic reprisal have often caused authors to express their views indirectly in the form of allegory rather than to name names and write openly, thereby risking political prosecution, accusations of libel, or even bodily harm. Hence, the double meanings of many allegories are based not just in the literary form but also in the reality of circumstances in our difficult world.

In studying allegory, determine whether all or part of a work can have an extended, allegorical meaning. The popularity of George Lucas's movie *Star Wars* and its sequels (in videotape and newly refurbished rereleases) and also its "prequel" (*The Phantom Menace*), for example, is attributable at least partly to its being an allegory about the conflict between good and evil. Obi Wan Kenobi (intelligence) assists Luke Skywalker (heroism, boldness) and instructs him in "the Force" (moral or religious faith). Thus armed and guided, Skywalker opposes the powers of Darth Vader (evil) to rescue the Princess Leia (purity and goodness) with the aid of the latest spaceships and weaponry (technology). The story has produced a set of popular adventure films, accompanied by dramatic music and ingenious visual and sound effects. With the obvious allegorical overtones, however, it stands for any person's quest for self-fulfillment.

To apply a part of the allegory more specifically, consider that for a time the evil Vader imprisons Skywalker and that Skywalker must exert all his skill and strength to get free and overcome Vader. In the allegorical application of the episode, this imprisonment signifies those moments of doubt, discouragement, and depression that people experience while trying to better themselves through education, work, self-improvement, friendship, marriage, and so on.

Almost from the beginning of recorded literature, similar heroic deeds have been represented in allegorical forms. From ancient Greece, the allegorical hero Jason sails the *Argo* to distant lands to gain the Golden Fleece (those who take risks are rewarded). From Anglo-Saxon England, the hero Beowulf saves King Hrothgar's throne by killing the monster Grendel and his even more monstrous mother (victory comes to those who rely on the forces of good). From seventeenth-century England, Bunyan's *The Pilgrim's Progress* tells how the hero Christian overcomes difficulties and temptations while traveling from this world to the next (belief, perseverance, and resistance to temptation save the faithful). As long as the parallel connections are close and consistent, such as those mentioned here, an allegorical interpretation is valid.

Fable, Parable, and Myth

Closely related to symbolism and allegory in the ability to extend and expand meaning are three additional forms—**fable**, **parable**, and **myth**.

A Fable Is a Short Tale with a Pointed Moral

The fable (from Latin *fabula*, a story or narration) is an old, brief, and popular form. Often but not always, fables are about animals that possess human traits (such fables are called **beast fables**). Past collectors and editors of fables have attached "morals" or explanations to the brief stories, as is the case with Aesop, the most enduringly popular of fable writers. Tradition has it that Aesop was a slave who composed fables in ancient Greece. His fable "The Fox and the Grapes" signifies the trait of belittling things we cannot have. More recent popular contributions to the fable tradition include Walt Disney's "Mickey Mouse," Walt Kelly's "Pogo," and Berke Breathed's "Bloom County." The adjective *fabulous* refers to the collective body of fables of all sorts, even though the word is often used as little more than a vague term of approval.

A Parable Is a Short Narrative Illustrating a Religious Concept

A parable (from Greek *parabolé*, a "setting beside" or comparison) is a short, simple story with a moral or religious bent. Parables are most often associated with Jesus, who used them to embody unique religious insights and truths. For example, his parables "The Prodigal Son" and "The Good Samaritan," as recorded by Luke, are interpreted to show God's understanding, forgiveness, concern, and love.

A Myth Is a Tale with Social, Political, Religious, or Philosophical Meanings

A myth (from Greek *muthos*, a "story" or "plot") is a traditional story that embodies and codifies the religious, philosophical, and cultural values of the civilization in which it is composed. Usually the central figures of mythical stories are heroes, gods, and demigods, such as the ancient figures Zeus, Hera, Prometheus, Athena, Sisyphus, Oedipus, Atalanta, Hercules, Venus, and Aeneas. Although most myths are fictional, many are based in historical truth. They are by no means confined to the past, for the word *myth* can also refer to abstractions and ideas that people today hold collectively, such as the concept of perpetual military supremacy or the idea that future problems can be deferred indefinitely. Sometimes the words *myth* and *mythical* are used with the meaning "fanciful" or "untrue." Such disparagement is misleading because the truths of mythology are not to be found literally in the myths themselves but rather in their symbolic and allegorical interpretations.

Allusion in Symbolism and Allegory

Cultural or universal symbols and allegories often allude to other works from our cultural heritage, such as the Bible, ancient history and literature, and works of the British and American traditions. Sometimes understanding a story may require knowledge of history and current politics.

If the meaning of a symbol is not immediately clear to you, you will need a dictionary or other reference work. The scope of your college dictionary will surprise you. If you cannot find an entry there, however, try one of the major encyclopedias, or ask your reference librarian, who can direct you to shelves loaded with helpful books. A few excellent guides are *The Oxford Companion to Classical Literature* (ed. M. C. Howatson and Ian Chilvers), *The Oxford Companion to English Literature* (ed. Margaret Drabble), *Merriam Webster's Encyclopedia of Literature*, Timothy Gantz's *Early Greek Myth: A Guide to Literary and Artistic Sources*, and Richmond Y. Hathorn's *Greek Mythology*.

Useful aids in finding biblical references are *Cruden's Complete Concordance*, which in various editions has been a reliable guide since 1737, and *The Strongest Strong's Exhaustive Concordance of the Bible* (2001), which has been revised and expanded regularly since it was first published in 1890. These concordances list all the major words used in the Bible (King James version), so you can easily locate the chapter and verse of any and all biblical passages. If you still have trouble after using sources like these, see your instructor.

Writing About Symbolism and Allegory

As you read, take notes and make all the observations you can about the presence of symbols or allusions or both. Explanatory notes will help you establish basic information, but you also need to explain meanings and create interpretations in your own words. Use a dictionary for understanding words or phrases that require further study. For allusions, you might check out original sources to determine original contexts. Try to determine the ways in which your poem is similar to, or different from, the original work or source, and then determine the purpose served by the allusion.

Raise Questions to Discover Ideas

Cultural or Universal Symbols

- What symbols that you consider cultural or universal can you discover in names, objects, places, situations, or actions in the work (e.g., the character Faith and the walking stick in "Young Goodman Brown," the funeral bells in "Anthem for Doomed Youth," the snow in "Desert Places," Bethlehem in "The Second Coming")?
- How are these symbols used? What do they mean, both specifically, in the poem, and universally, in a broader context? What would the poem be like without the symbolic meaning?

Contextual Symbols

- What contextual symbols can you locate in the work (e.g., boxes, children singing in the choir, yellow leaves in autumn)? How is the symbolism used specifically in the poem? What would the poem be like if the symbols were not taken to be symbolic?
- What causes you to conclude that the symbols are truly symbolic? What is being symbolized? What do the symbols mean? How definite or direct is the symbolism?

- Is the symbolism used systematically throughout the work, or is it used only once? How does the symbolism affect the work's ideas or emotions?

Other Forms

- What enables you to identify the story as a parable or fable? What lesson or moral is either clearly stated or implicit?
- What mythological identification is established in the work? What do you find in the story (names, situations, etc.) that enables you to determine its mythological significance? How is the myth to be interpreted? What symbolic value does the myth have? What current and timeless application does it have?

Organize Your Essay on Symbolism or Allegory

Introduction   Relate the central idea of your essay to the meaning of the major symbols or allegorical thrust of the story. An idea about "Young Goodman Brown," for example, is that fanaticism darkens and limits the human soul. An early incident in the story provides symbolic support for this idea. When Goodman Brown enters the woods, he resolves "to stand firm against the devil," and he then looks up toward "Heaven above him." As he looks, a "black mass of cloud" appears to hide the "brightening stars" (paragraph 47). Within the limits of our central idea, the cloud can be seen as a symbol, just like the widening path or the night walk itself. Look for ways to make solid connections like this when you designate something as a symbol or allegory.

Also, your essay will need to include justifications for your symbols or allegorical parallels. In Poe's "The Masque of the Red Death," for example, Prince Prospero's seemingly impregnable "castellated abbey" is a line of defense against the plague. But the Red Death in a human shape easily invades the castle and conquers Prospero and his ill-fated guests. If you treat the abbey as a symbol, it is important to apply it to measures that people take (medicine, escapist activity, etc.) to keep death distant and remote. In the same way, in describing the allegorical elements in "Young Goodman Brown," you need to establish a comprehensive statement such as the following: People lose ideals and forsake principles not because they are evil but because they misunderstand the people around them (see the second illustrative essay that follows).

Body   For the body of your essay there are a number of strategies for discussing symbolism and allegory. You might use just one or a combination.

Symbolism

1. **The meaning of symbols**. This approach is the most natural one to take for an essay on symbolism. If you have discovered a symbol or symbols, explain the meaning as best you can. What is the work's major idea? How do you know that your interpretation is valid? How do the work's symbols contribute to your interpretation? How pervasive, how applicable, are these devices? If you have discovered many symbols, which ones predominate?

What do they mean? Why are some more important than others? What connects them with each other and with the work's main ideas? How are you able to make conclusions about all this?

2. **The effect of symbols on the work's form**. Here the goal is to determine how symbolism is related to the work's structure. Where does the symbol occur? If it is early, how do the following parts relate to the ideas borne by the symbol? What logical or chronological function does the symbol serve in the work's development? Is the symbol repeated, and if so, to what effect? If the symbol is introduced later, has it been anticipated earlier? How do you know? Can the symbol be considered climactic? What might the structure of the work have been like if the symbolism had not been used?

3. **The relationship between the literal and the symbolic**. The object here is to describe the literal nature of the symbols, and then to determine their appropriateness to the work's context. If the symbol is part of a narrative, what is its literal function? If the symbol is a person, object, or setting, what physical aspects are described? Are colors included? Shapes? Sizes? Sounds? In light of this description, how applicable is the symbol to the ideas it embodies? How appropriate is the literal condition to the symbolic condition? The answers to questions like these should lead not so much to a detailed account of the meaning of the symbols but rather to an account of their appropriateness to the topics and ideas of the poem.

4. **The implications and resonances of symbols**. This type of essay is more personal than the others, for it is devoted to the suggestions and associations—the "implications and resonances"—that the work's symbols and allusions bring out. The object of the essay is to describe your own responses or chain of thinking that the work sets in motion. You are therefore free to move in your own direction as long as you base your discussion on the symbols you discover. If the writer is speaking in general terms about the end of an era, for example, as with the symbol of the rough beast in Yeats's "The Second Coming," then you could apply these symbols to your own thinking. It is not easy to summon the knowledge and authority to contradict the work of any poet, but if you can point out shortcomings in the thought of the symbols or allusions, you should do so.

Allegory

1. **The application and meaning of the allegory**. What is the subject of the story (allegory, fable, parable, myth)? How can it be more generally applied to ideas or to qualities of human character, not only of its own time but also of our own? What other versions of the story do you know, if any? Does it illustrate, either closely or loosely, particular philosophies or religious views? If so, what are these? How do you know?

2. **The consistency of the allegory**. Is the allegory used consistently throughout the story, or is it used intermittently? Explain and illustrate this use. Would it be correct to call your story *allegorical* rather than an *allegory*? Can you determine how parts of the story are introduced for their allegorical importance? Examples are the increasingly dark pathway to Farquhar's home in Bierce's "An Occurrence at Owl Creek Bridge" and the frozen preserves in Glaspell's *Trifles*, which we may take as allegorical equivalents of life's

destructive difficulties, and the Parisian street in Maupassant's "The Neck-lace" (in Chapter 1), which corresponds to the temptation to live beyond one's means.

Conclusion   You might summarize main points, describe general impressions, explain the impact of the symbolic or allegorical methods, indicate personal responses, or suggest further lines of thought and application. You might also assess the quality and appropriateness of the symbolism or allegory (such as Hawthorne's "Young Goodman Brown" opening in darkness and closing in gloom). If your poem is rich in symbols or allusions, you might also consider some of the elements that you have not discussed in the body and try to tie these together with those you have already discussed. It would also be appropriate to introduce any new ideas you developed as a result of your study.

Illustrative Essay

Symbolism in William Butler Yeats's "The Second Coming"°

[1]   Yeats's "The Second Coming" is a prophetic poem that lays out reasons for being scared about the future. The poem's symbolism combines traditional materials from ancient history and literature together with Yeats's own scheme for visualizing the rise and fall of civilizations. <u>This scheme is designed to explain both the disruption of our present but old culture, and also the installation of a frightening new one.</u>* To make his prophecies clear, Yeats uses his symbolism as a reflection of the horrors of the twentieth century.†

[2]   <u>Yeats's first major symbol, the gyre, or rather two interconnecting gyres, pervades the poem, for it outlines the cyclical nature of political changes.</u> Flying outward at the widest point of the gyre—symbolizing our present era—a falcon is used by Yeats to introduce the idea that "the center cannot hold." The "desert birds," hovering around the "lion body and the head of a man" (the sphinx-like figure) show a tighter circle in a second gyre, symbolizing a new stage of human existence. Thus the widening symbolic gyre in line 1 is interpenetrating with the narrowing gyre pointing at the "rough beast." This intersecting and blending show that new things both emerge and separate from old things. The spatial and geometrical symbolism thus illustrates that the past is breaking up while the future is about to take the shape of the past—but at its worst, not at its best.

[3]   <u>Embodying this horror-to-be, the second major symbol is the sphinx-like creature moving its "slow thighs" in the sands of the desert.</u> The attributes of the monstrous creature are blankness and pitilessness. Yeats describes it as a "rough beast," with the "indignant desert birds" flying in circles above it like

---

°For the text of this poem, see pages 383–384.
*Central idea.
†Thesis sentence.

vultures. This description symbolizes the brutal nature of the new age. Yeats wrote the poem in 1919, right after the conclusion of World War I, which had seen both the viciousness and mindlessness of trench warfare. The disruption of life caused by this war was a disturbing indicator of the repressiveness and brutality to come.

[4]   It is this brutality that makes ironic another of the poem's major symbols—the long-awaited "second coming" of Jesus. Yeats alludes to the second coming in the poem's title and also in lines 9 and 10:

> Surely some revelation is at hand;
> Surely the Second Coming is at hand.

The reference is to New Testament prophecies about the return of Christ at the end of historical time, when the Kingdom of God will come on earth. In the Bible, war and rumors of war are claimed as being the signs indicating that the return, or "Second Coming," is near. Thus far, both the biblical signs and the observations of Yeats coincide. The twist, however, is that Yeats is suggesting through the symbol that after the breakup of the present age, the new age will be marked not by God's Kingdom but by the "rough beast." Because Yeats describes the beast as a sphinx, his model is the kind of despotism known in ancient Egypt, when power was held absolutely by the pharaoh, and when freedom and civil rights were unknown to the mass of people.

[5]   A unique aspect of Yeats's symbolism is that he fuses his own symbolism with symbolism of paganism and Christianity. The "ceremony of innocence," for example (line 6), refers to the ritual of communion and also to its symbolic value of regeneration. By indicating that it is being drowned, he doubles the impact of his assertion that tradition is being lost and brutalized. The Spiritus Mundi is an abstract allusion to a common human bond of images and characteristics, but because of the image of brutality it produces, as a symbol it demonstrates that horror is a normal condition of human life. In addition, the "blood-dimmed tide" is an allusion to Shakespeare's Macbeth, who symbolically has stained the ocean red with King Duncan's blood. The "blood-dimmed tide" therefore both allusively and symbolically indicates the global scope of the evil age being born.

[6]   "The Second Coming" is rich in symbols that are both traditional and personal, and there are additional symbols. The most easily visualized of these is the falcon out of control, flying higher and higher and farther away from the falconer, to symbolize the anarchy that Yeats mentions in line 4 as being "loosed" in the world. An example of a symbol being used ironically is the reference to Bethlehem where, according to the Gospels of Matthew and Luke, Jesus, the "Prince of Peace," was born. In "The Second Coming," Yeats asserts that the new birth will not lead to peace, but instead will bring about a future age of repression and brutality. Yeats's poem thus offers a complex and disturbing fabric of symbolism.

Work Cited

Yeats, William Butler. "The Second Coming." Edgar V. Roberts. *Writing About Literature.* 11th ed. Upper Saddle River: Prentice Hall, 2006. 383–384.

Commentary on the Essay

The introduction of this essay briefly characterizes Yeats's poem and asserts that the arguments are made through the use of symbols. The central idea is about the replacement of the old by the new, and the thesis sentence states that Yeats combines major symbols to achieve an effect of horror. Paragraph 2 describes the shape of the symbol, thus illustrating strategy 2 as described on page 156, and also explains it, illustrating strategy 1 (page 155). Paragraph 3 considers the "rough beast" as a symbol of emerging brutality. Paragraph 4 treats the title's use of New Testament prophetic symbolism, showing that Yeats makes his point by reversing the outcome that tradition had predicted. Paragraph 5 demonstrates the complexity of Yeats's poem by stressing how he fuses symbolism and allusion. The sixth and last paragraph contains a brief summary and then proceeds to illustrate the richness of "The Second Coming" with brief references to additional symbols.

Illustrative Essay

The Allegory of Hawthorne's "Young Goodman Brown"°

[1]   Nathaniel Hawthorne's "Young Goodman Brown" is a nightmarish narrative. It allegorizes the process by which something good—religion—becomes a justification for intolerance and prejudice. The major character, Young Goodman Brown of Salem during colonial times, begins as a pious and holy person, but he takes a walk into a nearby darkening forest of suspicion and sanctimoniousness. The process is portrayed by Hawthorne as being originated by the devil himself, who leads Goodman Brown into the night, which becomes increasingly evil and sinful. By the end of the allegory Brown is transformed into an unforgiving, antisocial, dour, and dreary misanthrope.

[2]   Hawthorne's location for the story reminds us that it was in Salem, in the late seventeenth century, that religious zealousness became so extreme that a number of witch trials and public hangings took place solely on the basis of suspicion and false accusation. This setting indicates that Hawthorne's immediate allegorical target is the overzealous pursuit of religious principles. And so Goodman Brown's trip not only takes him into the gloom of night, but also marks a descent into the darkest dungeon of his soul.*

[3]   While the story directly details elements in the growth of religious zealotry, Hawthorne's allegory may also be applied more generally to the ways in which people uncritically follow any ideal that leads them to distrust and suspect others. The allegory is thus relevant to those who swallow political slogans, who believe in their own racial or ethnic superiority, or who justify super patriotism and super nationalism. As such persons persuade themselves of

---

°See pages 340–348 for this story.
*Central idea.

their own supremacy they ignore the greater need for love, understanding, toleration, cooperation, and forgiveness. Hawthorne's allegory is a realistic portrait of how people get into such a mental state, with Goodman Brown as the example of the attitude. <u>Such people push ahead even against their own good nature and background, and they develop their prejudices through delusion and suspicion.</u>[†]

[4]   <u>Young Goodman Brown's pathway into the night is not a direct plunge into evil, but Hawthorne shows that Brown is not without good nature because he has misgivings about what he is doing.</u> Many times early in the story we learn that he has doubts about the "evil purpose" of his allegorical walk. At the very beginning Faith calls him back and pleads with him to stay the night with her (paragraph 2), but even so, he leaves her. As he walks away he thinks of himself as "a wretch" for doing so (paragraph 7). He excuses himself with a promise that once the evening is over he will stick with Faith forever after, an "excellent resolve for the future," as the narrator ironically states (paragraph 8). When Goodman Brown is reproached by the devil for being late—we conclude that Brown's purpose was to keep this diabolical appointment—he gives the excuse "Faith kept me back a while" (paragraph 12), a sentence of ironic double meaning. Once he has kept his appointment with the devil, he states his intention to go no farther because he has "scruples," which remind him that "it is my purpose now to return whence I came" (paragraph 15). Even when Goodman Brown is standing before the altar of profanation deep within the forest, he appeals to Faith, "Look up to Heaven, and resist the Wicked One!" (paragraph 68). All this hesitation represents a true conscience in Goodman Brown even though he ignores it as he progresses deeper into the forest of sin. His failure is his inability or unwillingness to make his own insight and conscience his guides of conduct.

[5]   <u>It is important to remember that Goodman Brown is favored by his background, which might reasonably be expected to have kept him on a true path of goodness.</u> Almost as a claim of entitlement he cries out, "With Heaven above, and Faith below, I will yet stand firm against the devil" (paragraph 46). He also cries out for Faith even when he hears a voice resembling hers that is "uttering lamentations" within the darkening woods (paragraph 47). When he sees Faith's pink ribbon mysteriously flutter down, he exclaims, "My Faith is gone!" (paragraph 50). These instances show allegorically that Goodman Brown's previous way of life has given him the right paths to follow and the right persons in whom to believe. Even as he is tempted when he is standing before the "unhallowed altar" (paragraph 64), he asks the question "But, where is Faith?" as though he could reclaim the innocence that he has previously known (paragraph 57). Just as he ignores his conscience, he also ignores the power of his background, and it is this neglect that fuels his change into the "demoniac" who abandons himself to "the instinct that guides mortal man to evil" (paragraph 50).

[6]   <u>Another major element in Goodman Brown's allegorical path into darkness is that he develops the assumption that virtually all the people he knows have yielded their lives to sin and are therefore unworthy.</u> In the grips of this

---

[†]Thesis sentence.

distorted view of others, he believes not what he sees but what he thinks he is seeing. Thus he witnesses the encounter between the devil and Goody Cloyse shortly after he enters the forest, but what he sees is not the good woman who taught him his catechism but rather a witch who is bent on evil and who is friendly with the devil. He ignores the fact that he too is friendly with the devil (the image of his own father) and therefore, while ignoring the log in his own eye, he condemns Goody Cloyse for the speck in hers. After his transformation, when he walks back into his village from his allegorical walk into evil, he "snatche[s] away" a child from Goody as though she were preaching the words of the devil and not God (paragraph 70). He cannot believe that others possess goodness as long he is convinced by the devil's words that "the whole earth [is] one stain of guilt, one mighty blood-spot" (paragraph 63). For this reason he condemns both his minister and Deacon Gookin, whose conspiratorial voices he thinks he overhears on the pathway through the forest. In short, the process of Hawthorne's allegory about the growth of harmful pietism demonstrates that travelers on the pathway to prejudice accept suspicion and mistrust without trying to get at the whole truth and without recognizing that judgment is not in human but rather is in divine hands.

[7]   As Hawthorne allegorizes the development of religious discrimination he makes clear that, like any kind of discrimination, mistrust and suspicion form its basis. Certainly, as the devil claims, human beings commit many criminal and depraved sins (paragraph 63), but this does not mean that all human beings are equally at fault, and that they are beyond love and redemption. The key for Goodman Brown is that he exceeds his judgmental role and bases his condemnation of others solely on his own hasty and mistrustful conclusions. As long as he has faith he will not falter, but when he leaves his faith, or believes that he has lost his faith, he is adrift and will see only evil wherever he looks. For this reason he permits suspicion and loathing to distort his previous love for his wife and neighbors, and he becomes harsh and desperate forever after. Hawthorne devotes the concluding paragraph of the story to a brief summary of Brown's life after the fateful night. This conclusion completes the allegorical cycle beginning with Brown's initiation into evil and extending to his "dying hour" of "gloom" and his unhopeful tombstone (paragraph 72).

[8]   Hawthorne's "Young Goodman Brown" allegorizes the paradox of how noble beliefs become ignoble. Goodman Brown dies in gloom because he believes that his wrong vision is true. His form of evil is the hardest to stop because wrongdoers who are convinced of their own goodness are beyond reach. In view of such self-righteous evil, whether cloaked in the apparent virtues of Puritanism or of some other blindly rigorous doctrine, Hawthorne writes, "the fiend in his own shape is less hideous than when he rages in the breast of man" (paragraph 53). Young Goodman Brown is one of the many who are convinced that they alone walk in light, but who really create darkness.

Work Cited

Hawthorne, Nathaniel. "Young Goodman Brown." Edgar V. Roberts. *Writing About Literature.* 11th ed. Upper Saddle River: Prentice Hall, 2006. 340–348.

Commentary on the Essay

This essay deals with a major idea in "Young Goodman Brown," and it therefore illustrates the first approach described earlier (page 156). Unity in the essay is achieved by a number of means. For example, paragraph 2 extends a topic in paragraph 1. Also, a phrase in sentence 2 of paragraph 1 is echoed in sentence 1 of paragraph 8. Making additional connections within the essay are individual words such as "another," "while," "therefore," and the repetition of words throughout the essay that are contained in the thesis sentence.

The first three paragraphs of the essay constitute an extended introduction to the topics of paragraphs 4 through 8, for they establish "Young Goodman Brown" as an allegory. Paragraph 1 briefly treats the allegorical nature of the narrative. Paragraph 2 relates the historical basis of the topic to Hawthorne's purpose in writing the story, and it concludes with the essay's central idea. Paragraph 3 broadens the scope of Hawthorne's allegory by showing that it includes zealousness wherever it might appear. Paragraph 3 also concludes with the essay's thesis sentence.

Paragraph 4, the first in the body, deals with an important aspect of the allegory, and one that makes it particularly relevant and timely even today— namely, that people of basically good nature may grow to practice evil ways under the pretense of goodness. Similarly, paragraph 5 points out that such people usually come from good backgrounds and have benefited from good influences during their lives.

Paragraphs 6 and 7 locate the origins of evil in two major human qualities— first, the belief in one's own delusions; and second, the mental confusion that results from the conviction that appearance is more real and believable than reality itself. Paragraph 8 concludes the essay on the note that the finished "product"—a person who has become suspicious and misguided— demonstrates how good ideas, when pushed to the extreme by false imagination, can backfire.

Special Topics for Studying
and Discussing Symbolism and Allegory

1. Compare and contrast the symbolism in Blake's "The Tyger," Arnold's "Dover Beach," Hughes's "Negro," and Poe's "The Masque of the Red Death." To what degree do the works rely on contextual symbols? On universal symbols? On the basis of your comparison, what is the case for asserting that realism and fantasy are directly related to the nature of the symbolism employed by the writer?

2. Why do writers who advocate moral, philosophical, or religious issues frequently use symbolism or allegory? In treating this question, you might introduce references from Hawthorne's "Young Goodman Brown," Hardy's "Channel Firing," and Arnold's "Dover Beach."

3. Write an essay on the allegorical method of one or more of the parables included in the Gospel of St. Luke, such as "The Bridegroom" (5:34–35), "The Garments and the Wineskins" (5:36–39), "The Sower" (8:4–15), "The Good Samaritan" (10:25–37), "The Prodigal Son" (15:11–32), "The Ox in the Well" (14:5–6), "The Watering of Animals on the Sabbath" (13:15–17), "The Rich Fool" (12:16–21), "Lazarus" (16:19–31), "The Widow and the Judge" (18:1–8), and "The Pharisee and the Publican" (18:9–14).

4. What is the nature of the symbols pertaining to the role of single and married women in Mansfield's "Miss Brill," Chekhov's *The Bear*, Glaspell's *Trifles*, Chopin's "The Story of an Hour," and Browning's "My Last Duchess"?

5. Consider the meaning of the symbols of war in Arnold's "Dover Beach," Hardy's "The Man He Killed," Layton's "Rhine Boat Trip," Lowell's "Patterns," and Owen's "Anthem for Doomed Youth."

6. Compare the use of religious symbols in Randall's "The Ballad of Birmingham," Yeats's "The Second Coming," and Hawthorne's "Young Goodman Brown." What are the locations from which the poets draw their symbols? How do the symbols figure into the ideas and actions of the works?

7. Write a poem in which you develop a major symbol, as Maupassant does in "The Necklace" (with the necklace) and Layton does in "Rhine Boat Trip" (with the cattle cars). To get yourself started, you might think about the meaning of symbols like these:
   - A littered street or sidewalk
   - Coffee-hour after church
   - An athletic competition
   - A computer
   - The checkout counter at the neighborhood supermarket
   - The family dog looking out a window as the children leave for school

8. Write your own brief story using a widely recognized cultural symbol such as the flag (patriotism, love of country, a certain type of politics), water (life, sexuality, regeneration), or the population explosion (the end of life on earth). By arranging actions and dialogue, make clear the issues conveyed by your symbol, and also try to resolve conflicts the symbol might raise among your characters.

9. Using the card or computer catalogue of your library, discover a recent critical-biographical book or books about Hawthorne. Explain what the book says about Hawthorne's uses of symbolism. To what extent does the book relate Hawthorne's symbolism to his religious and family heritage?

11

Writing About Tone
The Writer's Control over Attitudes and Feelings

Tone refers to the methods by which writers and speakers reveal attitudes or feelings. It is an aspect of all spoken and written statements, whether earnest declarations of love, requests to pass a dinner dish, letters from students asking parents for money, or official government notices threatening penalties if taxes and fines are not paid. Because tone is often equated with *attitude*, it is important to realize that tone refers not so much to attitudes themselves but rather to *those techniques and modes of presentation that reveal or create attitudes*.

As a literary concept, *tone* is adapted from the phrase *tone of voice* in speech. Tone of voice reflects attitudes toward a particular object or situation, and also toward listeners. Let us suppose that Mary has a difficult assignment, on which she expects to work all day. Things go well, and she finishes quickly. She happily tells her friend Anne, "I'm so pleased. I needed only two hours for that." Then she decides to buy tickets for a popular play and must wait through a long and slow line. After getting her tickets, she tells the people at the end of the line, "I'm so pleased. I needed only two hours for that." The sentences are exactly the same, but by changing her emphasis and vocal inflection, Mary indicates her disgust and impatience with her long wait and also shows her sympathy with the people still in line. By controlling the *tone* of her statements, in other words, Mary conveys attitudes of satisfaction at one time, and indignation and also sympathy at another.

As this example indicates, an attitude itself may be summarized with a word or phrase (satisfaction or indignation, love or contempt, deference or command, etc.) but the study of tone examines those aspects of situation, language, action, and background that *bring out* the attitude. In the last two lines of Owen's "Anthem for Doomed Youth," for example (page 378), the speaker refers to the reactions of those at home for the young men who die in battle:

> Their flowers [shall be] the tenderness of patient minds,
> And each slow dusk a drawing-down of blinds.

These words suggest that the anguish of immediate sorrow is past, and those left at home must endure unending, lifelong, quiet sorrow, indicated by the "drawing down of blinds," which by shutting out light also symbolizes the termination of love and intimacy.

Tone and Attitudes

In most literary works, attitudes point in a number of directions, so that tone becomes a highly complex matter. The following things to look for, however, should help you in understanding and describing literary tone.

Determine the Writer's Attitude Toward the Material

By reading a work carefully, we may deduce the author's attitude or attitudes toward the subject matter. In "The Story of an Hour," for example, Chopin sympathetically portrays a young wife's secret wishes for freedom, just as she also humorously reveals the unwitting smugness that often pervades men's relationships with women. In "Echo," Rossetti's speaker addresses a lover who is long dead, and by this means Rossetti renders attitudes of yearning and sorrow. In a broader perspective, authors may view human beings with amused affection, as in Chekhov's *The Bear*, or with amused resignation, as in Hardy's "Channel Firing." All these works exhibit various degrees of irony, which is one of the most significant aspects of authorial tone.

Discover the Writer's Attitude Toward Readers

Authors recognize that readers participate in the creative act and that all elements of a story—word choice, characterization, allusions, levels of reality—must take readers' responses into account (note the discussion of "Reader-Response" criticism in Appendix A). When Hawthorne's woodland guide in "Young Goodman Brown" refers to "King Philip's War," for example, Hawthorne assumes that his readers know that this war was inhumane, greedy, and cruel. By allowing this assumption to stand, he indicates respect for the knowledge of his readers, and he also assumes their essential agreement with him. Chekhov in *The Bear* assumes that readers understand that Smirnov's speeches reveal him as irascible and petulant, but they also show him as both generous and funny. Authors always make such considerations about readers by implicitly complimenting them on their knowledge and also by satisfying their curiosity and desire to be interested, stimulated, and pleased.

Determine Other Dominant Attitudes

Beyond general authorial tone, there are many internal and dramatically rendered expressions of attitude. For example, the speaker of Lowell's "Patterns" is a decent and proper upper-class young woman. Yet at the news of her fiancé's death, her sorrowful meditation brings out that she had made a promise to him to make love outside, on a "shady seat" in the garden (lines 86–89). This personal confession symbolically reveals the inner warmth that her external appearance does not suggest, and it also makes the poem pathetically poignant.

In addition, as characters interact, their tone dramatically shows their judgments about other characters and situations. A complicated control of tone occurs at the end of Glaspell's *Trifles*, when the two major characters, Mrs. Hale and Mrs. Peters, cover up incriminating evidence about Minnie Wright. When the two women are examining the things in the kitchen, however, before they actually do the covering up, Mrs. Peters speaks not about illegality, but rather about the possible embarrassment of the action:

> MRS. PETERS. [*Takes the bottle, looks about for something to wrap it in; takes petticoat from the clothes brought from the other room, very nervously begins winding this around the bottle. In a false voice.*] My, it's a good thing the men couldn't hear us. Wouldn't they just laugh! Getting all stirred up over a little thing like a—dead canary. As if that could have anything to do with—with— wouldn't they *laugh*! (speech 137)

Notice that her words reveal her knowledge that men scoff at feminine concerns, like Minnie's quilting knots, and therefore she openly anticipates the men's amusement. The reader, however, knows that Mrs. Peters is joining Mrs. Hale in hiding the incriminating evidence about Minnie.

Tone and Humor

A major aspect of tone is humor. Everyone likes to laugh, and shared laughter is part of good relationships; but not everyone can explain why things are funny. Laughter resists close analysis; it is often unplanned, personal, idiosyncratic, and unpredictable. Nonetheless, there are a number of common elements:

1. **There must be an object to laugh at.** There must be something at which to laugh—a person, a thing, a situation, a custom, a habit of speech or dialect, or an arrangement of words.
2. **Laughter usually stems out of disproportion or incongruity**. People normally know what to expect under given conditions, and anything contrary to these expectations is *incongruous* and may therefore generate laughter. When the temperature is 100°F, you expect people to dress lightly, so if you were to see a man wearing a heavy overcoat, a warm hat, and large gloves, and waving his arms and stamping his feet as though to keep warm, he would violate your expectations. Because his garments and behavior are *inappropriate* or *incongruous*, you would think he was funny. A student in a basic English class once wrote about a "*congregation* of verbs" and also about parts of speech as "nouns, verbs, and *proverbs*." The student meant the *conjugation* of verbs, of course, and also (maybe) either *adverbs* or *pronouns*, but somehow his understanding slipped, and he created a comic incongruity. Such inadvertent verbal errors are called **malapropisms**, after Mrs. Malaprop, a character in Sheridan's eighteenth-century play *The Rivals*

(1775). In the literary creation of malapropisms, the tone is directed against the speaker, for the amusement of both readers and author alike.

3. **Safety and/or good will prevents harm and insures laughter**. Seeing a person slip on a banana peel and hurtle through the air may cause laughter, but only if we ourselves are not that person, for laughter depends on insulation from danger and pain. In comic situations that involve physical abuse—falling down stairs or being hit in the face by cream pies—the abuse never harms the participants. The incongruity of such situations causes laughter, and the immunity from pain and injury prevents responses of horror. Good will enters into humor in romantic comedy or in any other work where we are drawn into general sympathy with the major figures, such as Smirnov and Mrs. Popov in Chekhov's *The Bear*. As the author leads the characters toward their unexpected outburst of love, our involvement produces happiness, smiles, and sympathetic laughter.

4. **Unfamiliarity, newness, and uniqueness are needed to produce the spontaneity of laughter**. Laughter depends on seeing something new or unique, or on experiencing something familiar in a new light. Because laughter is prompted by flashes of insight or sudden revelations, it is always spontaneous, even when readers already know and understand the object of their laughter. Indeed, the task of the comic writer is to develop ordinary materials to that point when spontaneity frees readers to laugh. Thus you can read and reread Chekhov's *The Bear* and laugh each time because, even though you know what will happen, the play shapes your acceptance of how reconciliation penetrates a wall of anger and guilt. The concluding embraces by Smirnov and Mrs. Popov are and always will be comic because they are so spontaneous and incongruous.

Tone and Irony

The capacity to have more than one attitude toward someone or something is a uniquely human trait. We know that people are not perfect, but we love a number of them anyway. So we speak to them not only with love and praise, but also with banter and criticism. You may have given mildly insulting greeting cards to your loved ones, not to affront them but to amuse them. You share smiles and laughs, and at the same time you remind them of your affection.

The word **irony** describes such contradictory statements or situations. Irony is natural to human beings who are aware of life's ambiguities and complexities. It develops from the realization that life does not always measure up to promise, that friends and loved ones are sometimes angry at each other, that the universe contains incomprehensible mysteries, that the social and political structure is often oppressive rather than liberating, that even those with great love and the best of intentions are frequently imposed upon, that doubt exists even in the certainty of knowledge and faith, and that human character is built through chagrin, regret, and pain as much as through emulation and praise. In expressing an idea ironically, writers pay the greatest compliment to their audience, for they assume that readers have sufficient intelligence and skill to discover the real meaning of quizzical or ambiguous statements and situations.

Understand the Four Major Kinds of Irony:
Verbal, Situational, Cosmic, and Dramatic

Verbal Irony Depends on the Interplay of Words   In **verbal irony**, one thing is said, but the opposite is meant. In the example opening this chapter, Mary's ironic expression of pleasure after her two-hour wait for tickets really means that she is disgusted. There are important types of verbal irony. In **understatement** the expression does not fully describe the importance of a situation, and therefore makes its point by implication. In Bierce's "An Occurrence at Owl Creek Bridge," the condemned man contemplates the apparatus designed by the soldiers to hang him. After considering the method, the man's response is described by the narrator: "The arrangement commended itself to his judgment as simple and effective" (paragraph 4). These words would be appropriate for the appraisal of ordinary machinery, perhaps, but because the apparatus will cause the man's death, the understated observation is ironic.

By contrast, in **hyperbole**, or **overstatement**, the words are obviously and inappropriately excessive, and readers or listeners therefore understand that the true meaning is considerably less than what is said. An example is Smirnov's exaggerated dialogue with Mrs. Popov in *The Bear* (speech 69). Though Smirnov tells about the number of times he has jilted women and women have jilted him, readers understand that he is exaggerating his past romantic life to impress Mrs. Popov. The gulf between the exaggeration of what he says and the (probably) more modest reality creates smiles and chuckles.

Often verbal irony is ambiguous, having double meaning or **double entendre**. Midway through "Young Goodman Brown," for example, the woodland guide leaves Brown alone while stating, "when you feel like moving again, there is my staff to help you along" (paragraph 40). The word "staff" is ambiguous, for it refers to the staff that resembles a serpent (paragraph 13). The word therefore suggests that the devilish guide is leaving Brown not only with a real staff but also with the spirit of evil (unlike the divine "staff" of Psalm 23 that gives comfort). Ambiguity, of course, may be used in relation to any topic. Quite often *double entendre* is used in statements about sexuality, usually for the amusement of listeners or readers.

Situational Irony Fills the Gap Between Hope and Reality   **Situational irony**, or **irony of situation**, refers to the chasm between what we hope for or expect and what actually happens. It is often pessimistic because it emphasizes that human beings usually have little or no control over their lives or anything else. The forces of opposition may be psychological, social, cultural, political, or environmental. The situation is not temporary, one might add, but permanent and universal, as in Hardy's "Channel Firing," in which the topic is the omnipresence of war in the past, present, and future. Although situational irony often involves disaster, it need not always do so. For example, a happier occurrence of situational irony is in Chekhov's *The Bear*, for the two characters shift from anger to love as they fall into the grips of emotions that, as the saying goes, are "bigger than both of them."

Cosmic Irony Stems from the Power of Chance and Fate   A special kind of situational irony that emphasizes the pessimistic and fatalistic side of life is **cosmic irony**, or **irony of fate**. By the standard of cosmic irony, the universe is indifferent to individuals, who are subject to blind chance, accident, uncontrollable emotions, perpetual misfortune, and misery. Even if things temporarily go well, people's lives end badly, and their best efforts do not rescue them or make them happy. A work illustrating cosmic irony is Glaspell's *Trifles*, which develops out of the stultifying conditions of farm life experienced by Minnie Wright. She has no profession, no other hope, no other life except the lonely, dreary farm—nothing. After thirty years of wretchedness, she buys a canary that warbles for her to make her life pleasant. Within a year, her insensitive and boorish husband wrings the bird's neck, and she in turn gains revenge against him. Her situation is cosmically ironic, for the implication of *Trifles* is that human beings are caught in a web of adverse circumstances from which there is no escape.

Dramatic Irony Results from Misunderstanding and Lack of Knowledge   Like cosmic irony, **dramatic irony** is a kind of situational irony. It happens when a character either has no information about a situation or else misjudges it, but readers (and often some of the other characters) see everything completely and correctly. The classic model of dramatic irony is found in Sophocles' ancient Greek play *Oedipus the King*. In this play, everyone (other characters and readers alike) knows the truth long before Oedipus knows it. Writers of nondramatic works also make use of dramatic irony, as seen in Chopin's "The Story of an Hour," in which the doctors are ignorant of Louise's secret response to the report of her husband's death. We readers do know and understand her feelings, and therefore we conclude rightly that the medical diagnosis by the doctors of her sudden death shows not their skill but rather their masculine vanity.

Writing About Tone

Begin with a careful reading, noting those elements of the work that convey attitudes. Consider whether the work genuinely creates the attitudes it is designed to evoke. In Hughes's "Negro," for example, are the references to real slavery and wage slavery, together with Congolese atrocities, sufficiently real to support the poem's underlying sense of rage and threat? In Poe's "The Masque of the Red Death," do the bizarre rooms of Prince Prospero's castellated abbey clearly determine the Prince's pride and defiance? Depending on the work, your devising and answering such questions will help you understand an author's control over tone. Similar questions apply when you study internal qualities such as style and characterization.

Raise Questions to Discover Ideas

- How strongly do you respond to the work? What attitudes can you identify and characterize? What elements in the story elicit your concern, indignation, fearfulness, anguish, amusement, or sense of affirmation?

- What causes you to sympathize or not to sympathize with characters, situations, or ideas? What makes the circumstances in the work admirable or understandable (or deplorable)?

- In fiction and drama, what does the dialogue suggest about the author's attitudes toward the characters? How does it influence your attitudes? What qualities of diction permit and encourage your responses?

- To what degree, if any, does the work supersede any previous ideas you might have had about the same or similar subject matter? What do you think changed your attitude?

- What role does the narrator or speaker play in your attitudes toward the dramatic or fictional material? Does the speaker seem intelligent or stupid, friendly or unfriendly, sane or insane, idealistic or pragmatic?

- In an amusing or comic story, what elements of plot, character, and diction are particularly comic? How strongly do you respond to humor-producing situations? Why?

- What ironies do you find in the work (verbal, situational, cosmic)? How is the irony connected to philosophies of marriage, family, society, politics, religion, or morality?

- To what extent are characters controlled by fate, social or racial discrimination, limitations of intelligence, economic and political inequality, and limited opportunity?

- Do any words seem unusual or noteworthy, such as words in dialect, polysyllabic words, or foreign words or phrases that the author assumes you know? Are there any especially connotative or emotive words? What authorial assumptions about the readers do these words suggest?

Organize Your Essay on Tone

Introduction   Your introduction should describe the general situation of the work and its dominant moods, such as that the work leads to cynicism, as in "Channel Firing," or to laughter and delight, as in *The Bear*. Problems connected with describing the work's tone should also be introduced here.

Body   Your goal is to show how the author establishes the dominant moods of the work, such as the poignancy of "Patterns" or the hilarity of *The Bear*. Some possibilities are the use or misuse of language, the exposé of a pretentious speaker, the use of exact and specific descriptions, the isolation of a major character, the failure of plans, and the continuance of naiveté in a disillusioned world. You might find a convenient approach in one of these:

1. **Audience, situation, and characters**. Is any person or group directly addressed by the speaker? What attitude is expressed (love, respect, condescension, confidentiality, confidence, etc.)? What is the basic situation in the story? Do you find irony? If so, what kind is it? What does the irony show (optimism or pessimism, for example)? How is the situation controlled to shape your responses? That is, can actions, situations, or characters be seen as expressions of attitude, or as embodiments of certain

favorable or unfavorable ideas or positions? What is the nature of the speaker or persona? Why does the persona speak exactly as he or she does? How is the persona's character manipulated to show apparent authorial attitude and to elicit reader response? Does the story promote respect, admiration, dislike, or other feelings about character or situation? How?

2. **Descriptions and diction**. Descriptions or diction in the work should not be analyzed for themselves alone but should be related to attitude. *For descriptions*: To what degree do descriptions of natural scenery and conditions (snowstorms, cold, rain, ice, intense sunlight) convey an attitude that complements or opposes the circumstances of the characters? Are there any systematic references to colors, sounds, or noises that collectively reflect an attitude? *For diction*: Do connotative meanings of words control response in any way? To what degree does the diction require readers to have a large or technical vocabulary? Do speech patterns or the use of dialect evoke attitudes about speakers or their condition of life? Is the level of diction normal, slang, standard, or substandard? What is the effect of such a level? Are there unusual or particularly noteworthy expressions? If so, what attitudes do these show? Does the author use verbal irony? To what effect?

3. **Humor**. Is the work funny? How funny? How is the humor achieved? Does the humor develop out of incongruous situations or language, or both? Is there an underlying basis of attack in the humor, or are the objects of laughter still respected or even loved even though they cause amusement?

4. **Ideas**. Are ideas advocated, defended mildly, or attacked? How does the author clarify his or her attitude toward these ideas—directly, by statement, or indirectly, through understatement, overstatement, or a character's speeches? How does the story assume a common ground of assent between author and reader (i.e., what common assumptions do you find about history, religion, politics, morality, behavioral standards, etc.)? Is it easy to give assent (temporary or permanent) to these ideas, or is any concession needed by the reader to approach the work? (For example, a major subject of *Trifles* is the negative effects on a farm wife of the isolation and bleakness of life on an early twentieth-century farm. Things have changed since the time of the play, and the life of such women is certainly better, but sympathetic modern readers can readily understand the psychological situation of the play and can find Minnie Wright's situation important because of a common desire to learn as much as possible about human beings.)

5. **Unique characteristics of the work**. Each work has unique properties that contribute to the tone. Hardy's "Channel Firing," for example, develops from the comic idea that guns being fired at sea are so loud they waken the dead. In other works, there might be a recurring word or phrase that seems special, as in Rossetti's "Echo." In this poem the speaker's anguished memory of her dead lover and her yearning are emphasized through the repetitions of the words "Come," "Dream," and "long ago."

Conclusion In your conclusion, first summarize your main points and then go on to redefinitions, explanations, or afterthoughts, together with ideas reinforcing earlier points. You might also mention some other major aspect of the story's tone that you did not develop in the body.

Illustrative Essay

The Confident Tone of "Theme for English B" by Langston Hughes°

[1] "Theme for English B" grows from the situational irony of racial differences as seen by the speaker, an African-American college student. This situation might easily produce bitterness, anger, outrage, or vengefulness. However, the poem contains none of these. It is not angry or indignant; it is not an appeal for revenge or revolution. It is rather a declaration of personal independence and individuality. <u>The tone is one of objectivity, daring, occasional playfulness, and confidence.</u>* <u>These attitudes are made plain in the speaker's situation, the ideas, the poetic form, the diction, and the expressions.</u>†

[2] <u>Hughes's poetic treatment is objective, factual, and personal, not emotional or political.</u> The poem contains a number of clearly expressed factual details: The speaker is black in an otherwise all-white college English class. He has come from North Carolina and is now living alone at the Harlem YMCA, away from family and roots. He is also, at 22, an older student. All this is evidence of disadvantage, yet the speaker does no more than present the facts objectively, without comment.

[3] <u>Hughes's thoughts about equality—the idea underlying the poem—are presented in the same objective, cool manner.</u> The speaker writes to his instructor as an equal, not as an inferior. His idea is that all people are the same, regardless of race or background. In defining himself, therefore, he does not deal in abstractions, but emphasizes that he, like everyone else, has ordinary likes and needs, and that his abilities and activities are like those of everyone else. By causing the speaker to avoid emotionalism and controversy, Hughes makes counter argument difficult if not impossible.

[4] The argument for equality is carried out even in Hughes's actual use of the poetic form. The title here is the key, for it does not promise the most exciting of topics. Normally, in fact, one might expect nothing more than a short prose essay in response to an English assignment, but a poem is unexpected and therefore daring and original, particularly one like this that touches on the topic of equality and identity. <u>The wit, originality, and skill of the speaker's use of the form itself demonstrate the self-confidence and self-sufficiency that underlie the theoretical claim for equality.</u>

[5] <u>Hughes's diction is also in keeping with the poem's confidence and daring.</u> Almost all the words are short and simple—of no more than one or two syllables—showing the speaker's confidence in the truth and power of his ideas. This high proportion of short words reflects a conscious attempt to keep the diction clear and direct. A result is that Hughes avoids any possible ambiguities, as the following words in lines 21–24 show:

> Well, I like to eat, sleep, drink, and be in love.
> I like to work, read, learn, and understand life.

°See page 373 for this poem.
*Central idea.
†Thesis sentence.

I like a pipe for a Christmas present,
or records—Bessie, bop, or Bach.

With the exception of what it means to "understand life," these descriptive words are free of emotional overtones. They reflect the speaker's confident belief that equality should replace inequality and prejudice.

[6] A number of the speaker's phrases and expressions also show this same confidence. Although most of the language is simple and descriptive, it is also playful and ironic. In lines 18–20 there seems to be a deliberate use of confusing language to bring about a verbal merging of the identities of the speaker, the instructor, Harlem, and the greater New York area:

Harlem, I hear you:
hear you, hear me—we two—you, me talk on this page.
(I hear New York, too.) Me—who?

There is also a certain whimsicality in the way in which the speaker treats the irony of the black-white situation in line 27:

So will my page be colored when I write?

Underlying this last expression is an awareness that, despite the claim that people are equal and are tied to each other by common humanity, there are also strong differences among individuals. The speaker is confidently asserting grounds for independence as well as equality.

[7] Thus, an examination of "Theme for English B" reveals vitality and confidence. The poem is a statement of trust and an almost open challenge on the personal level to the unachieved ideal of equality. Hughes makes this point through the deliberate simplicity of the speaker's words and descriptions. Yet the poem is not without irony, particularly at the end, where the speaker mentions that the instructor is "somewhat more free" than he is. "Theme for English B" is complex and engaging. It shows the speaker's confidence through objectivity, daring, and playfulness.

Work Cited

Hughes, Langston. "Theme for English B." Edgar V. Roberts. *Writing About Literature.* 11th ed. Upper Saddle River: Prentice Hall, 2006. 373.

Commentary on the Essay

Because this essay embodies a number of approaches by which tone may be studied in any work (situation, common ground, diction, special characteristics), it is typical of many essays that use a combined, eclectic approach. The central idea is that the dominant attitude in "Theme for English B" is the speaker's confidence, and that this confidence is shown in the similar but separable attitudes of objectivity, daring, and playfulness.

Paragraph 2 deals with the situational irony of the social/political circumstances of racial discrimination (approach 1). Paragraph 3 considers the objectivity with which Hughes considers the idea of equality (approach 4).

Paragraph 4 shows how a topic that might be taken for granted, in this case the basic form or genre of expression, can be a unique feature of tone (approach 5). The paragraph contrasts the *expected* response (no more than a brief prose essay) with the *actual* response (the poem itself, with its interesting twists and turns). Since the primary tone of the poem is that of self-confidence, which is the unspoken basis for the speaker's assertion of independence and equality, the paragraph stresses that the speaker's choice of form embodies this attitude.

Paragraphs 5 and 6 consider how Hughes's word choices exhibit his attempts at clarity, objectivity, playfulness, and confidence (approach 2). The attention given in these paragraphs to Hughes's simple, direct words is justified by the importance of the speaker's diction in the poem's tone.

The concluding paragraph stresses the attitude of confidence in the poem and also notes attitudes of trust, challenge, irony, daring, and playfulness.

Special Topics for Studying and Discussing Tone

1. Consider a story or poem in which the speaker is the central character (e.g., Arnold's "Dover Beach," Frost's "Desert Places," Hardy's "The Man He Killed," Lowell's "Patterns," Rossetti's "Echo"). Write an essay showing how the language of the speaker affects your attitudes toward him or her (i.e., your sympathy for the speaker, your interest in the situation).

2. Write an essay comparing and contrasting attitudes toward two or more of these female characters: Louise in "The Story of an Hour," Mathilde in "The Necklace," Mrs. Popov in *The Bear*, and Minnie Wright in *Trifles*. How does the author's presentation control your understanding of them? What details of tone might be important in a feminist approach to these works?

3. In "First Confession," the narrator, Jackie, is describing events that happened to him as a child. What are your attitudes toward Jackie? What are O'Connor's attitudes toward him? Has Jackie separated himself from his childhood emotions? What does he say that might be considered residual childhood responses? What effect, if any, do such comments create?

4. Write a short story about a student, a supervisor, or a politician. Treat your main character with dramatic irony; that is, your character thinks he or she knows all the details about a situation but really does not (e.g., a male student declares interest in a female student without realizing that she is already engaged; a supervisor expresses distrust of one of the best workers in the firm; a politician accuses an opponent of actions that were done not by the opponent but by a supporter). What action, words, and situations do you think you should choose to make your irony clear, and why?

5. Write either (a) two character sketches, or (b) two descriptions of an action, as though you were planning to include them as part of a story. For either your sketches or your descriptions, make the first favorable, and the second negative. Analyze your word choices in the contrasting accounts: What kinds of words do you select, and on what principles? What words might you select if you wanted a neutral account? On the basis of your answers, what can you conclude about the development of a fiction writer's style?

12

Writing About a Problem
Challenges to Overcome in Reading

A **problem** is any question that you cannot answer easily and correctly about a body of material that you know. The question "Who is the major character in Shakespeare's tragedy *Hamlet*?" is not a problem, because the obvious answer is Hamlet.

Let us, however, ask another question: "Why is it *correct* to say that Hamlet is the major character?" This question is not as easy as the first, and for this reason it is a problem. It requires that we think about our answer, even though we do not need to search very far. Hamlet is the title character. He is involved in most of the actions of the play. He is so much the center of our interest, concern, and liking that his death causes sadness and regret. To "solve" this problem has required a set of responses, all of which provide answers to the question "why?"

More complex, however, and more typical of most problems, are questions such as these: "Why does Hamlet talk of suicide during his first major speech in the play?" "Why does he treat Ophelia so coarsely and insultingly?" "Why does he delay in avenging his father's death?" Essays on a problem are normally concerned with such questions, because they require a good deal of thought, together with a number of interpretations knitted together into a whole essay. More broadly, dealing with problems is one of the major tasks of the intellectual, scientific, social, and political disciplines. Being able to advance and then explain solutions is therefore one of the most important techniques that you can acquire.

Strategies for Developing an Essay About a Problem

Your major purpose is to convince your reader that your solution is a good one. This you do by using evidence correctly in making sound conclusions. In nonscientific subjects like literature you seldom or never find absolute proofs, so your conclusions will not be *proved* in the way you prove triangles congruent in geometry. But your organization, your use of facts from the text, your interpretations, and your application of general or specific knowledge should all make your conclusions convincing. Thus, your basic strategy is *persuasion*. Here are some strategies for developing an essay designed to persuade a reader to accept your solution to a problem.

Strategy 1: Demonstrate That Conditions for a Solution Are Fulfilled

Suppose that you are writing on the problem of why Hamlet delays revenge against his stepfather, King Claudius. Suppose also that you make the point that Hamlet delays because he is never sure that Claudius is guilty. This point is your "solution" to the problem. In your essay, you support your answer by challenging the credibility of the information that Hamlet receives about the crime (i.e., the visits from the Ghost and Claudius's distress at the play within the play). Once you have "attacked" these sources of data on the grounds that they are unreliable, you have been persuasive because your solution is consistent with the details of the play.

Strategy 2: Analyze Significant Words in the Phrasing of the Problem

Your object in this approach is to clarify important words in the statement of the problem, and then to determine if they are applicable or not. This kind of attention to words, in fact, might give you enough material for all or part of your essay. Thus, an essay on the problem of Hamlet's delay might focus in part on a treatment of the word *delay*: What, really, does *delay* mean? For Hamlet, is there a difference between delay that is reasonable and delay that is unreasonable? Does Hamlet delay unreasonably? Is his delay the result of a psychological fault? Would speedy revenge be more or less reasonable than the delay? By the time you have answered such pointed questions, you will also have sufficient material for your full essay.

Strategy 3: Refer to Literary Conventions or Expectations

The theory of this aspect of argument is that literary problems can be solved by reference either to the literary mode or conventions of a work, or to the limitations of the work itself. In other words, what appears to be a problem is really no more than a normal characteristic. For example, a question might be raised about why Mathilde in "The Necklace" (Chapter 1) does not tell her friend Jeanne Forrestier about the loss of the necklace. A plausible answer is that, all motivation aside, the story builds up to a surprise (at least for first-time readers) that could be spoiled by an early disclosure. To solve the problem, in other words, one has recourse to the structure of the story—to the literary convention that Maupassant observes in "The Necklace." Similarly, a student once raised a problem about the impossibility of skeletons speaking in Hardy's "Channel Firing" (page 370). The answer to this problem is that Hardy is playing with the idea that the noise of naval gunnery blasting away at sea is loud enough to waken the dead. Once this given circumstance is accepted, whatever problem there was actually vanishes.

Strategy 4: Argue Against Possible Objections

With this strategy, you raise your own objections and then argue against them. Called **procatalepsis** ("to consider beforehand") or **anticipation**, this approach helps you sharpen your arguments, because *anticipating* and dealing with objections forces you to make analyses and to use facts that you might otherwise overlook. Although procatalepsis can be used point by point throughout your essay, you may find it most useful at the end.

The situation to imagine is that someone is raising objections to your solution to the problem. It is then your task to show that the objections (1) are not accurate or valid; (2) are not strong or convincing; or (3) are based on unusual rather than usual conditions (on an exception and not the rule). Here are some examples of these approaches.

A. The Objection Is Not Accurate or Valid   You reject this objection by showing that either the interpretation or the conclusions are wrong and also by emphasizing that the evidence supports your solution.

> Although Hamlet's delay is reasonable, the claim might be made that his duty is to kill Claudius in revenge immediately after the Ghost's accusations. This claim is not persuasive because it assumes that Hamlet knows everything the audience knows. The audience accepts the Ghost's word that Claudius is guilty, but Hamlet has no certain reasons to believe the Ghost. Would it not seem insane for Hamlet to kill Claudius, who reigns legally, and then to claim he did it because of the Ghost's words? The argument for speedy revenge is not good because it is based on an incorrect view of Hamlet's situation.

B. The Objection Is Not Strong or Convincing   You *concede* that the objection has some truth or validity, but you then try to show that it is weak and that your own solution is stronger.

> One might claim that Claudius's distress at the play within the play is evidence for his guilt and that therefore Hamlet should carry out his revenge right away. This argument has merit, and Hamlet's speech after Claudius has fled the scene ("I'll take the Ghost's word for a thousand pound") shows that the "conscience of the king" has been caught. But the King's guilty behavior is not a strong cause for killing him. Hamlet could justifiably ask for an investigation of his father's death on these grounds, but he could not justify a revenge killing. Claudius could not be convicted in any court on the testimony that he was disturbed at seeing "the Murder of Gonzago." Even after the play within the play, the reasons for delay are stronger than for action.

C. The Objection Depends on Unusual Rather than Usual Conditions   You reject the objection on the grounds that it could be valid only if normal conditions were suspended. The objection depends on an exception, not a rule.

> The case for quick action is simple: Hamlet should kill Claudius right after seeing the Ghost (1.3), or else after seeing the King's reaction to the stage murder of Gonzago (3.2), or else after seeing the Ghost again in the Queen's

room (3.4). Redress under these circumstances, goes the argument, must be both personal and extralegal. This argument wrongly assumes that due process does not exist in the Denmark of Hamlet and Claudius. Nothing in the play indicates that the Danes, even though they carouse a bit, do not value legality and the rules of evidence. Thus Hamlet cannot rush out to kill Claudius, because he knows that the King has not had anything close to due process. The argument for quick action is poor because it rests on an exception being made from civilized law.

Writing About a Problem

Remember that writing an essay on a problem requires you to argue in favor of a position: Either there is a solution, or there is not. To develop your position requires that you show the steps to your conclusion. Your general thematic form is thus (1) to describe the conditions that need to be met for the solution you propose; and then (2) to demonstrate that these conditions exist. If you assert that there is no solution, then your form would be the same for the first part, but your second part—the development—would show that these conditions have *not* been met.

Organize Your Essay About a Problem

Introduction   Begin with a statement of the problem, and refer to the conditions that must be established for a solution. Your central idea is your answer to the question, and your thesis sentence indicates the main heads of your development.

Body   In developing your essay, use one or more of the strategies described in this chapter. These are, again: (1) to demonstrate that conditions for a solution are fulfilled; (2) to analyze the words in the phrasing of the problem; (3) to refer to literary expectations or limitations; and (4) to argue against possible objections. You might combine these. Thus, if we assume that your argument is that Hamlet's delay is reasonable, you might first consider the word *delay* (strategy 2); then you might use strategy 1 to explain the reasons for Hamlet's delay. Finally, to answer objections to your argument, you might show that he acts promptly when he believes he is justified (strategy 4). Whatever your topic, the important thing is to use the method or methods that best help you make a good argument for your solution.

Conclusion   In your conclusion, try to affirm the validity of your solution in view of the supporting evidence. You might do this by reemphasizing your strongest points by presenting a brief summary, or by thinking of your argument as still continuing and thus using the strategy of procatalepsis to raise and answer possible objections to your solution, as is done in the last paragraph of the following illustrative essay.

Illustrative Essay

The Problem of Frost's Use of the Term "Desert Places" in the Poem "Desert Places"°

[1] In the last line of "Desert Places," the meaning suggested by the title undergoes a sudden shift. At the beginning, it clearly refers to the snowy setting described in the first stanza, but in the last line it refers to a negative state of soul. The problem is this: Does the change happen too late to be effective? That is, does the new meaning come out of nowhere, or does it really develop naturally from the poem's details? To answer these questions, one must grant that the change cannot be effective if there is no preparation for it before the last line of the poem. If there is preparation—that is, if Frost does provide hints that the speaker feels an emptiness like that of the bleak, snowy natural world—then the shift is both understandable and effective even though it comes at the very end. <u>It is clear that Frost makes the preparation and therefore that the change is effective.</u>* <u>The preparation may be traced in Frost's references, word choices, and concluding sentences.</u>†

[2] <u>In the first two stanzas, Frost includes the speaker in his reference to living things being overcome.</u> His opening scene is one of snow that covers "weeds and stubble" (line 4) and that almost literally smothers hibernating animals "in their lairs" (line 6). The speaker then focuses on his own mental state, saying that he is "too absent-spirited to count," and that the "loneliness" of the scene "includes" him "unawares" (lines 7 and 8). This movement—from vegetable, to animal, to human—shows that everything alive is changed by the snow. Obviously, the speaker will not die like the grass or hibernate like the animals, but he indicates that the "loneliness" overcomes him. These first eight lines thus connect the natural bleakness with the speaker.

[3] <u>In addition, a number of words in the third stanza are preparatory because they may be applied to human beings.</u> The words "lonely" and "loneliness" (line 9), "more lonely" (line 10), "blanker" and "benighted" (line 11), and "no expression, nothing to express" (line 12) may all refer equally to human or to natural conditions. The word "benighted" is most important, because it suggests not only the darkness of night but also intellectual or moral ignorance. Since these words invite the reader to think of negative mental and emotional states, they provide a context in which the meaning of the conclusion is both logical and natural.

[4] <u>The climax of Frost's preparation for the last two words is in the sentences of the fourth stanza (lines 13–16).</u> All along, the speaker claims to feel an inner void that is similar to the bleakness of the cold, snowy field. This idea emerges as the major focus in the last stanza, where in two sentences the speaker talks about his feelings of emptiness or insensitivity:

°See pages 369–370 for this poem.
*Central idea.
†Thesis sentence.

> They cannot scare me with their empty spaces
> Between stars—on stars where no human race is.
> I have it in me so much nearer home
> To scare myself with my own desert places.

[5]   <u>In the context of the poem, therefore, these last two words are not sudden or illogical.</u> They rather pull together the two parts of the comparison that Frost has been building from the first line. Just as the phrase "desert places" refers to the snowy field, it also suggests human coldness, blankness, unconcern, insensitivity, and cruelty. The phrase does not spring out of nowhere but is the strong climax of the poem.

[6]   Although Frost's conclusion is effective, a critic might still claim that it is weak because Frost does not develop the thought about the negative soul. He simply uses the term "desert places" and then stops. But the poem is a poem, not a long and analytical psychological study. To ask for more than Frost gives would be to expect more than sixteen lines can provide. A better claim against the effectiveness of the concluding shift of meaning is that the phrase "desert places" is both vague and perhaps boastfully humble. If the phrase were taken away from the poem, this criticism might be acceptable. The fact is that the phrase is within the poem, and that it must be judged only within the poem. There, it crystallizes and acts as a symbol for the previous fifteen lines, and does so with freshness and surprise. <u>The shift of meaning is a logical necessity in "Desert Places."</u>

Work Cited

Frost, Robert. "Desert Places." Edgar V. Roberts. *Writing About Literature.* 11th ed. Upper Saddle River: Prentice Hall, 2006. 369–370.

Commentary on the Essay

The development of this essay illustrates strategy 1 described earlier in this chapter (page 176). The attention to the word *effective* in paragraph 1 briefly illustrates the second strategy (page 176). The concluding paragraph shows two approaches to the fourth strategy (page 177), using the arguments that the objections are not good because (4a) they are not accurate or valid (here the inaccuracy is related to strategy 3), and (4c) they are based on the need for an exception, namely that the phrase in question be removed from the context in the poem.

After introducing the problem, paragraph 1 emphasizes that a solution is available only if the poem prepares the reader for the problematic shift of meaning. The central idea is that the poem satisfies this requirement and that the shift is effective. The thesis sentence indicates three subjects for development.

Paragraph 2 asserts that there is preparation even early in the poem. The argument of paragraph 3, like that of paragraph 2, is that the texture of the poem, right from the start, demonstrates the central idea (stated in the introductory paragraph) that the conditions for a solution to the problem are met. The method in this paragraph is to show how particular words and expressions, because they are applicable to both nature and human beings, connect the bleak opening scene with the speaker's professed spiritual numbness. The word "benighted" (line 11) is the most illustrative, because it refers especially to cultural and intellectual bleakness. The paragraph hence demonstrates how the careful selection and analysis of key words can be part of a total argument.

Paragraph 4 asserts that the concluding sentences build toward a climax of Frost's pattern or development.

Paragraphs 5 and 6 form a two-part conclusion to the essay. Paragraph 5 summarizes the arguments and offers an interpretation of the phrase. Paragraph 6 raises and answers two objections. The essay thus shows that a careful reading of the poem eliminates the grounds for claiming that there is any problem about the poem's concluding words.

Special Topics for Studying and Discussing Literary Problems

1. In Arnold's "Dover Beach," the lines "Ah, love, let us be true / To one another!" have been read to refer not so much to the need for love as to the need for fidelity in all relationships. Which choice seems correct? Explain.

2. Coleridge was planning a much longer poem when he began writing "Kubla Khan," but he was interrupted and could write no more. Some critics, however, are satisfied that the poem is complete as it stands. Defend the judgment that the poem may be considered finished.

3. Even though Chekhov's *The Bear* is a farce, some observers have claimed that the passionate embraces of Smirnov and Mrs. Popov at the end happen suddenly and unexpectedly. Does this outcome spoil the play by making it too unrealistic, too arbitrary, too unnatural?

4. To what degree would more details describing the horrors of war make Owen's "Anthem for Doomed Youth" a more or less effective poem?

5. Some readers claim that the speaker's reactions to her fiancé's death in Lowell's "Patterns" are too reserved, not sufficiently angry or passionate. What is your response to this problem about the poem?

6. Because Poe often writes about lurid and sensational subjects, some critics have stated that his works do not embody ideas. Consider whether this observation is true of "The Masque of the Red Death."

7. A view that is sometimes expressed about Shakespeare's sonnets is that the "systems" that Shakespeare introduces, such as comparing moments of silent introspection to judgments in a law court in "Sonnet 30: When to the Sessions of Sweet Silent Thought," are so affected and pretentious that they detract from the ideas. With reference to Sonnet 30 particularly, how valid is this judgment? Do the comparisons add to or detract from the poem's ideas?

13

Writing About Prosody

Sound, Rhythm, and Rhyme in Poetry

Prosody (the pronunciation or accent of a song or poem, a song set to music) describes the study of poetic sounds and rhythms. Common alternative words are **metrics, versification, mechanics of verse**, and the **music of poetry**. Most readers, when reading poetry aloud, interpret the lines and develop an appropriate speed and expressiveness of delivery, a proper *rhythm*. Some think of rhythm and sound as the *music* of poetry because they convey musical rhythms and tempos. Like music, poetry often requires a regular beat, but the tempo and loudness of poetry may vary freely, and a reader may stop at any time to repeat the sounds and to think about the words and ideas. The music of poetry makes the speaking and hearing of poetry dramatic, exciting, and inspiring.

In considering prosody, we should recognize that poets, being especially attuned to language, blend words and ideas so that "the sound" becomes "an echo to the sense" (Pope, *An Essay on Criticism*, line 365). The consequence of this idea is that *prosodic technique cannot be separated from a poem's content*. For this reason, the study of prosody determines how poets control their words so that the sound of a poem complements its expression of emotions and ideas.

Important Definitions for Studying Prosody

To understand and discuss prosody, you need to be able to explain the various sounds of both speech and poetry. Let us grant that the subject is technical, detailed, and also subtle, and as a result, the study of vocal production can take, and has taken, entire careers. A basic knowledge of spoken sound, however, will enable you to analyze that aspect of the poet's craft that pertains to qualities of pronunciation and rhythm.

Vowel Sounds Create the Flow of Poetic Speech

The continuous stream of speech, whether conversation, oratory, or poetry, is provided mainly by **vowel sounds**. A vowel (from the Latin word *vox*, or "voice") results from vibrations resonating in the space between the tongue and the top of the mouth. As our tongues go up or down or forward or backward, or as they curl or flatten out, and as our lips move synchronously with our tongues, we form vowels. Some vowels are "long," such as $\bar{e}$ (fl*ee*), $\bar{a}$, (st*a*y), $\bar{o}$ (*o*pen), and *oo* (f*oo*d). Others are "short," such as $\breve{i}$ (f*i*t), $\breve{u}$ (f*u*n), and $\breve{e}$ (s*e*t). Some vowels are called "front" (e.g., s*ee*, pl*a*y) and some are called "back" (kn*o*wing, m*oo*n), depending on the position of the tongue in the production of the sound. Some are rounded (h*o*pe, h*oo*p) because their production requires pursed lips, but more are unrounded (gr*ee*n, sw*i*m).

Many of our English vowel sounds are pronounced as a *schwa*, or minimal vowel sound, despite their spellings (e.g., the *e* in "th*e* boy," the *a* in "*a*lone"). Thus, "*a*bout," "stag*e*s," "rap*i*d," "nati*o*n," and "circ*u*s" contain the vowels *a, e, i, o,* and *u,* but all the italicized letters make the same *schwa* sound.

Of special importance is the diphthong ("two voices," "two sounds"), that is, a meaningful sound that begins with one vowel sound and then is completed by the movement to another vowel sound. The three English diphthongs are *i* (tr*y*, appl*i*ance), *ou* (h*ou*se, sh*ou*t), and *oi* (f*oi*l, empl*oy*).

Consonant Sounds Are Meaningful Sounds Produced Through the Creation of Vocal Obstructions in the Mouth

Consonant sounds ("sounds made at the same time [as vowels]") result from the touching and near touching of various parts of the mouth (lips, tongue, teeth, hard palate, soft palate), thus producing meaningful sounds obstructing the flow of vowel sound. Some consonants might theoretically be prolonged (e.g., *m, h, sh*), while others are by nature no more than momentary (*t, k*). In combination, consonants and vowels make for understandable speech. The consonants are classified into three major groups.

1. **Stop Sounds, Also Called** *Plosives,* **Are Percussive and Abrupt.** There are six stop sounds, which are made by the momentary stoppage and release of breath either when the lips touch each other (*p* and *b*) or when the tongue touches the hard palate (the *k* and *g* in *keep* and *gear*) or soft palate (the *k* and *g* in *cool* and *goal*), or when the tongue touches the alveolar ridge immediately above the teeth (*t* and *d*).

2. **Continuant Sounds Are Smooth and Flowing.** They are produced by the steady release of the breath in conjunction with various positions of the tongue in relation to the lips, teeth, and palate, as in *n, ng, l, r, th* (as in *th*orn), *th* (as in *th*e), *f, v, s, z, sh* (as in *sh*arp), and *zh* (as in plea*s*ure); or with the touching of the lower lip and upper teeth for the sounds *f* and *v;* or with the touching of both lips for the sound *m.* Two special sounds called *affricates* begin with the stops *t* and *d* and then become the continuants *sh* and *zh* (as in *ch*ew and ju*dg*e).

3. **Semivowel Sounds Are More Like Consonants Than Vowels.** They are midway between vowels and consonants, and they move from an originating sound and then move to another vowel sound. They are *w* (*w*agon, *w*in, *w*eather), *y* (*y*es, *y*oung, *u*nion), and *h* (*h*ope, *h*eap).

*Consonants May Be Either **Voiced** or **Voiceless*** Voiced consonants are produced with the vibration of the vocal chords (e.g., *b, d, g, v, z, zh*), and voiceless consonants are produced by the breath alone, for this reason being
whispered sounds (e.g., *p, t, k, f, s, sh*). Among the semivowels, *w* and *y* are
voiced, but *h* is voiceless.

Nasal Consonants Result from the Release of Sound Through the Nose Three
consonants require the stoppage of the breath in the mouth so that the sound
can be released through the nose. The consonants, called **nasals,** are *n, m,* and
ng (as in su*n*, su*m*, and su*ng*). In English, the *n* and *m* sounds may begin and end
words or may appear in the middle of a word, whereas the *ng* sound may appear in the middle or end but may not begin a word. The nasals affect the pronunciation of adjoining consonants, as in words like *mountain* and *student*, in
which the *t* and *d* sounds are released nasally by many speakers of English. Adjoining consonants also affect the pronunciation of the nasal, as in words like *sink*
and *think*, in which the concluding *k* sound causes the preceding nasal to be an
ng sound, as in *sing* and *thing*, even though the sound is spelled with an *n* alone.

Segments: Individually Meaningful Sounds

Individual sounds in combination make up syllables and words, and separate
words in combination make up lines of poetry. Syllables and words are made
up of **segments**, or individually meaningful sounds (that linguists call
segmental phonemes). In the word *top*, there are three segments: *t, o,* and *p*. When
you hear these three sounds in order, you recognize the word *top*, as distinguished from *tape, tap, type,* and *taupe*. It takes three alphabetical letters—*t, o,*
and *p*—to spell (or **graph**) *top*, because each letter is identical with a segment.
Quite often, however, English uses more than one letter to spell a segment. For
example, in the word *enough*, there are four segments (*e, n, u, f*), although six
letters are required for the correct spelling: *e, n, ou,* and *gh*. The last two segments (*u* and *f*) require two letters each (two letters forming one segment are
called a *digraph*). In the word *through* there are three segments but *seven* letters.
To be spelled correctly in this word, the *oo* segment must have four letters
(*ough*). Note, however, that in the word *flute*, the *oo* segment requires only one
letter, *u*. When we study the effects of various segments in relationship to poetic rhythm, we deal with **sound**; usually our concern is with prosodic devices such as **alliteration, assonance,** and **rhyme.**

When segments are meaningfully combined, they make up syllables and
words. A **syllable**, in both prose and poetry, consists of a single meaningful
strand of sound such as the article *a* in "*a* table," the stem *lin* in "*lin*en," and
the entire word *screech*. The article *a*, which is both a syllable and a word, has
only one segment; *lin*, the first syllable of a two-syllable word, contains three
segments (*lin* does not occur alone but is used in combinations such as
lingerie and *linoleum*); *screech* is a complete word of one syllable consisting
of the five segments *s, k, r, ee,* and *tch*. The past tense of *screech* (*screeched*) adds

one meaningful sound, *t*, and two letters, *ed*, but this additional sound does not create a new syllable. The understanding of what constitutes syllables is important because poetic rhythm is determined by the positions of heavily stressed and less heavily stressed syllables.

Distinguish Between Spellings and the Actual Sounds of Words

It is important—vital—to understand the differences between spelling, or **graphics,** and pronunciation, or **phonetics**. Not all English sounds are spelled and pronounced in the same way, as with *top*. Thus the letter *s* has three very different sounds in the words *sweet, sugar,* and *flows: s, sh* (s*h*arp), and *z*. On the other hand, the words *shape, ocean, nation, sure, fissure, Eschscholtzia,* and *machine* use different combinations of letters to spell the *sh* sound.

Vowel sounds may also be spelled in different ways. The *e* sound, for example, can be spelled *i* in *machine*, *ee* in *speed*, *ea* in *eat*, *e* in *even*, and *y* in *funny*, yet the vowel sounds in *eat, break,* and *bear* are not the same even though they are spelled the same. Remember this: With both consonants and vowel sounds, *do not confuse spellings with sounds.*

Poetic Rhythm

Rhythm in speech is a combination of vocal speeds, rises and falls, starts and stops, vigor and slackness, and relaxation and tension. In ordinary speech and in prose, rhythm is not as important as the flow of ideas. In poetry, rhythm is significant because poetry is emotionally charged, compact, and intense. Poets invite us to change speeds while reading—to slow down and linger over some words and sounds and to pass rapidly over others. They also invite us to give more-than-ordinary vocal stress or emphasis to certain syllables and less stress to others. The more intense syllables are called **heavy stress** syllables, and it is the heavy stresses that determine the **accent** or **beat** of a poetic line. The less intense syllables receive **light stress**. In traditional verse, poets select patterns called **feet**, which consist of a regularized relationship of heavy stresses to light stresses.

Scansion Is the Systematic Study of Poetic Rhythm

To study the patterns of versification in any poem, you **scan** the poem. The act of scanning—**scansion**—lets you see how the poem establishes a prevailing metrical pattern, and also how and why there are variations in the pattern.

Determine Stresses, or Beats   In the scansion of a poem, it is important to use a commonly recognized notational system to record stresses or accents. A *heavy* or *primary* stress (also called an **accented syllable**) may be indicated by capital letters, as in "To BE or NOT to BE," or it may also be indicated by a prime mark or acute accent (´). A *light* stress (also called an **unaccented syllable**) has often been indicated by a bowl-like half circle called a **breve** (ˇ) or sometimes by a raised circle or degree sign (°). If you are using capital letters to indicate a heavy stress, use lowercase letters alone, without any diacritical marks, to indicate the light stress, as in Milton's "When I con-SID-er HOW my LIGHT is SPENT." To separate one foot from another, a **virgule** or slash (/) may be used. Thus, the following line, from Coleridge's "The Rime of the Ancient Mariner," may be schematized formally in this way:

WA – ter, / WA - ter, / EV - ery WHERE,

Here the virgules or slashes show that the line contains two two-syllable feet followed by a single three-syllable foot.

Determine the Meter or Measure   A major part of scansion is the determination of a poem's **meter**, or the number of feet in its lines. Lines containing five feet are **pentameter**, four are **tetrameter**, three are **trimeter**, two are **dimeter**, and one is **monometer.** (To these may be added the less common line lengths **hexameter**, a six-foot line; **heptameter** or the **septenary**, seven feet; and **octameter**, eight feet.) In terms of accent or beat, a trimeter line has three beats (heavy stresses), a pentameter line five beats, and so on.

The Major Metrical Feet

You are now ready to scan poems and to determine the patterns of metrical feet, which measure the relationships of syllables and stresses. In English the names of the feet are derived from Greek poetry. We may classify them as feet of two syllables, three syllables, and one syllable (or imperfect).

The Two-Syllable Foot

1. **Iamb** (*Light/Heavy*). The most important poetic foot in English is the iamb (a word of unknown origin), which contains a light stress followed by a heavy stress:

   the WINDS

   The iamb is the most important and most common foot because it most nearly duplicates natural speech while also elevating speech to poetry. It is the most versatile of English poetic feet, and it is capable of great variation. Even within the same line, iambic feet vary in intensity, thus supporting the shades of meaning designed by the poet. For example, in this line of iambic pentameter from Wordsworth's sonnet "The World Is Too Much with Us," each foot is unique;

   The WINDS / that WILL / be HOWL - / ing AT / all HOURS, /

   Even though "will" and "at" receive the heavy stress in their individual iambic positions, they are not as strongly emphasized as "winds," "howl-," and "hours" (indeed, they are also less strong than "all," which is in the light-stress position in the concluding iamb). Such variability, approximating the stresses and rhythms of actual speech, makes the iamb suitable for both serious and light verse, and it therefore helps poets to focus attention on ideas and emotions. If they use it with skill, it never becomes monotonous, for it does not distract readers by drawing attention to its own rhythm.

2. **Trochee** (*Heavy/Light*). The trochee ("running"), sometimes called the **choree** ("dancing"), consists of a heavy accent followed by a light one.

FLOW – er

Rhythmically, most two-syllable English words are trochaic (tro-KAY-ick), as may be seen in words like *author, early, follow, major, morning, often, singing, snowfall, something, story, water, walking, willow,* and *window.* A major exception is seen in many two-syllable words beginning with prefixes, such as *sublime, because,* and *impel.* Another exception is found in two-syllable words that are borrowed from another language but are still pronounced as in the original language, as with *machine, technique, garage,* and *chemise,* all of which are recent importations from French, in which an iambic structure prevails. Illustrating the strength of trochaic rhythms in English, however, the final stresses in many French words borrowed hundreds of years ago now accent the next-to-last syllable, as with *apartment, cherry, expression, language, lesson, nation,* and *very.*

Because trochaic rhythm has often been called *falling, dying, light,* or *anticlimactic,* and because iambic rhythm has been called *rising, elevating, serious,* and *climactic,* poets have preferred the iambic foot. They therefore have arranged various placements of single- and multiple-syllable words, and have also used a variety of other means, so that the heavy-stress syllable is at the end of the foot, as in Shakespeare's

With - IN / his BEND - / ing SICK - / le's COM - / pass COME, /

in which three successive trochaic words (*bending, sickle's,* and *compass*) are arranged to match the iambic meter.

3. **Spondee** (*Heavy/Heavy*). The spondee (originally two long notes played at the pouring of an offering)—also called a **hovering accent**—consists of two successive, equally heavy accents, as in "men's eyes" in Shakespeare's line

When IN / dis - GRACE / with FOR - / tune AND / MEN'S EYES

The spondee is mainly a substitute foot in English verse because successive spondees usually become iambs or trochees. An entire poem written in spondees would be unlikely within traditional metrical patterns and ordinary English syntax. As a substitute, however, the spondee creates emphasis, very often because the two stressed syllables of the spondee are next to a stressed syllable in a previous or following foot, thus in practice creating three successive strong stresses, and in some instances four. The effect is that in reading, the voice lingers on the stressed words, and the mind lingers on the idea expressed in the words. This kind of emphasis is seen in the first two iambic foot positions in line 9 of Keats's "Bright Star."

NO—YET / STILL STEAD - / fast, STILL / un - CHANGE - / a - BLE

4. **Pyrrhic** (*Light/Light*). The pyrrhic (a *foot*, a *war dance*) consists of two un-stressed syllables, even though one of them may be in a normally stressed position, as in "on their" in this line from Pope's *Pastorals* (4.5).

Now SLEEP - / ing FLOCKS / on their / SOFT FLEEC - / es LIE. /

The pyrrhic is usually made up of weakly accented words such as prepo-sitions (e.g., *on, to*) and articles (*the, a*). Like the spondee, it is a substitute foot for an iamb or a trochee. An entire poem could not be in pyrrhics be-cause most of the pyrrhics, like spondees, would be resolved as trochees and iambs. As a substitute foot, however, the pyrrhic acts as a rhythmic catapult to move the reader swiftly to the next heavy-stress syllable, and therefore it undergirds the ideas conveyed by more significant words.

The Three-Syllable Foot

1. **Dactyl** (*Heavy/Light/Light*). The dactyl (after the shape of a finger, which has a long joint and two shorter joints) has a heavy stress followed by two lights.

GREEN as our / HOPE in it, /
WHITE as our / FAITH in it. / (Swinburne)

2. **Anapest** (*Light/Light/Heavy*). The anapest (*beaten back* or *turned around;* the reverse of a dactyl) consists of two light accents followed by a heavy accent:

by the DAWN'S / ear - ly LIGHT. / (Key)

The Imperfect Foot

A single stressed syllable (´) by itself or an unstressed syllable (˘ or °) by itself creates an **imperfect foot**. This foot is a variant or substitute occurring in a poem in which one of the major feet forms the metrical pattern. The second line of Key's "The Star-Spangled Banner," for example, is anapestic, but it con-tains an imperfect foot at the end.

What so PROUD - / ly we HAILED /
at the TWI- / light's last GLEAM- / ing. /

Substitution

Most regular poems (i.e., poems written according to the "rules" of prosody) follow a formal pattern that may be analyzed according to the feet we have been describing here. Too much formal regularity, however, sometimes makes for monotony, and so for interest and emphasis (and also, especially, because of the natural rhythms of English speech), poets frequently alter and enlarge the regular patterns through the **substitution** of a dominant foot by a variant foot. Thus in an iambic line the poet may insert a spondee or an anapest and by this means provide a wider and more conversational rhythmical range than the unvarying use of the poem's chosen pattern. As an example, the pat-tern of Swift's "A Description of the Morning" is iambic pentameter (i.e., five

SPECIAL METERS

In many poems you will find meters other than those described earlier. Poets like Browning, Tennyson, Poe, and Swinburne introduce special or unusual meters. Other poets manipulate pauses or caesurae (discussed later) to create the effects of unusual meters. For these reasons, you should know about metrical feet such as the following:

1. **Amphibrach** (short at both ends). A light, heavy, and light:

   Ah FEED me / and FILL me / with PLEAS - ure / (Swinburne)

2. **Amphimacer** (long at both ends) or cretic (a song from the Island of Crete). A heavy, light, and heavy:

   LOVE is BEST. / (Robert Browning)

3. **Bacchius** or **Bacchic** (pertaining to Bacchus, the god of wine and conviviality). A light stress followed by two heavy stresses:

   Some LATE LARK / (William Ernest Henley)

4. **Dipodic measure** (literally, "two feet" combining to make one) or **syzygy** (a "yoking together"), or double duple meter. Dipodic measure develops in longer lines when a poet submerges two regular feet under a stronger beat, so that a "galloping" or "rollicking" rhythm results. The following line from Masefield's "Cargoes," for example, may be scanned as trochaic hexameter, with the concluding foot being an iamb:

   QUIN - que / REME of / NIN- e- /
   VEH from / DIS-tant / o - PHIR, /

   In reading, however, a stronger beat is superimposed, which makes one foot out of two—*dipodic measure* or *syzygy:*

   QUIN - quer - eme of / NIN - e - veh from / DIS – tant o –PHIR,

iambs per line). However, Swift introduces a formal substitution at the beginning of the following line.

DUNS at / his LORD- / ship's GATE / be - GAN / to MEET;

The first foot is a trochee, and the strong accent on *Duns* enables Swift to stress his comic assertion that even a member of the nobility, who supposedly has the money to pay his bills, does not do so and therefore is dunned by bill collectors. Note also that the light accent on *at* enables the voice to move rapidly through *at his lord.* Thus, although the first two feet are a trochee and an iamb, the rhythmical effect is that of an imperfect foot followed by an anapest. This fairly common substitution helps Swift emphasize and satirize the unglamorous side of London life early in the eighteenth century.

When studying rhythm, your main concern in noting substitutions is to determine the formal metrical pattern and then to analyze the variations on this pattern and their principal techniques and effects. Always show how these variations have enabled the poet to get points across and to achieve emphasis.

Accentual, Strong-Stress, and "Sprung" Rhythms

The foregoing descriptions of poetic feet will enable the analysis of most so-called traditional poetry. A number of poets, however, stretch the bounds of traditional feet, and use often unmeasured rhythms derived from accentual or strong stresses. Such lines are historically linked to English poetry as our language existed a thousand years ago. At that time, each line was divided in two, with two major alliterated stresses occurring in each half. In the nineteenth century, Gerard Manley Hopkins (1844–1889) developed what he called "sprung" rhythm, a rhythm in which the major stresses would be released or "sprung" from the line. The method is complex, but one of the primary characteristics is the placement together of one-syllable stressed words, as in the second of these lines from his poem "God's Grandeur":

> It gathers to a greatness, like the ooze of oil
> Crushed. Why do MEN THEN NOW NOT RECK his ROD°?

Here we find five successive heavy stresses. Many of Hopkins's lines combine alliteration and strong stresses to create the same powerful emphasis.

The Caesura: The Pause Creating Variety and Natural Rhythms in Poetry

Whenever we speak, we run words together rapidly, without pause, but we do stop briefly and almost unnoticeably between significant units or phrases. Intelligible conversation could not take place without these pauses, which, both grammatically and rhythmically, create separate units of meaning called **cadence groups.** In poetry using a regular meter, the cadence groups operate just as they do in prose to make ideas clear. That is, as we follow the poetic measures, we also pause briefly at the ends of phrases, and we pause longer, for emphasis, at the ends of sentences. In scansion, the name of these pauses, which linguists call *junctures,* is **caesura** (a "cutting off"), pluralized as **caesurae.** When writing out our scansion of a line, we use two diagonal slashes or virgules (/ /) to indicate a caesura so that the caesura can be distinguished from the single virgule separating feet. Often the caesura coincides with the end of a foot, as at the end of the second iamb in line 4 of Frost's "Desert Places":

> But a / FEW WEEDS // and STUB - / ble SHOW - / ing LAST. /

---

2 *rod:* royal scepter.

The caesura, however, may fall within a foot, and there may be more than one in a line, as within the second and fourth iambs in line 1 of "Desert Places":

Snow FALL - / ing // and / NIGHT FALL - / ing // FAST / oh, FAST /

When a caesura ends a line, usually marked by a comma, semicolon, or period, that line is **end-stopped,** as in this famous line opening Keats's "Endymion":

a THING / of BEAU - / ty // is / a JOY / for - EV - er. /

If a line has no punctuation at the end and the thought carries over to the next line, it is called **run-on**. A term also used to indicate run-on lines is **enjambement** ("straddling"). The following passage, a continuation of the poem by Keats, contains three run-on lines. Incidentally, Keats was widely criticized at this time for this use of enjambement.

> Its loveliness increases; // it will never
> Pass into nothingness; // but still will keep
> A bower quiet for us, // and a sleep
> Full of sweet dreams, // . . .

It is important to recognize that the formal rhythms of poetry are superimposed on the rhythms of natural speech, creating a tension between the two. By manipulating the placement of caesurae, the pauses that fall randomly in speech, poets create many of the variant rhythms that are provided by formal substitution. If the poet ends a cadence group within a foot, the pause, or caesura, may cause us actually to *hear* trochees, amphibrachs, and other variant feet even though the line may scan correctly and regularly in the established meter. This type of *de facto* variation is **rhetorical substitution**. A noteworthy example in an iambic pentameter line is this one from the first Epistle of Pope's *Essay on Man* (line 66):

His AC- / tions', // PAS-/sions', // BE-/ing's, // USE /and END; /

This is the second line in a "heroic" couplet, which theoretically requires that there should be only a single caesura following the fourth syllable. In this line, however, Pope provides us with great rhythmical variety. He uses not one but rather three caesurae, each of them producing an emphatic pause or juncture. Pope's line is regularly iambic, but the effect is different in actual reading or speaking. Because of the caesurae after the third, fifth, and seventh syllables, the rhythm produces an amphibrach, a trochee, another trochee, and an amphimacer. The effect is a skillful line containing two inner two-syllable feet, framed by two three-syllable feet, thus:

His AC-tions', // PAS-sions', // BE-ing's, // USE and END;
AMPHIBRACH   TROCHEE   TROCHEE   AMPHIMACER

The spoken substitutions effected by the caesurae in this regular line produce the effect of substitution—rhetorical substitution—and therefore tension and interest. Never believe that Pope did not know what he was doing with words and rhythms.

Segmental Poetic Devices

Once you have completed your analysis of rhythms, you should consider the segmental poetic devices in the poem. Usually these devices are used to create emphasis, but sometimes in context they may echo or imitate actions and objects. The segmental devices most common in poetry are *assonance, alliteration, onomatopoeia,* and *euphony and cacophony.*

Identical Vowel Sounds Create Assonance

Assonance (response *to a sound*) is the repetition of identical *vowel* sounds in different words—for example, the short *ĭ* in "swift Camilla skims" (Pope). It is a strong means of emphasis, as in the following line by Edmund Spenser, where the *ŭ* sound connects the two words *lull* and *slumber*, and the short *ĭ* connects *him, in,* and *his:*

> And more, to lull him in his slumber soft.

Identical Consonant Sounds Create Alliteration

Like assonance, **alliteration** (response *to a letter*) is a means of highlighting ideas by words containing the same consonant sound—for example, the repeated *m* in Spenser's "Mixed with a murmuring wind," or the *s* sound in Edmund Waller's praise of Oliver Cromwell, "Your never-failing sword made war to cease," which emphasizes the connection between the words *sword* and *cease.*

There are two kinds of alliteration. Most commonly, alliteration is regarded as the repetition of identical consonant sounds that usually (but not necessarily) begin syllables in close patterns—for example, in Pope's lines "Laborious, heavy, busy, bold, and blind," "While pensive poets painful vigils keep," and "brazen brainless brothers." When used judiciously, alliteration gives strength to ideas by emphasizing key words, but too much can cause comic and catastrophic consequences.

The second form of alliteration occurs when a poet repeats identical or similar consonant sounds that do not begin syllables but nevertheless create a pattern—for example, the *z* segment in the line "In these places freezing breezes easily cause sneezes," or the *m, b,* and *p* segments (all of which are made *bilabially*, that is, with both lips) in "The miserably mumbling and momentously murmuring bumpkin propels pegs and pebbles in the bubbling pool." Such clearly designed patterns are hard to overlook.

Verbal Imitation of Real Sounds Is
Onomatopoeia, or "Poetic Sound Effects"

Onomatopoeia ("the coining or creating of names") is a blend of consonant and vowel sounds designed to *imitate* or *suggest* a situation or an action. It is made possible in poetry because many English words are **echoic** in origin; that is, they are verbal echoes of the actions they describe, such as *buzz, bump, slap,* and so on. In "Anthem for Doomed Youth," Owen uses such words to create onomatopoeia. Through the combined use of assonance and alliteration, he imitates the repeating sounds of rifles in combat in the passage "Only the stuttering rifles' rapid rattle / Can patter out their hasty orisons." Here Owen's use of the *t, r,* and *k* sounds, together with the short *ă* vowel, accounts for his successful control of onomatopoeia.

Pleasing Sounds Create Euphony and Harsh Sounds Create Cacophony

Words describing smooth or jarring sounds, particularly those resulting from consonants, are euphony and cacophony. **Euphony** ("good sound") refers to words containing consonants that permit an easy and smooth flow of spoken sound. Although there is no rule that some consonants are inherently more pleasant than others, students of poetry often cite sounds like *m, n, ng, l, v,* and *z,* together with *w* and *y,* as being especially easy on the ears. The opposite of euphony is **cacophony** ("bad sound"), in which percussive and choppy sounds make for vigorous and noisy pronunciation, as in tongue twisters like "black bug's blood" and "shuffling shellfish fashioned by a selfish sushi chef." Obviously, unintentional cacophony is a mark of imperfect control. When a poet deliberately creates it for effect, however, as in Pope's "The hoarse, rough verse should like the torrent roar" (*An Essay on Criticism*), and in Coleridge's "Huge fragments vaulted like rebounding hail, / Or chaffy grain beneath the thresher's flail" ("Kubla Khan"), cacophony is a mark of poetic skill. Although poets generally aim at easily flowing, euphonious lines, cacophony does have a place, always depending on the poet's intention and subject matter.

Rhyme: The Duplication and Similarity of Sounds

Rhyme refers to words containing identical final syllables. One type of rhyme involves words with identical concluding vowel sounds, or assonance, as in *day, weigh, hey, bouquet, fiancé,* and *matinee.* A second type of rhyme is created by assonance combined with identical consonant sounds, as in *ache, bake, break,* and *opaque;* or *turn, yearn, fern, spurn,* and *adjourn;* or *double* and *trouble,* or *slippery* and *frippery.* Rhymes like these, because their rhyming sounds are identical, are called **exact rhymes.** It is important to note that rhymes result from *sound* rather than from spelling; words do not have to be spelled the same way or look alike to rhyme. All the words rhyming with *day,* for example, are spelled differently, but because they all contain the same "long ay" sound, they rhyme.

Rhyme, above all, gives delight and sustains interest, and it strengthens a poem's psychological impact. Through its network of similar sounds that echo and resonate in our minds, it promotes memory by clinching feelings and ideas. It has been an important aspect of poetry for hundreds of years, and, although many poets have shunned it because they find it restrictive and artificial, it is closely connected with how well particular poems move us or leave us flat. There are few restrictions on the types of words that poets may choose in making rhymes. Nouns may be rhymed with verbs, adjectives, adverbs, and other nouns or with any other rhyming word, regardless of part of speech.

Most often, rhymes are placed at the ends of lines. Two successive lines may rhyme, for example, or rhymes may appear in alternating lines. It is also possible to introduce rhyming words at intervals of four, five, or more lines. If rhyming sounds are too far away from each other, however, it is difficult for readers to recall them and they therefore lose their effectiveness. Sometimes poets use rhyme within individual lines—**internal rhyme**. Lowell uses internal rhyme effectively in "Patterns," a poem about the grief and sorrow of war. In lines two and three she rhymes *daffodils* and *squills*, a rhyme she repeats internally in line 22 (*daffodils and squills*) and also in line 95 (*squills and daffodils*), thus emphasizing these flowers, which might have been part of a wedding bouquet that is never to be. Internal rhyme is not common, but you should be alert for it and make note of it when it occurs.

Poets who are skillful and original rhymers are able to create fresh, unusual, and surprising turns of thought. We can therefore judge poets on their use of rhyme. Often poets are truly creative rhymers, putting together words like *bent 'em* and *Tarentem* or *masterly* and *dastardly*. Some rhymers, whom an anonymous sixteenth-century critic called a "rakehelly rout of ragged rhymers," are satisfied with easy rhymes, or **cliché rhymes**, like *trees* and *breeze* (a rhyme that Alexander Pope criticized in 1711 in *An Essay on Criticism*). But good rhymes and good poets go together, in creative cooperation. The seventeenth-century poet John Dryden, who wrote volumes of rhyming couplets, acknowledged that the need to find rhyming words inspired ideas he had not anticipated. In this sense, rhyme has been—and still is—a vital element of poetic creativity.

Rhyme and Meter

The effects of rhyme are closely bound to rhythm and meter. There is general agreement that rhymes coinciding with a strong accent are conducive to serious subjects. Commensurately, rhymes coinciding with syllables of light stress are appropriate for light and comic subject matter. There is no hard-and-fast rule about such matters, for the effects of rhyme always result from the poet's skill, regardless of rhymes. There is enough truth in the observations, however, to warrant considering the relationship of rhyme and accent.

Rising Rhymes Form the Climaxing Syllables of Iambs and Anapests

The most significant type of **rising rhyme** is **iambic rhyme**, which utilizes one-syllable words in an iambic foot (like *the west* and *in rest, more strong* and *ere long*) and two-syllable words in which the accent falls on the second syllable (like *away* and *today, demand* and *command*.) Such rhymes are also called **heavy-stress rhyme** or **accented rhyme**. Iambic rhyme is illustrated in the concluding lines of Keats's "Bright Star" (the rhymes are capitalized):

> Still, still to hear her tender-taken BREATH,
> And so live ever—or else swoon to DEATH.

Here, the rhyming sounds are produced by one-syllable words—*breath* and *death*—that occur in the final heavy-stress positions of the lines. The rhyme climaxing a final syllable can also involve spondees, as in lines 9–12 of Shakespeare's "Sonnet 18: Shall I Compare Thee to a Summer's Day?" (capitalized to show stress):

> But thy eternal summer shall NOT FADE,
> Nor lose possession of that fair THOU OWEST;
> Nor shall Death brag thou wander'st in HIS SHADE,
> When in eternal lines to time THOU GROWEST.

Falling Rhymes Conclude with One or Two or More Lightly Stressed Syllables.

Rhymes using words of two or more syllables in which the heavy stress is followed by light syllables are **trochaic rhyme** or **double rhyme** for two-syllable rhymes, and dactylic rhyme or **triple rhyme** for three-syllable rhymes. Less technically, these types of rhymes are also called **falling rhymes** or, sometimes, dying rhymes because the intensity of pronunciation decreases on the light accent or accents following the heavy accent. Coleridge's "Kubla Khan" (lines 17, 18) furnishes us with an example of trochaic rhyme (capitalized here):

> And from this chasm, with ceaseless turmoil SEETHING,
> As if this earth in fast thick pants were BREATHING

Here the rhyme almost pictorially describes the "fountain" that is bursting upward and then falling downward from the chasm in the scene that Coleridge makes verbally for us here.

Double rhymes can also be used to stress irony, as in *measure* and *pleasure* in Wordsworth's "Lines Written in Early Spring" (lines 13–16, caps added).

> The birds around me hopped and played
> Their thoughts I cannot MEASURE—
> But the least motion which they made,
> It seemed a thrill of PLEASURE.

In this poem Wordsworth contrasts the beauty and innocence of a natural scene with the inequality and injustice of the human scene. The effect of his trochaic rhyme is to complement his lamentation of the fact that human beings fail to make their own relationships as beautiful as the world that Nature has given us.

Dactylic or triple rhyme, even more than trochaic rhyme, is light or humorous because it tends to minimize the subject matter and maximize the rhythm. A poet noted for his cleverness in this regard is Ogden Nash (1902–1971), who created many comic triple rhymes. In "Very Like a Whale," for example, we find *better for* rhymed with *metaphor,* and *experience* with *Assyrians.* How many of us could be clever enough to create rhymes like these?

Variations in Rhyme Extend the Boundaries of Rhyming Poetry

Unlike poets writing in other languages (such as Italian, which offers virtually endless rhyming possibilities because most Italian words end in vowel sounds), English poets are limited in selecting rhymes because our language is short in identical word terminations. To compensate for this shortfall of English rhymes, a tradition has grown that many English words may be rhymed even if their sounds do not duplicate each other exactly.

Rhymes may therefore be created out of words with similar but not identical sounds—**inexact rhyme**. In most inexact rhymes, either the vowel segments are different while the consonants are the same, or vice versa. In addition to *inexact rhyme,* this type of rhyme is variously called **slant rhyme**, **near rhyme**, **half rhyme**, **off rhyme**, **analyzed rhyme**, or **suspended rhyme**. In employing slant rhyme, a poet can pair *bleak* with *broke* or *could* with *solitude.* We find slant rhymes in Coleridge's "Kubla Khan," where he rhymes *haunted* with *enchanted, ever* and *river,* and *forced* and *burst.*

Another common variation is **eye rhyme** or **sight rhyme**. In eye rhyme, the sounds to be eye-rhymed are *identical in spelling* but *different in pronunciation.* Entire words may be eye-rhymed, so that *wind* (verb) may be joined to *wind* (noun), and *cóntest* (noun) may be used with *contést* (verb). In most eye rhymes, however, it is only the relevant parts of words that must be spelled identically. Thus *stove* may pair with *prove* and *above,* and *bough* may match *cough, dough, enough,* and *through,* despite all the differing pronunciations. The following lines contain eye rhyme.

> Although his claim was not to praise but *bury,*
> His speech for Caesar roused the crowd to *fury.*

The different pronunciations of *bury* and *fury* make clear the contrast between exact rhyme and eye rhyme. In exact rhyme, *identical sound is crucial;* spelling is usually the same but may be different. In eye rhyme, the *eye-rhyming patterns must be spelled identically but the sounds must be different.*

An additional variation is **identical rhyme**; that is, the same words are placed into rhyming positions, such as *veil* and *veil* or *stone* and *stone.* Perhaps the most extreme variation is *vowel rhyme,* in which poets put words ending in vowels into rhyming positions, as in *day* and *sky* or *key* and *play.*

Rhyme Schemes

A **rhyme scheme** refers to a poem's pattern of rhyming sounds, which can be schematized by alphabetical letters. The first rhyming sounds, such as *love* and *dove*, are marked with an *a;* the next rhyming sounds, such as *swell* and *fell*, receive a *b;* the next sounds, such as *first* and *burst*, receive a *c;* and so on. Thus, a pattern of lines ending with the words *love, moon, thicket; dove, June, picket;* and *above, croon, wicket* can be schematized as *a b c, a b c, a b c.*

To formulate a rhyme scheme or pattern, you include the meter and the number of feet in each line as well as the letters indicating rhymes, as follows:

Iambic pentameter: a b a b, c d c d, e f e f

This scheme shows that all the lines in the poem are iambic, with five feet in each line. Commas are used here to mark a stanzaic pattern of three 4-line units, or **quatrains**, with the rhymes falling on the first and third, and the second and fourth, lines of each quatrain.

Should the number of feet in the lines of a poem or **stanza** vary, as in odes and songs, you show this fact by using a number in front of each letter:

Iambic: 4a 3b 4a 3b 5a 5a 4b

This formulation shows an intricate pattern of rhymes and line lengths in a stanza of seven lines. The first, third, fifth, and sixth lines rhyme and vary from four to five feet. The second, fourth, and seventh lines also rhyme and vary from three to four feet.

The absence of a rhyme sound is indicated by an *x*. Thus, you formulate the rhyme scheme of **ballad measure**, as in Randall's "Ballad of Birmingham," like this:

Iambic: 4x 3a 4x 3a

The formulation shows that the quatrain alternates iambic tetrameter (four feet) with iambic trimeter (three feet). In this ballad quatrain, only lines 2 and 4 rhyme; there is no end rhyme in lines 1 and 3.

Writing About Prosody

Because studying prosody requires a specific detail and description, it is best to limit your study to a short poem or to a short passage from a long poem. A sonnet, a stanza of a lyric poem, or a fragment from a long poem will often be sufficient. If you choose a fragment, it should be self-contained, such as an entire speech or a short episode or scene.

The analysis of even a short poem, however, can grow long because of the need to describe word positions and stresses and also to determine the various effects. For this reason you do not have to exhaust your topic. Try to make your discussion representative of the prosody of your poem or passage.

Your first reading in preparation for your essay should be for comprehension. On second and third readings, make notes of sounds, accents, and rhymes by reading the poem aloud. To perceive sounds, one student helped herself by reading aloud in an exaggerated way in front of a mirror. If you have privacy or are not self-conscious, you might do the same. Let yourself go a bit. As you dramatize your reading (maybe even in front of fellow students), you will find that heightened levels of reading also accompany the poet's expression of important ideas. Mark these spots for later analysis and discussion so that you will be able to make strong assertions about the relationship of sound to sense.

As a goal, you might try to determine whether and how the prosody of a poem may be used as an organizational element. In an Italian or Petrarchan sonnet, for example, the rhymes are important in tying together the development of ideas. In a Shakespearean sonnet there are three 4-line groups (quatrains), each containing the development of a particular idea or image or symbol, and the concluding two lines rhyme and at the same time create a "cap" or idea tying the previous ideas together.

Carry out your study of the passage in the following way. What counts in this preliminary study of prosody is that your analyses be clear enough to provide help in developing your actual discussion.

- Prepare a working copy of the poem or passage, and duplicate it three or four times. It is best to triple space your copy so that you will have plenty of room to mark your observations.

- Determine the formal pattern of metrical feet. You may wish to use lower case letters for light stresses, and capital letters for heavy stresses, as in Tennyson's "And ON / a SUD - /den, LO! / the LEV - / el LAKE." Capital letters bring out the strong accents, and are especially graphic in the indication of spondees. If your poem is spoken by an "I," for analytical purposes you may write the capital I as a small letter, as in "i SAID." There are other ways to mark the feet. A traditional way is to use a short acute accent or stress mark for heavily stressed syllables (´) and either a breve or a degree sign for unaccented or lightly stressed syllables (˘ or °), as in "And ón / a súd ' / den Ló! / the lév - / el Láke." Capital letters, however, are more noticeable, and are more easily managed.

- Indicate the separate feet by a diagonal slash or virgule (/). Indicate caesurae and end-of-line pauses by double virgules (//).

- Use colored pencils to underline, circle, make boxes, or otherwise mark the formal and rhetorical substitutions that you discover. Because such substitutions may occur throughout the poem, develop a numbering system for each type, as in 1 = anapest, 6 = trochee, etc. Provide a key to your numbers at the bottom of the page. Students have actually enjoyed the discovery of metrics and versification that the colored pencil system brings out.

- Do the same for alliteration, assonance, onomatopoeia, and rhyme. It has proved effective to draw lines to connect the repeating sounds, for these effects will be close together in the poem, and your connections will dramatize this closeness. The use of a separate color for each separate effect is helpful, for different colors make prosodic distinctions stand out clearly. You might also, if you use only one pen or pencil, wish to set up a system of dotted, wavy, cross-hatched, or double-cross-hatched lines in order to distinguish the patterns. Any easily recognized system that is convenient for you is acceptable. It is also a good idea to circle the regular and substitute metrical patterns. (Thus, anapests and trochees might be circled or underlined to help you in identifying them when you begin writing your essay.)

- At the bottom of your pages, provide a key to your circles and lines.
- It is good to use a standard pronunciation guide for your discussion of sounds. You may employ one of the standard collegiate dictionaries. If you have had formal linguistic study, use the phonemic or phonetic systems if you have these as symbols or special characters on your computer. If you have difficulty in using these systems when you are typing your essay or preparing it on the computer, you may wish to create your own method of indicating sounds. Thus *eh* would be the vowel sound in "yes," *sh* the consonant sound in "shake" or "nation," and so on.
- If you prepare your study sheets with care, half your job is over. All you need to do after this preparation is to describe what you have analyzed and noted. Here your connecting lines of the same types or colors can help you greatly, for the colors or special lines are obvious and will help you remember important characteristics of the sounds.

Once you have analyzed the various effects in your poem and have recorded these on your work sheets and in your notes, you will be ready to formulate a central idea and organization. The focus of your essay should reflect the most significant features of prosody in relationship to some other element of the poem, such as speaker, tone, or ideas.

Organize Your Essay on Prosody

Depending on your assignment, you might wish to discuss all aspects of rhythm or sound, or perhaps just one, such as the poet's use of regular meter, a particular substitution, alliteration, or assonance. It is possible, for example, to devote an entire essay to (1) regular meter; (2) one particular variation in meter, such as the anapest or spondee; (3) the caesura; (4) assonance; (5) alliteration; (6) onomatopoeia; or (7) rhyme.

Introduction After a brief description of the poem (e.g., it is a sonnet, a two-stanza lyric, a ballad, etc.), establish the scope of your essay. Your central idea will outline the thought that you wish to carry out through your prosodic analysis, such as that regularity of meter is consistent with a happy vision of love or life, or that frequent spondees emphasize the solidity of the speaker's wish to love, or that particular sounds echo some of the poem's actions.

Body The body may include all the following elements, or just one, depending on your instructor's assignment.

1. **Rhythm.** Establish the formal metrical pattern. What is the dominant metrical foot and line length? Are some lines shorter than the pattern? What relationship do the variable lengths have with the subject matter? If the poem is a lyric or a sonnet, are important words and syllables successfully

placed in stressed positions in order to achieve emphasis? Try to relate line lengths to exposition, development of ideas, and rising or falling emotions. It is also important to look for either repeating or varying metrical patterns as the subject matter reaches peaks or climaxes. Generally, deal with the relationship between the formal rhythmical pattern and the poet's ideas and attitudes.

When noting substitutions, analyze the formal variations and the principal effects of these. If you concentrate on only one substitution, describe any apparent pattern in its use, that is, its locations, recurrences, and effects on meaning.

For caesurae, treat the effectiveness of the poet's control. Can you see any pattern of use? Are the pauses regular or random? Describe noticeable principles of placement, such as (1) the creation of rhythmical similarities in various parts of the poem; (2) the development of particular rhetorical effects; or (3) the creation of interest through rhythmical variety. Do the caesurae lead to important ideas and attitudes? Are the lines all end-stopped, or do you discover enjambement? How do these rhythmical characteristics aid in descriptions and in the expressions of ideas?

2. **Segmental effects.** Here you might be discussing, collectively or separately, the use and effects of assonance, alliteration, onomatopoeia, and cacophony and euphony. Be sure to establish that the instances you choose have really occurred systematically enough within the poem to form a pattern. Illustrate sounds by including relevant words within parentheses. You might make separate paragraphs on alliteration, assonance, and any other seemingly important pattern. Also, because space is always at a premium, you might concentrate on only one noteworthy effect, like a representative pattern of assonance, rather than on everything. Throughout your discussion, always keep foremost the relationship between content and sound.

3. **Rhyme.** Your discussion of rhyme should describe the major features of the poem's rhymes, the basic scheme, the variants, the lengths and rhythms of the rhyming words, and anything else that is noteworthy. If you can discuss the grammar of the rhymes, note the kinds of words (i.e., verbs, nouns, etc.) used for rhymes: Are they all the same? Does one form predominate? Is there variety? Can you determine the grammatical positions of the rhyming words? How may these characteristics be related to the idea or theme of the poem?

You might also discuss the qualities of the rhyming words. Are the words specific? Concrete? Abstract? Are there any striking rhymes? Any surprises? Any rhymes that are particularly clever and witty? Do any rhymes give unique comparisons or contrasts? How?

Generally, note any striking or unique rhyming effects. Without becoming overly subtle or far-fetched, you can make valid and interesting conclusions. Do any sounds in the rhyming words appear in patterns of assonance or alliteration elsewhere in the poem? Do the rhymes enter into any onomatopoeic effects? Broadly, what aspects of rhyme are uniquely effective because they blend so fully with the poem's thought and mood?

Conclusion   In your conclusion, try to develop a short evaluation of the poet's prosodic performance. If we accept the premise that poetry is designed not only to stimulate emotions but also to provide information and transfer

---

REFERRING TO SOUNDS IN POETRY

To make illustrations clear, emphasize the sounds to which you are calling attention. If you use an entire word to illustrate a sound, underline
or italicize only the sound, not the entire word, and put the word within quotation marks (for example, "The poet uses a t sound ['tip,' 'top,'
and 'terrific,' or 'tip,' 'top,' and 'terrific']"). When you refer to entire
words containing particular segments, however, underline or italicize
these words (for example, "The poet uses a t in tip, top, and terrific," or
"The poet uses a *t* in *tip, top,* and *terrific*).

---

attitudes, to what degree do the prosodic techniques of your poem contribute
to these goals? Without going into excessive detail (and writing another essay),
what more can you say here? What has been the value of your study to your
understanding and appreciating the poem? If you think your analysis has
helped you to develop new awareness of the poet's craft, it would be appropriate to state what you have learned.

Illustrative Essay

Rhythm, Sound, and Rhyme in Robert Browning's "Porphyria's Lover"°

[1]   In Browning's dramatic monologue "Porphyria's Lover," the "lover" is the
      nameless speaker—a disaster for Porphyria, for he is a delusional psy-
      chopath. He is speaking early in the morning, and he describes the events
      of the night, his last night with her. Most probably he is speaking to no one at
      all, for we as readers seem to be overhearing his monologue. Porphyria
      seems to have been a golden-haired beauty who in the "wind and rain" (line
      30) had secretly left a social gathering to meet him for an evening of love. As
      a major aspect of the poem's drama, it appears that Porphyria gave this
      man her greatest trust. But she was horribly wrong. In his shocking confes-
      sion he states that he strangled Porphyria because in this way only he alone
      could have her love forever, with no fear that she might ever leave him. This
      delusion is so enormous that he claims that Porphyria herself wanted him to
      kill her so that she might give herself to him totally. His belief in divine ap-
      proval for this grisly act is shown in his claim that "God has not said a word"
      (line 60), a particularly sick statement. The way he tells his tale is expressive
      of his diseased mentality.* Specifically, the poem's rhythms, sound devices,
      and rhymes all reflect the disturbance of this demented character.†

°See pages 366–367 for this poem.
*Central idea.
†Thesis sentence.

[2] <u>The poem's metrical pattern and variations can be seen as a reflection of the</u>
<u>speaker's troubled mind.</u> The basic iambic tetrameter is not a "heroic" line like
iambic pentameter, but is a measure that is appropriate for satiric and more
common subjects. Browning's meter is established in the first four lines:

> The RAIN / set EAR- /ly IN / to – NIGHT, //
>   The SUL - / len WIND / was SOON / a - WAKE, //
> It TORE / the ELM- / tops DOWN / for SPITE, //
>   And DID / its WORST / to VEX / the LAKE: //

The fifth line begins to suggest the speaker's disturbance, for it may be analyzed in this way: "i LIST - / ened with / HEART FIT / to BREAK." Here the
second foot is a pyrrhic, and the third is a spondee. Variations of this sort
are used elsewhere in the poem, such as lines 41–45, where spondees
suggest the speaker's insistence on the correctness of his depraved actions. (Here only the spondees are marked):

> And strangled her. NO PAIN felt she;
>   I am QUITE SURE she felt NO PAIN.
> As a SHUT BUD that holds a bee,
>   I warily oped her lids: again.
>   Laughed the BLUE EYES without a stain.

The five spondees suggest a disruption that is appropriate in light of the
speaker's perverse admission that only after he has killed her is Porphyria
"without a stain"—that is, pure.

[3] <u>Another notable group is composed of the lines in which the speaker as-</u>
<u>sumes that he can read Porphyria's mind (lines 21–25), and then he states</u>
<u>that no matter how strongly she was "murmuring" that she loved him, she</u>
<u>nevertheless was too proud and too vain to give herself to him totally:</u>

> Murmuring how she loved ME—SHE
>   TOO WEAK, for all her heart's endeavor,
> To set its struggling passion free
>   From pride, and vainer ties dissever,
>   And give herself to me forever.

In this group there is only one regular line, the middle one (line 23). The
others show irregularity either through the use of spondees or, at the line
ends, amphibrachs (en-DEAV-or, dis-SEV-er, for-EV-er). One may conclude
that these metrical variations are consistent with the speaker's irregular
mental state.

[4] <u>Browning also presents an inventive use of segmental prosodic devices to</u>
<u>demonstrate the speaker's abnormality.</u> Throughout, there is a good deal of
assonance and alliteration. In lines 36 and 37 there is alliteration on *m* and
p sounds in "That *mom*ent she was *m*ine, *m*ine, fair, / *P*erfectly *p*ure . . ."
Under other circumstances, in other poems, alliteration is used to emphasize key words and ideas, but here the alliteration seems to suggest the
speaker's exhilaration when stating his weird and diseased fantasy about
possessing Porphyria and being "worshipped" by her.

[5]   The same excitement can be seen in the use of the *b* alliteration. In line
      43, Browning's speaker tells us of "a shut *b*ud that holds a *b*ee" in his de-
      scription of how he opened Porphyria's dead eyelids and seeing not
      death there but laughter. The plosive *b* sound, which is spoken with the
      lips being first closed and then opened, pictorially duplicates the action of
      the speaker's opening her eyelids. A few lines later (line 48), it should be
      stressed that the speaker is describing his own necrophilia. After he has
      strangled Porphyria, opened her eyes, and loosened her hair, he kisses
      her, and then he states that she "*B*lushed *b*right *b*eneath my *b*urning
      kiss." The *b*, a bilabial sound (the *m* in "my" is also bilabial), is appropriate
      in his description of actual kissing. Because the *b* occurs in four words of
      the line, the repetition suggests how his mad delusion excites him.

[6]   Just as with alliteration, the poem contains many examples of asso-
      nance. In lines 32 through 37, for example, there are a number of bal-
      ancing vowel sounds, as in "h*a*ppy" and "l*a*st," "Porph*y*ria" and
      "worsh*i*pped," "Wh*i*le" and m*i*ne" (twice), and "p*u*re" and "g*oo*d." In the
      phrase "shut bud," already discussed, there is assonance of the "uh"
      sound. Assonance occurs again on the "eh" sound in lines 46–49: "n*e*xt,"
      "tr*e*ss," "n*e*ck," and "h*e*ad." This same assonance, on *eh*, occurs again in
      five lines of the next group (51 to 55). It would appear that this killer be-
      comes uniquely expressive when his emotions are ignited by the memo-
      ry of his grisly act.

[7]   The poem's subtle cacophony, too, reflects the speaker's agitated mind.
      This can be seen in the first five lines, which, although they establish the
      regularity of the meter, contain words about the storm that better suggest
      the speaker's anger and hatred than an actual storm. Importantly, the
      sounds in a number of these words are percussive, and their cacophony
      suggests his abnormality: "*t*ore," "s*p*ite," "wors*t*," "ve*x*" (i.e., ve*k*s), "hear*t*
      fi*t*," and "*b*reak." This man is not shouting and raving, but he definitely is
      totally controlled by his compulsiveness. Also, the hissing "s" sounds in a
      number of words in the first five lines suggest that the threatening sounds
      of the wind and storm are like the raging tempest in his mind: "*s*ullen,"
      "*s*oon," "top*s*," "*s*pite," "wors*t*," "ve*x*" (i.e., vek*s*), "li*s*tened."

[8]   Browning also employs the rhymes of the poem to reflect the speaker's
      agitated state of mind. Although the four-stress iambic lines are not divid-
      ed into space-divided stanzas, they are grouped into twelve five-line pat-
      terns by Browning's rhyme scheme—*ababb*. These in effect are stanzas.
      The asymmetrical fifth lines of these stanza groupings are consistent with
      how the speaker's superficially balanced and calm description of his gris-
      ly crime may reveal the imbalance of his thought.

[9]   Many of the rhymes are consistent with the speaker's mental imbalance.
      For the most part, the rhyming sounds are separate and are unrepeated
      among the different groups of lines. Only two of the stanzas include
      rhyming sounds that also appear previously. In lines 41 and 43 we find
      the rhyme *she* and *bee,* which connect with the earlier *she* and *free* of
      lines 21 and 23. Also the rhymes *pain, again,* and *stain* in lines 42–45 re-
      call the earlier *restrain, vain,* and *rain* of lines 27–30. (This assumes that
      Browning pronounced "again" as a rhyme with the others.)

[10] <u>Interestingly, one of the most regular five-line stanzas (lines 16–20), with rhymes falling on the most ordinary words, is the one that seems to have set loose the speaker's internal demons:</u>

> She put my arm about her waist
> > And made her smooth white shoulder bare,
> And all her yellow hair displaced,
> > And stooping made my cheek lie there
> > And spread, o'er all, her yellow hair.

If we accept the accuracy of the speaker's description, the situation was warm and exciting. Porphyria's seductive enticements, however, did not free the speaker's love but rather triggered his insanity. Clearly, this character is emotionally incapable of dealing with a loving and assertive woman. He does not speak of returning her physical gestures of affection, but instead says he debated what to do under the circumstances. The rhymes here— *bare, there,* and *hair*—recur in the rhymes *fair* and *hair* (a repeated word) in lines 36–40. These last lines mark the climax of the poem's action, when the speaker says that he found what to do by strangling Porphyria with her own blonde tresses. It would seem that Browning is here using echoing rhymes to show that the crippling issue of this criminal mind is guilt about love and sexuality. The rhyming words connect the speaker's wish for total possession of Porphyria to his act of murder that fulfills this twisted wish.

[11] <u>"Porphyria's Lover" is a masterly poem in which subject and style fuse meaningfully together.</u> The meter is mostly regular, but it contains elements that may be taken as highlighting the speaker's disturbance. So also is it with Browning's segmental devices and rhymes, especially in those lines in which the speaker describes his insanely murderous act. Porphyria's only mistake was to love and trust this man whom she obviously did not really know. In virtually every way, the poem's regularities and variations complement both the speaker's addled character and his moments of pathological exhilaration.

Work Cited

Browning, Robert. "Porphyria's Lover." Edgar V. Roberts. *Writing About Literature.* 11th ed. Upper Saddle River: Prentice Hall, 2006. 366–367.

Commentary on the Essay

This essay presents a relatively full treatment of the prosody of Browning's "Porphyria's Lover." It is to be understood that there could be further analysis of the poem's prosody. If such analysis did no more than lengthen the essay, however, without adding significantly to the conclusions, it would be, in effect, superfluous.

Paragraph 1 is introductory and is concerned with establishing the poem's content—an essential purpose considering the extremity of the speaker's character. The central idea makes the connection between his madness and "The way he tells his tale."

In paragraphs 2 and 3 the essay concentrates on the poem's rhythms. Here, the spondee and the uncommon amphibrach in the poem are to be considered not as substitutions inserted for emphasis or variety but rather as evidence of the disruptions in the speaker's thoughts.

In paragraphs 4, 5, and 6 the topic is alliteration and assonance, which normally also, like meter, are elements that thrust individual words and lines into positions of emphasis. Here, however, the devices are shown to indicate the speaker's bizarre excitement at the memory of possessing Porphyria, strangling her, and then being able to kiss her passionately.

Paragraph 7 introduces the poem's "subtle cacophony." This is made apparent in the poem's first stanza, in which, even before we suspect the speaker of any wrongdoing, he describes the wind in words featuring sharp and painful sounds—words that can be interpreted to show that he is ascribing a malign influence to the rainstorm. The idea is that the malignity is his, not Nature's.

Paragraphs 8, 9, and 10 contain a discussion of the rhymes of "Porphyria's Lover." A principal idea is that the fifth rhyming line of each five-line group, together with other characteristics of the rhyme, is to be construed as suggestive of the speaker's abnormality. Of special note is paragraph 10, which emphasizes the regularity of the rhyming words, but which demonstrates the echoing connection of rhymes earlier in the poem and rhymes at that point when the speaker describes his act of demented murder. The point here, as in all the other paragraphs of the essay, is that the versification, along with the diction of the poem, is a major avenue by which Browning expresses the poem's portrait of the speaker.

The last paragraph, 11, is a summarizing statement speaking about the fusing together of subject and style and also asserting that the poem's prosodic regularities, irregularities, and variations are consistent with the speaker's disturbed mental state.

Of greatest importance for the clarity of the essay are many supporting examples. Some of these are embodied within the essay, and others are set off in block style, accurately marked, and numbered by line. In any essay about prosody, readers may be unsure of the validity of the writer's observations unless such examples are provided and are clearly located within the poem.

Special Topics for Studying and Discussing Rhythm and Rhyme in Poetry

1. For Shakespeare's "Sonnet 73: That Time of Year Thou Mayst in Me Behold," analyze the ways in which Shakespeare creates his iambics. That is, what is the relationship of lightly accented syllables to the heavily accented ones? Where does Shakespeare use articles (*the*), pronouns (*this, his*), prepositions (*upon, against, of*), relative clause markers (*which, that*), and adverb clause markers (*as, when*) in relation to syllables of heavy stress? On the basis of this study, how would you characterize Shakespeare's control of the iambic foot?

2. Analyze the rhymes in one of the Shakespeare sonnets, or else the rhymes in Coleridge's "Kubla Khan" or Arnold's "Dover Beach," or another poem of your choice. What is interesting or unique about the various rhyming words? What relationships can you discover between the rhymes and the topics of the poems?

3. Compare one of the rhyming poems with one of the nonrhyming poems included in this book. What differences in reading and sound can you discover as a result of the use or nonuse of rhyme? What benefits does rhyme give to the poem? What benefits does nonrhyme give?

4. Analyze Hardy's use of rhymes in "Channel Firing." What effects does he create by rhyming words with trochaic rhythm, like *hatters* and *matters*, and also by rhyming three-syllable words (dactylic rhythms) *saner be* and *century?* What is the relationship of such rhymes to the rhymes that fall on heavy stresses in the poem?

5. Write a short poem of your own using rhymes with trochaic words or dactylic words such as *computer, emetic, scholastic, remarkable, along with me, inedible, moron, anxiously, emotion, fishing,* and so on. If you have trouble with exact rhymes, see what you can do with slant rhymes and eye rhymes. The idea is to use your ingenuity.

6. Using the topical index in your library, take out a book on prosody, such as Harvey Gross's *Sound and Form in Modern Poetry* (1968) or *The Structure of Verse* (1966), or Gay Wilson Allen's *American Prosody* (1935, reprinted 1966). Select a topic (e.g., formal or experimental prosody) or a poet (e.g., Frost, Arnold, Shakespeare, or Blake), and write a summary of the ideas and observations that the writers make on your subject. What relationship do the writers make between prosody and the poet's ideas? How does prosody enter into the writers' thoughts or into the ways in which the poets emphasize ideas and images?

14

Writing Essays of Comparison-Contrast and Extended Comparison-Contrast

Learning by Seeing Literary Works Together

Comparison-contrast analysis is the act of putting things side by side—juxtaposing them, looking at them together—for a variety of purposes such as description, enhanced understanding, evaluation, and decision making. The technique underlies other important techniques, specifically (1) the analysis of causes and effects; and (2) the scientific method of constant-and-variable analysis. Significant questions of all these methods are, How is *A* both like and unlike *B*? What are the causes of *A*? How does a change in *A* affect *B*? These are all questions that call into play the technique of comparison and contrast.

The educational significance of the technique is to encourage you to make connections—*one of the major aspects of productive thought.* As long as things *seem* different and disconnected they in fact *are* different and disconnected. In practice, they are two separate and distinct entities. But when you can discover that they have similarities and connections, then you can make relationships clear. You are in a position both to stress points of likeness and also to demonstrate just what makes things distinct and unique. For all these reasons, it is vital for you to find similarities and differences through the technique of comparison and contrast.

The immediate goals of a comparison-contrast essay on literary works is to compare and contrast different authors; two or more works by the same author; different drafts of the same work; or characters, incidents, techniques, and ideas in the same work or in a number of separate works. Developing a comparison-contrast analysis enables you to study works in perspective. No matter what works you consider together, the method helps you get at the essence of a work or writer. Similarities are brought out by comparison; differences, by contrast. In other words, you can enhance your understanding of what a thing *is* by using comparison-contrast to determine what it *is not.*

For example, our understanding of Shakespeare's "Sonnet 30: When to the Sessions of Sweet Silent Thought" may be enhanced if we compare it with Christina Rossetti's poem "Echo." Both poems treat personal recollections of past experiences, told by a speaker to a listener who is not intended to be the reader. Both also refer to persons, now dead, with whom the speakers were closely involved. In these respects, the poems are comparable.

In addition to these similarities, there are important differences. Shakespeare's speaker numbers the dead persons as friends whom he laments generally, whereas Rossetti refers specifically to one person with whom the speaker was in love. Rossetti's topic is the sorrow of dead love, the irrevocability of the past, and the present loneliness of the speaker. Shakespeare includes the references to dead friends as a way of accounting for present sorrows, but then his speaker turns to the present and asserts that thinking about the "dear friend" being addressed enables him to restore past "losses" and end all "sorrows." In Rossetti's poem, there is no reconciliation of past and present; instead the speaker focuses entirely upon the sadness of the present moment. Though both poems are retrospective, Shakespeare's poem looks toward the present, and Rossetti's looks to the past. These differences show how the poems may be contrasted.

Guidelines for the Comparison-Contrast Method

The preceding example, although brief, shows how the comparison-contrast method makes it possible to identify leading similarities and distinguishing differences in two works. Frequently you can overcome the difficulties you might encounter in understanding one work by comparing and contrasting it with another work on a comparable subject. A few guidelines will help direct your efforts in writing comparison-contrast essays.

Clarify Your Intention

When planning a comparison-contrast essay, first decide on your goal, for you can use the method in a number of ways. One objective is the equal and mutual illumination of two (or more) works. For example, an essay comparing Hardy's "The Three Strangers" with Hawthorne's "Young Goodman Brown" might compare ideas, characters, or methods in these stories equally, without stressing or favoring either. For most purposes, this method will prove most useful. If you wish to emphasize just one of the works, you might also use the comparison-contrast technique. Thus you might highlight "Young Goodman Brown" by using comparable material in "The Three Strangers" (and vice versa). You might also show your liking of a particular story, poem, or play at the expense of another, or emphasize a method or idea in one work that you do not find in the other work. The illustrative essay on pages 214–216 shows how the essayist brings out the superiority of one work over the other, at least in certain chosen qualities.

Find Common Grounds for Comparison

The second stage in preparing a comparison-contrast essay is to select and articulate a common ground for discussion. It is pointless to compare dissimilar things, for the resulting conclusions will not have much value. Instead, compare like with like: idea with idea, characterization with characterization, setting with setting, point of view with point of view, tone with tone. Nothing much can be learned from a comparison of Frost's view of individuality and Chekhov's view of love; but a comparison of the relationship of individuality with identity and character in Frost and Chekhov suggests common ground, with the promise of significant ideas to be developed through the examination of similarities and differences.

In seeking common ground, you will need to be inventive and creative. For instance, if you compare Maupassant's "The Necklace" (Chapter 1) and Chekhov's *The Bear*, these two works at first may seem dissimilar. Yet common ground can be discovered, such as the treatment of self-deceit, the effects of chance on human affairs, and the authors' views of women. Although other works may seem even more dissimilar than these, it is usually possible to find a common ground for comparison and contrast. Much of your success in an essay of this type depends on your finding a workable basis—a common denominator—for comparison.

Integrate the Bases of Comparison

Let us assume that you have decided on your rhetorical purpose and on the basis or bases of your comparison. You have done your reading and taken notes, and you have a rough idea of what you want to say. The remaining problem is the treatment of your material.

One method is to make your points first about one work and then about the other. Unfortunately, such a comparison makes your paper seem like two separate lumps. ("Work 1" takes up one half of your paper to make one lump, and "Work 2" takes up the other half to make a second lump.) Also, the method involves repetition because you must repeat many points when you treat the second subject.

Therefore, a better method is to treat the major aspects of your main idea and to refer to the two (or more) works as they support your arguments. Thus you refer constantly to *both* works, sometimes within the same sentence, and remind your reader of the point of your discussion. There are reasons for the superiority of this method: (1) You do not repeat your points needlessly, for you develop them as you raise them; (2) By constantly referring to the two works, you make your points without requiring a reader with a poor memory to reread previous sections.

Here is a paragraph on "Natural References as a Basis of Comparison in Frost's 'Desert Places' and Shakespeare's 'Sonnet 73: That Time of Year Thou Mayst in Me Behold.'" The virtue of the paragraph is that it uses material from each of the poems simultaneously as the substance for the development of the ideas, as nearly as the time sequence of sentences allows.

(1) Both Shakespeare and Frost link their ideas to events occurring in the natural world. (2) Night as a parallel with death is common to both poems, with Frost speaking about it in his first line and Shakespeare introducing it in his

seventh. (3) Along with night, Frost emphasizes the onset of winter and snow as a time of death and desolation. (4) With this natural description, Frost also symbolically refers to empty, secret, dead places in the inner spirit—crannies of the soul where bleak winter snowfalls correspond to selfishness and indifference. (5) By contrast, Shakespeare uses the fall season, with the yellowing and dropping of leaves and the migrations of birds, to stress the closeness of real death and therefore the need to love fully during the time remaining. (6) Both poems thus share a sense of gloom because both present death as inevitable and final, just like the emptiness of winter. (7) Because Shakespeare's sonnet is addressed to a listener who is also a loved one, however, it is more outgoing than the more introspective poem of Frost. (8) Frost turns the snow, the night, and the emptiness of the universe inward in order to show the speaker's inner bleakness, and by extension, the bleakness of many human spirits. (9) Shakespeare instead uses the bleakness of season, night, and dying fire to state the need for loving "well." (10) The poems thus use common references for differing purposes.

This paragraph links Shakespeare's references to nature to those of Frost. Five sentences speak of both authors together; three speak of Frost alone and two of Shakespeare alone, but all the sentences are unified topically. This interweaving of references indicates that the writer has learned both poems well enough to consider them together, and it also enables the writing to be more pointed and succinct than if the works were separately treated.

You can learn from this example: If you develop your essay by putting your two subjects constantly together, you will write economically and pointedly (not only for essays but also for tests). Beyond that, if you digest the material as successfully as this method indicates, you demonstrate that you are fulfilling a major educational goal—the assimilation and *use* of material. Too often, because you learn things separately (in separate works and courses, at separate times), you tend also to compartmentalize them. Instead, you should always try to relate them, to *synthesize* them. Comparison and contrast help in this process of putting together, of seeing things not as fragments but as parts of wholes.

Avoid the Tennis-Ball Method

As you make your comparison, do not confuse an interlocking method with a "tennis-ball" method, in which you bounce your subject back and forth constantly and repetitively, almost as though you were hitting observations back and forth over a net. The tennis-ball method is shown in the following example from a comparison of the characters Mathilde (Maupassant's "The Necklace") and Mrs. Popov (Chekhov's *The Bear*).

Mathilde is a young married woman; Mrs. Popov is also young but a widow. Mathilde has a limited social life, and she doesn't have more than one friend; Mrs. Popov chooses to lead a life of solitude. Mathilde's daydreams about wealth are responsible for her misfortune, and Mrs. Popov's dedication to the memory of her husband is capable of ruining her life. Mathilde is made unhappy because of her shortcomings, but Mrs. Popov is rescued despite her shortcomings. In Mathilde's case the focus is on adversity not only causing trouble but also strengthening character. Similarly, in Mrs. Popov's case the focus is on a strong person realizing her strength regardless of her conscious decision to weaken herself.

Imagine the effect of an entire essay written in this invariable 1, 2, 1, 2, 1, 2 order. Aside from the inflexible patterning of subjects, the tennis-ball method does not permit much illustrative development. You should not feel so constrained that you cannot take two or more sentences to develop a point about one writer or subject before you include comparative references to another. If you remember to interlock the two subjects of comparison, however, as in the paragraph about Frost and Shakespeare, your method will give you the freedom to develop your topics fully.

The Extended Comparison-Contrast Essay

For a longer essay about a number of works—such as a limited research paper, comprehensive exam questions, and the sort of extended essay required at the end of a semester—comparison-contrast is an essential method. You may wish to compare the works on the basis of elements such as ideas, plot, language, structure, character, metaphor, point of view, or setting. Because of the larger number of works, however, you will need to modify the way in which you employ comparison-contrast. Suppose you are considering not just two works but rather six, seven, or more. You need first to find a common ground to use as your central, unifying idea, just as you do for a comparison of only two works. Once you establish the common ground, you can classify or group your works on the basis of the similarities and differences they exemplify with regard to the topic. The idea is to get two *groups* for comparison, not just two works.

Let us assume that three or four works treat a topic in one way but that two or three do it in another (e.g., either criticism or praise of wealth and trade, the joys or sorrows of love, the enthusiasm of youth, gratitude for life, or the disillusionment of age). In writing about these works, you might treat the topic itself in a straightforward comparison-contrast method but use details from the works within the groupings as the material that you use for illustration and argument.

To make your essay as specific as possible, it is best to stress only a small number of works with each of your subpoints. Once you have established these points, there is no need to go into detail about all the other works. Instead, you need to make no more than brief references to the other works, for your purpose should be to strengthen your points without bulking up your essay with more and more examples. Once you go to another subpoint, you might then use different works for illustration, so that by the end of your essay you will have given due attention to each work in your assignment. In this

---

CITING REFERENCES IN A LONGER COMPARISON-CONTRAST ESSAY

For the longer comparison-contrast essay, you may find a problem in making references to many different works. Generally you do not need to repeat references. For example, if you refer to Louise of Chopin's "The Story of an Hour" or to Minnie Wright of Glaspell's *Trifles*, you should make the full references only once and then refer later just to the character, story, or author, according to your needs.

When you quote lines or passages or when you cite actions or characters in special ways, you should use parenthetical line, speech, or paragraph references, as in the illustrative essay. Be guided by the following principle: If you make a specific reference that you think your reader might want to examine in more detail, supply the line, speech, or paragraph number. If you refer to minor details that might easily be unnoticed or forgotten, also supply the appropriate number. Your intention should be to include the appropriate location numbers whenever you are in doubt about references.

---

way—by treating many works in small comparative groups—you can keep your essay reasonably free of excessive detail.

The illustrative essay on pages 217–219 shows how this grouping may be done. In the first part of the body of this essay, six works are used comparatively to show how private needs conflict with social, public demands. The next part shows how three works can be compared and contrasted on the basis of how they treat the topic of public concerns as expressed through law.

Writing a Comparison-Contrast Essay

In planning your essay, you should first narrow and simplify your topic so that you can handle it conveniently. If your subject is a comparison of two poets (as in the comparison-contrast essay on Donne and Wordsworth beginning on page 214), choose one or two of each poet's poems on the same or a similar topic, and write your essay about these.

Once you have found an organizing principle, along with the relevant works, begin to refine and focus the direction of your essay. As you study each work, note common or contrasting elements and use these to form your central idea. You can also select the most illustrative works and classify them according to your topic, such as war, love, work, faithfulness, or self-analysis.

Organize Your Comparison-Contrast Essay

Introduction   Begin by stating the works, authors, characters, or ideas that you are considering; then show how you have narrowed the topic. Your central idea should briefly highlight the principal grounds of comparison and contrast, such as that both works treat a common topic, exhibit a similar idea, use a similar form, or develop an identical attitude, and also that major or minor differences help make the works unique. You may also assert that one work is superior to the other, if you wish to make this judgment and defend it.

Body   The body of your essay is governed by the works and your basis of comparison (presentations of ideas, depictions of character, uses of setting, qualities of style and tone, uses of poetic form, uses of comparable imagery or symbols, uses of point of view, and so on). For a comparison-contrast treatment on such a basis, your goal should be to shed light on both (or more) of the works you are treating. For example, you might examine stories written in the first-person point of view. An essay on this topic might compare the ways in which each author uses point of view to achieve similar or distinct effects; or it might compare poems that employ similar images, symbols, or ironic methods. Sometimes, the process can be as simple as identifying female or male protagonists and comparing the ways in which their characters are developed. Another obvious approach is to compare the *subjects*, as opposed to the *idea*. You might identify works dealing with general subjects such as love, death, youth, race, or war. Such groupings provide a basis for excellent comparisons and contrasts.

As you develop your essay, remember to keep comparison-contrast foremost. That is, your discussions of point of view, figurative language, or whatever should not so much explain these topics *as topics* but rather should explore *similarities and differences* of the works you are comparing. If your topic is an idea, for example, you need to explain the idea, but just enough to establish points of similarity or difference. As you develop such an essay, you might illustrate your arguments by referring to related uses of elements such as setting, characterization, symbolism, point of view, or metaphor. When you introduce these new subjects, you will be on target as long as you use them in the context of comparison-contrast.

Conclusion   In concluding, you might reflect on other ideas or techniques in the works you have compared, make observations about similar qualities, or summarize briefly the grounds of your comparison. If there is a point you have considered especially important, you might stress that point again in your conclusion. Also, your comparison might have led you to conclude that one work—or group of works—is superior to another. Stressing that point again would make an effective conclusion.

Illustrative Essay (Comparing and Contrasting Two Works)

The Use of the Word "Westward" in Wordsworth's "Stepping Westward" and Donne's "Good Friday, 1613, Riding Westward"°

[1] The reason for comparing the two poems is obvious from the titles, and the similarities become more obvious as a person reads the poems. Both employ "westward" as the direction in which the speakers are moving. As they move, they become aware of mortality, since the west—where the sun sets and the day dies—is the traditional direction symbolizing death. The reality of this situation causes the speakers to meditate on religion and philosophy. There is a difference in the ways in which the speakers move. William Wordsworth's speaker *is stepping* westward, while John Donne's is *riding* (i.e., being carried). If these actions are interpreted symbolically, Wordsworth suggests that his speaker is guided primarily by will, whereas Donne suggests that his speaker's will is guided by elements of greater complexity. The poems bear out this distinction. <u>The differences are more noteworthy than the similarities, and Donne's poem emerges as more forceful and realistic than Wordsworth's.</u>* <u>This difference can be seen clearly in the ideas that both poets have about the forces that govern life.</u>[†]

[2] <u>The idea of moving westward, away from the east, prompts both poets to be concerned with the nature of life once death has been taken into account.</u> It appears that Wordsworth is raising a question that Donne has already answered. Wordsworth's speaker asks whether we are governed by chance—the *"wildish* destiny" (line 2)—or whether we are controlled by *"heavenly"* forces (11). He opts for the "heavenly" destiny to guide him on his "endless way" (26). Donne's speaker does not raise this question, however, for to him the heavenly destiny indeed exists; his idea, instead, is that his speaker is riding away from his destiny, since God is in the East, and "pleasure" and "business" are whirling his "soul," like a "sphere" westward away from God (7–10). Thus Donne uses the opposition of East and West to bring out a conflict between faith, on the one hand, and both pleasures and business activities, on the other—a conflict that is far different from the greater calm in Wordsworth's poem.

[3] <u>Donne's poem is not only more agitated than Wordsworth's, but it contains images demonstrating that Donne's view of life is more complex and difficult than Wordsworth's.</u> Donne's first image is, "Let man's soul be a sphere" (line 1). The individual soul, from this image, is a world in itself over which the forces of good and evil contend, and the loss of any individual is of cosmic significance. Donne's other image, since he is deeply concerned with religious topic matter, is that of "Christ on this Cross" (13). In Donne's paradoxical view, it is Christ who by dying made death an entry way into life. The westward direction of travel therefore becomes not only the direction of

---

°See pages 382–383 and 368–369 for these poems.
*Central idea.
[†]Thesis sentence.

death but also, paradoxically, of east, of life—heavenly life—since it is the direction in which one must travel to see God (lines 9–14):

> Hence is it, that I am carried towards the west
> This day, when my soul's form bends towards the east.
> There I should see a sun, by rising set,
> And by that setting endless day beget;
> But that° Christ on this Cross, did rise and fall,
> Sin had eternally benighted all.

This passage, ending with the word *all*, demonstrates that it is all human souls, not only the speaker's soul, that are in the balance. The conflict is thus not just personal, it is common to all human beings. On the one hand they see the good, but on the other they do not follow it. As they avoid God, however, they move toward death, which is another and more permanent way toward God. Donne's world, in short, is much more complex and difficult than Wordsworth's.

[4] This is not to imply that Wordsworth interprets life as easy, for "In a strange Land and far from home" his speaker observes that "The dewy ground was dark and cold; / Behind, all gloomy to behold" (4, 9, 10). But Wordsworth's poem is not as forceful as Donne's. For example, after Wordsworth's speaker decides that his destiny is "heavenly," the dark, dewy ground is somehow transformed into a "region bright" (16). By contrast, Donne's sphere (the soul) is constantly "Subject to foreign motions," such as business and personal affairs, which drive it away from its heavenly destiny, corroding it and deforming it. His speaker therefore ends the poem in anguished prayer, asking God to purify his life so that he can withstand death (lines 39–42):

> O think me worth thine anger, punish me,
> Burn off my rusts, and my deformity,
> Restore thine Image, so much, by thy grace,
> That thou may'st know me, and I'll turn my face.

[5] Thus, for Donne, the only salvation in this difficult life is God's love, which enabled the pain of Jesus on the Cross, where His flesh was "raged and torn" (28). Paradoxically again, God dying on the Cross is a sight on which the speaker "durst not look." Consequently his ride westward is a direct result of his own weakness, for which God is the only remedy. These are contorted and tortuous ideas, which contrast sharply with Wordsworth's emphasis on "human sweetness" and "The very sound of courtesy" (24, 20). Both ideas are in accord in claiming the individual's dependency for support on something external. Donne's thought, however, is filled with visions of pain, uncertainty, anguish, and paradox, whereas Wordsworth's is characterized by greater calm, certainty, and simplicity.

[6] The principal difference between the two poems is that Donne's view of life is more difficult and anguished than Wordsworth's and thus Donne's poem is more comprehensive and more truthful. This difference is perhaps the same one that exists between an ending on the note that "they lived happily

---

°*But that:* unless.

ever after" and a psychological study that examines human problems and uncertainties. This is not to say that Wordsworth does not bring out personal conflicts elsewhere, as in *The Prelude* and the "Ode on the Intimations of Immortality," both of which deal with some of life's pain and anguish. Nor does Wordsworth direct our thought to the pain of the Crucifixion, as Donne's Good Friday poem does. With regard to these two poems, however, Wordsworth seems to end where Donne begins.

Work Cited

Donne, John, "Good Friday, 1613, Riding Westward," and William Wordsworth, "Stepping Westward." Edgar V. Roberts. *Writing About Literature.* 11th ed. Upper Saddle River: Prentice Hall, 2006. 382–383 and 368–369.

Commentary on the Essay

This essay shows how a writer can use comparison and contrast to emphasize the apparent superiority of one work over another. Words stressing similarity are *both employ, the poems bear out, both poets, in accord,* and *more.* Contrasts are stressed by *there is a difference, by contrast, more forceful and realistic, far different from,* and *however.* Transitions from paragraph to paragraph are not different in this type of essay from those in other essays. Thus, the phrases *prompts both poets, this is not to imply, not only . . . but also,* and *thus,* which are used here, could be used in any other essay, with necessary modifications for other topics, for the same transitional purpose.

The central idea—that the poems are inspired by a common topic but that Donne's poem is superior to Wordsworth's—is brought out in paragraph 1, together with the supporting idea that the poems differ on the issue of motivational complexity.

Paragraph 2, the first in the body, contrasts differences between the two poems. Paragraph 3 is actually mostly devoted to Donne, although there are also two comparative references to Wordsworth. This technique demonstrates that it is not necessary to provide exactly equal attention to each writer. Because Donne's poem develops the paradoxical nature of Donne's thought, more detail on Donne is necessary to develop the full comparison and contrast here. Similarly, paragraph 4 devotes virtually equal time to the two poems, but again, the emphasis is on the superiority of Donne.

Paragraph 5, the last in the body, begins with three sentences being devoted to Donne, but the last three sentences consider both poems together, weighing them and contrasting them in accord with the essay's central idea.

The conclusion, paragraph 6, summarizes the central idea, and it also treats both poems approximately equally while also stressing that Donne's poem, through its complex view of life, is more comprehensive and truthful than Wordsworth's.

Illustrative Essay (Extended Comparison-Contrast)

Literary Treatments of Conflicts Between Private and Public Life

[1] <u>The conflict between private or personal life, on the one hand, and public or civic and national life, on the other, is a topic common to many literary works.</u>° Authors show that individuals try to maintain their personal lives and commitments even though they are tested and stressed by public and external forces. Ideally, individuals should have the freedom to follow their own wishes independently of the outside world. It is a fact, however, that living itself causes people to venture into the public world and therefore to encounter conflicts. Getting married, following a profession, observing the natural world, looking at a person's possessions, taking a walk—all these draw people into the public world in which rules, regulations, and laws override private wishes. To greater and lesser degrees, such conflicts are found in Arnold's "Dover Beach," Bierce's "An Occurrence at Owl Creek Bridge," Chekhov's *The Bear*, Glaspell's *Trifles*, Chopin's "The Story of an Hour," Hardy's "Channel Firing," Hawthorne's "Young Goodman Brown," Keats's "Bright Star," Layton's "Rhine Boat Trip," Lowell's "Patterns," Shakespeare's "Sonnet 73: That Time of Year Thou Mayst in Me Behold," and Wordsworth's "Lines Written in Early Spring."* <u>In these works, conflicts are shown between interests of individuals and those of the social, legal, and military public.</u>†

[2] <u>One of the major private-public conflicts is created by the way in which characters respond to social conventions and expectations.</u> In Chekhov's *The Bear*, for example, Mrs. Popov has given up her personal life to memorialize her dead husband. She wears black, stays in her house for a whole year, and swears eternal fidelity; and she does all this to fulfill what she considers her public role as a grieving widow. Fortunately for her, Smirnov arrives on the scene and arouses her enough to make her give up this deadly pose. Not as fortunate is Hawthorne's Goodman Brown in "Young Goodman Brown." Brown's obligation is much less public and also more philosophical than Mrs. Popov's because his religiously inspired vision of evil fills him with lifelong gloom. Although Mrs. Popov is easily moved away from her position by the prospect of immediate life and vitality, Brown's mindless distrust locks him into a fear of evil from which not even his own faithful wife can shake him. The two characters therefore go in entirely different directions—one toward personal fulfillment, the other toward personal destruction.

[3] <u>A major idea in the various works is that philosophical or religious difficulties such as those of Goodman Brown force a crisis in an individual life.</u> In Arnold's "Dover Beach" the speaker expresses regret about uncertainty and the loss of religious faith that symbolically wear away civilization just like

---

°Central idea.
*See Appendix C for these works (except for Sonnet 73, which appears in Chapter 5).
†Thesis sentence.

surf beating on the stones of Dover Beach. This situation might be expected to make a person as dreary and depressed as Goodman Brown actually is. Arnold's speaker, however, in the lines "Ah, love, let us be true / To
one another," finds power in personal fidelity and commitment (lines
29–30). In other words, the public world of "human misery" and the dimin-
ishing "Sea of Faith" is beyond control, and therefore all that is left is personal commitment. This is not to say that "Young Goodman Brown," as a
story, is negative, for Hawthorne implies that a positive personal life lies in
the denial of choices like those made by Brown and in the acceptance of
choices like those made by Mrs. Popov and Arnold's speaker.

[4] To deny or to ignore the public world is a possible option that, under some
circumstances, can be chosen. For example, "Dover Beach" reflects a conscious decision to ignore the philosophic and religious uncertainty that the
speaker finds in the intellectual and public world. Even more independent
of such a public world, Shakespeare's "That Time of Year" and Keats's
"Bright Star" bring out their ideas as reflections on purely personal situations. Shakespeare's speaker deals with the love between himself and the
listener, whereas Keats's speaker, addressing a distant star, considers his
need for steadfastness in his relationship with his "fair love." Louise, the
major character in Chopin's "The Story of an Hour," embodies an interesting variation on the personal matters brought up in these two sonnets. At
first, Louise is prostrated by the news coming from the public world
through the medium of telegraph that her husband has been killed. Her
first vision of herself is that of a grieving, private widow. As she thinks
about things, however, she quickly begins to anticipate the liberation and
freedom—to become free to explore the public world—that widowhood will
give her. Ironically, it is the reappearance of her husband, who moves
freely in the public world, that causes her sudden heart failure and death.
What she looked forward to as the free choice to do what she wants and
to go where she wishes has suddenly been withdrawn from her by her renewed status within the publicly sanctioned system of marriage, and it is
her recognition of her abrupt loss of this private possibility that ends her
life.

[5] The complexity of the conflicts between private and public life is brought
out in the way in which structures secure their power through law and legality. With immense power, the law often acts as an arbitrary form of public judgment that disregards personal needs and circumstances. This idea
is brought out on the most personal level in Glaspell's *Trifles*, in which the
two major characters, both women, urgently confront the conflict between
their personal identification with the accused woman, Minnie, and their
public obligation to the law. One of the women, Mrs. Peters, is reminded
that she is "married to the law," but she and Mrs. Hale suppress the evidence that they know would condemn Minnie, even though technically—by
law, that is—their knowledge is public property. Their way of resolving the
conflict is therefore to accept personal obligations to the self rather than to
the public.

[6] The legal conflict is also treated more generally and philosophically in
some works. For example, Wordsworth deals with the morality—or

immorality—of the conflict in "Lines Written in Early Spring," when he says, "Have I not reason to lament / What man has made of man" (lines 15–16). "What man has made of man" in its most extreme form is legalized suppression and persecution, but Wordsworth does little more with the topic than to say that he laments it. Layton, however, in "Rhine Boat Trip," deals with the extremity of human cruelty. In this poem, Layton condemns the Nazi exterminations of "Jewish mothers" and "murdered rabbis" during the Holocaust of World War II. Ironically, the exterminations were carried out legally, for it has commonly been observed that the Nazis created laws to justify all their moral atrocities.

[7] <u>It is works about warfare that especially highlight how irreconcilable the conflicts between personal and public concerns can become.</u> A comic but nevertheless real instance is dramatized by Hardy in "Channel Firing." In this poem, set in a church graveyard, the skeleton of "Parson Thirdly" views "gunnery practice out at sea" (line 10) as evidence that his "forty year" dedication to serving his church was a total waste. His conclusion is that he would have been better off ignoring his public role and instead sticking "to pipes and beer." Although Thirdly is disillusioned, he has not been as deeply affected personally by warfare as the speaker of Lowell's "Patterns." Her fiancé, she learns, has been killed fighting abroad; and his death leads her to question—and by implication to doubt—the external "patterns" that destroy one's personal plans for life (line 107). Unlike both these characters, who are deeply touched by the effects of warfare, Peyton Farquhar, the main character in Bierce's "An Occurrence at Owl Creek Bridge," is actually killed by his commitment to a public concern—that of the Southern forces in the Civil War. As in "Channel Firing" and "Patterns," Farquhar's situation shows the absolute power of the public world over the private.

[8] The works examined here are in general agreement that, under ideal conditions, private life should be supreme over public life. They also demonstrate that in many ways, the public world invades the private world with a wide range of effects, from making people behave foolishly to destroying them utterly. Naturally, the tone of the works is shaped by the degree of seriousness of the conflict. Chekhov's *The Bear* is good-humored and farcical because the characters overcome the social roles in which they are cast. More sober are works such as "Dover Beach" and "Young Goodman Brown," in which characters either are overcome by public commitments or deliberately turn their backs on them. In the highest range of seriousness are works such as "Rhine Boat Trip," "Patterns," and "An Occurrence at Owl Creek Bridge," in which individuals are crushed by irresistible public forces. <u>The works compared and contrasted here show varied and powerful conflicts between public demands and personal interests.</u>

Work Cited

Roberts, Edgar V. *Writing About Literature.* 11th ed. Upper Saddle River: Prentice Hall, 2006. 363, 317–322, 384–392, 392–400, 323–324, 370–371, 340–348, 374, 375–377, 102–103, 381–382.

Commentary on the Essay

This essay, combining for discussion all three genres of fiction, poetry, and drama, is visualized as an assignment climaxing a unit of study. The expectation prompting the assignment is that a fairly large number of literary works can be profitably compared on the basis of a unifying subject, idea, or technique. For this essay, the works—seven poems, three stories, and two short plays—are compared and contrasted on the common topic of private-public conflicts. It is obviously impossible to discuss all the works in detail in every paragraph. The essay therefore demonstrates that a writer may introduce a large number of works in a straightforward comparison-contrast method without a need for detailed comparison of each work with every other work on each of the major subtopics (social, legal, military).

Thus, the first section, consisting of paragraphs 2–4, treats six of the works. In paragraph 2, however, only two works are discussed, and in paragraph 3 one of these works is carried over for comparison with only one additional work. The fourth paragraph springs out of the second, utilizing one of the works discussed there and then bringing out comparisons with three additional works.

The same technique is used in the rest of the essay. Paragraph 5 introduces only one work; paragraph 6 introduces two additional works; and paragraph 7 introduces three works for comparison and contrast. Each of the twelve works is then eventually discussed at least once in terms of how it contributes to the major topic. One might note that the essay concentrates on a relatively small number of the works, such as Chekhov's *The Bear* and Hawthorne's "Young Goodman Brown," but that as newer topics are introduced, the essay goes on to works that are more closely connected to these topics.

The technique of extended comparison-contrast used in this way shows how the various works can be defined and distinguished in relation to the common idea—the contrast between personal and public life. The concluding paragraph summarizes these distinctions by suggesting a continuous line along which each of the works may be placed.

Even so, the treatment of so many texts might easily cause crowding and confusion. The division of the major topic into subtopics, as noted, is a major means of trying to make the essay easy to follow. An additional means is the introduction of transitional words and phrases such as *also, choose,* and *one of the major conflicts.*

An extended comparison-contrast essay cannot present a full treatment of each of the works. The works are unique, and they deal independently with many things that are outside the topic of this essay. Ideas that are particularly important in Hardy's "Channel Firing," for example, are (1) that human beings need eternal rest and not eternal life; (2) that God is amused by—or indifferent to—human affairs; (3) that religious callings or vocations may be futile; and (4) that war itself is the supreme form of cruelty. All these topics could be treated in another essay, but they do not pertain to the goals of this particular essay. A topic compatible with the general private-public topic is needed, and the connection is readily made (paragraph 7) through the character of Hardy's Parson Thirdly. Because the essay deals with the conflicts brought out by Thirdly's comments, Hardy's poem is linked to all the other works for comparative purposes. So it is with the other works, each of which could also be the subject of analysis from many standpoints other than comparison-contrast. The effect of the comparison of all the works collectively, however, is the enhanced understanding of each of the works separately. To achieve such an understanding and to explain it are the major goals of the extended comparison-contrast method.

Special Topics for Studying and Discussing Comparison and Contrast

1. The use of the speaker in Arnold's "Dover Beach" and Wordsworth's "Lines Written in Early Spring."

2. The description of fidelity to love in Keats's "Bright Star" and Shakespeare's "Sonnet 73: That Time of Year Thou Mayst in Me Behold," or in Arnold's "Dover Beach" and Lowell's "Patterns."

3. The view of women in Chekhov's *The Bear* and Maupassant's "The Necklace" or in Glaspell's *Trifles* and Mansfield's "Miss Brill."

4. The use of descriptive scenery in Hawthorne's "Young Goodman Brown" and Lowell's "Patterns," or in Poe's "The Masque of the Red Death" and Bierce's "An Occurrence at Owl Creek Bridge."

5. Symbols of disapproval in Hardy's "Channel Firing" and Frost's "Desert Places."

6. The treatment of loss in Shakespeare's "Sonnet 30: When to the Sessions of Sweet Silent Thought" and Wagner's "The Boxes."

7. Treatments of racial prejudice and hate crime in Randall's "Ballad of Birmingham" and Hughes's "Negro."

8. Any of the foregoing topics applied to a number of separate works.

15

Writing a Review Essay

Developing Ideas and Evaluating Literary Works for General or Particular Audiences

The **review** is a general essay on a literary work. It may also be thought of as a "critique," a "critical review," an "evaluation," or simply an "essay." It is a free form, for in a review virtually everything is relevant—subject matter, technique, social and intellectual background, biographical facts, relationship to other works by the same author or by different authors, historical importance, and everything else. Unless you become a professional writer in the future, a review is the most likely kind of writing about literature that you may ever be called upon to do. Many businesses, associations, guilds, and other organizations issue regular newsletters or have meetings in which members are asked to discuss various subjects. Often, members of such groups are interested in learning about various works and authors—not only recent ones, but also well-known and well-established ones—and hence there is a need for good reviews.

A major aim of review writing is to provide a general overview of the work, especially including an evaluation of the author's performance, together with other elements of the work that you should mention, special difficulties that you explain, and special features that you note.

Since the review provides for freedom of topics and development, it is a challenge to the skills you have acquired thus far as a disciplined reader. Much of your experience has been *assimilation*—acquiring information and applying skills. Your tasks have been fulfilling assignments that you are given in your classes. But with a review, you are left to your own devices; you must decide what to write about as well as what to say. Freedom of choice is a constant goal, and your experience is equipping you to know what to do with this freedom. You should not only know how to answer questions but should also decide on the questions to be asked. You should be able to synthesize your knowledge.

Writing a Review Essay

Because reviews can be personal as well as objective, you may experiment with form and development. If you write about only a single topic, be sure to emphasize the various aspects with clear transitions. The third illustrative essay, for example, shows how the subject of faith or trust may be pursued throughout a review. Should you be writing a general review and select a number of topics, as in the first illustrative essay, be sure that your thesis sentence lists these topics.

Raise Questions to Discover Ideas

- Who are the people for whom you intend your review? Are they a general audience or part of a particular group? What are the special interests of the group? What general interests do people in the group have in common?

- How much detail, special or general, do you think you should include about the work itself? How much knowledge does your audience expect you to demonstrate in your review? Should you introduce references to comparable works by the same author or by different authors?

- Have the people who make up your audience read the work? Should you design your review to be a substitute for their reading the work? Should your review be designed to interest people in reading the work themselves?

- When was the work written? Just recently, or a long time ago? What is the nationality of the author (if he or she is of another nationality)? What kind of background knowledge is needed for an understanding of the work, or what kind, and how much, is supplied by the author (for example, a knowledge of military circumstances, of "old time" religion, of conditions in rural England or rural America)?

- To what genre does the work belong? What general issues need explaining before you begin your discussion of the work?

- What parts of the work are significant enough to warrant discussion in your review? What issues does the work bring out? What are the author's thoughts about these issues? How important are these thoughts? How timely is the work for today's readers?

- Do any particular characters, situations, or ideas stand out in the work you are reviewing? What are these? Why are they significant?

- What aspects of the writer's style and presentation are worthy of mention? How fully do you think you can refer to these without losing your audience's interest?

Organize Your Review Essay

Introduction In your introduction, you should place the work in perspective. Although most frequently you will be asked to review a play or novel, it is good to bear in mind that you may also be writing a review about acting techniques or play production. If you are reviewing a new edition of an old work, you may be judging the relevance of the past to the present, and you may also be judging the apparatus supplied by the editor. Always try to show that your work has relevance to the present group of readers.

Body   In the body, you should try either to arouse interest in the work or to discourage readers from reading the work if it seems to dictate this conclusion.

Beyond providing introductory information, your principal objective is to describe the strengths and weaknesses of the work. To write such a description, you must call into play just about everything you have learned about analyzing literature for ideas, form, and style. In a sense, the review can be as specific as you wish to make it, because the greatest part of the body should be given to analysis. In this analysis, you should try to bring out your own strengths and interests as a critical reader. It may be, for example, that you have become proficient in discussing ideas. Suppose that you observe intricately developed ideas in the work. You might choose to discuss that element in the body of your review, thereby appealing to your reader's interest in thought and ideas. You should always recognize, however, that your discussion should be of limited extent. There is no need for a detailed, word-by-word analysis. It is not an essay on ideas, style, or artistic qualities that you want, but a review emphasizing such elements.

For specialized reviews you might call into play those disciplines that have interested you thus far in your college career. For example, you may feel competent in handling ideas connected with sociology. Hence, in your review of a novel you might bring your sociological awareness to bear on the work. Or you may have developed an interest in psychology and might treat the characters in a work according to your understanding of psychological problems.

Whatever your personal interests and specialties may be, however, your best guide for subject matter is the work itself, which might well channel your thinking along definite lines. For example, the second illustrative essay relates the obvious character flaw of the hero of "Young Goodman Brown" to religious concerns (for an audience of people interested in religion). The third illustrative essay adopts the position that the same story literally compels readers to consider the psychological importance of personal certainty and security. In the work you are assigned, you may similarly find that certain features will point you in a specific direction (the humor, a connection with existential philosophy, reflections on economic or social conditions, the nature of life on the frontier, and so on).

Conclusion   Your conclusion should be an attempt to evaluate the work, certainly not extensively, but at least you should give an outline of your responses and a suggestion to your readers of how they might respond—assuming that you have shown that your interests coincide approximately with theirs. If the body of your review has emphasized evaluation, you should close your essay with a simple resumé of your points. If you are ever asked to review a work in, say no more than 150 words, the greatest part of the review should be devoted to evaluation.

Illustrative Essay (A Review for General Readers)

Hawthorne's Story "Young Goodman Brown":° A View of Mistaken Zeal

[1] "Young Goodman Brown" is an allegorical story by Nathaniel Hawthorne (1804–1864), the major American writer who probed deeply into the relationships between religion and guilt. Hawthorne's story is set in colonial Salem during the days of religious Puritanism. His major aim is to expose the weakness in the religious view that stresses the shortcomings and sins of human life.* Although this concern may seem narrow, the story itself is timely, presenting a dreamlike narrative, a realistic analysis of the growth of intolerance, and a number of questions of permanent importance.†

[2] On the surface, the apparent vagueness and dreamlike nature of Hawthorne's details may leave some readers a little baffled. The action is a nighttime trip by Young Goodman Brown to a mysterious satanic gathering in a deep forest just outside the village of Salem. Brown begins his walk as a friendly youth, just three months married to a young woman named Faith. The cult-gathering disillusions and embitters him, however. He loses his faith, and he spends the rest of his life in pessimism and gloom. This much is clear, but the precise nature of Brown's experience is not. Does he really make a trip into the woods? It would seem so, but by the story's end, Hawthorne states that the whole episode may have been no more than a dream or nightmare, and he speaks about it as such. Yet when the morning comes, Brown walks back into town as though he is returning from an overnight trip, and he recoils in horror from a number of his fellow villagers, including his wife. Just as uncertain is the identity of the stranger whom Brown encounters on the path. The man resembles Brown's father, but his serpentlike walking stick suggests the devil, who later presides at the satanic ritual deep within the forest.

[3] The fact is, however, that Hawthorne was clearly not interested in producing a realistic imitation of life in detail. Rather he wanted to get at the inward, psychological reality of persons like Goodman Brown, who mistakenly build a wall of anger and bitterness between themselves and the people around them. From this perspective, Brown's walk into the forest is a symbol of one of the ways in which people may turn sour. In Brown's case, he falls under the control of his will to condemn evil. So strong is his view that he rejects anyone not measuring up, even if he must live the rest of his life spiritually alone as a result. Although he is at the extreme edge, he is like many who cannot forgive and get along with anyone who is different.

°See pages 340–348 for this story.
*Central idea.
†Thesis sentence.

[4] Brown is thus anything but heroic, even if he is the story's major character. Nevertheless, the story is provocative and compelling, and it raises many timely questions. For example, how can something that is designed for human salvation, like the religious system that Brown inherited, lead its followers into disastrous mistakes? Does the failure result from the people who misunderstand the basic message of the system, or from the system itself? To what degree can the religious structure of the story be related to political and social institutions? Should any religious or political philosophy be given greater importance than the goodwill that is the cornerstone of society? Could any free society survive for long if it were composed of persons like Goodman Brown after his dream, or would it turn into some form of absolutism or despotism, and soon be reduced to persecution on moral, religious, or political grounds?

[5] Although the materials of the story belong to Salem during the late seventeenth century—the location, one might remember, of the infamous witchcraft trials—it has many layers. It is a memorable study in spiritual deterioration and a vivid example of the need for trust and goodwill in human relationships. Without such will, life itself would soon resemble the life lived by Goodman Brown, whose vision makes his world bleak and forbidding—a place controlled by negation and death rather than understanding and acceptance.

Work Cited

Hawthorne, Nathaniel. "Young Goodman Brown." Edgar V. Roberts. *Writing About Literature.* 11th ed. Upper Saddle River: Prentice Hall, 2006. 340–348.

Commentary on the Essay

This general review follows a normal pattern of exposition. The introduction briefly presents essential background, and it states a central idea about the timeliness of Hawthorne's ideas. Paragraph 2 deals with the problem of the dreamlike vagueness of the narrative. Paragraph 3 contains an explanation of the vagueness inasmuch as Hawthorne's point is to dramatize the way in which people become intolerant. Paragraph 4 treats the timeliness of this analysis in terms of important questions raised by the story. The last paragraph is a short tribute to the quality of Hawthorne's insights.

Throughout this illustrative review, the purpose is not to examine any of the points in great depth, but rather to give readers topics to consider in detail when they themselves consider the work.

Illustrative Essay (Designed for a Particular Group; Here, a Religious Group)

Religious Intolerance and Hawthorne's Story "Young Goodman Brown"°

[1] <u>Even though Hawthorne's allegorical story "Young Goodman Brown" is set in late seventeenth-century colonial Massachusetts, it continues to have great significance for religious people today.</u>* The tale is about the shattering of the principal character's illusions about human beings as a result of his witnessing a nightmarish witches' Sabbath in a forest. Brown becomes a despairing person and deprives those around him of love and light. This material could easily be interpreted psychologically or politically, but the Christian context of the story invites discussion of Hawthorne's religious ideas. <u>His significant message is both timely and biblically sound.</u>†

[2] <u>The story is timely because it deals with—rather exposes—the development of religious intolerance.</u> One would like to dismiss the topic as a dead issue in today's world. The reality is otherwise. Intolerance has not vanished along with seventeenth-century Salem, but it is still here and will continue to be as long as misperception and distrust like Brown's can exist. He sets up his own religious standards, and no one else can measure up. Surely this formula spells intolerance, no matter when it happens.

[3] <u>The Bible, a work that is at once both ancient and current, is the basis for "Young Goodman Brown."</u> It is true that scripture can be used to justify intolerant views like those by which Goodman Brown judges his fellow Salem residents. We may presume that people in Brown's day, like many in our own, have often been urged to seek perfection (for example, Genesis 17:1; Matthew 5:48). Almost all the letters of Paul, together with the Pastoral and General epistles, give advice to Christians to purify life (see Romans 12; Ephesians 5:6; I Timothy 5:22; James 4:8). There is no shortage of such advice. Indeed, there is so much that one might believe, as Brown does, that persons seemingly ignoring it cannot continue to call themselves Christian.

[4] <u>More positively, however, the rigorous side of things seems to represent no more than a partial view of the biblical message.</u> Nowhere does the Bible say that those who do not measure up should be condemned by *people*. The task of judgment, and even of vengeance if necessary, belongs to God alone (see Psalms 94:1 and Romans 12:19, for example). For human beings, the Bible constantly stresses forgiveness, and this is what Brown lacks. Here are only two of the many passages emphasizing forgiveness:

°See pages 340–348 for this story.
*Central idea.
†Thesis sentence.

> When ye stand praying, forgive, if ye have ought against any; that your Father also which is in heaven may forgive you your trespasses. (Mark 11:25)

> Forbearing one another, and forgiving one another, if any man have a quarrel against any: even as Christ forgave you, so also do ye. (Colossians 3:13)

One can go beyond advice like this to examples such as those of the Good Samaritan (Luke 10:29–31) and the Samaritan woman at the Well (John 4:7–42). These people were outsiders, not members of the same community, yet Jesus regarded them lovingly.

[5] <u>Charity, love, forgiveness, and toleration—these are virtues that people need today and that were needed in seventeenth-century Salem, but Goodman Brown ignores them totally.</u> He suffers from the "holier-than-thou" symptom that does nothing so well as to alienate others. It is no wonder that his offspring following him to his grave "carved no hopeful verse upon his tombstone, for his dying hour was gloom." Certainly we should all strive for perfection, but we should also leave judgment in greater hands, and rather spend our time working toward understanding. In "Young Goodman Brown," Hawthorne has dramatized this point vividly and powerfully.

Work Cited

Hawthorne, Nathaniel. "Young Goodman Brown." Edgar V. Roberts. *Writing About Literature.* 11th ed. Upper Saddle River: Prentice Hall, 2006. 340–348.

Commentary on the Essay

This illustrative review is intended for an audience concerned about religious issues. As such it considers the story not as a general work of art but as one with religious and moral implications. The essay works in two directions: first, as a presentation of arguments favoring religious tolerance; and second, as an attempt to supply enough Biblical background to show that the views in Hawthorne's story are based in scripture. The aim of the review is thus just as much persuasion as exposition and argument.

The first paragraph introduces the central idea about the story's religious significance, concluding with the essay's thesis sentence. Paragraph 2 demonstrates that misperceptions such as Brown's can occur at any time; therefore the story is about a permanent human condition. Paragraphs 3 and 4 deal with biblical passages that possibly have a bearing, first, on explaining Brown's conduct (3) and, second, criticizing it (4). This material is not the sort that one might bring out in an analysis of, say, the ideas in the work, because it deals more with the Bible than with the story. Nevertheless it is appropriate here because a review is to be considered as a much freer form than an analysis. The last paragraph utilizes the negative example of Brown as an incentive for tolerance.

Although this illustrative review deals with religious issues, it does so because of the intended audience. For an audience with other interests, a different treatment would be appropriate, even for the same work of literature.

Illustrative Essay (A Personal Review for a General Audience)

Security and Hawthorne's Story "Young Goodman Brown"°

[1] The major prop of life is security and certainty. These elements of stability stem from confidence in the people around us, secure laws, a sound economy, hope, and trust in ourselves and in the world generally. <u>The loss of any of these stabilizing props destroys our security and may produce panic.</u>* It is this kind of panic that Nathaniel Hawthorne portrays in his story "Young Goodman Brown." The major character is young Brown, who is a resident of seventeenth-century colonial Salem. Deep in a nighttime forest, he witnesses a nightmarish Satanic cult meeting, and because he sees his wife there together with the elders and dignitaries of the town, he loses the security that comes from confidence in others. <u>His story makes one think about the importance of the many things—personal, political, and natural—that provide us with a secure outlook on life.</u>†

[2] Personal security can depend on almost as many situations as there are people. Vital to Brown is his belief in the purity of his wife, Faith. Many people similarly base their lives on their confidence in those around them. But much can happen to disturb such security. Friends on whom we count might not be helpful when we need them because we badly misjudged them. A serious illness of someone close may have a devastating effect on confidence in the continuity of life itself. And, like Brown, we might imprison ourselves in our own suspicions and never again be able to trust anyone else. Personal security is delicate, even though the example of Brown, who does not try to explore the truth of his shattered illusions, shows that efforts at understanding might help to restore personal security that is mortally threatened.

°See pages 340–348 for this story.
*Central idea.
†Thesis sentence.

[3] <u>If personal security is fragile, political security is even more so.</u> At election times, there are always claims and counterclaims, so that we are never absolutely sure about the political wisdom we follow. Like many people, Brown loses faith in the local dignitaries, and he can never participate again with confidence in church and home. Today, on a world scale, we have even greater problems with our security, for happenings both abroad and in our nation disturb financial security and also threaten our very lives with distant hatreds and senseless attacks, which constantly verge on becoming big enough to cause the beginning of general wars. Certainly, political security is worth the many years of constant negotiating spent by diplomats in trying to gain it.

[4] <u>In the natural world, too, we assume a great deal on which we depend absolutely.</u> We cannot drive around a blind corner without the confidence that the road will continue, even though we cannot see it before we make our turns. We normally assume that the sun will rise and set, that rain will fall, that crops will grow (or at least appear in stores and cafés), that the air will be breathable, and that the earth generally will be a good place. But often there are fires, famines, tornadoes, earthquakes, floods, hurricanes, and volcanic eruptions. What occurs to Goodman Brown is, to him, a psychological equivalent, for his world is shattered by the dreams (or nightmares) of a single night. Such events can make people doubt the very ground they walk on.

[5] <u>The upshot of Hawthorne's story is that security—confidence about the world and people—is subject to accident and also design.</u> It is true, nevertheless, that people can work to make themselves more secure. Perhaps Brown's greatest flaw is that he apparently does not try to get to the bottom of what he has seen. He accepts his vision without question and, with his security destroyed, he descends into a life of "gloom" and depression. It is the possibility that people can always try at least to make things better that provides a gauge by which to measure Brown and also ourselves. One should be grateful to Hawthorne for having pointed the way so memorably to these ideas.

Work Cited

Hawthorne, Nathaniel. "Young Goodman Brown." Edgar V. Roberts. *Writing About Literature*. 11th ed. Upper Saddle River: Prentice Hall, 2006. 340–348.

Commentary on the Essay

This illustrative review is a personal essay on a topic—security—suggested by Hawthorne's story. The material from "Young Goodman Brown" is thus introduced as a part, although a major part, of the train of thought. The method of development is primarily illustration.

Unlike the religiously based audience visualized for the second illustrative essay, the audience intended here is a general one concerned with many broad topics, such as the personal, political, and natural ones discussed. The goal is to cause readers to reconsider and redefine the topic of security.

Paragraph 1 introduces security as a topic, attempts a definition, relates the topic to Hawthorne's story, and concludes with the essay's thesis sentence. Even though "Young Goodman Brown" is a religious story about how the hero's perceptions of life are destroyed by the Devil, the body of the illustrative essay does not deal with the story's religious issues, but instead goes into three separate though connected topics. Paragraph 2 deals with the first of these—personal situations that threaten personal security. Paragraph 3 considers political threats, and paragraph 4 brings in references to threats from the forces of nature. The concluding paragraph includes additional references to Goodman Brown, relating his passiveness to a need for a more aggressive pursuit of security.

Special Topics for Studying and Discussing the Writing of Reviews

Write reviews on any one of the following topics, being sure to consider the audiences for whom the review is intended.

1. A review of Glaspell's *Trifles* for people interested in law and the sentencing of offenders.
2. A review of Wagner's "The Boxes" for a group of young mothers.
3. A review of Lowell's "Patterns" for a group of women or men whose husbands, wives, sons, or daughters have been killed in war or police work.
4. A review of Chekhov's *The Bear* for people who like to laugh at humor and farce.
5. A review of Poe's "The Masque of the Red Death" for fans of mysteries and horror stories.
6. A review of Arnold's "Dover Beach" for a group of philosophers.
7. A review of Blake's "The Tyger" for a group of ministers.
8. A review of Frost's "Desert Places" for a group of psychologists.
9. A review of Layton's "Rhine Boat Trip" for people interested in World War II and the Holocaust.
10. A review of Randall's "Ballad of Birmingham" or of Hughes's "Negro" for people concerned with racial issues.
11. A review of Hardy's "The Three Strangers" for people interested in folkways or in the proper administration of law.

16

Writing About a Work in Its Historical, Intellectual, and Cultural Context

Everything written, spoken, painted, or composed reflects the period of its composition—its historical, intellectual, and cultural context, or milieu. Literature for the moment aside, we cannot open our mouths to speak without consciously or subconsciously taking into account the conditions in which we live, our ways of life, our intellectual goals, and our aims and aspirations. We are always a part of our greater culture, and our observations and thoughts are a constant function of the attitudes, idioms, ideas, and customs of our time and place. All things emerge from their own era, whether as a revolutionary idea, reaction, or synthesis; and a major job of the disciplined reader is to understand the relationship of historical times and artistic works. To study a work of literature in historical and cultural perspective is to determine the degree to which the work belongs in, and perhaps transcends, its period.

To carry out such a study you need to develop thoughts about the connections of literature to life. You might consider the obvious fact that as circumstances change, writers express attitudes toward these changes. You might also consider that artists themselves want to create new ideas from existing ones and also to suggest improvements and reforms in government and society. A permanent standard of judging art is therefore its newness, that is, its status of being different, and artists are always trying to meet this standard. To the degree that writers of the past (and present) have been successful, it is possible to place their works in historical perspective, in the light of change at least, if not of definite progress.

The idea of reading works in historical and sociological perspective is not to file them away in a historical pigeon-hole but to improve understanding of the entire work. The aim is to produce accuracy of reading and of judgments and to avoid errors that result from failure to see that artists respond to their own times, either by embracing the present or by probing idealistically into the past. An interesting example is Coleridge's poem "Kubla Khan." It was published in 1816, a time when scientists had begun the lengthy tasks of exploring the heavens with telescopes and everyday matter with microscopes.

Absolutely new descriptions of the elements and their properties had been made, and the known world was seemingly less awesome and more regular than it had ever seemed. But not everything was yielding to scientific discovery, and Coleridge was interested in evoking a less detailed but more mysterious past. And thus he based his poem on the distant, almost magical time of the great Chinese emperor Kublai Khan, who had ruled in the thirteenth century. It is as though Coleridge deliberately created his poem as an antithesis of the increasing scientism of his times.

History, Culture, and Multiculturalism

It is such connections that are formative in literary history, which is in effect the chronicling of the interaction of ideas, events, social and political conditions, and literary modes. Of particularly increasing interest has been the consideration of literature as it reflects the society from which the writers of literature have come and on which they have based their work. Recently, great attention has been devoted to multicultural studies and literary works; that is, works that are based in the stories of people who for the greater portion of modern history have been suppressed and also ignored. The United States is a unique place in the world, which during its relatively short existence has seen a virtually constant immigration of national groups and cultures.

The process is by no means over. The census of 1940 recorded about 130,000,000 Americans. At the present time our population is close to 285,000,000 and it is increasing daily. In addition to the massive numbers of African Americans, Chinese Americans, Central Europeans, and Scandinavians, much of whose immigration occurred before the twentieth century, new waves of people today have come from Asia, the Caribbean Islands, and Central and South America. As with all immigrants, many have arrived here with little or no knowledge of English but with strong memories of their native cultures. The second generations of these people have learned English but have had many of the traditional difficulties of integrating themselves into American life. They have encountered prejudice, hostility, segregation, and violence, for even though they were born on American soil they had much to overcome. A good deal of twentieth and early twenty-first century literature concerns the struggles of immigrants and their descendants as they have lived and worked and found a home in the United States.

As one might expect, this process of movement has stirred a not inconsiderable controversy. Politically, a traditional idea of long duration is that America is a "melting pot" of people of differing races and cultures, involving the blending and merging of the old world to create something entirely new. A contrary concept is that of multiculturalism, namely the idea that the members of each incoming group—on the basis of race, ethnicity, national origin, and culture—do not shed their unique qualities even though they have become American residents and citizens. Each group seeks to preserve its identity in the new land, and for this reason our culture is pluralistic. It is therefore diversity that should be celebrated, not assimilationism. Although there are profound political implications of this idea, including many possible divisions, our present focus is with the literature that has risen along with the many changes brought about by our unique nation of immigrants and their descendants.

Literature in Its Time and Place

Analyzing a literary work as a product of cultural and intellectual history is the task, first, of determining what can be clearly deducible as coming directly out of the major issues existing at the time it was written, and, second, of deciding what is new and permanent—that is, of determining what has been created by the author of the work from ideas prevalent at the time of composition. The concern is to see both the similarity and dissimilarity of a work and its period.

Such a study of literature is valuable because it promotes the realization that ideas and ways of seeing the universe change with time and place. Too often it is easy to read texts as though they were all written last week and to attribute to writers ideas that they never had. Shakespeare, for example, had a number of political ideas, but he had no experience with representative government as we know it today. Therefore, in considering works of his that touch the subject of politics, such as the *Henry IV* plays, *Richard II*, and *Henry V*, you should understand why he dramatizes the importance of a just and strong monarch or the necessity of a moral aristocracy. We can enthusiastically accept his idea that wise rulers and moral people are necessary in the creation of successful government, even though we today apply the principle not to monarchy—the form that Shakespeare knew—but to democracy.

Writing About a Work in Its Historical and Cultural Context

The first part of your task is to decide what is topical about the work on which you are going to write. Usually there is enough in a work's descriptions, actions, locations, customs, and cultural assumptions to find something there that is unique. Layton's "Rhine Boat Trip," for example, is derived from reflections about the unspeakable German atrocities and concentration camps during the Second World War.

Some works, however, may seem to offer a special challenge because of their apparent lack of currency; that is, they seem to be so closely connected with our own contemporary ideas and assumptions that you may not readily see them in historical and cultural perspective. At first, Arnold's poem "Dover Beach" might give this impression. But "Dover Beach" provides abundant symbolism about the loss of religious certainty in the nineteenth century, and this idea, which many people today also feel, would provide you with sufficient material on which to begin the thoughts for your essay.

Another problem might arise when the work assigned is remote either in history or in place. In such works, however, the subject matter brings out ideals and attitudes of the writer, and these can then be related to the time in which the work was written, just as it may also be related to our own times. Browning's poem "My Last Duchess" is such a work. It was published in 1842, but its subject is a Renaissance Italian nobleman who is callous and self-centered and who wields despotic power. Thus it is apparent that Browning is providing a timely idea that absolute power produces destructive results both on the individual wielding it and on those around him. This is an idea that is certainly up to date—in fact, it is up to the minute. Browning's presentation of the duke can therefore be analyzed as a good deal more than a dramatic study of a powerful and ruthless eccentric of past times.

Raise Questions to Discover Ideas

It is important to realize that the major source of your information is the work itself. In your reading you can discover a great deal about the period of the author, even our own period, and more importantly about the place of the work in that period. You need to ask, and answer, a number of questions.

- Are historical circumstances specifically mentioned? What are they? What does the author say about them?
- Does the writer describe conditions with photographic detail, or is he less concerned with pictorial details and more with human and political issues?
- To what national, ethnic, social, and economic class do the principal characters belong? What is their background? What values do they hold or represent?
- Are the characters religious or not? To what degree do religious or philosophical thoughts govern the actions of the characters?
- Is the principal character (or any character) an important part of the prevailing social and economic system as outlined in the work, or is he an outsider? If he is outside the system, what conditions have put and now keep him there? Are you made to feel pleased or angry with these conditions?
- Does the character eventually win a place in the system, or is he/she left out of the system, or is he/she broken by it?
- What assumptions do you think the author had about the literary interests of his audience? That is, does it seem that the author wrote for a sophisticated audience, a simple-minded one, or a sensation-seeking one?

- What conclusions can you draw, on the basis of your answers to these and like questions, about the author's attitudes toward his times? Does he/she attempt to give a complete view or a partial view? Does he/she seem to be recommending values that are similar, or contrary, to those held during his era?

From questions such as these you will soon discover a suitable topic, for there is need here as always for narrowing the focus of your discussion. For example, a question about the fortunes of particular characters can lead to an avenue of inquiry like the following: Does the popular thwarting of the hangman's wishes in Hardy's "The Three Strangers" reflect a romantic idea about the power of the folk—the strength of the mass—in nineteenth-century English society? Similarly, how can the unrealized talents of the characters in Anita Scott Coleman's "Unfinished Masterpieces" be shown to reflect Coleman's views about American racial politics in the early twentieth century? Events or situations themselves can be focused in the same way. The details about Jackie's home life in O'Connor's "First Confession" might suggest a topic like "The Negative Effect of Dublin Home Life on the Individual." Your creation of topics like these should enable you to develop an interesting and relevant essay.

This use of the work of literature itself as an authority for your remarks in the essay may seem open to the objection that literary works are often not reliable as actual source material for history. Sometimes works contain exaggerations made for comic or satiric effect, and sometimes they develop out of improbable circumstances. As history, therefore, the close study of a literary work is a weak substitute for more accurate documentation.

The answer to this objection—and an important realization for you to make—is that the focus of this assignment is the work itself. Your essay is about the historical period only as it is reflected in the work. Your concern is not to use the work for evidence in writing history but rather as evidence of a literary reaction to historical and cultural circumstances. Even if there are exaggerations and caricature or if conditions reported are brighter or darker than life, these very aspects of the work become an important part of the material you bring to your essay. Your aim should not be to use the work as a filter through which you attempt to acquire historical data but to determine to what use such observable data have been put within the work.

Some types of literature are more readily approached from the historical, intellectual, and cultural point of view than others. Usually novels, short stories, narrative poems, dramas, and essays are fairly obviously rooted in customs and ideas of their time. Many of these works can be discussed without extensive reading in secondary historical sources. By contrast, many short lyric poems are not obviously connected with their respective periods, and to write about these works may require more inferential efforts.

Organize Your Essay About a Work and Its Context

In the following plan, the introduction might be proportionately longer than usual because of the need for presenting detailed information about the work and what you know about its historical period.

Introduction   In addition to defining your central idea and thesis sentence, your aim here should be to place the work in its context. You should identify the work, state the time of its publication, and if known, its composition. You should also include any biographical data relevant to an understanding of the work and its background. You should also state whether there are any special problems in discussing the work, such as that it is a historical novel, or a work remote in time, or that there is some controversy about it.

You should also state the pertinent historical facts concerning the events and ideas that you have selected for discussion. There is no need for extensive explication, but only for those details that are relevant. If your work was written during or shortly after a recent war, for example, you may assume that your readers know as much generally about this war as you do and need only those details that will remind them of their knowledge. Thus, if you are discussing Hardy's "The Man He Killed," you might state that the poem is probably based on a soldier's view stemming out of the trench warfare on the Western front during World War I. You might then go on to state that this war was immensely complex, for it had implications for all the nations of Europe and also the United States; that it was fought not only on land but on the sea; that it was sometimes called the "Great War" and also "the war to end all wars"; that it was also seen as an ideological war in which nations felt their prestige to be at stake; that the war highlighted for many the idea that life and love were impermanent and fleeting; that the war was immensely wasteful and destructive; and that it was difficult to pinpoint the causes of the war and to explain the reasons for which opposing nations took sides. There is nothing unusual about these conclusions: The point about them is that they are general statements about the period rather than detailed descriptions.

Body   After dealing with introductory details, you should aim to show how they apply to the work you are studying. You may wish to include both of the following, or just one or the other.

A. A discussion of how the work embodies the facts, or of how the facts shape the work. Thus, Hardy's "The Man He Killed" not only demonstrates the common-sense quality of the speaker, but also exposes the sham of theoretical warfare when contrasted with the ordinary needs and wants of an average human being. The poem can be seen as an assertion that international political concerns, in human terms, are valueless. Similarly, in discussing Browning's "My Last Duchess," you might show that the duke's conversational manners (his preempting the discussion of marriage details by reflecting on the portrait of his former duchess and his stating that his "just pretense" for a dowry will be acceptable) can be related to the assertion that the poem is an effective counterargument against nineteenth-century claims that "great men" are needed to perform the great tasks that are required in public and political life. Browning's "great man" is so preoccupied with his own power that he listens to no one and abandons all human kindness.

B. As the first part of the body is concerned with ideas, the second is devoted to a discussion of literary matters (i.e., style, structure, tone, point of view, imagery, etc.) that can be related to the period. Thus, ideas about the need for personal freedom may be related to poems written in free verse. An awareness of the horror of discrimination may be related to the ballad structure of Randall's "Ballad of Birmingham," in which the simple poetic structure emphasizes the extreme to which such cruelty can go. The modern stress on psychology may account for the limited point of view story "Miss Brill," in which we as readers directly follow the thoughts and responses of the major character. The compact, brief stanzas of Hughes's "Negro" enables the poet to express a brief world history of the exploitation of blacks. What is important here is to apply the context of the work to its literary characteristics.

Conclusion   To conclude, you should try to determine which elements you have discussed seem out of date and which ones are still relevant and important. For purposes of your conclusion, you may assume that your own point of view is modern and up to date, although on this issue you should perhaps assert yourself humbly and emphasize your broadmindedness. Thus, in this section you might attempt to determine whether Browning's exposé of the ruthless Duke in "My Last Duchess" is still applicable, granted that many people in various nations have invented the title "President for Life," and continue to fill that role. Does Young Goodman Brown's preoccupation with the evil of others seem to be relevant today, or should we regard his ideas as having passed its time? What should be our responses to those young men of Gwendolyn Brooks who claim that they are "real cool"? It is questions such as these that you might ask and attempt to answer in your conclusion.

Illustrative Essay

Hughes's References to Black Servitude and Black Pride in "Negro"°

[1] Langston Hughes was a strong voice of the Harlem Renaissance, a twentieth-century movement that declared that the time had come to recognize the significance of African Americans in all phases of life. <u>In "Negro," Hughes propels this argument by showing that oppression against blacks is as old as human history.</u>* He might have chosen to develop his idea in a lengthy book study, with many supportive details and many references. Instead, his interest is to be brief and memorable—almost as though he is providing details for a political agenda—and he chooses to create a poem of six brief stanzas. The poem demonstrates how eloquent a spokesman and leader Hughes was for his people. <u>The poem is built on the contrast between what the heritage of blacks should be—the entitlement to equality and freedom—and what in fact it is and has been—the indignity of slavery and oppression.</u>†

[2] <u>The form of "Negro" is both simple and direct.</u> There are six stanzas in the poem, each beginning with the pronoun "I" followed by a grammatical form of the verb *to be.* The total number of lines is nineteen. The first and sixth stanzas identify the speaker as a representative Negro whose identity is the same as his race—black—"Black like the depths of my Africa" (lines 3, 19). These opening and concluding stanzas are not historical in scope, for they are in the present tense and they define the speaker's racial identity and pride in the color of his African heritage.

[3] <u>Stanzas 2, 3, and 5 are historical, however, briefly referring to the servitude and suffering that blacks have experienced.</u> The emphasis in these stanzas is on the past, and Hughes's use of the present-perfect tense bears out his continuing historical emphasis. These comprehensive stanzas jump time and place, from the slavery and oppression of ancient Rome and ancient Egypt, on the one hand, to Revolutionary War times and modern industrial times of the United States, on the other. Symbolically, the speaker says that in the palace of Caesar, he was a slave who kept the doorsteps clean, just as he cleaned the boots as a personal servant of America's first president, Washington. The idea is that the heights that these men (and others like them) reached were achieved by their dependence on the slavery of blacks. Similarly, the Belgian colonial regime in Africa was sustained by the oppressive cruelty against blacks, which is symbolized by the cutting off of the hands of slaves in the Congo (15). Hughes goes on to state that such colonial oppression is by no means over, for his speaker refers to the neo-colonial oppression of life in Mississippi (in 1958, the date of the poem), where lynching still occurred.

°See page 372 for this poem.
*Central idea.
†Thesis sentence.

[4] The most positive section of the poem is stanza four, where Hughes tells us that the narrator has sung his "sorrow songs" during the entire history of displacement from "Africa to Georgia" (11–12). This stanza is comparable to stanzas one and six, for in all three stanzas Hughes declares the positive identity and value of African Americans. In stanza four the idea is that there is a vast human talent among blacks that has already been realized, with the implication that there is much more to come. Here Hughes is emphasizing black pride, for the power of making music and providing musical beauty is a capacity that could never be suppressed, even through the long centuries of black oppression that date from the origin of history. The possibility of continued high achievement, Hughes implies, is endless.

[5] As we have seen, "Negro" concludes and ends on the importance of realizing the promises of history for the present time. The tenses of the verbs bring this out, for everything implies a current condition. The past has had its day, with its oppression, and is now over. The present is now the greatest concern. The time has come for African Americans to appreciate their own blackness, "like the depths of my Africa" (3, 19). Things are in some respects the same, yet they are changed because the time has come for liberation, for freedom. The idea is that it is time for the end of oppression—a time when African Americans can listen to themselves and their "sorrow songs," and can be themselves as they were meant to be when they were in their original homes in Africa.

[6] "Negro" is therefore a thoroughly modern poem. It recognizes the past, but emphasizes the significance of the present. In three of the poem's stanzas, Hughes refers to the past, which should be over and done with. The final stanza indicates that the present is the same as the past, but that African Americans have moved up from slavery and oppression and can build their new identity out of their past history. Even though this last stanza is identical word-for-word to the first, it suggests that it is time to move, to claim a new movement of history, a new direction. Hughes's argument is that this direction is forward.

Work Cited

Hughes, Langston. "Negro." Edgar V. Roberts. *Writing About Literature.* 11th ed. Upper Saddle River: Prentice Hall, 2006. 372.

Commentary on the Essay

As an essay about a literary work as it pertains to its historical period, this essay deals with the issues of black identity and liberation that have become a major ideal in American life during the preceding generations of Americans. All the descriptions and interpretations of "Negro" are based on this connection. Because the issues of African American life have such strongly political overtones, the essay treats the poem as a work of exhortation as well as description. The essay makes transitions with the key words *however* (paragraph 3), *most positive* (4), *as we have seen* (5), and *therefore* (6).

In the body, paragraph 2 deals with the poem's shape and its essential simplicity. Of special interest is the poet's use of the present tense to sustain the argument that the poem is directed at current readers, who can translate their attitudes and interpretations of life into direct political action.

Paragraphs 3 and 4 are the most extensive in the essay, for they are Hughes's historical stanzas, showing that he deals here with the historical indignities and horrors of black oppression. The unique analysis here is that the grammar of stanzas 2 through 5 is a major means by which Hughes sustains his argument. The idea in the essay here is to show that the past lives on in the present. Paragraph 4 follows Hughes's argument that the musical nature of African Americans is a positive symbol of their inherent human worthiness.

Paragraphs 5 and 6 emphasize once again the present implications of "Negro." Paragraph 5 especially emphasizes the present, while the concluding paragraph, 6, asserts that the poem is particularly modern. In this way the essay demonstrates how Hughes's poem has a place in the historical times when it was written. The essay's analysis and its central idea both emphasize this connection.

Special Topics for Studying and Discussing Works in Their Historical, Intellectual, and Cultural Context

1. Consider a story or poem in which the topics are connected with philosophy or politics, for example Arnold's "Dover Beach" (religion, philosophy), Frost's "Desert Places" (the cosmos), Hardy's "The Man He Killed" (politics and war), and Lowell's "Patterns" (war and human relationships). Write an essay about just one of these works showing how the topic reflects ideas and concerns of the time it was written and also of today's times.

2. Consider Blake's use of the image of the "Tyger" in "The Tyger." To what degree is the tyger a symbol of what Blake considered to be evil? How does he seem to define evil? How current is his use of what today is considered an endangered animal? How does his poem speak to today's concerns?

3. In the context of current relationships of human beings and the natural world, how significant is Wordsworth's "Lines Written in Early Spring"? Does the poem meet the same need for today's readers that it probably met for Wordsworth's readers?

4. The circumstances of farm life in the early twentieth century are reflected in Glaspell's *Trifles*. Consider the issues of loneliness, isolation, lack of communication, and marital abuse that are treated in these works. To what degree are these issues still significant in today's world?

5. Describe the timeliness of the issues Layton brings out in "Rhine Boat Trip."

6. Coleman's "Unfinished Masterpieces" deals with the issue of inadequate opportunity for minorities. Specifically, her topic is that ability is meaningless when there is no chance to develop it. Write an essay attempting to demonstrate that her idea is as vital now as it was in the 1920s, when she wrote her story.

7. The speaker of Salinas's "In a Farmhouse" is an eight-year-old boy who has been put to work picking cotton. What current issues are suggested by the speaker's plight?

8. Browning's "My Last Duchess" and Hardy's "The Three Strangers" touch upon the issue of political power. How do the works reflect political concerns of their times, and what contrasts between the works are you able to make?

17

Writing About Film

Drama on the Silver Screen, Television Set, and Computer Monitor

Film is the word most often used for motion pictures, although other common words are *movies, cinema, flicks,* and sometimes *pics.* It is a specialized type of drama, utilizing, like drama, the techniques of dialogue, monologue, and action. Also like drama, it employs movement and spectacle. For these reasons, film can be studied for aspects such as character, plot, structure, tone, and symbolism. Unlike drama, however, film embodies techniques from photography, film chemistry, electronic technology, sound, and editing. These techniques are extremely specialized, and for this reason they require special consideration.

A Thumbnail History of Film

Film arose out of technologies developed in the late nineteenth century. The first of these was the creation of a flexible substance—celluloid—that could accept the chemical emulsions that in the early years of photography could be applied only to glass. Other significant inventions were the motion picture camera and projector, together with screens coated with reflective silver iodide and on which the pictures were projected. Once these were in place, and once producers and directors decided to use the medium for full-length dramas, movies as we know them came into existence.

Although the earliest filmmakers thought of motion pictures as private entertainment, they soon recognized that the development of large filmmaking studios, national distribution, and a system of local movie theaters could become extremely lucrative. The history of film is hence just as much a history of the film business as of the art and development of film dramas and film acting. The enormous potential of the movie business was first realized with the production in 1915 of D. W. Griffith's landmark but still controversial film *Birth of a Nation,* which reaped an enormous profit on a small investment.

The first motion pictures were in black and white and were silent. Producers soon realized that large profits required easily recognized actors with "big names," and so the "star system" made national figures out of actors such as Mary Pickford, Charlie Chaplin, and Rudolph Valentino. In 1928 the first talking picture, *Lights of New York,* was made. Film as we know it today was substantially established in 1933 with the first Technicolor © film, *La Cucaracha,* a "short subject," and in 1935 with *Becky Sharp,* a feature film. Since then the use of color in films has undergone amazing refinement and improvement.

For a time after the end of World War II, the growth of television inhibited the power of the large studios. Soon, however, many films were developed specifically for television viewing, and popular pictures were released for television use. In the last decade or two, with the advent of videotape and then DVD technology, home viewing of films has become a normal feature of American life. Today, movie rental outlets can be found in shopping districts everywhere, with the result that most of the movies ever made are within the reach of anyone with a television set and the proper playing equipment. Early dramatists dreamed of filling their theaters for a number of consecutive performances, thus reaching perhaps several thousand persons. Film writers today, however, reach millions in first-run movie houses and many millions more on television reruns, videocassettes, and DVD.

Stage Plays and Film

Although film is a form of drama, there are a number of important differences between film and stage productions. Plays can be produced many times, in many different places, with many different people. In bringing a play to life, the producer and director use not only actors but also artists, scene designers, carpenters, painters, lighting technicians, costume makers, choreographers, music directors, and musicians. For the actual performance of a play, however, the stage itself limits what can be done. In each theater production, the actors, setting, and effects are all physically confined to the stage.

The stage for makers of film, however, is virtually infinite, and the absence of restrictions permits the inclusion of any details whatsoever—car chases, underwater adventures, flying geese following an airplane, wartime combat, legislative debates, executive discussions, scenes in living rooms, courtrooms, boxing rings, hotel rooms, football stadiums, and kitchens, and locations in cities and countrysides anywhere—domestic or foreign, modern or ancient. If the setting is a desert island, the filmmaker can travel to such an island and film it in all its reality, complete with beach, palm trees, huts, and authentic natives-turned-actors, and if additional scenery is desired, technicians can dub it in by computer enhancement, as in *Cast Away* (2000) by Robert Zemeckis. If the scene is a distant planet, the filmmaker can create an exotic planet location in the studio, with appropriate scenery, props, effects, lighting, and costumes for the space travelers. Additional special effects, in

---

DVD TECHNOLOGY AND FILM STUDY

DVD technology (*digital video disk* or *digital versatile disk*) promises a flourishing future for students of film. The video resolution of DVD is superior to that of videotape. DVDs often include many extra features that provide interesting background and sidelights for film study (including hidden "Easter Eggs"). Often the viewer is given the option to select a series of special scenes for study. Many DVDs include commentaries by the director, screenwriter, actors, and noted critics, who speak on alternate audio tracks. Also, frequently, there are special sections devoted to "bloopers," or spots where the actors did something funny and out of character, at which everyone on the set breaks into laughter.

The DVD for Jonathan Demme's *The Silence of the Lambs* (1990) is exemplary. It includes the entire film itself, together with a wide variety of additional material. The film is divided into "chapters" that can be selected, played, stopped, slowed, reversed, and enlarged as the viewer wishes. There are voice-overs by the principal actors, who comment on various scenes in which they are prominent. There is also frequent voice-over commentary by the director, the screenwriter, and an FBI consultant. Additional features for study are selected scenes that were reduced or omitted in the final editing, together with reports of research into abnormal psychology that were used in the creation of the film's diabolical villain.

Of comparable interest is the DVD remastered edition of Welles's *Citizen Kane*, which contains voice-over running analyses of the entire movie by both Roger Ebert and Peter Bogdanovich (Turner Home Video © 2001). In addition, many DVDs offer materials unobtainable elsewhere. The 1964 Richard Burton production of *Hamlet*, for example, is available only on DVD (in black and white). The DVD of Terry Gilliam's *Brazil* (1985) includes instructive interviews about the problems and controversies that preceded and followed the film's release.

---

which filmmakers often indulge too freely, are created by computers, which permit film scenes that were unimaginable for the greatest part of theater history. The freedom enjoyed by the filmmaker, in short, almost limitlessly exceeds the freedom of the play producer. Nothing is left to the audience's imagination.

The two types of dramatic productions, drama and film, are therefore vastly different. Each new production of a play is unlike every other production, because not only the actors but also the appurtenances of the staging are unique. Shakespeare's play *Hamlet,* for example, has been produced innumerable times since Shakespeare's actors at London's Globe Theatre first performed it at the beginning of the seventeenth century, and each subsequent production, including the various filmed versions, has been different from all the rest.

Paradoxically, this same variety cannot occur with film unless, of course, new generations of directors and producers decide to create new versions of particular films. Although filmmakers have great freedom in producing each individual movie, this freedom also imposes its own limitations. Because of high production costs and also because films reach a mass audience through wide distribution, films are generally released in only one version, perhaps with altered or dubbed versions for foreign audiences. Thus Orson Welles's *Citizen Kane* (1941) is in only one form, and although it was restored and reedited in 1991, and received additional changes and restorations for DVD in 2001, it remains in this form even though it is frequently shown and seen. Interestingly, no person can ever claim to have seen all the productions of plays like *Hamlet,* but everyone who sees a film like *Citizen Kane* can claim to have seen it in its entirety.

The Aesthetics of Film

To the degree that film is confined to a screen, it can be compared visually with the art of the painter and the still photographer. It uses the language of visual art. One object in a painting can take on special relationships to others as the artist directs the eyes of the observer. A color used in one part can be balanced with the same color, or its complement, in another part. Painters and photographers can introduce certain colors and details as symbols and can suggest allegorical interpretations through the inclusion of mythical figures or universally recognized objects. Particular effects can be achieved with the use of the textures of paint or with control over shutter speed, focus, and various techniques of development. The techniques and effects are extensive.

The filmmaker is able to utilize most of the resources of the still photographer and many of those of the painter, and can augment these with special effects. Artistically, the most confining aspect of film is the rectangular screen, but aside from that, film is unrestricted. Based in a dramatic text called a film-script or shooting script, the film uses words and their effects, but it also employs the language of visual art, and especially the particular vividness and power of moving pictures. When considering film, then, you should realize that film communicates not only with words but also by using various visual techniques. The visual presentation is inseparable from the medium of film itself.

The Techniques of Film

There are many techniques of film, and a full description and documentation of them can be—and has become—extensive.[1] In evaluating film, however, you need to familiarize yourself only with those aspects of technique that have an immediate bearing on your responses and interpretations.

Film Utilizes Special Visual Techniques

The Camera Is the Basic Tool of Film   Each film begins with the camera, which permits great freedom in the presentation of characters and actions. In a film, the visual viewpoint can shift. Thus, a film can begin with a distant shot of the actors—a "long shot"—much like the view of actors onstage. Then the camera can zoom in to show a close-up or zoom out to present a wide and complete panorama. Usually a speaking actor will be the subject of a close-up, but the camera can also capture other actors' reactions in close-up. You must interpret the effects of close-ups and long shots yourself, but it should be plain that the frequent use of either—or of middle-distance views—is a means by which film directors control viewer perception of characters and situations.

The camera can also move from character to character or from character to object. In this way, film can mark a series of reactions, concentrate your attention on a character's attitude, or comment visually on a character's actions. If a man and woman are in love, for example, the camera can shift, either directly or through montage, from the couple to flowers and trees, thus associating their love visually with objects of beauty and growth. Should the flowers be wilted and the trees leafless, however, the visual commentary might be that their love is doomed and hopeless.

The camera can also be used in the creation of unique effects. A common technique is slow motion, which can be used to emphasize a certain aspect of a person's character. The concentrated focus on a child running happily in a meadow (as in *The Color Purple* [1985] by Steven Spielberg) suggests the joy inherent in such movement. Surprisingly, speed is sometimes indicated by slow motion, which emphasizes strong muscular effort (as in the running scenes in Hugh Hudson's *Chariots of Fire* [1981]).

---

[1]See, for example, David Bleiler, *TLA Film, Video, and DVD Guide 2004: The Discerning Film Lover's Guide* (2003); Roger Ebert, *Roger Ebert's Movie Yearbook 2005* (2004); Roger Ebert, *The Great Movies* (2003); Roger Ebert, *The Great Movies II* (2005); Louis D. Giannetti, *Understanding Movies*, 9th ed. (2001); Leslie Halliwell, *Halliwell's Film, Video & DVD Guide 2005*, 20th ed. revised and updated, ed. John Walker (2004); Ephraim Katz, *The Film Encyclopedia*, 4th ed., revised by Fred Klein and Ronald Dean Nolan (2001); James Monaco, *How to Read a Film: The World of Movies, Media, and Multimedia: Language, History, Theory*, 3rd ed. (2000); Richard Beck Peacock, *The Art of Movie Making: Script to Screen* (2001); John Pym and Geoff Andrew, *Time Out Film Guide*, 13th ed. (2004); Robert Sklar, *A World History of Film* (2002); and David Thomson, *The New Biographical Dictionary of Film* (2002). See also the Internet Movie Data Base for complete data on films of all periods <www.imdb.com>.

Many other camera techniques bear on action and character. The focus can be sharp at one point, indistinct at another. Moving a speaking character out of focus can suggest that listeners are bored. Sharp or blurred focus can also show that a character has seen things exactly or inexactly. In action sequences, the camera can be mounted in a moving vehicle to "track" or follow running human beings or horses, speeding bicycles and cars (as in Woody Allen's *Annie Hall* [1977]), or moving sailboats, canoes, speedboats, or rowboats. A camera operator on foot can also be the tracker, or the camera may track ground movement from an aircraft. Movement can also be captured by a rotating camera that follows a moving object or character. Alternatively, the camera can be fixed while a character or object moves from one side to the other.

The Pictures in Film Involve Light, Shadow, and Color   As in the theater, the filmmaker uses light, shadow, and color to reinforce ideas and to create realistic and symbolic effects. Characters in bright light are presumably open and frank, whereas characters in shadow may be hiding something, particularly in black-and-white films. Flashing or strobe lights might indicate a changeable or sinister character or situation. A scene in sunshine, which brings out colors, and the same scene in rain and clouds or in twilight, all of which mute colors, create different moods. An example of such contrasts is the film *From Hell* (2001), directed by Albert and Allen Hughes, in which virtually the entire action takes place in darkness, and only the final scene is filmed in full light.

Colors, of course, have much the same meaning that they have in any other artistic medium. Blue sky and clear light suggest happiness, while greenish light can indicate something ghoulish. A memorable control of color occurs midway through David O. Selznick's *Gone with the Wind* (1939) when Scarlett O'Hara reflects upon the devastation of her plantation home, Tara. She resolves never to be hungry again, and as she speaks she is silhouetted against a darkened orange sky—a background that suggests how totally the way of life she knew as a young woman has been burned away. As in this example, you may expect colors to complement the story of the film. Thus, lovers may wear clothing with the same or complementary colors, whereas people who are not "right" for each other may wear clashing colors.

Action Is the Essence of Film

The strength of film is direct action. Actions of all sorts—running, swimming, driving a car, fighting, embracing and kissing, or even just sitting; chases, trick effects, ambushes—all these and more create a sense of immediate reality, and all are tied (or should be) to narrative development. Scenes of action can run on for several minutes, with little or no accompanying dialogue, to carry on the story or to convey ideas about the interests and abilities of the characters.

Camera Angles and Views of the Heads, Bodies, and Movements of Actors Are Related to a Film's Content

Closely related to the portrayal of action is the way in which film shows the human body (and animal bodies) together with bodily motion and gesture (or body language). The view or perspective that the filmmaker presents is particularly important. A torso shot of a character may stress no more than the content of that character's speech. A close-up shot, however, with the character's head filling the screen, may emphasize motives as well as content. The camera can also distort ordinary expectations of reality. Using wide-angle lenses and close-ups, for example, human subjects can be made to seem bizarre or grotesque, as are the faces in the crowd in Woody Allen's *Stardust Memories* (1980). Sometimes the camera creates other bodily distortions—for example, enlarging the limbs of the forest dweller in Ingmar Bergman's *The Virgin Spring* (1959) or throwing into unnatural prominence a scolding mouth or a suspicious eye. Distortion invites interpretation: The filmmaker may be asserting that certain human beings, even supposedly normal ones, are odd, sinister, intimidating, or psychopathic.

Sound Is Integral to the Presentation and Content of a Film

Dialogue and Music Complement Film Dramatizations   The first business of the sound track is the spoken dialogue, which is "mixed" in editing to be synchronized with the action. There are also many other elements in the sound track. Music, the most important, creates and augments moods. A melody in a major or minor key, or in a slow or fast tempo, can affect our perception of actions. If a character is thinking deeply, complementary music may be played by muted strings. But if the character is going insane, the music may become discordant and percussive.

Sometimes, music gives a film a special identity. Hudson's *Chariots of Fire* (1981), for example, includes music by Vangelis. Although this music is independently well known, it is always associated with the film. In addition, musical accompaniments can directly render dramatic statement, without dialogue. An example occurs in Welles's *Citizen Kane* (1941). Beginning that portion of the narrative derived from the autobiography of a character who is now dead (the scene first focuses on his statue), the musical sound track by Bernard Herrmann quotes the *Dies Irae* theme from the Catholic mass for the dead. The instrumentation, however, makes the music funny, and we smile rather than grieve. Herrmann, incidentally, varies the *Dies Irae* theme elsewhere in the film, usually for comic effect.

Film Uses Special and Often Ingenious Sound Effects   Special sound effects can also augment a film's action. The sound of a blow can be enhanced electronically to cause an impact similar to the force of the blow itself (as in the boxing scenes from the many *Rocky* films). At times some sounds, such as the noises

of wailing people, squeaking or slamming doors, marching feet, or moving vehicles, are filtered electronically to create weird or ghostly effects. Often a
character's words echo rapidly and sickeningly to show dismay or anguish.

Editing or Montage Is the Assembling
of a Film out of Separate Parts

A finished film is a composite, not a continuous work filmed from start to
end. The putting together of the film is the process of editing, or **montage** (assemblage, mounting, construction), which at one time involved cutting and
gluing, but which now takes place on specially programmed computers. Depending on the flexibility of the film-script, the various scenes of the film are
planned before shooting begins, but the major task of montage is accomplished
in a studio by editing specialists.

If we again compare film with a stage play, we note that a theatrical production moves continuously, with pauses only for intermissions and scene
changes. Your perception of the action is caused by your distance from the
stage (perhaps aided by opera glasses or binoculars). Also, even as you move
your eyes from one character to another, you still perceive the entire stage. In
a film, however, the directors and editors *create* these continuous perceptions
for you by piecing together different parts. The editors begin with many
"takes" (separately photographed scenes, including many versions of the
same scenes). What they select, or "mount," will be the film, and we never see
the discarded scenes (unless they appear on a DVD special edition). Thus, it
is editing that puts everything together.

Montage Creates Narrative Continuity   The first use of montage, already
suggested, is narrative continuity. For example, a climb up a steep cliff can be
shown at the bottom, middle, and top (with backward slips and falls to show
the danger of the climb and to make viewers catch their breath). All such narrative sequences result from the assembling of individual pieces, each one
representing phases of the activity. A classic example of a large number of
separate parts forming a narrative unit is the well-known shower murder in
Alfred Hitchcock's *Psycho* (1959), where a forty-five-second sequence is made
up of seventy-eight different shots (the woman in the shower, the murderer
behind the curtain, the attack, the slumping figure, the running water, the
dead woman's eye, the bathtub drain, etc.).

Montage Provides Explanation of Character and Motivation   Montage is used
in flashbacks to explain present, ongoing actions or characteristics; or in illustration of a character's thoughts and memories; or in brief examples from the
unremembered past of a character suffering from amnesia. It also supplies direct visual explanation of character. A famous example occurs in Welles's *Citizen
Kane*. The concluding scene shows overhead views of Kane's vast collection of
statuary and mementos. At the very end, the camera focuses on a raging furnace,

into which workmen have thrown his boyhood sled, which bears the brand name "Rosebud" (we have fleetingly seen Kane playing with the sled as a boy). Because "Rosebud" is Kane's last word, and everyone in the film is trying to decipher its meaning, this final scene reveals that Kane's dying thoughts were of his lost boyhood, before he was taken away from his parents, and that his unhappy life has resulted from early rejection and personal pain.

Montage Facilitates Directorial Commentary   Montage is also used symbolically as commentary, as in an early sequence in Charlie Chaplin's *Modern Times* (1936) that shows a group of workers rushing to their factory jobs. Immediately following this scene is a view of a milling herd of sheep. With this symbolic montage, Chaplin suggests that the men are being herded and dehumanized by modern industry. Thus, montage and editorial statement go hand in hand.

Montage Is Used in Many Other Ways   Montage can also produce other characteristics through camera work, development, and special effects of sound and light. For example, montage editors might reverse an action to emphasize its illogicality or ridiculousness. Editing can also speed up action (which makes even the most serious things funny) or slow things down. It can also blend one scene with another or juxtapose two or more actions in quick succession to show what people are doing while they are separated. The possibilities for creativity and innovation are extensive.

It bears stressing that montage should be thought of as the finishing stage in the readying of the film for presentation in movie theaters and DVD. When the photographic and other technical phases of filmmaking are over, there are not just many feet of film, but often many yards—thousands of yards—of film, a mile or more of film—enough to make a movie that would run for many hours and perhaps even days. The movie is definitely not yet ready for distribution.

It is therefore the montage editors who put everything together, sitting at their machines and trying, testing, arranging. They pick and choose to create many separate but connected scenes from the myriad various shots that have been taken. They might begin by selecting a longshot, and then they might pick out film footage that represents a closer view of the action. A character may begin a gesture as we see him or her from a distance. But by the time the gesture is completed there may be a number of closeup and semi-closeup views of that character. In addition, there may be responses of other characters to the action. Similarly, a group of people may be walking together over the countryside, and at first we see the entire group, maybe of twenty, or forty, or more. And then, through montage, the scene may focus on several characters together. And then one or two individually, and then one of them may stumble, and that in itself creates the group reactions. Then the characters may stop to have dinner. Or maybe the group may stop to rest while some of the characters seek their dinner by using fishing equipment, or rifles.

In such ways, the number of separate scenes that develop from any particular event can become magnified and modified and individualized, and the final narrative scene will have been selected and pieced together from many separate camera views. No film is ever complete until a considerable amount of montage work has been done on it. And even then what seems to be a final version may still be too long to present as a workable movie, and at that point the montage editors go back to their computers to shorten some scenes and to excise others.

By the time the finished film is presented to the public, it has been through the hands of one or more montage editors who, with the director and others closely involved in the process, have made innumerable artistic decisions about the final version that we see.

Writing About Film

The first requirement is to see the film, either in a theater, on videocassette, or on DVD. No matter how you see it, you should view it at least twice, making notes as you go, because your discussion takes on value the more thoroughly you know the material. Include the names of the scriptwriter, director, composer, special effects editor, chief photographer, and major actresses and actors. If particular speeches are worth quoting, remember the general circumstances of the quotation and also, if possible, key words. Take notes on costume and color or (if the film is in black and white) on light and shade. You may need to rely on memory, but if you have a videotape or a DVD, you can easily replay important sections of the film, and can verify important details.

Raise Questions to Discover Ideas

Action

- How important is action? Is there much repetition of action, say, in slow motion, or from different angles? Are actors (or animals) viewed closely or distantly? Why?
- What actions are stressed (chases, concealment, gun battles, lovemaking, etc.)? What does the type of action contribute to the film?
- What do close-ups (smiles and laughter, frowns, leers, anxious looks, etc.) show about character and motivation?
- What actions indicate seasonal conditions (e.g., cold by a character's stamping of feet, warmth by the character's removing a coat or shirt)? What connection do these actions have to the film's general ideas?
- Does the action show any changing of mood, say, from sadness to happiness or from indecision to decision?

Cinematographic Techniques

- What notable techniques are used (colors, lighting, etc.)? What is their relationship to the film's characterizations and themes?

- What characterizes the use of the camera (tracking, close-ups, distant shots, camera angles, etc.)? How do the camera perspectives reinforce or detract from the film's theme and plot?
- How does the editing (the sequencing of scenes) reinforce or detract from story and theme?
- What scene or scenes best exemplify how the cinematographic techniques interact with the theme, plot, characters, setting, and so on? Why?

Acting

- How well do the actors adapt to the medium of film? How well do they deliver their lines? How convincing are their performances?
- How well do the actors control their facial expressions and body movement? Are they graceful? Awkward?
- What does their appearance lend to your understanding of their characters?
- Does it seem that the actors are genuinely creating their roles, or are they just reading through the parts?

Organize Your Essay on Film

Introduction   State your central idea and thesis sentence. You should include the background necessary to support points you intend to make in the body of your essay and you should also name the major creative and performing persons of the film.

Body   Any of the organizing strategies discussed in this book's previous chapters, such as plot, structure, character, ideas, or setting, are equally valid for an essay on a film, except that you will need to consider them in a visual context. For example, if you choose to discuss the effects of a character on the plot (Chapters 3 and 5), you need to develop your argument using the evidence of camera techniques, montage, sound effects, and the like.

When discussing film techniques, be sure to have good notes so that your supporting details are accurate. A good method is to concentrate on technique in only a few scenes. If you analyze the effects of montage, for example, you can use a videocassette or DVD to repeat the scene a number of times.

Conclusion   In your conclusion, you might evaluate the effectiveness of the cinematic form to story and idea. Are all the devices of film used in the best possible way? Is anything overdone? Is anything underplayed? Is the film good, bad, or indifferent up to a point, and then does it change? How? Why?

Illustrative Essay

Welles's *Citizen Kane:* Whittling a Giant Down to Size

[1] *Citizen Kane* (1941) is a superbly crafted film in black and white. The script is by Herman Mankiewicz and Orson Welles, with photography by Gregg Toland, music by Bernard Herrmann, direction and production by Welles, and the leading role by Welles. It is the story of a wealthy and powerful man, Charles Foster Kane, who exemplifies the American Dream of economic self-sufficiency, self-determination, and self, period. <u>The film does not explore the "greatness" of the hero, however, but rather exposes him as a misguided, unhappy person who tries to buy love and manipulate reality.</u>° <u>All aspects of the picture—characterization, structure, and technique—are focused on this goal.</u>*

[2] <u>At the film's heart is the deterioration of Kane, the newly deceased newspaper magnate and millionaire.</u> He is not all bad, for he begins well before going tragically downward. For example, the view we see of him as a child, being taken away from home, invites sympathy. When we next see him as a young man, he idealistically takes over a daily newspaper, the *Inquirer.* This idealism makes him admirable but also makes his deterioration tragic. As he says to Thatcher in a moment of insight, he could have been a great person if he had not been wealthy. His corruption begins when he tries to alter the world to suit himself, as in his demented attempt to make an opera star out of his second wife, Susan, and his related attempt to shape critical praise for her. Even though he builds an opera house for her and also sponsors many performances, he cannot change reality. This tampering with truth indicates how completely he loses his youthful integrity.

[3] <u>The structure is progressively arranged to bring out such weaknesses.</u> The film flows out of the opening obituary newsreel, from which we learn that Kane's dying word was the name "Rosebud" (the brand name of his boyhood sled, which is spoken at the beginning by a person [Kane] whose mouth is shown in close-up). The newsreel director, wanting to get the inside story, assigns a reporter named Thompson to learn about "Rosebud." Thompson's search unifies the rest of the film; he goes from place to place and person to person to collect materials and conduct interviews that disclose Kane's increasing strangeness and alienation. At the end, although the camera abandons Thompson and focuses on the burning sled, he has been successful in uncovering the story of Kane's deterioration (even though he himself never learns what "Rosebud" means). Both the sled and the reporter therefore tie together the many aspects of the film.

[4] <u>It is through Thompson's searches that the film presents the flashback accounts of Kane's deterioration.</u> The separate persons being interviewed (including Thatcher's handwritten account) each contribute something different to the narrative because their experiences with Kane have all been unique.

°Central idea.
*Thesis sentence.

As a result of these individual points of view, the story is intricate. For example, we learn in the Bernstein section that Jedediah proudly saves a copy of Kane's declaration about truth in reporting. We do not learn in Jedediah's interview, however, that he, Jedediah (Joseph Cotten), sends the copy back to Kane as an indictment of Kane's betrayal of principle. Rather, it is in *Susan's* account that we learn about the return, even though she herself understands nothing about it. This subtlety, so typical of the film, marks the ways in which the biography of Kane is progressively revealed.

[5] Thus, the major importance of these narrating characters is to reveal and reflect Kane's disintegration. Jedediah is a man of principle who works closely with Kane, but after the lost election he rebels when he understands the falseness of Kane's personal life. He becomes alienated after Kane completes the unfinished attack on Susan's performance. Jedediah's change, or perhaps his assertion of principle, thus reveals Kane's increasing corruption. Susan, Kane's second wife (Dorothy Comingore), is naive, sincere, and warm, but her drinking, her attempted suicide, and her final separation show the harm of Kane's warped visions. Bernstein (Everett Sloane), the first person Thompson interviews, is a solitary figure who is uncritical of Kane, but it is he who first touches the theme about the mystery of Kane's motivations. Bernstein also takes on life when he speaks of his forty-five-year memory of the girl in white. Even though this revelation is brief, it suggests layers of feeling and longing.

[6] In addition to these perceptive structural characterizations, *Citizen Kane* is a masterpiece of film technique. The camera images are sharp, with clear depth of field. In keeping with Kane's disintegration and mysteriousness, the screen is rarely bright. Instead, the film makes strong use of darkness and contrasts, almost to the point at times of blurring distinctions between people. Unique in Gregg Toland's camera work are the many shots taken from waist height or below, distorting the bodies of the characters by distancing their heads—suggesting that the characters are preoccupied with their own concerns and oblivious to normal perspectives. Nowhere is this distortion better exemplified than in the scene between Kane and Jedediah in the empty rooms after the lost election, when Jedediah asks permission to leave for Chicago.

[7] As might be expected in a film so dominated by its central figure, the many symbols create strong statements about character. The most obvious is the sled, "Rosebud," the major symbol of the need for love and acceptance in childhood. Another notable symbol is glass and, in one scene, ice. In the party scene, two ice statues are in the foreground of the employees of the *Inquirer*. In another scene, a bottle looms large in front of Jedediah, who is drunk. In another, a pill bottle and drinking glass are in front of Susan, who has just used them in her suicide attempt. The suggestion of these carefully photographed symbols is that life is brittle and temporary. Particularly symbolic is the bizarre entertainment in the party scene. Because Kane joins the dancing and singing, the action suggests that he is doing no more than taking a role in life, never being himself or knowing himself. Symbols that frame the film are the wire fence and the "No Trespassing" sign at both beginning and end. These symbols suggest that even if we understand a little about Kane, or anyone else, there are boundaries we cannot pass, depths we can never reach.

[8] There are also amusing symbols that suggest the diminution not only of Kane but also of the other characters. An example is Bernstein's high-backed chair, which makes him look like a small child. Similarly, the gigantic fireplace at Xanadu makes both Kane and Susan seem like pygmies—a symbol of how great wealth dwarfs and dehumanizes people. Especially comic is Kane's picnic at Xanadu. In going into the country, Kane and his friends do not walk but ride in a long line of cars—more like a funeral procession than a picnic—and they stay overnight in a massive tent. Quite funny is the increasing distance between Kane and Emily, his first wife, in the rapid-fire shots that portray their developing separation. Even more comic is the vast distance at Xanadu between Kane and Susan when they discuss their life together. They are so far apart that they must shout to be heard. Amusing as these symbols of diminution and alienation are, however, they are also pathetic, because at first Kane finds closeness with both his wives.

[9] In all respects, *Citizen Kane* is a superb film. This is not to say that the characters are likable or that the amusing parts make it a comedy. Instead, the film pursues truth, suggesting that greatness and wealth cannot give happiness. It is relentless in whittling away at its major figure. Kane is likable at times, and he is enormously generous (as shown when he sends Jedediah $25,000 in severance pay). But these high moments show the contrasting depths to which Kane falls, with the general point being that people who are powerful and great may deteriorate even at their height. The goal of the newsreel director at the beginning is to get at the "real story" behind the public man. There is more to any person than a two-hour film can reveal, but within its limits, *Citizen Kane* gets at the real story, and the real story is both sad and disturbing.

Work Cited

Citizen Kane. By Orson Welles and Herman R. Mankiewicz. Dir. Orson Welles. Perf. Orson Welles et al. 1941. DVD. Turner Entertainment Co. and Warner Home Video. © 2001.

Commentary on the Essay

The major point of this essay is that the film diminishes the major figure, Kane. In this respect the essay illustrates the analysis of *character* (Chapter 3), and it therefore emphasizes how film can be considered as a form of literature. Also shown in the essay are other methods of literary analysis: *structure* (Chapter 5) and *symbolism* (Chapter 10). Of these topics, only the use of symbols, because they are visually presented in the film, is unique to the medium of film as opposed to the medium of words.

Any one of the topics might be developed as a separate essay. There is more than enough about the character of Susan, for example, to sustain a complete essay, and the film's structure could be extensively explored. *Citizen Kane* itself as a repository of film techniques is rich enough for an exhaustive, book-length account, and such accounts do, indeed, exist.

Because the essay is about a film, the unique aspect of paragraph 1 is the opening brief description (stressing the medium of black and white) and the credits to the scriptwriters, principal photographer, composer, and director. Unlike works written by a single author, film is a collaborative medium, and therefore it is appropriate to recognize the separate efforts of the principal contributors.

Paragraph 2 begins the body and carries out a brief analysis of the major character. Paragraphs 3 to 5 discuss various aspects of the film's structure (the second topic announced in the thesis sentence) as they bear on Kane. Paragraph 3 explains the unifying importance of the sled and the reporter, Thompson. Paragraph 4 focuses on the film's use of flashback as a structural technique, while paragraph 5 discusses three of the flashback characters as they either intentionally or unintentionally reveal Kane's flaws. In paragraphs 6 to 8, the topic is film technique, the third and last topic of the thesis sentence. Paragraph 6 focuses on light, camera angles, and distortion; paragraph 7 treats visual symbols; paragraph 8 continues the topic of symbols but extends it to amusing ones. The final paragraph restates the central idea and also relates the theme of deterioration to the larger issue of how great wealth and power affect character.

Special Topics for Studying and Discussing Film

1. Select a single film technique, such as the use of color, the control of light, or the photographing of action, and write an essay describing how it is used in a film. For best results, use a DVD or a videocassette for your study. As much as possible, try to explain how the technique is used throughout the film. Determine constant and contrasting features, the relationship of the technique to the development of story and character, and so on.

2. Write an essay explaining how all the film techniques of a particular part or section are employed (e.g., camera angles, close-ups or long shots, tracking, on-camera and off-camera speeches, lighting, depth of field). For your study, you will have to rerun the section a number of times, trying to notice elements for the first time and also reinforcing your first observations. To add a research element to this question, you might consult the works by Bleiler, Ebert, Giannetti, Halliwell, Katz, Monaco, Peacock, Pym, and Thomson listed in the footnote on page 247.

3. Pick out a news story and write a dramatic scene about it. Next, consider how to write the scene for a film, providing directions for actors and camera operators (e.g., "As Character A speaks, his face shows that he is lying; the camera zooms slowly in on his face, with a loss of focus," or "As Character A speaks, the camera focuses on Character B exchanging looks with Character C"). When you are done, write an explanation of how you intend your directions to bring out details about your story and characters.

18

Writing and Documenting
the Research Essay
Using Extra Resources for Understanding

Broadly, **research** is the act of systematic investigation, examination, and experimentation. It is the basic tool of intellectual inquiry for anyone engaged in any discipline—physics, chemistry, biology, psychology, anthropology, history, and literature, to name just a few disciplines. With research, our understanding and our civilization grow; without it, they die.

The major assumption of doing research is that the researcher is reaching out into new areas of knowledge. With each assignment the researcher acquires not only the knowledge gained from the particular task but also the skills needed to undertake further research and thereby to gain further knowledge. Some research tasks are elementary, such as using a dictionary to discover the meaning of a word and thereby aiding the understanding of an important passage. More involved research uses an array of resources: encyclopedias, biographies, introductions, critical studies, bibliographies, and histories. When you begin a research task you usually have little or no knowledge about your topic, but with such resources you can acquire expert knowledge in a relatively short time.

Although research is the animating spark of all disciplines, our topic here is **literary research**—the systematic use of primary and secondary sources in studying a literary problem. In doing literary research, you consult not only individual works themselves (*primary sources*) but also other works that shed light on them and interpret them (*secondary sources*). Typical research tasks are to learn important facts about a work and the period in which it was written; to learn about the lives, careers, and other works of authors; to discover and apply the comments and judgments of modern or earlier critics; to learn details that help explain the meaning of works; and to learn about critical and artistic taste.

Selecting a Topic

In most instances, your instructor assigns a research essay on a specific topic. Sometimes, however, the choice of a topic will be left in your hands. For such assignments, it is helpful to know the types of research essays you might find most congenial. Here are some possibilities.

1. **A particular work.** You might treat character (for example, "The Character of Louise in Chopin's 'The Story of an Hour'"or "The Question of Whether Young Goodman Brown Is a Hero or a Dupe in Hawthorne's 'Young Goodman Brown'") or tone, ideas, structure, form, and the like. A research paper on a single work is similar to an essay on the same work, except that the research paper takes into account more views and facts than those you are likely to have without the research.

2. **A particular author.** A project might focus on an idea or some facet of style, imagery, setting, or tone of the author, tracing the origins and development of the topic through a number of different stories, poems, or plays. Examples are "Hardy's Treatment of Local Country Folkways in His Short Stories" and "Frost's Conversational Speaker in Poetry Written Before 1920." This type of essay is suitable for a number of shorter works, although it is also applicable for a single major work, such as a longer story, novel, or play.

3. **Comparison and contrast** (see Chapter 14). There are two types.

   a. *An idea or quality common to two or more authors.* Here you show points of similarity or contrast, or else you show how one author's work can be taken to criticize another's. A possible subject is "Contrasting Uses of Dialogue in Chekhov and Glaspell" or "The Theme of Love and Sexuality in Shakespeare, Chekhov, and Arnold."

   b. *Different critical views of a particular work or body of works.* Sometimes much is to be gained from an examination of differing critical opinions on topics like "The Meaning of Poe's 'The Masque of the Red Death'" or "Various Views of Hawthorne's 'Young Goodman Brown.'" Such a study would attempt to determine the critical opinion and taste to which a work did or did not appeal, and it might also aim at conclusions about whether the work was in the advance or rear guard of its time.

4. **The influence of an idea, author, philosophy, political situation, or artistic movement on specific works of an author or authors.** An essay on influences can be specific and to the point, as in "Details of Black American Life as Reflected in Hughes's 'Negro,'" or else it can be more abstract and critical, as in "The Influence of Racial Oppression and the Goal of Racial Equality on the Speaker of Hughes's 'Negro.'"

5. **The origin of a particular work or type of work.** Such an essay might examine an author's biography to discover the germination and development of a work—for example, "'Kubla Khan' as an Outgrowth of Coleridge's Reading." Another way of discovering origins might be to relate a work to a particular type or tradition: "'The Masque of the Red Death' and Poe's Theory of the Short Story" or "'Patterns' and Its Relationship to Antiwar Literature of World War I."

If you consider these types, an idea of what to write may come to you. Perhaps you have particularly liked one author or several authors. If so, you might start to think along the lines of types 1, 2, or 3. If you are interested in influences or origins, then type 4 or 5 may suit you better.

If you still cannot decide on a topic after rereading the works you have liked, then you should carry your search for a topic into your school library. Look up your author or authors in the computer or card catalogue. Your first goal should be to find a relatively recent book-length critical study published by a university press. Look for a title indicating that the book is a general one dealing with the author's major works rather than just one work. Study those chapters relevant to the work or works you have chosen. Most writers of critical studies describe their purpose and plan in their introductions or first chapters, so begin with the first part of the book. If there is no separate chapter on the primary text, use the index as your guide to the relevant pages. Reading in this way will give you enough knowledge about the issues and ideas raised by the work to enable you to select a promising topic. Once you make your decision, you are ready to develop a working bibliography.

Setting up a Bibliography

The best way to develop a working bibliography of books and articles is to begin with major critical studies of the writer or writers. Again, go to the computer or card catalogue and find books that have been published by university presses. These books always contain comprehensive bibliographies. Be careful to read the chapters on your primary work or works and to look for the footnotes or endnotes, for often you can save time if you record the names of books and articles listed in these notes. Then refer to the bibliographies included at the ends of the books, and select likely looking titles. Now, look at the dates of publication of the scholarly books. Let us suppose that you have been looking at three, published in 1998, 2002, and 2004. Unless you are planning an extensive research assignment, you can safely assume that the writers of critical works will have done the selecting for you of important works published before the date of publication. These bibliographies will be reliable, and you can use them with confidence. Thus, the bibliography in a book published in 2002 will be complete up through about 2000–2001, for the writer will have finished the manuscript a year or two before the book was published. But such bibliographies will not go up to the present. For that, you will need to search for works published after the most recent of the books.

Consult Bibliographical Guides

Fortunately for students doing literary research, the Modern Language Association (MLA) of America has been providing a complete bibliography of literary studies for years, not only in English and American literatures but also in the literatures of many foreign languages. This is the *MLA International Bibliography of Books and Articles on the Modern Languages and Literatures* (*MLA Bibliography*). The *MLA Bibliography* started achieving completeness in the late 1950s. By 1969 the project had grown so large that it was published in many parts, which are bound together in library editions. University and college libraries have sets of this bibliography on open shelves or tables. The *MLA Bibliography* is also published on CD-ROM and on the Internet, formats accessible to you through your college library facilities. You will need to consult with a librarian about Internet access.

There are many other bibliographies useful for students doing literary research, such as the *Essay and General Literature Index*, the *International Index*, the *Reader's Guide to Periodical Literature*, *A Bibliography of Literary Theory, Criticism and Philology, 9th edition* (2004), available at <http://fyl.unizar.es/filologia_inglesa/bibliography.html>, and various specific indexes. The *MLA Bibliography* is more than adequate, however, for most purposes. Remember that as you progress in your reading, the notes and bibliographies in the works you consult will also constitute an unfolding selective bibliography. For the illustrative research essay in this chapter, a number of entries were discovered not from bibliographies like those just listed but from the reference lists in critical books.

The *MLA Bibliography*, in the traditional book format, is conveniently organized by period and author. Should you be doing research about Gwendolyn Brooks, look her up in *Volume I: British and Irish, Commonwealth, English, Caribbean, and American Literatures*, where you will also find references to most other authors of works in English, such as Shakespeare, Wordsworth, and Arnold. You will find most books and articles listed under the author's last name. In the *MLA Bibliography*, journal references are abbreviated, but a lengthy list explaining abbreviations appears at the beginning of the volume. Using the *MLA Bibliography* in the book format, begin with the most recent one and then go backward to your stopping point. If your library has machines dedicated to the electronic versions of the bibliography, you can do your searching by typing in the name of your author or subject. By whatever means you gain access to the bibliography, be sure to get the complete information, especially volume numbers and years of publication, for each article and book. You are now ready to find your sources and to take notes.

Online Library Services

Today, virtually all libraries have their own computerized catalogues, and card catalogues are growing rare. Through computer access, many college and university libraries are instantaneously connected to a vast array of local, national, and even international libraries, so that by using various online services, you can extend your research far beyond the capacities of your own library. You can use a personal computer to gain access to the catalogues of large research libraries, provided that you punch in the correct entry information, are able and willing to follow the program codes, and are patient and persistent.

Also, by registering an access code for <www.researchnavigator.com> and therefore by gaining entry to the Research Navigator system, many secondary sources are available to you as you use your own computer.[1] You will need, of course, to practice using the system.

In addition, by using search engines to gain access to sites on the World Wide Web, you can also discover special topics directly related to your subject—organizations devoted to making awards, for example, or clubs or other organizations that have been established in the home cities of particular authors, or works on topics inspired by various authors. The well-known Google search engine yields startling and overwhelming results. At the present time, it has been estimated that as many as eight billion Web pages are available through the regular Google service. This is a gross figure, of course, and refers to the entire range of all intellectual and scholarly disciplines, of which literature is only a part. The result is that more and more references are presently available, and thousands of pages are being added each day. The numbers of possible Google references are almost beyond comprehension.

The Google entry for Shakespeare, for example, yields 1,250,000 entries! The numbers for other writers are not as staggering, but they are staggering enough. Google lists 329,000 entries for Emily Dickinson, and 4,800 for David Wagoner. For Langston Hughes the number of entries is 153,000. Obviously the figures cited here are too massive for ordinary classroom purposes, and your principal task in the face of these overwhelming figures is to narrow your search. Look through a limited number of the titles, and pick out only those that you think will be most useful to you. You can also narrow your search by listing particular years of publication. For example, the year "2003" for Shakespeare's *Hamlet* in Google gives nine entries published that year on *Hamlet*, a number that facilitates the task of selection.

You can also connect with major libraries, though the ease with which you can gain access through a computer search is variable. Some library catalogues are friendly whereas others require a certain amount of trial and error.[2] In many cases you will need several tries to learn how to find what you are looking for, because the words some libraries use to categorize holdings are not immediately apparent. In all cases, practice with the various systems is essential, for you cannot expect to get the most out of an electronic search the first time you try.

After you have gained access, you can look up books by specific authors, or can select books about particular topics. A recent search for critical and interpretive works about Shakespeare in one of the major university libraries in the United States produced a list of 3,722 titles (not just in English but also in other languages). The same library listed 600 works (including videos) specifically about *Hamlet*. Another major university library produced 6,842 titles on Shakespeare biography and interpretation, and 411 titles exclusively on *Hamlet*.

---

[1]See Melissa Payton, *The Prentice Hall Guide to Evaluating Online Resources with Research Navigator* (Upper Saddle River: Prentice Hall, 2004).

[2]Libraries generally encourage access to their resources, so proper entry instructions are often attached to computer terminals, particularly for internal use. When you are hooked into catalogues of distant libraries, you will find that the computer screen itself contains instructions about what you need to do to continue your search.

Important Considerations About Computer-Aided Research

You must always keep in mind that online catalogues can give you only what has been entered into them. If one library classifies a work under "criticism and interpretation" and another classifies it under "characters," a search of "criticism and interpretation" at the first library will find the work but the same search at the second will not. Sometimes the inclusion of an author's life dates immediately following the name will throw off your search. Typographic errors in the system will cause additional search problems, although many programs try to forestall such difficulties by providing "nearby" entries to enable you to determine whether incorrectly entered topics may prove helpful to you. Also, if you use online services, be careful to determine the year when the computerization began. Many libraries have a recent commencement date—1978, for example, or 1985. For completeness, therefore, you would need assistance in finding catalogue entries for items published before these years.

Just a few years ago, the broadness of scope that electronic searches provide for most undergraduate students doing research assignments was not possible; today, it is commonplace. Even with the astounding possibilities of electronic resources, however, it is still necessary to take out actual books and articles—and read them and take notes on them—before you can begin and complete a research essay. The electronic services can help you locate materials, but they cannot do your reading, note taking, and writing. All that is still up to you, as it always has been.

Your list will make up a fairly comprehensive search bibliography, which you can use when you physically enter the library to begin collecting and using materials. A major convenience is that many associated libraries, such as state colleges and urban public libraries, have pooled their resources. Thus, if you use the services of a network of nearby county libraries, you can go to another library to use materials that are not accessible at your own college or branch. If distances are great, however, and your own library does not have a book that you think is important to your project, you can ask a librarian to get the book for you through the Interlibrary Loan Service. Usually, given time, the libraries will accommodate as many of your needs as they can.

A promising new feature in computer research became available in 2004. This is the <scholar.google.com> site, which contains general scholarly listings for the hard and social sciences as well as for literature. The listings refer to books, articles, and abstracts. For example, Google Scholar lists fifty two entries for Arnold's "Dover Beach," thirty-one for Glaspell's *Trifles*, and twenty-nine for Bierce's "An Occurrence at Owl Creek Bridge." One must hasten to add that Google Scholar provides a listing of works, not a collection. The articles themselves are only haphazardly available through the search engine, and you will often find a restriction on your right to access some of the listed materials. A particular convenience is that Google Scholar lists state libraries where particular books are part of the collection, so that if time is available you can go to the libraries or request interlibrary loans. As yet, however, Google Scholar is not comprehensive for literary topics.

Taking Notes

There are many ways of taking notes, but the consensus is that the best method is to use note cards.[3] If you have never used cards before, you might profit from consulting any one of a number of handbooks and special workbooks on research. The principal advantage of cards is that you can see them all together when you lay them out on a desk or other large surface. As a result, cards may be easily classified; numbered and renumbered; shuffled; tried out in one place, rejected, and then used in another place (or thrown away); and arranged in order when you start to write.

Take Complete and Accurate Notes

Write the Source on Each Card   As you take notes, write the source of your information on each card. This may seem bothersome, but it is easier than going back to the library to locate the correct source after you have begun your essay. You can save time if you take the complete data on one card—a "master card" for that source—and then create an abbreviation for the separate note cards you take from the source. Here is an example, which also includes the location where the reference was originally found (e.g., card catalogue, computer search, bibliography in a book, the *MLA Bibliography*, etc.). Observe that the author's last name goes first.

```
Donovan, Josephine, ed. Feminist            PN
    Literary Criticism: Explorations         98
    in Theory. 2nd ed. Lexington:           W64
UP of Kentucky. 1989                         F4

DONOVAN

Card Catalogue, "Women"
```

[3]See Muriel Harris, *Prentice Hall Reference Guide to Grammar and Usage.* 5th ed. (Upper Saddle River: Prentice Hall, 2003), 283–301.

If you take many notes from this book, the name *Donovan* will serve as identification. Be sure not to lose your master cards because you will need them when you prepare your list of works cited. If possible, record the complete bibliographical data in a computer file.

Record the Page Number for Each Note   It would be hard to guess how much exasperation has been caused by the failure to record page numbers in notes. Be sure to write the page number down first, *before* you begin to take your note, and, to be doubly sure, write the page number again at the end of your note. If the detail goes from one page to the next in your source, record the exact spot where the page changes, as in this example.

Heilbrun and Stimson, in DONOVAN, pp. 63–64

[63]After the raising of the feminist consciousness it is necessary to develop/[64] "the growth of moral perception" through anger and the "amelioration of social inequities."

The reason for such care is that you may wish to use only a part of a note you have taken, and when there are two pages you will need to be accurate in locating what goes where.

Record Only One Fact or Opinion on a Card   Record only one major detail on each card—one quotation, one paraphrase, one observation—*never two or more.* You might be tempted to fill up the entire card with many separate but unrelated details, but such a try at economy often gets you in trouble because you might want to use some of the details in other places. If you have only one entry per card, you will avoid such problems and also retain the freedom you need.

Use Quotation Marks for All Quoted Material   In taking notes it is extremely important—vitally important—to distinguish copied material from your own words. *Always put quotation marks around every direct quotation you copy verbatim from a source.* Make the quotation marks *immediately, before you forget,* so that you will always know that the words of your notes within quotation marks are the words of another writer.

Often, as you take a note, you may use some of your own words and some of the words from your source. In cases like this you should be even more cautious. Put quotation marks around *every word* that you take directly from the source, even if your note looks like a picket fence. Later, when you begin writing your essay, your memory of what is yours and not yours will be dim, and *if you use another's words in your own essay without proper acknowledgment, you are risking the charge of plagiarism.* Much of the time, plagiarism is caused not by deliberate deception but rather by sloppy note taking.

If Your Source Is Long, Make a Brief and Accurate Paraphrase

When you take notes, it is best to paraphrase the sources. A paraphrase is a re-statement in your own words, and because of this it is actually a first step in the writing of your essay. A big problem in paraphrasing is to capture the idea in the source without copying the words verbatim. The best way is to read and reread the passage you are noting. Turn over the book or journal—or put your computer screen to sleep—and write out the idea *in your own words* as accu-rately as you can. Once you have completed this note, compare it with the orig-inal and make corrections to improve your thought and emphasis. Add a short quotation if you believe it is needed, but be sure to use quotation marks. If your paraphrase is too close to the original, *throw out the note and write another one*. This effort may have its own reward because often you may be able to transfer some or even all of your note, word for word, directly to the appropriate place in your research essay.

To see the problems of paraphrasing, let us look at a paragraph of criticism and then see how a student doing research might take notes on it. The para-graph is by Richard F. Peterson, from an essay entitled "The Circle of Truth: The Stories of Katherine Mansfield and Mary Lavin," published in *Modern Fiction Studies* 24 (1978): 383–394. In the passage to be quoted, Peterson is considering the structures of two Mansfield stories, "Bliss" and "Miss Brill":

> "Bliss" and "Miss Brill" are flawed stories, but not because the truth they re-veal about their protagonists is too brutal or painful for the tastes of the common reader. In each story, the climax of the narrative suggests an arranged reality that leaves a lasting impression, not of life, but of the author's cleverness. This strategy of arrangement for dramatic effect or revelation, unfortunately, is com-mon in Katherine Mansfield's fiction. Too often in her stories a dropped remark at the right or wrong moment, a chance meeting or discovery, an intrusive fig-ure in the shape of a fat man at a ball or in the Cafe de Madrid, a convenient death of a hired man or a stranger dying aboard a ship, or a *deus ex machina* in the form of two doves, a dill pickle, or a fly plays too much of a role in/[386] cre-ating a character's dilemma or deciding the outcome of the narrative. 385–386

Because taking notes forces a shortening of this or any criticism, it also requires you to discriminate, judge, interpret, and select; good note taking is not easy. There are some things to guide you, however, when you go through the many sources you uncover.

Think about the Purpose of Your Research   You may not know exactly what you are "fishing for" when you start to take notes, for you cannot prejudge what your essay will contain. Research is a form of discovery. But soon you will notice subjects and issues that your sources constantly explore. If you can accept one of these as your major topic, or focus of interest, you can use that as your guide in all further note taking.

For example, suppose you start to take notes on criticism about Katherine Mansfield's "Miss Brill," and after a certain amount of reading, you decide to focus on the story's structure. This decision guides your further research and note taking. Thus, for example, Richard Peterson criticizes Mansfield's technique of arranging climaxes in her stories. With your topic being structure, it would therefore be appropriate to take a note on Peterson's judgment. The following note is adequate as a brief reminder of the content in the passage:

Peterson 385   structure: negative

Peterson claims that Mansfield creates climaxes that are too artificial, too unlifelike, giving the impression not of reality but of Mansfield's own "cleverness."   385

Let us now suppose that you want a fuller note, in the expectation that you need not just Peterson's general idea but also some of his supporting detail. Such a note might look like this:

Peterson 385   structure: negative

Peterson thinks that "Bliss" and "Miss Brill" are "flawed" because they have contrived endings that give the impression "not of life" but of Mansfield's "cleverness." She arranges things artificially, according to Peterson, to cause the endings in many other stories. Some of these things are chance remarks, discoveries, or meetings, together with other unexpected or chance incidents and objects. These contrivances make their stories imperfect.   385

In an actual research essay, any part of this note would be useful. The words are almost all the note taker's own, and the few quotations are within quotation marks. Note that Peterson, the critic, is properly recognized as the source of the criticism, so you could adapt the note easily when you are doing your writing. The key here is that your note taking should be guided by your developing plan for your essay.

Note taking is part of your thinking and composing process. You may not always know whether you will be able to use each note that you take, and you will exclude many notes when you write your essay. You will always find, however, that taking notes is easier once you have determined your purpose.

Title Your Notes   To help plan and develop the various parts of your essay, write a title for each of your notes, as in the examples in this chapter. This practice is a form of outlining. Let us continue discussing the structure of

Mansfield's "Miss Brill," the actual subject of the illustrative research essay (pages 278–286). As you do your research, you discover that there is a divergence of critical thought about how the ending of the story should be understood. Here is a note about one of the diverging interpretations:

> Daly 90   Last sentence of the story
>
> Miss Brill's "complete identification" with the shabby fur piece at the very end may cause readers to conclude that she is the one in tears but bravely does not recognize this fact, and also to conclude that she may never use the fur in public again because of her complete defeat. Everything may be for "perhaps the very last time."

Notice that the title classifies the topic of the note. If you use such classifications, a number of like-titled cards could underlie a section in your essay about how to understand the concluding sentence of "Miss Brill." In addition, once you decide to explore the last sentence, the topic itself will guide you in further study and note taking. (See the illustrative essay, in which paragraphs 19 to 24 concern this topic.)

Write Down Your Own Original Thoughts, and Be Sure to Mark Them as Your Own   As you take notes, you will be acquiring your own observations and thoughts. Do not push these aside in your mind, on the chance of remembering them later, but write them down immediately. Often you may notice a detail that your source does not mention, or you may get a hint for an idea that the critic does not develop. Often, too, you may get thoughts that can serve as "bridges" between details in your notes or as introductions or concluding observations. Be sure to title your comments and also to mark them as your own thought. Here is such a note, which is on the emphasis on character as opposed to action in "Miss Brill":

> My Own   Last sentence of the story
>
> Mansfield's letter of Jan. 17, 1921, indicates that action as such was less significant in her scheme for the story than the sympathetic evocation of Miss Brill's observations, impressions, and moods. She wanted to reveal character.

Observe that in paragraph 5 of the illustrative research essay, the substance of this note (also a good deal of the language) is used to introduce new material once the passage from the Mansfield letter has been quoted.

Classify Your Cards and Group Them

If you do a careful and thorough job of taking notes, your essay will already have been forming in your mind. The titles of your cards will suggest areas to be developed as you do your planning and initial drafting. Once you have assembled a stack of note cards derived from a reasonable number of sources (your instructor may have assigned an approximate number or a minimum number), you can sort them into groups according to the topics and titles. For the illustrative research essay, after some shuffling and retitling, the cards were assembled in the following groups:

1. Writing and publication
2. The title: amusement and seriousness
3. General structure
4. Specific structures: season, time of day, levels of cruelty, Miss Brill's own "hierarchies" of unreality
5. The concluding paragraphs, especially the last sentence
6. Concluding remarks

If you look at the major sections of the illustrative essay, you will see that the topics are closely adapted from these groups of cards. In other words, *the arrangement of the cards is an effective means of outlining and organizing a research essay.*

Make Logical Arrangements of the Cards in Each Group There is still much to do with each group of cards. You cannot use the details as they happen to fall randomly in your stack. You need to decide which notes are relevant. You might also need to retitle some cards and use them elsewhere. Those that remain will have to be arranged in a logical order for you to find use for them in your essay.

Once you have your cards in order, you can write whatever comments or transitions are needed to move from detail to detail. Write this material directly on the cards and be sure to use a different color ink so that you can distinguish later between the original note and what you add. Here is an example of such a "developed" note card:

Magalaner 39   Structure, general

Speaking of Mansfield's sense of form, and referring to "Miss Brill" as an example, Magalaner states that Mansfield has power to put together stories from "a myriad of threads into a rigidly patterned whole." 39

Some of these "threads" are the fall season, the time of day, examples of unkindness, the park bench sitters from the cupboards, and Miss Brill's stages of unreality (see Thorpe 661). Each of these is separate, but all work together to unify the story.

By adding such commentary to your note cards, you are also simplifying the writing of your first draft. In many instances, the note and the comment may be moved directly into the paper with minor adjustments (some of the content of this note appears in paragraph 6 of the illustrative essay, and almost all of the topics introduced here are developed in paragraphs 9 to 14).

Be Creative and Original Even Though You Are Doing Research   You will not always transfer your notes directly into your essay. The major trap to avoid in a research paper is that your use of sources can become an end in itself and therefore a shortcut for your own thinking and writing. Often, students make the mistake of introducing details the way a master of ceremonies introduces performers in a variety show. This is unfortunate because it is the *student* whose essay will be judged, even though the sources, like the performers, do all the work. Thus, it is important to be creative and original in a research essay and to do your own thinking and writing, even though you are relying heavily on your sources. Here are five ways in which research essays may be original.

1. **Your selection of material is original with you.** In each major part of your essay you will include many details from your sources. To be creative you should select different but related details and avoid overlapping or repetition. Your completed essay will be judged on the basis of the thoroughness with which you make your points with different details (which in turn will represent the completeness of your research). Even though you are relying on published materials and cannot be original on that score, your selection can be original because you bring these materials together for the first time, and because you emphasize some details and minimize others. Inevitably, your assemblage of details from your sources will be unique and therefore original.

2. **Your development of your essay is yours alone.** Your arrangement of your various points is an obvious area of originality: One detail seems naturally to precede another, and certain conclusions stem from certain details. As you present the details, conclusions, and arguments from your sources, you can also add an original stamp by introducing supporting details different from those in the source material. You can also add your own emphasis to particular points—an emphasis that you do not find in your sources.

3. **Your words are yours and yours alone.** Naturally, the words that you use will be original because they are yours. Your topic sentences, for example, will all be your own. As you introduce details and conclusions, you will need to write "bridges" to get yourself from point to point. These can be introductory remarks or transitions. In other words, as you write, you are not just stringing your notes together, but rather you are actively assembling and arranging your notes and thoughts in creative and unique ways.

4. **Explaining and contrasting controversial views is an original presentation of material.** Closely related to your selection is that in your research you may have found conflicting or differing views on a topic. If you make a point to describe and distinguish these views, and explain the reasons for the differences, you are presenting material originally. To see

how differing views can be handled, see paragraphs 19 through 21 of the illustrative essay.

5. **Your own insights and positions are uniquely your own.** There are three possibilities here, all related to how well you have learned the primary texts on which your research in secondary sources is based.

   a. *Weave your own interpretations and ideas into your essay.* An important part of taking notes is to make your own points *precisely when they occur to you.* Often you can expand these as truly original parts of your essay. Your originality does not need to be extensive; it may consist of no more than a single insight. Here is such a card, which was written during research on the structure of "Miss Brill."

My Own	Miss Brill's unreality

   It is ironic that the boy and girl sit down on the bench next to Miss Brill just when she is at the height of her fancies. By allowing her to overhear their insults, they introduce the harshness of reality to her. The result is that she is plunged instantly from the height of rapture to the depth of pain.

   The originality here is built around the contrast between Miss Brill's exhilaration and her rapid and cruel deflation. This observation is not unusual or startling, but it nevertheless represents original thought about the story. When modified and adapted (and put into full sentences with proper punctuation), the material of the card supplies much of paragraph 18 of the illustrative essay. You can see that your development of a "My Own" note card is an important part of the prewriting stage of a research essay.

   b. *Filling gaps in the sources enables you to present original thoughts and insights.* As you read your secondary sources, you may realize that an obvious conclusion is not being made or that an important detail is not being stressed. Here is an area that you can develop on your own. Your conclusions may involve a particular interpretation or major point of comparison, or they may rest on a particularly important but understressed word or fact. For example, paragraphs 21 to 24 in the illustrative essay form an argument based on observations that critics have overlooked, or have neglected to mention, about the conclusion of "Miss Brill." In your research, whenever you find such a critical "vacuum" (assuming that you cannot read all the articles about some of your topics, where your discovery may already have been made a number of times), it is right to include whatever is necessary to fill it.

   c. *By disputing your sources, you are being original.* Your sources may present arguments that you wish to dispute. As you develop your disagreement, you will be arguing originally, for you will be using details in a different way from that of the critic or critics whom you are disputing, and your conclusions will be your own. This area of originality is similar to the laying out of controversial critical views, except that you furnish one of the opposing views yourself. The approach is limited because it is difficult to find many substantive points of interpretation on which there are not already clearly delineated opposing views. Paragraph 13 of the illustrative research essay shows how a disagreement can lead to a different, if not original, interpretation.

Documenting Your Work

It is necessary and essential to acknowledge—to *document*—all sources from which you have *quoted or paraphrased* factual and interpretive information. This point cannot be overemphasized because of the need to avoid being challenged for plagiarism. As the means of documentation, various reference systems use parenthetical references, footnotes, or endnotes. Whatever system is used, documentation almost always includes a carefully prepared bibliography, or list of works cited.

We will first discuss the list of works cited and then review the two major reference systems for use in a research paper. Parenthetical references, preferred by the Modern Language Association (MLA) since 1984, are described in Joseph Gibaldi, *MLA Handbook for Writers of Research Papers*, 6th ed., 2003. Footnotes or endnotes, recommended by the MLA before 1984, are still required by many instructors.

A List of Works Cited (Bibliography) Is a List of the Works You Have Used

The key to any reference system is a carefully prepared list of works cited that is included at the end of the essay. "Works Cited" means exactly that; the list should include just those books and articles you have actually *used* in your essay. If, however, your instructor requires that you use footnotes or endnotes, you can extend your concluding list to be a complete bibliography both of works cited and also of works consulted but not actually used. *Always, always, always, follow your instructor's directions.*

The list of works cited should include the following information, in each entry, in the form indicated. If you are using a word processor with the capacity to make italics, you can italicize book and article titles rather than underline them.

For a Book

1. The author's name: last name first, followed by first name and middle name or initial. Period.
2. The title, italicized or underlined. Period.
3. The city of publication (not state or nation), colon; publisher (easily recognized abbreviations or key words can be used unless they seem awkward or strange; see the *MLA Handbook*, pp. 272–274), comma; year of publication. Period.

For an Article

1. The author's name: last name first, followed by first name and middle name or initial. Period.
2. The title of the article in quotation marks. Period.
3. The title of the journal or periodical, italicized or underlined, followed by the volume number in Arabic (*not* Roman) numbers with no punctuation, then the year of publication within parentheses. Colon. For a daily paper or weekly magazine, omit the parentheses and cite the date in the British style followed by a colon (day, month, year, as in *2 Feb. 2005:*). Inclusive page numbers (without any preceding *p.* or *pp.*). Period.

The works cited should be listed alphabetically according to the last names of authors, with unsigned articles included in the list alphabetically by titles. Bibliographical lists are begun at the left margin, with subsequent lines in hanging indentation, so that the key locating word—the author's last name or the first title word of an unsigned article—can be easily seen. Many unpredictable and complex combinations, including ways to describe works of art, musical or other performances, and films, are detailed extensively in the *MLA Handbook* (142–235). Here are two model entries.

Book: Alpers, Antony. *The Life of Katherine Mansfield.* New York: Viking, 1980.

Article: Hankin, Cheryl. "Fantasy and the Sense of an Ending in the Work of Katherine Mansfield." *Modern Fiction Studies* 24 (1978): 465–474.

Refer to Works Parenthetically as You Draw Details from Them

Within the text of your research essay, use parentheses in referring to works from which you are using facts and conclusions. This parenthetical citation system is recommended in the *MLA Handbook* (238–260), and its principle is to provide documentation without asking readers to interrupt their reading to find footnotes or endnotes. Readers wanting to see the complete reference can easily find it in your list of works cited. With this system, you incorporate the author's last name and the relevant page number or numbers directly, whenever possible, into the body of your essay. If the author's name is mentioned in your discussion, you need to give only the page number or numbers in parentheses. Here are two examples.

Alexander Pope believed in the idea that the universe is a whole, a totally unified body, which provides a "viable benevolent system for the salvation of everyone who does good" (Kallich 24).

Martin Kallich draws attention to Alexander Pope's belief in the idea that the universe is a whole, a totally unified body, which provides a "viable benevolent system for the salvation of everyone who does good" (24).

Footnotes and Endnotes Are Formal and Traditional Reference Formats

The most formal system of documentation still widely used is that of *footnotes* (references at the bottom of each page) or *endnotes* (references listed numerically at the end of the essay). If your instructor wants you to use one of these formats, do the following: Make a note the first time you quote or refer to a source, with the details ordered as outlined below.

For a Book

1. The author's name: first name or initials first, followed by middle name or initial, then last name. Comma.
2. The title, underlined or italicized for a book, no punctuation. If you are referring to a work in a collection (article, story, poem) use quotation marks for that, but italicize or underline the title of the book. No punctuation, but use a comma after the title if an editor, translator, or edition number follows.
3. The name of the editor or translator, if relevant. Abbreviate "editor" or "edited by" as *ed.*, "editors" as *eds.* Use *trans.* for "translator" or "translated by." No punctuation, but use a comma if an edition number follows.
4. The edition (if indicated), abbreviated thus: *2nd ed., 3rd ed.,* and so on. No punctuation.
5. The publication facts, within parentheses, without any preceding or following punctuation, in the following order:
   a. City (but not the state or nation) of publication, colon.
   b. Publisher (clear abbreviations are acceptable and desirable), comma.
   c. Year of publication.
6. The page number(s) with no *p.* or *pp.*, for example, 5, 6–10, 15–19, 295–307, 311–316. Period. If you are referring to longer works, such as novels or longer stories with division or chapter numbers, include these numbers for readers who may be using an edition different from yours.

For a Journal or Magazine Article

1. The author: first name or initials first, followed by middle name or initial, then last name. Comma.
2. The title of the article, in quotation marks. Comma.
3. The name of the journal, italicized or underlined. No punctuation.
4. The volume number, in Arabic letters. No punctuation.
5. The year of publication within parentheses. Colon. For newspaper and journal articles, omit the parentheses, and include day, month, and year (in the British style: *21 May 2005*). Colon.
6. The page number(s) with no *p.* or *pp.*: 5, 6–10, 34–36, 98–102, 345–347. Period.

For later notes to the same work, use the last name of the author as the reference unless you are referring to two or more works by the same author. Thus, if you refer to only one work by, say, Thomas Hardy, the name *Hardy* will be enough for all later references. Should you be referring to other works by Hardy, however, you will also need to make a short reference to the specific works to distinguish them, such as *Hardy, "The Three Strangers,"* and *Hardy, "The Man He Killed."*

Footnotes are placed at the bottom of each page, and endnotes are included on separate page(s) at the end of the essay. The first lines of both footnotes and endnotes should be paragraph indented, and continuing lines should be flush with the left margin. Both endnote and footnote numbers are set in a smaller font and positioned slightly above the line (as superior numbers) like this: [12]. You can single-space footnotes and endnotes and leave a line of space between them. Most computer programs have specially designed and consecutively numbered footnote formats. These are generally acceptable, but be sure to consult your instructor. (For more detailed coverage of footnoting practices, see the *MLA Handbook*, 298–313.)

Sample Footnotes　　In the examples below, book titles and periodicals are shown *italicized*, as they would be in an essay prepared on the computer. If the essay is typewritten or handwritten, these titles should be underlined.

[1]Blanche H. Gelfant, *Women Writing in America: Voices in Collage* (Hanover: UP of New England, for Dartmouth College, 1984): 110.

[2]Günter Grass, "Losses," *Granta* 42 (Winter 1992): 99.

[3]John O'Meara, "*Hamlet* and the Fortunes of Sorrowful Imagination: A Reexamination of the Genesis and Fate of the Ghost," *Cahiers Elisabéthains* 35 (1989): 21.

[4]Grass 104.

[5]Gelfant 141.

[6]O'Meara 17.

As a principle, you do not need to repeat in a footnote or endnote any material you have already mentioned in your own discourse. For example, if you recognize the author and title of your source, then the footnote or endnote should give no more than the data about publication. Here is an example:

In *The Fiction of Katherine Mansfield*, Marvin Magalaner points out that Mansfield was as skillful in the development of epiphanies (that is, the use of highly significant though perhaps unobtrusive actions or statements to reveal the depths of a particular character) as James Joyce himself, the "inventor" of the technique.

---

[9](Carbondale: Southern Illinois UP, 1971): 130.

Many Academic Disciplines Set Their Own Requirements for Documentation

Other reference systems and style manuals have been adopted by various disciplines (e.g., mathematics, medicine, psychology) to serve their own special needs. If you receive no instructions from your instructors in other courses, you can adapt the systems described here. If you need to use the documentation methods of other fields, however, use the *MLA Handbook,* pages 316–317 for guidance about which style manual to select.

When in Doubt, Consult Your Instructor

As long as all you want from a reference is the page number of a quotation or paraphrase, the parenthetical system described briefly here—and detailed fully in the *MLA Handbook*—is the most suitable and convenient one you can use. However, you may wish to use footnotes or endnotes if you need to add more details, provide additional explanations, or refer your readers to other materials that you are not using.

Whatever method you follow, *you must always acknowledge sources properly.* Remember that whenever you begin to write and cite references, you might forget a number of specific details about documentation, and you will certainly discover that you have many questions. Be sure, then, to ask your instructor, who is your final authority.

Strategies for Organizing Ideas in Your Research Essay

Introduction

In your research essay you may wish to expand your introduction more than usual because of the need to relate the problem of research to your topic. You may wish to bring in relevant historical or biographical information (see, for example, the introduction of the illustrative research essay on pages 278–280). You may also wish to summarize critical opinion or describe critical problems about your topic. The idea is to lead your reader into your topic by providing interesting and significant materials that you have found.

Because of the length of most research essays, some instructors require a topic outline, which is in effect a brief table of contents. This pattern is observed in the illustrative research essay. *Because the inclusion of an outline is a matter of the instructor's choice, be sure to learn whether your instructor requires it.*

Body and Conclusion

As you write the body and conclusion of your research essay, your development will be governed by your choice of topic. Consult the relevant chapters in this book about what to include for whatever approach or approaches you select (setting, ideas, point of view, character, tone, or any other).

In length, the research essay can be anywhere from five to fifteen or more pages, depending on your instructor's assignment. Obviously, an essay on a single work will be shorter than one based on several. If you narrow the scope of your topic, as suggested in the approaches described at the beginning of this chapter, you can readily keep your essay within the assigned length. The following illustrative research essay, for example, illustrates approach 1 (page 259) by being limited to only one character in one story. Were you to write on characters in a number of other stories by Mansfield or any other writer (approach 2), you could limit your total number of pages by stressing comparative treatments and by avoiding excessive detail about problems pertaining to only one work.

Although you limit your topic yourself in consultation with your instructor, you may encounter problems because you will deal not with one source alone but with many. Naturally the sources will provide you with details and also trigger many of your ideas. The problem is to handle the many strands without piling on too many details, and also without being led into digressions. It is important therefore to keep your central idea foremost; the constant stressing of your central idea will help you both to select relevant materials and to reject irrelevant ones.

It bears reemphasis that you need to distinguish between *your own work* and the *sources* you are using. Your readers will assume that everything you write is your own unless you indicate otherwise. Therefore, when blending your words with the ideas from sources, be clear about proper acknowledgments. Most commonly, if you are simply presenting details and facts, you can write straightforwardly and let parenthetical references suffice as your authority, as in the following sentence from the illustrative research essay:

> While Cheryl Hankin suggests that the structuring is perhaps more "instinctive" than deliberate (474), Marvin Magalaner, using "Miss Brill" as an example, speaks of Mansfield's power to weave "a myriad of threads into a rigidly patterned whole" (39).

Here there can be no question about plagiarism, for the names of the authors of the critical sources are fully acknowledged, the page numbers are specific, and the quotation marks clearly distinguish the words of the critics from the words of the essay writer. If you grant recognition as recommended here, no confusion can result about the authority underlying your essay. The words obviously belong to the writer of the essay, but the parenthetical references clearly indicate that the sentence is based on two sources.

If you use an interpretation unique to a particular writer, or if you rely on a significant quotation from your source, you should make your acknowledgment an essential part of your discussion, as in this sentence.

> Saralyn Daly, referring to Miss Brill as one of Mansfield's "isolatoes"—that is, solitary persons cut off from normal human contacts (88)—fears that the couple's callous insults have caused Miss Brill to face the outside world with her fur piece "perhaps for the very last time" (90).

Here the idea of the critic is singled out for special acknowledgment. If you indicate your sources in this way, no confusion can arise about how you have
used them.

Illustrative Research Essay

The Structure of Mansfield's "Miss Brill"°

I.   *Introduction*
   A.   *The Writing of "Miss Brill"*
   B.   *The Choice of the Name "Brill"*
   C.   *The Story's Structure*
II. *Season and Time as Structure*
III. *Insensitive or Cruel Actions as Structure*
IV. *Miss Brill's "Hierarchy of Unrealities" as Structure*
V.   *The Story's Conclusion*
VI. *Conclusion*

I.   *Introduction*
   A.   *The Writing of "Miss Brill"*

[1]   <u>Because Katherine Mansfield's "Miss Brill"</u>—one of the eighty-eight short stories and fragments she wrote in her brief life (Magalaner 5)—<u>succeeds so well
as a portrait of the protagonist's inner life, it has become well known and has
been frequently anthologized (Gargano).</u> She apparently wrote it on the
evening of November 11, 1920, when she was staying at Isola Bella, an island
retreat in northern Italy where she had gone in her desperate attempt to overcome tuberculosis. In her own words, she describes the night of composition:

> Last night I walked about and saw the new moon with the old moon
> in her arms and the lights in the water and the hollow pools filled
> with stars—and lamented there was no God. But I came in and
> wrote Miss Brill instead; which is my insect Magnificat now and al-
> ways. (Letters 594)

Her husband, J. Middleton Murry, who had remained in London, published
the story in the November 26, 1920, issue of the journal *Athenaeum,* which
he was then editing. In 1922, Mansfield included "Miss Brill" in her collection
entitled *The Garden Party and Other Stories* (Daly 134).

[2]   <u>She was particularly productive at the time of "Miss Brill" despite her illness,
for she wrote a number of excellent stories then.</u> The others, as reported by
her biographer Antony Alpers, were "The Lady's Maid," "The Young Girl," "The
Daughters of the Late Colonel," and "The Life of Ma Parker" (304–305). All
these stories share the common bond of "love and pity" rather than the
"harshness or satire" that typifies a number of her earlier stories (Alpers 305).

°See pages 348–351 for this story.

As with the later stories, "Miss Brill," in the words of Angela Smith, possesses a "tantalizing power to puzzle the reader" (150). There is little question that the story creates questions and ambiguities.

B.   The Choice of the Name "Brill"

[3]   <u>Although "Miss Brill" is a serious story, for example, it definitely contains at least a minor element of humor.</u> James W. Gargano notes that the title character is named after a lowly flatfish, the brill. This fish, with notoriously poor vision, is related to the turbot and the whiting (it is the whiting that the rude girl compares to Miss Brill's fur piece). *The Oxford English Dictionary* records that the brill is "inferior in flavour" to the turbot. One may conclude that Mansfield, in choosing the name, is establishing her heroine's insignificance in the larger scheme of things.

[4]   <u>Despite this small and deflating trick on poor Miss Brill, the story is neverthe-less both touching and powerful.</u> The title character is portrayed as one who has been excluded from "public history" (Gubar 31) because she lives exclusively in the "feminine world" (Maurois 337). Her main concerns, in other words, are not power and greatness but the privacy of personal moments, which may be upset by no more than a contemptuous giggle (Gubar 38). The story's touching poignancy stems from Miss Brill's eagerness to be "part of a scene that ruthlessly excludes her" and thus makes her "the loneliest of all . . . [characters in] Katherine Mansfield's stories about lonely women" (Fullbrook 103). The power of the story results from the feeling with which Mansfield renders the "inarticulate longings and the tumultuous feelings that lie beneath the surface of daily life" (McLaughlin 381). A mark of her skill is the way in which she enters the consciousness of the heroine, so much so that Claire Tomalin declares that the story is "conceived virtually as [a] dramatic" mono-logue (213). Mansfield's description in writing "Miss Brill" bears out these claims, for it shows how deeply she tried to create the pathetic inner life of her character:

> In *Miss Brill* I choose not only the length of every sentence, but even the sound of every sentence. I choose the rise and fall of every paragraph to fit her, and to fit her on that day at that very moment. After I'd written it I read it aloud—numbers of times—just as one would *play over* a musical composition—trying to get it nearer to the expression of Miss Brill—until it fitted her. (Letter to Richard Murry of January 17, 1921, qtd. in Sewell, 5–6)

C.   The Story's Structure

[5]   <u>Mansfield's description strongly indicates that action in the story was less significant in her narrative aim than the sympathetic evocation of Miss Brill's mood and impressions.</u> Such a design might lead readers to conclude that the story is not so much formed as forming, a free rather than planned de-velopment. In reference to Mansfield's talent generally, Edward Wa-genknecht reflects that the stories, including "Miss Brill," are "hardly even episodes or anecdotes. They offer reflections [instead] of some aspect of experience or express a mood" (163). This observation is true of "Miss Brill." The story grows from within the character, and it leaves the impression of

an individual who experiences a "crisis in miniature," a "deep cut into time" in which life changes and all hopes and expectations are reversed (Hankin 465). This concentration on such important cuts is a significant part of Mansfield's narrative skill. When writing in her journal, she called such moments "glimpses," which one may think of as insights into the mysterious core of human character:

> And yet one has these "glimpses" . . . The waves, as I drove home this afternoon, and the high foam, how it was suspended in the air before it fell, . . . What is it that happens in that moment of suspension? It is timeless. In that moment (what *do* I mean?) the whole life of the soul is contained [Sandley 71].

[6] It follows that Mansfield's achievement in "Miss Brill" is to fashion a credible character in an especially pathetic and shattering moment—to present a "glimpse" of a character in the extreme of vulnerability. <u>The story embodies an intricate set of structures that complement this downward movement.</u>* Whatever the source of Mansfield's control over form, critics agree that her power was great. Marvin Magalaner, using "Miss Brill" as an example, speaks of Mansfield's weaving of "a myriad of threads into a rigidly patterned whole" (39). Noting the same control over form, Cheryl Hankin suggests that her structuring is perhaps more "instinctive" than deliberate (474). <u>These complementary threads, stages, or "levels" of "unequal length"</u> (Harmat uses the terms "niveaux" and "longueur inégale," 49, 51) <u>are the fall season, the time of day, insensitive or cruel actions, Miss Brill's own unreal perceptions, and the final section or dénouement.</u>†

II.   *Season and Time as Structure*

[7] <u>A significant aspect of structure in "Miss Brill" is Mansfield's use of the season of the year.</u> Autumn and its movement toward winter is integral to the deteriorating circumstances of the heroine. In the first paragraph, we learn that there is a "faint chill" in the air (is the word "chill" chosen to rhyme with "Brill"?), and this phrase is repeated in paragraph 10. Thus the author establishes autumn and the approaching end of the year as the beginning of the movement toward dashed hopes. This seasonal reference is also carried out when we read that "yellow leaves" are "down drooping" in the local *Jardins Publiques* (paragraph 6) and that leaves are drifting "now and again" from almost "nowhere, from the sky" (paragraph 1). It is the autumn cold that has caused Miss Brill to take out her bedraggled fur piece at which the young girl later is so amused. The chill, together with the fur, forms a structural setting integrated with both the action and the mood of the story. The story both begins and ends with the fur (Sewell 25), which is the direct cause of Miss Brill's deep hurt at the conclusion.

[8] <u>Like this seasonal structuring, the times of day parallel Miss Brill's darkening existence.</u> At the beginning, the day is "brilliantly fine—the blue sky powdered with gold," and the light is "like white wine." This figurative language suggests

---

*Central idea.
†Thesis sentence.

the brightness and crispness of full sunlight. In paragraph 6, where we also learn of the yellow leaves, "the blue sky with gold-veined clouds" indicates that time has been passing as clouds accumulate during late afternoon. By the story's end, Miss Brill has returned in sadness to her "little dark room" (paragraph 18). In other words, the time moves from day to evening, from light to darkness, as an accompaniment to Miss Brill's psychological pain.

III. *Insensitive or Cruel Actions as Structure*

[9] Mansfield's most significant structural device, which is not emphasized by critics, is the introduction of insensitive or cruel actions. It is as though the hurt felt by Miss Brill on the bright Sunday afternoon is also being felt by many others. Because she is the spectator who is closely related to Mansfield's narrative voice, Miss Brill is the filter through whom these negative examples reach the reader. Considering the patterns that emerge, one may conclude that Mansfield intends the beauty of the day and the joyousness of the band as an ironic contrast to the pettiness and insensitivity of the people in the park.

[10] The first characters are a silent couple on Miss Brill's bench (paragraph 3) and the incompatible couple of the week before (paragraph 4). Because these seem no more than ordinary, they do not seem at first to be part of the story's pattern of cruelty and rejection. But their incompatibility, suggested by their silence and one-way complaining, establishes a structural parallel with the young and insensitive couple who insult Miss Brill. Thus the first two couples prepare the way for the third, and all show increasing insensitivity and cruelty.

[11] Almost unnoticed as a second level of negation is the vast group of "odd, silent, nearly all old" people filling "the benches and green chairs" (paragraph 5). They seem to be no more than a normal part of the Sunday afternoon landscape. But these people are significant structurally because the "dark little rooms—or even cupboards" that Miss Brill associates with them describe her own circumstances at the story's end (paragraphs 5, 18). The reader may conclude from Miss Brill's quiet eavesdropping that she herself is one of these nameless and faceless ones, all of whom lead similarly drab lives.

[12] Once Mansfield has set these levels for her heroine, she introduces examples—glimpses—of more active rejection and cruelty. The beautiful woman who throws down the bunch of violets is the first of these (paragraph 8). The causes of this woman's scorn are not made clear, and Miss Brill does not know what to make of the incident; but the woman's actions suggest that she has been involved in a relationship that has ended bitterly.

[13] The major figure involved in rejection, who is important enough to be considered a structural double of Miss Brill, is the woman wearing the ermine toque (paragraph 8). It is clear that she, like Miss Brill, is one of "the lonely and isolated women in a hostile world" that Mansfield is so skillful in portraying (Gordon, paragraph 6). This woman tries to please the "gentleman in grey," but this man insults her by blowing smoke in her face. It could be, as Peter Thorpe observes, that she is "obviously a prostitute" (661). More likely, from the conversation overheard by Miss Brill, the "ermine toque" has had a broken relationship with the gentleman. Being familiar with his Sunday habits,

she deliberately comes to the park to meet him, as though by accident, to attempt a reconciliation. After her rejection, her hurrying off to meet someone "much nicer" (there is no such person, for Mansfield uses the phrase "as though" to introduce the ermine toque's departure) is her way of masking her hurt. Regardless of the exact situation, however, Mansfield makes it plain that the encounter demonstrates vulnerability, unkindness, and pathos.

[14] Once Mansfield establishes this major incident, she introduces two additional examples of insensitivity. At the end of paragraph 8, the hobbling old man "with long whiskers" is nearly knocked over by the group of four girls, who show arrogance if not contempt. The final examples involve Miss Brill herself. These are the apparent indifference of her students and that of the old invalid "who habitually sleeps" when she reads to him.

[15] Although "Miss Brill" is a brief story, Mansfield creates a large number of structural parallels to the sudden climax brought about by the insulting young couple. The boy and girl do not appear until the very end, in other words (paragraphs 11–14), but actions like theirs have been fully anticipated in all the story's earlier parts. Mansfield's speaker does not take us to the homes of the other victims, as she does when we follow Miss Brill into her poor lodgings, but the narrative invites us to conclude that the silent couple, the complaining wife and long-suffering husband, the unseen man rejected by the young woman, the ermine toque, and the funny gentleman, not to mention the many silent and withdrawn people sitting like statues in the park, all return to comparable loneliness and personal pain.

IV. *Miss Brill's "Hierarchy of Unrealities" as Structure*

[16] The intricacy of the structure of "Miss Brill" does not end here. Of great importance is the structural development of the protagonist herself. Peter Thorpe notes a "hierarchy of unrealities" that govern the reader's increasing awareness of her plight (661). By this measure, the story's actions progressively bring out Miss Brill's failures of perception and understanding—failures that in this respect make her like her namesake fish, the brill (Gargano).

[17] These unrealities begin with Miss Brill's fanciful but harmless imaginings about her shabby fur piece. This beginning sets up the pattern of her pathetic inner life. When she imagines that the park band is a "single, responsive, and very sensitive creature" (Thorpe 661), we realize that she is simply making too much out of a band of ordinary musicians. Although she cannot interpret the actions of the beautiful young woman with the violets, she does see the encounter between the ermine toque and the gentleman in grey as a glimpse into rejection. Her response is correct, but then her belief that the band's drumbeats are sounding out "The Brute! The Brute!" indicates her vivid overdramatization of the incident. The "top of the hierarchy of unrealities" (Thorpe 661) is her fancy that she is an actor with a vital part in a gigantic drama played by all the people in the park. The most pathetic aspect of this daydream is her unreal imagining that someone would miss her if she were absent.

[18] In light of this structure, or hierarchy, of unrealities, it is ironic that the boy and girl sit down next to her just when she is at the height of her fancy about her own importance. When she hears the girl's insults, the couple introduces

objective reality to her with a vengeance, and she is plunged from rapture to pain. The story's concluding two paragraphs hence form a rapid dénouement to reflect her loneliness and despair.

V. *The Story's Conclusion*

[19] Of unique importance in the structure of "Miss Brill" are the final two paragraphs—the conclusion, or dénouement—in which Miss Brill, all alone, returns to her miserable tiny room. Saralyn Daly, referring to Miss Brill as one of Mansfield's "isolatoes"—that is, solitary persons cut off from normal human contacts—fears that the couple's callous insults have caused Miss Brill to face the outside world with her fur piece "perhaps for the very last time" (88, 90). Sydney Kaplan adds a political dimension to Miss Brill's defeat, asserting that here and in other stories Mansfield is expressing "outrage" against "a society in which privilege is so marked by indifference" to situations like those of Miss Brill (192). One must emphasize, however, that Mansfield's focus is not on social iniquities, but rather on Miss Brill herself. Her pathetic experience exemplifies a personal pattern in which the old are destroyed "by loneliness and sickness, by fear of death, by the thoughtless energy of the younger world around them" (Zinman 457). Mansfield herself considered this negative situation more generally as "the snail under the leaf," which also implies that disaster is waiting for everyone, not just those who are old (Meyers, 213). With such a crushing experience for the major character, "Miss Brill" may be fitted to the structuring of Mansfield stories described by André Maurois: "moments of beauty suddenly broken by contact with ugliness, cruelty, or death" (342–343).

[20] Because some critics have stated that Miss Brill's downfall is sudden, they have criticized the conclusion. Peterson complains that the ending is artificial and contrived because of the improbability that the young couple would appear at just that moment to make their insults (385). On much the same ground, Berkman declares that the ending is excessive, mechanical, and obvious (162, 175).

[21] Cheryl Hankin, however, hints at another way in which the conclusion may be taken, a way that makes the story seem both ironic and grimly humorous. In describing patterns to be found in Mansfield's stories, Hankin notes the following situation, which may account for the story's ending:

> [A]n impending disillusionment or change in expectations may be deflected by the central character's transmutation of the experience into something positive. (466)

There is no question that the ending indicates that Miss Brill has been totally shattered. Her deflation is shown by her dejection when she returns to her small "cupboard" room.

[22] The story's very last sentence, however, may be read as a way of indicating that Miss Brill is going back to her regularly established habit of reconstructing reality, in this respect indicating the "something positive" described by Hankin: "But when she put the lid on she thought she heard something crying" (paragraph 18). It is hard to read this last sentence without finding irony and pathos there. By hearing "something crying" Miss Brill may likely

be imagining that the fur piece, and not she, has been hurt. One might remember that the thoughtless young girl has laughed at the fur because it resembles a "fried whiting" (paragraph 14). <u>The irony here is that Miss Brill</u>
<u>forgets about the pain she has just experienced, and now slips back into her</u>
<u>life of fantasy.</u>

[23] <u>This pattern of evasion is totally in keeping with Miss Brill's character.</u> Despite
her poverty and loneliness, she has been holding a job (as a teacher of English, presumably to French pupils), and has also been regularly performing
her voluntary task of reading to the infirm old man. Her life has been restricted, but her Sunday afternoons of eavesdropping have enabled her, through
"the power of her imagination," to share the lives of many others (Hanson and
Gurr 81). Mansfield establishes this vicarious sociability as Miss Brill's major
strength, which Hanson and Gurr call "the saving grace of her life" (81). Her
method makes her both strange and pathetic, but nevertheless she has been
functioning. Within such a framework, the deflating insults of paragraphs 13
and 14 may be seen as another incentive for her to strengthen her fancy, not
to abandon it.

[24] This is not to interpret the story's conclusion as an indication that Miss Brill
has shaken off the couple's insults. She is first and foremost a "victim" (Zinman 457), if not of others, then of her own reality-modifying imagination. But
she is presented as a character with positive qualities. Indeed, Mansfield herself expressed her own personal liking of Miss Brill (despite the name "brill").
Her husband, J. Middleton Murry, shortly after receiving the story from her for
publication, sent her a letter in which he expressed his fondness for the protagonist. In a return letter to him of November 21, 1920, Mansfield wrote that
she shared this fondness. She went on in the same letter to say:

> One writes (<u>one</u> reason why is) because one does care so passion-
> ately that one <u>must show</u> it—one must declare one's love. (qtd. in
> Magalaner 17)

Surely the author could love her creation out of pity alone, but if she had
added an element of strength, such as the brave but sad ability to adjust to
"impossible and intolerable conditions" (Zinman 457), then her love would
have an additional cause. <u>Therefore it is plausible that the last sentence of</u>
<u>"Miss Brill" shows the resumption of the heroine's characteristic way of sur-</u>
<u>viving through the power of her own fantasies.</u>

VI. Conclusion

[25] <u>"Miss Brill" is a compact story intricately built up from a number of parallel</u>
<u>structures.</u> Its insight into the life of the heroine justifies the tribute of Antony
Alpers that it is a "minor masterpiece" (305). The structural contrast between
the protagonist and the world around her is derived from a deeply felt di-
chotomy about life attributed to Mansfield herself, a sense that the human
soul is beautiful, on the one hand, but that people are often vile, on the other
(Moore 245).

[26] The greater structure of "Miss Brill" may therefore be taken as a hard, disillusioned view of life itself, in which those who are lonely, closed out, and
hurt are wounded even more. This pattern of exclusion not only affects the

restricted lives of the lonely, but it also reaches directly into their minds and souls. Miss Brill's response is to retreat further and further into an inner world of unreality but also to continue life, even at an almost totally subdued level, within these confines. <u>It is Mansfield's "almost uncanny psychological insight" into the operation of this characteristic response that gives "Miss Brill" its structure and also its excellence (Hankin 467).</u>

Works Cited

Alpers, Antony. *Katherine Mansfield: A Biography.* New York: Knopf, 1953.

Berkman, Sylvia. *Katherine Mansfield: A Critical Study.* New Haven: Yale UP (for Wellesley College), 1951.

Daly, Saralyn R. *Katherine Mansfield.* New York: Twayne, 1965.

Fullbrook, Kate. *Katherine Mansfield.* Bloomington and Indianapolis: Indiana UP, 1986.

Gargano, James W. "Mansfield's Miss Brill." *Explicator* 19. 2 (1960): item 10 (one page, unpaginated).

Gordon, Ian A. "Katherine Mansfield: Overview." D. L. Kirkpatrick, ed., *Reference Guide to English Literature,* 2nd ed., St. James Press, 1991 (found at <www.galenet.com>).

Gubar, Susan. "The Birth of the Artist as Heroine: (Re)production, the *Kunstler-Roman* Tradition, and the Fiction of Katherine Mansfield." Carolyn Heilbrun and Margaret R. Higonnet, ed., *The Representation of Women in Fiction.* Selected Papers from the English Institute, 1981. Baltimore: Johns Hopkins UP, 1983, 19–58.

Hankin, Cheryl. "Fantasy and the Sense of an Ending in the Work of Katherine Mansfield." *Modern Fiction Studies* 24 (1978): 465–474.

Hanson, Clare, and Andrew Gurr. *Katherine Mansfield.* New York: St. Martin's, 1981.

Harmat, Andrée-Marie. "Essai D'Analyse Structurale d'une Nouvelle Lyrique Anglaise: 'Miss Brill' de Katherine Mansfield." *Les Cahiers de la Nouvelle* 1 (1983): 49–74.

Kaplan, Sydney Janet. *Katherine Mansfield and the Origins of Modernist Fiction.* Ithaca and London: Cornell UP, 1991.

Magalaner, Marvin. *The Fiction of Katherine Mansfield.* Carbondale: Southern Illinois UP, 1971.

Mansfield, Katherine. *Katherine Mansfield's Letters to John Middleton Murry, 1913–1922.* Ed. John Middleton Murry. New York: Knopf, 1951. Cited as "Letters."

———. *The Short Stories of Katherine Mansfield.* New York: Knopf, 1967.

Maurois, André. *Points of View from Kipling to Graham Greene.* 1935. New York: Ungar, 1968.

McLaughlin, Ann L. "The Same Job: The Shared Writing Aims of Katherine Mansfield and Virginia Woolf." *Modern Fiction Studies* 24 (1978): 369–382.

Meyers, Jeffrey. *Katherine Mansfield: A Darker View.* 1978. New York: Cooper Square Press, 2002.

Moore, Virginia. *Distinguished Women Writers.* 1934. Port Washington: Kennikat, 1962.

Peterson, Richard F. "The Circle of Truth: The Stories of Katherine Mansfield and Mary Lavin." *Modern Fiction Studies* 24 (1978): 383–394.

Sandley, Sarah. "The Middle of the Note: Katherine Mansfield's 'Glimpses.'" Roger
    Robinson, ed., *Katherine Mansfield: In from the Margin.* Baton Rouge:
    Louisiana State UP, 1994: 70–89.
Sewell, Arthur. *Katherine Mansfield: A Critical Essay.* Auckland: Unicorn, 1936.
Smith, Angela. *Katherine Mansfield: A Literary Life.* Houndmills, Basingstoke: Pal-
    grave, 2000.
Thorpe, Peter. "Teaching 'Miss Brill.'" *College English* 23 (1962): 661–663.
Tomalin, Claire. *Katherine Mansfield: A Secret Life.* New York: Knopf, 1988.
Wagenknecht, Edward. *A Preface to Literature.* New York: Holt, 1954.
Zinman, Toby Silverman. "The Snail Under the Leaf: Katherine Mansfield's Im-
    agery." *Modern Fiction Studies* 24 (1978): 457–464.

Commentary on the Essay

This essay fulfills an assignment of 2,500 to 3,000 words, with twenty to thirty sources. (There are actually twenty-six, not counting a dictionary reference.)
The bibliography was developed from a college library card catalogue, references in books of criticism (Magalaner, Daly, Berkman); the *MLA International Bibliography;* the *Essay and General Literature Index,* and the Literature
Resource Center available through Netscape and a county library system
<www.wls.lib.ny.us>. The sources themselves were found in a college library
with selective holdings, in a local public library, and in online resources. There
is only one rare source, an article (Harmat) obtained in photocopy through interlibrary loan from one of only two U.S. libraries holding the journal in which
it appears. The location was made through the national OCLS online service. For
most semester-long or quarter-long courses, you will likely not have time to
add to your sources by this method, but the article in question refers specifically
to "Miss Brill," and it was therefore desirable to examine it.

The sources consist of books, articles, and chapters or portions of books.
One article (Sewell) has been published as a separate short monograph. Also,
one of the sources is the story "Miss Brill" itself (with locations made by paragraph number) together with editions of Mansfield's letters and a collection of
her stories. The sources are used for facts, interpretations, reinforcement of conclusions, and general guidance and authority. All necessary thematic devices,
including overall organization and transitions, are unique to the illustrative
essay. The essay also contains passages taking issue with certain conclusions in
a few of the sources. Additional particulars about the handling of sources and
developing a research essay are included in the discussion of note taking and
related matters in this chapter.

The introduction to the illustrative essay contains details about the writing
of the story and the title as well as a pointed summary of critical appraisals of the
story itself. The idea explored here is that the story dramatizes Miss Brill's emotional responses first to exhilaration and then to pain. The central idea (paragraph 6) is built out of this idea, explaining that the movement of emotions in the
story is accompanied by an intricate and complementary set of structures.

Sections II to V examine various elements of the story for their structu relationship to Miss Brill's emotions. Section II details the structural uses of the tings of autumn and times of day, pointing out how they parallel experiences. The longest part, section III (paragraphs 9 to 15), is based on an idea not found in the sources—that a number of characters are experiencing difficulties and cruelties such as those that befall Miss Brill. Paragraph 10 cites the three couples of the story, paragraph 11 the silent old people, and paragraph 12 the woman with violets. Paragraph 13 is developed in disagreement with one of the sources, showing how a research essay may be original even though the sources form the basis for argument. Paragraph 14 contains brief descriptions of additional examples of insensitivity, two of them involving Miss Brill herself. Paragraph 15 summarizes the story's instances of insensitivity and cruelty, emphasizing again parallels to Miss Brill's situation.

Section IV (paragraphs 16 to 18) is based on ideas about the story's structure found in one of the sources (Thorpe). It is hence more derivative than the previous section. Section V (paragraphs 19 to 24) is devoted to the story's dénouement. Paragraphs 19 and 20 consider critical interpretations of the ending. In paragraph 21, however, a hint found in a source (Hankin) is used to interpret the story's final sentence. An argument in support of this original interpretation is developed in paragraphs 22 to 24, which conclude with a reference to Mansfield's own personal approval of the main character.

Section VI (paragraphs 25 and 26), the conclusion, relates the central idea to further biographical information and also to Mansfield's achievement in the story. Of the three sources cited in this section, two are used earlier in the essay, and one (Moore) is used for the first time here.

The list of works cited is the basis of all references in the essay, in accord with the *MLA Handbook for Writers of Research Papers*, 6th ed. By locating these references, a reader might readily examine, verify, and study any of the ideas and details drawn from the sources and developed in the essay.

Special Topics for Studying and Discussing How to Undertake Research Essays

In beginning research on any of the following topics, follow the steps in research described in this chapter.

1. Common themes in a number of stories by Hawthorne, Poe, Hardy, or Mansfield.
2. Various critical views of Chekhov's *The Bear*.
3. Glaspell's use of the narrative material in *Trifles*.
4. Hawthorne's use of religious and moral topic material.
5. Shakespeare's imagery in the Sonnets.
6. Views about women in Chopin, Glaspell, Mansfield, and Keats.
7. Poe's view of the short story as represented in "The Masque of the Red Death" and a number of other stories.

19

Writing Examinations on Literature

Succeeding on a literature examination is largely a result of intelligent and skillful preparation. Preparation means that you (1) study the material assigned, in conjunction with the comments made in class by your instructor and by fellow students in discussion; (2) develop and reinforce your own thoughts; (3) anticipate exam questions by creating and answering your own practice questions; and (4) understand the precise function of the test in your education.

First, realize that the test is not designed either to trap you or to hold down your grade. The grade you receive is a reflection of your achievement in the course. If your grades are high, congratulations; keep doing what you have been doing. If your grades are low, however, you can improve them through diligent and systematic study. Those students who can easily do satisfactory work might do superior work if they improved their habits of study and preparation. From whatever level you begin, *you can increase your achievement by improving your study methods.*

Your instructor has three major concerns in evaluating your tests (assuming the correct use of English): (1) to assess the extent of your command over the subject material of the course (How good is your retention?); (2) to assess how well you respond to a question or deal with an issue (How well do you separate the important from the unimportant?); and (3) to assess how well you draw conclusions about the material (How well are you educating yourself?).

Answer the Questions That Are Asked

Many elements go into writing good answers on tests, but *responsiveness* is the most important. A major cause of low exam grades is that students *often do not answer the questions asked*. Does that failure seem surprising? The problem is that some students do no more than retell a story or restate an argument, but they do not zero in on the issues in the question. This problem is not uncommon. Therefore, if you are asked, "Why does . . . ?," be sure to emphasize the *why* and use the *does* primarily to exemplify the *why*. If the question is about *organization,* focus on organization. If the question is about the

288

interpretation of an idea, deal with the interpretation of the idea. In short, *always respond directly to the question or instruction.* Answer what is asked. Compare the following two answers to the same question.

Question: How is the setting of Ambrose Bierce's "An Occurrence at Owl Creek Bridge" important in the story's development?

Answer A

The setting of Bierce's "An Occurrence at Owl Creek Bridge" is a major element in the story's development. The first scene is on a railroad bridge in northern Alabama, and the action is that a man, Peyton Farquhar, is about to be hanged. He is a southerner who has been surrounded and captured by Union soldiers. They are ready to string him up and they have the guns and power, so he cannot escape. He is so scared that his own watch seems to sound loudly and slowly, like a cannon. He also thinks about how he might escape, once he is hanged, by freeing his hands and throwing off the noose that will soon be choking and killing him. The scene shifts to the week before, at Farquhar's plantation. A Union spy deceives Farquhar, thereby tempting him to try to sabotage the Union efforts to keep the railroad open. Because the spy tells Farquhar about the punishment, the reader assumes that Farquhar had tried to sabotage the bridge, was caught, and now is going to be hanged. The third scene is also at the bridge, but it is about what Farquhar sees and thinks in his own mind: He imagines that he has been hanged and then escapes. He thinks he falls into the creek, frees himself from the ropes, and makes it to shore, from which he makes the long walk home. His final vision is of his wife coming out of the house to meet him, with everything looking beautiful in the morning sunshine. Then we find out that all this was just in his mind, because we are back on the bridge, from which Farquhar is swinging, hanged, dead, with a broken neck.

Answer B

The setting of Bierce's "An Occurrence at Owl Creek Bridge" is a major element in the story's development. The railroad bridge in northern Alabama, from which the doomed Peyton Farquhar will be hanged, is a frame for the story. The bridge, which begins as a real-life bridge in the first scene, becomes the bridge that the dying man imagines in the third. In between there is a brief scene at Farquhar's home, which took place a week before. The setting thus marks the progression of Farquhar's dying vision. He begins to distort and slow down reality—at the real bridge—when he realizes that there is no escape. The first indication of this distortion is that his watch seems to be ticking as slowly as a blacksmith's hammer. Once he is dropped from the bridge to be hanged, his perceptions slow down time so much that he imagines his complete escape before his death: falling into the water, freeing himself, being shot at, getting to shore, walking through a darkening forest, and returning home in beautiful morning sunshine. The final sentence of the story brutally restores the real situation at the railroad bridge and makes clear that Farquhar is hanging from it and is actually dead despite his imaginings. In all respects, therefore, the setting is essential to the story's development.

Answer A begins well and introduces important details of the story's setting, but it does not answer the question because it does not show how the details figure into the story's development. On the other hand, answer B focuses directly on the connection between the locations and the changes in the protagonist's perceptions. Because of this emphasis, B answers the question and is also shorter than A (287 words to 221); with the focus directly on the issue, there is no need for irrelevant narrative details. Thus, A is unresponsive and unnecessarily long, whereas B is responsive and includes details only if they exemplify the major points.

Systematic Preparation

Your challenge is how best to prepare yourself to have a knowledgeable and ready mind at examination time. If you simply cram facts into your head for the test in the hope that you can adjust to the questions, you will likely flounder. You need a systematic approach.

Read and Reread the Material on Which You Are to Be Examined

Above all, recognize that your preparation should begin as soon as the course begins, not on the night before the exam. Complete each assignment by the date it is due, for you will understand the classroom discussion only if you know the material (see also the guides for study in Chapter 1, pages 13–14). Then, about a week before the exam, review each assignment, preferably rereading everything completely. If particular passages were read and discussed in class, make a special point of studying the passages and referring to the notes you took at the time of the discussions. With this preparation, your study on the night before the exam will be fruitful because it is the climax of your preparation, not your entire preparation.

Construct Your Own Questions: Go on the Attack

To prepare yourself well for an exam, read *actively*, not passively. Read with a goal, and *go on the attack* by anticipating test conditions—creating and answering your own practice questions. Don't waste time, however, in trying to guess the questions you think your instructor might ask. Guessing correctly might happen (and wouldn't you be happy if it did?) but do not turn your study into a game of chance. Instead, arrange the subject matter by asking yourself questions that help you get things straight.

How can you construct your own questions? It is not as hard as you might think. Your instructor may have announced certain topics or ideas to be tested on the exam, and you might develop questions from these, or you might apply general questions to the specifics of your assignments, as in the following examples.

1. **Ideas about a character and the interactions of characters** (see also Chapter 3). What is character *A* like? How does *A* grow or change in the work? What does *A* learn or not learn that brings about the conclusion? To what degree does *A* represent a type or an idea? How does character *B* influence *A*? Does a change in character *C* bring about any corresponding change in *A*?

2. **Ideas about technical and structural questions.** These can be broad, covering everything from point of view (Chapter 4) to the meter of poetry (Chapter 13). The best guide here is to study those technical aspects that have been discussed in class, for it is unlikely that you will be asked to go beyond the levels considered in classroom discussion.

3. **Ideas about events or situations.** What relationship does episode *A* have to situation *B*? Does *C*'s thinking about situation *D* have any influence on the outcome of event *E*?

4. **Ideas about a problem** (see also Chapter 12). Why is character *A* or situation *X* this way and not that way? Is the conclusion justified by the ideas and events leading up to it?

Rephrase Your Notes as Questions

Because your classroom notes are the fullest record you have about your instructor's views, one of the best ways to construct questions is to develop them from these notes. As you select topics and phrase questions, refer to passages from the texts that were studied by the class and stressed by your instructor. If there is time, memorize as many important phrases or lines as you can from the studied works. Plan to incorporate these into your answers as evidence to support the points you make. Remember that it is useful to work not only with main ideas from your notes but also with matters such as character, setting, imagery, symbolism, ideas, and organization.

Obviously, you cannot make questions from all your notes, and you will therefore need to select from those that seem most important. As an example, here is a short note written by a student during a classroom discussion of Shakespeare's *Hamlet*: "A study in how private problems get public, how a court conspiracy can produce disastrous national and international consequences." Notice that you can devise practice questions from this note.

1. In what ways is *Hamlet* not only about private problems but also about public ones?

2. Why should the political consequences of Claudius's murder of Hamlet's father be considered disastrous?

The principle here is that most exam questions do not ask just about *what*, but rather get into the issues of *why*. Observe that the first question therefore introduces the words *in what ways* to the phrasing of the note. For the second, the word *why* has been used. Either question creates the need for you to study pointedly, and neither asks you merely to describe events from the play. Question 1 requires you to consider the wider political effects of Hamlet's hostility toward Claudius, including Hamlet's murder of Polonius and the subsequent madness of Ophelia. Question 2, with its emphasis on disaster, leads you to consider not only the ruination of the hopes and lives of those in the play but also the importance of young Fortinbras and the eventual establishment of Norwegian control over Denmark after Claudius and Hamlet have died. If you were to spend fifteen or twenty minutes writing practice answers to these questions, you could be confident in taking an examination on the material, for you could likely adapt, or even partially duplicate, your study answers to any exam question about the personal and political results of Claudius's murder of his brother.

Make Up Your Own Questions Even When Time Is Short

Whatever your subject, spend as much study time as possible making and answering your own questions. *Writing practice answers is one of the most important things you can do in preparing for your exam.* Remember also to work with your own remarks and the ideas you develop in the notebook or journal entries that you make when doing your regular assignments (see Chapter 1, page 14). Many of these will give you additional ideas for your own questions, which you can practice along with the questions you develop from your classroom notes.

Obviously, with limited study time, you will not be able to create your own questions and answers indefinitely. Even so, don't neglect asking and answering your own questions. If time is too short for full practice answers, write out the main heads, or topics, of an answer. When the press of time (or the need for sleep) no longer permits you to make even such a brief outline answer, keep thinking of questions and their answers as you go to the exam. *Never read passively or unresponsively; always read with a creative, question-and-answer goal.* Think of studying as a preliminary step leading to writing.

The time you spend in this way will be valuable, for as you practice, you will develop control and therefore confidence. Often those who have difficulty with tests, or claim a phobia about them, prepare passively rather than actively. Your instructor's test questions compel responsiveness, organization, thought, and insight. But a passively prepared student is not ready for this challenge and therefore writes answers that are unresponsive and filled with summary. The grade for such a performance is low, and the student's fear of tests is reinforced. The best way to break such long-standing patterns of fear or uncertainty is to study actively and creatively.

Study with a Classmate

Often the thoughts of another person can help you understand the material to be tested. Find a fellow student with whom you can work comfortably but also productively, for both of you together can help each other individually. In view of the need for steady preparation throughout a course, regular discussions about the material are a good idea. You might also make your joint study systematic by setting aside a specific evening or afternoon for work sessions. Many students have said that they encounter problems in taking examinations because they are unfamiliar with the ways in which questions are phrased. Consequently, they waste time in understanding and interpreting the questions before they begin their answers, and sometimes they lose all their time because they misunderstand the questions entirely. If you work with a fellow student, however, and trade questions, you will be gaining experience (and confidence) in dealing with this basic difficulty about exams. Working with someone else can be extremely rewarding, just as it can also be stimulating and instructive. Make the effort, and you'll never regret it.

Two Basic Types of Questions About Literature

Generally, there are two types of questions on literature exams. Keep them in mind as you prepare. The first type is *factual*, or *mainly objective*; and the second is *general*, *comprehensive*, *broad*, or *mainly subjective*. Except for multiple-choice questions, very few questions are purely objective in a literature course.

Anticipate the Kinds of Factual Questions That Might Be Asked

Multiple-Choice Questions Ask You to Pick the Most Accurate and Likely Answers   Multiple-choice questions are almost necessarily factual. Your instructor will most likely use them for short quizzes, usually on days when an assignment is due, to make sure that you are keeping up with the reading. Multiple-choice questions test your knowledge of facts and your ingenuity in perceiving subtleties of phrasing. On literature exams, however, this type of question is rare.

Identification Questions Ask for Accuracy, Explanation, and a Certain Amount of Interpretation   Identification questions are interesting and challenging because they require you both to know details and also to develop thoughts about them. This type of question is frequently used as a check on the depth and scope of your reading. In fact, an entire exam could be composed of only identification questions, each requiring perhaps five minutes for you to answer. Here are some typical examples of what you might be asked to identify.

1. **A character.** To identify a character, it is necessary to describe briefly the character's position, main activity, and significance. Let us assume that "Prince Prospero" is the character to be identified. Our answer should state that he is the prince (position) who invites a thousand followers to his castle to enjoy themselves while keeping out the plague of the Red Death in Edgar Allan Poe's "The Masque of the Red Death" (main activity). Prospero's egotism and arrogance are the major causes of the action, and he embodies the story's theme that pride is vain and that death is inescapable (significance). Under the category of "significance," of course,

you might develop as many ideas as you have time for, but the short example here is a general model for most identification questions.

2. **Incidents or situations.** In identifying an incident or a situation (for example, "A woman mourns the death of her husband"), first describe the circumstances and the principal character involved in them (Mrs. Popov's reaction to her widowhood in Chekhov's play *The Bear*). Then, describe the importance of this incident or situation in the work. For example, in *The Bear*, Mrs. Popov is mourning the death of her husband, and in the course of the play Chekhov uses her feelings to show amusingly that life and love with real emotion are stronger than allegiance to the dead.

3. **Things, places, and dates.** Your instructor may ask you to identify a hair ribbon (Nathaniel Hawthorne's "Young Goodman Brown") or a beach (Matthew Arnold's "Dover Beach"), or the date of Amy Lowell's "Patterns" (1916). For dates, you may be given a leeway of five or ten years. What is important about a date is not so much exactness as historical and intellectual perspective. The date of Lowell's "Patterns," for example, was the third year of World War I, and the poem consequently reflects a reaction against the protracted and senseless loss of life in war (even though details of the poem itself suggest an eighteenth-century war). To claim "World War I" as the date of the poem would be acceptable as an answer if it happens that you cannot remember the exact date.

4. **Quotations.** You should remember enough of the text to identify a passage taken from it, or at least to make an informed guess. Generally, you should (1) locate the quotation, if you remember it, or else describe what you think is the probable location; (2) show the ways in which the quotation is typical of the content and style of the work you have read; and (3) describe the importance of the passage. If you suffer a lapse of memory, write a reasoned and careful explanation of your guess. Even if your guess is not actually correct, the knowledge and cogency of your explanation should give you points.

Technical and Analytical Questions and Problems Require You to Relate Knowledge and Technical Understanding to the Issue   In a scale of ascending importance, the third and most difficult type of factual question relates to those matters of writing with which much of this book is concerned: technique and analysis. You might be asked to analyze the *setting, images, point of view,* or *important idea* of a work; you might be asked about the *tone and style* of a story or poem; or you might be asked to *explicate* a poem that may or may not be duplicated for your benefit (if it is not duplicated, woe to students who have not studied their assignments). Questions like these assume that you have technical knowledge, and they also ask you to examine the text within the limitations imposed by the directions.

Obviously, technical questions occur more frequently in advanced courses than in introductory ones, and the questions become more subtle as the courses become more advanced. Instructors of introductory courses may ask about ideas and problems but will likely not use many of the others unless they state their intentions to do so in advance or unless technical terms have been studied in class.

Questions of this type are fairly long, perhaps allowing from fifteen to twenty-five minutes apiece. If you have two or more of these questions, try to space your time sensibly; do not devote 80 percent of your time to one question and leave only 20 percent for the rest.

Understand How Your Responses Will Be Judged and Graded

Identification Questions Probe Your Understanding and Application of Facts In all factual questions, your instructor is testing (1) your factual command; and (2) your quickness in relating a part to the whole. Thus, suppose you are identifying the incident "A man kills a canary." It is correct to say that Susan Glaspell's play *Trifles* is the location of the incident, that the murdered farmer John Wright is the killer, and that the canary belonged to his wife, Minnie. Knowledge of these details clearly establishes that you know the facts. But a strong answer must go further. Even in the brief time you have for short answers, you should always connect the facts (1) to major causality in the work; (2) to an important idea or ideas; (3) to the development of the work; and (4) for a quotation, to the style. Time is short and you must be selective, but if you can make your answer move from facts to significance, you will always fashion superior responses. Along these lines, let us look at an answer identifying the action from *Trifles*:

> The action is from Glaspell's *Trifles*. The man who kills the bird is John Wright, the dead man, and the owner is his wife, Minnie, who, before the story begins, has been jailed on suspicion of murder. The wringing of the little bird's neck is important because it is shown as an indignity and outrage in Minnie Wright's desperate life, and it obviously has made her angry enough to put a rope around Wright's neck to strangle him in his sleep. It is thus the cause not only of the murder but also of the investigation bringing the two lawmen and their wives to the Wright kitchen. In fact, the killing of the bird makes the story possible because it is the wives who discover the dead bird's remains, and this discovery is the means by which Glaspell highlights them as the major characters of the action. Because the husband's cruelly brutal act shows how bleak the married life of Minnie Wright actually was, it dramatizes the lonely and victimized plight of women in a male-dominated way of life like that on the Wright farm. The discovery also raises the issue of legality and morality, because the women decide to conceal the evidence, therefore protecting Minnie Wright from conviction and punishment.

Any of the points in this answer could be developed as a separate essay, but the paragraph is successful as a short answer because it goes beyond fact to deal with significance. Clearly, such answers are possible at the time of an exam only if you have devoted considerable thought beforehand to the works on which you are tested. The more thinking and practicing you do before an exam, the better your answers will be. Remember this advice as an axiom: *You cannot write superior answers if you do not think extensively before the exam.* By ambitious advance study, you will be able to reduce surprise to a minimum.

Longer Factual Questions Probe Your Knowledge and Your Ability to Organize Your Thoughts   More extended factual questions also require more thoroughly developed organization. Remember that for these questions your skill in writing essays is important because the quality of your composition will determine a major share of your instructor's evaluation of your answers. It is therefore best to take several minutes to gather your thoughts before you begin to write. Remember, *a ten-minute planned answer is preferable to a twenty-five-minute unplanned answer.* You do not need to write every possible fact on each particular question. Of greater importance is the use to which you put the facts that you know and the organization and development of your answer. Use a sheet of scratch paper to jot down important facts and your ideas about them in relation to the question. Then put them together, phrase a thesis sentence, and use your facts to exemplify and support your thesis.

It is always necessary to begin your answer pointedly, using key words or phrases from the question or direction if possible, so that your answer will have thematic shape. You should *never* begin an answer with "Because" and then go on from there without referring again to the question. To be most responsive during the short time available for an exam, you should use the question as your guide for your answer. Let us suppose that you have the following question on your test: "How does Glaspell use details in *Trifles* to reveal the character of Minnie Wright?" The most common way to go astray on such a question—and the easiest thing to do also—is to concentrate on Minnie Wright's character rather than on how Glaspell uses detail to bring out her character. The word *how* makes a vast difference in the nature of the final answer, and hence a good method on the exam is to duplicate key phrases in the question to ensure that you make your major points clear. Here is an opening sentence that uses the key words and phrases (italicized here) from the question to organize thought and provide focus.

> Glaspell *uses details* of setting, marital relationships, and personal habits *to reveal the character of Minnie Wright* as a person of great but unfulfilled potential whom anger has finally overcome.

Because this sentence repeats the key phrases from the question and also because it promises to show *how* the details are to be focused on the character, it suggests that the answer to follow will be responsive.

General or Comprehensive Questions Require You to Connect a Number of Works to Broader Matters of Idea and Technique

General or comprehensive questions are particularly important on final examinations, when your instructor is testing your total comprehension of the course material. Considerable time is usually allowed for answering this type of question, which can be phrased in a number of ways (see top of page 297).

1. A *direct question* asking about philosophy, underlying attitudes, main ideas, characteristics of style, backgrounds, and so on. Here are some possible questions in this category.

   What use do _____, _____, and _____ make of the topic of _____?

   Define and characterize the short story as a genre of literature, using examples from the stories of _____, _____, and _____.

   Describe the use of dialogue by _____, _____, and _____.

   Contrast the technique of point of view as used by _____, _____, and _____.

2. A *"comment" question*, often based on an extensive quotation, borrowed from a critic or written by your instructor for the occasion, asking about a broad class of writers, a literary movement, or the like. Your instructor may ask you to treat this question broadly (taking in many writers) or else to apply the quotation to a specific writer.

3. A *"suppose" question*, such as "What advice might Minnie Wright of Glaspell's *Trifles* give the speakers of Lowell's 'Patterns' and Keats's 'Bright Star'?" or "What might the speaker of Rossetti's poem 'Echo' say if she were told that her dead lover was actually a person like Goodman Brown of Hawthorne's 'Young Goodman Brown'?" Although "suppose" questions seem whimsical at first sight, they have a serious design and should prompt original and radical thinking. The first question, for example, might cause a test writer to bring out, from Minnie Wright's perspective, that the love expressed by both speakers overlooks the possibilities of changes in character over a long period. She would likely sympathize with the speaker of "Patterns," a woman, but she might also say that the speaker's enthusiasm would need to be augmented by the constant exertion of kindness and mutual understanding. For the speaker of "Bright Star," a man, Mrs. Wright might say that the steadfast love he seeks should be linked to thoughtfulness and constant communication as well as passion.

Although "suppose" questions (and answers) are speculative, the need to respond to them requires a detailed consideration of the works involved, and in this respect the "suppose" question is a salutary means of learning. It is of course difficult to prepare for a "suppose" question, which you can therefore regard as a test not only of your knowledge but also of your adaptability, inventiveness, and ingenuity.

Understand How Your Responses to General and Comprehensive Questions Will Be Judged and Graded

When answering broad, general questions, you are dealing with an unstructured situation, and you must not only supply an answer but, equally important, also must create a *structure* within which your answer can have meaning. You might say that you make up your own specific question out of the original general question. If you were asked to consider the role of women as seen in works by Lowell, Maupassant, and Glaspell, for example, you would structure the question by focusing on a number of clearly defined topics. A possible way to begin answering such a question might be this:

> Lowell, Maupassant, and Glaspell present a view of female resilience by demonstrating the inner control, endurance, and power of adaptation of their major characters.

With this sort of focus, you would be able to proceed point-by-point, introducing supporting data as you form your answer.

As a general rule, the best method for answering a comprehensive question is comparison-contrast (see also Chapter 14). The reason is that in dealing with, say, a general question on Rossetti, Chekhov, and Keats, it is too easy to write *three* separate essays rather than *one*. Thus, you should try to create a topic such as "the treatment of real or idealized love" or "the difficulties in male-female relationships" and then develop your answer point by point rather than writer by writer. By creating your answer in this way, you can bring in references to each or all of the writers as they become relevant. If you were to treat each writer separately, your comprehensive answer would lose focus and effectiveness, and it would also be repetitive.

Remember that in judging your response to a general question, your instructor is interested in seeing (1) how effectively you perceive and explain the significant issues in the question; (2) how intelligently and clearly you organize your answer; and (3) how persuasively you link your answer to materials from the work as supporting evidence.

Bear in mind that in answering comprehensive questions, you do not have the freedom or license to write about anything at all. You must stick to the questions. The freedom you do have, however, is the freedom to create your own organization and development in response to the questions that your instructor has asked you. The underlying idea of the comprehensive, general question is that you possess special knowledge and insights that cannot be discovered by more factual questions. You must therefore formulate your own responses to the material and introduce evidence that reflects your own insights and command of information.

Two final words: Good luck.

Critical Approaches Important
in the Study of Literature

A number of critical theories or approaches for understanding and inter-preting literature are available to critics and students alike.[1] Many of these were developed during the twentieth century to create a discipline of lit-erary studies comparable with disciplines in the natural and social sciences. Literary critics have often borrowed liberally from other disciplines (e.g., his-tory, psychology, politics, anthropology) but have primarily aimed at devel-oping literature as a study in its own right.

At the heart of the various critical approaches are many fundamental questions: What is literature? What does it do? Is its concern only to tell sto-ries, or is it to express emotions? Is it private? Public? How does it get its ideas across? What more does it do than express ideas? How valuable was literature in the past, and how valuable is it now? What can it contribute to intellectu-al, artistic, and social history? To what degree is literature an art, as opposed to an instrument for imparting knowledge? How is literature used, and how and why is it misused? What theoretical and technical expertise may be in-voked to enhance literary studies?

Questions such as these indicate that criticism is concerned not only with reading and interpreting stories, poems, and plays but also with establishing theoretical understanding. Because of such extensive aims, you will under-stand that a full explanation and illustration of the approaches would fill the pages of a long book. The following descriptions are therefore intended as no more than brief introductions. Bear in mind that in the hands of skilled crit-ics, the approaches are so subtle, sophisticated, and complex that they are not only critical stances but also philosophies.

Although the various approaches provide divergent ways to study liter-ature and literary problems, they reflect major tendencies rather than absolute straitjacketing. Not every approach is appropriate for every work, nor are the approaches always mutually exclusive. Even the most devoted practitioners

---

[1]Some of the approaches described in this chapter are presented more simply in Chapter 1 as basic study techniques for writing about literary works.

of the methods do not pursue them rigidly. In addition, some of the approaches are more "user-friendly" than others for certain types of discovery. To a degree at least, most critics therefore take a particular approach but utilize methods that technically belong to one or more of the other approaches. A critic stressing the topical/historical approach, for example, might introduce the close study of a work that is associated with the method of the New Criticism. Similarly, a psychoanalytical critic might include details about archetypes. In short, a great deal of criticism is *pragmatic* or *eclectic* rather than rigid.

The approaches to be considered here are as follows: moral/intellectual; topical/historical; New Critical/formalist; structuralist; feminist; economic determinist/Marxist; psychological/psychoanalytic; archetypal/symbolic/mythic; deconstructionist; and reader-response.

The object of learning about these approaches, like everything else in this book, is to help you develop your own reading and writing. Accordingly, following each of the descriptions is a brief paragraph showing how Hawthorne's story "Young Goodman Brown" (Appendix C) might be considered in the light of the particular approach. The illustrative paragraph following the discussion of structuralism, for example, shows an application of the structuralist approach to Goodman Brown and his story, and so also with the feminist approach, the economic determinist approach, and the others. Whenever you are doing your own writing about literature, you are free to use the various approaches as part or all of your assignment, if you believe the approach may help you.

Moral/Intellectual

The **moral/intellectual critical approach** is concerned with content and values (see also Chapter 7). The approach is as old as literature itself, for literature is a traditional mode of imparting morality, philosophy, and religion. The concern in moral/intellectual criticism is not only to discover meaning but also to determine whether works of literature are both *true* and *significant*.

To study literature from the moral/intellectual perspective is therefore to determine whether a work conveys a lesson or a message and whether it can help readers lead better lives and improve their understanding of the world: What ideas does the work contain? How strongly does the work bring forth its ideas? What application do the ideas have to the work's characters and situations? How may the ideas be evaluated intellectually? Morally? Discussions based on such questions do not imply that literature is primarily a medium of moral and intellectual exhortation. Ideally, moral/intellectual criticism should differ from sermonizing to the degree that readers should always be left with their own decisions about whether to assimilate the ideas of a work and about whether the ideas—and values—are personally or morally acceptable.

Sophisticated critics have sometimes demeaned the moral/intellectual approach on the grounds that "message hunting" reduces a work's artistic value by treating it like a sermon or political speech; but the approach will be valuable as long as readers expect literature to be applicable to their own lives.

Example

"Young Goodman Brown" raises the issue of how an institution designed for human elevation, such as the religious system of colonial Salem, can be so ruinous. Does the failure result from the system itself or from the people who misunderstand it? Is what is true of religion as practiced by Brown also true of social and political institutions? Should any religious or political philosophy be given greater credence than good will and mutual trust? One of the major virtues of "Young Goodman Brown" is that it provokes questions like these but at the same time provides a number of satisfying answers. A particularly important one is that religious and moral beliefs should not be used to justify the condemnation of others. Another important answer is that attacks made from the refuge of a religion or group, such as Brown's Puritanism, are dangerous because the judge may condemn without thought and without personal responsibility.

Topical/Historical

The **topical/historical critical approach** stresses the relationship of literature to its historical period, and for this reason it has had a long life. Although much literature may be applicable to many places and times, much of it also directly reflects the intellectual and social worlds of the authors. When was the work written? What were the circumstances that produced it? What major issues does it deal with? How does it fit into the author's career? Keats's poem "On First Looking into Chapman's Homer," for example, is his excited response to his reading of one of the major literary works of Western civilization. Hardy's "Channel Firing" is an acerbic response to continued armament and preparation for war during the twentieth century.

The topical/historical approach investigates relationships of this sort, including the elucidation of words and concepts that today's readers may not immediately understand. Obviously, the approach requires the assistance of footnotes, dictionaries, library catalogues, histories, and handbooks.

A common criticism of the topical/historical approach is that in the extreme, it deals with background knowledge rather than with literature itself. It is possible, for example, for a topical/historical critic to describe a writer's life, the period of the writer's work, and the social and intellectual ideas of the time—all without ever considering the meaning, importance, and value of the work itself.

A reaction against such an unconnected use of historical details is the so-called **New Historicism**. This approach justifies the introduction of historical knowledge by integrating it with the understanding of particular texts. Readers of Arnold's "Dover Beach," for example, sometimes find it difficult to follow the meaning of Arnold's statement "The Sea of Faith/Was once, too, at the full." Historical background has a definite role to play here. In Arnold's time there developed a method of treating the Bible as a historical document rather than divinely inspired revelation. This approach has been called the Higher Criticism of the Bible, and to many thoughtful people of the time it undermined the concept that the Bible was divine, infallible, and inerrant. Therefore the "Sea of Faith" was thought to be not at full but rather at ebb tide. Because the introduction of such historical material is designed to facilitate the reading of the poem—and also the reading of other literature of the period—the New Historicism represents an integration of knowledge and interpretation. As a principle, New Historicism entails the acquisition of as much historical information as possible, because our knowledge of the relationship of literature to its historical period can never be complete. The practitioner of New Historicism must always seek new information on the grounds that it will be found to be relevant to literary works.

Example

"Young Goodman Brown" is an allegorical story by Nathaniel Hawthorne (1804–1864), a New England writer who probed deeply into the relationship between religion and guilt. His ancestors had been involved in religious persecutions, including the Salem witch trials, and he, living 150 years afterward, wanted to analyze the weaknesses and uncertainties of the sin-dominated religion of the earlier period, a tradition of which he was a resentful heir. Not surprisingly, therefore, "Young Goodman Brown" takes place in Puritan colonial Salem, and Hawthorne's implied judgments are those of a severe critic of how the harsh old religion destroyed personal and family relationships. Although the immediate concerns of the story belong to a vanished age, Hawthorne's treatment is still valuable because it is still timely.

New Critical/Formalist

New Criticism has been a dominant force in contemporary literary studies. It focuses on literary texts as formal works of art, and for this reason it can be seen as a reaction against the topical/historical approach. The objection raised by New Critics is that as topical/historical critics consider literary history, they evade direct contact with actual texts.

The inspiration for the **New Critical/formalist critical approach** was the French practice of *explication de texte,* a method that emphasizes detailed examination and explanation. The New Criticism is at its most brilliant in the formal analysis of smaller units such as entire poems and short passages. For the analysis of larger structures, the New Criticism also utilizes a number of techniques that have been selected as the basis of chapters in this book. Discussions of point of view, tone, plot, character, and structure, for example, are formal ways of looking at literature that are derived from the New Criticism.

The aim of the formalist study of literature is to provide readers not only with the means of explaining the content of works (what, specifically, does a work say?) but also with the insights needed for evaluating the artistic quality of individual works and writers (how well is it said?). A major aspect of New Critical thought is that content and form—including all ideas, ambiguities, subtleties, and even apparent contradictions—were originally within the conscious or subconscious control of the author. There are no accidents. It does not necessarily follow, however, that today's critic is able to define the author's intentions exactly, for such intentions require knowledge of biographical details that are irretrievably lost. Each literary work therefore takes on its own existence and identity, and the critic's work is to discover a reading or readings that explain the facts of the text. Note that the New Critic does not claim infallible interpretations and does not exclude the validity of multiple readings of the same work.

Dissenters from the New Criticism have noted a tendency by New Critics to ignore relevant knowledge that history and biography can bring to literary studies. In addition, the approach has been subject to the charge that stressing the explication of texts alone fails to deal with literary value and appreciation. In other words, the formalist critic, in explaining the meaning of literature, sometimes neglects the reasons for which readers find literature stimulating and valuable.

Example

A major aspect of Hawthorne's "Young Goodman Brown" is that the details are so vague and dreamlike that many readers are uncertain about what is happening. The action is a nighttime walk by the protagonist, Young Goodman Brown, into a deep forest where he encounters a mysterious satanic ritual that leaves him bitter and misanthropic. This much seems clear, but the precise nature of Brown's experience is not clear, nor is the identity of the stranger (father, village elder, devil) who accompanies Brown as he begins his walk. At the story's end Hawthorne's narrator states that the whole episode may have been no more than a dream or nightmare. Yet when morning comes, Brown walks back into town as though returning from an overnight trip, and he recoils in horror from his fellow villagers, including his wife Faith (paragraph 70). Could his attitude result from nothing more than a nightmare?

Even at the story's end these uncertainties remain. For this reason one may conclude that Hawthorne deliberately creates the uncertainties to reveal how people like Brown build defensive walls of judgment around themselves. The story thus implies that the real source of Brown's anger is as vague as his nocturnal walk, but he doesn't understand it in this way. Because Brown's vision and judgment are absolute, he rejects everyone around him, even if the cost is a life of bitter suspicion and spiritual isolation.

Structuralist

The principle of structuralism stems from the attempt to find relationships and connections among elements that appear to be separate and discrete. Just as physical science reveals unifying universal principles of matter such as gravity and the forces of electromagnetism (and is constantly searching for a "unified field theory"), the **structuralist critical approach** attempts to discover the forms unifying all literature. Thus a structural description of Maupassant's "The Necklace" stresses that the main character, Mathilde, is an *active* protagonist who undergoes a *test* (or series of tests) and emerges with a victory, though not the kind she had originally hoped for. The same might be said of Mrs. Popov and Smirnov in Chekhov's *The Bear*. If this same kind of structural view is applied to Bierce's "An Occurrence at Owl Creek Bridge," the protagonist is defeated in the test. Generally, the structural approach applies such configurations to other works of literature to determine that certain protagonists are active or submissive, that they pass or fail their tests, or that they succeed or fail at other encounters. The key is that many apparently unrelated works reveal many common patterns or contain similar structures with important variations.

The structural approach is important because it enables critics to discuss works from widely disparate cultures and historical periods. In this respect, critics have followed the leads of modern anthropologists, most notably Claude Lévi-Strauss (1908–1990). Along such lines, critics have undertaken the serious examination of folk and fairy tales. Some of the groundbreaking structuralist criticism, for example, was devoted to the structural principles underlying folktales of Russia. The method also bridges popular and serious literature, making little distinction between the two insofar as the description of the structures is concerned. Indeed, structuralism furnishes an ideal approach for comparative literature, and the method also enables critics to consolidate genres such as modern romances, detective tales, soap operas, and film.

Like the New Criticism, structuralism aims at comprehensiveness of description, and many critics would insist that the two are complementary and not separate. A distinction is that the New Criticism is at its best in dealing with smaller units of literature, whereas structuralism is best in the analysis of narratives and therefore larger units such as novels, myths, stories, plays, and films. Because structuralism shows how fiction is organized into various typical situations, the approach merges with the *archetypal* approach, and at times it is difficult to find any distinctions between structuralism and archetypalism.

Structuralism, however, deals not just with narrative structures but also with structures of any type, wherever they occur. For example, structuralism makes great use of linguistics. Modern linguistic scholars have determined that there is a difference between "deep structures" and "surface structures" in language. A structuralist analysis of style, therefore, emphasizes how writers utilize such structures. The structuralist interpretation of language also perceives distinguishing types or "grammars" of language that are recurrent in various types of literature. Suppose, for example, that you encounter opening passages like the following:

> Once upon a time a young prince fell in love with a young princess. He decided to tell her of his love, and early one morning he left his castle on his white charger, riding toward her castle home high in the mountains.

Early that morning, Alan had found himself thinking about Anne. He had believed her when she said she loved him, but his feelings about her were not certain, and his thinking had left him still unsure.

The words of these two passages create different and distinct frames of reference. One is a fairy tale of the past, the other a modern internalized reflection of feeling. The passages therefore demonstrate how language itself fits into predetermined patterns or structures. Similar uses of language structures can be associated with other types of literature.

Example

Young Goodman Brown is a hero who is passive, not active. He is a *witness*, a *receiver* rather than a *doer*. His only action—taking his trip in the forest—occurs at the story's beginning. After that point, he no longer acts but instead is acted upon, and his reactions to what he sees around him put his life's beliefs to a test. Of course, many protagonists undergo similar testing (such as rescuing victims and overcoming particularly terrible dragons), and they emerge triumphant. Not so with Goodman Brown. He is a responder who allows himself to be victimized by his own perceptions—or misperceptions. Despite all his previous experiences with his wife and with the good people of his village, he generalizes too hastily. He lets the single disillusioning experience of his nightmare govern his entire outlook on others, and thus he fails his test and turns his entire life into failure.

Feminist

The **feminist critical approach** holds that most of our literature presents a masculine-patriarchal view in which the role of women is negated or at best minimized. As an adjunct of the feminist movement in politics, the feminist critique of literature seeks to raise consciousness about the importance and unique nature of women.

Specifically, the feminist view attempts (1) to show that writers of traditional literature have ignored women and have also transmitted misguided and prejudiced views of them; (2) to stimulate the creation of a critical milieu that reflects a balanced view of the nature and value of women; (3) to recover the works of past women writers and to encourage the publication of present women writers so that the literary canon can be expanded to recognize women as thinkers and artists; and (4) to urge transformations in the language so as to eliminate inequities and inequalities that have resulted from centuries of linguistic inertia and antifeminist sensitivity.

In form, the feminist perspective requires the evaluation of literary works from the standpoint of the presentation of women. For works such as "The Necklace" (story) "Patterns" (poem), and *The Bear* (play), a feminist critique focuses on how such works treat women and also on either the shortcomings or enlightenment of the author as a result of this treatment: How important are the female characters and how individual in their own right? Are they credited with their own existence and their own character? In their relationships with men, how are they treated? Are they given equal status? Ignored? Patronized? Demeaned? Pedestalized? How much interest do the male characters exhibit about women's concerns?

Example

At the beginning of "Young Goodman Brown," Brown's wife, Faith, is only peripheral. In the traditional patriarchal spirit of wife-as-adjunct, she asks her husband to stay at home and take his journey at another time. Hawthorne does not give her the intelligence or dignity, however, to let her explain her concern (or might he not have been interested in what she had to say?) and she therefore remains in the background with her pink hair ribbon as her distinguishing symbol of submissive inferiority. During the mid-forest satanic ritual she appears again and is given power, but only the power to cause her husband to go astray. Once she is led in as a novice in the practice of demonism, her husband falls right in step. Unfortunately, by following her, Brown can conveniently excuse himself from guilt by claiming that "she" had made him do it, just as Eve, in some traditional views of the fall of humankind, compelled Adam to eat the apple (Genesis 3:16–17). Hawthorne's attention to the hero, in other words, permits him to neglect the possibility of a heroine.

Economic Determinist/Marxist

The concept of cultural and economic determinism is one of the major political ideas of the nineteenth century. Karl Marx (1818–1883) emphasized that the primary influence on life was economic, and he saw society as an opposition between the capitalist and working classes. The literature that emerged from this kind of analysis features individuals in the grips of the class struggle. Often called *proletarian literature*, it emphasizes persons of the lower class— the poor and oppressed who spend their lives in endless drudgery and misery, and whose attempts to rise above their disadvantages usually result in renewed suppression.

Marx's political ideas were never widely accepted in the United States and have faded still more in the aftermath of the political breakup of the Soviet Union, but the idea of economic determinism (and the related term *Social Darwinism*) is still credible. As a result, much literature can be judged from an economic perspective even though the economic critics may not be Marxian: What is the economic status of the characters? What happens to them as a result of this status? How do they fare against economic and political odds? What other conditions stemming from their class does the writer emphasize (e.g., poor education, poor nutrition, poor health care, inadequate opportunity)? To what extent does the work fail by overlooking the economic, social, and political implications of its material? In what other ways does economic determinism affect the work? How should readers consider the story in today's developed or underdeveloped world? Seemingly, Hawthorne's story "Young Goodman Brown," which we have used for analysis in these discussions, has no economic implications, but an **economic determinist/Marxist critical approach** might take the following turns:

Example

"Young Goodman Brown" is a fine story just as it is. It deals with the false values instilled by the skewed acceptance of sin-dominated religion, but it overlooks the economic implications of this situation. One suspects that the real story in the little world of Goodman Brown's Salem should be about survival and the disruption that an alienated member of society can produce. After Brown's condemnation and distrust of others forces him into his own shell of sick imagination, Hawthorne does not consider how such a disaffected character would injure the economic and public life of the town. Consider this, just for a moment: Why would the people from whom Brown recoils in disgust want to deal with him in business or personal matters? In town meetings, would they want to follow his opinions on crucial issues of public concern and investment? Would his preoccupation with sin and damnation make him anything more than a horror in his domestic life? Would his wife, Faith, be able to discuss household management with him, or how to take care of the children? All these questions of course are pointed toward another story—a story that Hawthorne did not write. They also indicate the shortcomings of Hawthorne's approach, because it is clear that the major result of Young Goodman Brown's selfish preoccupation with evil would be a serious disruption of the economic and political affairs of his small community.

Psychological/Psychoanalytic

The scientific study of the mind is a product of psychodynamic theory as established by Sigmund Freud (1856–1939) and of the psychoanalytic method practiced by his followers. Psychoanalysis provided a new key to the understanding of character by claiming that behavior is caused by hidden and unconscious motives. It was greeted as a revelation with far-reaching implications for all intellectual pursuits. Not surprisingly it has had a profound and continuing effect on post-Freudian literature.

In addition, its popularity produced a **psychological/psychoanalytic approach** to criticism.[2] Some critics use the approach to explain fictional characters, as in the landmark interpretation by Freud and Ernest Jones that Shakespeare's Hamlet suffers from an Oedipus complex. Still other critics use it as a way of analyzing authors and the artistic process. For example, John Livingston Lowes's study *The Road to Xanadu* presents a detailed examination of the mind, reading, and neuroses of Coleridge, the author of "Kubla Khan."

[2]See also Chapter 3, "Writing About Character: The People in Literature."

Critics using the psychoanalytic approach treat literature somewhat like information about patients in therapy. In the work itself, what are the obvious and hidden motives that cause a character's behavior and speech? How much background (e.g., repressed childhood trauma, adolescent memories) does the author reveal about a character? How purposeful is this information with regard to the character's psychological condition? How much is important in the analysis and understanding of the character?

In the consideration of authors, critics utilizing the psychoanalytic model consider questions like these: What particular life experiences explain characteristic subjects or preoccupations? Was the author's life happy? Miserable? Upsetting? Solitary? Social? Can the death of someone in the author's family be associated with melancholy situations in that author's work? All eleven brothers and sisters of the English poet Thomas Gray, for example, died before reaching adulthood. Gray was the only one to survive. In his poetry, Gray often deals with death, and he is therefore considered one of the "Graveyard School" of eighteenth-century poets. A psychoanalytical critic might make much of this connection.

Example

At the end of "Young Goodman Brown," Hawthorne's major character is no longer capable of normal existence. His nightmare should be read as a symbol of what in reality would have been lifelong mental subjection to the type of puritanical religion that emphasizes sin and guilt. Such preoccupation with sin is no hindrance to psychological health if the preoccupied people are convinced that God forgives them and grants them mercy. In their dealings with others, they remain healthy as long as they believe that other people have the same sincere trust in divine forgiveness. If their own faith is weak and uncertain, however, and if they cannot believe in forgiveness, then they are likely to transfer their own guilt—really a form of personal terror—to others. They remain conscious of their own sins, but they find it easy to claim that others are sinful—even those who are spiritually spotless, and even their own family, who should be dearest to them. When this process of projection or transference occurs, such people have created the rationale of condemning others because of their own guilt. The price that they pay is a life of gloom, a fate that Hawthorne designates for Goodman Brown after the nightmare about demons in human form.

Archetypal/Symbolic/Mythic

The **archetypal/symbolic/mythic critical approach**, derived from the work of the Swiss psychoanalyst Carl Jung (1875–1961), presupposes that human life is built up out of patterns, or *archetypes* ("first molds" or "first patterns") that are similar throughout various cultures and historical times.[3] The approach is

---

[3]Symbolism is also considered in Chapter 10.

similar to the structuralist analysis of literature, for both approaches stress the connections that may be discovered in literature written in different times and in vastly different locations in the world.

In literary evaluation, the archetypal approach is used to support the claim that the very best literature is grounded in archetypal patterns. The archetypal critic therefore looks for archetypes such as God's creation of human beings, the sacrifice of a hero, or the search for paradise. How does an individual story, poem, or play fit into any of the archetypal patterns? What truths does this correlation provide (particularly truths that cross historical, national, and cultural lines)? How closely does the work fit the archetype? What variations can be seen? What meaning or meanings do the connections have?

The most tenuous aspect of archetypal criticism is Jung's assertion that the recurring patterns provide evidence for a "universal human consciousness" that all of us, by virtue of our humanity, still retain in our minds and in our very blood.

Not all critics accept the hypothesis of a universal human consciousness, but they nevertheless consider the approach important for comparisons and contrasts (see Chapter 14). Many human situations, such as adolescence, dawning love, the search for success, the reconciliation with one's mother and father, and the encroachment of age and death, are similar in structure and can be analyzed as archetypes. For example, the following situations can be seen as a pattern or archetype of initiation: A young man discovers the power of literature and understanding (Keats's "On First Looking into Chapman's Homer"); a man determines the importance of truth and fidelity amidst uncertainty (Arnold's "Dover Beach"); a man and woman fall in love despite their wishes to remain independent (Chekhov's *The Bear*); a woman gains strength and integrity because of previously unrealized inner resources (Maupassant's "The Necklace"). The archetypal approach encourages the analysis of variations on the same theme, as in Glaspell's *Trifles* and Hardy's "The Three Strangers" when important characters conceal details that are relevant to a criminal investigation (one sort of initiation) and also, as a result, assert their own individuality and freedom (another sort of initiation).

Example

In the sense that Young Goodman Brown undergoes a change from psychological normality to rigidity, the story is a reverse archetype of the initiation ritual. According to the archetype of successful initiation, initiates seek to demonstrate their worthiness to become full-fledged members of society. Telemachus in Homer's *Odyssey*, for example, is a young man who in the course of the epic goes through the initiation rituals of travel, discussion, and battle. But in "Young Goodman Brown" we see initiation in reverse, for just as there is an archetype of successful initiation, Brown's initiation leads him into failure. In the private areas of life on which happiness depends, he falls short. He sees evil in his fellow villagers, condemns his minister, and shrinks even from his own family. His life is one of despair and gloom. His suspicions are those of a Puritan of long ago, but the timeliness of Hawthorne's story is that the archetype of misunderstanding and condemnation has not changed. Today's headlines of misery and war are produced by the same kind of intolerance that is exhibited by Goodman Brown.

Deconstructionist

The **deconstructionist critical approach**—which deconstructionists explain not as an approach but rather as a performance—was developed by the French critic Jacques Derrida (1930–2004). In the 1970s and 1980s it became a major but also controversial mode of criticism. As a literary theory, deconstructionism produces a type of analysis that stresses ambiguity and contradiction.

A major principle of deconstructionism is that Western thought has been *logocentric;* that is, Western philosophers have based their ideas on the assumption that central truth is knowable and entire (this view is incorrect, according to a deconstructionist). The deconstructionist view posits instead that there is no central truth because circumstances and time, which are changeable and sometimes arbitrary, govern the world of the intellect. This analysis leads to the declaration "All interpretation is misinterpretation." That is, literary works cannot be encapsulated as organically unified entireties, and therefore there is not *one correct interpretation* but only *interpretations,* each one possessing its own validity.

In "deconstructing" a work, therefore, the deconstructionist critic raises questions about what other critics have claimed about the work: Is a poem accepted as a model of classicism? Then it also exhibits qualities of romanticism. Is a story about a young Native American's flight from school commonly taken as a criticism of modern urban life? Then it may also be taken as a story of the failure of youth. In carrying out such criticism, deconstructionist critics place heavy emphasis on the ideas contained in terms such as *ambivalence, discrepancy, enigma, uncertainty, delusion, indecision,* and *lack of resolution,* among others.

The deconstructionist attack on "correct," "privileged," or "accepted" readings is also related to the principle that language, and therefore literature, is unstable. "Linguistic instability" means that the understanding of words can never be exact or comprehensive because there is a never-ending *play* between the words in a text and their many shades of meaning, including possible future meanings. That is, the words do not remain constant and produce a definite meaning but instead call forth the possibility of "infinite substitutions" of meaning. Each work of literature is therefore ambiguous and uncertain because its full meaning is constantly *deferred.* This infinite play or semantic tension renders language unstable and makes correct or accepted readings impossible.

A number of critics have found the deconstructionist position elusive and vague. They grant that literary works are often ambiguous, uncertain, and apparently contradictory, but they explain that the cause of these conditions is not linguistic instability but rather authorial intention. They also point out that the deconstructionist linguistic analysis is derivative, unoriginal, and incorrect. In addition, critics claim that the deconstructionist linguistic position does not support deconstructionist assertions about linguistic instability. Critics also draw attention to the contradiction that deconstructionism cannot follow its major premise about there being no "privileged readings" because it must recognize the privileged readings in order to invalidate or "subvert" them.

Example

There are many uncertainties in the details of "Young Goodman Brown." If one starts with the stranger on the path, one might conclude that he could be Brown's father because he recognizes Brown immediately and speaks to him jovially. On the other hand, the stranger could be the devil (he is recognized as such by Goody Cloyse) because of his wriggling walking stick. After disappearing, the stranger also takes on the characteristics of an omniscient cult leader and seer because at the satanic celebration he knows all the secret sins committed by Brown's neighbors and the community of greater New England. Additionally, he might represent a perverted conscience whose aim is to mislead and befuddle people by steering them into the holier-than-thou judgmentalism that Brown adopts. This method would be truly diabolical—to use religion in order to bring people to their own damnation. That the stranger is an evil force is therefore clear, but the pathways of his evil are not as clear. He seems to work his mission of damnation by reaching souls like that of Goodman Brown through means ordinarily attributed to conscience. If the stranger represents a satanic conscience, what are we to suppose that Hawthorne is asserting about what is considered real conscience?

Reader-Response

The **reader-response critical approach** is rooted in *phenomenology*, a branch of philosophy that deals with the understanding of how things appear. The phenomenological idea of knowledge is that reality is to be found not in the external world itself but rather in our *perception* of the external world. That is, all that we human beings can know—actual *knowledge*—is our collective and personal understanding of the world and our conclusions about it.

As a consequence of the phenomenological concept, reader-response theory holds that the reader is a necessary third party in the author-text-reader relationship that constitutes the literary work. The work, in other words, is not fully created until readers make a *transaction* with it by assimilating it and *actualizing* it in the light of their own knowledge and experience. The representative questions of the theory are these: What does this work mean to me, in my present intellectual and moral makeup? What particular aspects of my life can help me understand and appreciate the work? How can the work improve my understanding and widen my insights? How can my increasing understanding help me understand the work more deeply? The theory is that the free interchange or transaction that such questions bring about leads toward interest and growth so that readers can assimilate literary works and accept them as part of their lives.

As an initial way of reading, the reader-response method may be personal and anecdotal. In addition, by stressing response rather than interpretation, one of the leading exponents of the method (Stanley Fish) has raised the extreme question about whether texts, by themselves, have objective identity. These aspects have been cited as both a shortcoming and an inconsequentiality of the method.

It is therefore important to stress that the reader-response theory is *open*. It permits beginning readers to bring their own personal reactions to literature, but it also aims to increase their discipline and skill. The more that readers bring to literature through their interests and disciplined studies, the more "competent" and comprehensive their responses will be. With cumulative experience, the disciplined reader will habitually adjust to new works and respond to them with increasing expertise. If the works require special knowledge in fields such as art, politics, science, philosophy, religion, or morality, then competent readers will seek out such knowledge and utilize it in developing their responses. Also, because students experience many similar intellectual and cultural disciplines, it is logical to conclude that responses will tend not to diverge but rather to coalesce; agreements result not from personal but from cultural similarities. The reader-response theory, then, can and should be an avenue toward informed and detailed understanding of literature, but the initial emphasis is the *transaction* between readers and literary works.

Example

"Young Goodman Brown" is worrisome because it shows so disturbingly that good intentions may cause harmful results. I think that a person with too high a set of expectations is ripe for disillusionment, just as Goodman Brown is. When people don't measure up to this person's standard of perfection, they can be thrown aside as though they are worthless. They may be good, but their past mistakes make it impossible for the person with high expectations to endure them. I have seen this situation occur among some of my friends and acquaintances, particularly in romantic relationships. Goodman Brown makes the same kind of misjudgment, expecting perfection and turning sour when he learns about flaws. It is not that he is not a good man, because he is shown at the start as a person of belief and stability. He uncritically accepts his nightmare revelation that everyone else is evil, however, and he finally distrusts everyone because of this baseless suspicion. He cannot look at his neighbors without avoiding them like an "anathema," and he turns away from his own wife "without a greeting" (paragraph 70). Brown's problem is that he equates being human with being unworthy. By such a distorted standard of judgment, all of us fail, and that is what makes the story so disturbing.

MLA Recommendations
for Documenting Electronic Sources

Both students and instructors can now take advantage of the technology available to assist in research. While many libraries offer varied databases that enable researchers to locate information easily, the main thrust of technology is now the exploration of the World Wide Web. Through the use of various search engines, you need to enter the name of an author, a title, or a topic, upon which you will be linked to a host of resources from all over the world—home pages of specific authors, literary organizations, and works on various topics by contemporary writers. An important caveat is that many sources still remain in printed journals and magazines. Sometimes these may be included on the Internet, but quite often they are not. To make your searches thorough, *you must never neglect to search for printed information.*

Underlying these cautionary words is the vital concept of *refereed* material. Scholarly journals and publications are printed only after they have been refereed. That is, the manuscripts are studied by expert scholars—referees—who either recommend or do not recommend publication. You may thus be assured that journal articles and books from University Presses have undergone rigorous scrutiny. The facts you find in such publications are accurate, and the conclusions and interpretations are also reliably and soundly made. By contrast, a good deal of material on the Internet has been put there by interested persons, who may or may not be correct in their presentation of facts, or whose judgments may be based on insufficient or misunderstood data. You must always be sure that the sources you consult are as correct and as sound as human diligence can make them.

However, there is still much to be gained from the Internet. Accordingly, this appendix provides general guidelines for making electronic source citations, and is intended to augment the section titled "Documenting Your Work" in Chapter 18. For general information on citation recommendations by the Modern Language Association (MLA), see Joseph Gibaldi, *MLA Handbook for Writers of Research Papers,* 6th ed. (New York: MLA, 2003).

Because the available methods of obtaining electronic information are developing so rapidly, the printed style manuals have had difficulty keeping up with the changes. If you do a Web search looking for information on these styles, chances are that the information you find will vary from site to site. Therefore, you need to know the basics that are required for the citation of your sources.

When recovering electronic sources, it is vital to type every letter, number, symbol, dot, underline, and space accurately. Recovery systems are unforgiving, and mistakes or omissions of any sort will make it impossible for you to retrieve your source. The sources are often transitory because someone, somewhere, must maintain them (through the updating of information and the paying of fees). The sources are therefore not always reliable, so printing a copy of sources you plan to cite will make your citations both definite and accurate. If the uniform resource locator (URL) you have used does not turn up the material for which you are searching, you may be able to locate it simply by typing in the name of the author or the name of the article. You may often rely on this autofill mechanism to turn up the material for you.

By the same token, it is essential for you, when you are compiling your own list of works cited, to be absolutely accurate in reproducing the URL of your sources. You must assume that someone reading your essay and using your list will want to check out the sources themselves, and any errors in your transcription will at best create confusion and at worst create doubts about the quality of your research.

The style generally accepted in the "cyber" world, and the one recommended by the MLA, places angle brackets (< >) before and after Internet addresses and URLs. If you see such angle brackets around an address, do not use them as part of the address when you are seeking retrieval. Also, since a number of word-processing programs now support the use of italics, you can use italics as a regular practice. Some researchers, however, still prefer underlines, and if your programs (or typewriter) cannot produce italics, of course use underlines. If in doubt about which to use, consult your instructor.

MLA Style Guidelines

Many of the guidelines the MLA has authorized for the citation of electronic sources overlap with the MLA recommendations for printed sources, but to avoid ambiguity a number of recommendations bear repetition. Electronic materials are to be documented in basically the same style as printed sources. According to the sixth edition of the MLA Handbook, which illustrates most if not all the situations you will likely encounter (pages 207–235), the following items need to be included if they are available.

1. The name of the author, editor, compiler, or translator of the source (if available and relevant), last name first, followed by an abbreviation, such as *ed.,* if appropriate.

2. If there is no author listed in the source, then you should list the title first: the title of a poem, short story, article, or similar short work within a

scholarly project, database, or periodical (in quotation marks); or the title of a posting to a discussion list or forum (taken from the subject line and enclosed by quotation marks), concluded by the phrase "On-line posting."

3. The title of a book, underlined or italicized.

4. The name of the editor, compiler, or translator of the text (if relevant and if not cited earlier), preceded by (not followed by) any necessary abbreviations, such as *Ed.*

5. Publication information for any printed version of the source.

6. The title of the scholarly project, database, periodical, or professional or personal site, underlined or italicized; or, for a professional or personal site with no title, a description such as "Home page."

7. The name of the editor of the scholarly project or database (if available).

8. The version number of the source (if not part of the title), or, for a journal, the volume number, issue number, or other identifying number. All numbers should be in Arabic, not Roman, numerals.

9. The date of publication or posting that you find in your source. Sometimes the original date is no longer available because it has been replaced with an update; if so, cite that. Dates should be arranged by (a) day of the month; (b) month (months may be abbreviated); and (c) year.

10. For a work from a subscription service, the name of the service (and name, city, and state abbreviation if the subscriber is a library).

11. For a posting to a discussion list or forum, the name of the list or forum.

12. The number range or total number of pages, paragraphs, or other sections, if they are numbered. If you do your own numbering, include your numbers within square brackets [ ], and be sure to indicate what you have numbered.

13. The name of any institution or organization sponsoring or associated with the Web site.

14. The date when you consulted the source. If you have looked at the site a number of times, include the most recent date of use. The principle here is that the date immediately before the uniform resource locator (URL) will mark the last time you used the source.

15. The electronic address or URL of the source in angle brackets < >. Many programs now automatically include the angle brackets. If the URL is too long to fit on one line, it should be divided at a slash (/) if possible— do not introduce hyphenations into the URL as these may be mistaken for actual significant characters in that address.

The following examples show the formats you are likely to use most often.

For a Book

Shaw, Bernard. *Pygmalion.* 1912, 2001. *The Gutenberg Project.* 19 Aug. 2004 <http://gutenberg.org/etext/3825>.

For a Poem

Carroll, Lewis. *The Hunting of the Snark.* 1876. *Everypoet.com.* 20 Aug. 2004
<http://www.everypoet.com/archive/poetry/Lewis_Carroll/lewis_
carroll_the_hunting_of_the_snark.htm>.

For a Journal Article

Blair, Leslie. "Teaching Composition Online: No Longer the Second-Best
Choice." *Kairos* 8.2 (Fall 2003/Spring 2004). Multiple sections. 18 Aug.
2004 <http://english.ttu.edu/kairos/8.2/binder.html?praxis/blair/
index.html>.

For a Magazine Article

Jones, Kenneth. "Cue the Coffin: *Dracula the Musical* Opens Aug. 19 at the Be-
lasco." *Playbill* 19 Aug. 2004. 20 Aug. 2004. <http://www.playbill.com/
news/article/87940.html>.

Posting to a Discussion List

Kosinsky, Gary. "Re: Sonnet 15" Online posting. Google Groups. 18 Aug. 2004.
19 Aug. 2004. <http://groups.google.com/groups?dq=&hl=en&lr=&ie=
UTF-8&threadm=4123c90d.754639%40news.individual.net&prev=/groups
%3Fhl%3Den%26lr%3D%26ie%3DUTF-8%26group%3Dhumanities.lit.
authors.shakespeare>.

For a Scholarly Project

Voice of the Shuttle: Web Page for Humanities Research. Ed. Alan Liu. 19 Aug.
2004. U of California Santa Barbara. 20 Aug. 2004 <http://vos.ucsb.
edu/>.

For a Professional Site

Nobel e-Museum. The Nobel Foundation. 18 Aug. 2004. 19 Aug. 2004 <http://
www.nobel.se/>.

For a Personal Site

Barrett, Dan. *The Gentle Giant Home Page.* 16 July 2004. 20 Aug. 2004. <http://
www.blazemonger.com/GG/index.html>.

For Synchronous Communications (Such as MOOs, MUDs, and IRCs)

DU Educational Technology Services, Inc. Group Discussion. 15 Aug. 2004.
19 Aug. 2004 <moo.du.org>.

C

Works Used for References and Illustrative Essays

Stories

Ambrose Bierce (1842–1914?)

An Occurrence at Owl Creek Bridge (1891)

I

A man stood upon a railroad bridge in northern Alabama, looking down into the swift water twenty feet below. The man's hands were behind his back, the wrists bound with a cord. A rope closely encircled his neck. It was attached to a stout cross-timber above his head and the slack fell to the level of his knees. Some loose boards laid upon the sleepers supporting the metals of the railway supplied a footing for him and his executioners—two private soldiers of the Federal army, directed by a sergeant who in civil life may have been a deputy sheriff. At a short remove upon the same temporary platform was an officer in the uniform of his rank, armed. He was a captain. A sentinel at each end of the bridge stood with his rifle in the position known as "support," that is to say, vertical in front of the left shoulder, the hammer resting on the forearm thrown straight across the chest—a formal and unnatural position, enforcing an erect carriage of the body. It did not appear to be the duty of these two men to know what was occurring at the center of the bridge; they merely blockaded the two ends of the foot planking that traversed it.

Beyond one of the sentinels nobody was in sight; the railroad ran straight away into a forest for a hundred yards, then, curving, was lost to view. Doubtless there was an outpost farther along. The other bank of the stream was open ground—a gentle acclivity topped with a stockade of vertical tree trunks, loopholed for rifles, with a single embrasure through which protruded the muzzle of a brass cannon commanding the bridge. Midway of the slope between the bridge and fort were the spectators—a single company of infantry in line, at "parade rest," the butts of the rifles on the ground, the barrels inclining slightly backward against the right shoulder, the hands crossed upon the stock. A lieutenant stood at the right of the line, the point of his sword upon the ground, his left hand resting upon his right. Excepting the group of four at the center of the bridge, not a man moved. The company faced the bridge, staring stonily, motionless. The sentinels, facing the banks of the stream, might have been statues to adorn the bridge. The captain stood with folded arms, silent, observing the work of his subordinates, but making no sign. Death is a dignitary who when he comes announced is to be received with formal manifestations of respect, even by those most familiar with him. In the code of military etiquette silence and fixity are forms of deference.

The man who was engaged in being hanged was apparently about thirty-five years of age. He was a civilian, if one might judge from his habit, which was that of a planter. His features were good—a straight nose, firm mouth, broad forehead, from which his long, dark hair was combed straight back, falling behind his ears to the collar of his well-fitting frock coat. He wore a mustache and pointed beard, but no whiskers; his eyes were large and dark gray, and had a kindly expression which one would hardly have expected in one whose neck was in the hemp. Evidently this was no vulgar assassin. The liberal military code makes provision for hanging many kinds of persons, and gentlemen are not excluded.

The preparations being complete, the two private soldiers stepped aside and each drew away the plank upon which he had been standing. The sergeant turned to the captain, saluted and placed himself immediately behind that officer, who in turn moved apart one pace. These movements left the condemned man and the sergeant standing on the two ends of the same plank, which spanned three of the cross-ties of the bridge. The end upon which the civilian stood almost, but not quite, reached a fourth. This plank had been held in place by the weight of the captain; it was now held by that of the sergeant. At a signal from the former the latter would step aside, the plank would tilt and the condemned man go down between two ties. The arrangement commended itself to his judgment as simple and effective. His face had not been covered nor his eyes bandaged. He looked a moment at his "unsteadfast footing," then let his gaze wander to the swirling water of the stream racing madly beneath his feet. A piece of dancing driftwood caught his attention and his eyes followed it down the current. How slowly it appeared to move! What a sluggish stream!

5   He closed his eyes in order to fix his last thoughts upon his wife and children. The water, touched to gold by the early sun, the brooding mists under the banks at some distance down the stream, the fort, the soldiers, the piece of driftwood—all had distracted him. And now he became conscious of a new disturbance. Striking through the thought of his dear ones was a sound which he could neither ignore nor understand, a sharp, distinct, metallic percussion like the stroke of a blacksmith's hammer upon the anvil; it had the same ringing quality. He wondered what it was, and whether immeasurably distant or near by—it seemed both. Its recurrence was regular, but as slow as the tolling of a death knell. He awaited each stroke with impatience and—he knew not why—apprehension. The intervals of silence grew progressively longer; the delays became maddening. With their greater infrequency the sounds increased in strength and sharpness. They hurt his ear like the thrust of a knife; he feared he would shriek. What he heard was the ticking of his watch.

He unclosed his eyes and saw again the water below him. "If I could free my hands," he thought, "I might throw off the noose and spring into the stream. By diving I could evade the bullets and, swimming vigorously, reach the bank, take to the woods and get away home. My home, thank God, is as yet outside their lines; my wife and little ones are still beyond the invader's farthest advance."

As these thoughts, which have here to be set down in words, were flashed into the doomed man's brain rather than evolved from it the captain nodded to the sergeant. The sergeant stepped aside.

II

Peyton Farquhar was a well-to-do planter, of an old and highly respected Alabama family. Being a slave owner and like other slave owners a politician he was naturally an original secessionist and ardently devoted to the Southern cause. Circumstances of an imperious nature, which it is unnecessary to relate here, had prevented him from taking service with the gallant army that had fought the disastrous campaigns ending with the fall of Corinth,° and he chafed under the inglorious restraint, longing for the release of his energies, the larger life of the soldier, the opportunity for distinction. That opportunity, he felt, would come, as it comes to all in war time. Meanwhile he did what he could. No service was too humble for him to perform in aid of the South, no adventure too perilous for him to undertake if consistent with the character of a civilian who was at heart a soldier, and who in good faith and without too much qualification assented to at least a part of the frankly villainous dictum that all is fair in love and war.

One evening while Farquhar and his wife were sitting on a rustic bench near the entrance to his grounds, a grayclad soldier rode up to the gate and asked for a drink of water. Mrs. Farquhar was only too happy to serve him with her own white hands. While she was fetching the water her husband approached the dusty horseman and inquired eagerly for news from the front.

"The Yanks are repairing the railroads," said the man, "and are getting ready for another advance. They have reached the Owl Creek bridge, put it in order and built a stockade on the north bank. The commandant has issued an order, which is posted everywhere, declaring that any civilian caught interfering with the railroad, its bridges, tunnels or trains will be summarily hanged. I saw the order." 10

"How far is it to the Owl Creek bridge?" Farquhar asked.

"About thirty miles."

"Is there no force on this side of the creek?"

"Only a picket post half a mile out, on the railroad, and a single sentinel at this end of the bridge."

"Suppose a man—a civilian and student of hanging—should elude the picket post and perhaps get the better of the sentinel," said Farquhar, smiling, "what could he accomplish?" 15

The soldier reflected. "I was there a month ago," he replied. "I observed that the flood of last winter had lodged a great quantity of driftwood against the wooden pier at this end of the bridge. It is now dry and would burn like tow."

The lady had now brought the water, which the soldier drank. He thanked her ceremoniously, bowed to her husband and rode away. An hour later, after nightfall, he repassed the plantation, going northward in the direction from which he had come. He was a Federal scout.

III

As Peyton Farquhar fell straight downward through the bridge he lost consciousness and was as one already dead. From this state he was awakened—ages later, it seemed to him—by the pain of a sharp pressure upon his throat, followed by a sense of suffocation. Keen, poignant agonies seemed to shoot from his neck downward through every fiber of his body and limbs. These pains appeared to flash along well-defined

---

°*Corinth:* In the northeast corner of Mississippi, near the Alabama state line, Corinth was the site of a battle in 1862 won by the Union army.

lines of ramification and to beat with an inconceivably rapid periodicity. They seemed like streams of pulsating fire heating him to an intolerable temperature. As to his head, he was conscious of nothing but a feeling of fullness—of congestion. These sensations were unaccompanied by thought. The intellectual part of his nature was already effaced; he had power only to feel, and feeling was torment. He was conscious of motion. Encompassed in a luminous cloud, of which he was now merely the fiery heart, without material substance, he swung through unthinkable arcs of oscillation, like a vast pendulum. Then all at once, with terrible suddenness, the light about him shot upward with the noise of a loud plash; a frightful roaring was in his ears, and all was cold and dark. The power of thought was restored; he knew that the rope had broken and he had fallen into the stream. There was no additional strangulation; the noose about his neck was already suffocating him and kept the water from his lungs. To die of hanging at the bottom of a river!—the idea seemed to him ludicrous. He opened his eyes in the darkness and saw above him a gleam of light, but how distant, how inaccessible! He was still sinking, for the light became fainter and fainter until it was a mere glimmer. Then it began to grow and brighten, and he knew that he was rising toward the surface—knew it with reluctance, for he was now very comfortable. "To be hanged and drowned," he thought, "that is not so bad; but I do not wish to be shot. No; I will not be shot; that is not fair."

He was not conscious of an effort, but a sharp pain in his wrist apprised him that he was trying to free his hands. He gave the struggle his attention, as an idler might observe the feat of a juggler, without interest in the outcome. What splendid effort— what magnificent, what superhuman strength! Ah, that was a fine endeavor! Bravo! The cord fell away; his arms parted and floated upward, the hands dimly seen on each side in the growing light. He watched them with a new interest as first one and then the other pounced upon the noose at his neck. They tore it away and thrust it fiercely aside, its undulations resembling those of a water snake. "Put it back, put it back!" He thought he shouted these words to his hands, for the undoing of the noose had been succeeded by the direst pang that he had yet experienced. His neck ached horribly; his brain was on fire; his heart, which had been fluttering faintly, gave a great leap, trying to force itself out at his mouth. His whole body was racked and wrenched with an insupportable anguish! But his disobedient hands gave no heed to the command. They beat the water vigorously with quick, downward strokes, forcing him to the surface. He felt his head emerge; his eyes were blinded by the sunlight; his chest expanded convulsively, and with a supreme and crowning agony his lungs engulfed a great draught of air, which instantly he expelled in a shriek!

20   He was now in full possession of his physical senses. They were indeed, preternaturally keen and alert. Something in the awful disturbance of his organic system had so exalted and refined them that they made record of things never before perceived. He felt the ripples upon his face and heard their separate sounds as they struck. He looked at the forest on the bank of the stream, saw the individual trees, the leaves and the veining of each leaf—saw the very insects upon them: the locusts, the brilliant-bodied flies, the gray spiders stretching their webs from twig to twig. He noted the prismatic colors in all the dewdrops upon a million blades of grass. The humming of the gnats that danced above the eddies of the stream, the beating of the dragon flies' wings, the strokes of the water-spiders' legs, like oars which had lifted their boat— all these made audible music. A fish slid along beneath his eyes and he heard the rush of its body parting the water.

He had come to the surface facing down the stream; in a moment the visible world seemed to wheel slowly round, himself the pivotal point, and he saw the bridge, the fort, the soldiers upon the bridge, the captain, the sergeant, the two privates, his executioners. They were in silhouette against the blue sky. They shouted and gesticulated, pointing at him. The captain had drawn his pistol, but did not fire; the others were unarmed. Their movements were grotesque and horrible, their forms gigantic.

Suddenly he heard a sharp report and something struck the water smartly within a few inches of his head, spattering his face with spray. He heard a second report, and saw one of the sentinels with his rifle at his shoulder, a light cloud of blue smoke rising from the muzzle. The man in the water saw the eye of the man on the bridge gazing into his own through the sights of the rifle. He observed that it was a gray eye and remembered having read that gray eyes were keenest, and that all famous marksmen had them. Nevertheless, this one had missed.

A counter-swirl had caught Farquhar and turned him half round; he was again looking into the forest on the bank opposite the fort. The sound of a clear, high voice in a monotonous singsong now rang out behind him and came across the water with a distinctness that pierced and subdued all other sounds, even the beating of the ripples in his ears. Although no soldier, he had frequented camps enough to know the dread significance of that deliberate, drawling, aspirated chant; the lieutenant on shore was taking a part in the morning's work. How coldly and pitilessly—with what an even, calm intonation, presaging, and enforcing tranquillity in the men—with what accurately measured intervals fell those cruel words:

"Attention, company! . . . Shoulder arms! . . . Ready! . . . Aim! . . . Fire!"

Farquhar dived—dived as deeply as he could. The water roared in his ears like the *25* voice of Niagara, yet he heard the dulled thunder of the volley and, rising again toward the surface, met shining bits of metal, singularly flattened, oscillating slowly downward. Some of them touched him on the face and hands, then fell away, continuing their descent. One lodged between his collar and neck; it was uncomfortably warm and he snatched it out.

As he rose to the surface, gasping for breath, he saw that he had been a long time under water; he was perceptibly farther down stream—nearer to safety. The soldiers had almost finished reloading; the metal ramrods flashed all at once in the sunshine as they were drawn from the barrels, turned in the air; and thrust into their sockets. The two sentinels fired again, independently and ineffectually.

The hunted man saw all this over his shoulder; he was now swimming vigorously with the current. His brain was as energetic as his arms and legs; he thought with the rapidity of lightning.

"The officer," he reasoned, "will not make that martinet's error a second time. It is as easy to dodge a volley as a single shot. He has probably already given the command to fire at will. God help me, I cannot dodge them all!"

An appalling plash within two yards of him was followed by a loud, rushing sound, *diminuendo*, which seemed to travel back through the air to the fort and died in an explosion which stirred the very river to its deeps! A rising sheet of water curved over him, fell down upon him, blinded him, strangled him! The cannon had taken a hand in the game. As he shook his head free from the commotion of the smitten water he heard the deflected shot humming through the air ahead, and in an instant it was cracking and smashing the branches in the forest beyond.

They will not do that again," he thought; "the next time they will use a charge of *30* grape. I must keep my eye upon the gun; the smoke will apprise me—the report arrives too late; it lags behind the missile. That is a good gun."

Suddenly he felt himself whirled round and round—spinning like a top. The water, the banks, the forests, the now distant bridge, fort and men—all were commingled and blurred. Objects were represented by their colors only; circular horizontal streaks of color—that was all he saw. He had been caught in a vortex and was being whirled on with a velocity of advance and gyration that made him giddy and sick. In a few moments he was flung upon the gravel at the foot of the left bank of the stream—the southern bank—and behind a projecting point which concealed him from his enemies. The sudden arrest of his motion, the abrasion of one of his hands on the gravel, restored him, and he wept with delight. He dug his fingers into the sand, threw it over himself in handfuls and audibly blessed it. It looked like diamonds, rubies, emeralds; he could think of nothing beautiful which it did not resemble. The trees upon the bank were giant garden plants; he noted a definite order in their arrangement, inhaled the fragrance of their blooms. A strange, roseate light shone through the spaces among their trunks and the wind made in their branches the music of Æolian harps. He had no wish to perfect his escape—was content to remain in that enchanting spot until retaken.

A whiz and rattle of grapeshot among the branches high above his head roused him from his dream. The baffled cannoneer had fired him a random farewell. He sprang to his feet, rushed up the sloping bank, and plunged into the forest.

All that day he traveled, laying his course by the rounding sun. The forest seemed interminable; nowhere did he discover a break in it, not even a woodman's road. He had not known that he lived in so wild a region. There was something uncanny in the revelation.

By nightfall he was fatigued, footsore, famishing. The thought of his wife and children urged him on. At last he found a road which led him in what he knew to be the right direction. It was as wide and straight as a city street, yet it seemed untraveled. No fields bordered it, no dwelling anywhere. Not so much as the barking of a dog suggested human habitation. The black bodies of the trees formed a straight wall on both sides, terminating on the horizon in a point, like a diagram in a lesson in perspective. Overhead, as he looked up through this rift in the wood, shone great golden stars looking unfamiliar and grouped in strange constellations. He was sure they were arranged in some order which had a secret and malign significance. The wood on either side was full of singular noises, among which—once, twice, and again—he distinctly heard whispers in an unknown tongue.

35 His neck was in pain and lifting his hand to it found it horribly swollen. He knew that it had a circle of black where the rope had bruised it. His eyes felt congested; he could no longer close them. His tongue was swollen with thirst; he relieved its fever by thrusting it forward from between his teeth into the cold air. How softly the turf had carpeted the untraveled avenue—he could no longer feel the roadway beneath his feet!

Doubtless, despite his suffering, he had fallen asleep while walking, for now he sees another scene—perhaps he has merely recovered from a delirium. He stands at the gate of his own home. All is as he left it, and all bright and beautiful in the morning sunshine. He must have traveled the entire night. As he pushes open the gate and passes up the wide white walk, he sees a flutter of female garments; his wife, looking fresh and cool and sweet, steps down from the veranda to meet him. At the bottom of the steps she stands waiting, with a smile of ineffable joy, an attitude of matchless grace and dignity. Ah, how beautiful she is! He springs forward with extended arms. As he is about to clasp her he feels a stunning blow upon the back of the neck; a blinding white light blazes all about him with a sound like the shock of a cannon—then all is darkness and silence!

Peyton Farquhar was dead; his body, with a broken neck, swung gently from side to side beneath the timbers of the Owl Creek bridge.

Kate Chopin (1851–1904)

The Story of an Hour (1894)

Knowing that Mrs. Mallard was afflicted with a heart trouble, great care was taken to break to her as gently as possible the news of her husband's death.

It was her sister Josephine who told her, in broken sentences: veiled hints that revealed in half concealing. Her husband's friend Richards was there, too, near her. It was he who had been in the newspaper office when intelligence of the railroad disaster was received, with Brently Mallard's name leading the list of "killed." He had only taken the time to assure himself of its truth by a second telegram, and had hastened to forestall any less careful, less tender friend in bearing the sad message.

She did not hear the story as many women have heard the same, with a paralyzed inability to accept its significance. She wept at once, with sudden, wild abandonment, in her sister's arms. When the storm of grief had spent itself she went away to her room alone. She would have no one follow her.

There stood, facing the open window, a comfortable, roomy armchair. Into this she sank, pressed down by a physical exhaustion that haunted her body and seemed to reach into her soul.

She could see in the open square before her house the tops of trees that were all 5 aquiver with the new spring life. The delicious breath of rain was in the air. In the street below a peddler was crying his wares. The notes of a distant song which some one was singing reached her faintly, and countless sparrows were twittering in the eaves.

There were patches of blue sky showing here and there through the clouds that had met and piled one above the other in the west facing her window.

She sat with her head thrown back upon the cushion of the chair, quite motionless, except when a sob came up into her throat and shook her, as a child who has cried itself to sleep continues to sob in its dreams.

She was young, with a fair, calm face, whose lines bespoke repression and even a certain strength. But now there was a dull stare in her eyes, whose gaze was fixed away off yonder on one of those patches of blue sky. It was not a glance of reflection, but rather indicated a suspension of intelligent thought.

There was something coming to her and she was waiting for it, fearfully. What was it? She did not know; it was too subtle and elusive to name. But she felt it, creeping out of the sky, reaching toward her through the sounds, the scents, the color that filled the air.

Now her bosom rose and fell tumultuously. She was beginning to recognize this 10 thing that was approaching to possess her, and she was striving to beat it back with her will—as powerless as her two white slender hands would have been.

When she abandoned herself a little whispered word escaped her slightly parted lips. She said it over and over under her breath: "free, free, free!" The vacant stare and the look of terror that had followed it went from her eyes. They stayed keen and bright. Her pulses beat fast, and the coursing blood warmed and relaxed every inch of her body.

She did not stop to ask if it were or were not a monstrous joy that held her. A clear and exalted perception enabled her to dismiss the suggestion as trivial.

She knew that she would weep again when she saw the kind, tender hands folded in death; the face that had never looked save with love upon her, fixed and gray and dead. But she saw beyond that bitter moment a long procession of years to come that would belong to her absolutely. And she opened and spread her arms out to them in welcome.

There would be no one to live for during those coming years; she would live for herself. There would be no powerful will bending hers in that blind persistence with which men and women believe they have a right to impose a private will upon a fellow-creature. A kind intention or a cruel intention made the act seem no less a crime as she looked upon it in that brief moment of illumination.

15   And yet she had loved him—sometimes. Often she had not. What did it matter! What could love, the unsolved mystery, count for in face of this possession of self assertion which she suddenly recognized as the strongest impulse of her being!

"Free! Body and soul free!" she kept whispering.

Josephine was kneeling before the closed door with her lips to the keyhole, imploring for admission. "Louise, open the door! I beg; open the door—you will make yourself ill. What are you doing, Louise? For heaven's sake open the door."

"Go away. I am not making myself ill." No; she was drinking in a very elixir of life through that open window.

Her fancy was running riot along those days ahead of her. Spring days, and summer days, and all sorts of days that would be her own. She breathed a quick prayer that life might be long. It was only yesterday she had thought with a shudder that life might be long.

20   She arose at length and opened the door to her sister's importunities. There was a feverish triumph in her eyes, and she carried herself unwittingly like a goddess of Victory. She clasped her sister's waist, and together they descended the stairs. Richards stood waiting for them at the bottom.

Some one was opening the front door with a latchkey. It was Brently Mallard who entered, a little travel-stained, composedly carrying his grip-sack and umbrella. He had been far from the scene of accident, and did not even know there had been one. He stood amazed at Josephine's piercing cry: at Richards' quick motion to screen him from the view of his wife.

But Richards was too late.

When the doctors came they said she had died of heart disease—of joy that kills.

Anita Scott Coleman (1890–1960)

Unfinished Masterpieces (1927)

There are days which stand out clearly like limpid pools beside the dusty road; when your thoughts, crystal clear as water, are pinioned in loveliness like star-points. Solitary days, which come often, if you are given to browsing in fields of past adventure; or rarely, if you are seldom retrospective; and not at all, if you are too greatly concerned with rushing onward to a nebulous future. Days whereupon your experiences glimmer before you waveringly like motion-pictures and the people you have known stroll through the lanes of memory, arrayed in vari-colored splendor or in amusing disarray. Days like these are to be revered, for they have their humors and their whimsicalities. Hurry your thoughts and the gathering imageries take flight. Perplexity but makes the lens of introspection blur. And of annoyance beware, for it is an evil vapor that disseminates and drowns the visions in the sea of grim realities. Such days must be cultivated. Scenes for their reception must be set. Cushions perhaps, and warmth of fire. Above all, the warmth of sweet content. Ease and comfort, comfort and ease and moods of receptivity. Then hither, come hither the places and the people we have known, the associations that withstand time's effacements. Backward ho, through the mazes of the past.

STOP! "Why howdy, Dora Johns." Darling playmate of my child-years. With wooly hair a length too short for even pigtails. Mudspatters upon your funny black face. Mudspatters all over your dress and your little black hands mud-spattered too.

Why? What? Come on and see. And lo! I am a child again.

Hand in hand, unmindful of her muddy ones, we skip around the old ramshackle house, back to the furthest corner of an unkempt yard, impervious to the tin cans, the ash-heap, the litter, the clutter that impedes our way, our eyes upon, our thoughts bent upon one small clean-swept corner, where there is mud. More mud and water in a battered tin can. And row after row of mud. No, not mud—not merely mud, but things made out of mud. Row on row, drying in the sun.

Carefully, I sit down, doubling up, to be as small as possible, for only this corner   5
where mud things are drying is clean and corners are seldom, if ever, quite large enough. Besides, I must not touch the things made out of mud. If the dried ones fall, they break. If the moist ones are molested, be it with ever so gentle a finger, they lose their shape. Moreover I must not disturb Dora.

Her little hands are busied with the mud. Little molder's fingers are deftly plying their skill. Her child's face is alight. What has splashed her grave child's face with such a light? I wondered. I wonder now. The glitter of brittle talent, a gleam of sterling genius or the glow from artistic fires burning within the soul of a little black child?

Little Dora shaping figures out of mud. Vases and urns, dolls and toys, flying birds and trotting horses, frisking dogs and playing kittens, marvelous things out of mud. Crying aloud as though dealt a blow if one of the dried mud-figures is broken. Working in mud for endless hours, while the neighbor children play. Their hilarious merriment dropping like bombs into the quiet of our clean-swept corner. Deadly missiles seeking to find a mark. The insistent halloes of futile mirth forever bubbling on the other side of a highboard fence. The dividing fence and upon one side the clean-swept corner and the row on row of mud things drying in the sun. And Dora seeming not to heed the seething bubbles upon the other side, shaping, shaping marvelous things out of mud.

Yet, Oh Dora, now that the day is ours, will you not say, "When did the bombs of futile mirth strike their target? When did the tin-cans and the rags and the old ash-heap crowd you out from your clean-swept corner? What rude hand caused the dried mud shapes to fall and break? Who set a ruthless foot in the midst of your damp mud things?" Or were you too plastic, as plastic as your mud? You dare not tell. Only this you can whisper into the mists of our today. You are one of the Master's unfinished shapes which He will some day gather to mold anew into the finished masterpiece.

A lump of mud. Now, there is a sobriquet for you—you funny, funny man. Mr. William Williams. I saw you but once. We chanced to meet in the home of a mutual friend. I thought you so very funny then. Uncouth and very boorish, but ever, when these pageants of the past, these dumb shows of inarticulate folks arise before me upon retrospective days, you appear garbed in the tatters of pathos.

"I am fifty-one years old," you kept repeating. How pitiful those fifty-one years   10
are. You wear a child's simplicity, the sort that is so sad to see upon a man. Fifty-one and penniless. Fifty-one and possessed of naught else but the clothing you wore. Fifty-one and no place on earth you might call home. You confessed to being a vagabond though "bum" was the term you used and you were very proud of your one accomplishment, an ability to avoid all labor.

"I've given no man a full day's honest work in all my fifty-one years," you boast-ed. "I gambles. I ain't no cotton-pickin' nigger." Your one and only boast after hold-ing life, the fathomless fountain of eternal possibilities, in your possession for fifty-one priceless years.

Nevertheless you have lived and so intensely. You held us against our will. Clus-tered around you, listening to you talk. Relating clippings as it were from the scrap-book of your life.

Tales of the road, of the only places you knew. Roads leading away from plantations where the cotton waited to be picked by numberless "cotton-pickin' niggers." Roads leading to pool halls and gambling dens. Roads beginning and roads ending in "rid-ing the roads," carrying backward and forward, here and yon through the weird gob-lin land of the South's black belt.

With a hardened casualness you told stories that revolted and at the same time cheered us with an all sufficing glow of thankfulness that life had spared us the sordidness of yours. Offhandily, you gave us humorous skits that tempered our laughter with wish-es that we might know at least a bit of such a droll existence as had been yours. With mag-ical words you painted pictures so sharply they cut scars upon our hearts. You drew others so filled with rollicking delight their gladsomeness was contagious. With the non-chalance of a player shuffling cards you flipped your characters before us, drawn di-rectly from the cesspool of your contacts, and spellbound we listened.

15 Someone remarked how wonderful you talked and you replied, "Once, I sorter wanted to write books. Once, I uster read a heaps. See times when I was broke and no-body would stake me for a game. I'd lay around and read. I've read the Bible through and through and every Police Gazette I could lay my hands on. Yes, suh, I've read a heap. And I've wished a lot'er times I'd sense enough to write a book."

Lump of mud. Containing the you, the splendid artist in you, the soul of you, the unfinished you in the ungainly lump of you, awaiting the gathering-up to be molded anew into the finished masterpiece.

What a day! Here is my friend at whose fire-side I have lingered beholding Mr. William Williams, great lump of mud. To be sure, she also is an unfinished production. Though it is apparent that the Master had all but done when she slipped from his hands and dropped to earth to lie groping like the rest of us thereon.

Let us sit here together, friend, and enjoy this day.

I shall try to discover what recent gift you have given to the poor the while you are qui-etly stitching upon the garments, linens and scarlet, with which to clothe your household. Sit here and smile with the welcoming light in your eyes, knowing that your door is open to such as William Williams and Dora Johns, the Dora who is become as the mud beneath one's feet. Kind mistress of the widely opened door where white and black, rich and poor, of whatever caste or creed may enter and find comfort and ease and food and drink.

Thomas Hardy (1840–1928)

The Three Strangers (1888)

Among the few features of agricultural England which retain an appearance but little modified by the lapse of centuries may be reckoned the high, grassy and furzy downs, coombs, or ewe-leases, as they are indifferently called, that fill a large area of certain counties in the south and southwest. If any mark of human occupation is met with hereon, it usually takes the form of the solitary cottage of some shepherd.

Fifty years ago such a lonely cottage stood on such a down, and may possibly be standing there now. In spite of its loneliness, however, the spot, by actual measurement, was not more than five miles from a county-town. Yet that affected it little. Five miles of irregular upland, during the long inimical seasons, with their sleets, snows, rains, and mists, afford withdrawing space enough to isolate a Timon or a Nebuchadnezzar;° much less, in fair weather, to please that less repellent tribe, the poets, philosophers, artists, and others who "conceive and meditate of pleasant things."

Some old earthen camp or barrow, some clump of trees, at least some starved fragment of ancient hedge is usually taken advantage of in the erection of these forlorn dwellings. But, in the present case, such a kind of shelter had been disregarded. Higher Crowstairs, as the house was called, stood quite detached and undefended. The only reason for its precise situation seemed to be the crossing of two footpaths at right angles hard by, which may have crossed there and thus for a good five hundred years. Hence the house was exposed to the elements on all sides. But, though the wind up here blew unmistakably when it did blow, and the rain hit hard whenever it fell, the various weathers of the winter season were not quite so formidable on the coomb as they were imagined to be by dwellers on low ground. The raw rimes* were not so pernicious as in the hollows, and the frosts were scarcely so severe. When the shepherd and his family who tenanted the house were pitied for their sufferings from the exposure, they said that upon the whole they were less inconvenienced by "wuzzes and flames" (hoarses and phlegms) than when they had lived by the stream of a snug neighboring valley.

The night of March 28, 182–, was precisely one of the nights that were wont to call forth these expressions of commiseration. The level rainstorm smote walls, slopes, and hedges like the clothyard shafts of Senlac and Crécy.† Such sheep and outdoor animals as had no shelter stood with their buttocks to the winds; while the tails of little birds trying to roost on some scraggy thorn were blown inside-out like umbrellas. The gable-end of the cottage was stained with wet, and the eavesdroppings flapped against the wall. Yet never was commiseration for the shepherd more misplaced. For that cheerful rustic was entertaining a large party in glorification of the christening of his second girl.

The guests had arrived before the rain began to fall, and they were all now assembled in the chief or living room of the dwelling. A glance into the apartment at eight o'clock on this eventful evening would have resulted in the opinion that it was as cozy and comfortable a nook as could be wished for in boisterous weather. The calling of its inhabitant was proclaimed by a number of highly polished sheep crooks without stems that were hung ornamentally over the fireplace, the curl of each shining crook varying from the antiquated type engraved in the patriarchal pictures of old family Bibles to the most approved fashion of the last local sheep-fair. The room was lighted by half a dozen candles having wicks only a trifle smaller than the grease which enveloped them, in candlesticks that were never used but at high-days, holy-days, and family feasts. The lights were scattered about the room, two of them standing on the

5

°*Timon or a Nebuchadnezzar:* Both were proverbial for their solitude. The ancient Greek Timon withdrew from society because he did not get the advancement he expected. Nebuchadnezzar, a Babylonian king, suffered from the delusion that he was an ox, and was driven away from society (Daniel 4). *raw rimes:* coatings of frost.   †*clothyard shafts of Senlac and Crécy:* Cloth-yard shafts were thirty-six-inch arrows. At Senlac Hill, near Hastings in England, the Norman French defeated the English in 1066. In 1346, at Crécy in western France, the English defeated the French.

chimney piece. This position of candles was in itself significant. Candles on the chimney piece always meant a party.

On the hearth, in front of a back-brand° to give substance, blazed a fire of thorns, that crackled "like the laughter of the fool."*

Nineteen persons were gathered here. Of these, five women, wearing gowns of various bright hues, sat in chairs along the wall; girls shy and not shy filled the window-bench; four men, including Charley Jake the hedge-carpenter, Elijah New the parish-clerk, and John Pitcher, a neighboring dairyman, the shepherd's father-in-law, lolled in the settle; a young man and maid, who were blushing over tentative *pourparlers* on a life-companionship,† sat beneath the corner-cupboard; and an elderly engaged man of fifty or upward moved restlessly about from spots where his betrothed was not to the spot where she was. Enjoyment was pretty general, and so much the more prevailed in being unhampered by conventional restrictions. Absolute confidence in each other's good opinion begat perfect ease, while the finishing stroke of manner, amounting to a truly princely serenity, was lent to the majority by the absence of any expression or trait denoting that they wished to get on in the world, enlarge their minds, or do any eclipsing thing whatever—which nowadays so generally nips the bloom and *bonhomie* of all except the two extremes of the social scale.

Shepherd Fennel had married well, his wife being a dairyman's daughter from a vale at a distance, who brought fifty guineas in her pocket—and kept them there, till they should be required for ministering to the needs of a coming family. This frugal woman had been somewhat exercised as to the character that should be given to the gathering. A sit-still party had its advantages; but an undisturbed position of ease in chairs and settles was apt to lead on the men to such an unconscionable deal of toping that they would sometimes fairly drink the house dry. A dancing-party was the alternative; but this, while avoiding the foregoing objection on the score of good drink, had a counterbalancing disadvantage in the matter of good victuals, the ravenous appetites engendered by the exercise causing immense havoc in the buttery. Shepherdess Fennel fell back upon the intermediate plan of mingling short dances with short periods of talk and singing, so as to hinder any ungovernable rage in either. But this scheme was entirely confined to her own gentle mind: The shepherd himself was in the mood to exhibit the most reckless phases of hospitality.

The fiddler was a boy of those parts, about twelve years of age, who had a wonderful dexterity in jigs and reels, though his fingers were so small and short as to necessitate a constant shifting for the high notes, from which he scrambled back to the first position with sounds not of unmixed purity of tone. At seven the shrill tweedle-dee of this youngster had begun, accompanied by a booming ground-bass from Elijah New, the parish-clerk, who had thoughtfully brought with him his favorite musical instrument, the serpent. Dancing was instantaneous, Mrs. Fennel privately enjoining the players on no account to let the dance exceed the length of a quarter of an hour.

10   But Elijah and the boy, in the excitement of their position, quite forgot the injunction. Moreover, Oliver Giles, a man of seventeen, one of the dancers, who was enamored of his partner, a fair girl of thirty-three rolling years, had recklessly handed a new crown-piece to the musicians, as a bribe to keep going as long as they had muscle and wind. Mrs. Fennel, seeing the steam begin to generate on the countenances of her guests, crossed over and touched the fiddler's elbow and put her hand on the serpent's mouth.

°*back-brand:* a back-log or branch placed at the back of a fireplace.   **like the laughter of the fool:* Ecclesiastes 7:6.   †*pourparlors on a life-companionship:* conversations held prior to the negotiation of a marriage.

But they took no notice, and fearing she might lose her character of genial hostess if she were to interfere too markedly, she retired and sat down helpless. And so the dance whizzed on with cumulative fury, the performers moving in their planet-like courses, direct and retrograde, from apogee to perigee, till the hand of the well-kicked clock at the bottom of the room had traveled over the circumference of an hour.

While these cheerful events were in course of enactment within Fennel's pastoral dwelling, an incident having considerable bearing on the party had occurred in the gloomy night without. Mrs. Fennel's concern about the growing fierceness of the dance corresponded in point of time with the ascent of a human figure to the solitary hill of Higher Crowstairs from the direction of the distant town. This personage strode on through the rain without a pause, following the little-worn path which, further on in its course, skirted the shepherd's cottage.

It was nearly the time of full moon, and on this account, though the sky was lined with a uniform sheet of dripping cloud, ordinary objects out of doors were readily visible. The sad, wan light revealed the lonely pedestrian to be a man of supple frame; his gait suggested that he had somewhat passed the period of perfect and instinctive agility, though not so far as to be otherwise than rapid of motion when occasion required. At a rough guess, he might have been about forty years of age. He appeared tall, but a recruiting sergeant, or other person accustomed to the judging of men's heights by the eye, would have discerned that this was chiefly owing to his gauntness, and that he was not more than five-feet eight or nine.

Notwithstanding the regularity of his tread, there was caution in it, as in that of one who mentally feels his way; and despite the fact that it was not a black coat nor a dark garment of any sort that he wore, there was something about him which suggested that he naturally belonged to the black-coated tribes of men. His clothes were of fustian,° and his boots hobnailed, yet in his progress he showed not the mud-accustomed bearing of hobnailed and fustianed peasantry.

By the time that he had arrived abreast of the shepherd's premises the rain came down, or rather came along, with yet more determined violence. The outskirts of the little settlement partially broke the force of wind and rain, and this induced him to stand still. The most salient of the shepherd's domestic erections was an empty sty at the forward corner of his hedgeless garden, for in these latitudes the principle of masking the homelier features of your establishment by a conventional frontage was unknown. The traveler's eye was attracted to this small building by the pallid shine of the wet slates that covered it. He turned aside, and, finding it empty, stood under the pent-roof for shelter.

While he stood, the boom of the serpent within the adjacent house, and the lesser   15
strains of the fiddler, reached the spot as an accompaniment to the surging hiss of the flying rain on the sod, its louder beating on the cabbage-leaves of the garden, on the eight or ten beehives just discernible by the path, and its dripping from the eaves into a row of buckets and pans that had been placed under the walls of the cottage. For at Higher Crowstairs, as at all such elevated domiciles, the grand difficulty of housekeeping was an insufficiency of water; and a casual rainfall was utilized by turning out, as catchers, every utensil that the house contained. Some queer stories might be told of the contrivances for economy in suds and dishwaters that are absolutely necessitated in upland habitations during the droughts of summer. But at this season there were no such exigencies; a mere acceptance of what the skies bestowed was sufficient for an abundant store.

°*fustian:* a thick, coarse, and relatively inexpensive cloth.

At last the notes of the serpent ceased and the house was silent. This cessation of activity aroused the solitary pedestrian from the reverie into which he had elapsed, and, emerging from the shed, with an apparently new intention, he walked up the path to the house-door. Arrived here, his first act was to kneel down on a large stone beside the row of vessels, and to drink a copious draught from one of them. Having quenched his thirst, he rose and lifted his hand to knock, but paused with his eye upon the panel. Since the dark surface of the wood revealed absolutely nothing, it was evident that he must be mentally looking through the door, as if he wished to measure thereby all the possibilities that a house of this sort might include, and how they might bear upon the question of his entry.

In his indecision he turned and surveyed the scene around. Not a soul was anywhere visible. The garden path stretched downward from his feet, gleaming like the track of a snail; the roof of the little well (mostly dry), the well-cover, the top rail of the garden-gate, were varnished with the same dull liquid glaze; while, far away in the vale, a faint whiteness of more than usual extent showed that the rivers were high in the meads. Beyond all this winked a few bleared lamplights through the beating drops—lights that denoted the situation of the county-town from which he had appeared to come. The absence of all notes of life in that direction seemed to clinch his intentions, and he knocked at the door.

Within, a desultory chat had taken the place of movement and musical sound. The hedge-carpenter was suggesting a song to the company, which nobody just then was inclined to undertake, so that the knock afforded a not unwelcome diversion.

"Walk in!" said the shepherd, promptly.

20   The latch clicked upward, and out of the night our pedestrian appeared upon the door-mat. The shepherd arose, snuffed two of the nearest candles, and turned to look at him.

Their light disclosed that the stranger was dark in complexion and not unprepossessing as to feature. His hat, which for a moment he did not remove, hung low over his eyes, without concealing that they were large, open, and determined, moving with a flash rather than a glance round the room. He seemed pleased with his survey, and, baring his shaggy head, said, in a rich, deep voice: "The rain is so heavy, friends, that I ask leave to come in and rest awhile."

"To be sure, Stranger," said the shepherd. "And faith, you've been lucky in choosing your time, for we are having a bit of a fling for a glad cause—though, to be sure, a man could hardly wish that glad cause to happen more than once a year."

"Nor less," spoke up a woman. "For 'tis best to get your family over and done with, as soon as you can, so as to be all the earlier out of the fag o't."

"And what may be this glad cause?" asked the stranger.

25   "A birth and christening," said the shepherd.

The stranger hoped his host might not be made unhappy either by too many or too few of such episodes and, being invited by a gesture to a pull at the mug, he readily acquiesced. His manner, which, before entering, had been so dubious, was now altogether that of a careless and candid man.

"Late to be traipsing athwart this coomb—hey?" said the engaged man of fifty.

"Late it is, Master, as you say.—I'll take a seat in the chimney corner, if you have nothing to urge against it, Ma'am; for I am a little moist on the side that was next the rain."

Mrs. Shepherd Fennel assented, and made room for the self-invited comer, who, having got completely inside the chimney corner, stretched out his legs and arms with the expansiveness of a person quite at home.

30   "Yes, I am rather cracked in the vamp," he said freely, seeing that the eyes of the shepherd's wife fell upon his boots, "and I am not well fitted either. I have had some

rough times lately, and have been forced to pick up what I can get in the way of wearing, but I must find a suit better fit for working-days when I reach home."

"One of hereabouts?" she inquired.

"Not quite that—further up the country."

"I thought so. And so be I; and by your tongue you come from my neighborhood."

"But you would hardly have heard of me," he said quickly. "My time would be long before yours, Ma'am, you see."

This testimony to the youthfulness of his hostess had the effect of stopping her cross-examination.

"There is only one thing more wanted to make me happy," continued the newcomer, "and that is a little baccy, which I am sorry to say I am out of."

"I'll fill your pipe," said the shepherd.

"I must ask you to lend me a pipe likewise."

"A smoker, and no pipe about 'ee?"

"I have dropped it somewhere on the road."

The shepherd filled and handed him a new clay pipe, saying, as he did so, "Hand me your baccy-box—I'll fill that too, now I am about it."

The man went through the movement of searching his pockets.

"Lost that too?" said his entertainer, with some surprise.

"I am afraid so," said the man with some confusion. "Give it to me in a screw of paper." Lighting his pipe at the candle with a suction that drew the whole flame into the bowl, he resettled himself in the corner and bent his looks upon the faint steam from his damp legs, as if he wished to say no more.

Meanwhile the general body of guests had been taking little notice of this visitor by reason of an absorbing discussion in which they were engaged with the band about a tune for the next dance. The matter being settled, they were about to stand up when an interruption came in the shape of another knock at the door.

At sound of the same the man in the chimney corner took up the poker and began stirring the brands as if doing it thoroughly were the one aim of his existence; and a second time the shepherd said, "Walk in!" In a moment another man stood upon the straw-woven door-mat. He too was a stranger.

This individual was one of a type radically different from the first. There was more of the commonplace in his manner, and a certain jovial cosmopolitanism sat upon his features. He was several years older than the first arrival, his hair being slightly frosted, his eyebrows bristly, and his whiskers cut back from his cheeks. His face was rather full and flabby, and yet it was not altogether a face without power. A few grog-blossoms marked the neighborhood of his nose. He flung back his long drab greatcoat, revealing that beneath it he wore a suit of cinder-gray shade throughout, large heavy seals, of some metal or other that would take a polish, dangling from his fob as his only personal ornament. Shaking the water drops from his low-crowned glazed hat, he said, "I must ask for a few minutes' shelter, comrades, or I shall be wetted to my skin before I get to Casterbridge."

"Make yourself at home, Master," said the shepherd, perhaps a trifle less heartily than on the first occasion. Not that Fennel had the least tinge of niggardliness in his composition; but the room was far from large, spare chairs were not numerous, and damp companions were not altogether desirable at close quarters for the women and girls in their bright-colored gowns.

However, the second comer, after taking off his greatcoat, and hanging his hat on a nail in one of the ceiling-beams as if he had been specially invited to put it there, advanced and sat down at the table. This had been pushed so closely into the chimney corner, to give all available room to the dancers, that its inner edge grazed the elbow of the man who had ensconced himself by the fire; and thus the two strangers were brought into close companionship. They nodded to each other by way of breaking the ice of un-acquaintance, and the first stranger handed his neighbor the family mug—a huge ves-sel of brown ware, having its upper edge worn away like a threshold by the rub of whole generations of thirsty lips that had gone the way of all flesh, and bearing the following inscription burnt upon its rotund side in yellow letters:

THERE IS NO FUN

UNTIL i CUM.

The other man, nothing loath, raised the mug to his lips, and drank on, and on, and on—till a curious blueness overspread the countenance of the shepherd's wife, who had re-garded with no little surprise the first stranger's free offer to the second of what did not belong to him to dispense.

50   "I knew it!" said the toper to the shepherd with much satisfaction. "When I walked up your garden before coming in, and saw the hives all of a row, I said to myself, 'Where there's bees there's honey, and where there's honey there's mead.' But mead of such a truly comfortable sort as this I really didn't expect to meet in my older days." He took yet another pull at the mug, till it assumed an ominous elevation.

"Glad you enjoy it!" said the shepherd, warmly.

"It is goodish mead," assented Mrs. Fennel, with an absence of enthusiasm which seemed to say that it was possible to buy praise for one's cellar at too heavy a price. "It is trouble enough to make—and really I hardly think we shall make any more. For honey sells well, and we ourselves can make shift with a drop o' small mead and metheglin° for common use from the comb-washings."

"Oh, but you'll never have the heart!" reproachfully cried the stranger in cinder-gray, after taking up the mug a third time and setting it down empty. "I love mead, when 'tis old like this, as I love to go to church o' Sundays, or to relieve the needy any day of the week."

"Ha, ha, ha!" said the man in the chimney corner, who, in spite of the taciturnity in-duced by the pipe of tobacco, could not or would not refrain from this slight testimony to his comrade's humor.

55   Now the old mead of those days, brewed of the purest first-year or maiden honey, four pounds to the gallon—with its due complement of white of eggs, cinnamon, gin-ger, cloves, mace, rosemary, yeast, and processes of working, bottling, and cellaring—tasted remarkably strong; but it did not taste so strong as it actually was. Hence, presently, the stranger in cinder-gray at the table, moved by its creeping influence, un-buttoned his waistcoat, threw himself back in his chair, spread his legs, and made his presence felt in various ways.

"Well, well, as I say," he resumed, "I am going to Casterbridge, and to Casterbridge I must go. I should have been almost there by this time; but the rain drove me into your dwelling, and I'm not sorry for it."

"You don't live in Casterbridge?" said the shepherd.

"Not as yet; though I shortly mean to move there."

"Going to set up in trade, perhaps?"

60   "No, no," said the shepherd's wife. "It is easy to see that the gentleman is rich, and don't want to work at anything."

°*mead and metheglin:* Mead is an alcoholic drink made from honey. Metheglin is a cheaper drink made with spices and water rinsed from the honeycomb after the better honey is extracted.

The cinder-gray stranger paused, as if to consider whether he would accept that definition of himself. He presently rejected it by answering, "Rich is not quite the word for me, Dame. I do work, and I must work. And even if I only get to Casterbridge by midnight I must begin work there at eight tomorrow morning. Yes, het or wet, blow or snow, famine or sword, my day's work tomorrow must be done."

"Poor man! Then, in spite o' seeming, you be worse off than we," replied the shepherd's wife.

"'Tis the nature of my trade, men and maidens. 'Tis the nature of my trade more than my poverty. . . . But really and truly I must up and off, or I shan't get a lodging in the town." However, the speaker did not move, and directly added, "There's time for one more draught of friendship before I go; and I'd perform it at once if the mug were not dry."

"Here's a mug o' small," said Mrs. Fennel. "Small, we call it, though to be sure 'tis only the first wash o' the combs."

"No," said the stranger, disdainfully. "I won't spoil your first kindness by partaking o' your second." 65

"Certainly not," broke in Fennel. "We don't increase and multiply every day, and I'll fill the mug again." He went away to the dark place under the stairs where the barrel stood. The shepherdess followed him.

"Why should you do this?" she said, reproachfully, as soon as they were alone. "He's emptied it once, though it held enough for ten people; and now he's not contented wi' the small, but must needs call for more o' the strong! And a stranger unbeknown to any of us. For my part, I don't like the look o' the man at all."

"But he's in the house, my honey; and 'tis a wet night, and a christening. Daze it, what's a cup of mead more or less? There'll be plenty more next bee-burning."

"Very well—this time, then," she answered, looking wistfully at the barrel. "But what is the man's calling, and where is he one of, that he should come in and join us like this?"

"I don't know. I'll ask him again." 70

The catastrophe of having the mug drained dry at one pull by the stranger in cinder-gray was effectually guarded against this time by Mrs. Fennel. She poured out his allowance in a small cup, keeping the large one at a discreet distance from him. When he had tossed off his portion the shepherd renewed his inquiry about the stranger's occupation.

The latter did not immediately reply, and the man in the chimney corner, with sudden demonstrativeness, said, "Anybody may know my trade—I'm a wheelwright."

"A very good trade for these parts," said the shepherd.

"And anybody may know mine—if they've the sense they find it out," said the stranger in cinder-gray.

"You may generally tell what a man is by his claws," observed the hedge-carpenter, 75 looking at his own hands. "My fingers be as full of thorns as an old pincushion is of pins."

The hands of the man in the chimney corner instinctively sought the shade, and he gazed into the fire as he resumed his pipe. The man at the table took up the hedge-carpenter's remark, and added smartly, "True; but the oddity of my trade is that, instead of setting a mark upon me, it sets a mark upon my customers."

No observation being offered by anybody in elucidation of this enigma, the shepherd's wife once more called for a song. The same obstacles presented themselves as at the former time—one had no voice, another had forgotten the first verse. The stranger at the table, whose soul had now risen to a good working temperature, relieved the difficulty by exclaiming that, to start the company, he would sing himself. Thrusting one thumb into the armhole of his waistcoat, he waved the other hand in the air, and, with an extemporizing gaze at the shining sheepcrooks above the mantelpiece, began:

> *O my trade it is the rarest one,*
> *   Simple shepherds all—*
> *My trade is a sight to see;*
> *For my customers I tie, and take them up on high,*
> *And waft 'em to a far countree!*

The room was silent when he had finished the verse—with one exception, that of the man in the chimney corner, who at the singer's word, "Chorus!" joined him in a deep bass voice of musical relish:

> *And waft 'em to a far countree!*

Oliver Giles, John Pitcher the dairyman, the parish-clerk, the engaged man of fifty, the row of young women against the wall, seemed lost in thought not of the gayest kind. The shepherd looked meditatively on the ground, the shepherdess gazed keenly at the singer, and with some suspicion; she was doubting whether this stranger were merely singing an old song from recollection, or was composing one there and then for the occasion. All were as perplexed at the obscure revelation as the guests at Belshazzar's Feast,° except the man in the chimney corner, who quietly said, "Second verse, stranger," and smoked on.

The singer thoroughly moistened himself from his lips inward, and went on with the next stanza as requested:

> *My tools are but common ones,*
> *   Simple shepherds all—*
> *My tools are no sight to see:*
> *A little hempen string, and a post whereon to swing,*
> *Are implements enough for me!*

Shepherd Fennel glanced round. There was no longer any doubt that the stranger was answering his question rhythmically. The guests one and all started back with suppressed exclamations. The young woman engaged to the man of fifty fainted halfway, and would have proceeded, but finding him wanting in alacrity for catching her she sat down trembling.

"Oh, he's the———!" whispered the people in the background, mentioning the name of an ominous public officer. "He's come to do it! 'Tis to be at Casterbridge jail tomorrow—the man for sheep-stealing—the poor clockmaker we heard of, who used to live at Shottsford and had no work to do—Timothy Summers, whose family were astarving, and so he went out of Shottsford by the highroad, and took a sheep in open daylight, defying the farmer and the farmer's wife and the farmer's lad, and every man jack among 'em. He" (and they nodded toward the stranger of the deadly trade) "is come from up the country to do it because there's not enough to do in his own county-town, and he's got the place here now our own county-man's dead; he's going to live in the same cottage under the prison wall."

The stranger in cinder-gray took no notice of this whispered string of observations, but again wetted his lips. Seeing that his friend in the chimney corner was the only one who reciprocated his joviality in any way, he held out his cup toward that appreciative

---

°*Belshazzar's Feast:* At King Belshazzar's Feast the famous handwriting on the wall, predicting the downfall of the ancient Babylonian kingdom, magically appeared (Daniel 5).

comrade, who also held out his own. They clinked together, the eyes of the rest of the room hanging upon the singer's actions. He parted his lips for the third verse; but at that moment another knock was audible upon the door. This time the knock was faint and hesitating.

The company seemed scared; the shepherd looked with consternation toward the entrance, and it was with some effort that he resisted his alarmed wife's deprecatory glance, and uttered for the third time the welcoming words, "Walk in!"

The door was gently opened, and another man stood upon the mat. He, like those who had preceded him, was a stranger. This time it was a short, small personage, of fair complexion, and dressed in a decent suit of dark clothes.

"Can you tell me the way to———?" he began: when, gazing round the room to observe the nature of the company among whom he had fallen, his eyes lighted on the stranger in cinder-gray. It was just at the instant when the latter, who had thrown his mind into his song with such a will that he scarcely heeded the interruption, silenced all whispers and inquiries by bursting into his third verse:

> Tomorrow is my working day,
> > Simple shepherds all—
> Tomorrow is a working day for me:
> For the farmer's sheep is slain, and the lad who did it ta'en,
> And on his soul may God ha' merc-y!

The stranger in the chimney corner, waving cups with the singer so heartily that his mead splashed over on the hearth, repeated in his bass voice as before:

> And on his soul may God ha' merc-y!

All this time the third stranger had been standing in the doorway. Finding now that he did not come forward or go on speaking, the guests particularly regarded him. They noticed to their surprise that he stood before them the picture of abject terror—his knees trembling, his hand shaking so violently that the door-latch by which he supported himself rattled audibly: his white lips were parted, and his eyes fixed on the merry officer of justice in the middle of the room. A moment more and he had turned, closed the door, and fled.

"What a man can it be?" said the shepherd.

The rest, between the awfulness of their late discovery and the odd conduct of this third visitor, looked as if they knew not what to think, and said nothing. Instinctively they withdrew further and further from the grim gentleman in their midst, whom some of them seemed to take for the Prince of Darkness° himself, till they formed a remote circle, an empty space of floor being left between them and him—

> . . . *circulas, cujus centrum diabolus.**

The room was so silent—though there were more than twenty people in it—that nothing could be heard but the patter of the rain against the window-shutters, accompanied by the occasional hiss of a stray drop that fell down the chimney into the fire, and the steady puffing of the man in the corner, who had now resumed his pipe of long clay.

The stillness was unexpectedly broken. The distant sound of a gun reverberated through the air—apparently from the direction of the county-town.

"Be jiggered!" cried the stranger who had sung the song, jumping up.

85

°*Prince of Darkness:* the devil.
circulas . . . diabolus: circles, whose center [is] the devil.

90   "What does that mean?" asked several.

"A prisoner escaped from the jail—that's what it means."

All listened. The sound was repeated, and none of them spoke but the man in the chimney corner, who said quietly, "I've often been told that in this county they fire a gun at such times; but I never heard it till now."

"I wonder if it is *my* man?" murmured the personage in cinder-gray.

"Surely it is!" said the shepherd involuntarily. "And surely we've zeed him! That little man who looked in at the door by now, and quivered like a leaf when he zeed ye and heard your song!"

95   "His teeth chattered, and the breath went out of his body," said the dairyman.

"And his heart seemed to sink within him like a stone," said Oliver Giles.

"And he bolted as if he'd been shot at," said the hedge-carpenter.

"True—his teeth chattered, and his heart seemed to sink; and he bolted as if he'd been shot at," slowly summed up the man in the chimney corner.

"I didn't notice it," remarked the hangman.

100   "We were all awondering what made him run off in such a fright," faltered one of the women against the wall, "and now 'tis explained!"

The firing of the alarm-gun went on at intervals, low and sullenly, and their suspicions became a certainty. The sinister gentleman in cinder-gray roused himself. "Is there a constable here?" he asked, in thick tones. "If so, let him step forward."

The engaged man of fifty stepped quavering out from the wall, his betrothed beginning to sob on the back of the chair.

"You are a sworn constable?"

"I be, Sir."

105   "Then pursue the criminal at once, with assistance, and bring him back here. He can't have gone far."

"I will, Sir, I will—when I've got my staff. I'll go home and get it, and come sharp here, and start in a body."

"Staff!—never mind your staff; the man'll be gone!"

"But I can't do nothing without my staff—can I, William, and John, and Charles Jake? No; for there's the king's royal crown apainted on en in yaller and gold, and the lion and the unicorn, so as when I raise en up and hit my prisoner, 'tis made a lawful blow thereby. I wouldn't 'tempt to take up a man without my staff—no, not I. If I hadn't the law to gie me courage, why, instead o' my taking up him he might take up me!"

"Now, I'm a king's man myself, and can give you authority enough for this," said the formidable officer in gray. "Now then, all of ye, be ready. Have ye any lanterns?"

110   "Yes—have ye any lanterns?—I demand it!" said the constable.

"And the rest of you able-bodied—"

"Able-bodied men—yes—the rest of ye!" said the constable.

"Have you some good stout staves and pitchforks—"

"Staves and pitchforks—in the name o' the law! And take 'em in yer hands and go in quest, and do as we in authority tell ye!"

115   Thus aroused, the men prepared to give chase. The evidence was, indeed, though circumstantial, so convincing, that but little argument was needed to show the shepherd's guests that after what they had seen it would look very much like connivance if they did not instantly pursue the unhappy third stranger, who could not as yet have gone more than a few hundred yards over such uneven country.

A shepherd is always well provided with lanterns; and, lighting these hastily, and with hurdle-staves in their hands, they poured out of the door, taking a direction along the crest of the hill, away from the town, the rain having fortunately a little abated.

Disturbed by the noise, or possibly by unpleasant dreams of her baptism, the child who had been christened began to cry heart-brokenly in the room overhead. These notes of grief came down through the chinks of the floor to the ears of the women below, who jumped up one by one, and seemed glad of the excuse to ascend and comfort the baby, for the incidents of the last half-hour greatly oppressed them. Thus in the space of two or three minutes the room on the ground-floor was deserted quite.

But it was not for long. Hardly had the sound of footsteps died away when a man returned round the corner of the house from the direction the pursuers had taken. Peeping in at the door, and seeing nobody there, he entered leisurely. It was the stranger of the chimney corner, who had gone out with the rest. The motive of his return was shown by his helping himself to a cut piece of skimmer-cake that lay on a ledge beside where he had sat, and which he had apparently forgotten to take with him. He also poured out half a cup more mead from the quantity that remained, ravenously eating and drinking these as he stood. He had not finished when another figure came in just as quietly—his friend in cinder-gray.

"Oh—you here?" said the latter, smiling. "I thought you had gone to help in the capture." And this speaker also revealed the object of his return by looking solicitously round for the fascinating mug of old mead.

"And I thought you had gone," said the other, continuing his skimmer-cake with   120
some effort.

"Well, on second thoughts, I felt there were enough without me," said the first confidentially, "and such a night as it is, too. Besides, 'tis the business o' the Government to take care of its criminals—not mine."

"True; so it is. And I felt as you did, that there were enough without me."

"I don't want to break my limbs running over the humps and hollows of this wild country."

"Nor I neither, between you and me."

"These shepherd-people are used to it—simple-minded souls, you know, stirred up   125
to anything in a moment. They'll have him ready for me before the morning, and no trouble to me at all."

"They'll have him, and we shall have saved ourselves all labor in the matter."

"True, true. Well, my way is to Casterbridge; and 'tis as much as my legs will do to take me that far. Going the same way?"

"No, I am sorry to say! I have to get home over there" (he nodded indefinitely to the right), "and I feel as you do, that it is quite enough for my legs to do before bedtime."

The other had by this time finished the mead in the mug, after which, shaking hands heartily at the door, and wishing each other well, they went their several ways.

In the meantime the company of pursuers had reached the end of the hog's-back el-   130
evation which dominated this part of the down. They had decided on no particular plan of action; and, finding that the man of the baleful trade was no longer in their company, they seemed quite unable to form any such plan now. They descended in all directions down the hill, and straightway several of the party fell into the snare set by Nature for all misguided midnight ramblers over this part of the cretaceous formation. The "lanchets," or flint slopes, which belted the escarpment at intervals of a dozen yards, took the less cautious ones unawares, and losing their footing on the rubbly steep they slid sharply downward, the lanterns rolling from their hands to the bottom, and there lying on their sides till the horn was scorched through.

When they had again gathered themselves together, the shepherd, as the man who knew the country best, took the lead, and guided them round these treacherous inclines. The lanterns, which seemed rather to dazzle their eyes and warn the fugitive than to assist them in the exploration, were extinguished, due silence was observed; and in this more rational order they plunged into the vale. It was a grassy, briery, moist defile, affording some shelter to any person who had sought it; but the party perambulated it in vain, and ascended on the other side. Here they wandered apart, and after an interval closed together again to report progress. At the second time of closing in they found themselves near a lonely ash, the single tree on this part of the coomb, probably sown there by a passing bird some fifty years before. And here, standing a little to one side of the trunk, as motionless as the trunk itself appeared the man they were in quest of, his outline being well defined against the sky beyond. The band noiselessly drew up and faced him.

"Your money or your life!" said the constable sternly to the still figure.

"No, no," whispered John Pitcher. "'Tisn't our side ought to say that. That's the doctrine of vagabonds like him, and we be on the side of the law."

"Well, well," replied the constable, impatiently; "I must say something, mustn't I? and if you had all the weight o' this undertaking upon your mind, perhaps you'd say the wrong thing, too!—Prisoner at the bar, surrender in the name of the Father—the Crown, I mane!"

135   The man under the tree seemed now to notice them for the first time, and, giving them no opportunity whatever for exhibiting their courage, he strolled slowly toward them. He was, indeed, the little man, the third stranger; but his trepidation had in a great measure gone.

"Well, travelers," he said, "did I hear you speak to me?"

"You did; you've got to come and be our prisoner at once!" said the constable. "We arrest 'ee on the charge of not biding in Casterbridge jail in a decent proper manner to be hung tomorrow morning. Neighbors, do your duty, and seize the culprit!"

On hearing the charge, the man seemed enlightened, and, saying not another word, resigned himself with preternatural civility to the search-party, who, with their staves in their hands, surrounded him on all sides, and marched him back toward the shepherd's cottage.

It was eleven o'clock by the time they arrived. The light shining from the open door, a sound of men's voices within, proclaimed to them as they approached the house that some new events had arisen in their absence. On entering they discovered the shepherd's living-room to be invaded by two officers from Casterbridge jail, and a well-known magistrate who lived at the nearest county-seat, intelligence of the escape having become generally circulated.

140   "Gentlemen," said the constable, "I have brought back your man—not without risk and danger; but everyone must do his duty! He is inside this circle of able-bodied persons, who have lent me useful aid, considering their ignorance of Crown work.—Men, bring forward your prisoner!" And the third stranger was led to the light.

"Who is this?" said one of the officials.

"The man," said the constable.

"Certainly not," said the turnkey; and the first corroborated his statement.

"But how can it be otherwise?" asked the constable. "Or why was he so terrified at sight o' the singing instrument of the law who sat there?" Here he related the strange behavior of the third stranger on entering the house during the hangman's song.

145   "Can't understand it," said the officer coolly. "All I know is that it is not the condemned man. He's quite a different character from this one; a gauntish fellow, with dark hair and eyes, rather good-looking, and with a musical bass voice that if you heard it once you'd never mistake as long as you lived."

"Why, souls—'twas the man in the chimney corner!"

"Hey—what?" said the magistrate, coming forward after inquiring particulars from the shepherd in the background. "Haven't you got the man after all?"

"Well, Sir," said the constable, "he's the man we were in search of, that's true; and yet he's not the man we were in search of. For the man we were in search of was not the man we wanted, Sir, if you understand my everyday way; for 'twas the man in the chimney corner!"

"A pretty kettle of fish altogether!" said the magistrate. "You had better start for the other man at once."

The prisoner now spoke for the first time. The mention of the man in the chimney cor-   *150* ner seemed to have moved him as nothing else could do. "Sir," he said, stepping forward to the magistrate, "take no more trouble about me. The time is come when I may as well speak. I have done nothing; my crime is that the condemned man is my brother. Early this afternoon I left home at Shottsford to tramp it all the way to Casterbridge jail to bid him farewell. I was benighted, and called here to rest and ask the way. When I opened the door I saw before me the very man, my brother, that I thought to see in the condemned cell at Casterbridge. He was in this chimney corner; and jammed close to him, so that he could not have got out if he had tried, was the executioner who'd come to take his life, singing a song about it and not knowing that it was his victim who was close by, joining in to save appearances. My brother looked a glance of agony at me, and I know he meant, 'Don't reveal what you see; my life depends on it.' I was so terror-struck that I could hardly stand, and, not knowing what I did, I turned and hurried away."

The narrator's manner and tone had the stamp of truth, and his story made a great impression on all around. "And do you know where your brother is at the present time?" asked the magistrate.

"I do not. I have never seen him since I closed this door."

"I can testify to that, for we've been between ye ever since," said the constable.

"Where does he think to fly to?—what is his occupation?"

"He's a watch-and-clock-maker, Sir."   *155*

"'A said 'a was a wheelwright—a wicked rogue," said the constable.

"The wheels of clocks and watches he meant, no doubt," said Shepherd Fennel. "I thought his hands were palish for's trade."

"Well, it appears to me that nothing can be gained by retaining this poor man in custody," said the magistrate; "your business lies with the other, unquestionably."

And so the little man was released off-hand; but he looked nothing the less sad on that account, it being beyond the power of magistrate or constable to raze out the written troubles in his brain, for they concerned another whom he regarded with more solicitude than himself. When this was done, and the man had gone his way, the night was found to be so far advanced that it was deemed useless to renew the search before the next morning.

Next day, accordingly, the quest for the clever sheep-stealer became general and keen,   *160* to all appearance at least. But the intended punishment was cruelly disproportioned to the transgression, and the sympathy of a great many country-folk in that district was strongly on the side of the fugitive. Moreover, his marvelous coolness and daring in hob-and-nobbing with the hangman, under the unprecedented circumstances of the shepherd's party, won their admiration. So that it may be questioned if all those who ostensibly made themselves so busy in exploring woods and fields and lanes were quite so thorough when it came to the private examination of their own lofts and outhouses. Stories were afloat of a mysterious figure being occasionally seen in some old overgrown trackway or other, remote from turnpike roads, but when a search was instituted in any of these suspected quarters nobody was found. Thus the days and weeks passed without tidings.

In brief, the bass-voiced man of the chimney corner was never recaptured. Some said that he went across the sea, others that he did not, but buried himself in the depths of a populous city. At any rate, the gentleman in cinder-gray never did his morning's work at Casterbridge, nor met anywhere at all, for business purposes, the genial comrade with whom he had passed an hour of relaxation in the lonely house on the coomb.

The grass has long been green on the graves of Shepherd Fennel and his frugal wife; the guests who made up the christening party have mainly followed their entertainers to the tomb; the baby in whose honor they all had met is a matron in the sere and yellow leaf. But the arrival of the three strangers at the shepherd's that night, and the details connected therewith, is a story as well-known as ever in the country about Higher Crowstairs.

Nathaniel Hawthorne (1804–1864)

Young Goodman Brown (1835)

Young Goodman Brown came forth at sunset, into the street of Salem village,° but put his head back, after crossing the threshold, to exchange a parting kiss with his young wife. And Faith, as the wife was aptly named, thrust her own pretty head into the street, letting the wind play with the pink ribbons of her cap, while she called to Goodman Brown.

"Dearest heart," whispered she, softly and rather sadly, when her lips were close to his ear, "prithee, put off your journey until sunrise, and sleep in your own bed tonight. A lone woman is troubled with such dreams and such thoughts, that she's afeared of herself, sometimes. Pray, tarry with me this night, dear husband, of all nights in the year!"

"My love and my Faith," replied young Goodman Brown, "of all nights in the year; this one night must I tarry away from thee. My journey, as thou callest it, forth and back again, must needs be done 'twixt now and sunrise. What, my sweet, pretty wife, dost thou doubt me already, and we but three months married!"

"Then God bless you!" said Faith with the pink ribbons, "and may you find all well, when you come back."

5   "Amen!" cried Goodman Brown. "Say thy prayers, dear Faith, and go to bed at dusk, and no harm will come to thee."

So they parted; and the young man pursued his way, until, being about to turn the corner by the meeting-house, he looked back and saw the head of Faith still peeping after him, with a melancholy air, in spite of her pink ribbons.

"Poor little Faith!" thought he, for his heart smote him. "What a wretch am I, to leave her on such an errand! She talks of dreams, too. Methought, as she spoke, there was trouble in her face, as if a dream had warned her what work is to be done tonight. But no, no! 'twould kill her to think it. Well, she's a blessed angel on earth; and after this one night, I'll cling to her skirts and follow her to Heaven."

°*Salem village:* in Massachusetts, about fifteen miles north of Boston. The time of the story is the seventeenth or early eighteenth century.

With this excellent resolve for the future, Goodman Brown felt himself justified in making more haste on his present evil purpose. He had taken a dreary road, darkened by all the gloomiest trees of the forest, which barely stood aside to let the narrow path creep through, and closed immediately behind. It was all as lonely as could be; and there is this peculiarity in such a solitude, that the traveller knows not who may be concealed by the innumerable trunks and the thick boughs overhead; so that, with lonely foot-steps, he may yet be passing through an unseen multitude.

"There may be a devilish Indian behind every tree," said Goodman Brown to himself; and he glanced fearfully behind him, as he added, "What if the devil himself should be at my very elbow!"

His head being turned back, he passed a crook of the road, and looking forward again, beheld the figure of a man, in grave and decent attire, seated at the foot of an old tree. He arose at Goodman Brown's approach, and walked onward, side by side with him.   10

"You are late, Goodman Brown," said he. "The clock of the Old South° was striking, as I came through Boston; and that is full fifteen minutes agone."

"Faith kept me back a while," replied the young man, with a tremor in his voice, caused by the sudden appearance of his companion, though not wholly unexpected.

It was now deep dusk in the forest, and deepest in that part of it where these two were journeying. As nearly as could be discerned, the second traveller was about fifty years old, apparently in the same rank of life as Goodman Brown, and bearing a considerable resemblance to him, though perhaps more in expression than features. Still, they might have been taken for father and son. And yet, though the elder person was as simply clad as the younger, and as simple in manner too, he had an indescribable air of one who knew the world, and would not have felt abashed at the governor's dinner-table, or in King William's* court, were it possible that his affairs should call him thither. But the only thing about him that could be fixed upon as remarkable, was his staff, which bore the likeness of a great black snake, so curiously wrought, that it might almost be seen to twist and wriggle itself like a living serpent. This, of course, must have been an ocular deception, assisted by the uncertain light.

"Come, Goodman Brown!" cried his fellow-traveller, "this is a dull pace for the beginning of a journey. Take my staff, if you are so soon weary."

"Friend," said the other, exchanging his slow pace for a full stop, "having kept covenant by meeting thee here, it is my purpose now to return whence I came. I have scruples, touching the matter thou wot'st of."†   15

"Sayest thou so?" replied he of the serpent, smiling apart. "Let us walk on, nevertheless, reasoning as we go, and if I convince thee not, thou shalt turn back. We are but a little way in the forest, yet."

"Too far, too far!" exclaimed the goodman, unconsciously resuming his walk. "My father never went into the woods on such an errand, nor his father before him. We have been a race of honest men and good Christians, since the days of the martyrs.°° And shall I be the first of the name of Brown that ever took this path and kept—"

"Such company, thou wouldst say," observed the elder person, interrupting his pause. "Well said, Goodman Brown! I have been as well acquainted with your family as ever

---

°*Old South:* The Old South Church, in Boston, is still there.   *King William:* William III was king of England from 1688 to 1701 (the time of the story). William IV was king from 1830 to 1837 (the period when Hawthorne wrote the story).   †*thou wot'st:* you know (thou knowest).
°°*days of the martyrs:* the period of martyrdom of Protestants in England during the reign of Queen Mary (1553–1558).

a one among the Puritans; and that's no trifle to say. I helped your grandfather, the constable, when he lashed the Quaker woman so smartly through the streets of Salem. And it was I that brought your father a pitch-pine knot, kindled at my own hearth, to set fire to an Indian village, in King Philip's war.° They were my good friends, both; and many a pleasant walk have we had along this path, and returned merrily after midnight. I would fain be friends with you, for their sake."

"If it be as thou sayest," replied Goodman Brown, "I marvel they never spoke of these matters. Or, verily, I marvel not, seeing that the least rumor of the sort would have driven them from New England. We are a people of prayer, and good works to boot, and abide no such wickedness."

20   "Wickedness or not," said the traveller with twisted staff, "I have a very general acquaintance here in New England. The deacons of many a church have drunk the communion wine with me; the selectmen, of divers towns, make me their chairman; and a majority of the Great and General Court are firm supporters of my interest. The governor and I, too—but these are state secrets."

"Can this be so!" cried Goodman Brown, with a stare of amazement at his undisturbed companion. "Howbeit, I have nothing to do with the governor and council; they have their own ways, and are no rule for a simple husbandman like me. But, were I to go on with thee, how should I meet the eye of that good old man, our minister, at Salem village? Oh, his voice would make me tremble, both Sabbath-day and lecture-day!"

Thus far, the elder traveller had listened with due gravity, but now burst into a fit of irrepressible mirth, shaking himself so violently, that his snakelike staff actually seemed to wriggle in sympathy.

"Ha! ha! ha!" shouted he, again and again; then composing himself, "Well, go on, Goodman Brown, go on; but, prithee, don't kill me with laughing!"

"Well, then, to end the matter at once," said Goodman Brown, considerably nettled, "there is my wife, Faith. It would break her dear little heart; and I'd rather break my own!"

25   "Nay, if that be the case," answered the other, "e'en go thy ways, Goodman Brown. I would not, for twenty old women like the one hobbling before us, that Faith should come to any harm."

As he spoke, he pointed his staff at a female figure on the path, in whom Goodman Brown recognized a very pious and exemplary dame, who had taught him his catechism in youth, and was still his moral and spiritual adviser, jointly with the minister and Deacon Gookin.

"A marvel, truly, that Goody* Cloyse should be so far in the wilderness, at nightfall!" said he. "But, with your leave, friend, I shall take a cut through the woods, until we have left this Christian woman behind. Being a stranger to you, she might ask whom I was consorting with, and whither I was going."

"Be it so," said his fellow-traveller. "Betake you to the woods, and let me keep the path."

Accordingly, the young man turned aside, but took care to watch his companion, who advanced softly along the road, until he had come within a staff's length of the old

---

°*King Philip's war:* This war (1675–1676), infamous for the atrocities committed by the New England settlers, resulted in the suppression of Indian tribal life and prepared the way for unlimited settlement of New England by European immigrants. "Philip" was the English name of Chief Metacomet of the Wampanoag tribe.   *Goody:* shortened form of "goodwife," a respectful name for a married woman of low rank. "Goody Cloyse" was one of the women sentenced to execution by Hawthorne's great-grandfather, Judge John Hathorne.

dame. She, meanwhile, was making the best of her way, with singular speed for so aged a woman, and mumbling some indistinct words, a prayer, doubtless, as she went. The traveller put forth his staff, and touched her withered neck with what seemed the serpent's tail.

"The devil!" screamed the pious old lady.   30

"Then Goody Cloyse knows her old friend?" observed the traveller, confronting her, and leaning on his writhing stick.

"Ah, forsooth, and is it your worship, indeed?" cried the good dame. "Yea, truly is it, and in the very image of my old gossip,° Goodman Brown, the grandfather of the silly fellow that now is. But, would your worship believe it? My broomstick hath strangely disappeared, stolen, as I suspect, by that unhanged witch, Goody Cory,* and that, too, when I was all anointed with the juice of smallage and cinquefoil and wolf's-bane—"†

"Mingled with fine wheat and the fat of a new-born babe," said the shape of old Goodman Brown.

"Ah, your worship knows the recipe," cried the old lady, cackling aloud. "So, as I was saying, being all ready for the meeting, and no horse to ride on, I made up my mind to foot it; for they tell me there is a nice young man to be taken into communion tonight. But now your good worship will lend me your arm, and we shall be there in a twinkling."

"That can hardly be," answered her friend. "I will not spare you my arm, Goody   35
Cloyse, but here is my staff, if you will."

So saying, he threw it down at her feet, where, perhaps, it assumed life, being one of the rods which its owner had formerly lent to the Egyptian Magi.°° Of this fact, however, Goodman Brown could not take cognizance. He had cast up his eyes in astonishment, and looking down again, beheld neither Goody Cloyse nor the serpentine staff, but his fellow-traveller alone, who waited for him as calmly as if nothing had happened.

"That old woman taught me my catechism!" said the young man; and there was a world of meaning in this simple comment.

They continued to walk onward, while the elder traveller exhorted his companion to make good speed and persevere in the path, discoursing so aptly, that his arguments seemed rather to spring up in the bosom of his auditor, than to be suggested by himself. As they went he plucked a branch of maple, to serve for a walking-stick, and began to strip it of the twigs and little boughs, which were wet with evening dew. The moment his fingers touched them, they became strangely withered and dried up, as with a week's sunshine. Thus the pair proceeded, at a good free pace, until suddenly, in a gloomy hollow of the road, Goodman Brown sat himself down on the stump of a tree, and refused to go any farther.

"Friend," said he, stubbornly, "my mind is made up. Not another step will I budge on this errand. What if a wretched old woman do choose to go to the devil, when I thought she was going to Heaven! Is that any reason why I should quit my dear Faith, and go after her?"

"You will think better of this by and by," said his acquaintance, composedly. "Sit here   40
and rest yourself a while; and when you feel like moving again, there is my staff to help you along."

°*gossip:* from "good sib" or "good relative."   *Goody Cory:* the name of a woman who was also sentenced to execution by Judge John Hathorne.   †*smallage and cinquefoil and wolf's-bane:* plants commonly used by witches to make ointments.   °°*lent to the Egyptian Magi:* See Exodus 7:10–12.

Without more words, he threw his companion the maple stick, and was as speedily out of sight as if he had vanished into the deepening gloom. The young man sat a few moments by the roadside, applauding himself greatly, and thinking with how clear a conscience he should meet the minister, in his morning walk, nor shrink from the eye of good old Deacon Gookin. And what calm sleep would be his, that very night, which was to have been spent so wickedly, but purely and sweetly now, in the arms of Faith! Amidst these pleasant and praiseworthy meditations, Goodman Brown heard the tramp of horses along the road, and deemed it advisable to conceal himself within the verge of the forest, conscious of the guilty purpose that had brought him thither, though now so happily turned from it.

On came the hoof-tramps and the voices of the riders, two grave old voices, conversing soberly as they drew near. These mingled sounds appeared to pass along the road, within a few yards of the young man's hiding-place; but owing, doubtless, to the depth of the gloom, at that particular spot, neither the travellers nor their steeds were visible. Though their figures brushed the small boughs by the wayside, it could not be seen that they intercepted, even for a moment, the faint gleam from the strip of bright sky, athwart which they must have passed. Goodman Brown alternately crouched and stood on tiptoe, pulling aside the branches, and thrusting forth his head as far as he durst, without discerning so much as a shadow. It vexed him the more, because he could have sworn, were such a thing possible, that he recognized the voices of the minister and Deacon Gookin, jogging° along quietly, as they were wont to do, when bound to some ordination or ecclesiastical council. While yet within hearing, one of the riders stopped to pluck a switch.

"Of the two, reverend Sir," said the voice like the deacon's, "I had rather miss an ordination dinner than tonight's meeting. They tell me that some of our community are to be here from Falmouth and beyond, and others from Connecticut and Rhode Island; besides several of the Indian powwows,* who, after their fashion, know almost as much deviltry as the best of us. Moreover, there is a goodly young woman to be taken into communion."

"Mighty well, Deacon Gookin" replied the solemn old tones of the minister. "Spur up, or we shall be late. Nothing can be done, you know, until I get on the ground."

45   The hoofs clattered again, and the voices, talking so strangely in the empty air, passed on through the forest, where no church had ever been gathered, nor solitary Christian prayed. Whither, then, could these holy men be journeying, so deep into the heathen wilderness? Young Goodman Brown caught hold of a tree, for support, being ready to sink down on the ground, faint and over-burthened with the heavy sickness of his heart. He looked up to the sky, doubting whether there really was a Heaven above him. Yet, there was the blue arch, and the stars brightening in it.

"With Heaven above, and Faith below, I will yet stand firm against the devil!" cried Goodman Brown.

While he still gazed upward, into the deep arch of the firmament, and had lifted his hands to pray, a cloud, though no wind was stirring, hurried across the zenith, and hid the brightening stars. The blue sky was still visible, except directly overhead, where this black mass of cloud was sweeping swiftly northward. Aloft in the air, as if from the depths of the cloud, came a confused and doubtful sound of voices. Once, the listener

---

°*jogging:* riding a horse at a slow trot; not to be confused with the current meaning of "jogging," which refers to running slowly on foot.   *powwows:* a Narragansett Indian word describing a ritual ceremony of dancing, incantation, and magic.

fancied that he could distinguish the accents of town's people of his own, men and women, both pious and ungodly, many of whom he had met at the communion-table, and had seen others rioting at the tavern. The next moment, so indistinct were the sounds, he doubted whether he had heard aught but the murmur of the old forest, whispering without a wind. Then came a stronger swell of those familiar tones, heard daily in the sunshine, at Salem village, but never, until now, from a cloud at night. There was one voice, of a young woman, uttering lamentations, yet with an uncertain sorrow, and entreating for some favor, which, perhaps, it would grieve her to obtain. And all the unseen multitude, both saints and sinners, seemed to encourage her onward.

"Faith!" shouted Goodman Brown, in a voice of agony and desperation; and the echoes of the forest mocked him, crying—"Faith! Faith!" as if bewildered wretches were seeking her, all through the wilderness.

The cry of grief, rage, and terror was yet piercing the night, when the unhappy husband held his breath for a response. There was a scream, drowned immediately in a louder murmur of voices fading into far-off laughter, as the dark cloud swept away, leaving the clear and silent sky above Goodman Brown. But something fluttered lightly down through the air, and caught on the branch of a tree. The young man seized it and beheld a pink ribbon.

"My Faith is gone!" cried he, after one stupefied moment. "There is no good on earth, and sin is but a name. Come, devil! for to thee is this world given." 50

And maddened with despair, so that he laughed loud and long, did Goodman Brown grasp his staff and set forth again, at such a rate, that he seemed to fly along the forest path, rather than to walk or run. The road grew wilder and drearier, and more faintly traced, and vanished at length, leaving him in the heart of the dark wilderness, still rushing onward, with the instinct that guides mortal man to evil. The whole forest was peopled with frightful sounds; the creaking of the trees, the howling of wild beasts, and the yell of Indians; while, sometimes, the wind tolled like a distant church bell, and sometimes gave a broad roar around the traveller, as if all Nature were laughing him to scorn. But he was himself the chief horror of the scene, and shrank not from its other horrors.

"Ha! ha! ha!" roared Goodman Brown, when the wind laughed at him. "Let us hear which will laugh loudest! Think not to frighten me with your deviltry! Come witch, come wizard, come Indian powwow, come devil himself! and here comes Goodman Brown. You may as well fear him as he fear you!"

In truth, all through the haunted forest, there could be nothing more frightful than the figure of Goodman Brown. On he flew, among the black pines, brandishing his staff with frenzied gestures, now giving vent to an inspiration of horrid blasphemy, and now shouting forth such laughter, as set all the echoes of the forest laughing like demons around him. The fiend in his own shape is less hideous than when he rages in the breast of man. Thus sped the demoniac on his course, until, quivering among the trees, he saw a red light before him, as when the felled trunks and branches of a clearing have been set on fire, and throw up their lurid blaze against the sky, at the hour of midnight. He paused, in a lull of the tempest that had driven him onward, and heard the swell of what seemed a hymn, rolling solemnly from a distance, with the weight of many voices. He knew the tune. It was a familiar one in the choir of the village meeting-house. The verse died heavily away, and was lengthened by a chorus, not of human voices, but of all the sounds of the benighted wilderness, pealing in awful harmony together. Goodman Brown cried out; and his cry was lost to his own ear, by its unison with the cry of the desert.

In the interval of silence, he stole forward, until the light glared full upon his eyes. At one extremity of an open space, hemmed in by the dark wall of the forest, arose a rock, bearing some rude, natural resemblance either to an altar or a pulpit, and surrounded by four blazing pines, their tops aflame, their stems untouched, like candles at an evening meeting. The mass of foliage, that had overgrown the summit of the rock, was all on fire, blazing high into the night, and fitfully illuminating the whole field. Each pendent twig and leafy festoon was in a blaze. As the red light arose and fell, a numerous congregation alternately shone forth, then disappeared in shadow, and again grew, as it were, out of the darkness, peopling the heart of the solitary woods at once.

55   "A grave and dark-clad company!" quoth Goodman Brown.

In truth, they were such. Among them, quivering to-and-fro, between gloom and splendor, appeared faces that would be seen, next day, at the council-board of the province, and others which, Sabbath after Sabbath, looked devoutly heavenward, and benignantly over the crowded pews, from the holiest pulpits in the land. Some affirm that the lady of the governor was there. At least, there were high dames well known to her, and wives of honored husbands, and widows a great multitude, and ancient maidens, all of excellent repute, and fair young girls, who trembled lest their mothers should espy them. Either the sudden gleams of light, flashing over the obscure field, bedazzled Goodman Brown, or he recognized a score of the church members of Salem village, famous for their especial sanctity. Good old Deacon Gookin had arrived, and waited at the skirts of that venerable saint, his reverend pastor. But, irreverently consorting with these grave, reputable, and pious people, these elders of the church, these chaste dames and dewy virgins, there were men of dissolute lives and women of spotted fame, wretches given over to all mean and filthy vice, and suspected even of horrid crimes. It was strange to see, that the good shrank not from the wicked, nor were the sinners abashed by the saints. Scattered, also, among their pale-faced enemies, were the Indian priests, or powwows, who had often scared their native forest with more hideous incantations than any known to English witchcraft.

"But, where is Faith?" thought Goodman Brown; and, as hope came into his heart, he trembled.

Another verse of the hymn arose, a slow and mournful strain, such as the pious love, but joined to words which expressed all that our nature can conceive of sin, and darkly hinted at far more. Unfathomable to mere mortals is the lore of fiends. Verse after verse was sung, and still the chorus of the desert swelled between, like the deepest tone of a mighty organ. And, with the final peal of that dreadful anthem, there came a sound, as if the roaring wind, the rushing streams, the howling beasts, and every other voice of the unconverted wilderness were mingling and according with the voice of guilty man, in homage to the prince of all. The four blazing pines threw up a loftier flame, and obscurely discovered shapes and visages of horror on the smoke-wreaths, above the impious assembly. At the same moment, the fire on the rock shot redly forth, and formed a glowing arch above its base, where now appeared a figure. With reverence be it spoken, the apparition bore no slight similitude, both in garb and manner, to some grave divine of the New England churches.

"Bring forth the converts!" cried a voice, that echoed through the field and rolled into the forest.

60   At the word, Goodman Brown stepped forth from the shadow of the trees, and approached the congregation, with whom he felt a loathful brotherhood, by the sympathy of all that was wicked in his heart. He could have well-nigh sworn, that the shape of his own dead father beckoned him to advance, looking downward from a smoke-wreath, while a woman, with dim features of despair, threw out her hand to warn him back. Was it his mother? But he had no power to retreat one step, nor to resist, even in thought, when the minister and good old Deacon Gookin seized his arms, and led him to the

blazing rock. Thither came also the slender form of a veiled female, led between Goody Cloyse, that pious teacher of the catechism, and Martha Carrier, who had received the devil's promise to be queen of hell. A rampant hag was she! And there stood the prose-lytes, beneath the canopy of fire.

"Welcome, my children," said the dark figure, "to the communion of your race! Ye have found, thus young, your nature and your destiny. My children, look behind you!"

They turned; and flashing forth, as it were, in a sheet of flame, the fiend-worshippers were seen; the smile of welcome gleamed darkly on every visage.

"There," resumed the sable form, "are all whom ye have reverenced from youth. Ye deemed them holier than yourselves, and shrank from your own sin, contrasting it with their lives of righteousness and prayerful aspirations heavenward. Yet, here are they all, in my worshipping assembly! This night it shall be granted you to know their secret deeds; how hoary-bearded elders of the church have whispered wanton words to the young maids of their households; how many a woman, eager for widow's weeds, has given her husband a drink at bedtime, and let him sleep his last sleep in her bosom; how beardless youths have made haste to inherit their father's wealth; and how fair damsels— blush not, sweet ones!—have dug little graves in the garden, and bidden me, the sole guest, to an infant's funeral. By the sympathy of your human hearts for sin, ye shall scent out all the places—whether in church, bed-chamber, street, field, or forest—where crime has been committed, and shall exult to behold the whole earth one stain of guilt, one mighty blood-spot. Far more than this! It shall be yours to penetrate, in every bosom, the deep mystery of sin, the fountain of all wicked arts, and which inexhaustibly sup-plies more evil impulses than human power—than my power, at its utmost!—can make manifest in deeds. And now, my children, look upon each other."

They did so; and, by the blaze of the hell-kindled torches, the wretched man beheld his Faith, and the wife her husband, trembling before that unhallowed altar.

"Lo! there ye stand, my children," said the figure, in a deep and solemn tone, almost 65
sad, with its despairing awfulness, as if his once angelic nature° could yet mourn for our miserable race. Depending upon one another's hearts, ye had still hoped that virtue were not all a dream! Now are ye undeceived!—Evil is the nature of mankind. Evil must be your only happiness. Welcome, again, my children, to the communion of your race!"

"Welcome!" repeated the fiend-worshippers, in one cry of despair and triumph.

And there they stood, the only pair, as it seemed, who were yet hesitating on the verge of wickedness, in this dark world. A basin was hollowed, naturally, in the rock. Did it contain water, reddened by the lurid light? or was it blood? or, perchance, a liquid flame? Herein did the Shape of Evil dip his hand, and prepare to lay the mark of bap-tism upon their foreheads, that they might be partakers of the mystery of sin, more con-scious of the secret guilt of others, both in deed and thought, than they could now be of their own. The husband cast one look at his pale wife, and Faith at him. What polluted wretches would the next glance show them to each other, shuddering alike at what they disclosed and what they saw!

"Faith! Faith!" cried the husband. "Look up to Heaven, and resist the Wicked One!"

Whether Faith obeyed, he knew not. Hardly had he spoken, when he found himself amid calm night and solitude, listening to a roar of the wind, which died heavily away through the forest. He staggered against the rock, and felt it chill and damp, while a hanging twig, that had been all on fire, besprinkled his cheek with the coldest dew.

°*once angelic nature:* Lucifer ("light carrier"), another name for the Devil, led the traditional revolt of the angels and was thrown into hell as his punishment. See Isaiah 14:12–15.

70   The next morning, young Goodman Brown came slowly into the street of Salem village staring around him like a bewildered man. The good old minister was taking a walk along the grave-yard, to get an appetite for breakfast and meditate his sermon, and bestowed a blessing, as he passed, on Goodman Brown. He shrank from the venerable saint, as if to avoid an anathema. Old Deacon Gookin was at domestic worship, and the holy words of his prayer were heard through the open window. "What God doth the wizard pray to?" quoth Goodman Brown. Goody Cloyse, that excellent old Christian, stood in the early sunshine, at her own lattice, catechising a little girl, who had brought her a pint of morning's milk. Goodman Brown snatched away the child, as from the grasp of the fiend himself. Turning the corner by the meetinghouse, he spied the head of Faith, with the pink ribbons, gazing anxiously forth, and bursting into such joy at the sight of him that she skipt along the street, and almost kissed her husband before the whole village. But Goodman Brown looked sternly and sadly into her face, and passed on without a greeting.

Had Goodman Brown fallen asleep in the forest, and only dreamed a wild dream of a witch-meeting?

Be it so, if you will. But, alas! it was a dream of evil omen for young Goodman Brown. A stern, a sad, a darkly meditative, a distrustful, if not a desperate man did he become, from the night of that fearful dream. On the Sabbath day, when the congregation were singing a holy psalm, he could not listen, because an anthem of sin rushed loudly upon his ear, and drowned all the blessed strain. When the minister spoke from the pulpit, with power and fervid eloquence, and with his hand on the open Bible, of the sacred truths of our religion, and of saint-like lives and triumphant deaths, and of future bliss or misery unutterable, then did Goodman Brown turn pale, dreading lest the roof should thunder down upon the gray blasphemer and his hearers. Often, awaking suddenly at midnight, he shrank from the bosom of Faith, and at morning or eventide, when the family knelt down in prayer, he scowled, and muttered to himself, and gazed sternly at his wife, and turned away. And when he had lived long, and was borne to his grave, a hoary corpse, followed by Faith, an aged woman, and children and grandchildren, a goodly procession, besides neighbors not a few, they carved no hopeful verse upon his tombstone; for his dying hour was gloom.

Katherine Mansfield (1888–1923)

Miss Brill (1920)

Although it was so brilliantly fine—the blue sky powdered with gold and great spots of light like white wine splashed over the Jardins Publiques°—Miss Brill* was glad that she had decided on her fur. The air was motionless, but when you opened your mouth there was just a faint chill, like a chill from a glass of iced water before you sip, and now and again a leaf came drifting—from nowhere, from the sky. Miss Brill put up her hand

---

°*Jardins Publiques:* public gardens or park. The setting of the story is apparently a French seaside town.   **Miss Brill:* Brill is the name of a common deep-sea flatfish.

and touched her fur. Dear little thing! It was nice to feel it again. She had taken it out of its box that afternoon, shaken out the moth-powder, given it a good brush, and rubbed the life back into the dim little eyes. "What has been happening to me?" said the sad little eyes. Oh, how sweet it was to see them snap at her again from the red eider-down! . . . But the nose, which was of some black composition, wasn't at all firm. It must have had a knock, somehow. Never mind—a little dab of black sealing-wax when the time came—when it was absolutely necessary. . . . Little rogue! Yes, she really felt like that about it. Little rogue biting its tail just by her left ear. She could have taken it off and laid it on her lap and stroked it. She felt a tingling in her hands and arms, but that came from walking, she supposed. And when she breathed, something light and sad—no, not sad, exactly—something gentle seemed to move in her bosom.

There were a number of people out this afternoon, far more than last Sunday. And the band sounded louder and gayer. That was because the Season had begun. For although the band played all the year round on Sundays, out of season it was never the same. It was like some one playing with only the family to listen; it didn't care how it played if there weren't any strangers present. Wasn't the conductor wearing a new coat, too? She was sure it was new. He scraped with his foot and flapped his arms like a rooster about to crow, and the bandsmen sitting in the green rotunda blew out their cheeks and glared at the music. Now there came a little "flutey" bit—very pretty!—a little chain of bright drops. She was sure it would be repeated. It was; she lifted her head and smiled.

Only two people shared her "special" seat: a fine old man in a velvet coat, his hands clasped over a huge carved walking-stick, and a big old woman, sitting upright, with a roll of knitting on her embroidered apron. They did not speak. This was disappointing, for Miss Brill always looked forward to the conversation. She had become really quite expert, she thought, at listening as though she didn't listen, at sitting in other people's lives just for a minute while they talked round her.

She glanced, sideways, at the old couple. Perhaps they would go soon. Last Sunday, too, hadn't been as interesting as usual. An Englishman and his wife, he wearing a dread-ful Panama hat and she button boots. And she'd gone on the whole time about how she ought to wear spectacles; she knew she needed them; but that it was no good getting any; they'd be sure to break and they'd never keep on. And he'd been so patient. He'd sug-gested everything—gold rims, the kind that curved round your ears, little pads inside the bridge. No, nothing would please her. "They'll always be sliding down my nose!" Miss Brill had wanted to shake her.

The old people sat on the bench, still as statues. Never mind, there was always the   5
crowd to watch. To and fro, in front of the flower-beds and the band rotunda, the cou-ples and groups paraded, stopped to talk, to greet, to buy a handful of flowers from the old beggar who had his tray fixed to the railings. Little children ran among them, swoop-ing and laughing; little boys with big white silk bows under their chins, little girls, little French dolls, dressed up in velvet and lace. And sometimes a tiny staggerer came sud-denly rocking into the open from under the trees, stopped, stared, as suddenly sat down "flop," until its small high-stepping mother, like a young hen, rushed scolding to its res-cue. Other people sat on the benches and green chairs, but they were nearly always the same, Sunday after Sunday, and—Miss Brill had often noticed—there was something funny about nearly all of them. They were odd, silent, nearly all old, and from the way they stared they looked as though they'd just come from dark little rooms or even—even cupboards!

Behind the rotunda the slender trees with yellow leaves down drooping, and through them just a line of sea, and beyond the blue sky with gold-veined clouds.

Tum-tum-tum tiddle-um! tiddle-um! tum tiddle-um tum ta! blew the band.

Two young girls in red came by and two young soldiers in blue met them, and they laughed and paired and went off arm-in-arm. Two peasant women with funny straw hats passed, gravely, leading beautiful smoke-coloured donkeys. A cold, pale nun hurried by. A beautiful woman came along and dropped her bunch of violets, and a little boy ran after to hand them to her, and she took them and threw them away as if they'd been poisoned. Dear me! Miss Brill didn't know whether to admire that or not! And now an ermine toque° and a gentleman in grey met just in front of her. He was tall, stiff, dignified, and she was wearing the ermine toque she'd bought when her hair was yellow. Now everything, her hair, her face, even her eyes, was the same colour as the shabby ermine, and her hand, in its cleaned glove, lifted to dab her lips, was a tiny yellowish paw. Oh, she was so pleased to see him—delighted! She rather thought they were going to meet that afternoon. She described where she'd been—everywhere, here, there, along by the sea. The day was so charming—didn't he agree? And wouldn't he, perhaps? . . . But he shook his head, lighted a cigarette, slowly breathed a great deep puff into her face, and, even while she was still talking and laughing, flicked the match away and walked on. The ermine toque was alone; she smiled more brightly than ever. But even the band seemed to know what she was feeling and played more softly, played tenderly, and the drum beat, "The Brute! The Brute!" over and over. What would she do? What was going to happen now? But as Miss Brill wondered, the ermine toque turned, raised her hand as though she'd seen some one else, much nicer, just over there, and pattered away. And the band changed again and played more quickly, more gaily than ever, and the old couple on Miss Brill's seat got up and marched away, and such a funny old man with long whiskers hobbled along in time to the music and was nearly knocked over by four girls walking abreast.

Oh, how fascinating it was! How she enjoyed it! How she loved sitting here, watching it all! It was like a play. It was exactly like a play. Who could believe the sky at the back wasn't painted? But it wasn't till a little brown dog trotted on solemn and then slowly trotted off, like a little "theatre" dog, a little dog that had been drugged, that Miss Brill discovered what it was that made it so exciting. They were all on the stage. They weren't only the audience, not only looking on; they were acting. Even she had a part and came every Sunday. No doubt somebody would have noticed if she hadn't been there; she was part of the performance after all. How strange she'd never thought of it like that before! And yet it explained why she made such a point of starting from home at just the same time each week—so as not to be late for the performance—and it also explained why she had quite a queer, shy feeling at telling her English pupils how she spent her Sunday afternoons. No wonder! Miss Brill nearly laughed out loud. She was on the stage. She thought of the old invalid gentleman to whom she read the newspaper four afternoons a week while he slept in the garden. She had got quite used to the frail head on the cotton pillow, the hollowed eyes, the open mouth and the high pinched nose. If he'd been dead she mightn't have noticed for weeks; she wouldn't have minded. But suddenly he knew he was having the paper read to him by an actress! "An actress!" The old head lifted; two points of light quivered in the old eyes. "An actress—are ye?" And Miss Brill smoothed the newspaper as though it were the manuscript of her part and said gently: "Yes, I have been an actress for a long time."

10   The band had been having a rest. Now they started again. And what they played was warm, sunny, yet there was just a faint chill—a something, what was it?—not sadness— no, not sadness—a something that made you want to sing. The tune lifted, lifted, the

---

°*ermine toque:* close-fitting hat made of the white fur of an ermine; here the phrase stands for the woman wearing the hat.

light shone; and it seemed to Miss Brill that in another moment all of them, all the whole company, would begin singing. The young ones, the laughing ones who were moving together, they would begin, and the men's voices, very resolute and brave, would join them. And then she too, she too, and the others on the benches—they would come in with a kind of accompaniment—something low, that scarcely rose or fell, something so beautiful—moving. . . . And Miss Brill's eyes filled with tears and she looked smiling at all the other members of the company. Yes, we understand, we understand, she thought—though what they understood she didn't know.

Just at that moment a boy and girl came and sat down where the old couple had been. They were beautifully dressed; they were in love. The hero and heroine, of course, just arrived from his father's yacht. And still soundlessly singing, still with that trembling smile, Miss Brill prepared to listen.

"No, not now," said the girl, "Not here, I can't."

"But why? Because of that stupid old thing at the end there?" asked the boy. "Why does she come here at all—who wants her? Why doesn't she keep her silly old mug at home?"

"It's her fu-fur which is so funny," giggled the girl. "It's exactly like a fried whiting."

"Ah, be off with you!" said the boy in an angry whisper. Then: "Tell me, ma petite chérie—"   15

"No, not here," said the girl. "Not *yet*."

On her way home she usually bought a slice of honeycake at the baker's. It was her Sunday treat. Sometimes there was an almond in her slice, sometimes not. It made a great difference. If there was an almond it was like carrying home a tiny present—a surprise—something that might very well not have been there. She hurried on the almond Sundays and struck the match for the kettle in quite a dashing way.

But to-day she passed the baker's by, climbed the stairs, went into the little dark room—her room like a cupboard—and sat down on the red eiderdown. She sat there for a long time. The box that the fur came out of was on the bed. She unclasped the necklet quickly; quickly, without looking, laid it inside. But when she put the lid on she thought she heard something crying.

Frank O'Connor (1903–1966)

First Confession (1951)

All the trouble began when my grandfather died and my grandmother—my father's mother—came to live with us. Relations in the one house are a strain at the best of times, but, to make matters worse, my grandmother was a real old countrywoman and quite unsuited to the life in town. She had a fat, wrinkled old face, and, to Mother's great indignation, went round the house in bare feet—the boots had her crippled, she said. For dinner she had a jug of porter° and a pot of potatoes with—sometimes—a bit of salt fish, and she poured out the potatoes on the table and ate them slowly, with great relish, using her fingers by way of a fork.

°*porter:* a dark-brown beer.

Now, girls are supposed to be fastidious, but I was the one who suffered most from this. Nora, my sister, just sucked up to the old woman for the penny she got every Friday out of the old-age pension, a thing I could not do. I was too honest, that was my trouble; and when I was playing with Bill Connell, the sergeant-major's son, and saw my grandmother steering up the path with the jug of porter sticking out from beneath her shawl I was mortified. I made excuses not to let him come into the house, because I could never be sure what she would be up to when we went in.

When Mother was at work and my grandmother made the dinner I wouldn't touch it. Nora once tried to make me, but I hid under the table from her and took the bread-knife with me for protection. Nora let on to be very indignant (she wasn't, of course, but she knew Mother saw through her, so she sided with Gran) and came after me. I lashed out at her with the bread-knife, and after that she left me alone. I stayed there till Mother came in from work and made my dinner, but when Father came in later Nora said in a shocked voice: "Oh, Dadda, do you know what Jackie did at dinner time?" Then, of course, it all came out; Father gave me a flaking; Mother interfered, and for days after that he didn't speak to me and Mother barely spoke to Nora. And all because of that old woman! God knows, I was heart-scalded.

Then, to crown my misfortune, I had to make my first confession and communion. It was an old woman called Ryan who prepared us for these. She was about the one age with Gran; she was well-to-do, lived in a big house on Montenotte, wore a black cloak and bonnet, and came every day to school at three o'clock when we should have been going home, and talked to us of hell. She may have mentioned the other place as well, but that could only have been by accident, for hell had the first place in her heart.

5   She lit a candle, took out a new half-crown, and offered it to the first boy who would hold one finger—only one finger!—in the flame for five minutes by the school clock. Being always very ambitious I was tempted to volunteer, but I thought it might look greedy. Then she asked were we afraid of holding one finger—only one finger!—in a little candle flame for five minutes and not be afraid of burning all over in roasting hot furnaces for all eternity. "All eternity! Just think of that! A whole lifetime goes by and it's nothing, not even a drop in the ocean of your sufferings." The woman was really interesting about hell, but my attention was all fixed on the half-crown. At the end of the lesson she put it back in her purse. It was a great disappointment; a religious woman like that, you wouldn't think she'd bother about a thing like a half-crown.

Another day she said she knew a priest who woke one night to find a fellow he didn't recognize leaning over the end of his bed. The priest was a bit frightened—naturally enough—but he asked the fellow what he wanted, and the fellow said in a deep, husky voice that he wanted to go to confession. The priest said it was an awkward time and wouldn't it do in the morning, but the fellow said that last time he went to confession, there was one sin he kept back, being ashamed to mention it, and now it was always on his mind. Then the priest knew it was a bad case, because the fellow was after making a bad confession and committing a mortal sin. He got up to dress, and just then the cock crew in the yard outside, and—lo and behold!—when the priest looked round there was no sign of the fellow, only a smell of burning timber, and when the priest looked at his bed didn't he see the print of two hands burned in it? That was because the fellow had made a bad confession. This story made a shocking impression on me.

But the worst of all was when she showed us how to examine our conscience. Did we take the name of the Lord, our God, in vain? Did we honour our father and our mother? (I asked her did this include grandmothers and she said it did.) Did we love our neighbours as ourselves? Did we covet our neighbour's goods? (I thought of the way I felt about the penny that Nora got every Friday.) I decided that, between one thing and another, I must have broken the whole ten commandments, all on account of that old woman, and so far as I could see, so long as she remained in the house I had no hope of ever doing anything else.

I was scared to death of confession. The day the whole class went I let on to have a toothache, hoping my absence wouldn't be noticed; but at three o'clock, just as I was feeling safe, along comes a chap with a message from Mrs. Ryan that I was to go to confession myself on Saturday and be at the chapel for communion with the rest. To make it worse, Mother couldn't come with me and sent Nora instead.

Now, that girl had ways of tormenting me that Mother never knew of. She held my hand as we went down the hill, smiling sadly and saying how sorry she was for me, as if she were bringing me to the hospital for an operation.

"Oh, God help us!" she moaned. "Isn't it a terrible pity you weren't a good boy? Oh, Jackie, my heart bleeds for you! How will you ever think of all your sins? Don't forget you have to tell him about the time you kicked Gran on the shin."   *10*

"Lemme go!" I said, trying to drag myself free of her. "I don't want to go to confession at all."

"But sure, you'll have to go to confession, Jackie," she replied in the same regretful tone. "Sure, if you didn't the parish priest would be up to the house, looking for you. 'Tisn't, God knows, that I'm not sorry for you. Do you remember the time you tried to kill me with the bread-knife under the table? And the language you used to me? I don't know what he'll do with you at all, Jackie. He might have to send you up to the bishop."

I remember thinking bitterly that she didn't know the half of what I had to tell—if I told it. I knew I couldn't tell it, and understood perfectly why the fellow in Mrs. Ryan's story made a bad confession; it seemed to me a great shame that people wouldn't stop criticizing him. I remember that steep hill down to the church, and the sunlit hillsides beyond the valley of the river, which I saw in the gaps between the houses like Adam's last glimpse of Paradise.°

Then, when she had maneuvered me down the long flight of steps to the chapel yard, Nora suddenly changed her tone. She became the raging malicious devil she really was.

"There you are!" she said with a yelp of triumph, hurling me through the church door. "And I hope he'll give you the penitential psalms, you dirty little caffler."   *15*

I knew then I was lost, given up to eternal justice. The door with the coloured-glass panels swung shut behind me, the sunlight went out and gave place to deep shadow, and the wind whistled outside so that the silence within seemed to crackle like ice under my feet. Nora sat in front of me by the confession box. There were a couple of old women ahead of her, and then a miserable-looking poor devil came and wedged me in at the other side, so that I couldn't escape even if I had the courage. He joined his hands and rolled his eyes in the direction of the roof, muttering aspirations in an anguished tone, and I wondered had he a grandmother too. Only a grandmother could account for a fellow behaving in that heartbroken way, but he was better off than I, for he at least could go and confess his sins; while I would make a bad confession and then die in the night and be continually coming back and burning people's furniture.

Nora's turn came, and I heard the sound of something slamming, and then her voice as if butter wouldn't melt in her mouth, and then another slam, and out she came. God, the hypocrisy of women! Her eyes were lowered, her head was bowed, and her hands were joined very low down on her stomach, and she walked up the aisle to the side altar

---

°*Adam's last glimpse of Paradise:* Genesis 3:23–24.

looking like a saint. You never saw such an exhibition of devotion, and I remembered the devilish malice with which she had tormented me all the way from our door, and wondered were all religious people like that, really. It was my turn now. With the fear of damnation in my soul I went in, and the confessional door closed of itself behind me.

It was pitch-dark and I couldn't see the priest or anything else. Then I really began to be frightened. In the darkness it was a matter between God and me, and He had all the odds. He knew what my intentions were before I even started; I had no chance. All I had ever been told about confession got mixed up in my mind, and I knelt to one wall and said: "Bless me, father, for I have sinned; this is my first confession." I waited for a few minutes, but nothing happened, so I tried it on the other wall. Nothing happened there either. He had me spotted all right.

It must have been then that I noticed the shelf at about one height with my head. It was really a place for grown-up people to rest their elbows, but in my distracted state I thought it was probably the place you were supposed to kneel. Of course, it was on the high side and not very deep, but I was always good at climbing and managed to get up all right. Staying up was the trouble. There was room only for my knees, and nothing you could get a grip on but a sort of wooden moulding a bit above it. I held on to the moulding and repeated the words a little louder, and this time something happened all right. A slide was slammed back; a little light entered the box, and a man's voice said: "Who's there?"

20   "'Tis me, father," I said for fear he mightn't see me and go away again. I couldn't see him at all. The place the voice came from was under the moulding, about level with my knees, so I took a good grip of the moulding and swung myself down till I saw the astonished face of a young priest looking up at me. He had to put his head on one side to see me, and I had to put mine on one side to see him, so we were more or less talking to one another upside-down. It struck me as a queer way of hearing confessions, but I didn't feel it my place to criticize.

"Bless me, father, for I have sinned; this is my first confession," I rattled off all in one breath, and swung myself down the least shade more to make it easier for him.

"What are you doing up there?" he shouted in an angry voice, and the strain the politeness was putting on my hold of the moulding, and the shock of being addressed in such an uncivil tone, were too much for me. I lost my grip, tumbled, and hit the door an unmerciful wallop before I found myself flat on my back in the middle of the aisle. The people who had been waiting stood up with their mouths open. The priest opened the door of the middle box and came out, pushing his biretta back from his forehead; he looked something terrible. Then Nora came scampering down the aisle.

"Oh, you dirty little caffler!" she said. "I might have known you'd do it. I might have known you'd disgrace me. I can't leave you out of my sight for one minute."

Before I could even get to my feet to defend myself she bent down and gave me a clip across the ear. This reminded me that I was so stunned I had even forgotten to cry, so that people might think I wasn't hurt at all, when in fact I was probably maimed for life. I gave a roar out of me.

25   "What's all this about?" the priest hissed, getting angrier than ever and pushing Nora off me. "How dare you hit the child like that, you little vixen?"

"But I can't do my penance with him, father," Nora cried, cocking an outraged eye up to him.

"Well, go and do it, or I'll give you some more to do," he said, giving me a hand up. "Was it coming to confession you were, my poor man?" he asked me.

"'Twas, father," said I with a sob.

"Oh," he said respectfully, "a big hefty fellow like you must have terrible sins. Is this your first?"

"'Tis, father," said I. *30*

"Worse and worse," he said gloomily. "The crimes of a lifetime. I don't know will I get rid of you at all today. You'd better wait now till I'm finished with these old ones. You can see by the looks of them they haven't much to tell."

"I will, father," I said with something approaching joy.

The relief of it was really enormous. Nora stuck out her tongue at me from behind his back, but I couldn't even be bothered retorting. I knew from the very moment that man opened his mouth that he was intelligent above the ordinary. When I had time to think, I saw how right I was. It only stood to reason that a fellow confessing after seven years would have more to tell than people that went every week. The crimes of a lifetime, exactly as he said. It was only what he expected, and the rest was the cackle of old women and girls with their talk of hell, the bishop, and the penitential psalms. That was all they knew. I started to make my examination of conscience, and barring the one bad business of my grandmother it didn't seem so bad.

The next time, the priest steered me into the confession box himself and left the shutter back the way I could see him get in and sit down at the further side of the grille from me.

"Well, now," he said, "what do they call you?" *35*

"Jackie, father," said I.

"And what's a-trouble to you, Jackie?"

"Father," I said, feeling I might as well get it over while I had him in good humour, "I had it all arranged to kill my grandmother."

He seemed a bit shaken by that, all right, because he said nothing for quite a while.

"My goodness," he said at last, "that'd be a shocking thing to do. What put that into *40* your head?"

"Father," I said, feeling very sorry for myself, "she's an awful woman."

"Is she?" he asked. "What way is she awful?"

"She takes porter, father," I said, knowing well from the way Mother talked of it that this was a mortal sin, and hoping it would make the priest take a more favourable view of my case.

"Oh, my!" he said, and I could see he was impressed.

"And snuff, father," said I. *45*

"That's a bad case, sure enough, Jackie," he said.

"And she goes round in her bare feet, father," I went on in a rush of self-pity, "and she knows I don't like her, and she gives pennies to Nora and none to me, and my da sides with her and flakes me, and one night I was so heartscalded I made up my mind I'd have to kill her."

"And what would you do with the body?" he asked with great interest.

"I was thinking I could chop that up and carry it away in a barrow I have," I said.

"Begor, Jackie," he said, "do you know you're a terrible child?" *50*

"I know, father," I said, for I was just thinking the same thing myself. "I tried to kill Nora too with a bread-knife under the table, only I missed her."

"Is that the little girl that was beating you just now?" he asked.

"'Tis, father."

"Someone will go for her with a bread-knife one day, and he won't miss her," he said rather cryptically. "You must have great courage. Between ourselves, there's a lot of people I'd like to do the same to but I'd never have the nerve. Hanging is an awful death."

"Is it, father?" I asked with the deepest interest—I was always very keen on hanging. *55* "Did you ever see a fellow hanged?"

"Dozens of them," he said solemnly. "And they all died roaring."

"Jay!" I said.

"Oh, a horrible death!" he said with great satisfaction. "Lots of fellows I saw killed their grandmothers too, but they all said 'twas never worth it."

He had me there for a full ten minutes talking, and then walked out the chapel yard with me. I was genuinely sorry to part with him, because he was the most entertaining character I'd ever met in the religious line. Outside, after the shadow of the church, the sunlight was like the roaring of waves on a beach; it dazzled me; and when the frozen silence melted and I heard the screech of trams on the road my heart soared. I knew now I wouldn't die in the night and come back, leaving marks on my mother's furniture. It would be a great worry to her, and the poor soul had enough.

60   Nora was sitting on the railing, waiting for me, and she put on a very sour puss when she saw the priest with me. She was made jealous because a priest had never come out of the church with her.

"Well," she asked coldly, after he left me, "what did he give you?"

"Three Hail Marys," I said.

"Three Hail Marys," she repeated incredulously. "You mustn't have told him anything."

"I told him everything," I said confidently.

65   "About Gran and all?"

"About Gran and all."

(All she wanted was to be able to go home and say I'd made a bad confession.)

"Did you tell him you went for me with the bread-knife?" she asked with a frown.

"I did to be sure."

"And he only gave you three Hail Marys?"

"That's all."

She slowly got down from the railing with a baffled air. Clearly, this was beyond her. As we mounted the steps back to the main road she looked at me suspiciously.

"What are you sucking?" she asked.

"Bullseyes."

"Was it the priest gave them to you?"

"'Twas."

"Lord God," she wailed bitterly, "some people have all the luck! 'Tis no advantage to anybody trying to be good. I might just as well be a sinner like you."

Edgar Allan Poe (1809–1849)

The Masque of the Red Death (1842)

The "Red Death" had long devastated the country. No pestilence had ever been so fatal, or so hideous. Blood was its Avatar° and its seal—the redness and the horror of blood. There were sharp pains, and sudden dizziness, and then profuse bleeding at the pores, with dissolution. The scarlet stains upon the body and especially upon the face of the victim, were the pest ban which shut him out from the aid and from the sympathy of his

---

°*Avatar:* model, incarnation, manifestation.

fellow-men. And the whole seizure, progress, and termination of the disease, were the incidents of half an hour.

But the Prince Prospero° was happy and dauntless and sagacious. When his dominions were half depopulated, he summoned to his presence a thousand hale and light-hearted friends from among the knights and dames of his court, and with these retired to the deep seclusion of one of his castellated abbeys. This was an extensive and magnificent structure, the creation of the prince's own eccentric yet august taste. A strong and lofty wall girdled it in. This wall had gates of iron. The courtiers, having entered, brought furnaces and massy hammers and welded the bolts. They resolved to leave means neither of ingress nor egress to the sudden impulses of despair or of frenzy from within. The abbey was amply provisioned. With such precautions the courtiers might bid defiance to contagion. The external world could take care of itself. In the meantime it was folly to grieve, or to think. The prince had provided all the appliances of pleasure. There were buffoons, there were improvisatori, there were ballet-dancers, there were musicians, there was Beauty, there was wine. All these and security were within. Without was the "Red Death."

It was toward the close of the fifth or sixth month of his seclusion, and while the pestilence raged most furiously abroad, that the Prince Prospero entertained his thousand friends at a masked ball of the most unusual magnificence.

It was a voluptuous scene, that masquerade. But first let me tell of the rooms in which it was held. There were seven—an imperial suite. In many palaces, however, such suites form a long and straight vista, while the folding doors slide back nearly to the walls on either hand, so that the view of the whole extent is scarcely impeded. Here the case was very different; as might have been expected from the duke's love of the *bizarre*. The apartments were so irregularly disposed that the vision embraced but little more than one at a time. There was a sharp turn at every twenty or thirty yards, and at each turn a novel effect. To the right and left, in the middle of each wall, a tall and narrow Gothic window looked out upon a closed corridor which pursued the windings of the suite. These windows were of stained glass whose color varied in accordance with the prevailing hue of the decorations of the chamber into which it opened. That at the eastern extremity was hung, for example, in blue—and vividly blue were its windows. The second chamber was purple in its ornaments and tapestries, and here the panes were purple. The third was green throughout, and so were the casements. The fourth was furnished and lighted with orange—the fifth with white—the sixth with violet. The seventh apartment was closely shrouded in black velvet tapestries that hung all over the ceiling and down the walls, falling in heavy folds upon a carpet of the same material and hue. But in this chamber only, the color of the windows failed to correspond with the decorations. The panes here were scarlet—a deep blood color. Now in no one of the seven apartments was there any lamp or candelabrum, amid the profusion of golden ornaments that lay scattered to and fro or depended from the roof. There was no light of any kind emanating from lamp or candle within the suite of chambers. But in the corridors that followed the suite, there stood, opposite to each window, a heavy tripod, bearing a brazier of fire, that projected its rays through the tinted glass and so glaringly illumined the room. And thus were produced a multitude of gaudy and fantastic appearances. But in the western or black chamber the effect of the fire-light that streamed upon the dark hangings through the blood-tinted panes was ghastly in the extreme, and produced so wild a look upon the countenances of those who entered, that there were few of the company bold enough to set foot within its precincts at all.

°*Prospero:* "Prosperous." In Shakespeare's play *The Tempest*, the principal character is Prospero.

5   It was in this apartment, also, that there stood against the western wall, a gigantic clock of ebony. Its pendulum swung to and fro with a dull, heavy, monotonous clang; and when the minute-hand made the circuit of the face, and the hour was to be stricken, there came from the brazen lungs of the clock a sound which was clear and loud and deep and exceedingly musical, but of so peculiar a note and emphasis that, at each lapse of an hour, the musicians of the orchestra were constrained to pause, momentarily, in their performance, to hearken to the sound; and thus the waltzers perforce ceased their evolutions; and there was a brief disconcert of the whole gay company; and, while the chimes of the clock yet rang, it was observed that the giddiest grew pale, and the more aged and sedate passed their hands over their brows as if in confused revery or meditation. But when the echoes had fully ceased, a light laughter at once pervaded the assembly; the musicians looked at each other and smiled as if at their own nervousness and folly, and made whispering vows, each to the other, that the next chiming of the clock should produce in them no similar emotion; and then, after the lapse of sixty minutes (which embrace three thousand and six hundred seconds of the Time that flies), there came yet another chiming of the clock, and then were the same disconcert and tremulousness and meditation as before.

     But, in spite of all these things, it was a gay and magnificent revel. The tastes of the duke were peculiar. He had a fine eye for colors and effects. He disregarded the *decora*° of mere fashion. His plans were bold and fiery, and his conceptions glowed with barbaric lustre. There are some who would have thought him mad. His followers felt that he was not. It was necessary to hear and see and touch him to be *sure* that he was not.

     He had directed, in great part, the movable embellishments of the seven chambers, upon occasion of this great fête,* and it was his own guiding taste which had given character to the masqueraders. Be sure they were grotesque. There were much glare and glitter and piquancy and phantasm—much of what has been since seen in "Hernani."† There were arabesque figures with unsuited limbs and appointments. There were delirious fancies such as the madman fashions. There were much of the beautiful, much of the wanton, much of the *bizarre*, something of the terrible, and not a little of that which might have excited disgust. To and fro in the seven chambers there stalked, in fact, a multitude of dreams. And these—the dreams—writhed in and about, taking hue from the rooms, and causing the wild music of the orchestra to seem as the echo of their steps. And, anon, there strikes the ebony clock which stands in the hall of the velvet. And then, for a moment, all is still, and all is silent save the voice of the clock. The dreams are stiff-frozen as they stand. But the echoes of the chime die away— they have endured but an instant—and a light, half-subdued laughter floats after them as they depart. And now again the music swells, and the dreams live, and writhe to and fro more merrily than ever, taking hue from the many-tinted windows through which stream the rays from the tripods. But to the chamber which lies most westwardly of the seven there are now none of the maskers who venture; for the night is waning away; and there flows a ruddier light through the blood-colored panes; and the blackness of the sable drapery appalls; and to him whose foot falls upon the sable carpet, there comes from the near clock of ebony a muffled peal more solemnly emphatic than any which reaches *their* ears who indulge in the more remote gaieties of the other apartments.

°*decora:* schemes, patterns.   *fête:* party, festival, revel.   †*Hernani:* a tragedy (1830) by Victor Hugo (1802–1885), featuring elaborate scenes and costumes. The opera *Ernani* by Giusseppi Verdi (1813–1901), which was based on Hugo's play, was not produced until 1844, two years after "The Masque of the Red Death" appeared.

But these other apartments were densely crowded, and in them beat feverishly the heart of life. And the revel went whirlingly on, until at length there commenced the sounding of midnight upon the clock. And then the music ceased, as I have told; and the evolutions of the waltzers were quieted; and there was an uneasy cessation of all things as before. But now there were twelve strokes to be sounded by the bell of the clock; and thus it happened, perhaps that more of thought crept, with more of time, into the meditations of the thoughtful among those who revelled. And thus, too, it happened, perhaps that before the last echoes of the last chime had utterly sunk into silence, there were many individuals in the crowd who had found leisure to become aware of the presence of a masked figure, which had arrested the attention of no single individual before. And the rumor of this new presence having spread itself whisperingly around, there arose at length from the whole company a buzz, or murmur, expressive of disapprobation and surprise—then, finally, of terror, of horror, and of disgust.

In an assembly of phantasms such as I have painted, it may well be supposed that no ordinary appearance could have excited such sensation. In truth the masquerade license of the night was nearly unlimited; but the figure in question had out-Heroded Herod,° and gone beyond the bounds of even the prince's indefinite decorum. There are chords in the hearts of the most reckless which cannot be touched without emotion. Even with the utterly lost, to whom life and death are equally jests, there are matters of which no jest can be made. The whole company, indeed, seemed now deeply to feel that in the costume and bearing of the stranger neither wit nor propriety existed. The figure was tall and gaunt, and shrouded from head to foot in the habiliments of the grave. The mask which concealed the visage was made so nearly to resemble the countenance of a stiffened corpse that the closest scrutiny must have had difficulty in detecting the cheat. And yet all this might have been endured, if not approved, by the mad revellers around. But the mummer had gone so far as to assume the type of the Red Death. His vesture was dabbled in *blood*—and his broad brow, with all the features of the face, was besprinkled with the scarlet horror.

When the eyes of Prince Prospero fell upon this spectral image (which, with a slow and solemn movement, as if more fully to sustain its rôle, stalked to and fro among the waltzers) he was seen to be convulsed, in the first moment with a strong shudder either of terror or distaste; but, in the next, his brow reddened with rage. **10**

"Who dares"—he demanded hoarsely of the courtiers who stood near him—"who dares insult us with this blasphemous mockery? Seize him and unmask him—that we may know whom we have to hang, at sunrise, from the battlements!"

It was in the eastern or blue chamber in which stood the Prince Prospero as he uttered these words. They rang throughout the seven rooms loudly and clearly, for the prince was a bold and robust man, and the music had become hushed at the waving of his hand.

It was in the blue room where stood the prince, with a group of pale courtiers by his side. At first, as he spoke, there was a slight rushing movement of this group in the direction of the intruder, who, at the moment was also near at hand, and now, with deliberate and stately step, made closer approach to the speaker. But from a certain nameless awe with which the mad assumptions of the mummer had inspired the whole party, there were found none who put forth hand to seize him; so that, unimpeded, he passed within a yard of the prince's person; and, while the vast assembly, as if with one impulse, shrank from the centres of the rooms to the walls, he made his way uninterruptedly, but with the same solemn and measured step which had distinguished him from the first,

---

°*Herod*: quoted from Shakespeare's *Hamlet*, Act 3, scene 2, line 13, in reference to flamboyantly extreme overacting.

through the blue chamber to the purple—through the purple to the green—through the green to the orange—through this again to the white—and even thence to the violet, ere a decided movement had been made to arrest him. It was then, however, that the Prince Prospero, maddening with rage and the shame of his own momentary cowardice, rushed hurriedly through the six chambers, while none followed him on account of a deadly terror that had seized upon all. He bore aloft a drawn dagger, and had approached, in rapid impetuosity, to within three or four feet of the retreating figure, when the latter, having attained the extremity of the velvet apartment, turned suddenly and confronted his pursuer. There was a sharp cry—and the dagger dropped gleaming upon the sable carpet, upon which, instantly afterward, fell prostrate in death the Prince Prospero. Then, summoning the wild courage of despair, a throng of the revellers at once threw themselves into the black apartment, and, seizing the mummer, whose tall figure stood erect and motionless within the shadow of the ebony clock, gasped in unutterable horror at finding the grave cerements and corpse-like mask, which they handled with so violent a rudeness, untenanted by any tangible form.

And now was acknowledged the presence of the Red Death. He had come like a thief in the night,° And one by one dropped the revellers in the blood-bedewed halls of their revel, and died each in the despairing posture of his fall. And the life of the ebony clock went out with that of the last of the gay. And the flames of the tripods expired. And Darkness and Decay and the Red Death held illimitable dominion over all.

Mark Twain (1835–1910)

Luck° (1891)

It was at a banquet in London in honor of one of the two or three conspicuously illustrious English military names of this generation. For reasons which will presently appear, I will withhold his real name and titles and call him Lieutenant-General Lord Arthur Scoresby, Y.C., K.C.B., etc., etc. What a fascination there is in a renowned name! There sat the man, in actual flesh, whom I had heard of so many thousands of times since that day, thirty years before, when his name shot suddenly to the zenith from a Crimean battlefield to remain forever celebrated. It was food and drink to me to look, and look, and look at that demigod; scanning, searching, noting: the quietness, the reserve, the noble gravity of his countenance; the simple honesty that expressed itself all over him; the sweet unconsciousness of his greatness—unconsciousness of the hundreds of admiring eyes fastened upon him, unconsciousness of the deep, loving, sincere worship welling out of the breasts of those people and flowing toward him.

The clergyman at my left was an old acquaintance of mine—clergyman now, but had spent the first half of his life in the camp and field and as an instructor in the military school at Woolwich. Just at the moment I have been talking about a veiled and singular light glimmered in his eyes and he leaned down and muttered confidentially to me—indicating the hero of the banquet with a gesture:

"Privately—he's an absolute fool."

°*Thief in the night:* 2 Peter 3:10.
°This is not a fancy sketch. I got it from a clergyman who was an instructor at Woolwich forty years ago, and who vouched for its truth. [Twain's note.]

This verdict was a great surprise to me. If its subject had been Napoleon, or Socrates, or Solomon, my astonishment could not have been greater. Two things I was well aware of: that the Reverend was a man of strict veracity and that his judgment of men was good. Therefore I knew, beyond doubt or question, that the world was mistaken about this hero: he *was* a fool. So I meant to find out, at a convenient moment, how the Reverend, all solitary and alone, had discovered the secret.

Some days later the opportunity came, and this is what the Reverend told me: 5

About forty years ago I was an instructor in the military academy at Woolwich. I was present in one of the sections when young Scoresby underwent his preliminary examination. I was touched to the quick with pity, for the rest of the class answered up brightly and handsomely, while he—why, dear me, he didn't know *anything*, so to speak. He was evidently good, and sweet, and lovable, and guileless; and so it was exceedingly painful to see him stand there, as serene as a graven image, and deliver himself of answers which were veritably miraculous for stupidity and ignorance. All the compassion in me was aroused in his behalf. I said to myself, when he comes to be examined again he will be flung over, of course; so it will be simply a harmless act of charity to ease his fall as much as I can. I took him aside and found that he knew a little of Caesar's history; and as he didn't know anything else, I went to work and drilled him like a galley-slave on a certain line of stock questions concerning Caesar which I knew would be used. If you'll believe me, he went through with flying colors on examination day! He went through on that purely superficial "cram," and got compliments too, while others, who knew a thousand times more than he, got plucked. By some strangely lucky accident—an accident not likely to happen twice in a century—he was asked no question outside of the narrow limits of his drill.

It was stupefying. Well, all through his course I stood by him, with something of the sentiment which a mother feels for a crippled child; and he always saved himself—just by miracle, apparently.

Now, of course, the thing that would expose him and kill him at last was mathematics. I resolved to make his death as easy as I could; so I drilled him and crammed him, and crammed him and drilled him, just on the line of questions which the examiners would be most likely to use, and then launched him on his fate. Well, sir, try to conceive of the result: to my consternation, he took the first prize! And with it he got a perfect ovation in the way of compliments.

Sleep? There was no more sleep for me for a week. My conscience tortured me day and night. What I had done I had done purely through charity, and only to ease the poor youth's fall. I never had dreamed of any such preposterous results as the thing that had happened. I felt as guilty and miserable as Frankenstein. Here was a wooden-head whom I had put in the way of glittering promotions and prodigious responsibilities, and but one thing could happen: He and his responsibilities would all go to ruin together at the first opportunity.

The Crimean War° had just broken out. Of course there had to be a war, I said to my-   10
self. We couldn't have peace and give this donkey a chance to die before he is found out. I waited for the earthquake. It came. And it made me reel when it did come. He was actually gazetted to a captaincy in a marching regiment! Better men grow old and gray in the service before they climb to a sublimity like that. And who could ever have foreseen that they would go and put such a load of responsibility on such green and inadequate shoulders? I could just barely have stood it if they had made him a cornet; but a captain—think of it! I thought my hair would turn white.

°*Crimean War:* In the Crimean War (1853–1856), England was one of the allies that fought against Russia.

Consider what I did—I who so loved repose and inaction. I said to myself, I am responsible to the country for this, and I must go along with him and protect the country against him as far as I can. So I took my poor little capital that I had saved up through years of work and grinding economy, and went with a sigh and bought a cornetcy in his regiment, and away we went to the field.

And there—oh, dear, it was awful. Blunders?—why he never did anything but blunder. But, you see, nobody was in the fellow's secret. Everybody had him focused wrong, and necessarily misinterpreted his performance every time. Consequently they took his idiotic blunders for inspirations of genius. They did, honestly! His mildest blunders were enough to make a man in his right mind cry; and they did make me cry—and rage and rave, too, privately. And the thing that kept me always in a sweat of apprehension was the fact that every fresh blunder he made increased the luster of his reputation! I kept saying to myself, he'll get so high that when discovery does finally come it will be like the sun falling out of the sky.

He went right along, up from grade to grade, over the dead bodies of his superiors, until at last, in the hottest moment of the battle of ———— down went our colonel, and my heart jumped into my mouth, for Scoresby was next in rank! Now for it, said I: we'll all land in Sheol in ten minutes, sure.

The battle was awfully hot; the allies were steadily giving way all over the field. Our regiment occupied a position that was vital; a blunder now must be destruction. At this crucial moment, what does this immortal fool do but detach the regiment from its place and order a charge over a neighboring hill where there wasn't a suggestion of an enemy! "There you go!" I said to myself; "This is the end at last."

15   And away we did go, and were over the shoulder of the hill before the insane movement could be discovered and stopped. And what did we find? An entire and unsuspected Russian army in reserve! And what happened? We were eaten up? That is necessarily what would have happened in ninety-nine cases out of a hundred. But no; those Russians argued that no single regiment would come browsing around there at such a time. It must be the entire English army, and that the sly Russian game was detected and blocked, so they turned tail, and away they went, pell-mell, over the hill and down into the field, in wild confusion, and we after them; they themselves broke the solid Russian center in the field, and tore through, and in no time there was the most tremendous rout you ever saw, and the defeat of the allies was turned into a sweeping and splendid victory! Marshall Canrobert looked on, dizzy with astonishment, admiration, and delight; and sent right off for Scoresby, and hugged him, and decorated him on the field in presence of all the armies!

And what was Scoresby's blunder that time? Merely the mistaking his right hand for his left—that was all. An order had come to him to fall back and support our right; and, instead, he fell *forward* and went over the hill to the left. But the name he won that day as a marvelous military genius filled the world with his glory, and that glory will never fade while history books last.

He is just as good and sweet and lovable and unpretending as a man can be, but he doesn't know enough to come in when it rains. Now that is absolutely true. He is the supremest ass in the universe; and until half an hour ago nobody knew it but himself and me. He has been pursued, day by day and year by year, by a most phenomenal astonishing luckiness. He has been a shining soldier in all our wars for a generation; he has littered his whole military life with blunders, and yet has never committed one that didn't make him a knight or a baronet or a lord or something. Look at his breast; why, he is just clothed in domestic and foreign decorations. Well, sir, every one of them is the record of some shouting stupidity or other; and, taken together, they are proof that the very best thing in all this world that can befall a man is to be born lucky. I say again, as I said at the banquet, Scoresby's an absolute fool.

Poems

Matthew Arnold (1822–1888)

Dover Beach (1849)

The sea is calm tonight.
The tide is full, the moon lies fair
Upon the straits:—on the French coast the light
Gleams and is gone; the cliffs of England stand,
Glimmering and vast, out in the tranquil bay.   5
Come to the window, sweet is the night air!
Only, from the long line of spray
Where the sea meets the moon-blanched land,
Listen! You can hear the grating roar
Of pebbles which the waves draw back, and fling,   10
At their return, up the high strand,
Begin, and cease, and then again begin,
With tremulous cadence slow, and bring
The eternal note of sadness in.

Sophocles long ago   15
Heard it on the Ægean, and it brought
Into his mind the turbid ebb and flow
Of human misery; we
Find also in the sound a thought,
Hearing it by this distant northern sea.   20
The Sea of Faith
Was once, too, at the full, and round earth's shore
Lay like the folds of a bright girdle furled.
But now I only hear
Its melancholy, long, withdrawing roar,   25
Retreating, to the breath
Of the night wind, down the vast edges drear
And naked shingles of the world.

Ah, love, let us be true
To one another! for the world, which seems   30
To lie before us like a land of dreams,
So various, so beautiful, so new,
Hath really neither joy, nor love, nor light,
Nor certitude, nor peace, nor help for pain;
And we are here as on a darkling plain   35
Swept with confused alarms of struggle and flight
Where ignorant armies clash by night.

William Blake (1757–1827)

The Tyger° (1794)

Tyger! Tyger! burning bright
In the forests of the night,
What immortal hand or eye
Could frame thy fearful symmetry?

In what distant deeps or skies   5
Burnt the fire of thine eyes?
On what wings dare he aspire?
What the hand, dare seize the fire?

And what shoulder, & what art,
Could twist the sinews of thy heart?   10
And when thy heart began to beat,
What dread hand? & what dread feet?

What the hammer? what the chain?
In what furnace was thy brain?
What the anvil? what dread grasp   15
Dare its deadly terrors clasp?

When the stars threw down their spears,
And water'd heaven with their tears,
Did he smile his work to see?
Did he who made the Lamb make thee?   20

Tyger! Tyger! burning bright
In the forests of the night,
What immortal hand or eye
Dare frame thy fearful symmetry?

Gwendolyn Brooks (1917–2000)

We Real Cool (1959)

The Pool Players.
Seven at the Golden Shovel.

We real cool. We
Left school. We

Lurk late. We
Strike straight. We

Sing sin. We   5
Thin gin. We

Jazz June. We
Die soon.

°*Tyger:* Tyger here means not only a tiger but also a lion or similarly large and ferocious cat.

Robert Browning (1812–1889)

My Last Duchess (1842)

That's my last Duchess painted on the wall,
Looking as if she were alive. I call
That piece a wonder, now: Frà Pandolf's° hands
Worked busily a day, and there she stands.
Will't please you sit and look at her? I said   5
"Frà Pandolf" by design, for never read
Strangers like you that pictured countenance,
The depth and passion of its earnest glance,
But to myself they turned (since none puts by
The curtain I have drawn for you, but I)   10
And seemed as they would ask me, if they durst,*
How such a glance came there; so, not the first
Are you to turn and ask thus. Sir, 'twas not
Her husband's presence only, called that spot
Of joy into the Duchess' cheek: perhaps   15
Frà Pandolf chanced to say "Her mantle laps
Over my lady's wrist too much," or "Paint
Must never hope to reproduce the faint
Half-flush that dies along her throat": such stuff
Was courtesy, she thought, and cause enough   20
For calling up that spot of joy. She had
A heart—how shall I say?—too soon made glad,
Too easily impressed; she liked whate'er
She looked on, and her looks went everywhere.
Sir, 'twas all one! My favor at her breast,   25
The dropping of the daylight in the West,
The bough of cherries some officious fool
Broke in the orchard for her, the white mule
She rode with round the terrace—all and each
Would draw from her alike the approving speech,   30
Or blush, at least. She thanked men—good! But thanked
Somehow—I know not how—as if she ranked
My gift of a nine-hundred-years-old name
With anybody's gift. Who'd stoop to blame
This sort of trifling? Even had you skill   35
In speech—(which I have not)—to make your will
Quite clear to such a one, and say, "Just this
Or that in you disgusts me; here you miss,
Or there exceed the mark"—and if she let
Herself be lessoned so, nor plainly set   40
Her wits to yours, forsooth, and made excuse
—E'en then would be some stooping; and I choose
Never to stoop. Oh sir, she smiled, no doubt,
Whene'er I passed her; but who passed without

°*Frà Pandolf:* an imaginary painter and a monk.   *durst: dared.

Much the same smile? This grew, I gave commands;   45
Then all smiles stopped together. There she stands
As if alive. Will't please you rise? We'll meet
The company below, then. I repeat,
The Count your master's known munificence
Is ample warrant that no just pretense   50
Of mine for dowry will be disallowed;
Though his fair daughter's self, as I avowed
At starting, is my object. Nay, we'll go
Together down, sir. Notice Neptune,[†] though,
Taming a sea horse, thought a rarity,   55
Which Claus of Innsbruck[°°] cast in bronze for me!

Porphyria's Lover (1836)

The Rain set early in to-night,
   The sullen wind was soon awake,
It tore the elm-tops down for spite,
   And did its worst to vex the lake;
   I listened with heart fit to break.   5
When glided in Porphyria; straight
   She shut the cold out and the storm,
And kneeled and made the cheerless grate
   Blaze up, and all the cottage warm;
   Which done, she rose, and from her form   10
Withdrew the dripping cloak and shawl,
   And laid her soiled gloves by, untied
Her hat and let the damp hair fall,
   And, last, she sat down by my side
   And called me. When no voice replied,   15
She put my arm about her waist,
   And made her smooth white shoulder bare,
And all her yellow hair displaced,
   And, stooping, made my cheek lie there,
   And spread, o'er all, her yellow hair.   20
Murmuring how she loved me—she
   Too weak, for all her heart's endeavor,
To set its struggling passion free
   From pride, and vainer ties dissever,
   And give herself to me forever,   25
But passion sometimes would prevail,
   Nor could to-night's gay feast restrain
A sudden thought of one so pale
   For love of her, and all in vain:
   So, she was come through wind and rain.   30
Be sure I looked up at her eyes
   Happy and proud; at last I knew

[†]*Neptune:* statue of the Roman Sea God.   [°°]*Claus of Innsbrook:* an imaginary sculptor.

Porphyria worshipped me: surprise
   Made my heart swell, and still it grew
   While I debated what to do.   35
That moment she was mine, mine, fair,
   Perfectly pure and good: I found
A thing to do, and all her hair
   In one long yellow string I wound
   Three times her little throat around   40
And strangled her. No pain felt she;
   I am quite sure she felt no pain.
As a shut bud that holds a bee,
   I warily oped her lids: again
   Laughed the blue eyes without a stain.   45
And I untightened next the tress
   About her neck; her cheek once more
Blushed bright beneath my burning kiss:
   I propped her head up as before
   Only, this time my shoulder bore   50
Her head, which droops upon it still:
   The smiling rosy little head,
So glad it has its utmost will,
   That all it scorned at once is fled,
   And I, its love, am gained instead!   55
Porphyria's love: she guessed not how
   Her darling one wish would be heard.
And thus we sit together now,
   And all night long we have not stirred,
   And yet God has not said a word!   60

Samuel Taylor Coleridge (1772–1834)

Kubla Khan (1816)

In Xanadu did Kubla Kahn
A stately pleasure dome decree:
Where Alph, the sacred river, ran
Through caverns measureless to man
   Down to a sunless sea.   5
So twice five miles of fertile ground
With walls and towers were girdled round:
And there were gardens bright with sinuous rills,
Where blossomed many an incense-bearing tree;
And here were forests ancient as the hills,   10
Enfolding sunny spots of greenery.

But oh! that deep romantic chasm which slanted
Down the green hill athwart a cedarn cover!
A savage place! as holy and enchanted
As e'er beneath a waning moon was haunted   15
By woman wailing for her demon lover!

And from this chasm, with ceaseless turmoil seething,
As if this earth in fast thick pants were breathing,
A mighty fountain momently was forced:
Amid whose swift half-intermitted burst   20
Huge fragments vaulted like rebounding hail,
Or chaffy grain beneath the thresher's flail;
And 'mid these dancing rocks at once and ever
It flung up momently the sacred river.
Five miles meandering with a mazy motion   25
Through wood and dale the sacred river ran,
Then reached the caverns measureless to man,
And sank in tumult to a lifeless ocean:
And 'mid this tumult Kubla heard from far
Ancestral voices prophesying war!   30
   The shadow of the dome of pleasure
   Floated midway on the waves;
   Where was heard the mingled measure
   From the fountain and the caves.
It was a miracle of rare device,   35
A sunny pleasure dome with caves of ice!
   A damsel with a dulcimer
   In a vision once I saw:
   It was an Abyssinian maid,
   And on her dulcimer she played,   40
   Singing of Mount Abora.
Could I revive within me
   Her symphony and song,
To such a deep delight 'twould win me,
   That with music loud and long,   45
I would build that dome in air,
That sunny dome! those caves of ice!
And all who heard should see them there,
And all should cry, Beware! Beware!
His flashing eyes, his floating hair!   50
Weave a circle round him thrice,
And close your eyes with holy dread,
For he on honeydew hath fed,
And drunk the milk of Paradise.

John Donne (1572–1631)

Good Friday, 1613, Riding Westward (1613)

Let man's soul be a sphere, and then, in this,
The intelligence that moves, devotion is,
And as the other spheres, by being grown
Subject to foreign motions, lose their own,
And being by others hurried every day,   5
Scarce in a year their natural form obey:

Pleasure or business, so, our souls admit
For their first mover, and are whirled by it.
Hence is 't, that I am carried towards the West
This day, when my soul's form bends toward the East.   *10*
There I should see a sun, by rising set,
And by that setting endless day beget;
But that° Christ on this cross did rise and fall,
Sin had eternally benighted all.
Yet dare I almost be glad, I do not see   *15*
That spectacle of too much weight for me.
Who* sees God's face, that is self life,† must die;
What a death were it then to see God die?
It made his own Lieutenant Nature shrink,
It made his footstool crack, and the sun wink.°°   *20*
Could I behold those hands which span the poles,
And tune all spheres at once, pierced with those holes?
Could I behold that endless height which is
Zenith to us, and our Antipodes,
Humbled below us? or that blood which is   *25*
The seat of all our souls, if not of his,
Made dirt of dust, or that flesh which was worn
By God, for his apparel, raged and torn?
If on these things I durst not look, durst I
Upon his miserable mother cast mine eye,   *30*
Who was God's partner here, and furnished thus
Half of that sacrifice, which ransomed us?
Though these things, as I ride, be from mine eye,
They are present yet unto my memory,
For that looks towards them; and thou look'st towards me,   *35*
O Savior, as thou hang'st upon the tree;**
I turn my back to thee,‡ but to receive
Corrections, till thy mercies bid thee leave.
O think me worth thine anger, punish me,
Burn off my rests, and my deformity,   *40*
Restore thine image, so much, by thy grace,
That thou may'st know me, and I'll turn my face.

Robert Frost (1875–1963)

Desert Places (1936)

Snow falling and night falling fast, oh, fast
In a field I looked into going past,
And the ground almost covered smooth in snow,
But a few weeds and stubble showing last.

°*but that:* unless.   **Who:* whoever.   †*self life:* life itself.   °°. . . *the sun wink:* see Luke 23:44–45.
***the tree:* the cross.   ‡*I turn my back to thee:* to avoid death; see line 18.

The woods around it have it—it is theirs.   5
All animals are smothered in their lairs.
I am too absent-spirited to count;
The loneliness includes me unawares.

And lonely as it is that loneliness
Will be more lonely ere it will be less—   10
A blanker whiteness of benighted snow
With no expression, nothing to express.

They cannot scare me with their empty spaces
Between stars—on stars where no human race is.
I have it in me so much nearer home   15
To scare myself with my own desert places.

The Road Not Taken (1915)

Two roads diverged in a yellow wood,
And sorry I could not travel both
And be one traveler, long I stood
And looked down one as far as I could
To where it bent in the undergrowth;   5

Then took the other, as just as fair,
And having perhaps the better claim,
Because it was grassy and wanted wear;
Though as for that the passing there
Had worn them really about the same,   10

And both that morning equally lay
In leaves no step had trodden black.
Oh, I kept the first for another day!
Yet knowing how way leads into way,
I doubted if I should ever come back.   15

I shall be telling this with a sigh
Somewhere ages and ages hence:
Two roads diverged in a wood, and I—
I took the one less traveled by,
And that has made all the difference.   20

Thomas Hardy (1840–1928)

Channel Firing (1914)

That night your great guns unawares,
Shook all our coffins as we lay,
And broke the chancel window squares.
We thought it was the Judgment-day

And sat upright. While drearisome 5
Arose the howl of wakened hounds:
The mouse let fall the altar-crumb,
The worms drew back into the mounds.

The glebe° cow drooled. Till God called, "No;
It's gunnery practice out at sea 10
Just as before you went below;
The world is as it used to be:

"All nations striving strong to make
Red war yet redder. Mad as hatters
They do no more for Christés sake 15
Than you who are helpless in such matters.

"That this is not the judgment-hour
For some of them's a blessed thing,
For if it were they'd have to scour
Hell's floor for so much threatening . . . 20

"Ha, ha. It will be warmer when
I blow the trumpet (if indeed
I ever do; for you are men,
And rest eternal sorely need)."

So down we lay again. "I wonder, 25
Will the world ever saner be,"
Said one, "than when He sent us under
In our indifferent century!"

And many a skeleton shook his head.
"Instead of preaching forty year," 30
My neighbor Parson Thirdly said,
"I wish I had stuck to pipes and beer."

Again the guns disturbed the hour,
Roaring their readiness to avenge,
As far inland as Stourton Tower, 35
And Camelot, and starlit Stonehenge.*

The Man He Killed (1902)

"Had he and I but met
By some old ancient inn,
We should have sat us down to wet
Right many a nipperkin!°

°*glebe:* the land and cemetery surrounding and belonging to a church. Cows were kept there to keep the grass short.   **Stourton Tower . . . Stonehenge:* Places in the south of England associated with ancient Druids and also with the mythical King Arthur.   °*nipperkin:* a half-pint of ale.

"But ranged as infantry,   *5*
And staring face to face,
I shot at him as he at me,
And killed him in his place.

"I shot him dead because—
Because he was my foe.   *10*
Just so: my foe of course he was;
That's clear enough; although

"He thought he'd 'list,* perhaps,
Off-hand like—just as I—
Was out of work—had sold his traps†   *15*
No other reason why.

"Yes; quaint and curious war is!
You shoot a fellow down
You'd treat if met where any bar is
Or help to half-a-crown."°°   *20*

Langston Hughes (1902–1967)

Negro (1958)

I am a Negro:
   Black as the night is black,
   Black like the depths of my Africa.

I've been a slave:
   Caesar told me to keep his door-steps clean.   *5*
   I brushed the boots of Washington.

I've been a worker:
   Under my hand the pyramids arose.
   I made mortar for the Woolworth Building.

I've been a singer: *10*
   All the way from Africa to Georgia
   I carried my sorrow songs.
   I made ragtime.

I've been a victim:
   The Belgians cut off my hands in the Congo.   *15*
   They lynch me still in Mississippi.

I am a Negro:
   Black as the night is black,
   Black like the depths of my Africa.

'list: enlist.   †*traps:* personal possessions.   °°*half-a-crown:* perhaps as much as $10 or $20.

Theme for English B (1959)

The instructor said,

> Go home and write
> a page tonight.
> And let that page come out of you—
> Then, it will be true.   5

I wonder if it's that simple?

I am twenty-two, colored, born in Winston-Salem.
I went to school there, then Durham, then here
to this college on the hill above Harlem.°
I am the only colored student in my class.   10
The steps from the hill lead down to Harlem,
Through a park, then I cross St. Nicholas,
Eighth Avenue, Seventh, and I come to the Y,
The Harlem Branch Y, where I take the elevator
Up to my room, sit down, and write this page: 15

It's not easy to know what is true for you or me
at twenty-two, my age. But I guess I'm what
I feel and see and hear. Harlem, I hear you:
hear you, hear me—we two—you, me talk on this page.
(I hear New York, too.) Me—who?   20

Well, I like to eat, sleep, drink, and be in love.
I like to work, read, learn, and understand life.
I like a pipe for a Christmas present,
or records—Bessie,* bop,† or Bach.°°

I guess being colored doesn't make me not like   25
the same things other folks like who are other races.
So will my page be colored that I write?
Being me, it will not be white.
But it will be
a part of you, instructor.   30
You are white—
yet a part of me, as I am a part of you.
That's American.

Sometimes perhaps you don't want to be a part of me.
Nor do I often want to be a part of you.   35
But we are, that's true!
As I learn from you,
I guess you learn from me—
although you're older—and white—
and somewhat more free.   40

This is my page for English B.

°*college on the hill above Harlem:* Columbia University in New York City.   **Bessie:* Bessie Smith (ca.
1898–1937), U.S. jazz singer, the "Empress of the Blues."   †*bop:* type of music that was popular in
the 1940s–60s.   °°*Bach:* Johann Sebastian Bach (1685–1750), German composer of baroque music.

John Keats (1795–1821)

Bright Star (1819)

Bright star! would I were steadfast as thou art—
    Not in lone splendor hung aloft the night,
And watching, with eternal lids apart,
    Like Nature's patient, sleepless eremite,°
The moving waters at their priestlike task   5
    Of pure ablution round earth's human shores,
Or gazing on the new soft-fallen mask
    Of snow upon the mountains and the moors;
No—yet still steadfast, still unchangeable,
    Pillowed upon my fair love's ripening breast,   10
To feel forever its soft fall and swell,
    Awake forever in a sweet unrest,
Still, still to hear her tender-taken breath,
And so live ever—or else swoon to death.

Irving Layton (b. 1912)

Rhine Boat Trip° (1977)

The castles on the Rhine
are all haunted
by the ghosts of Jewish mothers
looking for their ghostly children

And the clusters of grapes   5
in the sloping vineyards
are myriads of blinded eyes
staring at the blind sun

The tireless Lorelei*
can never comb from their hair   10
the crimson beards
of murdered rabbis

However sweetly they sing
one hears only
the low wailing of cattle-cars[†]   15
moving invisibly across the land

°*eremite:* hermit.　°*Rhine Boat Trip:* The Rhine, Germany's best-known river, is virtually synonymous with German national history.　**Lorelei:* mythical shore nymphs who lured passing rivermen to their doom; subject of a famous poem by Heinrich Heine (1797–1856). [†]*cattle-cars:* During the Holocaust in World War II, the Nazis crowded their victims together into cattle-cars and transported them by rail to concentration and extermination camps in Germany and neighboring countries.

Amy Lowell (1874–1925)

Patterns (1916)

I walk down the garden paths,
And all the daffodils
Are blowing, and the bright blue squills.
I walk down the patterned garden-paths
In my stiff, brocaded gown. 5
With my powdered hair and jewelled fan,
I too am a rare
Pattern. As I wander down
The garden paths.

My dress is richly figured, 10
And the train
Makes a pink and silver stain
On the gravel, and the thrift
Of the borders.
Just a plate of current fashion 15
Tripping by in high-heeled, ribboned shoes.
Not a softness anywhere about me,
Only whalebone° and brocade.
And I sink on a seat in the shade

Of a lime tree. For my passion 20
Wars against the stiff brocade.
The daffodils and squills
Flutter in the breeze
As they please.
And I weep; 25
For the lime-tree is in blossom
And one small flower has dropped upon my bosom.

And the plashing of waterdrops
In the marble fountain
Comes down the garden-paths. 30
The dripping never stops.
Underneath my stiffened gown
Is the softness of a woman bathing in a marble basin,
A basin in the midst of hedges grown
So thick, she cannot see her lover hiding. 35
But she guesses he is near,

And the sliding of the water
Seems the stroking of a dear
Hand upon her.
What is Summer in a fine brocaded gown! 40

°*whalebone:* Baleen from whales was used to make corsets for women because it was strong and flexible, like an early plastic.

I should like to see it lying in a heap upon the ground.
All the pink and silver crumpled up on the ground.
I would be the pink and silver as I ran along the paths,
And he would stumble after,
Bewildered by my laughter.   45
I should see the sun flashing from his sword-hilt and buckles on his shoes.
I would choose
To lead him in a maze along the patterned paths,
A bright and laughing maze for my heavy-booted lover.
Till he caught me in the shade,   50
And the buttons of his waistcoat bruised my body as he clasped me,
Aching, melting, unafraid.
With the shadows of the leaves and the sundrops,
And the plopping of the waterdrops,
All about us in the open afternoon—   55
I am very like to swoon
With the weight of this brocade,
For the sun sifts through the shade.

Underneath the fallen blossom
In my bosom,   60
Is a letter I have hid.
It was brought to me this morning by a rider from the Duke.
Madam, we regret to inform you that Lord Hartwell
Died in action Thursday se'nnight.*
As I read it in the white, morning sunlight,   65
The letters squirmed like snakes.
"Any answer, Madam," said my footman.
"No," I told him.
"See that the messenger takes some refreshment.

No, no answer."   70
And I walked into the garden.
Up and down the patterned paths,
In my stiff, correct brocade.
The blue and yellow flowers stood up proudly in the sun,
Each one.   75
I stood upright too,
Held rigid to the pattern
By the stiffness of my gown.
Up and down I walked.
Up and down.   80

In a month he would have been my husband.
In a month, here, underneath this lime,
We would have broken the pattern;
He for me, and I for him,
He as Colonel, I as Lady,   85
On this shady seat.

---

se'nnight: on a Thursday, seven days before last Thursday.

He had a whim
That sunlight carried blessing.
And I answered, "It shall be as you have said."
Now he is dead. 90

In Summer and in Winter I shall walk
Up and down
The patterned garden-paths
In my stiff, brocaded gown.
The squills and daffodils 95
Will give place to pillared roses, and to asters, and to snow.
I shall go
Up and down,
In my gown.
Gorgeously arrayed, 100
Boned and stayed.
And the softness of my body will be guarded from embrace
By each button, hook, and lace.
For the man who should loose me is dead,
Fighting with the Duke in Flanders,† 105
In a pattern called a war.
Christ! What are patterns for?

John Masefield (1878–1967)

Cargoes 1902

Quinquereme° of Nineveh* from distant Ophir,†
Rowing home to haven in sunny Palestine,
With a cargo of ivory,
And apes and peacocks,°°
Sandalwood, cedarwood,** and sweet white wine. 5

Stately Spanish galleon coming from the Isthmus,‡
Dipping through the Tropics by the palm-green shores,
With a cargo of diamonds,
Emeralds, amethysts,
Topazes, and cinnamon, and gold moidores.°°° 10

Dirty British coaster with a salt-caked smoke-stack,
Butting through the Channel in the mad March days,
With a cargo of Tyne coal,***
Road-rails, pig-lead,
Firewood, iron-ware, and cheap tin trays. 15

---

†*Flanders:* a place of frequent warfare in Belgium (e.g., the Duke of Marlborough's Flanders campaigns of 1702–1710; The Battle of Waterloo, 1815, under the Duke of Wellington; battles with the Germans during World War I, 1914–1915). °*quinquereme:* largest of the ancient ships, with three tiers of oars operated by five men at each vertical oar station. *Nineveh:* the capital of ancient Assyria. †*Ophir:* Ophir, known for its gold, probably was in Africa. °°*apes and peacocks:* 1 Kings 10:22 and 2 Chronicles 9:21. **cedarwood:* 1 Kings 9:11. ‡*Isthmus:* the Isthmus of Panama. °°°*moidores:* coins (in Portugal and Brazil). ***Tyne coal:* coal from Newcastle upon Tyne, England.

Wilfred Owen (1893–1918)

Anthem for Doomed Youth (1920)

What passing-bells° for these who die as cattle?
Only the monstrous anger of the guns.
Only the stuttering rifles' rapid rattle
Can patter out their hasty orisons.*

No mockeries for them from prayers or bells,   5
Nor any voice of mourning save the choirs—
The shrill, demented choirs of wailing shells;
And bugles calling for them from sad shires.†

What candles may be held to speed them all?
Not in the hands of boys, but in their eyes   10
Shall shine the holy glimmers of good-byes.
The pallor of girls' brows shall be their pall;
Their flowers the tenderness of patient minds,
And each slow dusk a drawing-down of blinds.

Dudley Randall (b. 1914)

Ballad of Birmingham° (1966)

"Mother dear, may I go downtown
   Instead of out to play,
And march the streets of Birmingham
   In a Freedom March today?"

"No, baby, no, you may not go,   5
   For the dogs are fierce and wild,
And clubs and hoses, guns and jails
   Aren't good for a little child."

"But, mother, I won't be alone,
   Other children will go with me,   10
And march in the streets of Birmingham
   To make our country free."

"No, baby, no, you may not go,
   For I fear those guns will fire.
But you may go to church instead   15
   And sing in the children's choir."

She has combed and brushed her night-dark hair,
   And bathed rose petal sweet,

°*passing-bells:* church bells that are tolled at the entry of a funeral cortege into a church cemetery.
orisons: prayers. †*shires:* British counties. °Four black children were killed when the
Sixteenth Street Baptist Church in Birmingham, Alabama, was bombed in 1963. It was not until
May 2002, thirty-nine years later, that the last of the four bombers was convicted of the crime.

And drawn white gloves on her small brown hands,
    And white shoes on her feet.   *20*

The mother smiled to know her child
    Was in the sacred place,
But that smile was the last smile
    To come upon her face.

For when she heard the explosion   *25*
    Her eyes grew wet and wild.
She raced through the streets of Birmingham
    Calling for her child.

She clawed through bits of glass and brick,
    Then lifted out a shoe   *30*
"Oh, here's the shoe my baby wore,
    But, baby, where are you?"

Christina Rossetti (1830–1894)

Echo (1854)

Come to me in the silence of the night;
    Come in the speaking silence of a dream;
Come with soft rounded cheeks and eyes as bright
    As sunlight on a stream
        Come back in tears,   *5*
        O memory, hope, love of finished years.

O dream how sweet, too sweet, too bitter sweet,
    Whose wakening should have been in paradise,
Where souls brimful of love abide and meet;
    Where thirsty longing eyes   *10*
        Watch the slow door
        That opening, letting in, lets out no more.

Yet come to me in dreams, that I may live
    My very life again though cold in death;
Come back to me in dreams, that I may give   *15*
    Pulse for pulse, breath for breath:
        Speak low, lean low,
        As long ago, my love, how long ago!

Luis Omar Salinas (b. 1937)

In a Farmhouse (1973)

Fifteen miles
out of Robstown
with the Texas sun
fading in the distance

I sit in the bedroom   5
profoundly,
animated by the day's work
in the cottonfields.

I made two dollars and
thirty cents today   10
I am eight years old
and I wonder
how the rest of the Mestizos°
do not go hungry
and if one were to die   15
of hunger
what an odd way
to leave for heaven.

William Shakespeare (1564–1616)

Sonnet 30: When to the Sessions of Sweet Silent Thought (1609)

When to the sessions of sweet silent thought,
I summon up remembrance of things past,
I sigh the lack of many a thing I sought,
And with old woes new wail my dear time's waste:
Then can I drown an eye (un-used to flow)   5
For precious friends hid in death's dateless night,
And weep afresh love's long since cancelled woe,
And moan th' expense of many a vanished sight.
Then can I grieve at grievances foregone,
And heavily from woe to woe tell o'er   10
The sad account of fore-bemoaned moan,
Which I new pay, as if not paid before.
     But if the while I think on thee (dear friend)
     All losses are restored, and sorrows end.

Shelly Wagner (b. ca. 1950)

The Boxes (1991)

When I told the police I couldn't find you,
they began a search that included everything—
even the boxes in the house:
the footlockers of clothes in the attic,
the hamper in the bathroom,   5
and the Chinese lacquered trunk by the sofa.
They made me raise every lid.

°*Mestizos:* persons of mixed Spanish and Amerindian ancestry.

I told them you would never stay in a box,
not with all the commotion.
You would have jumped out,   *10*
found your flashlight
and joined the search.

Poor Thomas, taking these men
who don't know us
through our neighbors' garages   *15*
where you never played,
hoping they were right
and we were wrong
and he would find you and
snatch you home by the hand   *20*

so the police cars could
get out of our driveway
and the divers would
get out of our river
because it was certainly   *25*
past our bedtime.
We would double-bolt our doors
like always,
say longer prayers than usual
and go to bed. But during the night   *30*
I would have sat till morning
beside my sleeping boys.

But that's not what happened.
Thomas is still here, now older.
I still go to his room   *35*
when he is sleeping
just to look at him.
I still visit the cemetery,
not as often,
but the urge is the same: *40*
to lie down on the grass,
put my arm around the hump of ground
and tell you, "Get out of this box!
Put a stop to this commotion. Come home.
You should be in bed."   *45*

William Wordsworth (1770–1850)

Lines Written in Early Spring (1798)

I heard a thousand blended notes,
While in a grove I sat reclined,
In that sweet mood when pleasant thoughts
Bring sad thoughts to the mind.

To her fair works did Nature link   5
The human soul that through me ran;
And much it grieved my heart to think
What man has made of man.

Through primrose tufts, in that green bower,
The periwinkle trailed its wreaths;   10
And 'tis my faith that every flower
Enjoys the air it breathes.

The birds around me hopped and played,
Their thoughts I cannot measure—
But the least motion which they made,   15
It seemed a thrill of pleasure.

The budding twigs spread out their fan,
To catch the breezy air;
And I must think, do all I can,
That there was pleasure there.   20

If this belief from heaven be sent,
If such be Nature's holy plan,
Have I not reason to lament
What man has made of man?

Stepping Westward (1807)

While my Fellow-traveller and I were walking by the side of Loch Ketterine, one fine evening after sunset, in our road to a Hut where, in the course of our Tour, we had been hospitably entertained some weeks before, we met, in one of the loneliest parts of that solitary region, two well-dressed Women, one of whom said to us, by way of greeting, "What, you are stepping westward?"

> *"What, you are stepping westward?"—"Yea."*
> —'T would be a *wildish* destiny,
> If we, who thus together roam
> In a strange Land, and far from home,
> Were in this place the guests of Chance: 5
> Yet who would stop, or fear to advance,
> Though home or shelter he had none,
> With such a sky to lead him on?
>
> The dewy ground was dark and cold;
> Behind, all gloomy to behold;   10
> And stepping westward seemed to be
> A kind of heavenly destiny:
> I liked the greeting; 't was a sound
> Of something without place or bound;
> And seemed to give me spiritual right   15
> To travel through that region bright.
>
> The voice was soft, and she who spake
> Was walking by her native lake:

The salutation had to me
The very sound of courtesy: 20
Its power was felt; and while my eye
Was fixed upon the glowing Sky,
The echo of the voice enwrought
A human sweetness with the thought
Of travelling through the world that lay   25
Before me in my endless way.

William Butler Yeats (1865–1939)

The Second Coming° (1920)

Turning and turning in the widening gyre*
The falcon cannot hear the falconer;
Things fall apart; the center cannot hold;
Mere anarchy is loosed upon the world.
The blood-dimmed tide[†] is loosed, and everywhere   5
The ceremony of innocence is drowned;
The best lack all conviction, while the worst
Are full of passionate intensity.
Surely some revelation is at hand;

Surely the Second Coming is at hand.   10
The Second Coming! Hardly are those words out
When a vast image out of *Spiritus Mundi*[°°]
Troubles my sight; somewhere in sands of the desert
A shape with lion body and the head of a man,**
A gaze blank and pitiless as the sun,   15
Is moving its slow thighs, while all about it
Reel shadows of the indignant desert birds.
The darkness drops again; but now I know

°*Second Coming:* the return of Jesus Christ for the salvation of believers, as described in the Book of Revelation, which foretold that Christ's return would be preceded by famine, epidemics, war, and civil disturbances. Yeats believed that human history could be measured in cycles of 2,000 years (approx.), and that Jesus's birth ended the Greco-Roman cycle. In 1919, when Yeats wrote "The Second Coming," he thought the Christian period was ending. The New Testament expectation was that Jesus would reappear, but Yeats held that the disruptions of the twentieth century were preceding a takeover by the forces of evil.   *gyre:* a radiating spiral, cone, or vortex. Yeats refers to the intersection of two of these shapes as a visual symbol of his cyclic theory. As one gyre spiraled, widened, and disintegrated, a period of history would be ending. At the same time a new gyre would be beginning a reverse spiral:

The falcon is at the broadest, centrifugal point of the old gyre, symbolizing the end of a historic cycle. The desert birds "reel" in a tighter circle, symbolizing the beginning of the new age in the new gyre.   †*Blood-dimmed tide:* See Shakespeare's *Macbeth,* 2.2.60–63.   °°*Spiritus Mundi:* "the spirit of the world," a collective human consciousness that furnished a common fund of images and symbols; Yeats referred to it as "a great memory passing on from generation to generation."   **lion body and the head of a man:* a description of an Egyptian sphinx, which symbolized the Pharaoh as a sun spirit. Here the sphinx represents a monstrous satanic figure.

That twenty centuries of stony sleep
Were vexed to nightmare by a rocking cradle,   *20*
And what rough beast, its hour come round at last
Slouches towards Bethlehem to be born?

Plays

Anton Chekhov (1860–1904)

The Bear: A Joke in One Act (1888)

Cast of Characters

Mrs. Popov. *A widow of seven months,* Mrs. Popov *is small and pretty, with dimples. She is a landowner. At the start of the play, she is pining away in memory of her dead husband.*
Grigory Stepanovich Smirnov. *Easily angered and loud,* Smirnov *is older. He is a landowner, too, and a man of substance.*
Luka. Luka *is* Mrs. Popov's *footman (a servant whose main tasks were to wait table and attend the carriages, in addition to general duties). He is old enough to feel secure in telling* Mrs. Popov *what he thinks.*
Gardener, Coachman, Workmen, *who enter at the end.*

Scene. *The drawing room of* Mrs. Popov's *country home.*

[Mrs. Popov, in deep mourning, does not remove her eyes from a photograph.]

Luka. It isn't right, madam . . . you're only destroying yourself. . . . The chambermaid and the cook have gone off berry picking; every living being is rejoicing; even the cat knows how to be content, walking around the yard catching birds, and you sit in your room all day as if it were a convent, and you don't take pleasure in anything. Yes, really! Almost a year has passed since you've gone out of the house!
Mrs. Popov. And I shall never go out. . . . What for? My life is already ended. *He* lies in his grave; I have buried myself in these four walls . . . we are both dead.
Luka. There you go again! Your husband is dead, that's as it was meant to be, it's the will of God, may he rest in peace. . . . You've done your mourning and that will do. You can't go on weeping and mourning forever. My wife died when her time came, too. . . . Well? I grieved, I wept for a month, and that was enough for her; the old lady wasn't worth a second more. [*Sighs.*] You've forgotten all your neighbors. You don't go anywhere or accept any calls. We live, so to speak, like spiders. We never see the light. The mice have eaten my uniform. It isn't as if there weren't any nice neighbors—the district is full of them . . . there's a regiment stationed at Riblov, such officers—they're like candy—you'll never get your fill of them! And in the barracks, never a Friday goes by without a dance; and, if you please, the military band plays music every day. . . . Yes, madam, my dear lady: you're young, beautiful, in the full bloom of youth—if only you took a little pleasure in life . . . Beauty doesn't last forever, you know! In ten years' time, you'll be wanting to wave your fanny in front of the officers—and it will be too late.
Mrs. Popov. [*Determined.*] I must ask you never to talk to me like that! You know that when Mr. Popov died, life lost all its salt for me. It may seem to you that I am alive,

but that's only conjecture! I vowed to wear mourning to my grave and not to see the light of day. . . . Do you hear me? May his departed spirit see how much I love him. . . . Yes, I know, it's no mystery to you that he was often mean to me, cruel . . . and even unfaithful, but I shall remain true to the grave and show him I know how to love. There, beyond the grave, he will see me as I was before his death. . . .

LUKA. Instead of talking like that, you should be taking a walk in the garden or have   5
Toby or Giant harnessed and go visit some of the neighbors. . . .

MRS. POPOV. Ai! [*She weeps.*]

LUKA. Madam! Dear lady! What's the matter with you! Christ be with you!

MRS. POPOV. Oh, how he loved Toby! He always used to ride on him to visit the Korchagins or the Vlasovs. How wonderfully he rode! How graceful he was when he pulled at the reins with all his strength! Do you remember? Toby, Toby! Tell them to give him an extra bag of oats today.

LUKA. Yes, madam.

[*Sound of loud ringing.*]

MRS. POPOV. [*Shudders.*] Who's that? Tell them I'm not at home!   10

LUKA. Of course, madam. [*He exits.*]

MRS. POPOV. [*Alone. Looks at the photograph.*] You will see, Nikolai, how much I can love and forgive . . . my love will die only when I do, when my poor heart stops beating. [*Laughing through her tears.*] Have you no shame? I'm a good girl, a virtuous little wife. I've locked myself in and I'll be true to you to the grave, and you . . . aren't you ashamed, you chubby cheeks? You deceived me, you made scenes, for weeks on end you left me alone. . . .

LUKA. [*Enters, alarmed.*] Madam, somebody is asking for you. He wants to see you. . . .

MRS. POPOV. But didn't you tell them that since the death of my husband, I don't see anybody?

LUKA. I did, but he didn't want to listen; he spoke about some very important business.   15

MRS. POPOV. I am *not at home!*

LUKA. That's what I told him . . . but . . . the devil . . . he cursed and pushed past me right into the room . . . he's in the dining room right now.

MRS. POPOV. [*Losing her temper.*] Very well, let him come in . . . such manners! [*Luka goes out.*] How difficult these people are! What does he want from me? Why should he disturb my peace? [*Sighs.*] But it's obvious I'll have to go live in a convent. . . . [*Thoughtfully.*] Yes, a convent. . . .

SMIRNOV. [*Enters while speaking to LUKA.*] You idiot, you talk too much. . . . Ass! [*Sees MRS. POPOV and changes to dignified speech.*] Madam, may I introduce myself: retired lieutenant of the artillery and landowner, Grigory Stepanovich Smirnov! I feel the necessity of troubling you about a highly important matter. . . .

MRS. POPOV. [*Refusing her hand.*] What do you want?   20

SMIRNOV. Your late husband, whom I had the pleasure of knowing, has remained in my debt for two twelve-hundred-ruble notes. Since I must pay the interest at the agricultural bank tomorrow, I have come to ask you, madam, to pay me the money today.

MRS. POPOV. One thousand two hundred. . . . And why was my husband in debt to you?

SMIRNOV. He used to buy oats from me.

MRS. POPOV. [*Sighing, to LUKA.*] So, Luka, don't you forget to tell them to give Toby an extra bag of oats.

[*LUKA goes out.*]

[*To SMIRNOV.*] If Nikolai, my husband, was in debt to you, then it goes without saying that I'll pay; but please excuse me today. I haven't any spare cash. The day after tomorrow, my steward will be back from town and I will give him instructions to pay you what is owed; until then I cannot comply with your wishes. . . . Besides, today is the anniversary—exactly seven months ago my husband died, and I'm in such a mood that I'm not quite disposed to occupy myself with money matters.

25   SMIRNOV. And I'm in such a mood that if I don't pay the interest tomorrow, I'll be owing so much that my troubles will drown me. They'll take away my estate!

MRS. POPOV. You'll receive your money the day after tomorrow.

SMIRNOV. I don't want the money the day after tomorrow. I want it today.

MRS. POPOV. You must excuse me. I can't pay you today.

SMIRNOV. And I can't wait until after tomorrow.

30   MRS. POPOV. What can I do, if I don't have it now?

SMIRNOV. You mean to say you can't pay?

MRS. POPOV. I can't pay. . . .

SMIRNOV. Hm! Is that your last word?

MRS. POPOV. That is my last word.

35   SMIRNOV. Positively the last?

MRS. POPOV. Positively.

SMIRNOV. Thank you very much. We'll make a note of that. [*Shrugs his shoulders.*] And people want me to be calm and collected! Just now, on the way here, I met a tax officer and he asked me: why are you always so angry, Grigory Stepanovich? Goodness' sake, how can I be anything but angry? I need money desperately . . . I rode out yesterday early in the morning, at daybreak, and went to see all my debtors; and if only one of them had paid his debt . . . I was dog-tired, spent the night God knows where—a Jewish tavern beside a barrel of vodka. . . . Finally I got here, fifty miles from home, hoping to be paid, and you treat me to a "mood." How can I help being angry?

MRS. POPOV. It seems to me that I clearly said: My steward will return from the country and then you will be paid.

SMIRNOV. I didn't come to your steward, but to you! What the hell, if you'll pardon the expression, would I do with your steward?

40   MRS. POPOV. Excuse me, my dear sir, I am not accustomed to such profane expressions nor to such a tone. I'm not listening to you any more. [*Goes out quickly.*]

SMIRNOV. [*Alone.*] Well, how do you like that? "A mood.". . . "Husband died seven months ago"! Must I pay the interest or mustn't I? I ask you: Must I pay, or must I not? So, your husband's dead, and you're in a mood and all that finicky stuff . . . and your steward's away somewhere; may he drop dead. What do you want me to do? Do you think I can fly away from my creditors in a balloon or something? Or should I run and bash my head against the wall? I go to Gruzdev—and he's not at home; Yaroshevich is hiding, with Kuritsin it's a quarrel to the death and I almost throw him out the window; Mazutov has diarrhea, and this one is in a "mood." Not one of these swine wants to pay me! And all because I'm too nice to them. I'm a sniveling idiot, I'm spineless, I'm an old lady! I'm too delicate with them! So, just you wait! You'll find out what I'm like! I won't let you play around with me, you devils! I'll stay and stick it out until she pays. Rrr! . . . How furious I am today, how furious! I'm shaking inside from rage and I can hardly catch my breath. . . . Damn it! My God, I even feel sick! [*He shouts.*] Hey, you!

LUKA. [*Enters.*] What do you want?

SMIRNOV. Give me some beer or some water! [*LUKA exits.*] What logic is there in this! A man needs money desperately, it's like a noose around his neck—and she won't pay because, you see, she's not disposed to occupy herself with money matters! . . . That's the logic of a woman! That's why I never did like and do not like to talk to women. I'd rather sit on a keg of gunpowder than talk to a woman. Brr! . . . I even have goose pimples, this broad has put me in such a rage! All I have to do is see one of those spoiled bitches from a distance, and I get so angry it gives me a cramp in the leg. I just want to shout for help.

LUKA. [*Entering with water.*] Madam is sick and won't see anyone.

SMIRNOV. Get out! [*LUKA goes.*] Sick and won't see anyone! No need to see me . . . I'll   45
stay and sit here until you give me the money. You can stay sick for a week, and I'll stay for a week. . . . If you're sick for a year, I'll stay a year. I'll get my own back, dear lady! You can't impress me with your widow's weeds and your dimpled cheeks . . . we know all about those dimples! [*Shouts through the window.*] Semyon, unharness the horses! We're not going away quite yet! I'm staying here! Tell them in the stable to give the horses some oats! You brute, you let the horse on the left side get all tangled up in the reins again! [*Teasing.*] "Never mind" . . . I'll give you a never mind! [*Goes away from the window.*] Shit! The heat is unbearable and nobody pays up. I slept badly last night and on top of everything else this broad in mourning is "in a mood" . . . my head aches . . . [*Drinks, and grimaces.*] Shit! This is water! What I need is a drink! [*Shouts.*] Hey, you!

LUKA. [*Enters.*] What is it?

SMIRNOV. Give me a glass of vodka. [*LUKA goes out.*] Oaf! [*Sits down and examines himself.*] Nobody would say I was looking well! Dusty all over, boots dirty, unwashed, unkept, straw on my waistcoat. . . . The dear lady probably took me for a robber. [*Yawns.*] It's not very polite to present myself in a drawing room looking like this; oh well; who cares? . . . I'm not here as a visitor but as a creditor, and there's no official costume for creditors.

LUKA. [*Enters with vodka.*] You're taking liberties, my good man. . . .

SMIRNOV. [*Angrily.*] What?

LUKA. I . . . nothing . . . I only . . .   50

SMIRNOV. Who are you talking to? Shut up!

LUKA. [*Aside.*] The devil sent this leech. An ill wind brought him. . . . [*LUKA goes out.*]

SMIRNOV. Oh how furious I am! I'm so mad I could crush the whole world into a powder! I even feel faint! [*Shouts.*] Hey, you!

MRS. POPOV. [*Enters, eyes downcast.*] My dear sir, in my solitude, I have long ago grown unaccustomed to the masculine voice and I cannot bear shouting. I must request you not to disturb my peace and quiet!

SMIRNOV. Pay me my money and I'll go.   55

MRS. POPOV. I told you in plain language: I haven't any spare cash now; wait until the day after tomorrow.

SMIRNOV. And I also told you respectfully, in plain language: I don't need the money the day after tomorrow, but today. If you don't pay me today, then tomorrow I'll have to hang myself.

MRS. POPOV. But what can I do if I don't have the money? You're so strange!

SMIRNOV. Then you won't pay me now? No?

MRS. POPOV. I can't. . . .   60

SMIRNOV. In that case, I can stay here and wait until you pay. . . . [*Sits down.*] You'll pay the day after tomorrow? Excellent! In that case I'll stay here until the day after tomorrow. I'll sit here all that time . . . [*Jumps up.*] I ask you: Have I got to pay the interest tomorrow, or not? Or do you think I'm joking?

MRS. POPOV. My dear sir, I ask you not to shout! This isn't a stable!

SMIRNOV. I wasn't asking you about a stable but about this: Do I have to pay the interest tomorrow or not?

MRS. POPOV. You don't know how to behave in the company of a lady!

SMIRNOV. No, I don't know how to behave in the company of a lady!   65

MRS. POPOV. No, you don't! You are an ill-bred, rude man! Respectable people don't talk to a woman like that!

SMIRNOV. Ach, it's astonishing! How would you like me to talk to you? In French, perhaps? [*Lisps in anger.*] Madame, *je vous prie*° . . . how happy I am that you're not paying me the money. . . . Ah, pardon, I've made you uneasy! Such lovely weather we're having today! And you look so becoming in your mourning dress. [*Bows and scrapes.*]

MRS. POPOV. That's rude and not very clever!

SMIRNOV. [*Teasing.*] Rude and not very clever! I don't know how to behave in the company of ladies. Madam, in my time I've seen far more women than you've seen sparrows. Three times I've fought duels over women; I've jilted twelve women, nine have jilted me! Yes! There was a time when I played the fool; I became sentimental over women, used honeyed words, fawned on them, bowed and scraped. . . . I loved, suffered, sighed at the moon; I became limp, melted, shivered. . . . I loved passionately, madly, every which way, devil take me, I chattered away like a magpie about the emancipation of women, ran through half my fortune as a result of my tender feelings; but now, if you will excuse me, I'm on to your ways! I've had enough! Dark eyes, passionate eyes, ruby lips, dimpled cheeks; the moon, whispers, bated breath—for all that I wouldn't give a good goddamn. Present company excepted, of course, but all women, young and old alike, are affected clowns, gossips, hateful, consummate liars to the marrow of their bones, vain, trivial, ruthless, outrageously illogical, and as far as this is concerned [*taps on his forehead.*], well, excuse my frankness, any sparrow could give pointers to a philosopher in petticoats! Look at one of those romantic creatures: muslin, ethereal demigoddess, a thousand raptures, and you look into her soul—a common crocodile! [*Grips the back of a chair; the chair cracks and breaks.*] But the most revolting part of it all is that this crocodile imagines that she has, above everything, her own privilege, a monopoly on tender feelings. The hell with it—you can hang me upside down by that nail if a woman is capable of loving anything besides a lapdog. All she can do when she's in love is slobber! While the man suffers and sacrifices, all her love is expressed in playing with her skirt and trying to lead him around firmly by the nose. You have the misfortune of being a woman, you know yourself what the nature of a woman is like. Tell me honestly: Have you ever in your life seen a woman who is sincere, faithful, and constant? You never have! Only old and ugly ladies are faithful and constant! You're more liable to meet a horned cat or a white woodcock than a faithful woman!

70 MRS. POPOV. Pardon me, but in your opinion, who is faithful and constant in love? The man?

SMIRNOV. Yes, the man!

MRS. POPOV. The man! [*Malicious laugh.*] Men are faithful and constant in love! That's news! [*Heatedly.*] What right have you to say that? Men are faithful and constant! For that matter, as far as I know, of all the men I have known and now know, my late husband was the best. . . . I loved him passionately, with all my being, as only a young intellectual woman can love; I gave him my youth, my happiness, my life, my fortune; he was my life's breath; I worshipped him as if I were a heathen, and . . . and, what good did it do—this best of men himself deceived me shamelessly at every step of the way. After his death, I found his desk full of love letters; and when he was alive— it's terrible to remember—he used to leave me alone for weeks at a time, and before my eyes he flirted with other women and deceived me. He squandered my money, made a mockery of my feelings . . . and, in spite of all that, I loved him and was true to him . . . and besides, now that he is dead, I am still faithful and constant. I have shut myself up in these four walls forever and I won't remove these widow's weeds until my dying day. . . .

°*Madame, je vous prie:* Madam, I beg you.

SMIRNOV. [*Laughs contemptuously.*] Widow's weeds! . . . I don't know what you take me for! As if I didn't know why you wear that black outfit and bury yourself in these four walls! Well, well! It's no secret, so romantic! When some fool of a poet passes by this country house, he'll look up at your window and think: "Here lives the mysterious Tamara, who, for the love of her husband, buried herself in these four walls." We know these tricks!

MRS. POPOV. [*Flaring.*] What? How dare you say that to me?

SMIRNOV. You may have buried yourself alive, but you haven't forgotten to powder 75
yourself!

MRS. POPOV. How dare you use such expressions with me?

SMIRNOV. Please don't shout. I'm not your steward! You must allow me to call a spade a spade. I'm not a woman and I'm used to saying what's on my mind! Don't you shout at me!

MRS. POPOV. I'm not shouting, you are! Please leave me in peace!

SMIRNOV. Pay me my money and I'll go.

MRS. POPOV. I won't give you any money! 80

SMIRNOV. Yes, you will.

MRS. POPOV. To spite you, I won't pay you anything. You can leave me in peace!

SMIRNOV. I don't have the pleasure of being either your husband or your fiancé, so please don't make scenes! [*Sits down.*] I don't like it.

MRS. POPOV. [*Choking with rage.*] You're sitting down?

SMIRNOV. Yes, I am. 85

MRS. POPOV. I ask you to get out!

SMIRNOV. Give me my money . . . [*Aside.*] Oh, I'm so furious! Furious!

MRS. POPOV. I don't want to talk to impudent people! Get out of here! [*Pause.*] You're not going? No?

SMIRNOV. No.

MRS. POPOV. No? 90

SMIRNOV. No!

MRS. POPOV. We'll see about that. [*Rings.*]

[*LUKA enters.*]

Luka, show the gentleman out.

LUKA. [*Goes up to SMIRNOV.*] Sir, will you please leave, as you have been asked. You mustn't . . .

SMIRNOV. [*Jumping up.*] Shut up! Who do you think you're talking to? I'll make mince-meat out of you!

LUKA. [*His hand to his heart.*] Oh my God! Saints above! [*Falls into chair.*] Oh, I feel ill! 95
I feel ill! I can't catch my breath!

MRS. POPOV. Where's Dasha? Dasha! [*She shouts.*] Dasha! Pelagea! Dasha! [*She rings.*]

LUKA. Oh! They've all gone berry picking . . . there's nobody at home . . . I'm ill!
Water!

MRS. POPOV. Will you please get out!

SMIRNOV. Will you please be more polite?

MRS. POPOV. [*Clenches her fist and stamps her feet.*] You're nothing but a crude bear! A 100
brute! A monster!

SMIRNOV. What? What did you say?

MRS. POPOV. I said that you were a bear, a monster!

SMIRNOV. [*Advancing toward her.*] Excuse me, but what right do you have to insult me?

MRS. POPOV. Yes, I am insulting you . . . so what? Do you think I'm afraid of you?

105   SMIRNOV. And do you think just because you're one of those romantic creations, that you have the right to insult me with impunity? Yes? I challenge you!

LUKA. Lord in Heaven! Saints above! . . . Water!

SMIRNOV. Pistols!

MRS. POPOV. Do you think just because you have big fists and you can bellow like a bull, that I'm afraid of you? You're such a bully!

SMIRNOV. I challenge you! I'm not going to let anybody insult me, and I don't care if you are a woman, a delicate creature!

110   MRS. POPOV. [*Trying to get a word in edgewise.*] Bear! Bear! Bear!

SMIRNOV. It's about time we got rid of the prejudice that only men must pay for their insults! Devil take it, if women want to be equal, they should behave as equals! Let's fight!

MRS. POPOV. You want to fight! By all means!

SMIRNOV. This minute!

MRS. POPOV. This minute! My husband had some pistols. . . . I'll go and get them right away. [*Goes out hurriedly and then returns.*] What pleasure I'll have putting a bullet through that thick head of yours! The hell with you! [*She goes out.*]

115   SMIRNOV. I'll shoot her down like a chicken! I'm not a little boy or a sentimental puppy. I don't care if she is delicate and fragile.

LUKA. Kind sir! Holy father! [*kneels.*] Have pity on a poor old man and go away from here! You've frightened her to death and now you're going to shoot her?

SMIRNOV. [*Not listening to him.*] If she fights, then it means she believes in equality of rights and emancipation of women. Here the sexes are equal! I'll shoot her like a chicken! But what a woman! [*Imitates her.*] "The hell with you! . . . I'll put a bullet through that thick head of yours! . . ." What a woman! How she blushed, her eyes shone . . . she accepted my challenge! To tell the truth, it was the first time in my life I've seen a woman like that. . . .

LUKA. Dear sir, please go away! I'll pray to God on your behalf as long as I live!

SMIRNOV. That's a woman for you! A woman like that I can understand! A real woman! Not a sour-faced nincompoop but fiery, gunpowder! Fireworks! I'm even sorry to have to kill her!

120   LUKA. [*Weeps.*] Dear sir . . . go away!

SMIRNOV. I positively like her! Positively! Even though she has dimpled cheeks, I like her! I'm almost ready to forget about the debt. . . . My fury has diminished. Wonderful woman!

MRS. POPOV. [*Enters with pistols.*] Here they are, the pistols. Before we fight, you must show me how to fire. . . . I've never had a pistol in my hands before . . .

LUKA. Oh dear Lord, for pity's sake. . . . I'll go and find the gardener and the coachman. . . . What did we do to deserve such trouble? [*Exit.*]

SMIRNOV. [*Examining the pistols.*] You see, there are several sorts of pistols . . . there are special dueling pistols, the Mortimer with primers. Then there are Smith and Wesson revolvers, triple action with extractors . . . excellent pistols! . . . they cost a minimum of ninety rubles a pair. . . . You must hold the revolver like this . . . [*Aside.*] What eyes, what eyes! A woman to set you on fire!

125   MRS. POPOV. Like this?

SMIRNOV. Yes, like this . . . then you cock the pistol . . . take aim . . . put your head back a little . . . stretch your arm out all the way . . . that's right . . . then with this finger press on this little piece of goods . . . and that's all there is to do . . . but the most important thing is not to get excited and aim without hurrying . . . try to keep your arm from shaking.

MRS. POPOV. Good . . . it's not comfortable to shoot indoors. Let's go into the garden.

SMIRNOV. Let's go. But I'm giving you advance notice that I'm going to fire into the air.

MRS. POPOV. That's the last straw! Why?

SMIRNOV. Why? . . . Why . . . because it's my business, that's why.   130

MRS. POPOV. Are you afraid? Yes? Aahhh! No, sir. You're not going to get out of it that easily! Be so good as to follow me! I will not rest until I've put a hole through your forehead . . . that forehead I hate so much! Are you afraid?

SMIRNOV. Yes. I'm afraid.

MRS. POPOV. You're lying! Why don't you want to fight?

SMIRNOV. Because . . . because you . . . because I like you.

MRS. POPOV. [*Laughs angrily.*] He likes me! He dares say that he likes me! [*Points to the*   135
door.] Out!

SMIRNOV. [*Loads the revolver in silence, takes cap and goes; at the door, stops for half a minute while they look at each other in silence; then he approaches MRS. POPOV hesitantly.*] Listen. . . . Are you still angry? I'm extremely irritated, but, do you understand me, how can I express it . . . the fact is, that, you see, strictly speaking . . . [*He shouts.*] Is it my fault, really, for liking you? [*Grabs the back of a chair, which cracks and breaks.*] Why the hell do you have such fragile furniture! I like you! Do you understand? I . . . I'm almost in love with you!

MRS. POPOV. Get away from me—I hate you!

SMIRNOV. God, what a woman! I've never in my life seen anything like her! I'm lost! I'm done for! I'm caught like a mouse in a trap!

MRS. POPOV. Stand back or I'll shoot!

SMIRNOV. Shoot! You could never understand what happiness it would be to die   140
under the gaze of those wonderful eyes, to be shot by a revolver which was held by those little velvet hands. . . . I've gone out of my mind! Think about it and decide right away, because if I leave here, then we'll never see each other again! Decide . . . I'm a nobleman, a respectable gentleman, of good family. I have an income of ten thousand a year. . . . I can put a bullet through a coin tossed in the air . . . I have some fine horses. . . . Will you be my wife?

MRS. POPOV. [*Indignantly brandishes her revolver.*] Let's fight! I challenge you!

SMIRNOV. I'm out of my mind . . . I don't understand anything . . . [*Shouts.*] Hey, you, water!

MRS. POPOV. [*Shouts.*] Let's fight!

SMIRNOV. I've gone out of my mind. I'm in love like a boy, like an idiot! [*He grabs her hand, she screams with pain.*] I love you! [*Kneels.*] I love you as I've never loved before! I've jilted twelve women, nine women have jilted me, but I've never loved one of them as I love you. . . . I'm weak, I'm a limp rag. . . . I'm on my knees like a fool, offering you my hand. . . . Shame, shame! I haven't been in love for five years, I vowed I wouldn't; and suddenly I'm in love, like a fish out of water. I'm offering my hand in marriage. Yes or no? You don't want to? You don't need to! [*Gets up and quickly goes to the door.*]

MRS. POPOV. Wait!   145

SMIRNOV. [*Stops.*] Well?

MRS. POPOV. Nothing . . . you can go . . . go away . . . wait . . . No, get out, get out! I hate you! But—don't go! Oh, if you only knew how furious I am, how angry! [*Throws revolver on table.*] My fingers are swollen from that nasty thing. . . . [*Tears her handkerchief furiously.*] What are you waiting for? Get out!

SMIRNOV. Farewell!

MRS. POPOV. Yes, yes, go away! [*Shouts.*] Where are you going? Stop. . . . Oh, go away! Oh, how furious I am! Don't come near me! Don't come near me!

150   SMIRNOV. [*Approaching her.*] How angry I am with myself! I'm in love like a student. I've been on my knees. . . . It gives me the shivers. [*Rudely.*] I love you! A lot of good it will do me to fall in love with you! Tomorrow I've got to pay the interest, begin the mowing of the hay. [*Puts his arm around her waist.*] I'll never forgive myself for this. . . .

    MRS. POPOV. Get away from me! Get your hands away! I . . . hate you! I . . . challenge you!

[*Prolonged kiss, LUKA enters with an ax, the GARDENER with a rake, the COACHMAN with a pitchfork, and WORKMEN with cudgels.*]

    LUKA. [*Catches sight of the pair kissing.*] Lord in heaven! [*Pause.*]

    MRS. POPOV. [*Lowering her eyes.*] Luka, tell them in the stable not to give Toby any oats today.

CURTAIN

Susan Glaspell (1882–1948)

Trifles (1916)

Cast of Characters

George Henderson, *county attorney*

Henry Peters, *sheriff*

Lewis Hale, *a neighboring farmer*

Mrs. Peters

Mrs. Hale

SCENE. *The kitchen in the now abandoned farmhouse of JOHN WRIGHT, a gloomy kitchen, and left without having been put in order—unwashed pans under the sink, a loaf of bread outside the breadbox, a dish-towel on the table—other signs of incompleted work. At the rear the outer door opens and the SHERIFF comes in followed by the COUNTY ATTORNEY and HALE. The SHERIFF and HALE are men in middle life, the COUNTY ATTORNEY is a young man; all are much bundled up and go at once to the stove. They are followed by the two women—the SHERIFF'S wife first; she is a slight wiry woman, a thin nervous face. MRS. HALE is larger and would ordinarily be called more comfortable looking, but she is disturbed now and looks fearfully about as she enters. The women have come in slowly, and stand close together near the door.*

    COUNTY ATTORNEY. [*Rubbing his hands.*] This feels good. Come up to the fire, ladies.

    MRS. PETERS. [*After taking a step forward.*] I'm not—cold.

    SHERIFF. [*Unbuttoning his overcoat and stepping away from the stove as if to mark the beginning of official business.*] Now, Mr. Hale, before we move things about, you explain to Mr. Henderson just what you saw when you came here yesterday morning.

    COUNTY ATTORNEY. By the way, has anything been moved? Are things just as you left them yesterday?

5   SHERIFF. [*Looking about.*] It's just the same. When it dropped below zero last night I thought I'd better send Frank out this morning to make a fire for us—no use getting pneumonia with a big case on, but I told him not to touch anything except the stove—and you know Frank.

    COUNTY ATTORNEY. Somebody should have been left here yesterday.

SHERIFF. Oh—yesterday. When I had to send Frank to Morris Center for that man who went crazy—I want you to know I had my hands full yesterday. I knew you could get back from Omaha by today and as long as I went over everything here myself—

COUNTY ATTORNEY. Well, Mr. Hale, tell just what happened when you came here yesterday morning.

HALE. Harry and I had started to town with a load of potatoes. We came along the road from my place and as I got here I said, "I'm going to see if I can't get John Wright to go in with me on a party telephone." I spoke to Wright about it once before and he put me off, saying folks talked too much anyway, and all he asked was peace and quiet—I guess you know about how much he talked himself; but I thought maybe if I went to the house and talked about it before his wife, though I said to Harry that I didn't know as what his wife wanted made much difference to John—

COUNTY ATTORNEY. Let's talk about that later, Mr. Hale. I do want to talk about that,   10
but tell now just what happened when you got to the house.

HALE. I didn't hear or see anything; I knocked at the door, and still it was all quiet inside. I knew they must be up, it was past eight o'clock. So I knocked again, and I thought I heard somebody say, "Come in." I wasn't sure, I'm not sure yet, but I opened the door—this door [*Indicating the door by which the two women are still standing.*] and there in that rocker—[*Pointing to it.*] sat Mrs. Wright.

[*They all look at the rocker.*]

COUNTY ATTORNEY. What—was she doing?

HALE. She was rockin' back and forth. She had her apron in her hand and was kind of—pleating it.

COUNTY ATTORNEY. And how did she—look?

HALE. Well, she looked queer.   15

COUNTY ATTORNEY. How do you mean—queer?

HALE. Well, as if she didn't know what she was going to do next. And kind of done up.

COUNTY ATTORNEY. How did she seem to feel about your coming?

HALE. Why, I don't think she minded—one way or other. She didn't pay much attention. I said, "How do, Mrs. Wright, it's cold, ain't it?" And she said, "Is it?"—and went on kind of pleating at her apron. Well, I was surprised; she didn't ask me to come up to the stove, or to set down, but just sat there, not even looking at me, so I said, "I want to see John." And then she—laughed. I guess you would call it a laugh. I thought of Harry and the team outside, so I said a little sharp: "Can't I see John?" "No," she says, kind o' dull like. "Ain't he home?" says I. "Yes," says she, "he's home." "Then why can't I see him?" I asked her, out of patience. "'Cause he's dead," says she. "*Dead?*" says I. She just nodded her head, not getting a bit excited, but rockin' back and forth. "Why—where is he?" says I, not knowing what to say. She just pointed upstairs—like that. [*Himself pointing to the room above.*] I got up, with the idea of going up there. I walked from there to here—then I says, "What did he die of?" "He died of a rope round his neck," says she, and just went on pleatin' at her apron. Well, I went out and called Harry. I thought I might—need help. We went upstairs and there he was lyin'—

COUNTY ATTORNEY. I think I'd rather have you go into that upstairs, where you can   20
point it all out. Just go on now with the rest of the story.

HALE. Well, my first thought was to get that rope off. It looked . . . [*Stops, his face twitches.*] . . . but Harry, he went up to him, and he said, "No, he's dead all right, and we'd better not touch anything." So we went back downstairs. She was still sitting that same way. "Has anybody been notified?" I asked. "No," says she, unconcerned. "Who did this, Mrs. Wright?" said Harry. He said it businesslike—and she stopped pleatin' of her apron.

"I don't know," she says. "You don't *know*?" says Harry. "No," says she. "Weren't you sleepin' in the bed with him?" says Harry. "Yes," says she, "but I was on the inside." "Somebody slipped a rope round his neck and strangled him and you didn't wake up?" says Harry. "I didn't wake up," she said after him. We must 'a looked as if we didn't see how that could be, for after a minute she said, "I sleep sound." Harry was going to ask her more questions but I said maybe we ought to let her tell her story first to the coroner, or the sheriff, so Harry went fast as he could to Rivers' place, where there's a telephone.

COUNTY ATTORNEY. And what did Mrs. Wright do when she knew that you had gone for the coroner?

HALE. She moved from that chair to this one over here [*Pointing to a small chair in the corner.*] and just sat there with her hands held together and looking down. I got a feeling that I ought to make some conversation, so I said I had come in to see if John wanted to put in a telephone, and at that she started to laugh, and then she stopped and looked at me—scared. [*The COUNTY ATTORNEY, who has had his notebook out, makes a note.*] I dunno, maybe it wasn't scared. I wouldn't like to say it was. Soon Harry got back, and then Dr. Lloyd came, and you, Mr. Peters, and so I guess that's all I know that you don't.

COUNTY ATTORNEY. [*Looking around.*] I guess we'll go upstairs first—and then out to the barn and around there. [*To the SHERIFF.*] You're convinced that there was nothing important here—nothing that would point to any motive.

25   SHERIFF. Nothing here but kitchen things.

[*The COUNTY ATTORNEY, after again looking around the kitchen, opens the door of a cupboard closet. He gets up on a chair and looks on a shelf. Pulls his hand away, sticky.*]

COUNTY ATTORNEY. Here's a nice mess.

[*The women draw nearer.*]

MRS. PETERS. [*To the other woman.*] Oh, her fruit; it did freeze. [*To the LAWYER.*] She worried about that when it turned so cold. She said the fire'd go out and her jars would break.

SHERIFF. Well, can you beat the women! Held for murder and worryin' about her preserves.

COUNTY ATTORNEY. I guess before we're through she may have something more serious than preserves to worry about.

30   HALE. Well, women are used to worrying over trifles.

[*The two women move a little closer together.*]

COUNTY ATTORNEY. [*With the gallantry of a young politician.*] And yet, for all their worries, what would we do without the ladies? [*The women do not unbend. He goes to the sink, takes a dipperful of water from the pail and pouring it into a basin, washes his hands. Starts to wipe them on the roller-towel, turns it for a cleaner place.*] Dirty towels! [*Kicks his foot against the pans under the sink.*] Not much of a housekeeper, would you say, ladies?

MRS. HALE. [*Stiffly.*] There's a great deal of work to be done on a farm.

COUNTY ATTORNEY. To be sure. And yet [*With a little bow to her.*] I know there are some Dickson county farmhouses which do not have such roller towels.

[*He gives it a pull to expose its full length again.*]

MRS. HALE. Those towels get dirty awful quick. Men's hands aren't always as clean as they might be.

35   COUNTY ATTORNEY. Ah, loyal to your sex, I see. But you and Mrs. Wright were neighbors. I suppose you were friends, too.

MRS. HALE. [*Shaking her head.*] I've not seen much of her of late years. I've not been in this house—it's more than a year.

COUNTY ATTORNEY. And why was that? You didn't like her?

MRS. HALE. I liked her all well enough. Farmers' wives have their hands full, Mr. Henderson. And then—

COUNTY ATTORNEY. Yes?

MRS. HALE. [*Looking about.*] It never seemed a very cheerful place. 40

COUNTY ATTORNEY. No—it's not cheerful. I shouldn't say she had the homemaking instinct.

MRS. HALE. Well, I don't know as Wright had, either.

COUNTY ATTORNEY. You mean that they didn't get on very well?

MRS. HALE. No, I don't mean anything. But I don't think a place'd be any cheerfuller for John Wright's being in it.

COUNTY ATTORNEY. I'd like to talk more of that a little later. I want to get the lay of 45
things upstairs now.

[*He goes to the left, where three steps lead to a stair door.*]

SHERIFF. I suppose anything Mrs. Peters does'll be all right. She was to take in some clothes for her, you know, and a few little things. We left in such a hurry yesterday.

COUNTY ATTORNEY. Yes, but I would like to see what you take, Mrs. Peters, and keep an eye out for anything that might be of use to us.

MRS. PETERS. Yes, Mr. Henderson.

[*The women listen to the men's steps on the stairs, then look about the kitchen.*]

MRS. HALE. I'd hate to have men coming into my kitchen, snooping around and criticizing.

[*She arranges the pans under the sink which the* LAWYER *had shoved out of place.*]

MRS. PETERS. Of course it's no more than their duty. 50

MRS. HALE. Duty's all right, but I guess that deputy sheriff that came out to make the fire might have got a little of this on. [*Gives the roller towel a pull.*] Wish I'd thought of that sooner. Seems mean to talk about her for not having things slicked up when she had to come away in such a hurry.

MRS. PETERS. [*Who had gone to a small table in the left rear corner of the room, and lifted one end of a towel that covers a pan.*] She had bread set.

[*Stands still.*]

MRS. HALE. [*Eyes fixed on a loaf of bread beside the breadbox, which is on a low shelf at the other side of the room. Moves slowly toward it.*] She was going to put this in there. [*Picks up loaf, then abruptly drops it. In a manner of returning to familiar things.*] It's a shame about her fruit. I wonder if it's all gone. [*Gets up on the chair and looks.*] I think there's some here that's all right, Mrs. Peters. Yes—here; [*Holding it toward the window.*] this is cherries, too. [*Looking again.*] I declare I believe that's the only one. [*Gets down, bottle in her hand. Goes to the sink and wipes it off on the outside.*] She'll feel awful bad after all her hard work in the hot weather. I remember the afternoon I put up my cherries last summer.

[*She puts the bottle on the big kitchen table, center of the room. With a sigh, is about to sit down in the rocking-chair. Before she is seated realizes what chair it is; with a slow look at it, steps back. The chair which she has touched rocks back and forth.*]

MRS. PETERS. Well, I must get those things from the front room closet. [*She goes to the door at the right, but after looking into the other room, steps back.*] You coming with me, Mrs. Hale? You could help me carry them.

[*They go in the other room; reappear,* MRS. PETERS *carrying a dress and skirt,* MRS. HALE *following with a pair of shoes.*]

55   MRS. PETERS. My, it's cold in there.

[*She puts the clothes on the big table, and hurries to the stove.*]

MRS. HALE. [*Examining the skirt.*] Wright was close. I think maybe that's why she kept so much to herself. She didn't even belong to the Ladies Aid. I suppose she felt she couldn't do her part, and then you don't enjoy things when you feel shabby. She used to wear pretty clothes and be lively, when she was Minnie Foster, one of the town girls singing in the choir. But that—oh, that was thirty years ago. This all you was to take in?

MRS. PETERS. She said she wanted an apron. Funny thing to want, for there isn't much to get you dirty in jail, goodness knows. But I suppose just to make her feel more natural. She said they was in the top drawer in this cupboard. Yes, here. And then her little shawl that always hung behind the door. [*Opens stair door and looks.*] Yes, here it is.

[*Quickly shuts door leading upstairs.*]

MRS. HALE. [*Abruptly moving toward her.*] Mrs. Peters?

MRS. PETERS. Yes, Mrs. Hale?

60   MRS. HALE. Do you think she did it?

MRS. PETERS. [*In a frightened voice.*] Oh, I don't know.

MRS. HALE. Well, I don't think she did. Asking for an apron and her little shawl. Worrying about her fruit.

MRS. PETERS. [*Starts to speak, glances up, where footsteps are heard in the room above. In a low voice.*] Mr. Peters says it looks bad for her. Mr. Henderson is awful sarcastic in a speech and he'll make fun of her sayin' she didn't wake up.

MRS. HALE. Well, I guess John Wright didn't wake when they was slipping that rope under his neck.

65   MRS. PETERS. No, it's strange. It must have been done awful crafty and still. They say it was such a—funny way to kill a man, rigging it all up like that.

MRS. HALE. That's just what Mr. Hale said. There was a gun in the house. He says that's what he can't understand.

MRS. PETERS. Mr. Henderson said coming out that what was needed for the case was a motive; something to show anger, or—sudden feeling.

MRS. HALE. [*Who is standing by the table.*] Well, I don't see any signs of anger around here. [*She puts her hand on the dish towel which lies on the table, stands looking down at table, one half of which is clean, the other half messy.*] It's wiped to here. [*Makes a move as if to finish work, then turns and looks at loaf of bread outside the breadbox. Drops towel. In that voice of coming back to familiar things.*] Wonder how they are finding things upstairs. I hope she had it a little more red-up° up there. You know, it seems kind of *sneaking*. Locking her up in town and then coming out here and trying to get her own house to turn against her!

MRS. PETERS. But Mrs. Hale, the law is the law.

70   MRS. HALE. I s'pose 'tis. [*Unbuttoning her coat.*] Better loosen up your things, Mrs. Peters. You won't feel them when you go out.

[*MRS. PETERS takes off her fur tippet,* goes to hang it on hook at back of room, stands looking at the under part of the small corner table.*]

MRS. PETERS. She was piecing a quilt.

[*She brings the large sewing basket and they look at the bright pieces.*]

MRS. HALE. It's a log cabin pattern. Pretty, isn't it? I wonder if she was goin' to quilt it or just knot it?

°*red-up:* neat, arranged in order.   *tippet:* scarf-like garment of fur or wool for the neck and shoulders.

[*Footsteps have been heard coming down the stairs. The* SHERIFF *enters followed by* HALE *and the* COUNTY ATTORNEY.]

SHERIFF. They wonder if she was going to quilt it or just knot it!

[*The men laugh; the women look abashed.*]

COUNTY ATTORNEY. [*Rubbing his hands over the stove.*] Frank's fire didn't do much up there, did it? Well, let's go out to the barn and get that cleared up.

[*The men go outside.*]

MRS. HALE. [*Resentfully.*] I don't know as there's anything so strange, our takin' up our   75 time with little things while we're waiting for them to get the evidence. [*She sits down at the big table smoothing out a block with decision.*] I don't see as it's anything to laugh about.

MRS. PETERS. [*Apologetically.*] Of course they've got awful important things on their minds.

[*Pulls up a chair and joins* MRS. HALE *at the table.*]

MRS. HALE. [*Examining another block.*] Mrs. Peters, look at this one. Here. This is the one she was working on, and look at the sewing! All the rest of it has been so nice and even. And look at this! It's all over the place! Why, it looks as if she didn't know what she was about!

[*After she has said this they look at each other, then start to glance back at the door. After an instant* MRS. HALE *has pulled at a knot and ripped the sewing.*]

MRS. PETERS. Oh, what are you doing, Mrs. Hale?

MRS. HALE. [*Mildly.*] Just pulling out a stitch or two that's not sewed very good. [*Threading a needle.*] Bad sewing always made me fidgety.

MRS. PETERS. [*Nervously.*] I don't think we ought to touch things.   80

MRS. HALE. I'll just finish up this end. [*Suddenly stopping and leaning forward.*] Mrs. Peters?

MRS. PETERS. Yes, Mrs. Hale?

MRS. HALE. What do you suppose she was so nervous about?

MRS. PETERS. Oh—I don't know. I don't know as she was nervous. I sometimes sew awful queer when I'm just tired. [*MRS. HALE starts to say something, looks at* MRS. PETERS, *then goes on sewing.*] Well I must get these things wrapped up. They may be through sooner than we think. [*Putting apron and other things together.*] I wonder where I can find a piece of paper, and string.

MRS. HALE. In that cupboard, maybe.   85

MRS. PETERS. [*Looking in cupboard.*] Why, here's a birdcage. [*Holds it up.*] Did she have a bird, Mrs. Hale?

MRS. HALE. Why, I don't know whether she did or not—I've not been here for so long. There was a man around last year selling canaries cheap, but I don't know as she took one; maybe she did. She used to sing real pretty herself.

MRS. PETERS. [*Glancing around.*] Seems funny to think of a bird here. But she must have had one, or why would she have a cage? I wonder what happened to it.

MRS. HALE. I s'pose maybe the cat got it.

MRS. PETERS. No, she didn't have a cat. She's got that feeling some people have about   90 cats—being afraid of them. My cat got in her room and she was real upset and asked me to take it out.

MRS. HALE. My sister Bessie was like that. Queer, ain't it?

MRS. PETERS. [*Examining the cage.*] Why, look at this door. It's broke. One hinge is pulled apart.

MRS. HALE. [*Looking too.*] Looks as if someone must have been rough with it.

MRS. PETERS. Why, yes.

[*She brings the cage forward and puts it on the table.*]

95   MRS. HALE. I wish if they're going to find any evidence they'd be about it. I don't like this place.

MRS. PETERS. But I'm awful glad you came with me, Mrs. Hale. It would be lonesome for me sitting here alone.

MRS. HALE. It would, wouldn't it? [*Dropping her sewing.*] But I tell you what I do wish, Mrs. Peters. I wish I had come over sometimes when *she* was here. I—[*Looking around the room.*] I—wish I had.

MRS. PETERS. But of course you were awful busy, Mrs. Hale—your house and your children.

MRS. HALE. I could've come. I stayed away because it weren't cheerful—and that's why I ought to have come. I—I've never liked this place. Maybe because it's down in a hollow and you don't see the road. I dunno what it is, but it's a lonesome place and always was. I wish I had come over to see Minnie Foster sometimes. I can see now—

[*Shakes her head.*]

100   MRS. PETERS. Well, you mustn't reproach yourself, Mrs. Hale. Somehow we just don't see how it is with other folks until—something comes up.

MRS. HALE. Not having children makes less work—but it makes a quiet house, and Wright out to work all day, and no company when he did come in. Did you know John Wright, Mrs. Peters?

MRS. PETERS. Not to know him; I've seen him in town. They say he was a good man.

MRS. HALE. Yes—good; he didn't drink, and kept his word as well as most, I guess, and paid his debts. But he was a hard man, Mrs. Peters. Just to pass the time of day with him—[*Shivers.*] Like a raw wind that gets to the bone. [*Pauses, her eye falling on the cage.*] I should think she would 'a wanted a bird. But what do you suppose went with it?

MRS. PETERS. I don't know, unless it got sick and died.

[*She reaches over and swings the broken door, swings it again, both women watch it.*]

105   MRS. HALE. You weren't raised round here, were you? [*MRS. PETERS shakes her head.*] You didn't know—her?

MRS. PETERS. Not till they brought her yesterday,

MRS. HALE. She—come to think of it, she was kind of like a bird herself—real sweet and pretty, but kind of timid and—fluttery. How—she—did—change. [*Silence; then as if struck by a happy thought and relieved to get back to everyday things.*] Tell you what, Mrs. Peters, why don't you take the quilt in with you? It might take up her mind.

MRS. PETERS. Why, I think that's a real nice idea, Mrs. Hale. There couldn't possibly be any objection to it, could there? Now, just what would I take? I wonder if her patches are in here—and her things.

[*They look in the sewing basket.*]

MRS. HALE. Here's some red. I expect this has got sewing things in it. [*Brings out a fancy box.*] What a pretty box. Looks like something somebody would give you. Maybe her scissors are in here. [*Opens box. Suddenly puts her hand to her nose.*] Why—[*MRS. PETERS bends nearer, then turns her face away.*] There's something wrapped up in this piece of silk.

110   MRS. PETERS. Why, this isn't her scissors.

MRS. HALE. [*Lifting the silk.*] Oh, Mrs. Peters—it's—

[*MRS. PETERS bends closer.*]

MRS. PETERS. It's the bird.

MRS. HALE. [*Jumping up.*] But, Mrs. Peters—look at it! Its neck! Look at its neck! It's all—other side *to*.

MRS. PETERS. Somebody—wrung—its—neck.

[*Their eyes meet. A look of growing comprehension, of horror. Steps are heard outside. MRS. HALE slips box under quilt pieces, and sinks into her chair. Enter SHERIFF and COUNTY ATTORNEY. MRS. PETERS rises.*]

COUNTY ATTORNEY. [*As one turning from serious things to little pleasantries.*] Well, ladies, 115
have you decided whether she was going to quilt it or knot it?

MRS. PETERS. We think she was going to—knot it.

COUNTY ATTORNEY. Well, that's interesting, I'm sure. [*Seeing the bird-cage.*] Has the bird flown?

MRS. HALE. [*Putting more quilt pieces over the box.*] We think the—cat got it.

COUNTY ATTORNEY. [*Preoccupied.*] Is there a cat?

[*MRS. HALE glances in a quick covert way at MRS. PETERS.*]

MRS. PETERS. Well, not *now*. They're superstitious, you know. They leave. 120

COUNTY ATTORNEY. [*To SHERIFF PETERS, continuing an interrupted conversation.*] No sign at all of anyone having come from the outside. Their own rope. Now let's go up again and go over it piece by piece. [*They start upstairs.*] It would have to have been someone who knew just the—

[*MRS. PETERS sits down. The two women sit there not looking at one another, but as if peering into something and at the same time holding back. When they talk now it is in the manner of feeling their way over strange ground, as if afraid of what they are saying, but as if they cannot help saying it.*]

MRS. HALE. She liked the bird. She was going to bury it in that pretty box.

MRS. PETERS. [*In a whisper.*] When I was a girl—my kitten—there was a boy took a hatchet, and before my eyes—and before I could get there—[*Covers her face an instant.*] If they hadn't held me back I would have—[*Catches herself, looks upstairs where steps are heard, falters weakly.*]—hurt him.

MRS. HALE. [*With a slow look around her.*] I wonder how it would seem never to have had any children around. [*Pause.*] No, Wright wouldn't like the bird—a thing that sang. She used to sing. He killed that, too.

MRS. PETERS. [*Moving uneasily.*] We don't know who killed the bird. 125

MRS. HALE. I knew John Wright.

MRS. PETERS. It was an awful thing was done in this house that night, Mrs. Hale. Killing a man while he slept, slipping a rope around his neck that choked the life out of him.

MRS. HALE. His neck. Choked the life out of him.

[*Her hand goes out and rests on the birdcage.*]

MRS. PETERS. [*With rising voice.*] We don't know who killed him. We don't know.

MRS. HALE. [*Her own feeling not interrupted.*] If there'd been years and years of noth- 130
ing, then a bird to sing to you, it would be awful—still, after the bird was still.

MRS. PETERS. [*Something within her speaking.*] I know what stillness is. When we home-steaded in Dakota, and my first baby died—after he was two years old, and me with no other then—

MRS. HALE. [*Moving.*] How soon do you suppose they'll be through, looking for the evidence?

MRS. PETERS. I know what stillness is. [*Pulling herself back.*] The law has got to punish crime, Mrs. Hale.

MRS. HALE. [*Not as if answering that.*] I wish you'd seen Minnie Foster when she wore a white dress with blue ribbons and stood up there in the choir and sang. [*A look around the room.*] Oh, I *wish* I'd come over here once in a while! That was a crime! That was a crime! Who's going to punish that?

135 MRS. PETERS. [*Looking upstairs.*] We mustn't—take on.

MRS. HALE. I might have known she needed help! I know how things can be—for women. I tell you, it's queer, Mrs. Peters. We live close together and we live far apart. We all go through the same things—it's all just a different kind of the same thing. [*Brushes her eyes; noticing the bottle of fruit, reaches out for it.*] If I was you I wouldn't tell her her fruit was gone. Tell her it *ain't*. Tell her it's all right. Take this in to prove it to her. She—she may never know whether it was broke or not.

MRS. PETERS. [*Takes the bottle, looks about for something to wrap it in; takes petticoat from the clothes brought from the other room, very nervously begins winding this around the bottle. In a false voice.*] My, it's a good thing the men couldn't hear us. Wouldn't they just laugh! Getting all stirred up over a little thing like a—dead canary. As if that could have anything to do with—with—wouldn't they *laugh*!

[*The men are heard coming down stairs.*]

MRS. HALE. [*Under her breath.*] Maybe they would—maybe they wouldn't.

COUNTY ATTORNEY. No, Peters, it's all perfectly clear except a reason for doing it. But you know juries when it comes to women. If there was some definite thing. Something to show—something to make a story about—a thing that would connect up with this strange way of doing it—

[*The women's eyes meet for an instant. Enter HALE from outer door.*]

140 HALE. Well, I've got the team around. Pretty cold out there.

COUNTY ATTORNEY. I'm going to stay here a while by myself. [*To the SHERIFF.*] You can send Frank out for me, can't you? I want to go over everything. I'm not satisfied that we can't do better.

SHERIFF. Do you want to see what Mrs. Peters is going to take in?

[*The COUNTY ATTORNEY goes to the table, picks up the apron, laughs.*]

COUNTY ATTORNEY. Oh, I guess they're not very dangerous things the ladies have picked out. [*Moves a few things about, disturbing the quilt pieces which cover the box. Steps back.*] No, Mrs. Peters doesn't need supervising. For that matter, a sheriff's wife is married to the law. Ever think of it that way, Mrs. Peters?

MRS. PETERS. Not—just that way.

145 SHERIFF. [*Chuckling.*] Married to the law. [*Moves toward the other room.*] I just want you to come in here a minute, George. We ought to take a look at these windows.

COUNTY ATTORNEY. [*Scoffingly.*] Oh, windows!

SHERIFF. We'll be right out, Mr. Hale.

[*HALE goes outside. The SHERIFF follows the COUNTY ATTORNEY into the other room. Then MRS. HALE rises, hands tight together, looking intensely at MRS. PETERS, whose eyes make a slow turn, finally meeting MRS. HALE'S. A moment MRS. HALE holds her, then her own eyes point the way to where the box is concealed. Suddenly MRS. PETERS throws back quilt pieces and tries to put the box in the bag she is wearing. It is too big. She opens box, starts to take bird out, cannot touch it, goes to pieces, stands there helpless. Sound of a knob turning in the other room. MRS. HALE snatches the box and puts it in the pocket of her big coat. Enter COUNTY ATTORNEY and SHERIFF.*]

COUNTY ATTORNEY. [*Facetiously.*] Well, Henry, at least we found out that she was not going to quilt it. She was going to—what is it you call it, ladies?

MRS. HALE. [*Her hand against her pocket.*] We call it—knot it, Mr. Henderson.

CURTAIN

A Glossary of Important Literary Terms

This glossary presents brief definitions of terms that are bold-faced in the text. Page references indicate where readers may find additional detail and illustration, together with discussions about how the concepts may be utilized in studying and writing about literature.

accent or **beat**   The heavy stresses or accents in lines of poetry. Because *heavy stresses* are paired with *light stresses* to compose metrical *feet*, the numbers of accents or beats in a line usually govern the meter of the line (five beats in a *pentameter* line, four in a *tetrameter* line, etc.). (185)

accented rhyme   See *heavy-stress rhyme.*

accented syllable   A syllable receiving a major, or heavy, stress. (185)

acute accent   In scansion, the prime mark (´) indicating a heavy stress. (185)

allegory   A complete narrative that may also be applied to a parallel set of moral, philosophical, political, religious, or social situations. (149–163)

alliteration   The repetition of identical consonant sounds (most often the sounds beginning words) in close proximity (e.g., "*p*ensive *p*oets," "*s*omewhere *s*afe to *s*ea," "*g*racious, *g*olden, *g*littering *g*leams," "*d*eath once *d*ead, there's no more *d*ying then"). (184)

allusion   Unacknowledged references and quotations that authors make while assuming that readers will recognize the original sources and relate their meanings to the new context. Allusions are hence compliments that the author pays to readers for their perceptiveness, knowledge, and awareness. (153)

amphibrach   A three-syllable foot consisting of a light, heavy, and light stress, as in "my SING-ing." (189)

amphimacer or **cretic**   A three-syllable foot consisting of a heavy, light, and heavy stress, as in SING-*ing* SONGS. (189)

analytical sentence outline   A scheme or plan for an essay, arranged according to topics (A, B, C, etc.) and with the topics expressed in sentences. (32)

analyzed rhyme   See *inexact rhyme.*

anapest   A three-syllable foot consisting of two light stresses climaxed by a heavy stress, as in *ear-ly LIGHT*. (188)

antagonist   The person, idea, force, or general set of circumstances opposing the *protagonist;* an essential element of *plot*. (68)

anticipation   See *procatalepsis.*

archetypal/symbolic/mythic critical approach   An interpretive literary approach explaining literature in terms of archetypal patterns (e.g., God's creation of human beings, the search for paradise, the initiation of a young person). (308)

argument   The development of a pattern of interpretation or thought with an intent to persuade. In most cases of writing about literature, the persuasive situation is to show the validity of a particular idea or circumstance in a story, poem, or play. More broadly, the term *argument* applies to any situation about which there may be disagreement. Although sometimes argumentative discourse may become disputatious, one should never forget that true arguments should stem from the reasonable interpretation of correct and accurate data. (21, 45, 47)

assonance   The repetition of identical vowel sounds in different words in close proximity, as in the d*ee*p gr*ee*n s*ea*. (184, 192)

atmosphere or **mood**   The emotional aura invoked by a work. (112)

auditory images   References to sounds. (131)

authorial symbol   See *contextual symbol*.

authorial voice   The *voice* or *persona* used by authors when seemingly speaking for themselves. The use of the term makes it possible to discuss a narration or presentation without identifying the ideas absolutely with those of the author. See also *speaker, point of view,* and *third-person point of view.* (83)

Bacchius or **Bacchic**   A three-syllable foot consisting of a light stress followed by two heavy stresses, as in "*a NEW SONG*" and "*the OLD WAYS.*" (189)

ballad, ballad measure   A narrative poem composed of quatrains in *ballad measure;* that is, a pattern of iambic tetrameter alternating with iambic trimeter and rhyming *x-a-x-a.* (3, 197)

beast fable   A fable featuring animals with human characteristics. (152)

beat   See *accent.*

brainstorming   The exploration, discovery, and development of details to be used in a composition. (18)

breve   In traditional poetic scansion, a mark in the shape of a bowl-like half circle (˘) to indicate a light stress or unaccented syllable. (185)

cacophony   Meaning "bad sound," *cacophony* refers to words combining sharp or harsh sounds, as in Pope's "When Ajax strives some rock's vast weight to throw." (193)

cadence group   A coherent word group spoken as a single rhythmical unit, such as a noun phrase ("our sacred honor") or prepositional phrase ("of parting day"). (190)

caesura, caesurae   The pause(s) or juncture(s) separating words and phrases within lines of poetry, as in Pope's line "Trees, where you sit, shall crowd into a shade" (Second Pastoral, "Summer," line 74), in which there is a caesura after "Trees" and also after "sit." In poetic *scansion* the caesura is marked by a double *virgule* (//). The control of caesurae is a vital aspect of poetic *rhythm.* (193)

central idea or **central argument**   (1) The thesis or main idea of an essay. (2) The *theme* of a literary work. (27)

character   An extended verbal representation of a human being, the inner self that determines thought, speech, and behavior. (3, 64–76)

chronology (the "logic of time")   The sequence of events in a work, with emphasis on the intertwining of cause and effect. (93)

climax (Greek for *ladder*)   The high point of *conflict* and tension preceding the resolution of a story or play; the point of decision, of inevitability and no return. The climax is sometimes merged with the *crisis* in the consideration of dramatic and narrative structure. (99)

close reading   The detailed study of a poem or passage, designed to explain characters, motivations, situations, ideas, style, organization, word selections, settings, similarities, and contrasts of sound, etc. (53–63)

close-up (film)   A camera view of an actor's head and upper body, designed to emphasize the psychological makeup and reactions of the character being portrayed; contrasted with *long shot.* (247)

comparison-contrast   A technique of analyzing two or more works in order to determine similarities and differences in topic, treatment, and quality. (207–221)

complication   A stage of narrative and dramatic structure in which the major *conflicts* are brought out; the *rising action* of a *drama.* (99)

conflict   The opposition between two characters, between large groups of people, or between *protagonists* and larger forces such as natural objects, ideas, modes of behavior, public opinion, and the like. Conflict may also be internal and psychological, involving choices facing a *protagonist.* The resolution of conflict is the essence of *plot.* (93)

consonant sounds or **consonant segments**   Consonant sounds (i.e., sounds that accompany ["con"] the sound ["sonant," i.e., vowel sounds]) are produced as a result of the touching or close proximity of the tongue or the lips in relation to the teeth or palate (e.g., *m, n, p, f, sh, ch*); to be compared with *vowel sounds.* (183)

contextual, private, or **authorial symbol**   A symbol that is derived not from common historical, cultural, or religious materials, but that is rather developed within the context of an individual work. See also *cultural symbol.* (150, 154)

cosmic irony (irony of fate)   Situational irony that is connected to a pessimistic or fatalistic view of life. (169)

couplet   Two lines that may be unified by rhyme or, in Biblical poetry, by content. (3)

creative nonfiction   A type of literature that is technically nonfiction, such as diaries, journals, and news features, but that nevertheless involves high degrees of imaginative and literary skill. (4)

cretic   See *amphimacer.*

crisis   The point of uncertainty and tension—the turning point—that results from the *conflicts* and difficulties brought about through the *complications* of the plot. The crisis leads to the *climax*—that is, to the decision made by the protagonist to resolve the conflict. Sometimes the crisis and the climax are considered as two elements of the same stage of *plot* development. (99)

cultural context   See *historical context.*

cultural or **universal symbol**   A symbol that is recognized and shared as a result of a common political, social, and cultural heritage. See also *contextual symbol.* (150)

dactyl   A three-syllable foot consisting of a heavy stress followed by two lights, as in the words *QUOT-a-ble* and *PAR-a-ble.* (188)

deconstructionist critical approach   An interpretive literary approach that rejects absolute interpretations and stresses ambiguities and contradictions. (310)

dénouement ("untying") or **resolution**   The final stage of plot development, in which mysteries are explained, characters find their destinies, lovers are united, sanity is restored, and the work is completed. Usually the dénouement is done as speedily as possible, for it occurs after all conflicts are ended, and little that is new can be begun to hold the interest of readers. (100)

dilemma   A situation presenting a character with two choices, each one of which is unacceptable, dangerous, or even lethal. (94)

dimeter   A line of two metrical feet. (186)

dipody, dipodic foot, or **syzygy**   A strong beat that creates a single foot out of two normal feet—usually iambs or trochees—so that a "galloping" or "rollicking" rhythm results. (189)

documentation   Granting recognition to the ideas and words of others, either through textual, parenthetical, or footnote references. (272)

double entendre ("double meaning")   Deliberate ambiguity, usually humorous, and often sexual. (168)

double rhyme   See *trochaic rhyme.*

drama   An individual play; also plays considered as a group; one of the three major genres of *imaginative literature.* (3)

dramatic irony   A special kind of *situational irony* in which a character perceives his or her plight in a limited way while the audience and one or more of the other characters understand it entirely. (169)

dramatic or **objective point of view**   A *third-person narration* reporting speech and action, but excluding commentary on the actions and thoughts of the characters. (83)

dynamic character   A character who undergoes adaptation, change, or growth, unlike the *static character,* who remains constant. In a *short story,* there is usually only one dynamic character, whereas in a *novel* there may be a large number. (68)

echoic words   Words echoing the actions they describe, such as *buzz, bump,* and *slap;* important in the device of *onomatopoeia.* (193)

economic determinist/Marxist critical approach   An interpretive literary approach based on the theories of Karl Marx (1818–1883), stressing that literature is to be judged from the perspective of economic and social class inequality and oppression. (306)

editing   See *montage.*

enclosing setting   See *framing setting.*

end-stopped line   A line ending in a full pause, usually indicated with a period or semicolon. (191)

enjambement or **run-on line**   A line having no end punctuation but running over to the next line. (191)

epic   A long narrative poem elevating character, speech, and action. (3)

essay   A short and tightly organized written composition dealing with a topic such as a character, setting, or point of view. (16)

euphony   Meaning "good sound," *euphony* refers to word groups containing consonants that permit an easy and pleasant flow of spoken sound. See also *cacophony.* (193)

exact rhyme   Also sometimes called *perfect rhyme.* Exact rhyme is the placement of rhyming words in which both the vowel and concluding consonant sounds, if any, are identical, as in "done" and "run," and "see" and "be." It is important to judge rhymes on the basis of *sound* rather than spelling, as in these examples. Words do not have to be spelled the same way to be exact rhymes. (193)

examination   A written or oral test or inquiry designed to discover a person's understanding and capacity to deal with a particular topic or set of topics. (288–298)

exposition   The stage of dramatic or narrative structure that introduces all things necessary for the development of the plot. (99)

eye rhyme or **sight rhyme**   Words that seem to rhyme because parts of them are spelled identically but pronounced differently (e.g., *bear, fear; fury, bury; stove, shove; wonder, yonder*). (196)

fable   A brief *story* illustrating a moral truth, most often associated with the ancient Greek writer Aesop. (152)

falling rhyme   Trochaic rhymes, such as *dying* and *crying,* and also dactylic rhymes, such as *flattery* and *battery,* and *slippery* and *frippery.* (195)

feet   See *foot.*

feminist critical approach   An interpretive literary approach designed to raise consciousness about the importance and unique nature of women in literature. (305)

fiction   *Narratives* based in the imagination of the author, not in literal, reportorial facts; one of the three major genres of imaginative literature. (2)

figurative devices   See *figures of speech.*

figurative language   Words and expressions that conform to a particular pattern or form, such as *metaphor, simile,* and *parallelism.* (138)

figures   See *figurative language.*

figures of speech   See *figurative language.*

film   Motion pictures, movies. (243–257)

film script   The written dramatic text on which a film is based, including directions for movement and expression. (246)

first-person point of view   The use of an "I," or first-person, speaker or narrator who tells about things that he or she has seen, done, spoken, heard, thought, and also learned about in other ways. (81, 84, 87)

flashback   A method of *narration* in which past events are introduced into a present action. Also called *selective recollection.* (101)

flat character   A character, usually minor, who is not individual, but rather useful and structural, static and unchanging; distinguished from *round character.* (68)

foot, feet   A poetic foot consists of the measured combination of heavy and light *stresses,* such as the *iamb,* which contains a light followed by a heavy stress (e.g., "*of YEAR*"). In poetic scansion, the feet are separated by a *virgule* or single slash mark (/), as in Shakespeare's "That time / of year / thou mayst / in me / behold." (185)

formal substitution   See *substitution.*

formalist critical approach   See *New Critical/formalist critical approach.*

framing (enclosing) setting   The same features of topic or setting used at both the beginning and ending of a work so as to "frame" or "enclose" the work. (112)

freewriting   See *brainstorming.*

genre   One of the types of literature, such as *fiction* and *poetry.* Also, a type of work, such as detective fiction, epic poetry, tragedy, etc. (2)

graph, graphics (spelling)   Writing or spelling; the appearance of words on a page, as opposed to their actual sounds. Thus the *sh* sound may be spelled in many different ways, such as "*sh*ip," "na*tion*," "o*cean*," "fi*ss*ion," and "Fu*chs*ia." (184)

gustatory images   References to impressions of taste. (131)

haiku   A poetic form derived from Japanese, traditionally containing three lines of 5, 7, and 5 syllables, in that order. (3)

half rhyme   See *inexact rhyme.*

heavy-stress rhyme or **rising rhyme**   A rhyme, such as rhyming iambs or anapests, ending with a strong stress. The rhymes may be produced with one-syllable words, like *SKY* and *FLY,* or with multisyllabic words in which the accent falls on the last syllable, such as *deCLINE* and *conFINE.* (185)

heptameter or **the septenary**   A line consisting of seven metrical feet. (186)

hero, heroine   The major male and female *protagonists* in a narrative or drama. The terms are often used to describe leading characters in adventures and romances. (68)

hexameter   A line consisting of six metrical feet. (186)

historical context (also **cultural** or **intellectual context**)   The historical times when a work was written, together with the intellectual and cultural ideas of this period. To study a work of literature in this perspective is to determine the degree to which the work spoke not only to people of its own times, but continues to speak to people of current times (and perhaps to people of all times). (232–242)

historical critical approach   See *topical/historical critical approach.*

hovering accent   See *spondee.*

humor   The feature or features of a situation or expression to provoke laughter and amusement. (166)

hyperbole or **overstatement**   A rhetorical figure in which emphasis is achieved through exaggeration. (168)

iamb   A two-syllable *foot* consisting of a light stress followed by a heavy stress (e.g., *the WINDS, have FELT, of MAY*). The iamb is the most common metrical foot in English poetry because it closely resembles natural speech while it also follows measured poetic accents. (186)

iambic rhyme   A *heavy-stress rhyme* that is built from rhyming *iambs* such as "the west" and "in rest," or from rhyming two-syllable words such as "admire" and "desire." (195)

idea or **theme**   A concept, thought, opinion, or belief; in literature, a unifying, centralizing conception or theme. (119–128)

identical rhyme   The use of the same words in rhyming positions, such as *veil* and *veil,* or *stone* and *stone.* (196)

image, imagery   Images are references that trigger the mind to fuse together memories of sights (*visual*), sounds (*auditory*), tastes (*gustatory*), smells (*olfactory*), and sensations of touch (*tactile*). "Image" refers to a single mental creation. "Imagery" refers to images throughout a work or throughout the works of a writer or group of writers. Images may be *literal* (descriptive and pictorial) and *metaphorical* (figurative and suggestive). (129–137)

imaginative literature   *Literature* based in the imagination of the writer; the genres of imaginative literature are *fiction, poetry,* and *drama.* (2, *passim*)

imperfect foot   A metrical foot consisting of a single syllable, either heavily or lightly stressed, as the "ing" in "the twilight's last gleaming." There is nothing imperfect about an imperfect foot. It is so named because, having only one syllable, it does not fit into the patterns of the other poetic feet. (188)

incidents   See *actions.*

incongruity   A discrepancy between what is ordinarily or normally expected and what is actually experienced. The resulting gap is a major cause of amusement. (166)

inexact rhyme   Rhymes that are created from words with similar but not identical sounds. In most of these instances, either the vowel segments are different while the consonants are the same, or vice versa. This type of rhyme is variously called *slant rhyme, near rhyme, half rhyme, off rhyme, analyzed rhyme,* or *suspended rhyme.* (196)

intellectual critical approach   See *topical/intellectual critical approach.*

internal rhyme   The occurrence of rhyming words within a single line of verse. (194)

irony   Broadly, a means of indirection. *Verbal irony* is language that states the opposite of what is intended. *Dramatic irony* describes the condition of characters who do not know the nature, seriousness, and extent of their circumstances. An emphasis on ineffectiveness and powerlessness is *situational irony.* (112, 167)

irony of fate   See *cosmic irony.*

irony of situation   See *situational irony.*

journal   A notebook or word-processor file for recording responses and observations that, for purposes of writing, may be used in the development of essays. (13)

kinesthetic images   Words describing human or animal motion and activity. (132)

kinetic images   Words describing general motion. (132)

light stress   In speech and in metrical scansion, the less-emphasized syllables, as in Shakespeare's "That time of year," in which *that* and *of* are pronounced less emphatically than *TIME* and *YEAR.* (185)

limited point of view or **limited third-person point of view** or **limited-omniscient point of view**   A third-person narration in which the actions and thoughts of the protagonist are the primary focus of attention. (84)

line   The basic poetic unit of length, appearing as a row of words on a page or else, sometimes, as a single word or even as a part of a word, and cohering grammatically through phrases and sentences. Lines in closed-form poetry are composed of determinable numbers of metrical feet; lines in open-form poetry are variable, depending on content and rhythmical speech patterns. (186)

literary research   See *research.*

literature   Written or oral compositions that tell stories, dramatize situations, express emotions, and analyze and advocate ideas. Literature is designed to engage readers emotionally as well as intellectually, with the major genres being *fiction, poetry, drama,* and *nonfiction prose,* and with many separate subforms. (1, *passim*)

long shot (film)   A distant camera view, including not only characters but also their surroundings; contrasted with a *close-up.* (247)

lyric   A short poem or *song* written in a fixed stanzaic form. If the poem is set to music for performance, the repeating lyric stanza allows for the words to be sung in verses to an appropriately fixed melody. (3)

major mover   A major participant in a work's action who either causes things to happen or who is the subject of major events. If the first-person narrator is also a major mover, such as the *protagonist,* that fact gives first-hand authenticity to the narration. (79)

malapropism   The comic use of an improperly pronounced word, so that what comes out is a real but also incorrect word. Examples are *odorous* for *odious* (Shakespeare) or *pineapple* for *pinnacle* (Sheridan). The new word must be close enough to the correct word so that the resemblance is immediately recognized, along with the error. See also *pun.* (166)

Marxist critical approach   See *economic determinist/Marxist critical approach.*

mechanics of verse   See *prosody.*

metaphor ("carrying out a change")   *Figurative language* that describes something as though it actually were something else, thereby enhancing understanding and insight. (3, 138–148)

metaphorical language   See *figures of speech.*

meter   The number of feet within a line of traditional verse, such as *iambic pentameter* referring to a line containing five *iambs.* (186)

metrical foot   See *foot.*

metrics   See *prosody.*

monometer   A line consisting of one metrical foot. (186)

montage or **editing**   The editing or assembling of the various camera "takes," or separately filmed scenes, to make a continuous film. (250)

mood   See *atmosphere.*

moral/intellectual critical approach   An interpretive literary approach that is concerned primarily with content and values. (300)

music of poetry   See *prosody.*

myth, mythology, mythos   A myth is a story that deals with the relationships of gods to humanity, or with battles among heroes. A myth may also be a set of beliefs or assumptions among societies. *Mythology* refers collectively to the stories and beliefs either of a single group or number of groups. A system of beliefs and religious or historical doctrine is a *mythos.* (2, 153)

mythic critical approach   See *archetypal/symbolic/mythic critical approach.*

narration, narrative fiction   The relating or recounting of a sequence of events or actions. Whereas a narration may be reportorial and historical, *narrative fiction* is primarily creative and imaginative. See also *prose fiction* and *creative nonfiction.* (77, 93)

narrative fiction   See *prose fiction.*

narrator   See *speaker.*

near rhyme   See *inexact rhyme.*

New Critical/formalist critical approach   An interpretive literary approach based on the French practice of *explication de texte,* stressing the form and details of literary works. (302)

new historicism   A type of literary criticism that emphasizes the integration of literature and historical background and culture. (301)

nonfiction prose   A *genre* consisting of essays, articles, and books about real as opposed to fictional occurrences and objects; one of the major *genres* of literature. (3)

novel   A long work of prose fiction. (2)

objective point of view   See *dramatic point of view.*

octameter   A line of eight metrical *feet.* (186)

off rhyme   See *inexact rhyme.*

olfactory imagery   Images referring to impressions of smell. (131)

omniscient point of view   A *third-person narrative* in which the *speaker* or *narrator,* with no apparent limitations, may describe intentions, actions, reactions, locations, and speeches of any or all of the characters, and may also describe their innermost thoughts (when necessary). (83)

onomatopoeia   A blending of consonant and vowel sounds designed to imitate or suggest the object or activity being described, as in Pope's line "That like a wounded snake, drags its slow length along." (193)

outline   See *analytical sentence outline.*

overstatement   See *hyperbole.*

parable   A short *allegory* designed to illustrate a religious truth, most often associated with Jesus as recorded in the Gospels. (2, 153)

pastoral   A traditional poetic form with topical material drawn from the often idealized lives and vocabularies of rural and shepherd life. Famous English pastorals are Milton's "Lycidas," Arnold's "Thyrsis," Pope's *Pastorals,* and Spenser's *The Shepherd's Calendar.* (2)

pentameter   A line of five metrical *feet.* (186)

perfect rhyme   See *exact rhyme.*

persona   See *speaker.*

phonetic, phonetics   The actual pronunciation of sounds, as distinguished from spelling or *graphics.* (185)

plausibility   See *probability.*

plot   The plan or groundwork for a story or a play, with the actions resulting from believable and authentic human responses to a *conflict.* It is causality, conflict, response, opposition, and interaction that make a plot out of a series of actions. (93–108)

poem, poet, poetry A variable literary genre that is, foremost, characterized by the rhythmical qualities of language. While poems may be short (including *epigrams* and *haiku* of just a few lines) or long (*epics* of thousands of lines), the essence of poetry is compression, economy, and force, in contrast with the expansiveness of prose. There is no bar to the topics that poets may consider, and poems may range from the personal and lyric to the public and discursive. A *poem* is one poetic work. A *poet* is a person who writes poems. *Poetry* may refer to the poems of one writer, to poems of a number of writers, to all poems generally, or to the aesthetics of poetry considered as an art. (3)

point of view The *speaker, voice, narrator,* or *persona* of a work; the position from which details are perceived and related; a centralizing mind or intelligence; not to be confused with *opinion* or *belief.* (77–92)

point-of-view character The central figure or *protagonist* in a *limited-point-of-view narration,* the character about whom events turn, the focus of attention in the narration. (84)

private or **contextual symbol** See *cultural symbol.*

probability or plausibility The standard that literature should be concerned with what is likely, common, normal, and usual. (69)

problem A question or issue about the interpretation or understanding of a work. (175–181)

procatalepsis or **anticipation** A rhetorical strategy whereby the writer raises an objection and then answers it; the idea is to strengthen an argument by anticipating and forestalling objections. (177)

prose fiction *Imaginative* prose narratives (*short stories* and *novels*) that focus on one or a few characters who undergo a change or development as they interact with other characters and deal with their problems. (2)

prosody Metrics and versification; the sounds, rhythms, rhymes, and general qualities of poetry; the relationships between content and sound in poetry. (182–206)

protagonist The central character and focus of interest in a narrative or drama. (68)

psychological/psychoanalytic critical approach An interpretive literary approach stressing how psychology may be used in the explanation of both authors and literary works. (307)

pyrrhic A metrical foot consisting of two unaccented syllables, as in the words "on their" in Pope's line "Now sleeping flocks on their soft fleeces lie." (186)

quatrain (1) A four-line stanza or poetic unit. (2) In an *English* or *Shakespearean* sonnet, a group of four lines united by rhyme. (3, 197)

reader-response critical approach An interpretive literary approach based on the proposition that literary works are not fully created until readers make *transactions* with them by *actualizing* them in the light of their particular knowledge and experience. (311)

realism or **verisimilitude** The use of true, lifelike, or probable situations and concerns. Also, the theory underlying the use of reality in literature. (69, 111)

reliable narrator A speaker who has nothing to hide by making misstatements and who is untainted by self-interest. This speaker's narration is therefore to be accepted at face value; contrasted with an *unreliable narrator.* (81, 85)

representative character A *flat character* with the qualities of all other members of a group (i.e., clerks, cowboys, detectives, etc.); a *stereotype.* (69)

research, literary The systematic use of primary and secondary sources for assistance in studying a literary *problem.* (258–287)

resolution See *dénouement.*

response A reader's intellectual and emotional reactions to a literary work. (311)

review A free-ranging essay on a literary work. (222–231)

rhetorical figure See *figurative language.*

rhetorical substitution See *substitution.*

rhyme The repetition of identical or closely related sounds in the syllables of different words, most often in concluding syllables at the ends of lines, such as Shakespeare's *day* and *May* and Swinburne's *forever* and *never.* (184, 193, 200)

rhyme scheme   A pattern of rhyme, usually indicated by the assignment of a letter of the alphabet to each rhyming sound, as in *a b b a* as the rhyming pattern of the first quatrain of an Italian or Petrarchan sonnet. (197)

rhythm   The varying speed, intensity, elevation, pitch, loudness, and expressiveness of speech, especially poetry. (199)

rising rhyme   See *heavy-stress rhyme.*

romance   (1) Lengthy Spanish and French stories of the sixteenth and seventeenth centuries; (2) Modern formulaic stories describing the growth of an impulsive, passionate, and powerful love relationship. (2)

round character   A literary character, usually but not necessarily the *protagonist* of a story or play, who is three-dimensional, rounded, authentic, memorable, original, and true to life. A round character is the center of our attention, and is both individual and unpredictable. A round character profits from experience, and in the course of a story or play undergoes change or development. (68)

run-on line   See *enjambement.*

scan, scansion   The act of determining the prevailing *rhythm* and poetic characteristics of a poem. (185)

second-person point of view   A narration in which a second-person listener ("you") is the protagonist and the speaker is someone (e.g., doctor, parent, rejected lover, etc.) with knowledge that the protagonist does not possess or understand about his or her own actions. (82, 85, 87)

segment   The smallest meaningful unit of sound, such as the *l*, *uh*, and *v* sounds making up the word "love." Segments are to be distinguished from spellings. Thus, the *oo* sound may be spelled as *ui* in "fruit," *u* in "flute," *oo* in "foolish," *o* in "lose," *uu* in "vacuum," or *ou* in "troupe." (184)

selective recollection   See *flashback.*

septenary   See *heptameter.*

setting   The natural, manufactured, and cultural environment in which characters live and move, including their possessions, homes, ways of life, and assumptions. (109–118)

short story   A compact, concentrated work of *narrative fiction* that may also contain description, dialogue, and commentary. Poe used the term "brief prose tale" for the short story, and emphasized that it should create a powerful and unified impact. (2)

sight rhyme   See *eye rhyme.*

simile   A figure of comparison, using "like" with nouns and "as" with clauses, as in "the trees were bent by the wind *like actors bowing after a performance.*" (138–148)

situational irony or **irony of situation**   A type of *irony* emphasizing that human beings are enmeshed in forces beyond their comprehension and control. (168)

slant rhyme   A *near rhyme* in which the concluding consonant sounds (but not the vowels) are identical, as in "should" and "food," "slim" and "ham." See also *inexact rhyme.* (196)

song   See *lyric.*

sound   The phonetics of language, separately and collectively considered. See also *prosody.* (184)

speaker   The *narrator* of a story or poem, the *point of view*, often an independent character who is completely imagined and consistently maintained by the author. In addition to narrating the essential events of the work (justifying the status of narrator), the speaker may also introduce other aspects of his or her knowledge, and may express judgments and opinions. Often the character of the speaker is of as much interest in the story as the *actions* or *incidents.* (77)

spondee   A two-syllable *foot* consisting of successive, equally heavy *accents* (e.g., *slow time, men's eyes*). (187)

stanza   A group of poetic lines corresponding to paragraphs in prose; stanzaic me ters and rhymes are usually repeating and systematic. (102)

static character   A character who undergoes no change, a *flat character;* contrasted with a *dynamic character.* (68)

stereotype   A character who is so ordinary and unoriginal that he or she seems to have been cast in a mold; a *representative* character. (69)

stock character   A *flat character* in a standard role with standard *traits,* such as the irate police captain, the bored hotel clerk, the sadistic criminal, etc.; a *stereotype.* (69)

story   A narrative, usually fictional, centering on a major character, and rendering a complete action. (2)

stress   The emphasis given to a syllable, either strong or light. See also *accent.* (185)

strong-stress rhythm   See *heavy-stress rhythm.*

structuralist critical approach   An interpretive literary approach attempting to find relationships and similarities among elements that appear to be separate and discrete. (303)

structure   The arrangement and placement of materials in a work. (93–108)

substitution   The presence of a variant poetic *foot* within a poem in which a particular metrical foot is dominant. *Formal substitution* is the use of an actual variant foot within a line, such as an *anapest* being used in place of an *iamb. Rhetorical substitution* is the manipulation of the caesura to create the effect of a series of differing feet. (188)

suspended rhyme   See *inexact rhyme.*

syllable   A separately pronounced part of a word (e.g., the *sing* and *ing* parts of "singing"; the *sub, sti, tu,* and *tion* parts of "substitution"). Some words consist of only one syllable (e.g., *a, an, man, girl, the, when, screeched*). (184)

symbol, symbolism   A specific word, idea, or object that may stand for ideas, values, persons, or ways of life. (149–163)

syzygy   See *dipody.*

tactile imagery   *Images* of touch and responses to touch. (131)

tenor   The ideas conveyed in a *metaphor* or *simile.* See also *vehicle.* (142)

tetrameter   A line of four metrical *feet.* (186)

theme   (1) The major or central idea of a work. (2) An essay, a short composition developing an interpretation or advancing an argument. (3) The main point or idea that a writer of an essay asserts and illustrates. (119)

thesis sentence or **thesis statement**   An introductory sentence that names the topics to be developed in the body of an essay. (30)

third-person point of view   A third-person method of *narration* (i.e., *she, he, it, they, them,* etc.), in which the *speaker* or *narrator* is not a part of the story, unlike the involvement of the narrator of a *first-person point of view.* Because the third-person speaker may exhibit great knowledge and understanding, together with other qualities of character, he or she is often virtually identified with the author, but this identification is not easily decided. See also *authorial voice, omniscient point of view.* (83, 85, 87)

third-person objective point of view   See *dramatic point of view.*

tone   The techniques and modes of presentation that reveal or create attitudes. (164–174)

topic sentence   The sentence determining or introducing the subject matter of a paragraph. (30)

topical/historical critical approach   An interpretive literary approach that stresses the relationship of literature to its historical period. (301)

trait, traits   A typical mode of behavior; the study of major traits provides a guide to the description of *character.* (64)

trimeter   A line of three metrical *feet.* (186)

triple rhyme   See *dactylic rhyme.*

trochaic (double) rhyme   Rhyming trochees such as *FLOW-er* and *TOW-er.* (195)

trochee trochaic   A two-syllable foot consisting of a heavy stress followed by a light stress (e.g., *RUN-ning, SING-ing, EAT-ing*). (187)

unaccented syllable   A syllable receiving a light stress. (185)

understatement   Rhetorically, the deliberate underplaying or undervaluing of an assertion or idea to create emphasis; a form of *irony.* (168)

universal symbol   See *cultural symbol.*

unreliable narrator   A speaker who through ignorance, self-interest, or lack of capacity may tell lies and otherwise distort details. For the reader to locate truth in the unreliable narrator's story requires careful judgment and not inconsiderable skepticism; contrasted with *reliable narrator.* (81, 85)

unstressed syllable   See *light stress.*

value, values   The attachment of worth, significance, and desirability to an *idea* so that the idea is judged not only for its significance as thought but also for its importance as a goal, ideal, or standard. (120)

vehicle   The image or reference of figures of speech, such as a *metaphor* or *simile;* it is the vehicle that carries or embodies the *tenor.* See also *tenor.* (142)

verbal irony   Language stressing the importance of an idea by stating the opposite of what is meant. (168)

verisimilitude ("like truth")   A characteristic whereby the setting, circumstances, characters, dialogue, actions, and outcomes in a work are designed to seem true, lifelike, real, plausible, and probable. See also *realism.* (69, 111)

versification   See *prosody.*

virgule   A slash mark (/) used in poetic *scansion* to mark the boundaries of poetic *feet.* A double virgule (//) is commonly used to indicate the placement of a *caesura.* See *caesura.* (186)

visual image   Language describing visible objects and situations. (130)

voice   See *speaker.*

vowel sounds or **vowel segments**   Meaningful continuant sounds produced by the resonation of the voice in the space between the tongue and the top of the mouth, such as the *ee* in "feel," the *eh* in "bet," and the *oo* in "cool." (182)

Acknowledgments

Gwendolyn Brooks, "We Real Cool" from *Blacks*. Reprinted by Consent of Brooks Permissions.

Anita Scott Coleman, "Unfinished Masterpieces" from *The Crisis*, March 1927. The editor wishes to thank The Crisis Publishing Co., Inc., the publisher of the magazine of the National Association for the Advancement of Colored People, for authorizing the use of this work.

"Desert Places" from *The Poetry of Robert Frost*, edited by Edward Connery Lathem. Copyright 1936 by Robert Frost, copyright 1964 by Lesley Frost Ballantine, © 1969 by Henry Holt and Company. Reprinted by permission of Henry Holt and Company, LLC.

"Theme for English B" and "Negro" from *The Collected Poems of Langston Hughes* by Langston Hughes, copyright © 1994 by The Estate of Langston Hughes. Used by permission of Alfred A. Knopf, a division of Random House, Inc.

"Rhine Boat Trip" from *The Collected Poems of Irving Layton* by Irving Layton. Used by permission of McClelland & Stewart Ltd.

"Rhine Boat Trip" by Irving Layton, from *The Selected Poems of Irving Layton*, copyright © 1977 by New Directions Publishing Corp. Reprinted by permission of New Directions Publishing Corp.

John Masefield, "Cargoes" from *Selected Poems* (New York: Macmillan Publishing Company, 1978). Reprinted with the permission of The Society of Authors as the Literary Representative of the Estate of John Masefield.

MLA Style Guidelines are reprinted by permission of the Modern Language Association (MLA) <http://www.mla.org/main.stl.htm>.

"First Confession" from *The Collected Stories of Frank O'Connor* by Frank O'Connor, copyright © 1981 by Harriet O'Donovan Sheehy, Executrix of the Estate of Frank O'Connor. Used by permission of Alfred A. Knopf, a division of Random House, Inc. and Writer's House, LLC, New York on behalf of the proprietors.

Richard F. Peterson, *The Circle of Truth: The Stories of Katherine Mansfield and Mary Lavin*. *Modern Fiction Studies* 24 (1978), 385–386. © Purdue Research Foundation. Reprinted by permission of the Johns Hopkins University Press.

Dudley Randall, "Ballad of Birmingham" from *Poem Counter Poem*. Copyright © 1966 by Dudley Randall. Reprinted with the permission of Broadside Press.

Luis Omar Salinas, "In a Farmhouse." Reprinted with permission of the author.

Shelly Wagner, "The Boxes" from *The Andrew Poems*. Copyright © 1994 by Shelly Wagner. Reprinted with the permission of Texas Tech University Press.

"The Second Coming" is reprinted with permission of Scribner, an imprint of Simon & Schuster Adult Publishing Group, from *The Collected Works of W. B. Yeats, Volume 1: The Poems*, revised, edited by Richard J. Finneran. Copyright © 1924 by The Macmillan Company; copyright renewed © 1952 by Bertha Georgie Yeats.

Index of Authors and Titles, Topics, Directors, Producers, and Chapter Titles

Authors are listed alphabetically, followed by the titles of their works. In some instances, such as the Oxford Companions, the titles are listed separately. The titles of films follow the names of the director or, in one instance, the producer, and film titles are also indexed here. Anonymous works and films are indexed under the titles. For brief definitions of important terms and concepts used in the text, please consult the Glossary on pages 401–411.